Guide to Charts, Lists, and Tables

(continued on reverse)

The Holt Handbook

The Holt Handbook

Second Edition

Laurie G. Kirszner
Philadelphia College of Pharmacy and Science

Stephen R. Mandell
Drexel University

Holt, Rinehart and Winston, Inc.
Fort Worth   Chicago   San Francisco
Philadelphia   Montreal   Toronto   L
Sydney   Tokyo

Publisher/Acquisitions Editor   Charlyce Jones Owen
Senior Project Manager   Françoise Bartlett
Senior Production Manager   Nancy Myers
Art Director   Gloria Gentile
Interior Design   Caliber Design Planning, Inc.
Cover Design   Caliber Design Planning, Inc.

Library of Congress Cataloging-in-Publication Data

Kirszner, Laurie G.
    The Holt handbook.

    Includes index.
    1. English language—Rhetoric.   2. English
language—Grammar—1950–   I. Mandell, Stephen R.
II. Title.
PE1408.K675   1989   808′.042   88-13176

ISBN 0-03-021702-4

Printed in the United States of America

9   0   1   2   071   9   8   7   6   5   4   3   2

Holt, Rinehart and Winston, Inc.
The Dryden Press
Saunders College Publishing

Acknowledgments are on page 775.

Preface to the Instructor

When we planned the *The Holt Handbook*, our aim was to create a true writer's handbook, one that would serve not only as a text and a reference guide but also as a companion. In preparing the first edition we concentrated on making the book inviting, accessible, useful, and interesting to both students and teachers. Although we relied extensively on new research in composition, we were careful to apply the results of this research in a practical and straightforward manner. Our hope was that its organization, its process approach, its emphasis on revision, and its focus on student writing would make *The Holt Handbook* truly a writing-centered text. In addition, we hoped that its descriptive approach to grammar and its nonthreatening tone would make it particularly appealing to students. Now, three years after publication, we are delighted to see that our book has been warmly and enthusiastically received.

As we began to revise *The Holt Handbook*, our goal was to retain the features that made the book so successful while fine-tuning it to make it an even more valuable resource. Its overall organization remains unchanged. As in its first edition, *The Holt Handbook* is divided into eight sections and two appendices. Section I, "Composing an Essay," discusses the writing process, moving from planning, shaping, and writing and revising an essay to writing paragraphs, thinking logically, and writing an argumentative essay. Section II, "Composing Sentences," concentrates on crafting sentences, paying particular attention to the rhetorical choices that writers can make as they build and combine sentences. Section III, "Solving Common Sentence Problems," helps students to identify and revise problem sentences in their own writing. Throughout this section, the emphasis is on revision and experimentation, not on error. Section IV, "Using Words Effectively," contains detailed chapters on word choice, using the dictionary, building a vocabulary, and improving spelling. Section V, "Understanding Grammar," and Section VI, "Understanding Punctuation and Mechanics," together comprise an editor's handbook. Section VII, "Writing with Sources," is a comprehensive four-chapter unit that places emphasis on nonlibrary research (observation, interviews, field trips, and other nonprint sources) as well as on print sources. This section devotes separate chapters to conducting research, working with source material, documentation (MLA, APA, CBE, and other styles), and writing a research paper. process approach follows a student's research through plann ing, and writing and revising, culminating with an ann paper that illustrates current MLA documentation. S

Special Assignments," includes detailed chapters on writing essay examinations, writing about literature, and writing business letters and memos. Following these sections are informative and timely appendices on composing on a computer and manuscript preparation; the book ends with glossaries of usage and of grammatical terms.

In addition to treating grammar, mechanics, and style, *The Holt Handbook* gives detailed coverage to many subjects usually treated fully only in a rhetoric—for instance, writing short essays, research papers, examinations, and critical papers about literature. Unlike other handbooks, *The Holt Handbook* follows the development of a single student essay—from choice of topic to completion of a final draft—through three chapters. The four-chapter section devoted to research, paying particular attention to nonlibrary research, also deserves special attention. Throughout *The Holt Handbook* we include abundant practice exercises, including sentence combining and imitation exercises. Most exercises and examples represent a wide variety of disciplines and subject matter. At the end of many chapters is a "Student Writer at Work" exercise, a draft of a student writing assignment that students are asked to revise. These are not presented as models of good writing; rather, they are working drafts, naturally flawed. As such, the "Student Writer at Work" pieces provide a context in which students can identify key problems associated with chapters or chapter clusters.

Thoughtful comments from users of the first edition and our own careful reevaluation of each element of the book have led us to make a number of changes in the second edition. In Section I, we have chosen a new, more challenging student essay, "The Kuomboka Ceremony," to illustrate the writing process. A reorganized treatment, enhanced by a new design, makes the discussion sections and the student essay-in-progress segments genuinely complementary. In response to suggestions from readers, the instructor's comments now accompany the student's second draft. Elsewhere in Section I, we have significantly expanded the treatment of outlining and have given additional coverage to developing a thesis and to the discussion of editing and proofreading. We have streamlined and condensed Chapter 4's treatment of paragraphing and have added a new section on when to paragraph.

We have also expanded our discussion of argument. Two full chapters are now devoted to the principles of argument. Chapter 5, "Thinking Logically," explains the principles of deductive reasoning (considering validity versus truth and the enthymeme) and of inductive reasoning; the chapter goes on to explain and illustrate many common logical fallacies. Chapter 6, "Writing an Argumentative Essay," traces a student's progress as she plans, shapes, writes, and revises an essay on the controversial topic of pit bull terriers. This chapter includes expanded coverage of such topics as gathering evidence and making inferences.

We have carefully revised Section II, "Composing Sentences," expanding the chapters on sentence fragments; misplaced and modifiers; faulty parallelism; and shifts, mixed constructions, ion. Throughout Sections II, III, V, and VI, we have

p[...]
room[...]
write to:[...]
New York, N[...]

y
phis-
groups of
instead of in

edited and redesigned the chapters on style, grammar, and punctuation and mechanics so that definitions, guidelines, notes, and other key information are emphasized visually as well as stylistically. We have carefully scrutinized every example and exercise in these sections, and we have edited, revised, eliminated, or replaced material when necessary. The changes in Section IV, while perhaps less obvious, are no less important. For example, Chapter 17 now includes expanded coverage of sexist language, plus five new exercises.

We have also given Section VII, "Writing with Sources," significant attention. We have reorganized Chapter 37, "Research for Writing," so that it now begins with an explanation of the search strategy likely to be most useful for beginning researchers. We have updated and expanded the list of print sources. In Chapter 38, "Working with Source Material," new material on reading sources and on evaluating both print and nonprint sources now precedes the discussions of taking notes, interpreting source material, and avoiding plagiarism. In Chapter 39, "Documentation," the coverage of MLA style remains comprehensive and up-to-date, and a helpful reference guide now makes it easier for readers to locate particular examples. In addition, we offer an expanded treatment of APA style and of documentation styles used in other academic disciplines. We retain the self-contained process-oriented Chapter 40, "Writing a Research Paper," which we have reorganized so that it conforms to the search strategy introduced in Chapter 37. The four-chapter research section remains unusually thorough, comprehensive, and usable.

In Section VIII, "Writing Special Assignments," we have extensively revised Chapter 42, "Writing About Literature." The chapter now follows two students through the process of writing essays about literature—one on a short story and one on a poem. The chapter includes examples of student work-in-progress, a glossary of literary terms, and three helpful checklists.

We have taken special care to make the second edition of *The Holt Handbook* even more teachable for the instructor—and more usable for the student—than the first edition was. Throughout the text, we have added boxed lists, summaries, and other design elements that highlight the material that teachers and students will consult most often. We have taken special care to word headings so that they are clear and descriptive and to position them logically in the text. The result, we believe, is a superior reference work that enables writers to find and apply information quickly and easily.

In this edition *The Holt Handbook* continues to approach writing as a recursive process, giving students the opportunity to practice planning, shaping, and writing and revising. This approach, consistent with recent research, encourages students to become involved with every stage of the process and to view revision as a natural and ongoing part of their writing. The style, grammar, and mechanics and punctuation chapters present clear, concise definitions of key concepts followed examples and exercises that gradually increase in difficulty tication. Whenever possible, sentence-level skills are t related sentences that focus on a single high-inte isolated sentences. This pedagogically sound methodology allows students to learn incrementally, practicing each skill as it is introduced. In this way students learn to recognize and revise sentence-level problems within longer units of discourse, duplicating the way that they must actually interact with their own writing. This approach has been useful to the thousands of students who have used the first edition, and we continue to believe in its effectiveness.

Throughout, the second edition of *The Holt Handbook* reflects our conviction that virtually all college assignments call for critical thinking. Students apply critical thinking when they use reasoning in an argumentative essay, when they read and respond to works of literature, when they evaluate sources for a research assignment, and in countless other writing tasks. In a more general sense, students must think critically when they read and highlight material, take notes, recognize inferences, identify errors in logic, analyze connections, or evaluate arguments and supporting evidence. Because critical thinking is such an important part of the writing process, we have decided not to isolate a discussion of it in a single catch-all chapter. Instead, we discuss it when it is relevant at various points in this text—for instance, in sections treating argumentation, writing an interpretation, and evaluating research sources. To help you and your students find these sections, we have listed them in the index under the entry "Critical thinking."

The Holt Handbook is a classroom text, a reference guide, and above all, a writing companion that students can turn to for advice and guidance as they write in college and beyond. Our goal throughout remains the same: to translate the best of research in composition theory into practice. In addition, we still believe that we have an obligation to give not just the rule but the rationale behind it. Accordingly, we are careful to explain the principles that writers must understand to make informed choices about grammar, usage, rhetoric, and style. The result is a book that students and instructors can continue to use with ease, confidence, and, we hope, pleasure.

With this edition, an even more comprehensive ancillary package is available for instructors and students: an *Instructor's Handbook* on teaching composition, with reprints of important scholarly articles on composition and current issues in teaching, and answers to the exercises in the text; *The Holt Workbook*, second edition; *The Holt Research Workbook*; *The Holt Guide to Documentation*, second edition (which is free to students with every copy of *The Holt Handbook*); *Supplementary Exercises; Diagnostic Tests, Computerized Diagnostic Tests* for Apple, Macintosh, and IBM computers; *The Writing Tutor*, an eight-disk interactive software program for Apple, Macintosh, and IBM computers; *Processwriter*, a unique word-processing program for Macintosh and IBM computers; *Processwriter Guide to Writing*, a writing workbook to mpany the *Processwriter* software; and sixty transparency acetates checklists and exercises for overhead projection in the class- mplimentary copies of these teaching and learning aids, ditor, Holt, Rinehart and Winston, 111 Fifth Avenue, 0003.

We wish to thank the following colleagues for their valuable comments and sound advice on this revision:

Chris Abbott, University of Pittsburgh (PA)

Lois Avery, Houston Community College (TX)

Julia Bates, St. Mary's College of Maryland (MD)

Larry Beason, Texas A & M University (TX)

Al Bell, St. Louis Community College at Florissant Valley (MO)

Debra Boyd, Winthrop College (NC)

Pat Bridges, Grand Valley State College (MI)

Wayne Buchman, Rose State College (OK)

David Carlson, Springfield College (MA)

Faye Chandler, Pasadena City College (CA)

Sharon Gibson, University of Louisville (KY)

Owen Gilman, St. Joseph's University (PA)

Margaret Goddin, Davis and Elkins College (VA)

Ruth Greenberg, University of Louisville (KY)

Iris Rose Hart, Santa Fe Community College (FL)

Michael Herzog, Gonzaga University (WA)

Clela Hoggatt, Los Angeles Mission College (CA)

Anne Jackets, Everett Community College (WA)

LaVinia Jennings, University of North Carolina/Chapel Hill (NC)

George Kennedy, Washington State University (WA)

William King, Bethel College (TN)

Ed Kline, University of Notre Dame (IN)

Marsha McDonald, Belmont College (TN)

Vivien Minshull-Ford, Wichita State University (KS)

Robert Moore, SUNY/Oswego (NY)

George Murphy, Villanova University (PA)

Robert Noreen, California State University/Northridge (CA)

L. Sam Phillips, Gaston College (NC)

William Pierce, Prince George's Community College (MD)

Robbie Pinter, Belmont College (TN)

Nancy Posselt, Midlands Technical College (SC)

Robert Post, Kalamazoo Valley Community College (MI)

Mike Riherd, Pasadena City College (CA)

Barbara Stevenson, Kennesaw College (GA)

Jim Stick, Des Moines Area Community College (IA)

James Sodon, St. Louis Community College at Florissant Valley (MO)

Kathleen Tickner, Brevard Community College/Melbourne (FL)

George Trail, University of Houston (TX)

Connie White, Salisbury State College (MD)

Branson Woodard, Liberty University (VA)

Peter Zoller, Wichita State University (KS)

Among the many people at Holt who contributed to this
we would like to single out Fran Bartlett, whose care and
reflected on every page; Nancy Myers and Gloria Gent
uted so much to the book's production and desig
who skillfully prepared the answers to the ex

indebted to Charlyce Jones Owen, friend and editor, who is, quite simply, the best there is.

Finally, we would like to thank our families—Mark, Adam, and Rebecca Kirszner and Demi, David, and Sarah Mandell—who gave us no editorial assistance, did not type the manuscript, and offered no helpful suggestions, but whose love and understanding helped make it all possible.

Philadelphia   L.G.K.
November 1988   S.R.M.

Preface to the Student

The Holt Handbook is a comprehensive guide that you can consult whenever you have a question about grammar, usage, style, or rhetoric. We suggest that you read Section I of the book to become acquainted with the stages of the writing process and the techniques that good writers use when they write. Only after you are familiar with the choices that you have as a writer will you be able to place information about grammar, usage, sentence structure, and mechanics into perspective. As you use *The Holt Handbook*, you will notice that whenever possible we give advice, not rules. We believe that student writers do best when they have the freedom to make informed choices about their writing and are able to take into consideration the demands of varying audiences, purposes, and writing situations.

You can find material in *The Holt Handbook* in a number of ways. Individual chapters offer in-depth discussions of a wide variety of topics, and cross references in the text point you to definitions and discussions of unfamiliar terms. Throughout the text, helpful **charts** and **summary boxes** highlight important material. These boxes are shaded in blue for easy identification. As you write, they can help you locate information quickly and efficiently. (An index to these charts appears on the right inside front cover of your text.)

The Holt Handbook has a number of other special features that will help you locate material.

The **left inside front cover** contains a list of Correction Symbols that your instructor may use to help you edit and revise your papers. These symbols consist of an abbreviation (*agr* for agreement, for example) and a combination of numbers and letters (such as 24a) that refer you to a specific section of the text (section twenty-four, subsection a). You can locate the section of the book that you need by looking at the red tabs in the margin of each page.

The **"Guide to the Plan of the Book,"** at the very end of the handbook, highlights key elements of the table of contents on pages xv to xxiv and gives an overview of the entire book. Use this guide when you are looking for a specific subject or a discussion that you know is part of a specific chapter. On page xiii is an alphabetical list of topics for quick reference and review.

The **index** presents a detailed alphabetical listing of all subje covered in the book. Because it lists all major topics, subtopi cross references, the index is the most comprehensive guide contents.

The **glossary of usage** offers an alphabetica confused words (*continually/continuously*, for lems in usage (*data/datum*, for instance). Although this section does not eliminate the need to consult a dictionary, it enables you to solve many common problems.

The **glossary of grammatical terms** provides definitions of the grammatical and rhetorical terms that appear throughout *The Holt Handbook* as well as cross references to the sections of the book that contain more detailed discussion of the terms.

When you use *The Holt Handbook*, keep in mind that at best it is a guide, not a final authority. To determine what is appropriate for a specific writing situation you must ultimately rely on your own sense of the language and your own assessment of your purpose and audience. Used with this principle in mind, *The Holt Handbook* should serve you well for the writing that you will do both in college and in your life beyond your years as a student.

Philadelphia   L.G.K.
November 1988   S.R.M.

For Quick Reference and Review

Contents

SECTION IV   Using Words Effectively   271

17   Choosing Words   272

18   Using the Dictionary   303

19   Building a Vocabulary   320

20   Improving Spelling   332

SECTION V   Understanding Grammar   347

21   Identifying the Parts of Speech   348

Contents

SECTION VIII   Writing Special Assignments   661

SECTION I

Composing an Essay

1

Planning an Essay

Writing is a constant process of decision-making, of selecting, deleting, and rearranging material. When *planning* an essay, you consider your audience, your purpose, and the possibilities suggested by the assignment, and you discover materials to write about. When *shaping* your material, you decide how to organize your essay. When *writing and revising,* you write a first draft; then you "re-see" what you have written and, reworking content, organization, and style, take your essay through one or more additional drafts. And, even after you have gone through these stages, you will go on to *edit* and *proofread* your essay.

But these neatly defined stages really do not communicate either the complexity or the flexibility of the writing process. Although we will examine these stages separately, they actually overlap: as you seek ideas you begin to shape your material; as you shape your material you begin to write; as you write a first draft you change your organization; as you revise you continue to discover more material.

During your college years, and in the years that follow, you will develop your own version of the writing process and use it whenever you write, adapting it to your audience, purpose, and writing situation.

1a Thinking About Writing

Writing presents many situations in which you must think critically—make judgments, weigh alternatives, analyze, compare, question, evaluate, and engage in other decision-making activities. Two writing activities that require you to apply these critical skills are deciding on ideas to write about—selecting some ideas, rejecting others, determining what else you need to include—and analyzing where a draft has led and what you can do to make it stronger. Virtually all writing demands that you make informed choices about your subject matter and about the manner in which you present your ideas. The writing process itself is a series of decisions, a constant process of choosing among different options for selecting and arranging material. In this sense it requires that you use your critical faculties at every stage: during planning, shaping, writing, and revising.

Planning your essay—thinking about what you want to say and how you want to say it—begins well before you actually put your thoughts on paper in any organized way. This planning is actually as important a part of the writing process as the writing itself. Two factors—your purpose and your audience—influence your planning and help you make choices as you shape, write, revise, edit, and proofread your material. As you move through the process, you develop a clearer focus on what material to include, how to organize it, and how to express it.

(1)   Determining your purpose

We write for a variety of purposes. One purpose in composing a particular piece of writing might be simply to *express feeling or attitudes*, as in a diary, an autobiography, or a personal letter. Another might be to *persuade*. In this case you would try to convince your audience to agree with certain ideas and, often, to take some action, as in advertisements, proposals, editorials, and sermons. Another purpose might be to *convey information*, as in reports, news articles, textbooks, and encyclopedia entries. Still another could be to *give pleasure*, as in short stories, plays, novels, poems, and so on. You may also have additional, more spe-

---

Purposes for Writing

• to express feelings or attitudes	• to satirize
• to persuade	• to speculate
• to convey information	• to warn
• to give pleasure	• to reassure
• to evaluate	• to amuse
• to discover	• to take a stand
• to analyze	• to identify problems
• to debunk	• to suggest solutions
• to criticize	• to speculate about causes
	• to predict effects

cific aims or a combination of purposes. The preceding chart lists some of the most common purposes for writing.

The material you choose and the way you arrange and express it are determined by your purpose. For instance, a paper on summer camps could *inform*—explain how camping has changed in the last twenty years, for example. Such a paper would present pertinent facts and statistics straightforwardly. An advertisement designed to recruit potential campers would *persuade* by enumerating the benefits of the camping experience. Such an advertisement would stress positive details—the opportunity to meet new friends, for example—and deemphasize the possibilities of homesickness and rainy weather. A letter from a camper to a friend might try to *amuse*, describing all the things that would not appear in the promotional literature—mosquitoes, poison ivy, institutional food, shaving cream fights, and so on. To *evaluate* the camping experience a writer would aim for a balanced discussion of such things as recreational programs and sports facilities. In each case, your purpose determines what material you choose and how you present it.

College writing may call for any of a wide variety of approaches, but your general purpose is usually to convey information. As you do so, you try to demonstrate that you understand your subject and that you can make valid points about it.

☐   **EXERCISE 1**

This brief article presents information in an entertaining manner. How would you change it to convince readers that the federal government is needlessly extravagant in a time of high unemployment and that it should focus on more critical issues? Would you omit any details? Would you rearrange any information? Would you add anything? Explain.

Squirrel Census

The Government put out a call for volunteers last November to help with its newest census: a study of squirrels in Lafayette Park, across the street from the White House.

The National Park Service wanted the volunteers to count the squirrels, observe their habits and take photos.

"They had lots of volunteers and finally settled on 35," reports Duncan Morrow, a spokesman for the park agency. The group has "wrapped up the training phase," he says, and for the next few months will be in the "serious data collection phase."

"They have nice little forms to fill out," Mr. Morrow notes, including one that "calls for them to pick an individual squirrel and follow it for five minutes, recording exactly what it's doing each minute." Another duty is to keep track of squirrel traffic into and out of the 8.2 acre park. It goes without saying that a computer will be used to help analyze the data.

Why is the department doing it?

"What they're focusing on is why there is such a concentration of squirrels there," Mr. Morrow says, adding that there never has been any "really good study" on how city squirrels live.

Some residents suspect the squirrels have become hardcore welfare cases, subsidized not only by kind taxpayers but even the White House.

"There are a number of White House staff people," Mr. Morrow notes, "who show up pretty regularly with stuff they feed the squirrels." *(New York Times)*

(2) Identifying your audience

Writing is often such a solitary activity that it is easy to forget about your audience. But except for diaries, journals, or letters written to let off steam (but not to mail), everything you write addresses an audience—a particular set of readers.

When you write, you may address many different kinds of audiences. As a citizen, consumer, and member of a community or civic, political, or religious group, you may respond to society's most pressing issues by writing letters to a newspaper editor, a public official, a representative of a special interest group, business, or corporation, or another recipient you do not know well or at all. In your personal life you write notes and letters to friends and family and perhaps diary or journal entries to yourself. As an employee, you may write letters, memos, and reports to your superiors, to workers you supervise, or to workers on your level; you may also be called on to address customers or critics, board members or stockholders, funding agencies or the general public. As a student, you write essays, reports, and other papers addressed to one or more instructors and sometimes to other students or outside evaluators.

As you work through the writing process, you shape your paper increasingly in terms of what you believe your audience needs and expects. Your decisions about your readers' interests, educational level, biases, and expectations determine not only what information you include but also what emphasis, arrangement of material, and style or tone you choose.

A student very often writes for an audience of one: the instructor who assigns the paper. But instructors have different interests and expertise, attitudes and beliefs, assumptions and values, concerns and standards. How, then, do you identify your audience? You generalize. When addressing an instructor, you assume he or she represents a class of readers who apply accepted standards of academic writing.

What are these standards? Basically, instructors expect correct information, standard grammar and spelling, logical organization, and some stylistic fluency. Instructors further ask that you define your terms and support your generalizations with specifics. They want to know what you know and whether you can express what you know clearly and accurately. Instructors assign written work to encourage you to use critical thinking skills, so the way you organize and express your ideas can be as important as the ideas themselves.

Of course, each of your instructors is also a unique person with special knowledge and interests. Even though instructors generally have similar overall requirements concerning the quality of your work, many will look for a particular emphasis or approach. Your assessment of these special requirements also influences what and how you write. You can assume that all your instructors are specialists in their fields, so you can safely omit long overviews and basic definitions unless your instructor will need them to see how you have arrived at your ideas. But outside their areas of expertise, most instructors are simply general readers. If you think you may know more about a subject than your instructor does, be sure to provide ample background and definitions, examples, and analogies to make your ideas clear. Considering these factors helps you make the best possible writing choices.

The course for which you are writing will also influence your choices. If you decide to write about the underground mine fires that for years have been burning out of control near your hometown of Centralia, Pennsylvania, you would focus on different aspects of the topic for different courses. For chemistry, you might consider the origins of the fires; for sociology, you could examine what kind of people have left the area and what kind plan to remain; for economics, you could consider how local business and real estate have been affected; for psychology, you could focus on the emotional impact of the spreading fires on the town's children; for political science, you could recommend the role the federal government should take in relocating people or putting out the fires. In each case your subject would be the same, but you would choose the details and points to stress according to your audience's interest in and knowledge of the subject.

Different academic disciplines also use their own formats, documentation styles, methods of collecting and reporting data, systems of formulas and symbols, technical vocabularies, and stylistic conventions. Instructors in different disciplines may therefore have somewhat different expectations.

Audience Checklist

Is your audience
- an individual?
- a member of a group?
- specialized?
- general?

Can you identify your audience's
- needs?
- expectations?
- education?
- biases?
- interests?

Do you need to supply your audience with
- definitions?
- overviews?
- examples?
- analogies?

What special conventions does your audience expect concerning
- format?
- documentation style?
- methods of collecting and reporting data?
- systems of formulas and symbols?
- specialized vocabulary?
- writing style?

☐   **EXERCISE 2**

Different audiences call for differences in the content and emphasis of your writing.

1. Think for a moment about the best—or worst—teacher you ever had. What made this teacher so perfect or so dreadful?
   a. Explore this question in a one-page diary entry written for your eyes only.
   b. In a few paragraphs, tell your composition instructor about this teacher's strengths or weaknesses.
   c. Reread the two pieces of writing. List the most obvious differences in content and emphasis between the two.
2. Be prepared to discuss how you might revise the material you have presented when writing.
   a. A letter to the school board, which is considering whether or not to renew the teacher's contract
   b. A short paper for an introductory education course
   c. Notes for a speech at the teacher's retirement dinner

Setting your tone

ur **tone** is the attitude you adopt as you write. This attitude, or mood, may be serious or frivolous, respectful or condescending, intimate or detached. Your tone, which usually emerges during the planning stage, should remain consistent with your purpose and your audience as you shape, write, and revise your material. It gives your readers clues about your feelings toward your material, and this in turn helps them understand what you have to say.

How you feel about your readers—sympathetic or superior, concerned or indifferent, friendly or critical—is also revealed by your tone. For instance, if you identify with your readers or feel close to them, you use a personal and conversational tone. When you address a generalized, distant reader indirectly or anonymously, you use a more formal, impersonal tone.

When your audience is an instructor and your purpose is to inform, you should strive for an objective tone, neither too personal and informal nor too detached and formal (unless you are told otherwise). This paragraph from a student paper on the resistance to various drugs of a specific group of microorganisms achieves an appropriate tone for its audience (students in a medical technology lab) and purpose (to present information).

> One of the major characteristics of streptococci is that they are gram-positive. This means that after a series of dyes and rinses they take on a violet color. (Gram-negative organisms take on a red color.) Streptococci are also non-spore forming and non-motile. Most strains produce a protective shield called a capsule. They use organic substances instead of oxygen for their metabolism. This process is called fermentation.

This student expresses no personal feelings about her subject, conveys no judgments, and carefully maintains her distance from her audience. This kind of objective tone is appropriate in much college writing.

An English composition assignment asking students to write a short, informal essay expressing their feelings about the worst job they had ever had calls for an entirely different tone. Here is how a student chose to write about his work during cucumber season.

> Every day I followed the same boring, monotonous routine. After clocking in like a good little laborer, I proceeded over to a grey file cabinet, forced open the half-caved-in doors, and removed a staple gun, various packs of size cards, and a blue ballpoint pen. Now here comes the excitement! Each farmer had a specific number assigned to his name. As his cucumbers were

being sorted into their particular size, they were loaded into two-hundred-pound bins which I had to label with a stapled size card with the farmer's number on it. I had to complete a specific size card for every bin containing that size cucumber. Doesn't it sound wonderful? Any second grader could have handled it. And all the time I worked the machinery moaned and rattled and the odor of cucumbers filled the air.

This students's sarcastic tone effectively conveys his attitude toward his job, and his use of the first person encourages audience identification. Ironic comments ("good little laborer," "Now here comes the excitement") further involve the reader.

In a letter applying for another job, however, both his distance from his audience and his purpose (to impress readers with his qualifications) demanded a much more objective and straightforward tone.

My primary duty at Germaine Produce was to label cucumbers as they were sorted into bins. I was responsible for making sure each 200-pound bin bore the name of the farmer who had grown those cucumbers and also for keeping track of the cucumbers' sizes. Accuracy was extremely important in this task.

☐   **EXERCISE 3**

Use the list that follows to write two paragraphs: one informing curious readers of the nature of the Domestic Abuse Project's services and clientele and one convincing a skeptical audience that the project deserves continued funding.

Before you write, consider how these different purposes dictate different organizations. You may add brief remarks as you write, but in each paragraph be sure to use *all* the information provided below and *only* this information. Your choice of language (*not* your choice of content) will help you achieve the desired effect.

The Domestic Abuse Project

Agency's purpose: to aid the victims of mental and physical abuse
Located in small room in Chester Police Department
Offers support groups and advice hotlines
Started when police began receiving excessive number of reports of abuse
Most clients from low-income families
Staff of two professionals and eight volunteers
Funded by State Civil Service Welfare Program
Future plans include new programs (especially counseling) and hiring of more workers

☐   **EXERCISE 4**

Take as your general subject a book that you liked or disliked very much. How would each of the following writing situations affect the content, style, organization, tone, and emphasis of an essay on this book? Write an opening paragraph for each.

A journal entry recording your informal impressions of the book
An examination question that asks you to summarize the book
A book review for a composition class in which you evaluate both the book's strengths and its weaknesses
A letter to your local school board in which you try to convince your readers that, regardless of the book's style or content, it should not be banned from the local public library
An editorial for your school newspaper in which you try to persuade other students that the book is not worth reading

1b   Getting Started

Before you begin any writing task, make sure you understand the exact requirements of your assignment. It is very important that you keep these guidelines in mind as you write and revise. What is the word, paragraph, or page limit? How much time do you have to complete your assignment? Is the assignment to be done in class or at home? Can you make notes or do research? If the assignment requires a specific format, do you know what its conventions are? Do not make any guesses—and do not assume anything. Ask questions and make sure you understand the answers.

Sometimes an assignment allows you to choose your own topic. If so, consider your audience and purpose carefully in light of what you know about the assignment—length, format, and so on. Then choose a topic you know something about or want to learn about. Perhaps a class discussion or assigned reading suggests a topic; maybe you have seen a movie or television special or had a provocative conversation about an interesting subject. If so, you are off to a good start. If not, your instructor may be able to help you develop an unfocused idea into a workable topic.

(1)   Choosing a topic

Though you are sometimes able to choose your topic, your instructor's assignment generally limits your options. Sometimes it asks a specific question for you to answer: "How did the boundaries of Europe change following World War I?" "What are the advantages and disadvantages of the Federal Guaranteed Student Loan Program?'' More often, it specifies a length, format, and particular subject area or list of subjects to choose from.

> Write a two-page critical analysis of a film. (Specifies subject area)
> Write an essay explaining the significance of *one* of these court decisions: *Marbury* v. *Madison, Baker* v. *Carr, Brown* v. *Board of Education, Roe* v. *Wade.* (Gives list of specific subjects to choose from)

Even here you cannot start to write immediately. You must narrow down the assignment to a workable topic that suits your purpose and audience. What examples will you choose? What aspects of the subject will you include? What will you emphasize? How much detail should you go into? Given the assigned time and length, how will you limit your topic?

Look at these typical broad assignments:

Course	Assignment
Public Health	Analyze one effect of AIDS (Acquired Immune Deficiency Syndrome) on the American people.
Sociology	Identify and evaluate one resource available to the homeless population of one major American city.
Freshman Composition	Describe a place that is very important to you.
Psychology	Write a three- to five-page paper assessing one method of treating depression.

How could you hope to cover all AIDS research, all the problems of the homeless, all important places, or all treatments for depression in one short paper? Clearly you must make some choices. You must choose an area that fits within the limits of the assignment while meeting the demands of your audience and suiting your purpose.

Here are some narrower topics that could emerge from the assignments listed above.

- How has the spread of AIDS affected metropolitan-area blood banks?
- The role of the Salvation Army in providing for Chicago's homeless
- Cape May: A town that never changes
- How dogs interact with severely depressed patients

Whatever your assignment, begin by reviewing your options. Consider your assignment, your audience, and your purpose; also consider the things you know best and like best. If your assignment is to write about a place that is important to you, do not write about your dorm room because it is the first thing you think of or about the treasures of the Metropolitan Museum of Art because you think the topic sounds important. But if your dorm room represents your first taste of independence and your essay is about making a new start, it could be an ideal topic. If you know the collections at the Metropolitan well and plan to study art, you may legitimately use this knowledge in a paper about how your career goals developed. Still, do not automatically settle for a routine glance at the Mississippi River when you can describe Catfish Creek vividly.

Consider both what you *can* write about and what you *want* to write about. You may be very much interested in the Yukon but have nothing interesting to say about it; you may know more than you care to admit about McDonald's but not have the faintest desire to write about it. Your goal is to fill both requirements.

When George Panacheril, a freshman composition student who spent the first fourteen years of his life in Zambia, was assigned an essay to write, he had some decisions to make. The assignment was, "Write a short essay about a rite, ritual, or ceremony of a religion or an ethnic or community group with which you are familiar. Be sure your essay has a clearly stated thesis." The class had one week to complete the assignment, and the instructor asked the students not to do library research. The instructor explained that she would be requiring peer criticism, so students knew that their classmates would read and react to their papers. The purpose of the essay was to help readers to understand the ritual and its significance.

George began to think about the assignment right away, and he had no trouble thinking of several possible topics. He first considered rituals he observed and participated in during his years as a secondary school student in the United States. These ceremonies—his first American Thanksgiving and Christmas, for instance—were freshest in his mind, so he thought he would best be able to write about them. But when he began to think more carefully about what to include in an essay on one of these topics, or on a community block party or a religious service, he realized that he was not very interested in such topics. Moreover, he decided that his American audience would be most interested in something less familiar to them—for example, a ritual he had witnessed in Zambia. Once he narrowed his focus to Zambia, he was able to decide on the perfect topic for his essay: the Kuomboka Ceremony, a yearly ritual during which the Lozi people, who live on a floodplain of the Zambezi River, move their village to higher ground for the duration of the rainy season.

☐ **EXERCISE 5**

Read the following excerpt from Ron Kovic's autobiographical *Born on the Fourth of July*. Then list ten possible essay topics about your own childhood suggested by Kovic's memories of his. Each topic should be suitable for a short essay directed to your composition instructor. Your purpose is to give your audience a sense of what some aspect of your childhood was like. Finally, choose the one topic you feel best qualified to write about and explain the reasons for your choice.

When we weren't down at the field or watching the Yankees on TV, we were playing whiffle ball and climbing trees checking out birds' nests, going down to Fly Beach in Mrs. Zimmer's old car that honked the horn every time it turned the corner, diving underwater with our masks, kicking with our rubber frog's feet, then running in and out of our sprinklers when we got home, waiting for our turn in the shower. And during the summer nights we were all over the neighborhood, from Bobby's house to Kenny's, throwing gliders, doing handstands and backflips off fences, riding to the woods at the end of the block on our bikes, making rafts, building tree forts, jumping across the streams with tree branches, walking and balancing along the back fence like Houdini, hopping along the slate path all around the back yard seeing how far we could go on one foot.

And I ran wherever I went. Down to school, to the candy store, to the deli, buying baseball cards and Bazooka bubblegum that had the little fortunes at the bottom of the cartoons.

When the Fourth of July came, there were fireworks going off all over the neighborhood. It was the most exciting time of year for me next to Christmas. Being born on the exact same day as my country I thought was really great. I was so proud. And every Fourth of July, I had a birthday party and all my friends would come over with birthday presents and we'd put on silly hats and blow these horns my dad brought home from the A&P. We'd eat lots of ice cream and watermelon and I'd open up all the presents and blow out the candles on the big red, white, and blue birthday cake and then we'd all sing "Happy Birthday" and "I'm a Yankee Doodle Dandy." At night everyone would pile into Bobby's mother's old car and we'd go down to the drive-in, where we'd watch the fireworks display. Before the movie started, we'd all get out and sit up on the roof of the car with our blankets wrapped around us watching the rockets and Roman candles going up and exploding into fountains of rainbow colors, and later after Mrs. Zimmer dropped me off, I'd lie on my bed feeling a little sad that it all had to end so soon. As I closed my eyes I could still hear strings of firecrackers and cherry bombs going off all over the neighborhood. . . .

The whole block grew up watching television. There was Howdy Doody and Rootie Kazootie, Cisco Kid and Gabby Hayes, Roy Rogers and Dale Evans. The Lone Ranger was on Channel 7. We watched cartoons for hours on Saturdays—Beanie and Cecil, Crusader Rabbit, Woody Woodpecker—and a show with puppets called Kukla, Fran, and Ollie. I sat on the rug in the living room watching Captain Video take off in his spaceship and saw thousands of savages killed by Ramar of the Jungle.

I remember Elvis Presley on the Ed Sullivan Show and my sister Sue going crazy in the living room jumping up and down. He kept twanging this big guitar and wiggling his hips, but for some reason they were mostly showing just the top of him. My mother was sitting on the couch with her hands folded in her lap like she was praying, and my dad was in the other room talking about how the Church had advised us all that Sunday that watching Elvis Presley could lead to sin.

(2)   Finding something to say

Once you have a topic, you can begin to discover ideas for your paper. Ideas seldom spring magically from your pen, so you will usually have to rely on more systematic ways of finding them. One or several of the following strategies should help you in your college writing.

> **Strategies for Finding Something to Say**
>
> - Brainstorming
> - Freewriting
> - Keeping a Journal
> - Reading and Observing
> - Asking Journalistic Questions
> - Asking In-depth Questions

Brainstorming   One of the most useful ways to accumulate ideas is **brainstorming**. This strategy encourages you to recall pieces of information you have stored away and to see connections among the pieces.

Begin by listing all the points you can think of that seem pertinent to your topic. Keeping your topic in mind, write down all the ideas that surface—comments, questions, single words, symbols, or diagrams—as quickly as you can. As the ideas begin to flow, write them down without pausing to consider their relevance or explain their significance. At this stage, crossing out ideas or rearranging them will not be helpful. Your main goal is to let one idea suggest another, so do nothing to slow down your momentum. Only when you finish your brainstorming should you begin to group, sort, and classify the information on your list.

You can also brainstorm with your classmates in small groups that your instructor sets up, or you can enlist some friends to help you work through some ideas. Sometimes you can meet individually with your instructor and brainstorm about your paper. As others suggest ideas, write them down uncritically; you will sort through and evaluate them later. For now, unlock your mind and let your ideas flow freely, and do not be afraid to explore lines of thought that may at first seem unproductive. The unexpected perspectives or sudden shifts of thought that occur when you brainstorm can shed new light on your topic and suggest some interesting and original ideas.

Freewriting If you find that you are having trouble coming up with ideas, you can try **freewriting.** When you freewrite, you fix your mind on your topic and write *nonstop,* as quickly as you can, for a certain period of time—say, five minutes—without worrying about punctuation, spelling, or grammar, or about whether your mind is wandering. The momentum generated by this strategy encourages your mind to make connections and frees ideas that you may not be aware you have. If you run out of things to say about your topic, write about *anything*—the weather, the spot on the wall—until you pick up your subject again. When your time is up, look over what you have written and see if you have anything you can use. Occasionally you have nothing at all, but often you will see new details, a new approach to your topic, or even a new topic. Frequently you will find one good idea that you can use as the center of a new freewriting exercise.

Keeping a Journal Professional writers sometimes keep **journals,** writing in them regularly whether or not they have a specific project in mind. Such a record of your own thoughts and reactions is a storehouse of information when you run short of ideas. Journals, unlike diaries, do more than record personal experiences and reactions. In a journal you explore ideas as well as events and emotions, thinking on paper and drawing conclusions. You might, for example, explore the evolution of your position on a political issue or solve on paper a problem you find difficult to work through in your mind. A journal is an excellent place to record the evolution of your ideas about an assignment. You can also record quotations that mean something special to you or summarize important news events, films, or conversations. A good journal is a scrapbook of ideas that you can leaf through in search of new material and new ways of looking at old material.

Reading and Observing It is unlikely that all the ideas you need for your essay will already be in your mind, just waiting to be set free. For this reason, it is important that you keep your eyes and ears open from the time you receive your assignment until you turn it in. As you read textbooks in various subjects or look through magazines and newspapers, be on the lookout for new ideas that pertain to your topic. Also, make a point of talking with friends or family about your topic.

If your instructor encourages you to do formal research, you can use material from nonprint sources such as films and television programs as well as material from books and articles. Interviews, telephone calls, letters, and questionnaires can be as fruitful as library research. But remember to document ideas that are not your own. (See Section VII for detailed information on doing research.)

For his essay on the Kuomboka Ceremony, George Panacheril made the brainstorming list shown in Figure 1. Looking over his list, George saw that he had plenty of material to work with. He immediately saw some logical and sequential links among the events he planned to describe, and he noticed that his brainstorming had uncovered a few interesting ideas—for instance, the importance of the drums, and music in general, to the ceremony, and the ceremony's blending of old and new elements. Not every item on the brainstorming list would appear in his essay, but the list did include some useful material and suggest some promising directions for further exploration.

George's brainstorming was so productive that he did not feel a need to freewrite. One additional step he did take, though, was to write an entry about his assignment in the journal he kept for his composition class. Here he began to explore the problems he might face as he continued the writing process.

> I know I can write about the Kuomboka. I have a
> good topic, interesting and unusual, I think. I
> remember how things looked, the first time at least,
> but I'm not sure I can describe what I saw to this
> audience. It will be very strange to them. I need to
> really create a scene, with a lot of visual detail,
> and I need to describe what the drums, the chief,
> and the barge look like. Also, how much of my
> feelings should I include?

This brief entry, in combination with others he would add as he continued to plan, write, and revise his essay, would eventually help George to crystallize his ideas about his topic.

Meanwhile, George had to decide what kind of additional information on his topic he might need. He knew that his aunt, a journalist, would be a good source of information because she had taken him to see the Kuomboka Ceremony. He knew that he could ask her about the history of the ceremony, or its significance, but he decided that the paper he was planning would not need such background. Later on, in response to the

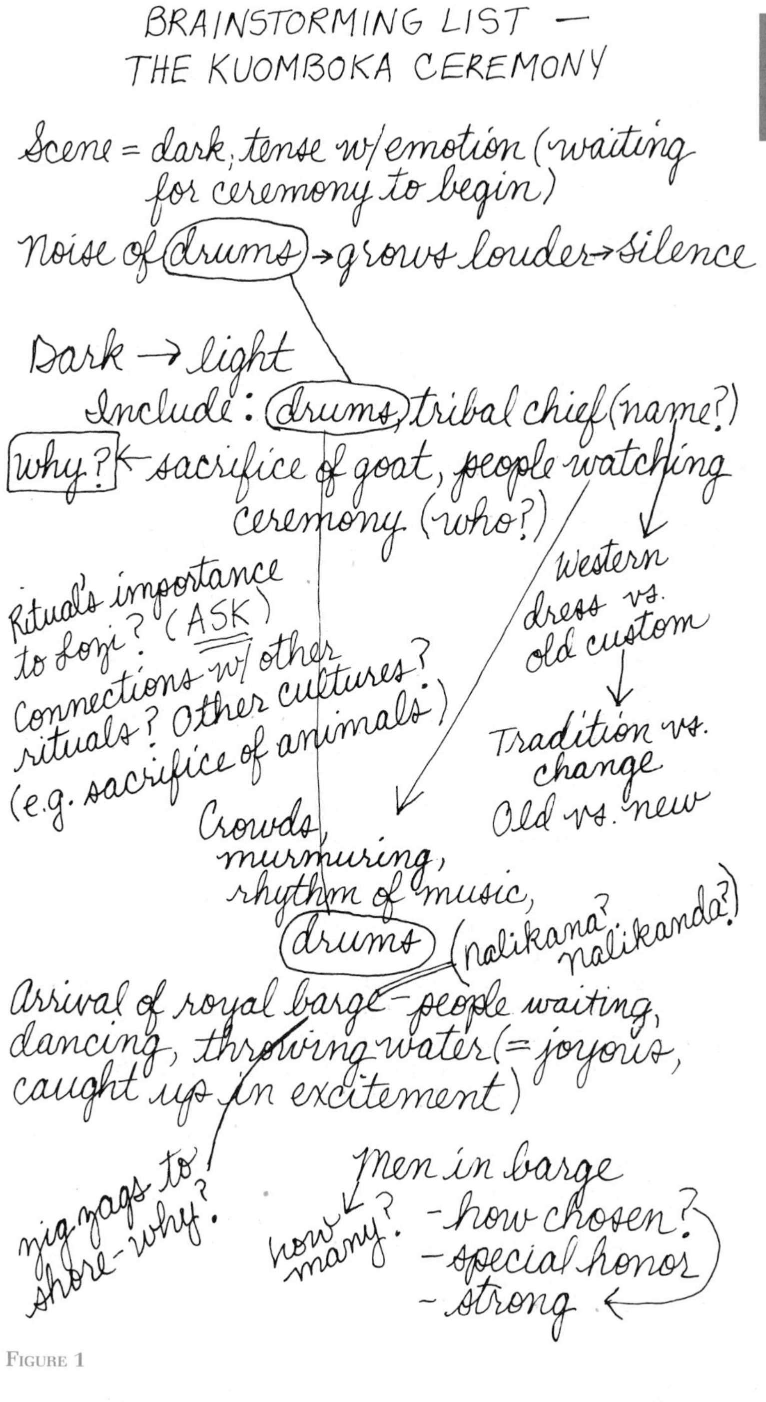

BRAINSTORMING LIST —
THE KUOMBOKA CEREMONY

plan
1b

Scene = dark, tense w/ emotion (waiting
        for ceremony to begin)
Noise of (drums) → grows louder → silence

Dark → light
  Include: (drums), tribal chief (name?)
why? ← sacrifice of goat, people watching
           ceremony. (who?)

Ritual's importance
to Lozi? (ASK)   Western
Connections w/ other   dress vs.
rituals? Other cultures?   old custom
(e.g. sacrifice of animals)
                                        Tradition vs.
                                           change
            Crowds,   Old vs. new
            murmuring,
          rhythm of music,
          (drums) (nalikana? nalikanda?)

Arrival of royal barge – people waiting,
dancing, throwing water (= joyous,
caught up in excitement)

zig-zags to   Men in barge
shore – why?   how   – how chosen?
               many? – special honor
                      – strong ←

FIGURE 1

comments of his peer critics, he would have to return to his aunt to ask her more about the ceremony. For the time being, however, he asked only the two questions that occurred to him as he reviewed his brainstorming list. First, he asked his aunt to spell the words for tribal chief (Litunga) and royal barge (Nalikwanda). Second, he asked her to explain the significance of one element of the ritual that puzzled him: why the barge zigzags as it approaches the shore. When he had her answers, he recorded the information in his journal so that he could refer to it when he wrote his first draft.

☐   **EXERCISE 6**

Make a brainstorming list on the topic you selected in Exercise 5. If you have trouble thinking of material to write about, try freewriting. Then write a journal entry assessing your progress.

☐   **EXERCISE 7**

List all the sources you encounter in one day (people, books, magazines, observations, and so on) that could provide you with relevant information for the essay you are writing.

Asking Journalistic Questions Another way of finding something to say about your topic is to ask questions. Your answers to these questions will enable you to explore your topic in an orderly and systematic fashion. One strategy involves asking six simple questions: *Who? What? Why? Where? When? How?* Journalists often use these questions to assure themselves that they have touched on all angles of a story. You can use them to see whether you have considered all sides of your topic too.

Asking In-Depth Questions If you have time, and if you still need more material, you can explore your topic in greater detail by asking questions that suggest familiar ways of organizing material. These questions can not only give you a great deal of information about your topic but can also help you shape your ideas into paragraphs and whole essays. (As you review these questions, keep in mind that not every question will apply to every topic.)

What happened? When did it happen? Where did it happen?	Suggests narration (account of your first day of school; a summary of Emily Dickinson's life)
What does it look like? What are its characteristics?	Suggests description (of the Louvre; of the electron microscope)

What are some typical cases or examples of it?	Suggests exemplification (three infant day-care settings; four popular fad diets)
How did it happen? What makes it work? How is it made?	Suggests process (how to apply for financial aid; how a bill becomes a law)
Why did it happen? What caused it? What does it cause? What are its effects?	Suggests cause and effect (events leading to the Korean War; the results of Prohibition; the impact of a new math curriculum on slow learners)
How is it like other things? How is it different from other things?	Suggests comparison and contrast (compare the music of the 1950's and the 1960's; compare two paintings)
What are its parts or types? Can they be separated or grouped? Do they fall into a logical order? Can they be categorized?	Suggests division and classification (components of the catalytic converter; kinds of occupational therapy; kinds of dietary supplements)
What is it? How does it resemble other members of its class? How does it differ from other members of its class?	Suggests definition (What is Marxism? What is photosynthesis? What is schizophrenia?)

If the questions that suggest *process* seem most productive, consider organizing your essay as a step-by-step explanation of a procedure; if the questions that suggest *cause and effect* yield the most material, perhaps you should devote your essay to tracing causes or predicting effects. (For a full discussion of patterns of development, see 4f.)

    In a search for additional material to write about, George Panacheril decided to engage in questioning exercises. He began by asking himself the journalistic questions, with the following results.

Who started the Kuomboka tradition? *Who* is most concerned with preserving the tradition? *Who* participates in the ceremony? *Who* witnesses it?
What is the ceremony? *What* does it mean?
Why does it take place? *Why* does it continue to take place?

Where does it take place?
When does it take place? *When* did it begin?
How is the chief chosen? *How* are the rowers chosen? *How* has
    the ceremony changed over the years?

These questions suggested both possible answers and additional questions. They encouraged George to begin thinking about including material about the ceremony's history and meaning and perhaps exploring the idea of how the ceremony had changed over the years.

As he grew more involved with his topic, George kept his purpose, audience, and assignment firmly in mind. He knew that his audience—his instructor and fellow students—would know nothing about the ceremony and that one of his most important goals was to help them visualize it; in addition, his assignment required him to communicate the significance of the ritual to his readers. Now he had to decide on the most effective way to do this.

After he had collected most of his ideas, George thought that a systematic review of the in-depth questions might help him to explore possibilities for shaping his essay. A number of choices were available to him. For instance, he could give *examples* of the ceremony's most interesting features or analyze the *causes* of its endurance or its *effects* on the Lozi people. He could *compare and contrast* the ceremony with other rituals, or he could define the ceremony, trying to explain its unique role in the community. Or, he could combine several of these patterns. A quick review of the in-depth questions showed George that he would best be able to *describe* the ceremony and recount the stages in the *process*. When he asked himself the questions relevant to description and process, he came up with a number of useful responses which he added to his notes.

What does it look like? What are its characteristics?

(suggests   Drums are wood covered with cowhide. Sky is black, then
description)   gray. Chief: white-haired, dressed in black. Barge: men with
                       long wooden poles, thatched cabin for chief.

How did it happen?

(suggests   It has happened the same way every time, for many years.
process)   The repeated process has become a ritual for the Lozi people. This predictable process and other familiar rituals may
                       be what helps them keep their sense of identity.

With all this material, George felt ready to put his notes into a tentative order and start to shape his ideas into an essay.   ▇

☐   **EXERCISE 8**

Using the question strategies described earlier to supplement the work you did in Exercises 6 and 7, compile enough information for a short essay on your topic from Exercise 5.

2

shap
2a

Shaping Your Material

2a Grouping Ideas

When you begin to see the direction your ideas are taking, it is time to sort your notes, to sift through your ideas and choose those you can use to build the most effective essay. One way to do this is to make a **topic tree,** a diagram that enables you to group ideas logically, develop an overview of your topic, and see relationships among ideas.

Begin your topic tree by reviewing all your notes and writing down the three or four basic categories of information that seem most pertinent to your essay. Write these categories across the top of a piece of paper. Then go through your notes again, select points that are related to each category, and write each point under the relevant heading, drawing lines to connect each point to the more general heading above. Continue going through your notes and adding related points, skipping those that seem irrelevant. As you move down the page, you should move from general information to increasingly specific details.

Of course you will add to, delete from, rearrange, and rewrite the points on your topic tree as you review your brainstorming list and other notes. When you finish, you can begin to see how your ideas are related and which are subordinate and which dominant. Seeing these relationships will help you to develop a tentative thesis.

Steps for Making a Topic Tree

- Review notes carefully.
- Identify the three or four general categories of information most pertinent to your emerging essay.
- Copy these points across the top of a piece of paper.
- Review notes again to select points related to each category.
- Copy points under relevant headings, moving from general information to increasingly specific details as you move down the page.
- Draw branches to connect points in each category.

George Panacheril's topic tree, shown in Figure 2, consisted of four divisions that he could treat individually in an essay. When he reviewed his tree, he considered adding an additional category, representing another stage in the ritual: the aftermath of the ceremony. He decided against this addition, however, because it did not seem consistent with his purpose, which was to communicate the significance of the event itself. He decided to limit his essay's scope to the four categories on his topic tree.

Now George felt well on his way toward writing an effective essay. But before he could begin drafting his paper, he needed to bring his ideas into sharper focus: to find a thesis or central idea for his essay.

☐   **EXERCISE 1**

Construct a topic tree from the work you did for Exercises 6, 7, and 8 in Chapter 1.

2b   Developing a Thesis

(1)   Defining an effective thesis

Your **thesis** is the main idea of your essay, the central point your essay supports.

An effective thesis clearly communicates your essay's main idea: it tells your readers not only what your essay's topic is but also how you will approach that topic and what you will say about it. Thus the thesis reflects your essay's purpose, and because your purpose for writing can vary, the nature of your thesis can too. If your aim is to persuade, your thesis will take a strong stand (see 6b.3). If your purpose is to convey information, your thesis can present the specific points you will discuss or give an overview that suggests how the essay will be organized. A labora-

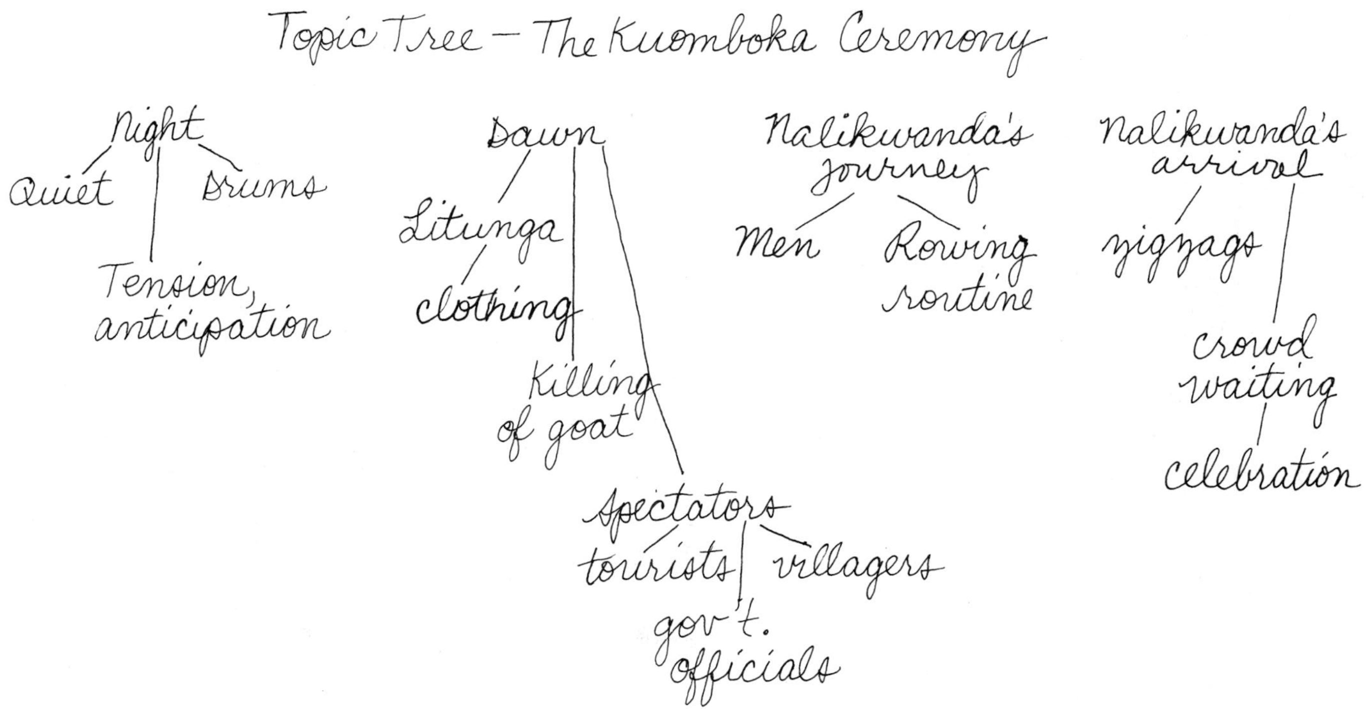

Topic Tree — The Kuomboka Ceremony

night
Quiet / Drums

Tension,
anticipation

dawn

Litunga
/
clothing

Killing
of goat

Nalikwanda's
journey

Men / Rowing
routine

Spectators
tourists / villagers
gov't.
officials

Nalikwanda's
arrival

zigzags
/
crowd
waiting
/
celebration

FIGURE 2

23

tory report, for instance, simply explains a process and does not take a position. To impose an argumentative thesis on such a report could be confusing or distracting. A descriptive or narrative essay may be written to express feelings or convey impressions; its purpose may be simply to describe a scene or recount an experience, not to argue a point about that scene or experience. In such an essay, the thesis might reflect the organizing principle or dominant impression.

Neither a title, a statement of fact, nor an announcement of your subject can take the place of a thesis. Consider the differences among the following statements.

Title	Statement of Fact	Announcement
The Draft	The United States currently has no peacetime draft.	In this essay I will discuss our country's need for a draft.

Thesis   As our statesmen talk again of resisting aggression and demonstrating our will—as they talk, that is, of sending someone's sons (or daughters) to bear arms overseas—the only fair and decent answer to that question lies in a return to the draft. (James Fallows, "The Draft: Why Our Country Needs It")

Title	Statement of Fact	Announcement
Intelligence Tests	Intelligence tests are used extensively in some schools.	The paragraphs that follow will advance the idea that intelligence tests may be inaccurate.

Thesis   My intelligence, then, is not absolute but is a function of the society I live in and of the fact that a small subsection of that society has managed to foist itself on the rest as an arbiter of such matters. (Isaac Asimov, "Intelligence")

Title	Statement of Fact	Announcement
Music Videos	Music videos can enhance record sales.	As I will argue in this paper, music videos are an important part of our culture.

Thesis   The proliferation of music videos threatens to produce an entire generation of people who will all but miss out on the sublime, extremely personal element of music. (Eric Zorn, "Memories Aren't Made of This")

Title	Statement of Fact	Announcement
Math Anxiety	Math anxiety is a problem for many young girls.	My paper will attempt to show why young girls have problems with mathematics.

Thesis   Since ability in mathematics is considered by many to be unfeminine, perhaps fear of success, more than any bodily or mental dysfunction, may interfere with girls' ability to learn math. (Sheila Tobias, "Who's Afraid of Math, and Why?")

Title	Statement of Fact	Announcement
Prize Fighting and the Death of Benny Paret	Prize fighting is an inherently dangerous sport that resulted in the death of Benny Paret.	It is my opinion that prize fighting is a dangerous sport, and I intend to explain here how it caused Benny Paret's death.

Thesis   Put the blame [for Paret's death] where it belongs—on the prevailing mores that regard prize fighting as a perfectly proper enterprise and vehicle of entertainment. (Norman Cousins, "Who Killed Benny Paret?")

In order to communicate your main idea, an effective thesis should be clearly and accurately worded, with careful phrasing that makes your meaning and emphasis apparent to your readers. Often, it is expressed in a single concise sentence. Your thesis should be direct and straightforward, avoiding vague, abstract language and overly complex terminology. Although your thesis cannot enumerate every point your essay will develop, it may list your most important points; in any case, it should be specific enough to give readers a good idea of the essay's scope and direction.

Your thesis should give an accurate overview of your essay, including no unnecessary details that might confuse or mislead readers and making no promises that the essay will not fulfill. If a paper about the benefits of microcomputers will cover only the advantages of particular software programs for preschoolers, do not promise to discuss the benefits for adults—or anything else.

The following thesis statement clearly communicates the writer's main idea and gives readers an accurate sense of the essay to follow.

Several new software programs developed for microcomputers give young children more than just an opportunity for game playing:

such software can enable even preschoolers to improve hand-eye coordination and problem-solving skills.

This thesis not only identifies the main point the essay will support but also suggests how the essay could be organized. The writer could first briefly describe the new software available for microcomputers and then explain how such programs could improve children's hand-eye coordination and problem-solving skills.

Checklist for Identifying an Effective Thesis

- Does your thesis express your essay's main idea?
- Does your thesis suggest the approach you will take toward your material?
- Does your thesis communicate your essay's purpose?
- Is your thesis more than a title, a statement of fact, or an announcement of your subject?
- Is your thesis clearly and concisely worded?
- Does your thesis use specific, concrete language?
- Does your thesis give a realistic indication of your essay's content and emphasis?

---

(2)   Developing a thesis

Occasionally—especially if you know a lot about your topic—you may begin writing with a thesis in mind. Most often, however, your thesis evolves out of the reading, questioning, and grouping of ideas you do early in the writing process. If you have difficulty finding a thesis, try reviewing your notes or brainstorming. Some writers find that doing focused freewriting at this stage helps. By concentrating on a key idea about your topic and then freewriting about it, you can frequently uncover a possible thesis.

The thesis you develop as you plan your essay is only a tentative thesis. It gives you sufficient focus to guide you through your first draft, but you should expect to modify it in subsequent drafts. As you write and rewrite, you often see new connections and change your emphasis several times. It stands to reason, then, that you will constantly change and sharpen your thesis to keep it consistent with your paper's changing goals. Notice how the following pairs of thesis statements changed as the writers moved through successive drafts of their essays.

Tentative Thesis	Revised Thesis
Professional sports can easily be corrupted by organized crime.	Although proponents of legalized gambling argue that organized crime cannot make inroads into professional sports, the way in which underworld figures compromised the 1919 World Series suggests the opposite.
Fast-food restaurants tell us a lot about today's society.	In the next ten years, as the American population grows older, fast-food restaurants are likely to continue declining in popularity.
Laboratory courses provide valuable educational experiences.	By providing students with the actual experience of doing scientific work, laboratory courses encourage precise thinking, careful observation, and creativity.
It is difficult to understand Henry James's short novel *The Turn of the Screw* without examining the personality of the governess.	A careful reading of Henry James's *The Turn of the Screw* suggests that the governess is an unreliable narrator, incapable of distinguishing appearance from reality.

(3)   Stating your thesis

As a beginning writer, you may find it helpful to state your thesis early in your paper. Not only will this placement immediately signal the context of your discussion to your readers, but it will also serve as a constant reminder to you of your essay's direction. Your thesis can appear anywhere in your essay, however, as long as it makes your essay's main idea clear to your readers. Where you state your thesis largely depends on the effect you wish your essay to have on a particular audience. In an argument you may have to lead your readers gradually to your controversial thesis instead of stating it at once. To do otherwise could alienate a segment of your audience. In a research paper, you may have to present several paragraphs of background material before your audience is able to understand your thesis.

Although many of the essays you write in college will include a thesis, not all require it to be explicitly stated. Sometimes your thesis can be *implied* through the arrangement of the points in your essay. Like an explicit thesis, an implied thesis must clearly and specifically convey your essay's main idea to your readers. Professional writers often use this technique, preferring to make their points in a more subtle manner that allows readers to arrive at their own conclusions. For example, in "Letter from Birmingham Jail," Martin Luther King, Jr., prefers to let a chain of reasoning supported by many descriptive examples lead his readers to the implied thesis that people of goodwill should support his demonstrations in Birmingham, Alabama.

As George reviewed his topic tree and notes and analyzed his thoughts, several possible thesis statements came to mind. At first he considered "The Kuomboka Ceremony is extremely important to many people," but he quickly realized that this statement was far too general: it said nothing about why the ceremony was so important. Next he tried "The Kuomboka Ceremony is important both because it is fascinating to watch and because it represents a long-standing tradition to many people." This statement was closer to what he wanted to express, but it was still too vague. What he wanted to communicate, he knew, was the significance of the ritual, but he could not seem to identify what qualities made the ceremony so important. He had gathered plenty of useful information, but now he found himself wondering what the point of all the details was. He tried "If rituals like the Kuomboka Ceremony are allowed to die, the world will lose something vitally important," but he rejected this at once as inappropriately argumentative and impersonal. After considering and rejecting several additional statements, George finally decided on this one.

What is most amazing about the Kuomboka Ceremony is the way it has lasted through the years, maintaining tradition in the face of change.

This thesis statement was specific enough to give George direction, and it was an idea he felt his description of the process could support. Now he could proceed to outline and draft his essay.

☐   EXERCISE 2

Analyze the following statements or topics, and determine why none of them qualifies as an effective thesis. Be prepared to explain your criticisms and to discuss how each could be improved.

1. In the pages that follow, I will examine the use of pesticides in the Great Plains states.
2. The development of the nuclear freeze movement
3. How to apply for a civil service position
4. ROTC: Pro and Con
5. Medicare benefits many senior citizens, but it has some drawbacks.
6. The feminist position on pornography
7. Unemployment is rising steadily in the auto industry.
8. Welfare reform is sorely needed.
9. Benjamin Franklin was a statesman and scientist.
10. Most of my friends like running or skiing, but I prefer tennis.

☐   EXERCISE 3

For three of the following topics, formulate a clearly worded thesis statement.

1. An embarrassing moment
2. The continuing appeal of Elvis Presley
3. How to use the library
4. Is corporal punishment ever justified?
5. The role of women in the military
6. Why the drinking age should be lowered/raised
7. Does vitamin C affect the common cold?
8. The rise of Japanese industry
9. The perfect vacation spot
10. Private vs. public education

☐   EXERCISE 4

Read the following sentences excerpted from the essay "Territoriality and Dominance" by René Dubos. Then develop a thesis that will tie together the information in the sentences. Make sure that your thesis is well constructed and follows the requirements outlined in this chapter.

- Whenever the population density of a group increases beyond a safe limit, many of the low-ranking animals in the social hierarchy are removed from the reproductive pool.
- The remarkable outcome of these automatic mechanisms is that, in the case of many animal species, animal populations in the wild remain on the average much more stable than would be expected from the maximum reproductive potential.
- When males fight, the combat is rarely to the death.
- The losing animal in a struggle saves itself . . . by an act of submission, an act usually recognized and accepted by the winner.
- The view that destructive combat is rare among wild animals . . . is at variance with the "Nature, red in tooth and claw" legend. . . .
- Since ritualization of behavior is widespread among the higher apes, it is surprising that humans differ from them, as well as from most other animals, in practicing warfare extensively with the intent to kill.

☐   EXERCISE 5

Review the topic tree you made in Exercise 1. Use it to help you to develop a thesis for an essay on the topic you chose in Exercise 5 in Chapter 1.

2c   Preparing a Working Plan ————————————

A **working plan** is a blueprint for an essay, an informal outline
that can give you more detailed, specific guidance than a thesis
statement. You need not always prepare such a plan; a short
essay on a topic with which you are familiar may require nothing
beyond a thesis and a mental outline of supporting points. More
often, however, you need additional help. A working plan ar-
ranges your main ideas and supporting points in an informal but
orderly way to guide you as you write.

Preparing a Working Plan ————————————————

- Write down the categories and subcategories from your
  topic tree.
- Arrange the categories and subcategories in the order in
  which you will use them.
- Flesh out the plan with additional material from your
  brainstorming list, journal, or any other notes you may
  have.

Reviewing his notes and topic tree carefully, George selected material he could use and prepared the following working plan.

WORKING PLAN: THE KUOMBOKA CEREMONY

Thesis: What is most amazing about the Kuomboka
Ceremony is the way it has lasted through the years,
maintaining tradition in the face of change.

```
Night (before ceremony)
   Quiet
      —insects
      —animals?
      —low rumble of drums
   Drums get louder
      —like kettle drum
      —wood and cowhide
   Fires start around the camp
Dawn (preparation for ceremony)
   People gather
      —tourists
      —villagers
      —government officials
   Litunga
      —black clothing
      —dignity
```

```
        Killing of goat
Nalikwanda's journey
    Men
        —strong warriors
        —honor
    Cabin for Litunga
    Rowing
        —men in unison, singing
        —boat speeds up
Nalikwanda's arrival
    Waiting crowd
        —dancing
        —drums
    Boat zigzags to shore
    Celebration
```

shap
2d

This working plan guided George as he wrote his first draft.

2d Preparing a Formal Outline

A **formal outline** indicates the order in which you will present your ideas and the relationship of main ideas to supporting details. A formal outline is more polished than a working plan. It is more strictly parallel and more precise, pays more attention to form, and presents points in the exact order in which you plan to present them in your draft. A working plan is not inaccurate or illogical, but it is informal; neither the order of ideas nor their exact relationship is firmly established.

Although many writers prefer not to make a formal outline for a short essay, others find outlines valuable. A formal outline can be useful at any stage of the writing process. Early in the writing process, even when your ideas have not yet fully taken shape, a formal outline can reveal inconsistencies, suggest possibilities for rearrangement, highlight points that need greater emphasis or further development, or identify ideas that are irrelevant and should not be included in your draft. Instructors know how much outlines can reveal, to them as well as to you, and they may assign outlines at this stage so that they can review the completeness and the logic of the paper you are planning. Remember, your outline is only a guide, not an inflexible blueprint for your finished essay. As you write, you will probably discover new ideas and new directions. This is the way writing works, and you should feel free to depart from your outline to explore new territory.

Later in the writing process, after you have written one or more drafts, preparing a more detailed formal outline (or revising an earlier one) can help you to revise your paper's structure (see 3d.1). When you have completed your final draft, your instructor may ask you to submit a formal outline as a guide for your readers. If you decide to prepare an outline early in the writing process and if you are also required to hand in an outline with your finished paper, be sure to revise your outline whenever you revise your essay. The outline and the paper can serve as checks for each other, and you can be certain that your outline reflects the structure and content of your paper.

A formal outline may be a topic outline or a sentence outline. In a **topic outline** each entry consists of a single word or a short phrase; in a **sentence outline** each entry is a complete sentence. Each of these outline forms has advantages and disadvantages. Because it uses complete sentences, a sentence outline is a more fully developed guide for your paper: you have a head start on your paper when you are able to use the sentences of your outline in your draft. This completeness, however, makes the sentence outline more difficult to construct, especially at an early stage of the writing process. A topic outline provides less precise guidance, but it is easier to construct. Many writers prefer to use topic outlines for relatively brief, uncomplicated essays and reserve sentence outlines for long or complex papers. Some writers prefer to make a topic outline at an early stage, use it to guide them through their first draft, and then construct a more thorough, polished topic outline, or even a sentence outline, as they revise the draft. This outline can in turn guide them as they create a new draft. (See 40i for a sample sentence outline.)

(1)   Structure

Formal outlines follow a prescribed structure. The standard outline format uses indentation and a system of Roman numerals, Arabic numerals, and upper-case and lower-case letters to indicate relationships among ideas. Each number or letter is followed by a period. Roman numerals indicate major headings and are placed flush with the left margin of the page. Upper-case letters precede headings of secondary importance and are indented slightly. Arabic numerals, which signal major supporting examples, are indented further. Lower-case letters, indicating specific supporting details, are indented still further. Only the first word of each heading (or a proper noun) is capitalized. No punctuation is placed at the end of any heading in a topic outline, but each entry in a sentence outline ends with a period. This structure tells you at a glance which ideas are of equal importance because all ideas on a given level have the same level of specificity—a heading preceded by an Arabic numeral, for example, is more specific than an entry preceded by an upper-case letter.

Two additional rules apply to the structure of a formal outline. First, each heading should establish a category that is separate and distinct from any other; no categories, and therefore no headings, should overlap. Headings that overlap should be combined. For example, consider this section of a topic outline.

  I. Imported goods
    A. Automobiles
    B. Textiles
    C. Electronics
    D. Stereo components
 II. American-made goods

Because *stereo components* and *electronics* overlap, they should be combined under one heading—electronics—that can describe both.

Second, no heading can contain only one subheading. If heading A has a subheading 1, then it must have a subheading 2; if heading 1 has a subheading a, it must also have a subheading b. After all, you cannot subdivide an entity into one part. If you find a heading with a single subdivision, either delete the subdivision (perhaps revising the larger category to include it) or add another one. (For information on using a computer to help you construct an outline, see Appendix A.)

(2)   Content

A formal outline focuses only on the body of your essay, the section that presents your supporting ideas. The introduction and conclusion are not part of your essay's logical development, and they are often undeveloped or even absent in early drafts. Nevertheless, the outline always includes your essay's thesis statement, placed above the first entry (Roman numeral I). Even if you decide not to state your thesis explicitly in your essay, your outline must include it. You will not be able to check the logic of your ideas or the relationship between thesis and support if your thesis is not part of your outline.

Headings should be as specific and concrete as possible, and they should be descriptive—that is, they should clearly indicate the meaning of the point to be developed in the draft. An outline for a paper about a meaningful ritual would not be very helpful with headings like *Atmosphere, Events,* or *Reactions.* More useful guides are headings that describe the atmosphere, list the events, and identify the reactions.

(3) Style

All headings of the same rank in an outline should be expressed in grammatically parallel terms. Be careful not to mix sentence and topic outline formats in a single outline. In a topic outline you can use either single words or phrases; however, all entries on the same level of the outline must use the same parts of speech—for instance, all nouns or noun phrases.

INCORRECT: I. Importing goods
         A. Importing automobiles
         B. Textiles
         C. Electronics
      II. American-made goods

CORRECT: I. Imported goods
         A. Automobiles
         B. Textiles
         C. Electronics
      II. American-made goods

In a sentence outline, use complete sentences throughout, with all sentences in the same tense. Using parallel phrasing ensures that ideas of equal weight are presented in similar fashion and gives balance and logic to your outline—and to your paper.

If you follow the conventions of outlining carefully, your formal outline can help you to see that you have covered all relevant ideas in an effective order, with appropriate emphasis, within a logical system of subordination. The chart below lists the conventions of outlining.

The Conventions of Outlining

Structure

- Outline format should be followed strictly:

   I. First major division of your paper
      A. First secondary division
      B. Next secondary division
         1. First supporting example
         2. Next supporting example
            a. First specific detail
            b. Next specific detail
   II. Second major division

- Headings should not overlap.
- Each heading should have at least two subheadings.
- Each entry should be introduced by an appropriate letter or number, with the letter or number followed by a period.
- The first word of each entry should be capitalized.

- In a sentence outline, each entry should end with a period.
- In a topic outline, entries should not be followed by end punctuation.

Content

- Outline should include thesis statement.
- Outline should focus only on the body of the essay.
- Headings should be specific and concrete.
- Headings should be descriptive, clearly related to the topic to which they refer.

Style

- Headings should be grammatically parallel.
- Sentence outlines should use complete sentences, with all sentences in the same tense.
- Topic outlines should use words or short phrases, with all headings of the same rank using the same parts of speech.

A formal outline for George's paper follows. At this early stage of the writing process, George thought it best to prepare a topic outline rather than a sentence outline. Notice that all entries are grammatically parallel (all are nouns or noun phrases) and that this outline presents points in the exact order in which George plans to discuss them in the draft.

Thesis: What is most amazing about the Kuomboka Ceremony is the way it has lasted through the years, maintaining tradition in the face of change.

```
    I. Night
        A. Quiet
            1. Insects
            2. Animals
                a. Hyena
                b. Baboon
        B. Drums
            1. Sound
            2. Description
                a. Large
                b. Wood and cowhide
            3. Rhythms
        C. Fires
   II. Dawn
        A. Observers
            1. Tourists
```

```
        2. Villagers
        2. Government officials
     B. Participants
        1. Litunga
           a. Black clothing
           b. Dignified expression
           c. Cane
           d. Fly—whisk
        2. Killer of goat
III. Nalikwanda's journey
     A. Men
        1. Elite
        2. Strong
     B. Cabin
     C. Ritual rowing
        1. Singing
        2. Rowing in unison
     D. Increasing speed
  IV. Nalikwanda's arrival
     A. Waiting crowd
        1. Drums
        2. Dancing
        3. Water play
     B. Zigzag motion of boat
     C. Celebration
```

☐   **EXERCISE 6**

Review your notes and prepare a working plan for a paper on the thesis
you developed in Exercise 5. Then prepare a topic outline.

3

Writing and Revising

3a Using Thesis and Support

With a tentative thesis and a working plan or formal outline to guide you, you are ready to write a first (or rough) draft. Although you will arrive at new insights about your material as you write, this draft will have a focus that freewriting, brainstorming, and other planning strategies do not have.

Most college instructors expect you to support a thesis with specific examples. As you write your rough draft, then, you should be familiar with one of the most common methods of presenting information: **thesis and support.** Knowing this method helps you as you begin to write and simplifies later revision.

A thesis-and-support paper begins with an **introduction.** If you want your audience to see the direction of your essay at the outset—and in many cases you will—include your thesis in your introduction.

In the **body** of a thesis-and-support paper you present the facts, reasons, arguments, or examples that support your thesis.

In the **conclusion** of your thesis-and-support paper you review your major points, sum up your evidence, and perhaps restate your thesis in different words.

Thesis and support is simply a general type of essay structure. How you present your support—how you arrange the reasons, examples, and arguments offered in your body paragraphs—will vary. Your thesis is one tool that helps you visualize the most effective way to structure your essay. It suggests how your points are related, in what order your major points should be introduced, and where you should place your emphasis.

The following thesis statement conveys a good deal of information.

> Widely ridiculed as escape reading, romance novels are becoming increasingly important as a proving ground for many never-before-published writers and, most significantly, as a showcase for strong heroines.

First, this thesis tells you that this essay focuses primarily on what the writer considers to be the two major new roles of the romance novel: providing markets for new writers and (most importantly) presenting strong female characters. To a lesser extent, the role of the romance as escapist fiction may also be treated. The thesis statement even suggests a possible order for the various ideas discussed.

> Introduction: Romance formulas; general settings
> Body: plots and characters; thesis
> • Romance novels as escapist reading
> • Romance novels as an outlet for unpublished writers
> • Romance novels as a showcase for strong heroines
>
> Conclusion: Review of major points; significance of recent developments; restatement of thesis

In an essay written according to this plan, the body paragraphs would provide the evidence necessary to support the thesis.

In the following example the thesis suggests not only the order of the ideas but also a specific pattern of development.

> Romance novels may be extremely popular, but science fiction contributes more to the art of popular fiction.

The phrasing of the thesis clearly indicates that the essay *compares and contrasts* two kinds of popular fiction and concludes something about their relative merits. (For a full discussion of patterns of development, see 4f.)

■ What did George Panacheril's tentative thesis predict about the structure of his essay? Consider it once again.

> What is most amazing about the Kuomboka Ceremony is the way it has lasted through the years, maintaining tradition in the face of change.

This tentative thesis, which emphasizes the continuity of the ritual, gave George a good sense of where his essay was heading. It also suggested an order in which he felt he could present his ideas, proceeding from the first stage of the ceremony to the last. Now he felt ready to write a rough draft. ■

3b   Writing a Rough Draft ————————————

Because the purpose of a rough draft is to get your thoughts down on paper so you can react to them, a rough draft is often messy and full of false starts. Experienced writers know that they will generally rewrite a paper several times. They expect to cross out words and sentences and to produce choppy, disconnected paragraphs. They realize that they will correct these problems when they revise.

As you write your draft, you may discover new questions and new perspectives. These represent departures from the paper you are planning, but they should not present a problem. If new ideas occur to you, follow them through. They may lead you to a better paper than the one you were planning.

In most cases, a rough draft focuses on the body paragraphs of your essay, with only a weak—or even nonexistent—introduction and conclusion. This is as it should be. In fact, students who struggle to write perfect opening and closing paragraphs are usually wasting their time: the effort slows them down, and these paragraphs are likely to change substantially in subsequent drafts. For these reasons, many experienced writers write their introductions and conclusions last.

The following suggestions should make writing rough drafts easier.

Prepare your work area. Once you begin to write, you should not have to stop because you need a sharp pencil, important notes, or anything else. Unscheduled breaks can ruin your concentration.

Fight writer's block. **Writer's block**—an inability to start (or continue) writing—may be caused by fear that you will not write well or that you have nothing to say. If you really do not feel ready to write, taking a short break may give your ideas time to incubate, which in turn may unlock new ideas. If you decide that you really do not have enough material to get you started, return to one of the strategies for finding something to say (1b.2). But remember, the least productive response to writer's block is procrastination.

Get your ideas down on paper as quickly as you can. Do not worry about sentence structure, spelling, or finding exactly the right word. Concentrate on recording your points. Writing quickly helps you uncover new ideas or new connections between ideas.

Take regular breaks as you write. Write one section of your essay at a time. When you have completed a section, take a break.

Your unconscious mind may continue to focus on your assignment while you do other things. When you return to your essay, writing may be easier.

Leave yourself enough time to revise. A single draft does not make an essay. All writing benefits from revision, so be sure you have time to reconsider your work and to write as many drafts as necessary.

Prepare to revise extensively. You will probably be revising much of what you write, and careful preparation of your first draft will make these revisions less painful.

1. Write on every other line. (If you type, triple space). This makes seeing errors easier. It also gives you plenty of room to add new material or to try out new versions of sentences.
2. Develop a system of symbols, each indicating a different type of revision. For instance, you can circle individual words or box longer groups of words (or even entire paragraphs) that you want to relocate. You can use an arrow to indicate the new location, or you can use asterisks or matching numbers or letters to indicate how you want to rearrange ideas. When you want to add words, use a caret like $^{this}_{\wedge}$.
3. Write on only one side of a sheet of paper. This technique enables you to reread your pages side by side. Writing on one side only also allows you to cut and paste without destroying material on the other side of the page. This strategy gives you the flexibility to keep reorganizing the sections or paragraphs of your paper until you find their most effective arrangement.

If you are composing on a computer, revision is easier. You can delete words and sentences or relocate paragraphs just by touching a few keys. But be careful not to discard information that you may need later. (For detailed information on composing and revising on a computer, see Appendix A.)

■   Notice that in this typed version of his first draft, George Panacheril set up four body paragraphs to correspond to the four major headings in his working plan and topic outline.

First Draft: The Kuomboka Ceremony

¹   Of all the rituals I have observed or participated in, the one that I found the most interesting is the Kuomboka Ceremony. It is a truly important, even momentous event. What is most amazing about the Kuomboka Ceremony is the

way it has lasted through the years, maintaining tradition in the face of change.

2   All was still in the inky darkness of the African night, the silence punctuated by the sounds of various insects. Occasionally the inane laugh of the hyena or the screech of a baboon split the night. As I stood motionless, together with hundreds of others, a low throbbing sound filled the air. Soft, almost inaudible at first, the sound gradually increased in intensity as more and more drummers joined in. They were playing big drums which were essentially an African equivilant of the kettle drum. Made from wood, it was covered with stretched cowhide. The rhythms they played were complex, highly intricate patterns which took years of practice to master. It was now midnight and the drums would not stop beating until the chief left the next morning, some seven hours later. This served as a signal and within minutes a number of fires had sprung up around the camp as the whole village came to life. The Kuomboka Ceremony had begun.

3   The sky was a dusky gray as the first rays of soft sunlight heralded the dawn. Slowly people began to gather around the Litunga's hut. There were all kinds of people there, from foreign tourists with their cameras and tape recorders, to villagers dressed in animal skins and dilapidated, cast-off Western clothing. Looking through the crowd I was not surprised to see a few cabinet ministers and other top government officials present. Inside the thatched mud hut the Litunga was being prepared for the journey by the tribal elders. And then, for the first time since they had started, the big drums missed a beat; and then another. Then as they had started they gradually faded off until there was silence. In fact after the many hours of drumming you could almost hear the silence. All eyes turned expectantly toward the door of the chief's hut. As the Litunga stepped out into the

light there was an explosion of smaller drums in a rapid, staccato beat that was very much like a high-speed pneumatic drill. Suddenly all around me people were clapping and dancing in time to the drums. The chief was an elderly man with white hair who walked with the help of a cane. In his left hand he carried a fly-whisk. He was dressed in black robes that hung down to his knees and black trousers and shoes, and carried himself with the dignity due his age and position. As the Litunga walked away from the hut a warrior standing a short distance away raised his knife to kill a goat.

4   As the crowd moved toward the river I caught my first glimpse of the royal barge, "the Nalikwanda." The two sides of the boat were lined with men who were all adjusting their costumes or fidgeting with the long wooden poles they each held. They were an elite group of men in the tribe, a select group of warriors with the power and stamina to row nonstop for ten hours. It was in fact a great privilege because in the many years to come they would be able to boast to their children and grand-children about how they had rowed on the Nalikwanda. In the centre of the boat was a small thatched cabin which was where the Litunga would sit during the journey. Finally after much singing and dancing the chief stepped into the boat and in a flurry of paddles the boat cast off from the bank. Then on a given signal all the poles lifted as one, and plunged into the water in perfect unison as the boat began to move off. They sang as they rowed. One man would sing a line of a song while they all lifted their poles out of the water and then they would all sing the second line as they completed the downward stroke. It was an incredible sight—one hundred or so ten foot poles rising and falling in perfect harmony as the spray flew. The Nalikwanda slowly picked up speed until it was flying along at an

incredible pace. As far as we were concerned this was the
last we would see of the Nalikwanda until it reached the
winter palace where we would be waiting for it. Meanwhile
a whole fleet of smaller boats set out as the Lozi
followed their chief to their new homes.

5   The waiting crowd rushed forward as the boat appeared
on the horizon. As the boat drew closer the drumming grew
more frenzied and people would spontaneously break into
dance. Women would dance down to the water's edge, scoop
up a handful of water and dance back, sprinkling the water
on those around them as a way of showing everyone how
happy they were. As the boat drew closer it suddenly
stopped and started to move backward. Then it moved
forward and again reversed direction. According to
tradition a direct approach to the shore would bring bad
luck, and so the boat zigzagged in this manner for about
half an hour before coming in to dock. In the winter
village the feast had been prepared and the potent local
beer had been brewed. That night the Lozi people
celebrated the successful completion of yet another
Kuomboka Ceremony.

6   This was one of several times I observed the Kuomboka
Ceremony. I still remember how moved I was and how much
it meant to me to witness this age-old ritual.

☐   **EXERCISE 1**

Write a rough draft of the essay you began planning in Chapter 1.

3c   Understanding Revision

Revision makes your writing conform to your goals as defined by
your purpose, audience, and assignment. In your rough draft
you may write for yourself. In your next draft, you begin to shape
your writing for others. Now you "re-see" what you have written
and make the changes necessary to enable your readers to understand and appreciate your ideas. This difference in approach
is basic to revision.

Revision does not simply follow planning, shaping, and writing as the next step in a sequence. Rather, it is a process you engage in from the moment you begin to discover ideas for your essay. As you work you are constantly rethinking your topic or thesis and reconsidering your ideas, their order, and the pattern in which you arrange them. Revision is a creative and individual aspect of the writing process, and everyone does it somewhat differently. You will have to do a lot of experimenting before you find the particular techniques that work best for you.

As you review the drafts of your essay, you may find that you want to revise your thesis, look for new ideas, or reconsider your essay's organization. This shifting back to earlier stages in the writing process is to be expected. Experienced writers do this routinely.

Inexperienced writers sometimes believe they have failed if their first drafts are not perfect, but more experienced writers expect to revise. They also differ from inexperienced writers in *how* they revise. Inexperienced writers tend to concentrate on words, spelling, and grammar. They might do little more than refine word choices, correct grammatical or mechanical errors, or recopy their papers to make them neater. Experienced writers, however, see revision as a series of internal upheavals. They are willing to rethink a thesis and to disassemble and reassemble an entire essay. Only by doing so can they find a voice and a shape for their writing.

Revision reflects not just your private criticism of your first draft but also your response to outside influences—peer reaction, teachers' comments, new observations and experiences. You revise to satisfy yourself, of course, but also to accommodate your readers. Revision, in fact, should bring you closer and closer to your readers.

One of your goals is to write in a readable fashion. All your changes should make what you say clearer and more interesting and keep readers moving forward. Certain strategies help make your ideas more accessible.

Present one idea at a time and summarize regularly. When you overload your paper with more information than readers can take in, you lose them. Readers should not have to backtrack constantly to understand your message.

Fulfill your readers' expectations. Readers expect your paper to do what your thesis says it will do, with major points introduced in an understandable order and appropriate support developed in your body paragraphs. They also expect style, grammar, punctuation, and mechanics to be correct.

Provide clear signals to establish your essay's direction. Repeating key points regularly, constructing clear topic sentences, using transitional words and phrases to link ideas logically, and identifying dominant and subordinate ideas accurately all help provide continuity.

3d   Applying Strategies for Revision

Everyone revises differently, and every writing task demands a slightly different kind of revision. Three specific strategies, however, can help you revise.

(1)   Outlining

Making a formal outline of a draft helps you to check the structure of your paper. (For specific instructions on outlining, see 2d.) An outline reveals at once whether points are irrelevant or poorly placed—or, worse, missing. It also reveals the hierarchy of your ideas—which points are dominant and which subordinate. This strategy is especially helpful early in revision, when you are reworking the larger structural elements of your essay.

(2)   Peer criticism

Instead of trying to imagine your audience, you can address a real audience by asking a friend, classmate, or relative to read your draft and comment on it (with your instructor's permission, of course). The response should tell you whether or not your essay has the effect you intended and perhaps why it succeeds or fails. **Peer criticism** can also be more formal. Your instructor may ask you to exchange essays with other students and may even require you to write evaluations of their work.

In either case, take the analysis of your essay seriously. If your writing fails to communicate your ideas, it hardly matters how sharp your observations are.

Suggested Questions for Peer Criticism
1. What is the main point of the essay? Is the thesis stated? If so, is it clearly worded? If not, how can the wording be improved? Is the thesis stated in an appropriate place?
2. Is the essay arranged logically? Do the body paragraphs appear in an appropriate order?
3. What ideas support the thesis? Does each body paragraph develop one of these ideas?
4. Does each body paragraph have a unifying idea? Do you need topic sentences to summarize the information in the

paragraphs? Are the topic sentences clearly related to the thesis?

5. Is any additional supporting information needed? List any missing points. Is any information irrelevant? If so, indicate possible deletions.

6. Are all the necessary transitions provided? Or would additional links between sentences or paragraphs help? If so, where are such links needed?

7. Does the introductory paragraph attract your attention? Would another kind of introduction work better?

8. Does the conclusion add interest to the essay and reinforce the thesis? Would another kind of conclusion be more appropriate?

9. Is anything unclear or confusing?

10. What is the essay's greatest strength?

11. What is the essay's greatest weakness?

(3) Checklists

Using a **revision checklist**—either one your instructor prepares or one you devise yourself—is a systematic way of examining your writing. A checklist helps you focus on revising one element at a time: the whole essay; paragraphs; individual sentences, phrases, and words; tone and style; or spelling, punctuation, mechanics, and the like. Depending upon the problems you have and the time you have to deal with them, you can survey your paper using all the questions on the checklist or only some of them.

On pages 46–49 is a comprehensive checklist that parallels the normal revision process, moving in four stages from largest to smallest elements and then considering the issues of tone and style. This checklist may be more helpful when you have become familiar with concepts discussed later in the book. For now, you can certainly use the questions listed under "The Whole Essay." You may also know from experience which questions apply to your current writing problems. As your understanding of the writing process increases and you are better able to identify the strengths and weaknesses of your writing, you can narrow the focus of your revision. Perhaps you will even add points to the checklist. You can also use your teachers' comments to tailor this checklist to your own needs.

Revision Checklist

The Whole Essay
Does your essay have an overall organizational pattern? Is it

appropriate to your topic, purpose, and audience? Consider alternative ways of arranging your ideas. (See Chapter 2, 3e.1.)

rev
3d

- Does each body paragraph support your thesis? Revise paragraphs or thesis to make them consistent. (See 2b, 3a, 3e.1.)
- Are your thesis and supporting points easily understood? Make sure they are correctly placed and worded. (See 2b, 3a, 3e.1.)
- Have you drawn explicit connections between your thesis and your supporting information? Make sure your support is clearly related to your thesis. (See 2b, 3a, 3e.1.)
- Did you present your ideas in a logical sequence? Can you think of a different arrangement that might be more appropriate for your purpose? If so, reorder your ideas. (See 2d, 3e.1.)
- Have you discussed everything promised in your thesis? Develop additional points if necessary. (See 2b, 3a, 3e.1.)
- Have you included any irrelevant points? If so, delete. (See 3e.1.)
- Did you present enough information—reasons, examples, arguments—to make your point? Add support if necessary. (See 3a, 3e.1.)
- Do clear transitions between paragraphs allow your readers to follow your essay's structure? If not, add transitions or modify existing ones. (See 4d.5.)
- Have you stressed your key points through judicious use of repetition? Emphasize major concepts as necessary. (See 3c.)
- Did you summarize your progress as you went along? Be sure to take stock of your ideas at regular intervals. (See 3c.)

Paragraphs
- Does each body paragraph have one unifying idea? Delete or relocate extraneous information, and make sure topic sentences identify the unifying idea of each paragraph. (See 4c.1.)
- Are topic sentences clearly recognizable and linked to the thesis? Make a brief outline to check. (See 4c.1.)
- Do your body paragraphs contain enough detail—reasons, facts, examples—to support your ideas? Add more information if necessary. (See 4e.)
- Are your paragraphs constructed according to familiar patterns? Be sure to use patterns your readers will recognize and understand. (See 4f.)
- Are the relationships of sentences within paragraphs clear? If not, add the linking words or phrases your audience needs to follow your ideas. (See 4d.)
- Do your introductory paragraphs arouse reader interest and prepare them for what is to come? Consider other introductory strategies. (See 4g.1.)
- Do your concluding paragraphs sum up your main points? Be sure that they provide a sense of completion. (See 4g.2.)

Sentences
- Are sentences overloaded with too many clauses? Break long, hard-to-follow sentences into simpler, more comprehensible units. (See 10c.)

- Have you used correct sentence structure? Revise to eliminate sentence fragments, comma splices, and fused sentences. (See Chapters 12 and 13.)
- Have you placed modifiers clearly and logically? Make sure each modifier is clearly related to the word or word group it modifies. (See Chapter 14.)
- Have you made potentially confusing shifts in tense, voice, mood, person, or number? Revise to eliminate them. (See 16a–d.) Are your sentences constructed logically? Revise to eliminate mixed constructions and faulty predication. (See 16f–l.)
- Have you strengthened sentences through repetition, balance, and parallelism? Reconsider ways to use these strategies. (See 9c, 9d, 15a.)
- Have you used emphatic word order? Revise sentences to place stress where you want it. (See 9a.)
- Have you used the passive voice appropriately? Eliminate it wherever it may be confusing and wherever the active voice will work more effectively. (See 9e.)
- Have you used sentence structure to signal the relative importance of clauses in a sentence and their logical relationship to one another? Revise sentences when necessary. (See 9b.)
- Can you find nonessential words and needless repetition? Delete empty expressions that may obscure your meaning and distract or annoy your readers. (See 10a, 10b.)
- Have you varied your sentence structure? Experiment with different structures to make your presentation interesting. (See Chapter 11.)
- Have you combined sentences where ideas are closely related? Link sentences to clarify relationships between ideas and to avoid monotony. (See 11b.)

Words

- Have you selected words that accurately reflect your intentions? Consider both the denotations and connotations of your words and make sure you are saying what you want to say. (See 17c.1.)
- Is your level of diction appropriate for your audience and your purpose? If not, revise to make it suitable and consistent. (See 17b.)
- Have you chosen words that are specific, concrete, and unambiguous? Replace any words that are not precise. (See 17c.3, 17c.4.)
- Have you enriched your writing with figurative language? Add figurative language where appropriate. (See 17e.)
- Have you eliminated jargon, neologisms, pretentious diction, clichés, ineffective figures of speech, and offensive language from your writing? Delete all such language from your writing. (See 17d, 17f, 17g.)

Tone and Style

- Is your tone consistent with your purpose? If your purpose is to inform, use a balanced, objective tone. If you are writing to in-fluence your readers, consider ways in which to appeal to their emotions without alienating them. (See 1a.)

* Have you maintained the proper distance from your readers? Reconsider your purpose and audience when assessing this point. (See 1a.)
* Is your style appropriate for your subject, purpose, and audi-ence? Decide whether a formal or informal style is most appro-priate, and make sure to use that style consistently throughout. (See 17a.)

3e Revising Your Drafts

(1) Revising the first draft

Set your rough draft aside for a day, if possible. When you look back over it, you will probably spot problems that need attention. You cannot solve every problem at once, however. You must focus on only a few areas at a time and rework your essay in several drafts. As you review your first draft, focus on your essay's *content, organization,* and *thesis.* Once you have fixed problems in these areas, you can attend to other problems more easily.

As you reread your draft, consider carefully the items in the first section of the revision checklist on pages 46–47. Begin by evaluating your essay's content. Should you discuss additional ideas? Does all the material you included seem relevant?

Next, reconsider your paper's organization. Do you want to reorder your paragraphs or rearrange the information within paragraphs? Does your essay follow your working plan or out-line? Do you need to outline your draft to help you see whether your essay's organization is logical? Do you need to shape your material further to bring it into line with a particular organiza-tional pattern?

Finally, reconsider your paper's thesis. Is it clearly worded? Is it specific? Check to make certain that your body paragraphs support your thesis. If they do not, revise your thesis or your supporting material.

As you review your first draft, you may have the benefit of peer criticism or a conference with your instructor. If you do, consider these readers' comments carefully, focusing for now on their suggestions about content, organization, and thesis.

George Panacheril worked hard to revise his first draft. He decided to begin by reviewing the first section of the revision checklist on pages

46–47. He quickly decided that his essay included all the information that he felt was important and treated no irrelevant points. He also felt his organization was logical enough: it made sense to discuss the ceremony in chronological order, and the process pattern and transitions between stages was so clear that he could tell no stages had been omitted or presented out of order. As a result, he did not think it would be necessary for him to outline his draft.

Reviewing his thesis, George felt satisfied that it was consistent with his purpose and assignment and that it was worded clearly. He also believed that the body paragraphs of his essay, which emphasized the ceremony's tradition, supported his thesis quite well. All in all, he was satisfied with his draft.

However, when George discussed his essay with the three students with whom he exchanged peer criticism exercises, he discovered that he had a lot of work left to do. What the criticism revealed was that although the students who read his paper agreed with George's own assessment of the essay's organization and thesis, they had many concerns about its content. Because the students knew little about his subject, George's paper raised many questions. Among the comments his peer critics had were the following.

> Where is all this taking place?
> Paragraphs are too long, and this makes the story hard to follow.
> What is a Litunga?
> You didn't tell the meaning of the ceremony. We need more background.
> Why is the goat killed?
> Why is the chief carrying a fly-whisk?
> You need more on how things looked to you—the chief, the warriors, the barge, etc.
> I think you should focus more on how you felt at the time—maybe add a paragraph about how this is an emotional event for you as a resident of that country. You seem to be just giving a description of the event instead of expressing your feelings about what you've learned from it.
> I think you expected us to know too much.

After reading and discussing his classmates' critiques of his draft, George decided not to add a separate paragraph about his feelings but rather to inject brief comments about his reactions wherever it seemed to be appropriate. His assignment did not ask him to tell what he had learned from the ritual or how he felt about it, so he thought a full paragraph on either of these subjects would be inconsistent with his purpose. He did decide to add a background paragraph explaining the ritual's significance and to add more description of the scene and its participants. Now George went on to edit his first draft to reflect these decisions.

First Draft: The Kuomboka Ceremony

1   Of all the rituals I have observed

or participated in, the one that I

found the most interesting is the
Kuomboka Ceremony. It is a truly
important, even momentous event. What
is most amazing about the Kuomboka
Ceremony is the way it has lasted
through the years, maintaining
tradition in the face of change.
2   All was still in the inky darkness
of the African night, the silence
punctuated by the sounds of various
insects. Occasionally the inane laugh
of the hyena or the screech of a baboon
split the night. As I stood
motionless, together with hundreds of
others, a low throbbing sound filled
the air. Soft, almost inaudible at
first, the sound gradually increased in
intensity as more and more drummers
joined in. They were playing big drums
which were essentially an African
equivilant of the kettle drum. Made
from wood, it was ^covered with *shaped like a giant gourd and was*
stretched cowhide. The rhythms they
played were complex, highly intricate
patterns which took years of practice
to master. It was now midnight and the
drums would not stop beating until the
chief left the next morning, some seven
hours later. This served as a signal
and within minutes a number of fires
had sprung up around the camp as the
whole village came to life. The
Kuomboka Ceremony had begun.
⟶ add new ¶ from last page
3   The sky was a dusky gray as the
first rays of soft sunlight heralded
the dawn. Slowly people began to

**rev
3e**

gather around the Litunga's hut. There
were all kinds of people there, from
foreign tourists with their cameras and
tape recorders, to villagers dressed in
animal skins and dilapidated, cast-off
Western clothing. Looking through the
crowd I was not surprised to see a few
cabinet ministers and other top
government officials present. Inside
the thatched mud hut the Litunga was
being prepared for the journey by the
tribal elders. And then, for the first
time since they had started, the big
drums missed a beat; and then another.
Then as they had started they gradually
faded off until there was silence. In
fact after the many hours of drumming
you could almost hear the silence. All
eyes turned expectantly toward the door
of the chief's hut. ¶ *new par.* As the Litunga
stepped out into the light there was an
explosion of smaller drums in a rapid,
staccato beat that was very much like a
high-speed pneumatic drill. Suddenly
all around me people were clapping and *The emotionally*
dancing in time to the drums. ∧ The   *charged atmosphere*
chief was an elderly man with white   *affected all of us*
hair who walked with the help of a   *and I could feel*
cane. In his left hand he carried a *the*   *my feet twitching*
                                             to the rhythm.
fly-whisk. ∧ *that is to a Lozi chief what* He was dressed in black   *the sceptre in the*
robes that hung down to his knees and   *crown jewels is to*
                                             a British monarch.
black trousers and shoes, and carried
himself with the dignity due his age

and position. ∧As the Litunga walked *I remember thinking how anachronistic his clothing was in a ceremony of such symbolic importance. It was a measure of how the influence of Western culture had started eroding the age-old customs of these people.*

away from the hut a warrior standing a
short distance away raised his knife to
kill a goat. *At the blade of the panga swept up and down I shivered as I thought about the stories of how in days gone by a man had stood where the goat now lay.*

4   As the crowd moved toward the
river I caught my first glimpse of the
royal barge, "the Nalikwanda." The two
sides of the boat were lined with men
who were all adjusting their costumes
or fidgeting with the long wooden poles
they each held. *They were all clad in different arrangements of animal skins, their meticulously oiled bodies, bare from the waist upward, glistening in the sunlight. Each rower wore a head dress made from the feathers of jacanas, maribou storks, herons, King-fisher, fish-eagles and other birds of the plains.*

It was a long, relatively narrow boat that sat low in the water. It was painted in a zebra-like pattern of vertical black and white stripes.

They were an elite group
of men in the tribe, a select
group of warriors with the power and
stamina to row nonstop for ten hours.
It was in fact a great privilege
because in the many years to come they
would be able to boast to their
children and grand-children about how

they had rowed on the Nalikwanda. In
the centre of the boat was a small
thatched cabin which was where the
Litunga would sit during the journey.

¶ *new par* Finally after much singing and dancing
the chief stepped into the boat and in
a flurry of paddles the boat cast off
from the bank. Then on a given signal
all the poles lifted as one, and
plunged into the water in perfect
unison as the boat began to move off.
They sang as they rowed. One man would
sing a line of a song while they all
lifted their poles out of the water and
then they would all sing the second
line as they completed the downward
stroke. It was an incredible sight—one
hundred or so ten foot poles rising and
falling in perfect harmony as the spray
flew. The Nalikwanda slowly picked up
speed until it was flying along at an
incredible pace. As far as we were
concerned this was the last we would
see of the Nalikwanda until it reached
the winter palace where we would be
waiting for it. Meanwhile a whole
fleet of smaller boats set out as the
Lozi followed their chief to their new
homes.

5   The waiting crowd rushed forward
as the boat appeared on the horizon.
As the boat drew closer the drumming
grew more frenzied and people would
spontaneously break into dance, ∧ Women *which is the Zambian's way of expressing joy.*
would dance down to the water's edge,

scoop up a handful of water and dance
back, sprinkling the water on those
around them as a way of showing
everyone how happy they were. As the
boat drew closer it suddenly stopped
and started to move backward. Then it
moved forward and again reversed
direction. According to tradition a
direct approach to the shore would
bring bad luck, and so the boat
zigzagged in this manner for about half
an hour before coming in to dock. In
the winter village the feast had been
prepared and the potent local beer had
been brewed. That night the Lozi
people celebrated the successful
completion of yet another Kuomboka
Ceremony.

6   This was one of several times I
observed the Kuomboka Ceremony. I
still remember how moved I was and how
much it meant to me to witness this
age—old ritual.

* add after ¶ 2

The Lozi people live on the Basuto Plains in the
Western Province of the Republic of Zambia. This
region which constitutes a section of the floodplain of the Zambezi River is subject to
seasonal flooding and as a result every year
these people have to move their village to
higher ground in the rainy season. The
annual trek from low to high ground is a
ritual that goes as far back as the beginning

rev
3e

of the Lozi. The mass population movement is ceremonially initiated when the tribal chief, the Litunga, travels from his summer palace to his winter palace in a grand ceremony called the "Kuomboka"

☐   **EXERCISE 2**

Consulting 2d, make a formal topic outline of your completed first draft, and use this outline to check the logic of your organization. Then compare the outline with the one you made before you began your first draft. Account for any differences and explain why you departed from your original outline.

☐   **EXERCISE 3**

Revise the large structure—content, organization, and thesis—of your essay, following the guidelines listed on pages 46–49, and write a second draft reflecting your changes.

(2) Revising the second draft

■   Following is George's second draft, recopied from the edited first draft on pages 50–55. It was submitted to his instructor, whose comments appear on the manuscript.

Second Draft: The Kuomboka Ceremony

1   Of all the rituals I have observed
or participated in, the one that I
found the most interesting is the
Kuomboka Ceremony. It is a truly
important, even momentous event. What   *Do you really*
is most amazing about the Kuomboka   *need all this?*
Ceremony is the way it has lasted
through the years, maintaining
tradition in the face of change.
2   All was still in the inky darkness
of the African night, the silence

punctuated by the sounds of various
insects. Occasionally the inane laugh
of the hyena or the screech of a baboon
split the night. As I stood
motionless, together with hundreds of
others, a low throbbing sound filled
the air. Soft, almost inaudible at
first, the sound gradually increased in
intensity as more and more drummers
joined in. They were playing big drums
which were essentially an African
(equivilant) of the kettledrum. Made   *sp*
from wood, it was shaped like a giant
gourd and was covered with stretched
cowhide. The rhythms they played were
complex, highly intricate patterns
which took years of practice to
master. It was now midnight and the
drums would not stop beating until the
chief left the next morning, some seven
hours later. (This) served as a signal   *ref ?*
and within minutes a number of fires
had sprung up around the camp as the
whole village came to life. The
Kuomboka Ceremony had begun.
 3   The Lozi people live on the Basuto
Plains in the Western Province of the
Republic of Zambia. This region which
constitutes a section of the
flood—plain of the Zambezi River is
subject to seasonal flooding and as a   *good — This*
result every year these people have to   *background*
move their village to higher ground in   *really helps*
the rainy season. The annual trek from
low to high ground is a ritual that

goes as far back as the beginning of the Lozi. The mass population movement is ceremonially initiated when the tribal chief, the Litunga, travels from his summer palace to his winter palace in a grand ceremony called the "Kuomboka."

4   The sky was a dusky gray as the first rays of soft sunlight <u>heralded</u>   *cliché* <u>the dawn</u>. Slowly people began to gather around the Litunga's hut. There were all kinds of people there, from foreign tourists with their cameras and tape recorders, to villagers dressed in animal skins and dilapidated, cast-off Western clothing. Looking through the crowd I was not surprised to see a few cabinet ministers and other top government officials present. Inside the thatched mud hut the Litunga was being prepared for the journey by the tribal elders. And then, for the first time since they had started, the big drums missed a beat; and then another. Then as they had started they gradually faded off until there was silence. In fact after the many hours of drumming you could almost hear the silence. All eyes turned expectantly toward the door of the chief's hut.

5   As the Litunga stepped out into the light there was an explosion of smaller drums in a rapid, staccato beat that was very much like a high-speed pneumatic drill. Suddenly all around

me people were clapping and dancing in
time to the drums. The emotionally
charged atmosphere affected all of us
and I could feel my feet twitching to
the rhythm. The chief was an elderly
man with white hair who walked with the
help of a cane. In his left hand he
carried the fly—whisk that is to a Lozi
chief what the (sceptre) in the crown   → *use American*
jewels is to a British monarch. He was   *spelling (scepter)*
dressed in black robes that hung down
to his knees and black trousers and
shoes, and carried himself with the
dignity due his age and position. I
remember thinking how anachronistic his
clothing was in a ceremony of such   *This helps*
symbolic importance. It was a measure   *support*
of how the influence of Western culture   *your thesis*
had started eroding the age—old customs
of these people. As the Litunga walked
away from the hut a warrior standing a
short distance away raised his knife to
kill a goat. As the blade of the panga
swept up and down I shivered as I
thought about the stories of how in
days gone by a man had stood where the
goat now lay.

6   As the crowd moved toward the
river I caught my first glimpse of the
royal barge, "the Nalikwanda." It was
a long, relatively narrow boat that sat
low in the water. It was painted in a   *good*
zebra—like pattern of vertical black   *description*
and white stripes. The two sides of
the boat were lined with men who were

all adjusting their costumes or
fidgeting with the long wooden poles
they each held. They were all clad in
different arrangements of animal skins,
their meticulously oiled bodies, bare
from the waist upward, glistening in
the sunlight. Each rower wore a head   *great detail*
dress made from the feathers of
jacanas, maribou storks, herons,
king-fishers, fish-eagles and other
birds of the Plains. They were an
elite group of men in the tribe, a
select group of warriors with the power
and stamina to row nonstop for ten
hours. It was in fact a great
privilege because in the many years to
come they would be able to boast to
their children and grand-children about
how they had rowed on the Nalikwanda.
In the centre of the boat was a small   *use American*
thatched cabin which was where the   *spelling (center)*
Litunga would sit during the journey.
7   Finally after much singing and
dancing the chief stepped into the boat
and in a flurry of paddles the boat
cast off from the bank. Then on a
given signal all the poles lifted as
one, and plunged into the water in
perfect unison as the boat began to
move off. They sang as they rowed.
One man would sing a line of a song
while they all lifted their poles out
of the water and then they would all
sing the second line as they completed
the downward stroke. It was an

incredible sight—one hundred or so
ten_foot poles rising and falling in

use two unspaced hyphens

perfect harmony as the spray flew. The
Nalikwanda slowly picked up speed until
it was flying along at an incredible
pace. As far as we were concerned this
was the last we would see of the
Nalikwanda until it reached the winter
palace where we would be waiting for
it. Meanwhile a whole fleet of smaller
boats set out as the Lozi followed
their chief to their new homes.

8   The waiting crowd rushed forward
as the boat appeared on the horizon.
As the boat drew closer the drumming
grew more frenzied and people would
spontaneously break into dance, which
is the Zambian's way of expressing
joy. Women would dance down to the
water's edge, scoop up a handful of
water and dance back, sprinkling the
water on those around them as a way of
showing everyone how happy they were.
As the boat drew closer it suddenly
stopped and started to move backward.
Then it moved forward and again
reversed direction. According to
tradition a direct approach to the
shore would bring bad luck, and so the
boat zigzagged in this manner for about
half an hour before coming in to dock.
In the winter village the feast had
been prepared and the potent local beer
had been brewed. That night the Lozi
people celebrated the successful

completion of yet another Kuomboka
Ceremony.

9   This was one of several times I
observed the Kuomboka Ceremony. I
still remember how moved I was and how
much it meant to me to witness this
age-old ritual.

Are you sure this ¶ is necessary?

Very interesting essay. Some things to think about before conference:

— Choice of tense (past, as though relating the experience of your eyewitness rather than present to describe a habitual action) is problematic. Using present throughout might make the essay more immediate.

— Introduction and conclusion seem somehow tacked on.

— You have numerous missing commas, especially in compound sentences and after introductory phrases.

— Essay is wordy at times.

In this draft George had corrected many of his first draft's most obvious shortcomings in content and organization. Now he would be able to move on to consider elements like sentence structure and word choice, tone and style. To guide his revision he would have the benefit of his instructor's written comments on his draft and a full discussion of those comments in a conference. He would also review the balance of the revision checklist.

Although George had added new material, occasionally changing words or phrasing, the style and tone of his second draft remained much the same as those of his first draft. Following the advice of his instructor, George decided to aim for a less wordy style and to carefully review his punctuation. Also, he decided to edit or even perhaps delete his introduction and conclusion and to rewrite his essay in the present tense.

☐   **EXERCISE 4**

Review the second draft of your paper, paying particular attention to topic sentences and transitions and to the way you structure your sen-

tences and select your words. If possible, ask a friend to read your draft
and respond to the peer criticism questions in 3d.2. Then revise your
draft, incorporating any suggestions you find helpful.

**rev
3e**

(3) Preparing the final draft: editing and proofreading

After you have revised your drafts to your satisfaction, one final
step remains: editing and proofreading your paper. When you
edit, you concentrate not on organization, content, or style, but
on surface features: grammar and spelling, punctuation and
mechanics. You will have done some of this work as you revised
previous drafts; what is different now is that your *focus* is on
editing. Approach your work as a critical reader would, reading
each sentence carefully. As you proceed, you may find it helpful
to review the items on the editing checklist that follows. Keep
your preliminary notes, any sources you have used, and reference books (such as this handbook and an up-to-date college
dictionary) nearby as you edit. If you are typing your paper on a
computer, now is the time to run spelling and style checks (see
Appendix A).

  When you have completed your editing, you will type a final
draft. Even when it is complete, however, you are still not finished with your essay. Now you must proofread it, rereading
every word carefully to make sure you did not make any errors as
you typed. You must also ensure that the final typed copy of your
paper conforms to your instructor's requirements. (See Appendix
B for general information on preparing your papers.)

Editing Checklist

Grammar
- Have you used the appropriate case for pronouns (22a–d)?
- Are pronoun references clear and unambiguous (22e–f)?
- Are verb forms correct (23a–b)?
- Are tense, mood, and voice of verbs logical and appropriate (23c–l)?
- Do subjects and verbs agree (24a–h)?
- Do pronouns and antecedents agree (24i–j)?
- Are adjectives and adverbs used correctly (25a–d)?

Punctuation
- Is end punctuation used correctly (26a–c)?
- Are commas used correctly (27a–g)?
- Are semicolons used correctly (28a–f)?
- Is an apostrophe used everywhere one is needed (29a–d)?
- Are quotation marks used where they are required (30a–e)?

- Are quotation marks used correctly with other punctuation marks (30f)?
- Are other punctuation marks—colons, dashes, parentheses, brackets, slashes, and ellipsis marks—used correctly (31a–q)?

Mechanics
- Is capitalization consistent with standard English usage (32a–f)?
- Are italics used correctly (33a–e)?
- Are hyphens used where required and placed correctly within and between words (34a–b)?
- Are abbreviations used where convention calls for their use (35a–d)?
- Are numerals and spelled-out numbers used appropriately (36a–e)?

Spelling
- Are all words spelled correctly? (Check a dictionary if necessary.)

Having revised his second draft, George Panacheril edited his essay, referring to the editing checklist as he corrected grammar, spelling, punctuation, and mechanics. Then he retyped his essay. When he had finished, he proofread his paper carefully, checking to make sure that it was free of typographical errors and that its format conformed to his instructor's requirements. His final draft appears below.

Final Draft: The Kuomboka Ceremony

1   All is still in the inky darkness of the African night, the silence punctuated by the sounds of various insects. Occasionally, the inane laugh of the hyena or the screech of a baboon splits the night. As I stand motionless, huddled together with hundreds of others, a low throbbing sound fills the air. The people who have been talking stop to listen. Almost inaudible at first, the sound gradually increases in intensity as more and more drummers join in. As time goes on and I listen to more and more of the hypnotic throbbing, it begins to feel as though the drumming is within my own body. They are playing big drums, the African equivalent of kettle drums. Made from wood, they are shaped like giant gourds and covered with stretched cowhide. The rhythms the drummers play are complex, highly intricate patterns which

take years of practice to master. It is now midnight and
the drums will not stop beating until the chief leaves the
next morning, about seven hours from now. The drums serve
as a signal, and within minutes fires spring up around the
camp as the whole village comes to life. The Kuomboka
Ceremony has begun.

2   The Lozi people live on the Basuto Plains in the
Western Province of the Republic of Zambia. This region,
which constitutes a section of the flood plain of the
Zambezi River, is subject to seasonal flooding and, as a
result, every year these people have to move their village
to higher ground in the rainy season. The annual trek
from low to high ground is a ritual that goes as far back
as the beginning of the Lozi. The mass population
movement is ceremonially initiated when the tribal chief,
the Litunga, travels from his summer palace to his winter
palace in a grand ceremony called the "Kuomboka." Knowing
that this ceremony has continued for so many years,
maintaining tradition in the face of change, gives me
confidence that the rituals of the Lozi people will
endure.

3   The sky is a dusky gray as the first rays of soft
sunlight appear. Slowly, people begin to gather around
the Litunga's hut. All kinds of people are there, from
foreign tourists with their cameras and tape recorders to
villagers dressed in animal skins and dilapidated cast-off
Western clothing. Looking through the crowd I am not
particularly surprised to see a few cabinet ministers and
other top government officials present, for at the
Kuomboka there are no racial, tribal, or social
distinctions.

4   Inside the thatched mud hut the Litunga is being
prepared by the tribal elders for the journey. Suddenly,
for the first time since they started, the big drums miss
a beat, and then another. Then they gradually fade off

until there is silence. After the many hours of drumming,
you can almost hear the silence. All eyes turn
expectantly toward the door of the chief's hut.

5   As the Litunga steps out into the light, there is an
explosion of smaller drums in a rapid, staccato beat that
is very much like a high-speed pneumatic drill. Now all
around me people are clapping and dancing in time to the
drums. The emotionally charged atmosphere affects all of
us, and I can feel my feet inadvertently moving to the
rhythm. The chief, an elderly man with white hair, has to
walk with the help of a cane. In his left hand he carries
the fly-whisk that is to a Lozi chief what the scepter in
the Crown Jewels is to a British monarch. He is dressed
in black robes that hang down to his knees, and black
trousers and shoes. He stands tall and proud and carries
himself with the dignity due his age and position. It
seems odd that he should wear Western clothes in a ceremony
of such symbolic importance; it is a measure of how the
influence of Western culture has started eroding the
age-old customs of these people. As the Litunga walks
away from the hut, a warrior standing a short distance
away raises his knife to kill a goat. As the blade of the
panga swishes through the air, my body twitches
involuntarily. Originally, by tradition, a man would have
knelt where the butchered goat now lies.

6   As the crowd moves toward the river, I catch my first
glimpse of the royal barge, the Nalikwanda. A long,
relatively narrow boat that sits low in the water, it is
painted in a zebra-like pattern of vertical black and
white stripes. The two sides of the boat are lined with
men who are all adjusting their costumes or fidgeting with
the long wooden poles each one holds. They are all clad
in different arrangements of animal skins, and their
meticulously oiled bodies, bare from the waist up, glisten
in the sunlight. Each rower wears a headdress made from

the feathers of jacanas, maribou storks, herons,
kingfishers, fisheagles, and other birds of the plains.
They are an elite group of tribesmen, a select group of
warriors with the power and stamina to row nonstop for ten
hours. There are smiles on their faces as they dream of
the day when they will be able to boast to their children
and grandchildren about how they rowed on the Nalikwanda.
In the center of the boat is a small thatched cabin, which
is where the Litunga will sit during the journey.

7   Finally, after much singing and dancing, the chief
steps into the boat, and in a flurry of paddles the boat
casts off the bank. Then, on a given signal, all the
poles lift as one and plunge into the water in perfect
unison as the boat begins to move off. The men sing as
they row. One man sings a line of the song while they all
lift their poles out of the water, and then they all sing
the second line as they complete the downward stroke. It
is an awe-inspiring sight--one hundred or so ten-foot
poles rising and falling in perfect harmony. The
Nalikwanda slowly picks up speed until it is flying along
at an incredible pace. The water around the boat turns
white as it smashes its way through the powerful mid-river
currents. This is the last we will see of the Nalikwanda
until it reaches the winter palace where we will be
waiting for it. Meanwhile, a whole fleet of smaller boats
sets out as the Lozi follow their chief to their new
homes.

8   The waiting crowd at the winter palace rushes forward
as the boat appears on the horizon. As the boat draws
closer, the drumming grows more frenzied and people
spontaneously break into dance, which is the Zambian's way
of expressing joy. Women dance down to the water's edge,
scoop up handfuls of water, and dance back, sprinkling the
water on those around them as a way of showing everyone
how happy they are. Their joy is such that at this time

there is no distinction between those of the tribe and the
spectators. As people we all celebrate the success of a
great event and the continuation of a great tradition.

9   As the boat approaches the shore, it suddenly stops
and starts to move backward. Then it moves forward and
again reverses direction. According to tradition a direct
approach to the shore will bring bad luck, and so the boat
zigzags in this manner for about half an hour before
coming in to dock. In the winter village the feast has
been prepared, and the potent local beer has been brewed.
Tonight the Lozi people will celebrate the successful
completion of yet another Kuomboka Ceremony.

☐   EXERCISE 5

What exactly has George changed between his second and third drafts?
List each of these changes and evaluate them as any careful reader
would. Are all his changes for the better? Are any other changes called
for?

☐   EXERCISE 6

Using the revision checklist in 3d.3 as a guide, create a checklist that
reflects the specific concerns you need to consider to revise your essay.
Then revise your essay according to this checklist.

☐   EXERCISE 7

Edit your essay, and then prepare a final draft, making sure to proofread
it carefully.

4

Writing Paragraphs

A **paragraph** is a group of related sentences, complete in itself, which forms a distinct unit of a longer piece of writing. Paragraphs serve three important functions in an essay. First, they group sentences into units of thought that work as a whole to support an essay's main idea. Second, they provide visual breaks in the text that give readers a chance to pause and assimilate each idea. Finally, they signal the movement of ideas in the essay. In most short essays each paragraph presents a specific point contributing to a more general thesis. In longer essays, groups of related paragraphs, called **paragraph clusters,** may present the points. By reinforcing your overall purpose, paragraphs help you control the organization of your paper and convey your ideas clearly to your readers.

4a Determining When to Paragraph

Beginning a new paragraph signals a major shift in emphasis or subject matter. By breaking your text into paragraphs you are able to isolate information and emphasize ideas so that your readers will be able to follow your discussion. In general, you use paragraphs breaks as described in the guidelines on page 70.

69

¶
4b

When to Paragraph

- **To signal a shift in focus** Whenever you move from one major idea to another in your essay, you begin a new paragraph. In general these shifts correspond to the major divisions of your outline.

- **To signal a shift in time or place** In narrative or descriptive sections of an essay, you may begin a new paragraph whenever you want to move your readers from one time or place to another. For example, if you were describing the Metropolitan Museum of Art, you might devote one paragraph to describing the steps leading up to it and then begin a new paragraph to describe the front of the building.

- **To signal a shift in sequence** In enumerating points or tasks, you may change paragraphs every time you begin discussing a new point in a sequence or list or a new stage in a process. These shifts are typically signaled by transitional words and phrases such as *first, second, in the first case,* or *in the second case.*

- **To signal a shift in emphasis** Writers underscore ideas by putting them in separate paragraphs. Sometimes several ideas or examples could be discussed in a single paragraph, but for the sake of clarity and emphasis, each is assigned its own paragraph.

- **To signal a shift in dialogue** When recording dialogue, convention requires that you begin a new paragraph every time a new person speaks (see 30e).

- **To signal introductions and conclusions** Set off your paper's introduction and conclusion. Begin a new paragraph to signal the end of your introduction, and begin your conclusion with a new paragraph.

4b Charting Paragraph Structure

Charting the ideas in a paragraph helps you to recognize its underlying structure. You begin by assigning the sentence that expresses the main or **unifying idea** of the paragraph to level 1. If no sentence in the paragraph expresses the unifying idea, compose a sentence that does. Then, read each sentence of the paragraph. Assign to level 1 sentences as important as the one containing the unifying idea. Indent and assign to level 2 more specific sentences that qualify or limit the unifying idea. Indent again and assign to level 3 any sentences that support level-2 sentences. Do this for every sentence in the paragraph, assigning increasingly higher numbers to more specific sentences. Notice how charting reveals the structure of the following paragraph.

1 My grandmother told me that fifty years ago life was not easy for a girl in rural Italy.
  2 At the age of six a girl was expected to help her mother with household chores.
    3 Girls of this age were no longer permitted to play games or to indulge in childish activities.
  2 At the age of twelve, a girl assumed most of the responsibilities of an adult.
    3 She worked in the fields, prepared meals, carried water, and took care of the younger children.
    3 Education was usually out of the question; it was an unusual family that allowed a girl to enroll in one of the few convent schools that took peasant children.

All the level-2 and 3 sentences in the paragraph explain and expand the unifying idea. They provide the supporting details that strengthen and clarify the topic sentence. The first sentence (level 1) of this paragraph introduces the unifying idea, and each level-2 sentence gives an illustration of that idea. The level-3 sentences support these examples with specifics. Note that in a properly constructed paragraph you will probably have only one level-1 sentence.

By charting the pattern of sentences as you revise your paragraphs, you can make certain your paragraphs are *unified, coherent,* and *well developed.*

☐   **EXERCISE 1**

Chart the underlying structure of the following paragraphs.

Two kinds of movies are characteristic of the 1930's. The first and most popular kind is escapist movies. This category includes big-budget musicals, and to some extent gangster and horror films. *The Wizard of Oz* falls into this category and so do *Frankenstein* and *Dracula.* The second, and certainly less popular, group comprises movies that focus on the Depression. This includes limited-distribution documentaries and a small number of films made by major studios. *Power and the Land* and *The Plow That Broke the Plains* fall into this category.   (Student)

Antipathy to the city goes back a long way. When industrialization drove the European workingman into the major cities of that continent, books and pamphlets appeared attacking the city as a source of crime, corruption, filth, disease, vice, licentiousness, subversion and high prices. The theme of some of the earliest English novels—*Moll Flanders* abounds in it—is that of the innocent country youth coming to the big

¶
4c

city and being subjected to all forms of horror until justice—and a return to the pastoral life—follows.   (John V. Lindsay, *The City*)

Ursula K. LeGuin grew up in a stimulating environment. Her father, Alfred Kroeber, was a distinguished anthropologist, and her mother was a successful author. Her parents' interests included history and biology as well as art and literature. Her father could speak several languages. The family lived in Berkeley during the school year, but every summer they went to the forty acres they owned in the hills of the Napa Valley. For the Kroebers summer was a time for exploring, working, and creating in an environment where a variety of intellectuals gathered.
(Student)

4c Writing Unified Paragraphs

Readers expect a paragraph to focus on a single idea and to develop it. A paragraph without such a unifying idea is confusing and hard to follow.

You can create unified paragraphs in two ways: by using a topic sentence carefully and by making sure that all the sentences in your paragraph support the unifying idea this topic sentence expresses.

(1) Using topic sentences

Your paragraph's unifying idea is easiest to identify when it is stated in a topic sentence, as it is in the following paragraph.

> Bananas, like many other kinds of fruit, are always picked in their green, or unripened, state. This is not, however, for reasons of marketing convenience, as is the case with most other fruits and vegetables. Gourmet hearsay to the contrary, a banana is not at its best when freshly picked from the tree. A tree-ripened banana lacks the melting sweetness and velvety texture for which the store-bought banana is relished. Bananas ripen properly only after picking. They must, moreover, be picked at a certain stage of maturity. There is a period, usually set at about three weeks, during which they must be cut in order to ripen satisfactorily. The distance the banana must travel to market determines the moment of cutting. Bananas consigned to the most distant markets are cut on the earliest possible days, for a day, even a few hours, can be important in their fragile market life. Few fruits (the strawberry, perhaps, and the raspberry) are more sensitive than the banana to the destructiveness of time. (Berton Roueché, *The River World and Other Explorations*)

The writer of this paragraph stays with his purpose. The topic sentence states the unifying idea of the paragraph: that bananas are always picked in their green, or unripened, state. Sentence 2 limits the topic sentence. The rest of the paragraph develops the topic sentence by telling why bananas are picked before they ripen. None of the sentences in this paragraph distracts readers with irrelevant information. The clear relationship of each subsequent sentence to the topic sentence gives the paragraph its unity.

Although many experienced writers do not use topic sentences in all their paragraphs, they do organize each of their paragraphs around a single unifying idea. In some paragraphs the topic sentence is **implied**. However, it makes good sense for you as a beginning writer to use topic sentences because they make your unifying idea clear both to you and to your readers.

Placement of a topic sentence and the decision whether or not to use one vary according to your purpose. A topic sentence at the beginning of a paragraph immediately establishes the focus of the paragraph. A topic sentence in the middle of a paragraph enables you to present background information before you state your topic sentence. A topic sentence at the end of a paragraph draws information together. An implied topic sentence enables readers to infer the point of a paragraph when a direct statement would be awkward or out of place.

Topic Sentence at the Beginning   When you use this option, you begin with a topic sentence and follow with support.

Using a topic sentence at the beginning of each paragraph is effective when you want your readers to grasp your meaning immediately. Beginning with topic sentences also helps you stay focused on your subject and follow a line of thought without trailing off into irrelevant discussions.

In the following paragraph the topic sentence tells readers what the paragraph will be about and keeps the writer focused on her topic.

> A Hindoo temple is a conglomeration of adornment. The lines of the building are completely hidden by the decorations. Sculptured figures and ornaments crowd its surface, stand out from it in thick masses, break it up into a bewildering series of irregular tiers. It is not a unity but a collection, rich, confused. It looks like something not planned but built this way and that as the ornament required. The convictions underlying it can be perceived: each bit of exquisitely wrought detail had a mystical meaning, and the temple's exterior was important only as a means for the artist to ascribe thereon the symbols of truth. It is decoration, not architecture. (Edith Hamilton, *The Greek Way*)

Topic Sentence in the Middle Placing a topic sentence in the middle of a paragraph enables you to build up to a point or give background information before you state your position and then go on to expand your ideas. This strategy is especially effective if you are refuting opposing points of view or presenting unfamiliar or unexpected information. In these situations you have to explain your point to your readers before you can present it or discuss it in any detail. Notice how the topic sentence in the middle of the following paragraph enables the writer to lead his readers gradually toward the paragraph's central point.

> Black servicemen have played a role in the United States military since Revolutionary times. In the years before World War II, however, they were employed chiefly as truck drivers, quartermasters, bakers, and cooks. Then, in July 1941, a program was set up at Alabama's Tuskegee Institute to train black fighter pilots. Eventually, nearly one thousand flyers—about half of whom fought overseas—were trained there; sixty-six of these men were killed in action. Ironically, even as black servicemen were fighting valiantly against fascism in Europe, they continued to experience discrimination in the United States military. Black officers encountered hostility and even violence at officers' clubs. Enlisted men and women were frequently the target of bigoted remarks. Throughout the war, in fact, black servicemen were placed in separate all-black units. This segregation was official army policy until 1948, when President Harry S. Truman signed an executive order to desegregate the military. (Student)

Topic Sentence at the End Using a topic sentence at the end of a paragraph enables you to present controversial issues effectively. Leading off with a controversial statement can alienate an audience. However, if you lead your readers through a logical and carefully thought out argument and *then* present your conclusion, you are more likely to convince them that your conclusion is reasonable.

Notice how Rachel Carson maintains interest by placing her topic sentence at the end of the following paragraph. By doing so, she effectively introduces an idea that not all of her audience would readily accept.

> These sprays, dusts and aerosols are now applied almost universally to farms, gardens, forests, and homes—nonselective chemicals that have the power to kill every insect, the "good" and the "bad," to still the song of birds and the leaping of fish in the streams, to coat the leaves with a deadly film, and to linger on in soil—all this though the intended target may be only a few weeds or insects. Can anyone believe it is possible to lay down such a

barrage of poisons on the surface without making it unfit for life? They should not be called "insecticides," but "biocides." ("The Obligation to Endure," *Silent Spring*)

Topic Sentence Implied   At times you will want to avoid a direct statement of your unifying idea. In some situations—especially narrative or descriptive paragraphs—a topic sentence can seem forced or artificial. In the following paragraph Alice Walker wants readers to share her experience. To accomplish this goal, she implies her paragraph's unifying idea: that because she was a girl, she was considered inferior.

I am eight years old and a tomboy. I have a cowboy hat, cowboy boots, checkered shirt and pants, all red. My playmates are my brothers, two and four years older than I. Their colors are black and green, the only difference in the way we are dressed. On Saturday nights we all go to the picture show, even my mother; Westerns are her favorite kind of movie. Back home, "on the ranch," we pretend we are Tom Mix, Hopalong Cassidy, Lash LaRue (we've even named one of our dogs Lash LaRue); we chase each other for hours rustling cattle, being outlaws, delivering damsels from distress. Then my parents decide to buy my brothers guns. These are not "real" guns. They shoot "BBs," copper pellets my brothers say will kill birds. Because I am a girl, I do not get a gun. Instantly I am relegated to the position of Indian. Now there appears a great distance between us. They shoot and shoot at everything with their new guns. I try to keep up with my bow and arrows. ("Beauty: When the Other Dancer Is the Self," *In Search of Our Mothers' Gardens*)

(2)   Supporting the unifying idea

Each sentence in a paragraph should support its unifying idea. When you revise your paragraphs, look carefully for sentences that do not do so. You can bring your paragraph into focus by rewriting these sentences or, in some cases, by deleting them. The following paragraph contains sentences that wander from the subject.

One of the first problems that freshmen have is learning to use a microcomputer. All freshmen were required to buy a computer before school started. Throughout the first semester we took a special course to teach us to use a computer. The Apple Macintosh has a large memory and can do word processing and spreadsheets. It has an eighty-character screen and a disk drive. My parents were happy that I had a computer, but they were concerned about the price. Tuition was high, and when they added in the price of the computer, it was almost out of reach. To

offset expenses, I arranged for a part-time job in the school library. Now I am determined to overcome my "computer anxiety"
and to master my Apple Macintosh by the end of the semester.
(Student)

The opening statement that freshmen have problems learning to
use a microcomputer seems to be the topic sentence, so readers
expect the rest of the paragraph to develop this idea. The next
two sentences seem to do so. But sentence 4 shifts to a description of the Apple Macintosh, and this digression continues in
sentence 5. Sentence 6 introduces a new subject—the parents'
problem of paying tuition, an idea further developed in sentences 7 and 8. Sentence 9 returns to the idea introduced in
sentence 1, but by this time the subject has shifted so often that
readers cannot be sure what the paragraph is about.

This lack of unity becomes obvious when you chart the
paragraph.

1 One of the first problems that freshmen have is learning to
use a microcomputer.
  2 All freshmen were required to buy a computer before
  school started.
    3 Throughout the first semester we took a special course
    to teach us to use a computer.
1 The Apple Macintosh has a large memory and can do word
processing and spreadsheets.
  2 It has an eighty-character screen and a disk drive.
1 My parents were happy that I had a computer, but they
were concerned about the price.
  2 Tuition was high, and when they added in the price of
  the computer, it was almost out of reach.
    3 To offset expenses, I arranged for a part-time job in the
    school library.
1 Now I am determined to overcome my "computer anxiety"
and to master my Apple Macintosh by the end of the semester.

Since each level-1 sentence represents a topic that should be
developed in its own paragraph, this paragraph has not one but
four topics. Instead of writing one unified paragraph, the writer
simply made a series of false starts.

To unify this paragraph around the subject of learning to
use his computer, the writer decided to take out the sentences
about his parents' financial situation and the computer's characteristics, keeping only those details related to the unifying idea.
Here is his revision.

One of the first problems I had as a freshman was learning to use my computer. All freshmen were required to buy a computer before school started. Throughout the first semester, we took a special course to teach us to use the computer. In theory this system sounded fine, but in my case it was a disaster. In the first place, the closest I had ever come to a computer was the hand-held calculator I used in math class. In the second place, I could not type. And to make matters worse, many of the people in my computer orientation course already knew how to operate a computer. By the end of the first week I was convinced that I would never be able to work with my Apple Macintosh.

☐   **EXERCISE 2**

Each of the following paragraphs is unified by a central idea, but that idea is not explicitly stated. Identify the unifying idea of each paragraph, write a topic sentence that expresses it, and decide where in the paragraph to place it.

A. For one thing the cost of paper has gone up dramatically. The shortage of wood and increased labor costs have contributed to this increase. Another problem is the high cost of upgrading equipment. The expense of complex computer-assisted systems has put many publishers on the brink of bankruptcy. Finally, publishers work on very small profit margins. With competition from nonprint sources most publishers feel that they cannot set prices of books at a level that makes them profitable. As one publisher observes, "People are just not ready for the thirty-five-dollar best-seller."

B. The Department of Transportation has done a lot to clarify federal regulations. The DOT is concerned with safety and realized the need for clear and coherent regulations. The Coast Guard has also tried to recodify and rewrite regulations. Although not as successful as the DOT, it has made inroads, considering the task. The largest agency to attempt to clarify its regulations using plain English was the Social Security Administration. Because their regulations have a great impact on the public, their task was especially important. The SSA program was carried out by in-house editors who were told to cut out the government gobbledygook.

C. Spray the hinges with a silicone lubricating compound or a light oil. You can buy these products in any hardware store. Be sure the spray soaks into the hinges, and work the door back and forth as you spray. If this does not stop the squeak, you will have to remove the hinges and clean them of rust and dirt. You can do this by soaking them in oil for several hours and then scouring them with fine steel wool.

D. The sun came up early. Both of us got up, washed, and walked to the stream. We fished for several hours and then returned to camp to cook our catch. After breakfast we swam and then hiked through the woods that began about a hundred yards from our camp. That evening we drank beer and ate the cheese we had brought from home.

We went to bed early and slept until it was time to leave for home the next morning.

4d Writing Coherent Paragraphs

A paragraph is unified if all its sentences are related to a single idea. A paragraph is **coherent** if all its sentences are logically related to one another.

You can use a number of strategies to achieve coherence in your paragraphs. You can signal relationships with pronoun reference, parallelism, repeated key words, and transitional words and phrases.

(1) Using pronouns

Because **pronouns** refer to nouns or other pronouns, they establish connections among sentences. Clear, well-placed pronoun references can lead readers through a paragraph. Unclear pronoun references, like those in the paragraph that follows, can make a writer's ideas difficult to follow.

> Like Martin Luther, John Calvin wanted to return [1] to principles of early Christianity described in the New Testament. Martin Luther founded the evangelical [2] churches in Germany and Scandinavia, and he founded a number of reformed churches in other countries. A [3]
> *Inexact pronoun reference* third Protestant branch, episcopacy, developed in England. They rejected the word *Protestant* because they [4] agreed with Roman Catholicism on most points. They [5] rejected the primacy of the Pope. They accepted the [6] Bible as the only source of revealed truth, and they held that faith, not good works, defined a person's relationship to God. (Student)

Unclear pronoun references make the paragraph confusing. Does *he* in sentence 2 refer to Luther or Calvin? Does *they* in sentence 4 refer to Luther and Calvin or to the three Protestant branches?

In this revised version, clear pronoun references draw ideas together and establish coherence.

[1] Like Martin Luther, John Calvin wanted to return to the principles of early Christianity described in the New Testament.
[2] Martin Luther founded the evangelical churches in Germany and Scandinavia, and John Calvin founded a number of reformed
[3] churches in other countries. A third Protestant branch, episcopacy,
[4] developed in England. Its members rejected the word *Protestant*

5 because they agreed with Roman Catholicism on most points. All
6 these sects rejected the primacy of the Pope. They accepted the
Bible as the only source of revealed truth, and they held that faith,
not good works, defined a person's relationship to God. (Student)

The writer has replaced *he* in sentence 2 with *John Calvin* and
changed *they* in sentence 4 to *its members*, to which the sentence's second *they* now clearly refers. By adding the phrase *all
these sects*, the writer makes clear that *they* in sentence 6 refers
to sects, not the episcopacy. Correct pronoun usage has pulled
the paragraph together.

(2)   Using parallel structure

Parallelism—the repeated use of similar grammatical structures—
can help to establish coherence (see 15a). Consider the following
paragraph.

*Without
parallel
structure*

> Thomas Jefferson was born in 1743 and died at Mon-
> ticello, Virginia, on July 4, 1826. During his eighty-four years
> he accomplished a number of things. Although best known
> for his draft of the Declaration of Independence, Jefferson
> was a delegate to the Continental Congress. Not only was
> Jefferson a patriot, he was also a profound thinker. During
> the Revolution he drafted the Statute for Religious Freedom.
> He drafted an ordinance for governing the West, and he for-
> mulated the first decimal monetary system. After being
> elected president, he abolished internal taxes, reduced the
> national debt, and made the Louisiana Purchase. Jefferson
> also designed Monticello and the University of Virginia.
> (Student)

This paragraph is unified and fairly coherent. It presents information straightforwardly if not memorably. The following revision shows how parallelism can strengthen paragraph coherence.

> Thomas Jefferson was born in 1743 and died at Monticello,
> Virginia, on July 4, 1826. During his eighty-four years he accom-
> plished a number of things. Although best known for his draft of
> the Declaration of Independence, Jefferson was a man of many
> talents who had a wide intellectual range. He was a patriot who
> was one of the revolutionary founders of the United States. He
> was a reformer who, when he was governor of Virginia, drafted
> the Statute for Religious Freedom. He was an innovator who
> drafted an ordinance for governing the West and devised the first
> decimal monetary system. He was a president who abolished in-
> ternal taxes, reduced the national debt, and made the Louisiana
> Purchase. And finally he was an architect who designed Monti-
> cello and the University of Virginia.

Now the same basic sentence structure introduces each of Jefferson's accomplishments: *He was a patriot who . . . ; He was an innovator who . . . ; He was a president who . . . ; And finally he was an architect who. . . .* This presentation in parallel form helps the reader comprehend the material and at the same time adds emphasis (see 9c).

(3) Repeating key words

Repeating **key words** or phrases—those essential to the meaning—throughout a paragraph aids coherence by reminding readers how the sentences relate to one another and to the paragraph's unifying idea.

You should not repeat words and phrases monotonously—a well-written paragraph must have variety. But you have to balance this need to vary your vocabulary against your audience's need to understand what you have written. Whenever your readers may be in danger of losing sight of your topic, you can repeat a key word relating to the topic. In the following paragraph, the absence of repeated key words or phrases that point to the paragraph's subject makes the discussion difficult to follow.

Without repeated key words or phrases

Mercury poisoning is a problem that has long ¹ been recognized. "Mad as a hatter" refers to the condi- ² tion prevalent among nineteenth-century workers who manufactured felt hats. Workers in many other indus- ³ tries, such as mining, chemicals, and dentistry, were also affected. In the 1950's and 1960's there were cases ⁴ of poisoning in Minamata, Japan. Research showed that ⁵ there were high levels of pollution in streams and lakes surrounding the village. In the United States in 1969 a ⁶ New Mexico family got sick from eating tainted food. Since then certain pesticides have been withdrawn from ⁷ the market, and chemical wastes can no longer be dumped into the ocean. (Student)

This paragraph demands a lot from readers. Sentence 1 introduces mercury poisoning as the topic of the paragraph, but sentences 2 through 7 never mention it. Readers must decide for themselves how the examples relate to the topic sentence. The following revision shows how repetition of key words can help readers focus on the subject.

¹   Mercury poisoning is a problem that has long been recog-
²   nized. "Mad as a hatter" refers to the condition prevalent among
    nineteenth-century workers who were exposed to mercury during
³   the manufacturing of felt hats. Workers in many other industries,
    such as mining, chemicals, and dentistry, were similarly affected.

4 In the 1950's and 1960's there were cases of mercury poisoning in
5 Minamata, Japan. Research showed that there were high levels of
6 mercury pollution in streams and lakes surrounding the village. In
   the United States this problem came to light in 1969 when a New
   Mexico family got sick from eating food tainted with mercury.
7 Since then pesticides containing mercury have been withdrawn
   from the market, and chemical wastes can no longer be dumped
   into the ocean.

The words *mercury* and *mercury poisoning* throughout the paragraph now remind readers of the subject. Notice that to avoid monotony the writer sometimes refers indirectly to this subject with phrases such as *similarly affected* (sentence 3) and *this problem came to light* (sentence 6).

(4)   Using transitional words and phrases

Transitional words and phrases—*but, similarly, also, on the other hand, moreover, in contrast, the same as, therefore, however,* and so on—aid coherence by indicating the relationships among sentences. By establishing these connections, transitional words and phrases tie together ideas in a paragraph. The following paragraph shows how the omission of transitional words and phrases can make a passage difficult to understand.

Without transitional words and phrases

Napoleon certainly made a change for the worse by leaving his small kingdom of Elba. He went back to Paris, and he abdicated for a second time. He fled to Rochfort in hope of escaping to America. He gave himself up to the English captain of the ship *Bellerophon.* He suggested that the Prince Regent should grant him asylum, and he was refused. All he saw of England was the Devon coast and Plymouth Sound as he passed on to the remote island of St. Helena. He died on May 5, 1821, at the age of fifty-two.

Although the unifying idea of this paragraph is clearly stated, the exact chronological relationships among events is not. With no transitional words or phrases, the paragraph reads like a list of unconnected events. In the following revision, words and phrases like *after, finally, once again,* and *in the end* provide the links that clarify the chronological order of the events in the passage.

Napoleon certainly made a change for the worse by leaving his small kingdom of Elba. After Waterloo, he went back to Paris, and he abdicated for a second time. A hundred days after his return from Elba, he fled to Rochfort in hope of escaping to America. Finally, he gave himself up to the English captain of the ship

Transitional Expressions

Transitions That Signal Sequence or Addition

and	besides
again	finally
also	furthermore
too	in addition
moreover	one . . . another
next	first . . . second . . . third
last	still

Transitions That Signal Time

at first, second (etc.)	afterward
soon	at length
earlier	at the same time
before	now
after	as soon as
finally	meanwhile
then	in the meantime
later	until
next	immediately
during	eventually
subsequently	

Transitions That Signal Comparison

similarly	in comparison
likewise	also
by the same token	

Transitions That Signal Contrast

however	nevertheless
but	instead
yet	even though
still	on the one hand . . . on the other hand
nonetheless	in contrast
on the contrary	although
despite	meanwhile

Transitions That Signal Examples

for example	thus
for instance	namely
to illustrate	specifically
the following example . . .	

Transitions That Signal Narrowing of Focus

after all	specifically
in fact	that is
indeed	in other words
in particular	

Transitions That Signal Conclusions or Summaries

in summary	consequently
in conclusion	in other words
to conclude	thus
therefore	as a result

Transitions That Signal Concession

although it is true that . . .	admittedly
granted	certainly
naturally	
although you could say that . . .	
of course	

Transitions That Signal Causes or Effects

because	consequently
hence	then
since	thus
therefore	as a result
so	accordingly

Bellerophon. Once again, he suggested that the Prince Regent grant him asylum, and once again, he was refused. In the end, all he saw of England was the Devon coast and Plymouth Sound as he passed on to the remote island of St. Helena. After six years of exile, he died on May 5, 1821, at the age of fifty-two. (Norman Mackenzie, *The Escape from Elba*)

(5)   Achieving coherence among paragraphs

The same methods you use to establish coherence within paragraphs—pronoun reference, parallelism, repeated key words, and transitional words and phrases—may also be used to link paragraphs. The following paragraph cluster shows how some of these strategies work.

A language may borrow a word directly or indirectly. A direct borrowing means that the borrowed item is a native word in the language it is borrowed from. The native Middle French word *festa* (Modern French *fête;* the Old French was *feste* from Latin *festa*) was directly borrowed by Middle English, and has become Modern English *feast.* On the other hand, the word *algebra* was borrowed from Spanish, which in turn was borrowed from Arabic. English borrowed *algebra* indirectly from Arabic, with Spanish as an intermediary.

Some languages are heavy borrowers. Albanian has borrowed so heavily that few native words are retained. On the other hand, many American Indian languages have borrowed but lightly from their neighbors.

English has borrowed extensively. Of the 20,000 or so words in common use, about three-fifths are borrowed. However, the figure is misleading. Of the 500 most frequently used words, only two-sevenths are borrowed, and since these "common" words are used over and over again in sentences, the actual frequency of appearance of native words is much higher than the statistics on borrowing would lead one to believe. "Little" words such as *and, be, have, it, of, the, to, will, you, on, that,* and *is* are all native to English, and constitute about one-fourth of the words regularly used. Thus it is not unreasonable to suppose that more than four-fifths of the words commonly used in speaking English are native to the language. (Victoria Fromkin and Robert Rodman, *An Introduction to Language,* 3d ed.)

These three paragraphs form a tightly knit unit, and the topic sentences reinforce the structure. Each establishes coherence by including a variation of the phrase *A language may borrow.* In addition, some form of the key words *language* and *borrow* appears in almost every sentence.

☐ **EXERCISE 3**

A. Read the following paragraph and determine how the author achieves coherence. Identify parallel elements, pronouns, repeated words, and transitional words and phrases that link sentences.

Some years ago the old elevated railway in Philadelphia was torn down and replaced by the subway system. This ancient El with its barnlike stations containing nut-vending machines and scattered food scraps had, for generations, been the favorite feeding ground of flocks of pigeons, generally one flock to a station along the route of the El. Hundreds of pigeons were dependent upon the system. They flapped in and out of its stanchions and steel work or gathered in watchful little audiences about the feet of anyone who rattled the peanut-vending machines. They even watched people who jingled change in their hands, and prospected for food under the feet of the crowds who gathered between trains. Probably very few among the waiting people who tossed a crumb to an eager pigeon realized that this El was like a food-bearing river, and that the life which haunted its banks was dependent upon the running of the trains with their human freight. (Loren Eiseley, *The Night Country*)

B. Supplying the missing transitional words and phrases, revise the following paragraph to make it coherent.

> The theory of continental drift was first put forward by Alfred Wegener in 1912. The continents fit together like a gigantic jigsaw puzzle. The opposing Atlantic coasts, especially South America and Africa, seem to have been attached. He believed that at one time, probably 225 million years ago, there was one supercontinent. This continent broke into parts that drifted into their present positions. The theory stirred controversy during the 1920's and eventually was ridiculed by the scientific community. In 1954 the theory was revived. The theory of continental drift is accepted as a reasonable geologic explanation of the continental system.

4e   Writing Well-Developed Paragraphs ⸺

A paragraph is **well developed** when it contains the support—examples, statistics, opinions, and so on—readers need to understand the unifying idea. Without adequate development a paragraph gives readers only a partial picture.

Unfortunately, no rule exists to determine *adequate*. The amount of support you need in a paragraph depends on your purpose, your audience, and the scope of your unifying idea. Just as charting structure can help you see whether a paragraph is unified, it can also help you determine if it is well developed.

The following paragraph is not adequately developed.

> From Thanksgiving until Christmas, children are saturated with ads for violent toys. Advertisers persist in thinking that only toys that appeal to children's aggressiveness will sell. Far from improving the situation, video games have escalated the arms race. The real question is why toy manufacturers continue to pour millions of dollars into violent toys, especially in light of the success of toys that promote learning and cooperation. (Student)

Looking at the underlying structure of the paragraph above, we are able to see where the problem lies.

1 From Thanksgiving until Christmas, children are saturated with ads for violent toys.
   2 Advertisers persist in thinking that only toys that appeal to children's aggressiveness will sell.
   2 Far from improving the situation, video games have escalated the arms race.

¶/dev
4f

2 The real question is why toy manufacturers continue to pour millions of dollars into violent toys, especially in light of the success of toys that promote learning and cooperation.

The level-1 sentence of this paragraph is the topic sentence. The level-2 sentences expand the discussion, but the paragraph offers no level-3 examples. What kinds of toys appeal to a child's aggressive tendencies? Exactly what video games does the writer object to? In the following revision, the writer adds specific examples that convincingly support his topic sentence.

From Thanksgiving until Christmas, children are saturated with ads for violent toys. Advertisers persist in thinking that only toys that appeal to children's aggressiveness will sell. One television commercial praises the merits of an Eagle Force commando team that attacks and captures a miniature enemy base. Toy soldiers wear realistic uniforms and carry automatic rifles, pistols, knives, grenades, and ammunition. Another commercial shows laughing children shooting one another with plastic rocket fighters and tanklike "walkers." Far from improving the situation, video games have escalated the arms race. The most popular video games involve children in realistic combat situations. One game, Star Raiders, lets children search out and destroy enemy rocket fighters in outer space. Other best-selling games simulate attacks on enemy fortresses or fight off an array of hostile creatures. The real question is why toy manufacturers continue to pour millions of dollars into violent toys, especially in light of the success of toys that promote learning and cooperation.

4f Using Patterns of Development

The pattern of a paragraph, like the pattern of an entire essay, reflects the way the writer thinks. These patterns, like the in-depth questions discussed in 1b.2, may be used to develop a topic. Most of the time writers do not consciously decide in advance on a particular pattern of development and then write their paragraphs accordingly. Only in revision do they see the patterns their thoughts fall into. When you see the direction a paragraph is taking, you can revise the topic sentence and rearrange information to support the unifying idea more effectively.

Of course, some paragraphs, like some essays, have more than one pattern of development. As a beginning writer, however, you should practice each pattern separately. After you have developed good paragraph skills, you can combine strategies to express your ideas.

(1)   What happened? (Narration)

¶/dev
4f

Narrative paragraphs tell a story. They do not, however, have to follow strict chronological order. Sometimes a narrative can begin in the middle of a story or even at the end and then move back to the beginning. Careful use of transitions that signal sequence and time (see 4d.4) keep the chronology clear.

In the following paragraph the topic sentence introduces the narrative. The sequence of events is signaled by expressions like *By midterms, By the end of the semester,* and *At the beginning of my second semester.*

> My academic career almost ended as soon as it began. Three weeks after I arrived at college, I decided to pledge a fraternity. By midterms I was wearing a straw hat and saying "Yes sir" to every fraternity brother I met. I ate lunch at the fraternity house, and when classes were over I ran errands for the fraternity members. After dinner I socialized and worked on projects with the other people in my pledge class. In between these activities I tried to study. Somehow I managed to write papers, take tests, and attend lectures. By the end of the semester, though, my grades had slipped and I was exhausted. It was then that I began to ask myself some important questions. Why was I putting myself through this? Why did I want to join a fraternity? I realized that I wanted to be popular, but not at the expense of my grades and my future career. At the beginning of my second semester I dropped out of the fraternity and volunteered to work in the biology lab. Looking back, I realize that it was then that I actually began to grow up. (Student)

Not every narrative paragraph has—or needs—a topic sentence. For instance, the following narrative paragraph by an eighteenth-century naturalist is unified not by a topic sentence but by the orderly sequence of events.

> About midnight, having fallen asleep, I was awakened and greatly surprised at finding the most of my companions up in arms, and furiously engaged with a large alligator but a few yards from me. One of our company, it seems, awoke in the night, and perceived the monster within a few paces of the camp; when giving the alarm to the rest, they readily came to his assistance, for it was a rare piece of sport. Some took fire-brands and cast them at his head, whilst others formed javelins of saplings, pointed and hardened with fire; these they thrust down his throat . . . which caused the monster to roar and bellow hideously; but his strength and fury were so great, that he easily wrenched or twisted them out of their hands, and wielding and brandishing them about, kept his enemies at a distance for a time. Some were for putting an end to his life and sufferings with a rifle ball, but the majority

thought this would too soon deprive them of the diversion and pleasure of exercising their various inventions of torture: they at length grew tired, and agreed in one opinion, that he had suffered sufficiently; and put an end to his existence. (William Bartram, *Travels of William Bartram*)

(2)   What does it look like? (Description)

To **describe** something you must first see it, and to see it you must first look at it part by part. You then present your perception of these separate parts in such a way that they form a pattern for your audience. The most natural arrangement of details reflects the way you actually look at a scene or object: near to far, top to bottom, side to side, or front to back. The arrangement of details is made clear by transitions that identify the spatial relationships. Although many descriptive paragraphs do not have topic sentences, they must be unified by a dominant impression to which all the details contribute.

The following descriptive paragraph begins with a distant view of the Great Beach on Cape Cod and then moves closer. This organization makes it easy for readers to see the details, and the paragraph is unified by the writer's sense of the sand bar's mystery.

The sand bar of Eastham is the sea wall of the inlet. Its crest overhangs the beach, and from the high, wind-trampled rim, a long slope well overgrown with dune grass descends to the meadows on the west. Seen from the tower at Nauset, the land has an air of geological simplicity; as a matter of fact, it is full of hollows, blind passages and amphitheatres in which the roaring of the sea changes into the far roar of a cataract. I often wander into these curious pits. On their floors of sand, on their slopes, I find patterns made of the feet of visiting birds. Here, in a little disturbed and claw-marked space of sand, a flock of larks has alighted; here one of the birds has wandered off by himself; here are the deeper tracks of hungry crows; here the webbed impressions of a gull. There is always something poetic and mysterious to me about these tracks in the pits of the dunes; they begin at nowhere, sometimes with the faint impression of an alighting wing, and vanish as suddenly into the trackless nowhere of the sky. (Henry Breston, *The Outmost House*)

(3)   What are some typical cases or examples of it? (Exemplification)

One of the basic ways we explain something or prove a point is with **examples,** specific illustrations that clarify a general statement. Carefully chosen examples often can be much more convincing than pages of analysis. In the following paragraph a series of well-chosen examples support the topic sentence, with the movement from one example to the next clearly signaled by the transitions *In addition* and *finally.*

> From an engineering standpoint alcohol could supplement oil as a fuel source. Alcohol could easily be substituted for diesel fuel if engineers implemented simple engine modifications and made ignition timing and fuel tank capacity changes. In addition, alcohol could be diluted with as much as thirty percent water and still burn in a home furnace. A farmer could use animal and plant waste to make enough fuel for his own consumption or could use the dried distiller's grain as a feed supplement. Finally, studies have shown that industrial consumers of fuel oil could, with little or no trouble, adapt their furnaces to use alcohol. (Student)

In the following paragraph a single extended example gives readers enough detail to help them accept the author's point about hormone secretion and aggressiveness.

> The influence of aggressiveness and dominance on hormones and sex reaches its peak in the case of small tropical fish called "cleaners," which feed off parasites that they remove from the skin of other fish. One species, studied on the Australian Great Barrier Reef, lives in groups of one male with a harem of three to six females; the male dominates the females and the larger, older females dominate the smaller, younger ones. If the male dies or is removed from the group, the largest of the females almost immediately begins to act like a male, carrying out typical male aggressive displays toward the other females. And within a couple of weeks *she actually turns into a male,* producing sperm instead of eggs! I am not suggesting, of course, that anything of the sort could occur in primates or other mammals; for one thing, most or all cleaner-fish females possess rudimentary testes, as mammalian females do not. Nonetheless, I find rather mind-blowing the fact that a female can change into a male simply by acting like one. (Robert Claiborne, *God or Beast*)

(4) How did—or does—it happen? (Process)

Process paragraphs describe how something works, presenting a series of steps in strict chronological order. The topic sentence (when there is one) identifies the process, and the rest of the paragraph itemizes the steps involved. Throughout the paragraph, transitional terms like *first, next, then,* and *finally* signal the organizational pattern and hold the paragraph together. Here, for example, is an explanation of the process by which members of the Supreme Court decide whether or not to grant an appeal.

> Members of the court have disclosed, however, the general way the conference is conducted. It begins at ten A.M. and usually runs on until late afternoon. At the start each justice, when he enters the room, shakes hands with all others there (thirty-six handshakes altogether). The custom, dating back generations, is evidently designed to begin the meeting at a friendly level, no matter how heated the intellectual differences may be. The conference takes up, first, the applications for review—a few appeals, many more petitions for certiorari. Those on the Appellate Docket, the regular paid cases, are considered first, then the pauper's applications on the Miscellaneous Docket. (If any of these are granted, they are then transferred to the Appellate Docket.) After this the justices consider, and vote on, all the cases argued during the preceding Monday through Thursday. These are tentative votes, which may be and quite often are changed as the opinion is written and the problem thought through more deeply. There may be further discussion at later conferences before the opinion is handed down. (Anthony Lewis, *Gideon's Trumpet*)

Sometimes a process paragraph *instructs;* in this case its purpose is to enable readers to actually perform the process. Instructions are written in the present tense and, like commands, in the imperative mood: "Remove the cover . . . and check the valve." This directness of both tense and mood helps readers follow the directions more easily. The following paragraph presents a set of instructions.

> If you have a photograph that hasn't been framed or mounted, sooner or later it will ripple or curl up at the corners. But you *can* treat the malady. Put the picture in a pan of room-temperature water. Take the photograph out after a few minutes. Shake the water droplets off it, then gently insert it in a folded paper towel. Put this flat packet on your ironing board. Cover the picture-side with more clean, white paper toweling. *Note:* Do not use a decorated towel! If you do, you'll transfer the design to your photograph. Set your *dry* iron on a low temperature, then iron across the towel. Now take the towel off. Lo and behold! A flat, ready-to-frame photograph! (Marcia D. Liles and Robert M. Liles, *Good Housekeeping Guide to Fixing Things Around the House*)

(5)   What caused it? What are its effects? (Cause and effect)

Like narrative and process, **cause and effect** is concerned with events in time. But instead of focusing on the order in which events occur, cause-and-effect paragraphs explore why they occur and what happens because of them. Cause-and-effect relationships are often complicated, so you must take care to use topic sentences and transitional words and phrases *(one cause, another cause, a more important result, because, as a result)* to help mark these relationships.

Often a paragraph focuses on either causes or effects. In the following paragraph the writer suggests a *cause* of thumb-sucking and then summarizes a study to support his assertion.

> The main reason that a young baby sucks his thumb seems to be that he hasn't had enough sucking at the breast or bottle to satisfy his sucking needs. Dr. David Levy pointed out that babies who are fed every 3 hours don't suck their thumbs as much as babies fed every 4 hours, and that babies who have cut down on nursing time from 20 minutes to 10 minutes . . . are more likely to suck their thumbs than babies who still have to work for 20 minutes. Dr. Levy fed a litter of puppies with a medicine dropper so that they had no chance to suck during their feedings. They acted just the same as babies who don't get enough chance to suck at feeding time. They sucked their own and each other's paws and skin so hard that the fur came off. (Benjamin Spock, *Baby and Child Care*)

In the next paragraph a student identifies the *effects* of Saturday cartoon-watching on her younger brother. She begins by identifying the effects she will examine and then gives her examples and draws her conclusions.

> Although I have not carried out a scientific study, I have noticed the effects of television violence on my younger brother. Every Saturday he goes on a four-hour television cartoon binge. His diet includes *Rambo, G.I. Joe, Ghostbusters, Dungeons and Dragons,* and occasionally *The Smurfs.* (He sneaks this one because he thinks he is too old for it.) As my brother watches the cartoons, he gets more and more excited. He runs and jumps around the room and has mock battles with furniture and imaginary enemies. Later, after he has finished watching, he and his friends act out things they have seen in the cartoons. Their games always involve fighting, shooting, stabbing, and killing. Even though some people might say that this aggressive behavior is normal for a nine-year-old boy, I feel that television cartoons cause his play to be excessively violent. (Student)

(6)   How is it like other things? How is it different? (Comparison and contrast)

Comparison-and-contrast paragraphs examine the similarities and differences between two subjects. Comparison emphasizes similarities, while contrast deals with differences. When using this pattern of development, be sure that the subjects you compare have elements in common and that you compare the same or similar qualities of both. Do not forget to use transitional words and phrases (*similarly, likewise, however, but, on the contrary, nevertheless*) to signal comparison or contrast and to indicate movement from one subject to another.

Comparison and contrast can be organized in one of two ways. First, you can compare and contrast the subjects point by point. This organization is especially useful in a complex paragraph in which your readers may have trouble keeping track of your points. To compare and contrast two automobiles, for example, your paragraph pattern looks like this.

Mileage
    Automobile A
    Automobile B

Safety
    Automobile A
    Automobile B

Warranty
    Automobile A
    Automobile B

A second way to organize a comparison-and-contrast paragraph is to treat one subject in its entirety in the beginning of your paragraph and the other subject in its entirety at the end. This organization works well when you feel certain that your readers can remember what you have said about the first subject while they read about the second. The pattern looks like this.

Automobile A
    Mileage
    Safety
    Warranty

Automobile B
    Mileage
    Safety
    Warranty

The following paragraph uses point-by-point comparison. Notice how the author handles his complex subjects as he compares them.

> There are two Americas. One is the America of Lincoln and Adlai Stevenson; the other is the America of Teddy Roosevelt and the modern superpatriots. One is generous and humane, the other narrowly egotistical; one is self-critical, the other self-righteous; one is sensible, the other romantic; one is good-humored, the other solemn; one is inquiring, the other pontificating; one is moderate, the other filled with passionate intensity; one is judicious and the other arrogant in the use of great power. (J. William Fulbright, *The Arrogance of Power*)

By repeating *one* and *the other* the writer sets up a parallel structure. Not only does this technique aid coherence, it also emphasizes the ideas the writer wants to convey.

In the next paragraph the writer treats all of one subject before going on to the next. He signals the shift from one subject to the other with the transitional word *now*.

> This seems to be an era of gratuitous inventions and negative improvements. Consider the beer can. It was beautiful—as beautiful as the clothespin, as inevitable as the wine bottle, as dignified and reassuring as the fire hydrant. A tranquil cylinder of delightfully resonant metal, it could be opened in an instant, requiring only the application of a handy gadget freely dispensed by every grocer. Who can forget the small, symmetrical thrill of those two triangular punctures, the dainty *pffff*, the little crest of suds that foamed eagerly in the exultation of release? Now we are given, instead, a top beetling with an ugly, shmoo-shaped "tab," which, after fiercely resisting the tugging, bleeding fingers of the thirsty man, threatens his lips with a dangerous and hideous hole. However, we have discovered a way to thwart Progress, usually so unthwartable. *Turn the beer can upside down and open the bottom.* The bottom is still the way the top used to be. True, this operation gives the beer an unsettling jolt, and the sight of a consistently inverted beer can might make people edgy, not to say queasy. But the latter difficulty could be eliminated if manufacturers would design cans that looked the same whichever end was up, like playing cards. What we need is Progress with an escape hatch. (John Updike, *Assorted Prose*)

(7) What are its parts? (Division) Into what categories can its parts be arranged? (Classification)

In **division,** you take a single item and break it into its components. You could, for instance, divide blood into its various parts: plasma, white cells, red cells, and so on. In **classification,** you take many separate items and group them into categories according to qualities or characteristics they have in common. You could, for instance, group books according to subject, author, or size.

In the following paragraph from a laboratory manual, a student *divides* blood into several components.

> The blood can be divided into four distinct components: plasma, red cells, white cells, and platelets. Plasma is 90 percent water and holds a great number of substances in suspension. It contains proteins, sugars, fat, and inorganic salts. Plasma also contains urea and other by-products from the breaking down of proteins, hormones, enzymes, and dissolved gasses. In addition, plasma contains the red blood cells that give it color, the white cells, and the platelets. The red cells are most numerous; they get oxygen from the lungs and release it in the tissues. The less numerous white cells are part of the body's defense against invading organisms. The platelets, which occur in almost the same number as white cells, are responsible for clotting. (Student)

The opening sentence identifies the subject the paragraph will analyze. Subsequent sentences identify the components of blood, moving from the most frequently to the least frequently found elements.

The paragraph below establishes the subject, scientific frauds, and then goes on to *classify* frauds into three categories.

> Charles Babbage, an English mathematician, reflecting in 1830 on what he saw as the decline of science at the time, distinguished among three major kinds of scientific fraud. He called the first "forging," by which he meant complete fabrication—the recording of observations that were never made. The second category he called "trimming"; this consists of manipulating the data to make them look better, or, as Babbage wrote, "in clipping off little bits here and there from those observations which differ most in *excess* from the mean and in sticking them on to those which are too small." His third category was data selection, which he called "cooking"—the choosing of those data that fitted the researcher's hypothesis and the discarding of those that did not. To this day, the serious discussion of scientific fraud has not improved on Babbage's typology. (Morton Hunt, *New York Times Magazine*)

Whether you classify or divide, your groups should be mutually exclusive; that is, items in one category should not also fit in another category.

(8) What is it? (Definition)

A **formal definition** includes the term you are defining, the class to which it belongs, and its attributes—the details that distinguish it from other members of its class.

Carbon is a nonmetallic element.
(term)   *(class to which it belongs)*
occurring as diamond, graphite, and charcoal.
                          (distinguishing details)

A puck is a rubber disk
(term)   *(class to which it belongs)*
used in ice hockey.
(distinguishing details)

An **extended definition**, which builds on this format, can be a paragraph or more in length. Such discussions may develop the definition with other patterns. You can define *happiness*, for instance, by telling a story (narration). You can define a diesel engine by telling how it works (process). Extended definitions may also include the background or origins of a term. Finally, you can define terms by telling what they are like (using synonyms) or what they are not (using negation).

The following paragraph develops an extended definition by exemplification. It begins with a straightforward definition of *gadget* and then cites an example.

A gadget is nearly always novel in design or concept and it often has no proper name. For example, the semaphore which signals the arrival of the mail in our rural mailbox certainly has no proper name. It is a contrivance consisting of a piece of shingle. Call it what you like, it saves us frequent frustrating trips to the mailbox in winter when you have to dress up and wade through snow to get there. That's a gadget! *(Smithsonian)*

The next paragraph uses narration to define. The writer tells a story to convey a clear idea of what *fear* means to him.

I never knew what fear meant until the day I went on my first cave descent. Because I was a novice, I entered last. For the first hour things went smoothly; then, as I squeezed through a narrow passageway, I got stuck. I had always thought of myself as being calm in emergencies, but when I realized I couldn't move, I panicked. I forgot everything I had been taught during my orientation. All I could think of was that I was wedged in so tightly that I couldn't move forward or backward. I must have been screaming because almost at once the leader of the descent crawled up to me. It took him about ten minutes to calm me down and to convince me to let out a deep breath. As soon as I exhaled, he was able to pull me free. (Student)

☐   **EXERCISE 4**

A. Go through several of your own essays and find examples of the basic patterns of paragraph development we have discussed.

B. Determine one possible method of development for a paragraph on each of these topics. Then write a paragraph on one of the topics.

1. What love is
2. How to cope with stress
3. What kinds of people attend rock concerts
4. My worst job
5. American vs. Japanese cars
6. The connection between sleep and memory
7. Dressing for success
8. Responsibility
9. Making the perfect meal
10. Drinking and driving

C. Write a well-developed paragraph on one of the following topics.

1. Learning to drive (process)
2. Studying (cause and effect)
3. Types of friends (classification)
4. A vacation you took (narration)
5. Smokers vs. nonsmokers (comparison and contrast)
6. What is success? (definition)
7. Something right or wrong with television (exemplification)
8. A picture of a person, place, or thing (description)

4g Writing Special Kinds of Paragraphs

So far we have been talking only about the paragraphs that carry the weight of your discussion by presenting your ideas to your readers. Other paragraphs have different functions, however, and do not follow all the principles we have discussed. Even so, they have a significant impact on how readers respond to your ideas.

(1) Writing introductions

An **introduction** prepares an audience for your essay. The preparation needed will depend on your subject, your audience, and the effect you want your paper to have. A strong introduction brings readers into the world of your essay. A weak one leaves them outside.

Many writers like to present their thesis statements in their introductions. Whether or not it includes a thesis, your introduction should lead naturally into the subject of your paper. It cannot be at odds with your subject or seem imposed on it. It must also be consistent with the purpose, tone, and style of the rest of your essay. A serious, formal discussion should have the same kind of introduction. If your discussion is relaxed and informal, your introduction should be so, too.

Some introductions are straightforward, concerned primarily with presenting information. They begin by announcing the subject, limiting it, and then stating the thesis. The following introduction is an example of this pattern.

Although modern architecture is usually not intricate in design, it often involves remarkable engineering accomplishments. Most people do not realize the difficulties an architect encounters when designing a "great" modern structure. The new wing of the Smithsonian in Washington, in its simplicity, is such a masterpiece of engineering and design. (Student)

¶
4g

Not all subjects appeal to all readers, so at times you must find a way to capture your audience's attention. Several strategies for arranging effective introductions are listed below.

QUOTATION

"It's far easier to explain why the moon shouldn't be there," says M.I.T. geophysicist Nafi Toksoz, "than to explain its existence." That may sound strange when the data amassed by the manned Apollo lunar missions should have settled, it seems, the age-old question of the moon's origin once and for all. But that just did not happen. Even after a decade of intensive study, lunar scientists are still trying to recreate the story of how the moon came to be. (Ben Patrusky, "Where Did the Moon Come From?")

QUESTION

What kind of person goes to the movies at least three times a week? A film buff, that's who. Film buffs will go anywhere, almost any time, to see a movie they have missed. They spend much of their lives sitting in uncomfortable seats in darkened movie theaters. Even so, their hobby can be interesting, exciting, and rewarding. (Student)

DEFINITION

Moles are collections of cells that can appear on any part of the body. With occasional exceptions, moles are absent at birth. They first appear in the early years of life, between ages two and six. Frequently moles appear at puberty. New moles, however, can continue to appear throughout life. During pregnancy new moles may appear and old ones darken. There are three major designations of moles, each with its own characteristics. (Student)

UNUSUAL COMPARISON

Once a long time ago, people had special little boxes called refrigerators in which milk, meat, and eggs could be kept cool. The grandchildren of these simple devices are large enough to store whole cows, and they reach temperatures comparable to those at the South Pole. Their operating costs increase each year, and they are so complicated that few home handymen attempt to repair them on their own. Why has this change in size and complexity occurred in America? It has not taken place in many areas of the technologically advanced world (the average West German refrigerator is about a yard high and less than a yard wide, yet refrigeration technology in Germany is quite advanced). Do we

¶
4g

really need (or even want) all that space and cold? (Appletree Rodden, "Why Smaller Refrigerators Can Preserve the Human Race")

CONTROVERSIAL POSITION

Most men live in harness. Richard was one of them. Typically he had no awareness of how his male harness was choking him until his personal and professional life and his body had nearly fallen apart. (Herb Goldberg, *The Hazards of Being Male*)

(2)   Writing conclusions

Most essays have a **conclusion,** a carefully constructed ending that reinforces major ideas and gives readers a sense of completion. In short essays, the conclusion is usually just one paragraph; in longer essays, however, it can run two paragraphs or more. By restating your thesis or reviewing your main points, the conclusion gives readers the chance to make sure that they have understood your essay.

Your conclusion should be a logical extension of your essay. It should fulfill the promises you make in your introduction, not introduce new points or go off in new directions. Your conclusion is your last word, and readers base their impressions of your writing on it. A weak or uninteresting ending detracts from an otherwise strong essay. Therefore, do not apologize ("I may not be an expert" or "At least this is my opinion") or in any way undercut your concluding points. Some options for developing conclusions appear below.

REVIEW OF MAIN POINTS

As you can see, my grandmother is an unusual person. She is a dedicated nurse and a loving parent and grandparent. She has fought for the rights of others all her life, and she has raised children—both male and female—who follow her example. I am glad that I have had the opportunity to know her and to use her as a model for my own life. (Student)

PREDICTION

Looking ahead, prospects may not be quite as dismal as they seem. As a matter of fact, we are not doing so badly. It is something of a miracle that creatures who evolved as nomads in an intimate, small-band, wide-open-spaces context manage to get along at all as villagers or surrounded by strangers in cubicle apartments. Considering that our genius as a species is adaptability, we may yet learn to live closer and closer to one another, if not in utter peace, then far more peacefully than we do today. (John Pheiffer, "Seeking Peace, Making War")

OPINION
 A piece of writing is never finished. It is delivered to a deadline, torn out of the typewriter on demand, sent off with a sense of accomplishment and shame and pride and frustration. If only there were a couple more days, time for just another run at it, perhaps then . . . (Donald Murray, "The Maker's Eye: Revising Your Own Manuscripts")

QUOTATION
 "Curiouser and curiouser," says Alice as she journeys through Wonderland. The same can be said by anyone who wanders through the maze of regulations contained in the tax code. Possibly someday our lawmakers will remedy this situation, but until then we are all victims of a tax system that is too complex for most people to understand and too unwieldy for the government to control. (Student)

(3)   Writing transitional paragraphs

Longer essays frequently include one or more **transitional paragraphs** whose function is to signal a change in subject and provide a bridge between one section of an essay and another.

 At their simplest, transitional paragraphs can be single sentences that move readers from one point to the next.

Let us examine this point further.

This idea works better in theory than in practice.

Of course there are other avenues we can explore.

Let us begin with a few estimates.

 Sometimes writers use a transitional paragraph to present a concise summary of what they have already said. This technique reinforces important concepts by allowing readers to pause to consider what they have read before moving on to a new point. The following transitional paragraph uses a series of questions to restate some frightening points about overpopulation. The author goes on to answer these questions in the next part of his essay.

 Can we bleed off the mass of humanity to other worlds? Right now the number of human beings on Earth is increasing by 80 million per year, and each year that number goes up by 1 and a fraction percent. Can we really suppose that we can send 80 million people per year to the Moon, Mars, and elsewhere, and engineer those worlds to support those people? And even so, nearly remain in the same place ourselves? (Isaac Asimov, "The Case Against Man")

□   **EXERCISE 5**

¶
4g

The following draft of a student essay has a weak introduction and conclusion. Rewrite them to increase their effectiveness.

There are a number of things we can do to reduce
traffic deaths.

A passive restraint system automatically protects both
driver and passenger in the event of a collision. Almost
twenty years ago the government funded air bag research
that it hoped would fill the need for such a system. The
air bag, which is supposed to inflate upon impact, would
automatically shield collision victims from injury. A
decline in American auto sales and pressure from auto
manufacturers have caused the government to pull back from
its commitment. Interestingly, Chrysler plans to
introduce driver-side air bags as standard equipment on
all its new cars by 1990. This is not to say, however,
that air bags do not have critics. Some people feel that
they are both costly and unreliable. There is no way of
knowing for certain that air bags will work until an
accident occurs. Even so, many experts feel that the
problems with this system can be solved if they are
deployed.

Combination seat belt and shoulder harnesses are the
best and simplest way to protect passengers in a crash.
Volkswagen has perfected an interlock system that
automatically buckles people into place when the door of
the car closes. Most American and Japanese car
manufacturers have not adopted this system, preferring
instead the driver-fastened harness. Whatever system
manufacturers use, government studies show that seat belts
could reduce the annual auto death rate by ten to twelve
thousand people. The problem, however, is that many
people just will not use seat belts. Insurance statistics
show that in states where seat belt use is not mandatory

only eleven to seventeen percent of all drivers wear their
seat belts regularly.

What can be done? First, the federal government
should move ahead with the air bag system, offering tax
subsidies or credits to consumers who buy it. The money
saved in medical costs alone would more than offset the
cost to the government. Second, more state governments
should pass laws requiring riders to use seat belts.
People riding without fastened seat belts would receive
tickets, just as they would if they were speeding. In the
states where laws like this are already in effect,
automobile injuries and deaths have decreased
significantly.

Certainly all these things would help.

5

Thinking Logically

As you now have learned, the major purpose of many essays is to convey information. In these essays you use factual statements for support and expect readers to accept them at face value. In argument, however, although factual statements are used to support assertions, you assume that your audience needs to be convinced that your claims are valid.

The rules of logic are central to argument, and the first step toward understanding arguments is to understand the basic techniques of logical thinking. An argument proceeds logically from facts to conclusions in two basic ways: **inductively,** starting with observations or experiences and reaching a probable conclusion, or **deductively,** starting with general statements held to be true or self-evident and moving to more specific conclusions. Whether you proceed inductively or deductively depends on your topic, purpose, and audience. Many—probably most—arguments involve a combination of deductive and inductive reasoning, relying both on well-established beliefs and on conclusions drawn from evidence. For now, however, we will consider induction and deduction separately.

5a Reasoning Inductively

An inductive argument begins with observations or experiences and moves toward a conclusion. By basing your generalization on a number of specific examples, you have an excellent chance of overcoming your readers' resistance and gaining support.

(1)   Moving from hypothesis to conclusion

Despite its variety of detail, an inductive argument frequently follows a certain general pattern. An inductive argument begins with the **hypothesis**, the idea the writer wants to investigate. Next, it examines the hypothesis by presenting a broad sample of evidence, usually examples. Finally, the writer draws a conclusion based on the evidence. Consider the following examples from a passage in which the author explores the idea of how important SAT scores are for admission to college. The writer begins by presenting the hypothesis that he will examine and goes on to cite a number of examples. In his final sentence, he states his conclusion.

HYPOTHESIS

SAT's may not be very important to a particular college's admissions procedures.

EVIDENCE

- At Princeton University 50 percent of the admission decision is based on academic credentials and 50 percent on nonacademic factors.
- The academic portion is based on grades and rank in high school, SAT scores, achievement-test scores, and recommendations.
- Nonacademic factors include "leadership activities," school activities, sports, and personal interviews.
- Special attention is given to prospective engineers, athletes, minorities, and alumni and faculty children, the admissions department admits.
- The SAT is used as an admission requirement that cuts across all applicants.
- Less than 52 percent of the applicants for the class of 1984 with SAT verbal scores between 750 and 800 were accepted.
- Less than 39 percent of those with similar SAT math scores were offered admission.
- Approximately 18 percent of those with SAT verbal scores between 550 and 599 and over 19 percent of those with similar SAT math scores were admitted.

CONCLUSION

While important, the SAT scores are not always determining factors in the admission process. (Adapted from Jay Amberg, "The SAT")

No matter how much evidence you present, inductive conclusions are never absolutely certain, only highly probable. They are arrived at by what is called an **inductive leap.** The more observations you make, the narrower the gap between your observations and your conclusion and the better your chances of drawing a convincing conclusion. When, for example, a small child looks out the window, sees dark clouds, and predicts it will rain, he or she is making an inductive leap. The conclusion is sound because the child has made similar observations in the past. As the following passage shows, induction is central to scientific inquiry. Notice how the writer presents his observations and then makes the inductive leap to his conclusion that the songs of swamp sparrows are an example of learned behavior.

> Male swamp sparrows brought into the laboratory as nestlings learn readily from taped songs of their species when these are played from the third to the eighth week of life. Full song develops some 9 months later and often contains a certain proportion of "syllables" that match the components on the training tapes. The diverse morphology of swamp sparrow syllables permits choice of a great variety of training patterns. Exposure to different syllables in infancy results in different patterns of adult singing. The conclusion that songs are learned is based on this capacity to match acoustic models and on the abnormality of songs of birds reared without exposure to the species song. (Peter Marler and Susan Peters, "Sparrows Learn Adult Song and More from Memory")

(2) Using evidence

The evidence you use to support the conclusion of your inductive arguments can come from a number of sources. Although you may use personal experiences or observations as evidence, more often you rely on facts and opinions drawn from outside your own experience.

Facts One source of evidence is **facts**—verifiable statements that something is true or that something happened. We accept many facts because our senses confirm them: the sky is blue, water is wet. However, an individual's experience is limited, and we have to accept facts we are not able to verify personally. We accept that the planet Jupiter is 483 million miles from the sun and that it has an atmosphere of helium, hydrogen, methane, and ammonia because we trust the reference sources that give us this information. Keep in mind, however, that facts change as new information is uncovered or as situations change. To most Europeans who lived during the late fifteenth century, it was a *fact* that there was no sea route to India. Several years ago it was a *fact* that a person could not be given an artificial heart.

Most factual evidence you use will be either *examples* or *statistics*.

Examples An **example** is a specific illustration of a more general claim. Because examples focus on an individual case, they illuminate arguments and can be quite convincing. To be effective, an example must clearly establish a connection between an observable event and a more general assertion. For instance, a recent article in the newspaper made the claim that a plane crash which resulted in great loss of life was the result of negligence on the part of the plane's crew. To support this claim, the article presented the following examples.

- The plane's flaps were not in the correct position at takeoff.
- A member of the crew had apparently turned off the alarm that would have signaled that the flaps were in the wrong position.
- The pilot had tried to take off from the wrong runway.
- The air traffic controller reported that the pilot seemed distracted when she told him of his error.

Together these examples give strong support for the article's general assertion and create a high level of certainty that the crash was due to the crew's negligence. Keep in mind, though, that you can accept the examples without granting the truth of the conclusion.

For readers to accept your conclusion, they have to feel sure that your examples are *relevant, representative,* and *sufficient.*

When evaluating the examples you offer as evidence you should first determine that the examples you present are **relevant**—that they actually relate to the issue. It is easy in the heat of debate to get caught up in your material and to lose sight of your original intention. But irrelevant evidence and tangential points will only cloud the issue and confuse your readers. In arguing for mandatory AIDS testing by the federal government, for example, one student mentioned the fact that all children entering the public schools must be vaccinated against the polio virus. Although interesting, this point has nothing to do with testing for AIDS, a disease for which there is no vaccine. As you write, remember to use strong topic sentences and clear transitional words and phrases to remind your readers how your information relates to your overall argument.

Next, make certain that the examples you present are **representative**—that they are typical of the situation you are discussing, not aberrant. For instance, in an essay arguing against a proposal for year-round schooling in your county, suppose you support your thesis by offering the example of a California county that tried and abandoned year-round schooling during the 1980's. To be valid, your example must be typical of all the counties that tried year-round schooling. Ask yourself if there was anything about the California experience that made it unique. Did other school districts using this system have success? If so, is California an unrepresentative example that does not adequately support your thesis?

Finally, determine whether the examples you present are **sufficient**—that there are enough to support your conclusion. How do you know whether you have enough examples? In general, the nature and complexity of your claim determine the number of examples you need. When writing, you constantly run the risk of basing your conclusion on too few examples. If you say that all Sony television sets are defective because the two you bought were, you have made a *hasty generalization*. Two examples do not make a rule or warrant this conclusion. Furthermore, your two sets do not represent the entire line of products.

Occasionally one or two examples do lead to a valid conclusion: just one case of food poisoning convinces most people that the condition is unpleasant (although you would not be likely to argue this point). More often, however, you must present additional evidence to support a conclusion.

Statistics A **statistic** summarizes in numerical form a large number of specific examples. The major advantage of statistics is that they give readers confidence that they are getting a general sampling of information. In addition, statistical information presented in the form of charts, graphs, and tables makes data easy to understand. A graph illustrating the government's spending of each tax dollar it receives, for example, is more accessible than a paragraph-length discussion of the same material.

Before you use statistics, consider several criteria. First, determine the source of the statistics. Were the statistics published in a journal known for its balanced treatment of the issues or one noted for its support of a particular cause? A newspaper poll that attempts to predict the outcome of an election is usually more accurate than one commissioned by an individual candidate, who may wish to use the results of a poll to influence voters.

Next, attempt to find out if the questions used to gather the statistics were biased or fair. Consider the following pair of questions. One is biased because it is worded so that it is likely to elicit a certain response. The other is fair because it attempts to evoke a more accurate response.

BIASED: Do you believe that the federal government should be allowed to take guns away from law-abiding citizens and deprive them of the ability to protect themselves and their families?

FAIR: Should the federal government be allowed to control the sale of handguns across state lines?

Finally, consider whether the statistical sample of the study to which you are referring is large enough to justify a researcher's conclusion. An article in the *Journal of the American Medical Association* recently complained that some researchers were publishing studies using as few as ten participants. In most cases, said the journal, this practice is misleading and does not further the cause of responsible medical research. A team of scientists claiming to have discovered a cure for a type of cancer would have to offer many examples—in the form of statistics—to convince colleagues that their conclusion was valid.

Expert Opinion   **Expert opinion**—the testimony of experts in the field you are writing about—can also support your claims. Notice how Rachel Carson uses the words of a noted entomologist to substantiate her argument.

> Yet such a world is pressed upon us. The crusade to create a chemically sterile, insect-free world seems to have engendered a fanatic zeal on the part of many specialists and most of the so-called control agencies. On every hand there is evidence that those engaged in spraying operations exercise a ruthless power. "The regulatory entomologists . . . function as prosecutor, judge and jury, tax assessor and collector and sheriff to enforce their own orders," says Connecticut entomologist Neely Turner. The most flagrant abuses go unchecked in both state and federal agencies. (*Silent Spring*)

To be useful, an authority's words must pertain specifically to your topic. Furthermore, the opinion of the authority has value only in his or her field. In other areas the individual's testimony should have no more weight than that of any other reasonably intelligent person.

Even though the views of authorities in a field are acceptable as evidence, these opinions must still be supported by facts. When an expert opinion is presented without anything to back it up, it does not constitute acceptable evidence. For example, an argument that contains as its only evidence the opinion of a former secretary of state that a nuclear test ban treaty is not in the best interests of the United States is weak. To strengthen this argument, the writer must include the facts that led to the expert's conclusion, as well as his or her own analysis of the subject.

In your writing you may cite the opinions of experts, but you should make certain they support *your* assertions. Your own interpretations of your source, not your sources alone, should form the basis of your discussion.

Finally, the authority whose information you use should be unbiased. Apologists for a particular cause or organization have been known to ignore evidence and to slant opinions to further their own ends. Naturally, using biased arguments from unreliable sources can undercut the effectiveness of your own case. (See 38b for information on evaluating sources.)

Checklist for Evaluating Evidence

I. Facts
Examples

- Are the examples relevant?
- Are the examples representative?
- Are the examples sufficient?

Statistics

- What is the source of the statistics?
- How were the statistics gathered?
- Is the statistical sample sufficiently large?

II. Expert Opinion

- Do the authority's words pertain specifically to your topic?
- Is the authority an expert in the field about which you are writing?
- Does the authority support his or her assertions with evidence?
- Do your own interpretations form the basis of your discussion?
- Is your authority biased?

□   **EXERCISE 1**

Read this essay carefully.

As Deerfield Academy, following Lawrenceville, departs from its traditional mission of single-sex education for boys, I, like others involved in girls' schools, am saddened that few voices were apparently raised to defend a mission I cannot help comparing to our own.

Advocates of single-sex education for girls are enthusiastic defenders of the cause. We feel validated every day in our classrooms, dormitories, councils of student government, science and computer laboratories and yearbook editing offices. We see growth, developing self-esteem, individuality and leadership all around us.

It is not that good co-educational schools cannot offer girls these things; it is that girls' schools do so consistently. We are a fail-safe producer of first-class citizenship for girls in a world in which they are not guaranteed this opportunity elsewhere. We, like the women's colleges, provide not only "equal opportunity, but every opportunity," to quote Dr. Nannerl Keohane, the president of Wellesley College.

A colleague of mine described a vignette in her all-girls kindergarten class: A small girl surveyed the room, arms akimbo and sized up the situation. "Thank heavens," she said. "No boys in the block corner." No, there aren't. She won't have to establish her right to build with blocks, just as later on she won't have to elbow her way to the computer terminals or perhaps feel out of place spending extra time in the physics lab.

Her voice will be heard in class, her opinion sought—on every topic—and taken seriously. Whatever the athletic facilities, they are for her alone. Moreover, leadership roles are more available: Girls get experience in managing radio stations, editing student newspapers and literary magazines, heading the debate and mathematics teams—all without having to fight for a place in the sun, because sex stereotyping does not complicate life in the school.

Since failure is less threatening, risk-taking becomes more bearable. For example, like many girls' schools we have a wonderful dance program, but our dancers don't have to care if they don't have figures like the models in Seventeen magazine—and few teen-agers do. Like most people, they come in various shapes and sizes, yet they know no one will laugh at them or make disparaging remarks. So they learn to carry themselves with poise and grace, to be proud of their bodies—and stand a chance of becoming good dancers besides.

Relationships can flourish, both among peers and between students and adults. Communication with teachers and other adults is open and warm. Friendships grow strong and last long into adult life, as I have observed time and again by watching the alumnae of women's schools and colleges network and support each other in myriad ways. All this creates a learning and teaching atmosphere that is almost tangible: Our classrooms are lively, exciting places.

A graduate, finishing her sophomore year at a major New England (formerly all-male) college, visited Miss Porter's School last summer. She and I had known each other somewhat, had talked during her years with us but had never discussed the roles and expectations of women as such.

She and her friends were fighting for better health services for women at her college and were frustrated with their lack of progress. They were not being heard, she said. People were not taking them seriously. She talked about the climate of the classrooms, which she found alienating, and the effort she felt she must continually make to claim her equal place. The intensity and warmth of the conversation surprised me. "I wanted to talk to you," she said. "I knew you'd understand." That solidarity and that strength is what a women's single-sex school or college can provide.

We are sorry that Lawrenceville, and now Deerfield, did not feel that they could raise their voices in support of their historic educational environments. This is not a judgment—it is a sentiment—because women's schools, like women's colleges, find their mission constantly validated.

Ours is a co-educational world—no doubt about it—and single-sex education needs its defenders, promoters, believers and proselytizers. Yes, some people think girls' schools are anachronisms, but they succeed, better than most people realize, and remain necessary in a world where men and women still do not work equally together as professionals. (Rachel Phillips Belash, "Why Girls' Schools Remain Necessary," *New York Times*)

A. Answer the following questions about the essay above.

1. What is Belash's hypothesis?
2. Do you think the audience's knowledge that Belash is the head of a girls' school would make them more or less likely to accept her arguments? Explain.
3. What evidence does Belash offer to support her hypothesis? What additional kinds of evidence would strengthen her argument?
4. Are the examples relevant? representative? sufficient? What additional examples could be offered in support of the hypothesis?
5. Where does Belash make an inductive leap?
6. What is Belash's conclusion? Is this conclusion warranted in light of the evidence she presents?

B. Imagine that you are writing an argument that takes a stand against Belash's hypothesis. Your audience consists of the students in your composition class. What kinds of evidence would you present? From what sources could you draw evidence to support your position? List some of the specific points you might use as evidence.

5b Reasoning Deductively

Unlike induction, deduction begins with a general statement or proposition and establishes a chain of reasoning that leads to a conclusion. In order to study the process of deduction, we rely on a formal schematic called a syllogism. Devised by Aristotle, a **syllogism** is a three-part set of statements or propositions that contains a *major premise*, a *minor premise*, and a *conclusion*.

MAJOR PREMISE: All books from that store are new.

MINOR PREMISE: These books are from that store.

CONCLUSION: Therefore, these books are new.

In deduction the premises contain all the information expressed in the conclusion: no terms are introduced that have not already appeared in the major and minor premises.

In a deductive argument, then, your conclusion must follow from your premises. Suppose you believe that the government should take steps to protect people who live near nuclear power plants. You begin by stating the general assumption that the government is obliged to protect its citizens. You then say that people who live near nuclear power plants are citizens. Your conclusion—that the safety of these residents should therefore be ensured—follows from these assumptions. Stated as a syllogism, your argument looks like this.

MAJOR PREMISE: All citizens should be protected by the government.

MINOR PREMISE: People who live around nuclear power plants are citizens.

CONCLUSION: Therefore, people who live around nuclear power plants should be protected by the government.

The strength of a deductive argument is that if your readers accept your premises, they usually grant your conclusion. At times your readers will accept both your major and minor premises. At other times you must present evidence to persuade readers to accept one or more of your premises. Because your major premise is so important, it is a good idea to choose an idea that your audience already accepts. Once you have established your premises, the force of logic alone should lead readers to accept your conclusion.

When you construct a deductive argument, you may state your conclusion at the beginning or at the end. Your choice depends on whether you want to state a conclusion explicitly and then support it or to lead up to a conclusion that is implied throughout. If your audience is likely to agree with your conclusion, state it at the outset. If not, proceed gradually. Here is an example of a deductive argument whose conclusion appears at the end.

> The primary function of a university is to discover and disseminate knowledge by means of research and teaching. To fulfill this function a free interchange of ideas is necessary not only within its walls but with the world beyond as well. It follows that the university must do everything possible to ensure within it the fullest degree of intellectual freedom. The history of intellectual growth and discovery clearly demonstrates the need for unfettered freedom, the right to think the unthinkable, discuss the unmentionable, and challenge the unchallenged. To curtail free expression strikes twice at intellectual freedom, for whoever deprives another of the right to state unpopular views necessarily also deprives others of the right to listen to those views. (Yale Committee, "Freedom of Expression at Yale")

The author begins this argument with the major premise. The

rest of the paragraph establishes the minor premise and then leads logically to the conclusion, stated in the final sentence.

(1) Distinguishing validity from truth

Before continuing we should distinguish between arguments that are valid and arguments that are true. A **valid** argument is one whose conclusion logically follows from its premises. In other words, *validity* depends on the form of a syllogism. A **true** argument is one that makes accurate claims—that is, one in which the information contained by the propositions is in agreement with the facts. A **sound** argument must be both valid and true. However, an argument may be valid without being true or true without being valid. In the following example the syllogism's argument is valid but not true.

MAJOR PREMISE: All politicians are male.

MINOR PREMISE: Patricia Schroeder is a politician.

CONCLUSION: Therefore, Patricia Schroeder is male.

As odd as it may seem, this syllogism's argument is valid. In the major premise the phrase "all politicians" establishes that the entire class *politicians* is male. Once Patricia Schroeder is identified as a politician, the conclusion that she is male automatically follows. Represented graphically, the logic of this syllogism becomes clear.

Politicians = Males
Patricia Schroeder = Politician
Patricia Schroeder = Male

Common sense tells us, however, that Patricia Schroeder is female. Because the major premise of this syllogism is not true, any argument based on this premise also cannot be true. For this reason, even though the logic of the syllogism is correct, its argument is not.

(2) Constructing valid arguments

Just as a syllogism can be valid but not true, it can also be true but not valid.

- A syllogism in which the middle term is not distributed cannot have a valid conclusion.

MAJOR PREMISE: All fathers are male.

MINOR PREMISE: John Updike is a male.

CONCLUSION: Therefore, John Updike is a father.

Even though the premises of this syllogism are true, the conclusion—John Updike is a father—does not follow logically because the construction of the syllogism is faulty. The rule of logic is that the middle term, the term used in both the major and minor premises, must be *distributed*—that is, it must refer to all members of the group. In the preceding syllogism, however, this is not the case. In the major premise, *all fathers* is distributed because it refers to *all* individuals in the class designated as fathers. The term *male*, however, is undistributed and for this reason cannot be used as the middle term. Therefore, you cannot go on to conclude that because John Updike is male, he is therefore a father.

Consider this version of the preceding syllogism.

MAJOR PREMISE: All fathers are male.

MINOR PREMISE: John Updike is a father.

CONCLUSION: Therefore, John Updike is a male.

Now the distributed term *fathers* appears in both the major and the minor premises. Since *John Updike* is equated with the distributed middle term *fathers*, the conclusion that he is a male logically follows.

- A syllogism in which the meaning of a key term shifts cannot have a valid conclusion.

MAJOR PREMISE: Only man contemplates the future.

MINOR PREMISE: No woman is a man.

CONCLUSION: Therefore, no woman contemplates the future.

In the major premise *man* is used to denote all human beings. In the minor premise, however, *man* refers to gender. As a result of this shift, the conclusion cannot be valid. You can correct this problem by making certain that the key terms in the syllogism remain the same.

MAJOR PREMISE: Only human beings contemplate the future.

MINOR PREMISE: No dog is a human being.

CONCLUSION: Therefore, no dog contemplates the future.

- A syllogism in which one of the premises is negative cannot have a valid affirmative conclusion.

MAJOR PREMISE: No handicapped persons may be denied employment because of their handicap.

MINOR PREMISE: Deaf persons are handicapped.

CONCLUSION: Therefore, no deaf persons may be denied employment because of their handicap.

In the preceding syllogism, you cannot infer from the premises an affirmative relationship between *employment* and *deaf persons*. The only conclusion possible is a negative one.

- A syllogism in which both of the premises are negative cannot have a valid conclusion.

MAJOR PREMISE: Injured workers may not be denied workers' compensation.

MINOR PREMISE: Frank is not an injured worker.

CONCLUSION: Therefore, Frank may not be denied workers' compensation.

The two negative premises of this syllogism provide no links in the chain of reasoning established by the syllogism. Only if one of the premises is positive can a valid conclusion be reached.

MAJOR PREMISE: Injured workers may not be denied workers' compensation.

MINOR PREMISE: Frank is an injured worker.

CONCLUSION: Therefore, Frank may not be denied workers' compensation.

(3)   Recognizing enthymemes

As intellectually challenging as syllogisms can be, they do not present a realistic picture of how people actually form arguments. Many deductive arguments occur as statements in which assumptions are implied rather than stated. Recognizing this fact, Aristotle developed the concept of the enthymeme. An **enthymeme** is a syllogism in which one of the premises—often the major premise—is implied rather than stated. Because you often encounter enthymemes in your assignments, you should learn to identify them. Consider these assertions.

Melissa is on the Dean's List.

She is intelligent.

These statements contain the minor premise and the conclusion of a syllogism. The writer feels that the major premise is so self-evident that he need not mention it. In other words, the reader will fill in the missing term and arrive at the following syllogism.

MAJOR PREMISE: All students on the Dean's List are intelligent.

MINOR PREMISE: Melissa is on the Dean's List.

CONCLUSION: Therefore, Melissa is intelligent.

Enthymemes often occur as compound sentences which contain words that signal conclusions—*therefore, consequently, for this reason, for, so, since,* or *because.* Notice how *so* in the following sentence indicates the presence of an enthymeme.

Deer are intelligent creatures, *so* they should not be hunted.

After the major premise is supplied, the structure of the argument becomes clear.

MAJOR PREMISE: Intelligent creatures should not be hunted.

MINOR PREMISE: Deer are intelligent creatures.

CONCLUSION: Therefore, deer should not be hunted.

Once you recognize an enthymeme, you can identify any unstated assumptions and determine the argument is sound.

Used when people can readily identify the unstated premises, enthymemes are effective and appropriate means of persuasion. Some writers and speakers, however, deliberately use enthymemes in an attempt to unfairly influence an audience. Bumper stickers like "Guns don't kill, people do" commonly use this technique. By keeping their basic assumptions ambiguous, they hope to persuade an unwitting audience to accept their conclusions even though these conclusions are based on faulty logic or are unjustified by the facts.

☐   **EXERCISE 2**

Read this essay carefully.

A nation succeeds only if the vast majority of its citizens succeed. It therefore stands to reason that with immigrants accounting for about 40 percent of our population growth, the future economic and social success of the United States is bound up with the success of these new Americans. Demography, in a word, is destiny.

This is an important principle to keep in mind as we try to come to grips with the problems and opportunities presented by the flood of legal and illegal immigrants from Mexico and other parts of South and Central America, who now constitute by far our largest immigrant group.

How are we doing in our efforts to assimilate these largely Hispanic newcomers and provide them with a bright future? Some signs are disturbing.

John Garcia, associate professor of political science at the University of Arizona, writing in International Migration Review, finds that the average rate of naturalization of Mexican immigrants is one-tenth that of other immigrant naturalization rates. The Select Commission on Immigration and Refugee Policy made a similar finding. Increasingly, immigrants are separated from everyone else by language, geography, ethnicity and class.

The future success of this country is closely linked to the ability of our immigrants to succeed. Yet 50 percent of our children of Hispanic background do not graduate from high school. Hispanic students score 100 points under the average student on Scholastic Aptitude Test scores. Hispanics have much higher rates of poverty, illiteracy and need for welfare than the national average. This engenders social crisis.

Not all the indicators of assimilation are pessimistic: the success of many Indochinese immigrants has been gratifying. But the warning signs of nonassimilation are increasing and ominous.

America must make sure the melting pot continues to melt: immigrants must become Americans. Seymour Martin Lipset, professor of political science and sociology at the Hoover Institution, Stanford University, observes: "The history of bilingual and bicultural societies that do not assimilate are histories of turmoil, tension and tragedy. Canada, Belgium, Malaysia, Lebanon—all face crises of national existence in which minorities press for autonomy, if not independence. Pakistan and Cyprus have divided. Nigeria suppressed an ethnic rebellion. France faces difficulties with its Basques, Bretons and Corsicans."

The United States is at a crossroads. If it does not consciously move toward greater integration, it will inevitably drift toward more fragmentation. It will either have to do better in assimilating all of the other peoples in its boundaries or it will witness increasing alienation and fragmentation. Cultural divisiveness is not a bedrock upon which a nation can be built. It is inherently unstable.

The nation faces a staggering social agenda. We have not adequately integrated blacks into our economy and society. Our education system is rightly described as "a rising tide of mediocrity." We have the most violent society in the industrial world; we have startlingly high rates of illiteracy, illegitimacy and welfare recipients.

It bespeaks a hubris to madly rush, with these unfinished social agendas, into accepting more immigrants and refugees than all of the rest of the world and then to still hope to keep a common agenda.

America can accept additional immigrants, but we must be sure that they become American. We can be a Joseph's coat of many nations, but we must be unified. One of the common glues that hold us together is language—the English language.

We should be color-blind but linguistically cohesive. We should be a rainbow but not a cacophony. We should welcome different peoples but not adopt different languages. We can teach English through bilingual education, but we should take great care not to become a bilingual society.   (Richard D. Lamm, "English Comes First," *New York Times*)

A. Answer the following questions about the essay above.

1. In developing the preceding argument, Richard D. Lamm relies on a number of basic premises, assumptions about his subject which he expects his audience to share. What are some of these assumptions on which he bases his argument?

2. In paragraph 1 Lamm presents a deductive argument. Express this argument as a syllogism.
3. What kinds of evidence does Lamm use to support his position? What other kinds of evidence could he have used?
4. Where does Lamm state his conclusion? Restate the conclusion in your own words.

B. Evaluate the soundness of these arguments. (If the argument is in the form of an enthymeme, supply the missing term before evaluating the argument.)

1. All immigrants should speak English. If they do not, they are not real Americans.
2. Richard Lamm was born in the United States and grew up in an English-speaking household. Therefore, he has no credibility on the subject of bilingualism.
3. Spanish-speaking immigrants should be required by law to learn English. After all, most Eastern European immigrants who came to this country early in the twentieth century learned English.
4. If immigrants do not care enough about our country to learn English, we should not allow them to become citizens.
5. Some immigrants have become financially successful even though they did not learn English. Obviously, then, learning English does not increase an immigrant's chances for success.
6. All Cuban immigrants speak Spanish. Former San Antonio Mayor Henry Cisneros speaks Spanish, so he must be a Cuban immigrant.
7. As Seymour Martin Lipset points out, bilingual societies can be threatened by tension and political unrest. Therefore, it is important that immigrants not be bilingual.

5c   Recognizing Logical Fallacies

Fallacies are indefensible flaws in arguments. Because they closely resemble sound arguments, fallacious arguments can seem convincing. Unscrupulous writers intentionally use such arguments, but well-intentioned writers sometimes slip into them without realizing it. When readers detect these fallacies, they see the writer as illogical—or, worse, dishonest. Here are some common fallacies to watch for when you revise your own arguments and when you evaluate the arguments of others.

(1)   Equivocation

You are guilty of **equivocation** when you shift the meaning of a key word during an argument so that your conclusion seems to follow logically from your premises.

Equivocation can be subtle. Consider this statement.

It is in the public interest for the government to provide for the welfare of those who cannot help themselves. The public's interest becomes aroused, however, when it hears of welfare recipients getting thousands of dollars by cheating or by fraud.

In the first sentence, *public interest* refers to social good, and *welfare* to well-being. In the second sentence, *the public's interest* refers to self-interest and *welfare* to financial assistance provided by the government.

Do not shift the meaning of key terms from one statement to another. To see if you have equivocated, reread your paper with your intended definition in mind.

(2)   The either/or fallacy

The **either/or fallacy** occurs when you analyze a complex situation as if it has only two sides when actually it has more. If you ask whether American involvement in Central America is beneficial or harmful, you admit only two possibilities, ruling out all others. In fact, American involvement in some Central American countries may be beneficial, but in others it may be harmful. Or in any given country it may be *both* beneficial and harmful. Avoid the either/or fallacy by acknowledging the complexity of an issue. Do not misrepresent issues by limiting them.

Of course, *some* either/or situations lead to valid conclusions. In biology lab a test either will or will not indicate the presence of a certain enzyme. To be valid, an either/or statement must encompass *every* possible alternative. The premise "Either Kim took the test or she did not" is valid. There are no other possibilities. But the premise "Either Kim took the test or she went to the health service" is an example of the either/or fallacy. To disprove it, all someone has to do is to point out that Kim went somewhere else.

(3)   *Post hoc, ergo propter hoc*

Post hoc, ergo propter hoc is Latin for "after this, therefore because of this." The *post hoc* fallacy occurs when you mistakenly infer that because one event follows another in time, the events are causally related. Many arguments depend on establishing cause-and-effect relationships, but the link between the causes and effects presented must actually exist. In some arguments this is not the case. For example, after the United States sold wheat to the U.S.S.R., the price of wheat and wheat products rose dramatically. Many people blamed the wheat sale for this rapid increase. One event followed another closely in time, so they falsely assumed that the first event caused the second. In fact, a complicated series of farm-price controls that had been in effect for years was the actual cause of increases in wheat prices.

Make certain that you identify the actual causes and effects of the events you discuss. Cause-and-effect relationships are difficult to prove, so you may have to rely on expert testimony to support your claim.

(4) Begging the question

You are **begging the question** when you state a debatable premise as if it were true instead of offering proof for it. Readers may assume in error that something has been proved when it has not.

> Experimentation on helpless animals clearly constitutes cruel and unusual punishment.

> It is obvious that animal experimentation is justified as a necessary part of scientific research.

The preceding statements use the words *clearly* and *obvious* and emotionally loaded language to make the audience believe they are factual. However, the statements require proof. If you encounter an example of begging the question when you revise an argument, delete the loaded words and provide the proof necessary for its defense.

(5) False analogy

Analogies—extended comparisons—are useful in arguments. They enable you to explain something unfamiliar by comparing it to something familiar. By itself an analogy establishes nothing; it is no substitute for evidence. Skillfully used, however, an analogy can be quite convincing. Henry David Thoreau illustrates the futility of welfare by comparing an ant battle to a human battle. In a freshman essay you might compare students at registration to rats in a maze: both are rewarded if they succeed and punished if they do not. But people are not rats, and you would still have to provide evidence if your purpose is to criticize the registration process.

A **false analogy** (or faulty analogy) assumes that because issues or concepts are similar in some ways, they are similar in other ways. On a television talk show recently a psychiatrist was asked to explain why people commit crimes.

"Some people," he said, "commit crimes because they are selfish

or psychotic. Others are like pregnant women who know they
shouldn't smoke but do anyway. They have a craving that they
have to give in to. The answer is not to punish this group of criminals, but to understand their behavior and to try to change it."

Admittedly, this analogy is convincing. However, it oversimplifies
the issue. A pregnant woman does not intend to harm her un-
born child by smoking; many criminals do intend to harm their
victims. To undercut the doctor's whole argument you need only
point out the shortcomings of his analogy.

(6)   Red herring

The **red herring** fallacy occurs when you change the subject to
distract your audience from the actual issue. Consider, for example, "This company may charge high prices, but they do give a
great deal of money to charity each year." The latter observation
has nothing to do with the former but somehow manages to
obscure it.

   Many people use this fallacy when backed into a corner.
By switching the subject, they hope to change direction and
begin their argument on safer ground. Here is an example from
a student essay.

> The appeals court should uphold the lower court's decision to
> allow females to attend previously all-male Central High School. A
> number of experts agree that Central High provides the best sec-
> ondary education in the city. One can only wonder if the school
> board members who oppose this decision do not have more
> pressing things to do. Perhaps they should spend more time won-
> dering how they will finance public education in this city next
> year.

This argument avoids discussing what it sets out to prove.
Instead of supporting the assertion about women attending
Central High, the writer introduces an irrelevant point about
financing public education.

(7)   *Argumentum ad ignorantiam*

In Latin **argumentum ad ignorantiam** means "argument to ignorance." This fallacy occurs when you say that something is true
because you cannot prove it false or that something is false because you cannot prove it true. This fallacy occurred recently
during a debate about allowing children who have been infected
with AIDS to attend public school. A parent asked an AIDS researcher, "How can you tell me to send my child to school where

there are children with AIDS? After all, you doctors can't say for sure that my child won't catch AIDS from these children." In other words, the parent was saying, "My children will contract AIDS from other children in school because it has never been proven that they cannot." As persuasive as this line of reasoning can sometimes be, it is logically flawed. The fact remains that no evidence has been presented to support the speaker's conclusion.

(8)   *Consensus gentium*

The fallacy of **consensus gentium** ("agreement of people") occurs when you try to establish that something is true or worthwhile because everyone believes that it is ("20 million Frenchmen can't be wrong!"). This appeal is the same as saying that a television program must be good because it has high ratings. A recent newspaper editorial makes the point that the state should raise the speed limit on its highways to sixty-five miles an hour because nearly everyone exceeds the present fifty-five mile an hour limit. Instead of focusing on the lack of merit of the present limit, the editorial relies on an appeal to numbers. Certainly the fact that many people ignore the speed limit is important, but this fact does not in itself establish that the speed limit should be raised.

(9)   Skewed sample

The **skewed sample** is a problem that can occur during the collection of statistical evidence. To present accurate results a statistical sample should be *representative*; that is, it should be typical of the broader population it represents. When a statistical sample is collected so that it favors one segment of the population over others, it is said to be *skewed*. For example, a study of the spending habits of Americans would most likely be skewed in favor of relatively affluent individuals if it were based on respondents chosen from lists of luxury car owners. In the same respect, census questions asked only in English would disproportionately skew results in favor of English-speaking respondents.

(10)   *Tu quoque*

In Latin *tu quoque* means "you also." This fallacy occurs when you say that a point has no merit because the person making it does not follow his or her own advice. Such an argument is irrel-

evant because it focuses attention on the person rather than on
the issue being debated.

> If you think that I should exercise, why are you so fat?

> You're telling me to invest wisely? Look at how much money you
> lost in the commodities market last year.

In argumentative essays, *tu quoque* is not usually so
straightforward. Frequently, it takes the form of "You would do it
too if you had the opportunity."

> It is difficult to understand why Congress wants to limit the au-
> thority of the CIA. After all, the KGB operates all over the world
> without any restraints.

> Why should Joey Coyle go to jail? Wouldn't you have taken a mil-
> lion dollars if it dropped out of a truck in front of you?

When you revise, keep in mind that the *tu quoque* fallacy does
not prove anything.

(11)   Argument *ad hominem*

Arguments **ad hominem** ("to the man" in Latin) attack a person
rather than an issue. By casting aspersions on an opponent, you
turn attention from the facts of the case. Here are some examples.

> That woman has criticized the president's commitment to equal
> rights for women. But she believes in parapsychology. She thinks
> that she can communicate with the dead.

> Senator Rodriguez supports the deployment of the MX missile.
> What do you expect from a man who worked for a defense con-
> tractor before he ran for public office?

When a topic is controversial, this tactic can work. But although
you may persuade some people, others will recognize the fallacy
and withdraw their support.

(12)   Argument *ad populum*

Arguments **ad populum** ("to the people") appeal to people's prejudices. A presidential candidate seeking support in a state
whose textile industry has been hurt by foreign competition may
allude to "foreign hordes who are attempting to overrun our
shores." By exploiting prejudices of the audience, the candidate
is able to avoid the concrete issues of the campaign. Of course,
many political speeches contain emotional appeals—to patriotism, for instance—and this is fine. These appeals should

Guide to Logical Fallacies

- **Equivocation** Shifting the meaning of a key word during an argument
- **The Either/Or Fallacy** Treating a complex issue as if it has only two sides
- *Post Hoc* Establishing an improper link between cause and effect
- **Begging the Question** Stating a debatable premise as if it were true
- **False Analogy** Assuming that because things are similar in some ways they are similar in other ways
- **Red Herring** Changing the subject to distract your audience from the issue
- **Argument *ad Ignorantiam*** Saying that something is true because it cannot be proven false, or vice versa
- *Consensus Gentium* Trying to establish that something is true because everyone believes it is true
- **Skewed Sample** Collecting a statistical sample so that it favors one population over another
- *Tu Quoque* Accusing a person of not upholding the position that he or she advocates
- **Argument *ad Hominem*** Attacking the person and not the issue
- **Argument *ad Populum*** Appealing to the prejudices of the people

be taken for what they are—an effort to establish good will—and should not substitute for specific assertions supported by concrete evidence.

☐   **EXERCISE 3**

Identify the fallacies in the following statements. In each case name the fallacy and rewrite the statement to correct the problem.

1. Dr. Spock is a brilliant physician. He should use his education to help the sick instead of criticizing the administration's nuclear policy.
2. My opponent says that he wants to be mayor. He has been divorced twice. Obviously, he should get his own life in order before he thinks of running for public office.
3. How can we not support railroads? Railroads are the arteries of our nation, and the trains are the life blood that bring sustenance to all parts of the country.
4. The school's mail-in registration program will either make things easier for students or result in total chaos.

5. During the last flight of the space shuttle, there was heavy rainfall throughout the entire Northeast. Therefore the launch must have disturbed the weather patterns for that region of the country.

6. I just received a pamphlet that urges people to buy savings bonds. How can the government talk about saving? Look how much money it wastes on cost overruns each year.

7. What former President Nixon did was wrong, but many people in public office have done a lot worse.

8. No truly intelligent person would deny that the government's welfare programs are shamefully mismanaged.

9. All of us must accept responsibility for the actions of the utility company. Therefore we should make certain that everyone gets heat this winter.

10. No responsible scientist has been able to establish that smoking will definitely cause lung cancer in a particular individual. Therefore, we can ignore the warnings of the surgeon general.

6

Writing an Argumentative Essay

When you set out to persuade an audience, you may rely on various appeals—to the emotions, to reason, and to ethics. But although most effective arguments also appeal to the emotions to some degree, their primary appeal is to reason.

When you write an argumentative essay, you follow the same process you use to construct any essay. Your purpose, however, makes necessary some special strategies. Argument requires you to use **critical thinking:** to define your terms, to take a stand, to pay special attention to readers' attitudes and values as well as to their knowledge of your subject, to deal with opposing arguments, to martial evidence, to refute opposing points of view, and to draw logical and fair conclusions. If you find that your ideas do not hold up to your audience's scrutiny, you must change them. Argument thus asks you not only to evaluate your own ideas but also to evaluate the ideas of others.

6a   Planning an Argumentative Essay

When you plan an argumentative essay you must choose an arguable—and defensible—topic, take a stand, define your terms, accommodate your audience, deal with opposing arguments, gather evidence, make inferences from the evidence that you have gathered, and present your points fairly.

125

**arg
6a**

(1) Choosing a topic

You should base your argumentative essay on a *debatable* topic. Any topic about which people disagree is suitable for argument. "Chromium is a metallic element" is not debatable; it is a fact. Like it or not, people have to accept it. But "We should not do business with South Africa even though we need South African chromite" is debatable. Reasonable people could dispute this statement by presenting evidence for or against it.

It helps if you care about your topic, but that is not an absolute requirement. In fact, when you feel very strongly about something, you may not view it clearly. If this is the case, consider another topic, or consider writing an argument for the other side. Dr. Samuel Johnson, the eighteenth-century lexicographer and critic, said that he preferred to argue on the wrong side of an issue because all the interesting things were to be said there.

You should also know something about your topic. The more evidence you can provide the more likely you are to sway your audience. General knowledge is seldom convincing by itself, so you will probably have to do some reading and perhaps some research (see Chapter 37). If you find as you read that your topic is too broad, you will have to narrow it. Your topic should also allow you to do more than rehash tired arguments that everyone has already heard. Unless you have something new to say, stay away from topics such as abortion, nuclear war, legalization of marijuana, and the death penalty.

Finally, you should understand what you want to accomplish in your essay. Your purpose is to change or clarify your readers' view of an issue; unclear, unfair, or unrealistic approaches will not achieve this end. At the very least, you must be able to define both sides of an issue, isolate crucial points, and state your own ideas. If you cannot do so, you probably do not have a good grasp of your topic.

(2) Taking a stand

Your next step is to take a stand. As in other types of writing, you may state your position in a single declarative sentence, or you may leave your thesis unstated but implied. Your thesis should be arguable: it should reflect your purpose by asserting or denying something about your topic. Properly cast, this thesis lays the foundation for the rest of your argument.

Just when you arrive at your thesis depends on how much you know about your topic. If you already know a lot about something, you may have a thesis in mind before you do any reading or writing. (Of course you will modify your thesis if you uncover information that causes you to change your mind.) But usually you will have to read, review your notes, and possibly do some brainstorming to find a thesis. Think carefully about what you want to say before you work up a thesis. If you are having problems settling on one, read some more. If you are still having trouble, begin writing without a thesis. Freewriting often helps you draw out your ideas and discover what you want to say (see 1b.2).

(3)   Defining your terms

You and your readers must agree about the terms you use in your argument. Words convey different meanings to different people. An argument that one rock group is superior to another means nothing unless your audience knows how you define *superior rock group*. Never assume that everybody will know exactly what you mean.

As a rule you should avoid words that convey a moral judgment. When you decide on a thesis, watch for the use of such words as *wrong, bad, good, right,* and *immoral,* which involve judgments that cannot be supported because they are based on beliefs. You may give your reasons for believing what you do, but simply stating your beliefs is not likely to convince a skeptical reader. You should revise a thesis that relies on loaded terms.

ORIGINAL: Censorship of pay TV would be wrong.

REVISED: Censorship of pay TV would unfairly limit free trade.

In the first sentence above, the thesis rests on a moral judgment; the revised thesis focuses on an issue that can be debated. Whatever you believe, you can debate the question of censorship and free trade using such evidence as court decisions, and expert testimony, and make a good case.

(4)   Accommodating your audience

Whatever you write, always consider what your audience knows about your subject (see 1a.2). When writing arguments you should also assess your readers' opinions, attitudes, and values. Before you attempt to convince people to consider your position, give serious thought to their concerns.

arg
6a

Plan your strategy with a specific audience in mind. The ideal situation is to address an audience with which you are familiar, but ideal situations are rare. Who are your readers? Are they unbiased observers or people deeply involved in the issue you plan to discuss? Can they be cast in a specific role—concerned parents, victims of discrimination, irate consumers—or are they so diverse that they cannot be categorized? If you cannot be certain who your readers are, you will have to direct your arguments to a general audience.

In an argument your aim is to bring your audience to a position closer to your own. You cannot do this effectively if you expect your readers to accept what you say without question. You must instead deal with their objections and use evidence to support your conclusion.

(5) Dealing with opposing arguments

To argue effectively, you must know how to refute opposing arguments. By addressing obvious objections to your thesis, you can defuse them before stating your case. You thereby present yourself as a reasonable person who has considered all sides of an issue before reaching a conclusion. When you acknowledge an opposing view, do not distort it or present it as ridiculously weak. This tactic, called creating a **straw man**, will not fool careful readers.

You can refute opposing views by showing that they are untrue, unfair, illogical, unimportant, or irrelevant. In an essay criticizing the unfair practices associated with whaling, a student refutes an argument against her position.

> Of course there are some who say Sea World only wants to capture a few whales. George Will makes this point in his commentary in *Newsweek*, pointing out how valuable the research on whales would be. Unfortunately, Will downplays the fact that Sea World wants to capture a hundred whales, not just "a few." And after releasing ninety whales, Sea World intends to keep ten for "further work." At hearings in Seattle last week, several noted marine biologists went on record condemning Sea World's research program. We must wonder, as they do, why Sea World needs such a large number of whales to carry out its project. (Student)

After acknowledging her opponent's position, the student questions its accuracy and supports her case by summarizing the testimony of several marine biologists.

When an opponent's position is so strong that it cannot be dismissed, admit that the point is well taken, and then, if possible, discuss its limitations. Martin Luther King, Jr., uses this tactic in his "Letter from Birmingham Jail."

> You express a great deal of anxiety over our willingness to break laws. This is certainly a legitimate concern. Since we so diligently urge people to obey the Supreme Court's decision of 1954 outlawing segregation in the public schools, at first glance it may seem rather paradoxical for us consciously to break laws. One may well ask: "How can you advocate breaking some laws and obeying others?" The answer lies in the fact that there are two types of laws: just and unjust. I would be the first to advocate obeying just laws. One has not only a legal but a moral responsibility to obey just laws. Conversely, one has a moral responsibility to disobey unjust laws. I would agree with St. Augustine that "an unjust law is no law at all."

King first acknowledges his audience's legitimate concern about his willingness to break laws. He then counters their objections by distinguishing between just and unjust laws. With this tactic King hopes to overcome audience resistance and gain support for his views.

When you are planning your argument, list the major arguments against your thesis and identify those you can refute. Experienced writers know that only after recognizing their opposition can they construct a persuasive argument.

(6)   Gathering evidence

Most arguments are built on **assertions** (claims you make about your topic) backed by **evidence** (facts—examples and statistics—or expert opinion that reinforces your argument). You could, for instance, assert that law-enforcement techniques have improved in the past few years. You could then support this assertion by referring to a government report stating that violent crime in the ten largest U.S. cities has declined during that time. This report would be one piece of persuasive evidence.

Certain assertions need no proof: statements that are *self-evident* ("All human beings are mortal"), statements that are true by *definition* (2 + 2 = 4), and *statements of fact* that you can expect the average person to know ("The Atlantic Ocean separates England and America"). Other kinds of assertions need supporting evidence.

Remember that an argumentative essay never proves a thesis conclusively—if it did, there would be no argument. The best you can do is to establish a high probability that your thesis is correct or establish that it is reasonable. Choose your evidence with this idea in mind (see 5a.2).

(7)   Making inferences

Whereas facts are bits of information you can verify, **inferences** are observations about the unknown that are based on already known information. For example, we commonly infer the amount of people's incomes from the kinds of cars they drive or the sizes of the houses they occupy. Similarly, an engineer infers the cause of a bridge's collapsing after finding signs of metal fatigue on a supporting girder. A physician infers the condition of a patient by carrying out a series of tests and basing conclusions on test results.

The process of inference is complex and can only be sketched out here. The philosopher John Dewey called an inference "a jump from the known to the unknown." In general, an inference starts with a feeling of confusion or perplexity. You encounter a problem and feel the need to discover a solution. After evaluating each possible solution, you infer the best possible one for the problem.

Suppose you are considering writing a paper about keeping your state free of the many soda bottles and cans that litter its towns and cities. Your research indicates that a number of possible solutions exist for this problem. The state could hire unemployed teenagers to pick up the litter. Brightly colored refuse containers could be placed prominently around the state to encourage people to dispose of bottles and cans properly. Finally, the state could enact a law that required a deposit from all those who bought beverages in bottles or cans. Reviewing your research, you find that your first two solutions had no long-term effect on litter in the states that tried them. However, mandatory deposit laws, along with a prohibition of plastic beverage containers, significantly decreased the number of discarded bottles and cans in two states that instituted such programs. Naturally, the conditions in your state are different from those in the states that you studied. For this reason, you must make a leap from a known situation—the states you studied—to an unknown situation—your state. As a result of your analysis, you infer that the mandatory deposit law is probably a good solution to your problem.

Effective arguments often require inductive leaps in which you connect evidence to your own original conclusions. The next section shows how you can make sure that the inferences you reach are fair.

(8)   Being fair

The line between being persuasive and being unfair is a fine one and, unfortunately, there are no clear-cut rules to help you make this distinction. Writers of effective and sometimes brilliant argumentative essays are often less than fair to their opponents. We could hardly call Jonathan Swift "fair" when, in "A Modest Proposal," he implies that the English are cannibals. A supporter of George III would argue that Thomas Jefferson and the other writers of the Declaration of Independence were less than fair when they criticized British policy in America.

Of course, "A Modest Proposal" is bitter satire, and Swift employs overstatement to express his rage at social conditions. In justifying their break with England, the writers of the Declaration of Independence did not intend to be fair to the king. Argument promotes one point of view, so it is seldom objective. Even so, writers of effective arguments know that they must seem fair and reasonable to their readers.

College writing requires that you stay within the bounds of fairness. To be sure that your evidence is not misleading or distorted, you should learn to avoid the following.

Distorting Evidence Distortion is misrepresentation. Writers sometimes intentionally misrepresent their opponents' views by exaggerating them and then attacking this extreme position. For example, Senator Fratori delivered a speech in which he said that unless something was done soon, the Social Security Trust Fund would run out of money in ten years. He added that a possible solution was to eliminate certain cost-of-living increases that were due to go into effect. His opponent, Ms. Ryan, attacked him by saying that clearly he was in favor of curtailing benefits to older Americans. Where would he stop? Would he eliminate benefits? Would he scrap the whole Social Security system? What about Medicare? Medicaid? Welfare? Anyone who could support such actions, Ms. Ryan said, did not deserve public office.

Senator Fratori said only that something had to be done to keep the Social Security system solvent. Ms. Ryan could have challenged Senator Fratori's assertion and his proposed solution with facts, figures, and other data. Instead, by distorting his position she attacked it unfairly.

Quoting Out of Context A writer or speaker quotes out of context by taking someone's words from their original setting and using them in another. When you select certain words from a statement and ignore others, you can change the meaning of what someone has said or implied. Consider this example.

Mr. N, township resident

> I don't know why you are opposing the new highway. According to your own statements the highway will increase land value and bring more business into the area.

Ms. L, township supervisor

> I think you should look at my statements more carefully. I have a copy of the paper that printed my interview and what I said was [*reading*]: "The highway will increase land values a bit and bring some business to the area. But at what cost? One hundred and fifty families will be displaced, and the highway will divide our township in half." My comments were not meant to support the new highway but to underscore the problems that its construction will cause.

By repeating only some of Ms. L's remarks, Mr. N alters her meaning to suit his purpose. In context, Ms. L's words indicate that although she acknowledges the highway's few benefits, she believes that its drawbacks outweigh them.

Slanting Evidence When you select information that supports your case and ignore information that does not, you are slanting evidence. For example, if you support your position that smoking should not be prohibited in public places by choosing only evidence provided by the American Tobacco Institute, you are guilty of slanting evidence. Inflammatory language also biases your writing. A national magazine slanted evidence, to say the least, when it described a reputed criminal as "a hulk of a man who looks as if he could burn out somebody's eyes with a propane torch." Although one-sided presentations do appear in newspapers and magazines, you should avoid such distortions when you seek to present a rational argument.

6b Shaping an Argumentative Essay

In its simplest form, an argument consists of a thesis and the evidence to support this thesis. However, argumentative essays contain additional elements calculated to win audience approval and to overcome potential opposition. Depending upon your purpose and audience, you may choose to arrange these elements in various ways; in some cases, you may decide to omit one or more elements entirely. Still, using these elements as a guide will help you make sure that you have included enough evidence, that you have presented it effectively, and that you have dealt with opposing points of view.

(1)   The introduction

The introduction of your argumentative essay orients your audience to your subject and helps to convince them that your sub-

Elements of an Argumentative Essay

1. The Introduction
2. The Background Statement
3. The Thesis Statement
4. The Points or Steps in the Argument
5. The Refutation of Opposing Arguments
6. The Conclusion

ject is something about which they should be concerned. Here you can show how your subject concerns the reader, note why it is interesting, or explain how it has been misunderstood (see 4g.1 for a discussion of specific strategies for writing introductions). In your introduction you try to present yourself as a reasonable person whose views deserve to be considered. You may also include any special qualifications that you have to write about your subject. For example, if you are writing a paper in which you argue against a proposed design for a new library for your college, you should let readers know in your introduction if you are a fourth-year architecture student.

(2) The background statement

In this section of your essay you present the background of the subject you will discuss. By giving readers an overview, you enable them to understand the more detailed points and refutations that you will present later. This section may include a narrative of past events, a summary of others' opinions on your subject, or a statement of the basic facts of an issue. Keep your background statement short; long, drawn-out discussions at this point will distract your readers from the focus of your argument. Include only the material you think your readers need to know about your subject. If your audience is already well informed about your subject, you may decide to omit this section. Often, however, it is helpful to include background information—even in abbreviated form—just to establish for your readers the context of your discussion.

(3) The thesis statement

Your thesis statement can appear anywhere in your argumentative essay, depending on the strategy you are employing and the nature of your audience. Frequently, you present your thesis after you have given your readers an overview of your subject. However, in highly controversial arguments—those to which your audience might react negatively—you may postpone your thesis until the end of your essay. Whatever the case, your thesis should clearly convey your position to your readers.

Because the purpose of an argumentative essay is to convince readers to accept your position, your thesis must take a stand. One way to make sure that your thesis actually does take a stand is to formulate an **antithesis,** a statement that takes an arguable position opposite from yours. If you can create an antithesis, your main idea takes a stand. If you cannot, your statement needs further revision to make it an argumentative thesis.

Thesis	Antithesis
Put the blame [for prize-fighter Benny Paret's death] where it belongs—on the prevailing mores that regard prize-fighting as a perfectly proper enterprise and vehicle of entertainment.	Paret's death cannot be blamed on the prevailing mores that regard prize-fighting as a perfectly proper enterprise and vehicle of entertainment.

(4)   The points or steps in the argument

This section is the center of your essay; it contains the deductive or inductive arguments, or a combination of the two, that you will use to support your thesis. Here you present your points and the evidence you have gathered to support them. One problem that you have at this stage is deciding on the arrangement of your points. Most often, you begin with your weakest argument and work up to your strongest. (An alternate plan is to begin with your *second* best argument and then end with your strongest.) To move in the opposite direction is anticlimactic. Not only would you emphasize your weakest arguments by putting them last, but you would also make it appear as if these arguments are afterthoughts. If all your arguments are equally strong, you can arrange them in any way; however, you might want to begin with points with which your readers are already familiar and are likely to accept and then move on to relatively unfamiliar points. In this way, the familiar paves the way for the unfamiliar.

(5)   The refutation of opposing arguments

In a face-to-face debate, you are confronted by the arguments against your thesis, and you have the opportunity to refute them. In an argumentative essay, however, you must bring these points up yourself: you must anticipate these arguments and question their soundness. If you do not confront these opposing arguments, doubts about your case will remain in the minds of your readers. If strong opposing arguments exist, admit their strengths and then refute them early in your paper, before you present your own points. If the opposing arguments are relatively weak, refute them after you have made your case. In this situation, the strength of your arguments will further undermine the opposing arguments. Keep in mind that your audience, purpose, and subject determine what constitutes appropriate refutation. What will convince one audience that an argument is weak may alienate another. Using a humorous anecdote, for example, to refute a point about a serious subject may convince some segments of your audience, but it will probably alienate more people than it convinces.

(6) The conclusion

The conclusion of a syllogism is the proposition that is deduced from the major and the minor premises (see 5b). The conclusion of your essay rounds out your argument and provides closure. Without a conclusion your essay would just stop, leaving your readers hanging. Because readers remember best what they encounter last, your conclusion has an important function in your argument. It can summarize facts, restate your thesis, reinforce the weaknesses of opposing arguments, or underscore the logic of your position (see 4g.2). Most often the conclusion restates in general terms the major arguments that you have marshaled in support of your thesis. This tactic brings your argument into focus and, for this reason, can have a powerful effect on readers. Many writers like to end their conclusions with a strong last line, one calculated to stay in the minds of their readers. An apt quotation or a statement that crystallizes the sentiments or captures the intensity of your argument works well. As with introductions, your evaluation of your purpose and audience should determine how elaborate or how simple your conclusion should be.

6c Writing and Revising an Argumentative Essay

You write your argumentative essay just as you would any other essay. As with planning and shaping, you keep the special concerns of argument in mind as you draft and revise.

(1) Writing an argumentative essay

The following draft of an essay contains many of the components discussed earlier. The student, Lauren Sklar, was asked by her instructor to write an argument about a controversial subject. She was told not to do library research but to use her own experiences to support her arguments; however, she was given permission to include expert opinion supplied by her father, an amateur dog breeder.

In Defense of Pit Bulls

Introduction   1   Throughout this coming year, many state legislatures will consider laws that if passed will result in the persecution of an entire group of individuals. These laws make possible the confiscation of private property, the imposition of fines, and the criminal prosecution of people who are guilty of nothing more than owning a dog. As difficult as it may be to believe, these things are already happening to the thousands of people all over the United States who own a breed of dog commonly referred to as "pit bulls."

Background statement   2   The term pit bull is applied to a number of mixed breeds related to the American bull terrier. This animal is sleek, agile, strong, loyal--and yes, lovable. Lately, these animals have achieved notoriety--especially on the television evening news--because of their attacks against human beings. The reports are usually accompanied by lurid pictures of the mangled limbs of victims and by adjectives such as "vicious" and "bloodthirsty." As a result of this publicity, many states have proposed laws that would make it a crime to own a pit bull. The penalty for violating these laws is often severe--destruction of the animal, stiff fines, and sometimes even imprisonment of the owner.

Thesis   Not only are these prohibitions unconstitutional, but they also reflect ideas about pit bulls that are not supported by the facts.

Refutation of opposing arguments

3   It cannot be denied that the pit bull is a formidable fighter and can be frightening when provoked. Both adults and children have been mauled by these animals, most often when they unknowingly encroach on a pit bull's territory. All dogs have strong territorial instincts and will fight to protect their property. The pit bull is no different. It will lunge from behind a fence or actually attack an individual whom it thinks is threatening an area that it has marked.

Refutation of opposing arguments

4   Although it is true that pit bulls have been bred to be fighters, they are not people-haters. As most owners will testify, attacking humans is against the nature of pit bulls, just as it is against the nature of most dogs. Certainly, pit bulls have been used as weapons by some individuals—inner-city gang members and drug dealers immediately come to mind. But the fact that these misguided owners abuse their animals does not mean that the whole breed is bad and should be outlawed. Outlawing pit bulls would make as much sense as outlawing all automobiles because just a few are used to commit crimes.

Deductive argument

5   In America a person is considered innocent until proven guilty. This principle is one of the cornerstones of our democratic system of government. Most people would agree that any law that violated this precept is unjust and, therefore, unconstitutional. Much of the legislation that is aimed at pit bull owners, however, subjects them to penalties <u>before</u> any harm has been done. One ordinance in Massachusetts makes it a crime to own the

"Staffordshire pit bull terrier or bull terrier or any mixture thereof." This law mandates that pit bulls be destroyed, even if they are gentle animals. By indiscriminately condemning all pit bulls, such statutes clearly violate the owners' rights.

Inductive argument supported by expert testimony

6   What is most disturbing about the recent movement to legislate against pit bull owners is how misinformed lawmakers seem to be. Take, for example, the charge that pit bulls are more vicious than other breeds. My father, who is an amateur breeder and who has handled pit bulls, says that no scientific evidence exists to support this claim. I myself have handled pit bulls and find them to be no more prone to bite than other dogs. In fact, statistics from the Humane Society of the United States indicate that German shepherds, Labrador retrievers, rottweilers, and assorted mongrels bite more frequently than do pit bulls.

Inductive argument supported by examples

7   Another area of misinformation concerns the severity of the injuries caused by pit bulls. Many dogs have the ability to inflict damage with their teeth. Every year thousands of dog bites are reported; most are minor, but some are quite severe. Although pit bulls have very powerful jaws and bite using a ripping motion, their bites are no more severe than those of many other breeds. Collies and cocker spaniels, for example, not only bite more frequently, but also are responsible for many more serious injuries each year than are pit bulls. These breeds are high-strung, nervous, and unpredictable. In contrast, pit bulls, despite their reputations, are generally even-tempered, calm, and loyal.

Conclusion   8   It is understandable that state legislators
                  want to protect people from the attacks of
                  vicious dogs. But unlike existing laws that hold
                  owners responsible for the actions of their pets,
                  laws that apply to a single breed will not help
                  the public. This shortsighted approach ignores
                  the fact it is the individual dog, not the entire
                  breed, that is dangerous. Outlawing an entire
                  breed not only violates the rights of owners, but
                  also undermines the freedom of all individuals.

Strong last   By so doing, these proposed laws would seem to be
line   more dangerous to the public than a pit bull
                  could ever be.

In paragraph 1 Lauren introduces her essay by orienting her readers to her subject. She creates interest by indicating that although what she is saying seems farfetched, it is nonetheless true. In her background statement in paragraph 2 Lauren gives an overview of the problem she is going to discuss. She presents a definition of *pit bull* and outlines the circumstances that have brought this animal to the public's attention. She ends this section with her thesis that the laws against the pit bull are both unconstitutional and misguided.

Paragraphs 3 and 4 refute the major arguments against Lauren's thesis. Because these arguments are compelling, she decides to refute them at the beginning of her essay, before she presents her own arguments. The attacks of pit bulls have been well documented in the press, so Lauren concedes the point in paragraph 3. She then points out that all dogs will attack if their territory is invaded. In paragraph 4 Lauren also concedes that some pit bulls have been misused by their owners. This fact is no reason, she says, to outlaw the entire breed. Lauren ends paragraph 4 with an analogy that underscores this point.

Paragraph 5 is a deductive argument that begins with the major premise that no law should violate the precept of "innocent until proven guilty." According to Lauren, laws that prohibit ownership of pit bulls do violate this precept, and therefore they violate the owners' rights.

Paragraphs 6 and 7 present inductive arguments against the legislation outlawing pit bulls. In paragraph 6, Lauren introduces the expert testimony of her father who is an amateur breeder and who, along with Lauren, has handled pit bulls. With this evidence she establishes that pit bulls do not bite more often than other breeds. In paragraph 7 Lauren admits that pit bulls can inflict severe injuries but offers evidence to establish that the bites of pit bulls are no more severe than those of other breeds.

Lauren establishes herself as a reasonable person in her conclusion by granting the benevolent intention of the legislation that she opposes. She goes on to say, however, that unlike existing laws that focus on vicious animals, laws outlawing a specific breed are shortsighted. She ends with a statement that sums up her feelings and that is calculated to stay with her readers.

(2) Revising an argumentative essay

You revise your argumentative essay using the same criteria you consider for any essay (see 3d.3). In addition, you concentrate on the specific concerns of argument that are listed in the following checklist.

Revision Checklist for Writing an Argumentative Essay

* Is your topic debatable?
* Have you stated your thesis?
* Have you adequately defined the terms you use in your argument?
* Have you considered the opinions, attitudes, and values of your audience?
* Have you identified and refuted opposing arguments?
* Have you supported your assertions with evidence? (see the "Checklist for Evaluating Evidence," p. 108)
* Have you made reasonable inferences from your evidence?
* Have you been fair?
* Are your arguments logically constructed?
* Does the structure of your essay suit your material and your audience?
* Have you provided your readers with enough background information?
* Do you need to make additional points?
* Do you have an interesting introduction and a strong conclusion?

Once you are satisfied that your essay meets these criteria, review your argument carefully to make certain it contains none of the fallacies listed in 5c.

☐   **EXERCISE**

The following paragraph was deleted by Lauren Sklar from her essay "In Defense of Pit Bulls" (p. 136). Was Lauren right to delete it? If it belongs in the essay, where would it go? Is it relevant? logical? Jot down your responses in the margins of the essay, and be prepared to discuss them in class.

> Another problem with these ordinances is that they ignore the fact that every decade seems to have its canine villains. During the nineteen forties the German shepherd achieved notoriety because of its use in concentration camps by the Nazis. In the nineteen fifties the chow was reputed to be a vicious animal that would turn without provocation on its owner. The seventies saw the Doberman pinscher take its place in the public mind as a fierce killer. No doubt several years from today the public will fix its gaze on another breed, and the pit bull will regain the anonymity that it formerly enjoyed. Although the laws that focus on a specific breed like the pit bull may be politically expedient, they do little to protect the public or to identify unsafe animals.

Student Writer at Work: Writing an Argumentative Essay

Revise the following draft of an argumentative essay, paying particular attention to the essay's logic and to the use of evidence. Be prepared to explain the changes you made and how they make the essay more convincing. If necessary, revise further to strengthen coherence, unity, and style.

The Gun Question

Years ago, guns were essential for obtaining food to feed many families. However, since we started domesticating animals, guns have become less important for obtaining food. Instead, they have been widely used for crimes and have caused many accidents. When respected and

used properly, however, guns can improve, protect, and
even save many people's lives.

Some people feel that if guns were outlawed, fewer
murders, robberies, and gun-related accidents would
occur. These people do not know what they are talking
about. If guns were taken away, only the honest citizens
would give up their guns. The criminals and the
government would be the only people who had guns. We would
be at the mercy of outlaws and the goodwill of the
government. Perhaps the people who oppose guns should
worry more about tyranny than about criminals who have
their rights violated.

Opponents of guns often suggest that all firearms in
this country should be registered. The registration of
firearms, however, is the first step toward confiscation.
If firearms were confiscated, this would be the first step
toward an authoritarian government. There would be no
armed citizenry to ensure that the Bill of Rights is
enforced. Would the people who favor the registration of
guns like it if the government took away their houses,
their cars, or even their money?

The Constitution guarantees all citizens the right to
bear arms. The Founding Fathers realized that an armed
citizenry is the best defense against tyranny. Look at
some of the countries that have forbidden private citizens
from owning guns. In Nazi Germany only the army could
have guns. If a citizen was caught with a gun, he or she
was killed. In Russia only certain people can own
weapons. Anyone else who has a gun is thought to be an
enemy of the state. The same holds true for Uganda,
Chile, Iran, and China.

In addition to protecting our rights, guns enable
citizens to protect their lives. Every issue of The
American Rifleman presents at least a dozen or more
examples of honest people using guns to protect their

lives and their possessions. These articles show how different types of people have been able to stop criminals. Store owners, housewives, and even children have used guns for protection against criminals. Anyone who cannot accept this evidence obviously has trouble accepting the truth.

Although some people fear guns and their misuse, guns are an important and beneficial factor in our lives. If guns were outlawed, only the criminals and the government would have guns. This fact should be enough to convince anyone how necessary guns are.

SECTION II

Composing Sentences

Building Simple Sentences

7a Identifying the Basic Sentence Elements

A **sentence** is an independent grammatical unit that contains a subject and a predicate and expresses a complete thought.

My sister decided to major in business.

It came from outer space.

Easter Island is a Chilean island in the South Pacific.

In these three sentences, the simple subjects are *sister*, *it*, and *Easter Island*, and the simple predicates are *decided*, *came*, and *is*. A **simple subject** is a noun or noun substitute that tells who or what the sentence is about. A **simple predicate**, a verb or verb phrase, tells or asks something about the subject. The **complete subject** of a sentence, however, includes all the words associated with the subject, and the **complete predicate** includes not just the verb or verb phrase but all the words associated with it.

7b Constructing Basic Sentence Patterns

In its basic form, a simple sentence consists of one subject and one predicate. The most basic English sentences may be built from one of the following five patterns.

(1) Subject and intransitive verb (s + v)

The simplest sentence pattern consists of just a subject and a verb or verb phrase.

$$s \qquad\qquad v$$
The price of gold rose.

$$s \qquad\qquad v$$
Stock prices may fall.

In both sentences the verbs (*rose, may fall*) are **intransitive**—that is, they have no direct objects. (A dictionary can tell you which verbs are transitive, which are intransitive, and which may be either, depending on context.)

(2) Subject + transitive verb + direct object (s + v + do)

In another pattern the sentence consists of the subject, a transitive verb, and a direct object. A **transitive** verb is one that requires an object to complete its meaning in the sentence. A **direct object** indicates where the verb's action is directed and who or what is affected by it.

$$s \qquad\quad v \qquad\qquad do$$
Van Gogh created "The Starry Night."

$$s \qquad\quad v \quad\; do$$
Caroline saved Jake.

In each sentence the direct object tells *who* or *what* received the verb's action.

(3) Subject + transitive verb + direct object + object complement (s + v + do + oc)

This pattern, similar to the one above, includes an **object complement** that renames or describes the direct object.

$$s \qquad\quad v \qquad do \qquad oc$$
The class elected Bridget treasurer.

$$s \quad v \qquad\quad do \quad\; oc$$
I found the exam easy.

In the first sentence the object complement is a noun that renames the object; in the second it is an adjective that describes the object.

(4) Subject + linking verb + subject complement (s + v + sc)

This kind of sentence consists of a subject, a **linking verb** (a verb that connects a subject to its complement) and the **subject com-**

plement (the word or phrase that describes or renames the subject).

The *injection* was painless.
`s`   `v`   `sc`

The *animals* seemed restless.
`s`   `v`   `sc`

Thatcher became prime minister.
`s`   `v`   `sc`

In the first two sentences the subject complement is an adjective, called a **predicate adjective,** that describes the subject; in the third sentence, the subject complement is a noun, called a **predicate nominative,** that renames the subject. In each case the linking verb can be seen as an equal sign, equating the subject with its complement (*Thatcher = prime minister*).

(5) Subject + transitive verb + indirect object + direct object (s + v + io + do)

In this sentence pattern the **indirect object** tells to or for whom the verb's action was done.

Cyrano wrote *Roxanne* a poem. (Cyrano wrote a poem for Roxanne.)
`s`   `v`   `io`   `do`

The *officer* handed *Frank* a ticket. (The officer handed a ticket to Frank.)
`s`   `v`   `io`   `do`

☐   **EXERCISE 1**

In each of the following sentences underline the subject once, and underline the verb twice. Then label direct objects, indirect objects, subject complements, and object complements.

EXAMPLE: *Scarlett O'Hara* wore a green velvet dress.
`do`

1. Metro-Goldwyn-Mayer released the film version of Margaret Mitchell's novel *Gone with the Wind* in 1939.
2. Vivien Leigh played the fiery Scarlett O'Hara, a beautiful Southern belle.
3. Clark Gable co-starred as Rhett Butler.
4. Scarlett loved her home, the plantation called Tara.
5. Yankee soldiers looted and vandalized Tara.

6. Scarlett was angry.
7. She was also desperate.
8. She paid Rhett Butler a visit.
9. Scarlett requested a $300 loan from Rhett to pay Tara's taxes.
10. She painted Rhett an optimistic picture.
11. Rhett called her a liar.
12. Moreover, he refused her the loan.

7c   Forming Questions and Commands

The five basic sentence patterns are alike in one respect: all are statements that present first the subject and then the predicate. This standard word order varies for questions and commands.

(1)   Questions

Questions in English can be formed in several ways. Most often, we invert subject and verb (This is Maggie's farm. → Is this Maggie's farm?). Sometimes we invert and add a form of *do* before the subject (Maggie lives here. → Does Maggie live here?). Sometimes we also indicate a question by beginning a sentence with *who, what, why, where, when,* or *how.* (Wes was late again. → Why was Wes late again?). In some cases we can simply add a question mark to a statement (This is Maggie's farm? Wes was late again?) or add a phrase with inverted subject and verb at the end of the sentence (This is Maggie's farm, isn't it? Wes was late again, wasn't he?). In these instances, the word order of the original statement remains unchanged.

(2)   Commands

To form commands, either use the second person singular (You stop that!) or simply leave out the sentence's subject (you), which is understood.

Go to your room.
March.
Stop that!

7d   Identifying Phrases and Clauses

Individual words may be joined to build *phrases* and *clauses.*

(1)   Identifying phrases

A **phrase** is a grammatically ordered group of related words that lacks a subject or predicate or both and functions as a single part of speech.

A **verb phrase** consists of an auxiliary verb and a main verb. (Time *is running* out.)

A **noun phrase** includes a noun or pronoun plus all related modifiers. (I'll climb *the highest mountain*.)

A **prepositional phrase** consists of a preposition, its object, and any modifiers of that object (see 7f.1).

They discussed the ethical implications of the operation.

He was last seen heading into the sunset.

A **verbal phrase** consists of a verbal and its related objects, modifiers, or complements (see 7f.2). A verbal phrase may be a **participial phrase**, a **gerund phrase**, or an **infinitive phrase**.

Encouraged by the voter turnout, the candidate predicted a victory. (participial phrase)

Taking it easy always makes sense. (gerund phrase)

The jury recessed to evaluate the evidence. (infinitive phrase)

An **absolute phrase** usually consists of a noun or pronoun and a participle, accompanied by modifiers (see 7f.3).

Their toes tapping, they watched the auditions.

(2)   Identifying clauses

A **clause** is a group of related words that includes a subject and a predicate. An **independent** (main) **clause** may stand alone as a sentence, but a **dependent** (subordinate) **clause** must always be accompanied by an independent clause.

[Lucretia Mott was an abolitionist.] [She was also a pioneer for women's rights.] (two independent clauses)

[Lucretia Mott was an abolitionist] [who was also a pioneer for women's rights.] (independent clause, dependent clause)

[Although Lucretia Mott was most widely known for her support of women's rights,] [she was also a prominent abolitionist.] (dependent clause, independent clause)

Depending on how they function in a sentence, dependent clauses may be classified as adjective, adverb, or noun clauses.

Adjective clauses, sometimes called **relative clauses**, modify nouns or pronouns. They are introduced by relative pronouns (see 8b). The adverbs *where* and *when* can be used as relative pronouns when the adjective clause modifies a place or time.

> The television series *M*A*S*H*, which depicted life in an army hospital in Korea during the Korean War, ran for eleven years. (Adjective clause modifies the noun *M*A*S*H*.)

> Celeste's grandparents, who were born in Rumania, speak little English. (Adjective clause modifies the noun *grandparents*.)

> The Pulitzer Prizes for journalism are prestigious awards that are presented in areas like editorial writing, photography, editorial cartooning, and national and international reporting. (Adjective clause modifies the noun *awards*.)

> *Sophie's Choice* is set in Brooklyn, where the narrator lives in a house painted pink. (Adjective clause modifies the noun *Brooklyn*.)

NOTE: Adjective clauses follow the nouns or pronouns they modify.

Adverb clauses modify single words (verbs, adjectives, or adverbs) or entire phrases or clauses. They are always introduced by subordinating conjunctions (see 8b). Adverb clauses provide information to answer the questions *how? where? when? why?* and *to what extent?*

> Exhausted after the match was over, Kim decided to take a long nap. (Adverb clause modifies the participle *exhausted*.)

> To get to the coach before it turned into a pumpkin, Cinderella had to hurry. (Adverb clause modifies the infinitive phrase *to get to the coach*.)

> Because 75 percent of its exports are fish products, Iceland's economy is heavily dependent on the fishing industry. (Adverb clause modifies independent clause, telling *why* the fishing industry is so important.)

> Her unemployment insurance benefits were reduced when she found a part-time job. (Adverb clause modifies independent clause, telling *when* benefits were reduced.)

Noun clauses act as nouns (as subjects, direct objects, indirect objects, or complements) in a sentence. A noun clause may be introduced by a relative pronoun or by *whether, when, where, why,* or *how.*

> Whatever happens to us will be for the best. (Noun clause serves as subject of sentence.)

> They finally decided which candidate was best. (Noun clause serves as direct object of verb *decided*.)

> What you see is what you get. (Noun clause serves as subject complement.)

Elliptical clauses are grammatically incomplete—that is, a part of the subject or predicate or the entire subject or predicate is missing. If the missing part can be easily inferred from the context of the sentence, such constructions are acceptable.

Although [they were] full, they could not resist dessert.

He has never been able to read maps as well as his brother [can read maps].

☐   **EXERCISE 2**

Which of the following groups of words are independent clauses? Which are dependent clauses? Which are phrases? Mark each word group IC, DC, or P.

EXAMPLE: Coming through the rye. (P)

1. Beauty is truth.
2. When knights were bold.
3. In a galaxy far away.
4. He saw stars
5. I hear a symphony.
6. Whenever you are near.
7. The clock struck ten.
8. The red planet.
9. Slowly I turned.
10. For the longest time.

7e Building Simple Sentences with Individual Words

A simple sentence can consist of as little as a subject and a predicate.

Jessica fell.

Simple sentences can also be considerably more elaborate.

Jessica fell in love.

Jessica fell in love with Henry.

Jessica almost immediately fell in love with Henry.

Jessica and her sister almost immediately fell in love with Henry.

Jessica and her younger sister Victoria almost immediately fell in love with the dashing Henry Goodyear.

Jessica and her lively younger sister Victoria almost immediately fell hopelessly in love with the very dashing and mysterious Henry Goodyear.

The addition of modifying words (*older, dashing*, and so on) and phrases (*with the dashing Henry Goodyear*) and the creation of compounds (*Jessica and her sister, dashing and mysterious*) have changed the substance and the meaning of *Jessica fell* quite substantially.

(1)   Building simple sentences with adjectives and adverbs

Descriptive adjectives and adverbs enrich the meaning of a sentence. Reread our sample sentence.

> Jessica and her lively younger sister Victoria almost immediately fell hopelessly in love with the very dashing and mysterious Henry Goodyear.

In this sentence, four adjectives describe nouns.

Adjective	*Noun*
lively	sister
younger	sister
dashing	Henry Goodyear
mysterious	Henry Goodyear

The four adverbs in the sentence describe the action of verbs or modify adjectives or other adverbs.

Adverb	
almost	immediately (adverb)
immediately	fell (verb)
hopelessly	fell (verb)
very	dashing and mysterious (adjectives)

(For a more complete discussion of adjectives and adverbs, see Chapter 25.)

☐   **EXERCISE 3**

Label all descriptive adjectives and adverbs in the following sentences.

EXAMPLE: The red house perched unsteadily on the edge of the hill.
           adj   *adv*

1. The matchmaker appeared one night out of the dark fourth-floor hallway of the graystone rooming house where Finkle lived, grasping a black, strapped portfolio that had been worn thin with use. (Bernard Malamud, "The Magic Barrel")
2. During these last decades the interest in professional fasting has markedly diminished. It used to pay very well to stage such great performances under one's own management, but today that is quite impossible. We live in a different world now.   (Franz Kafka, "A Hunger Artist")
3. A school of minnows swam by, each minnow with its small individual shadow, doubling the attendance, so clear and sharp in the sunlight. (E. B. White, "Once More to the Lake")
4. Poetry is as universal as language and almost as ancient.   (Laurence Perrine, *Sound and Sense*)
5. Every town and village along that vast stretch of double river frontage had a best dwelling, finest dwelling, mansion—the home of its

wealthiest and most conspicuous citizen.   (Mark Twain, *Life on the Mississippi*)

☐   **EXERCISE 4**

Using these five sentences as models, write five original simple sentences. Use adverbs and adjectives where the model sentences use them, and then underline and label these modifiers.

>   *adv*   *adj*
> EXAMPLE: Cathy carefully put the baby bird in the nest.
>   *adv*   *adj*
>   He angrily called the old man into the kitchen.

1. Nick turned his head carefully away smiling sweatily.   (Ernest Hemingway, *In Our Time*)
2. Outside, the fire-red, gas-blue, ghost-green signs shone smokily through the tranquil rain.   (F. Scott Fitzgerald, "Babylon Revisited")
3. The pavement was wet, glassy with water.   (Willa Cather, "The Old Beauty")
4. The therapy used for treating burns has been improved considerably in recent years.   (Lewis Thomas, "On Medicine and the Bomb")
5. There was a strange, inflamed, flurried, flighty recklessness of activity about him.   (Herman Melville, *Bartleby the Scrivener*)

(2)   Building simple sentences with nouns and verbals

Words other than adjectives and adverbs can help you build richer simple sentences. These include nouns and verbals.

Nouns   Nouns can sometimes act as adjectives modifying other nouns.

> He needed the cake pans for the layer cake.
> "Silent Night" is a Christmas carol.
> Dave is a soccer coach.

Verbals   **Verbals** include present and past participles, infinitives, and gerunds (see 21c).
> Verbals may act as modifiers.

> All three living former presidents attended the funeral. (Present participle serves as adjective.)
> The Grand Canyon is the attraction to visit. (Infinitive serves as adjective.)
> The puzzle was impossible to solve. (Infinitive serves as adverb.)
> Or verbals may act as nouns.

When the <u>going</u> gets tough, the tough get going. (Gerund serves as noun.)

To err is human. (Infinitive serves as noun.)

It took me an entire three-hour lab period to identify my <u>unknown</u>. (Past participle serves as noun.)

☐   **EXERCISE 5**

1. List ten nouns that can be used as modifiers.

   EXAMPLES: <u>word</u> processor, <u>truck</u> stop, <u>peanut</u> butter

2. List ten participles that can be used as modifiers.

   EXAMPLES: crushed, ringing

3. Choosing words from your lists, write five original sentences, each of which includes both a noun and a participle used as modifiers.

   EXAMPLE: The <u>word</u> processor was a <u>crushed</u> mass of metal and plastic.

4. Then add adjectives and adverbs to enrich the sentence further.

   EXAMPLE: The <u>new</u> word processor was a <u>gruesomely</u> crushed mass of metal and plastic.

☐   **EXERCISE 6**

For additional practice in building simple sentences using individual words, combine each of the following groups of sentences into one simple sentence that contains several modifiers. You will have to add, delete, or reorder words.

   EXAMPLE: The night was cold. The night was wet.
   The night scared them. They were terribly scared.

   REVISED: The cold, wet night scared them terribly.

1. The ship landed. The ship was from space. The ship was tremendous. It landed silently.
2. It landed in a field. The field was grassy. The field was deserted.
3. A dog appeared. The dog was tiny. The dog was abandoned. The dog was a stray.
4. The dog was brave. The dog was curious. He approached the spacecraft. The spacecraft was burning. He approached it carefully.
5. A creature emerged from the spaceship. The creature was smiling. He was purple. He emerged slowly.
6. The dog and the alien stared at each other. The dog was little. The alien was purple. They stared meaningfully.
7. The dog and the alien walked. They walked silently. They walked carefully. They walked toward each other.
8. The dog barked. He barked tentatively. He barked questioningly. The dog was uneasy.

9. The alien extended his hand. The alien was grinning. He extended it
slowly. The hand was hairy.
10. In his hand was a bag. The bag was of canvas. The bag was green.
The bag was for laundry.

7f   Building Simple Sentences with Phrases

You can also enrich your sentences by building with phrases (see
7d.1). Because a phrase lacks a subject or predicate (or both), it
cannot stand alone as a sentence. But within a sentence phrases
add information and provide connections between ideas.

(1)   Building simple sentences with prepositional phrases

A **preposition** relates a noun or noun substitute to the rest of the
sentence. (For a list of the most commonly used prepositions, see
21f.) A **prepositional phrase** consists of the preposition, its object
(the noun or noun substitute), and any modifiers of that object.

> *prep   obj*   *modifier*
> Cumulus clouds are towers on bases that extend thousands of
> feet. (Phrase functions as adjective modifying the noun *towers*.)

In this example the preposition *precedes* its object. Occasionally
in writing and often in speech, however, the preposition appears
after the object.

> *obj*   *prep*
> He is the person you are looking for.

Prepositional phrases can function in a sentence as adjectives or as adverbs.

> Carry Nation was an agitator for temperance. (Prepositional phrase
> functions as adjective modifying the noun *agitator*.)

> The Madeira River flows into the Amazon. (Prepositional phrase
> functions as adverb modifying the verb *flows*.)

☐   EXERCISE 7

Read the following sentences. Underline each prepositional phrase, and
then connect it with an arrow to the word it modifies. Finally, tell
whether each phrase functions as an adjective or an adverb.

> EXAMPLE: Herz looked harassed enough to be the father of three or
> four small, mean, colicky children. (Philip Roth, *Letting
> Go*) (Prepositional phrase functions as an adjective.)

1. He stumbled down the back steps, hugging the thick book under his arm.   (Richard Wright, "The Man Who Was Almost a Man")
2. She looked at me, sitting in the chair before the cold stove, the sailor hat on her head.   (William Faulkner "That Evening Sun")
3. It was Paul's afternoon to appear before the faculty of the Pittsburgh High School to account for his various misdemeanors.   (Willa Cather, "Paul's Case")
4. It struck the trunk of the apple tree, bounced back at an angle, and rolled steadily and stupidly onto the cement apron in front of the firehouse, where one of the trucks was parked.   (Richard Wilbur, "A Game of Catch")
5. Outside the town, along the tracks, there were barren trees and bushes below the embankment, snow-gray in the dark. And down among the trees and bushes there were makeshift houses made out of boxes and tin and old pieces of wood and canvas. You couldn't see them in the dark, but you knew they were there if you'd ever been on the road, if you had ever lived with the homeless and hungry in a depression.   (Langston Hughes, "On the Road")

☐   **EXERCISE 8**

For additional practice in using prepositional phrases, combine each pair of sentences to create one simple sentence that includes a prepositional phrase. You may add, delete, or reorder words. Some sentences may have more than one correct version.

> EXAMPLE: America's drinking water is being contaminated. Toxic substances are contaminating it.
>
> America's drinking water is being contaminated by toxic substances.

1. Toxic waste disposal presents a serious problem. Americans have this problem.
2. Hazardous chemicals pose a threat. People are threatened.
3. Some towns, like Times Beach, Missouri, have been completely abandoned. Their residents have abandoned them.
4. Dioxin is one chemical. It has serious toxic effects.
5. Dioxin is highly toxic. The toxicity affects animals and humans.
6. Toxic chemical wastes like dioxin may be found. Over fifty thousand dumps have them.
7. Industrial parks contain toxic wastes. Open pits, ponds, and lagoons are where the toxic substances are.
8. Toxic wastes pose dangers. The land, water, and air are endangered.
9. In addition, toxic substances are a threat. They threaten our public health and our economy.
10. Immediate toxic waste cleanup would be a tremendous benefit. Americans are the ones who would benefit.

(2) Building simple sentences with verbal phrases

A **verbal phrase** consists of a verbal (participle, gerund, or infinitive) and its related objects, modifiers, or complements. Like verbals, verbal phrases can also help you build sentences.

Some verbal phrases act as nouns. Gerund phrases, for example, like gerunds themselves, are always used as nouns, and infinitive phrases may also be used as nouns.

> Making a living isn't always easy. (Gerund phrase serves as sentence's subject.)
>
> Wendy appreciated Tom's being honest. (Gerund phrase serves as object of verb *appreciated*.)
>
> The entire town was shocked by their breaking up. (Gerund phrase is object of preposition *by*.)
>
> To know him is to love him. (Infinitive phrase *To know him* serves as sentence's subject; infinitive phrase *to love him* is subject complement.)

Some verbal phrases are also used as modifiers. Participial phrases are always used to modify nouns or pronouns, and infinitive phrases may function as adjectives or as adverbs.

> Fascinated by Scheherazade's story, they waited anxiously for the next installment. (Participial phrase modifies pronoun *they*.)
>
> The next morning young Goodman Brown came slowly into the street of Salem Village, staring around him like a bewildered man. (Nathaniel Hawthorne) (Participial phrase modifies noun *Goodman Brown*.)
>
> Henry M. Stanley went to Africa to find Dr. Livingstone. (Infinitive phrase modifies verb *went*.)
>
> It wasn't the ideal time to do homework. (Infinitive phrase modifies noun *time*.)

NOTE: When you use verbal phrases as modifiers, be especially careful not to create misplaced or dangling modifiers (see 14b and 14e).

□   **EXERCISE 9**

For practice in using verbal phrases, combine each of these sentence pairs to create one simple sentence that contains a participial phrase, a gerund phrase, or an infinitive phrase. Underline and label the verbal phrase in your sentence. You will have to add, delete, or reorder words, and you may find more than one way to combine each pair.

EXAMPLE: Judy decorated her new pair of jeans.

She painted them with pink and yellow flowers.

participial phrase

Judy decorated her new pair of jeans, painting them with pink and yellow flowers.

1. In 1912 the textile workers of Lawrence, Massachusetts, went on strike. They were demonstrating for "Bread and Roses, too."
2. The workers wanted higher wages and better working conditions. They felt trapped in their miserable jobs.
3. Mill workers toiled six days a week. They earned about $1.50 for this.
4. Most of the workers were women and children. They worked up to sixteen hours a day.
5. The mills were dangerous. They were filled with hazards.
6. Many mill workers joined unions. They did this to fight exploitation by their employers.
7. They wanted to improve their lives. This was their goal.
8. Finally, twenty-five thousand workers walked off their jobs. They knew they were risking everything.
9. The police and the state militia were called in. Attacking the strikers was their mission.
10. After 63 days, the American Woolen Company surrendered. This ended the strike with a victory for the workers.   (Adapted from William Cahn, *Lawrence 1912: The Bread and Roses Strike*)

(3)   Building simple sentences with absolute phrases

An **absolute phrase** is usually composed of a noun or pronoun and a past or present participle, along with its modifiers. Sometimes, however, an infinitive phrase functions as an absolute phrase. Absolute phrases act as modifiers, but they are not connected grammatically to any particular word or phrase in a sentence. Instead, an absolute phrase modifies the whole independent clause to which it is linked.

To make a long story short, our team lost.

She smiled, her lips curling up, her eyes blinking rapidly.

All things considered, I prefer Maine's cold winters to California's smog.

NOTE: When the participle in an absolute phrase is a form of the verb *be*, it is usually omitted.

They worked frantically, their time [being] almost up.

☐   **EXERCISE 10**

For practice in using absolute phrases, combine each group of sentences to create one simple sentence that includes an absolute phrase. You will have to change, add, delete, or reorder some words.

EXAMPLE: Paris was beautiful.
                    Its streets were exceptionally clean.

                    Paris was beautiful, its streets exceptionally clean.

1. Notre Dame stood majestically.
   Its Rose Window glowed in the darkness.
2. We took a boat ride down the Seine.
   Our feet were tired.
3. The Louvre is open six days a week.
   Its doors are closed on Tuesdays.
4. The Jeu de Paume displays Impressionist paintings. Its exhibits
   showcase Manet, Degas, Renoir, and van Gogh.
5. We were forced to cut our vacation short.
   Our francs were spent.

(4)   Building simple sentences with appositives

An **appositive** is a noun or a noun phrase that identifies, in different words, the noun or pronoun it follows. In these two sentences, for instance,

> Roy Rogers's horse Trigger was a golden palomino.

> Farrington hated his boss, a real tyrant.

Trigger is an appositive that identifies the noun *horse,* and *a real
tyrant* is an appositive that identifies the noun *boss.*

Appositives expand a sentence by defining the nouns or
pronouns they modify, giving them new names or adding identifying detail. Appositives can substitute for the nouns or pronouns to which they refer.

> Francie Nolan, the protagonist of Betty Smith's novel *A Tree Grows
> in Brooklyn*, is determined to finish high school and make a better
> life for herself. (Francie Nolan = the protagonist of the novel)

> Grant, the son of a tanner on the Western frontier, was everything
> Lee was not. (Bruce Catton) (Grant = the son of a tanner)

As in the examples above, appositives are frequently used
without special introductory phrases. They may also be introduced by *such as, or, that is, for example,* or *in other words.*

> Regional airlines, such as Piedmont and Western, frequently ac-
> count for more than half the departures at so-called second-tier
> airports.

> Rabies, or hydrophobia, was nearly always fatal until Pasteur's
> work.

(For information on punctuation with appositives, see 27d.2.)

☐   **EXERCISE 11**

For practice in using appositives when you write, build ten new simple sentences by combining each of the following pairs. Make one sentence in each pair an appositive. You may need to delete or reorder words in some cases.

EXAMPLE: Rasputin was a religious mystic and faith healer.
           Rasputin died in Russia just before the Revolution.

           Rasputin, <u>a religious mystic and faith healer</u>, died in Russia just before the revolution.

1. The Rocky Mountains are a mountain range over 300 miles long.
   The Rocky Mountains extend from Mexico to Alaska.
2. Joyce Carol Oates is a prolific fiction writer.
   She often develops the themes of violence and madness.
3. Grant and Lee were two Civil War generals.
   Grant was a Northerner and Lee was a Southerner.
4. Many dangerous diseases have all but disappeared in the United States.
   These include such diseases as measles and polio.
5. India and Sri Lanka are neighboring countries.
   Before 1972, Sri Lanka was known as Ceylon.

(5)   Building simple sentences with compound constructions

Compound constructions consist of two or more grammatically equivalent words or phrases, parallel in importance. These equivalent parts may be joined in one of three ways.

With commas (see 27b.2)

He took one <u>long, loving</u> look at his '57 Chevy.

With the coordinating conjunctions *and, but, nor, or,* or *yet* (see 21g)

He is <u>strong but gentle</u>.

She was not <u>glib or quick</u> in a world where glibness and quickness were easily confused with ability to learn. (Tillie Olsen, "I Stand Here Ironing")

They <u>reeled, whirled, flounced, capered, gamboled, and spun</u>. (Kurt Vonnegut, Jr., "Harrison Bergeson")

With a pair of correlative conjunctions (*both/and, not only/but also, either/or, neither/nor, whether/or*) (see 21g)

<u>Neither Sylvia Plath nor Emily Dickinson</u> achieved recognition during her lifetime.

Both milk and carrots contain Vitamin A.

(For information on parallelism with correlative conjunctions, see 15a.2.)

☐   **EXERCISE 12**

A. Expand each of the following sentences by using compound subjects and/or predicates.

> EXAMPLE: The kitten yawned.
>   The kitten and the mother cat yawned and stretched.

B. Then expand your simple sentence with modifying words and phrases, using compound phrases whenever possible.

> EXAMPLE: Absorbed in their ritual and paying no attention to us,
>   the kitten and the mother cat yawned and stretched.

1. Columbus set sail for the East Indies.
2. The Yankees competed.
3. The Beach Boys performed.
4. The miller's daughter could spin straw into gold.
5. Dracula wore a black cape.

☐   **EXERCISE 13**

To practice building sentences with compound subjects, predicates, and modifiers, combine the following groups of sentences into one.

> EXAMPLE: Lester laughed. Ted laughed. They laughed loudly.
>   They laughed heartily.
>   Lester and Ted laughed loudly and heartily.

1. John McEnroe plays tennis. Jimmy Connors plays tennis. Ivan Lendl plays tennis. Chris Evert Lloyd plays tennis. Martina Navratilova plays tennis.
2. Professional tennis players compete in tournaments. They play exhibition games.
3. Tennis superstars earn money by making personal appearances. They earn money by endorsing tennis-related products. They earn money by endorsing products unrelated to tennis.
4. Top players endorse tennis racquets. They endorse tennis clothing. They endorse sneakers.
5. Tennis players appear in magazine ads. They appear in television commercials. They sell all kinds of products.

8

Building Compound and Complex Sentences

8a Building Compound Sentences

The pairing of similar elements—words, phrases, or clauses—to give equal weight to each is called **coordination.** Coordination can be used in simple sentences, linking similar elements to form compound subjects, predicates, complements, or modifiers. It can also link two independent clauses to form a **compound sentence.**

Compound sentences most often communicate addition (through *and, in addition to, not only. . . but also,* or the use of a semicolon); contrast *(but, however)*; cause and effect *(so, therefore, consequently)*; or a choice of alternatives *(or, either . . . or).* A compound sentence is formed when two or more simple sentences (independent clauses) are connected with coordinating conjunctions, conjunctive adverbs, correlative conjunctions, semicolons, or colons.

(1) Using coordinating conjunctions

When two independent clauses are joined by a coordinating conjunction, the first is nearly always followed by a comma. The comma may be omitted in very short sentences (see 27a.2). The seven coordinating conjunctions are *and, or, nor, but, for, so,* and *yet* (see 21g).

[The cowboy is a workingman], yet [he has little in common with the urban blue-collar worker]. (John R. Erickson, *The Modern Cowboy*)

163

[In the fall the war was always there], but [we did not go to it anymore]. (Ernest Hemingway, "In Another Country")

[She carried a thin, small cane made from an umbrella], and [with this she kept tapping the frozen earth in front of her]. (Eudora Welty, "A Worn Path")

(2) Using conjunctive adverbs and other transitional expressions

When two independent clauses are joined by a conjunctive adverb or by any other transitional expression to form a compound sentence, the transitional phrase is always preceded by a semicolon and usually followed by a comma.

[Peter dropped Modern History]; instead, [he decided to take Educational Methods].

[The saxophone does not belong to the brass family]; in fact, [it is a member of the woodwind family].

[Aerobic exercise can help lower blood pressure]; however, [those with high blood pressure should still limit salt intake].

Commonly used conjunctive adverbs include *consequently, finally, still,* and *thus.* For a complete list, see 21e. Other commonly used transitional expressions include *for example, in fact, on the other hand,* and *for instance.* (A complete list of transitional expressions appears in 4d.4.)

(3) Using correlative conjunctions

Correlative conjunctions can connect two independent clauses to form a compound sentence (see 21g).

Sharon not only passed the exam, but she also received the highest grade in the class.

Either he left his coat in his locker, or he left it on the bus.

(4) Using semicolons

A semicolon can link two closely related independent clauses (see 28a).

[Alaska is the largest state]; [Rhode Island is the smallest].

[Theodore Roosevelt was president after the Spanish American War]; [Andrew Johnson was president after the Civil War].

(5)   Using colons

A colon can sometimes link two independent clauses (see 31a.2 and 31a.3).

> He got his orders: he was to leave for France on Sunday.
>
> They thought they knew the outcome: Truman would lose to Dewey.

☐   **EXERCISE 1**

Bracket the independent clauses in these compound sentences.

> EXAMPLE: [He was a man of few words], but [those few words were judiciously selected, weighed for quality, and delivered with expertise].   (Anita Brookner, *Hotel du Lac*)

1. We stand on the threshold of a great age of science; we are already over the threshold; it is for us to make that future our own.   (Jacob Bronowski, *Science and Human Values)*
2. The players were not two persons, but two illustrious families; the game had been going on for centuries.   (Jorge Luis Borges, "The Secret Miracle")
3. He blew the candle out suddenly, and we went inside.   (Joseph Conrad, *Heart of Darkness*)
4. They had not shown much interest in the elephant when he was merely ravaging their homes, but it was different now that he was going to be shot.   (George Orwell, "Shooting an Elephant")
5. The contempt of joggers and runners for the rest of humanity is often quite sincere, but I am not sure that it is deserved.   (Joseph Epstein, *Familiar Territory*)

☐   **EXERCISE 2**

After reading the following paragraph, use coordination to build as many compound sentences as you think your readers need to understand the links between ideas. When you have finished, bracket the independent clauses and underline the coordinating conjunctions, correlative conjunctions, or punctuation marks that link clauses.

The case of Alan Bakke presents an interesting footnote to the history of affirmative action legislation. Bakke applied to medical school at the University of California at Davis. He was rejected in 1973 and 1974. Bakke's grades were good. He said he was the victim of reverse discrimination. The medical school had designated sixteen out of every hundred slots for minority students. Bakke is white. Bakke said some minority students, less qualified than he, had been admitted. Bakke sued the University of California. The case went to the Supreme Court. In 1978, Bakke won his suit. Today, Bakke is a doctor.

☐   **EXERCISE 3**

Add appropriate coordinating conjunctions, conjunctive adverbs, or correlative conjunctions as indicated to combine each pair of sentences into one well-constructed compound sentence that retains the meaning of the original pair. Be sure to use correct punctuation.

> EXAMPLE: *Mad* was first published in 1952. It did not become a true magazine until July 1955. (coordinating conjunction)
>
> *Mad* was first published in 1952, but it did not become a true magazine until July 1955.

1. The average American consumes 128 pounds of sugar each year. Most of us eat much more sugar than any other food additive, including salt. (conjunctive adverb)
2. Many of us are determined to reduce our sugar intake. We have consciously eliminated sweets from our diets. (conjunctive adverb)
3. Unfortunately, sugar is not found only in sweets. It is also found in many processed foods. (correlative conjunction)
4. Processed foods like puddings and cake contain sugar. Foods like ketchup and spaghetti sauce do, too. (coordinating conjunction)
5. We are trying to cut down on sugar. We find limiting sugar intake extremely difficult. (coordinating conjunction)
6. Processors may use sugar in foods for taste. They may also use it to help prevent foods from spoiling and to improve their texture and appearance. (correlative conjunction)
7. Sugar comes in many different forms. It is easy to overlook it on a package label. (coordinating conjunction)
8. Sugar may be called sucrose or fructose. It may also be called corn syrup, corn sugar, brown sugar, honey, or molasses. (coordinating conjunction)
9. No sugar is more nourishing than the others. It really doesn't matter which is consumed. (conjunctive adverb)
10. Sugars contain empty calories. Whenever possible, they should be avoided. (conjunctive adverb)   (Adapted from *Jane Brody's Nutrition Book*)

☐   **EXERCISE 4**

Write two sentences imitating the following. Use the same parts of speech in making substitutions, and retain the function words (articles, prepositions, and conjunctions) of the model.

His clothes were a trifle outgrown, and the tan velvet on the collar of his open overcoat was frayed and worn; but for all that there was something of the dandy about him, and he wore an opal pin in his neatly knotted black four-in-hand, and a red carnation in his buttonhole. (Willa Cather, "Paul's Case")

8b   Building Complex Sentences ──────────

When you want to indicate that one idea is less important than another, you subordinate the secondary idea to the primary one. You might put the secondary idea in a modifying phrase or in another, less emphatic position in the sentence (see 9a). Another way to subordinate one idea to another is to place the main idea in an independent clause and the less important idea in a dependent clause. The result is a complex sentence.

A **complex sentence** consists of one simple sentence, which functions as an independent or main clause in the complex sentence, and at least one dependent or subordinate clause. **Independent clauses** can stand alone as sentences.

The hurricane began.

The town was evacuated.

Dependent clauses, introduced by subordinating conjunctions or relative pronouns, cannot stand alone.

<u>After</u> the town was evacuated.

<u>Which</u> threatened to destroy the town

Dependent clauses must be combined with independent clauses to form sentences. The subordinating conjunction or relative pronoun links the independent and dependent clauses and shows the relationship between them.

> *dependent clause*   *independent clause*
> [After the town was evacuated], [the hurricane began].
> *independent clause*   *dependent clause*
> [Officials watched the storm], [which threatened to destroy the town].

Sometimes, a dependent clause may be placed within an independent clause.

> *dependent clause*
> Town officials, [who were very concerned], watched the storm.

Depending on their function in a sentence, dependent clauses may be adverb, adjective, or noun clauses. Adverb clauses function in a sentence as adverbs, adjective clauses as adjectives, and noun clauses as nouns (see 7d.2).

<u>When the school board voted to ban Judy Blume's books</u>, parents protested. (adverb clause)

The Graduate was the film that launched Dustin Hoffman's career. (adjective clause)

How the fight started remained a mystery. (noun clause)

Subordinating conjunctions introduce adverb clauses.

Commonly Used Subordinating Conjunctions

after	rather than
although	since
as	so that
as if	that
as though	though
because	unless
before	until
even though	when
if	whenever
in order that	where
now that	wherever
once	while

Relative pronouns introduce adjective clauses.

Relative Pronouns

that	who (whose, whom)
what	whoever (whomever)
whatever	
which	

Noun clauses may be introduced by relative pronouns or by *whether, when, where, why,* or *how.*

☐   **EXERCISE 5**

Bracket and label the independent and dependent clauses in these sentences, and then underline and label the subordinating conjunctions or relative pronouns. Finally, indicate the function of each dependent clause.

EXAMPLE: ["Jet-stream art" is created] [when paint thrown into the exhaust of a jet engine is spattered onto a giant canvas].
(subordinate clause serves as an adverb)

1. The people were clustered thickly about the old man, all of them intermittently flicking glances toward me as they talked animatedly in their Mandinka tongue. (Alex Haley, *Roots*)

2. When professional writers complete a first draft, they usually feel that they are at the start of the writing process.   (Donald M. Murray, "The Maker's Eye")
3. We cannot help regarding a camel as aloof and unfriendly because it mimics, quite unwittingly and for other reasons, the "gesture of haughty rejection" common to so many human cultures.   (Stephen Jay Gould, *The Panda's Thumb*)
4. These are both hopeful and frustrating times for those who want to improve the nation's science and math education.   (Arlen J. Large, *Wall Street Journal*)
5. Although there was always generosity in the Negro neighborhood, it was indulged on pain of sacrifice.   (Maya Angelou, *I Know Why the Caged Bird Sings*)

☐   **EXERCISE 6**

Bracket the independent and dependent clauses in the following complex sentences. Then, using these sentences as models, create two new complex sentences in imitation of each. For each set of new sentences, use the same subordinating conjunction or relative pronoun that appears in the original.

1. Life is what happens while you're making other plans.
2. Mercury is the planet that is closest to the sun.
3. After she returned from the ball, Leila felt exhausted but exhilarated.
4. That vocational programs were becoming more important was obvious to the accreditation team.
5. Gertrude remarried before Hamlet had accepted his father's death.

☐   **EXERCISE 7**

Use a subordinating conjunction or relative pronoun to combine each of the following pairs of sentences into one well-constructed sentence. The conjunction or pronoun you select must indicate the relationship between the two sentences. You will have to change or reorder words, and in most cases you have a choice of connecting words.

EXAMPLE: College admissions requirements are tightening.

The pool of students is growing smaller.

Although the pool of students is growing smaller, college admissions requirements are tightening.

1. Some twelve million people are currently out of work. They need new skills for new careers.
2. In the 1960's and 1970's, talented high school students were encouraged to go to college. Some high school graduates are now starting to see that a college education may not guarantee them a job.
3. A college education can cost a student more than $50,000. Vocational education is becoming increasingly important.

4. Students complete their work in less than four years. They can enter the job market more quickly.
5. Nurses' aides, paralegals, travel agents, and computer technicians do not need college degrees. They have little trouble finding work.
6. Some four-year colleges are experiencing growth. Public community colleges and private trade schools are growing much more rapidly.
7. Vocational schools are responsive to the needs of local businesses. They train students for jobs that actually exist.
8. For instance, a school in Detroit might offer advanced automotive design. A school in New York City might focus on fashion design.
9. Other schools offer courses in horticulture, respiratory therapy, and computer programming. They are able to place their graduates easily.
10. Laid-off workers, returning housewives, recent high-school graduates, and even college graduates are reexamining vocational education. They all hope to find rewarding careers.

8c Building Compound-Complex Sentences

A **compound-complex sentence** consists of two or more independent clauses and at least one dependent clause.

dependent clause
[When small foreign imports began dominating the U.S.
independent clause
automobile industry], [consumers were very responsive],
independent clause
but [American auto workers were dismayed].

dependent clause   *independent clause*
[As the ferry entered the harbor], [she stood up and made her way down the deck against the light salt wind], and
dependent clause within independent clause
[Baxter], [who had returned to the island indifferently],
independent clause
[felt that summer had begun]. (John Cheever, "The Chaste Clarissa")

☐   **EXERCISE 8**

In each of these sentences, identify subjects and verbs; bracket and label dependent and independent clauses; and identify each sentence as simple, compound, complex, or compound-complex.

1. Use of the telephone involves personal risk because it involves exposure; for some, to be "hung up on" is among the worst fears; others dream of a ringing telephone and wake up with a pounding heart. (John Brooks, *Telephone: The First Hundred Years*)

2. Although Intourist, the government travel organization, has made great strides in improving tourist facilities and the variety of things to do, the Soviet state still regards the foreign tourist as a blend of spy and ideological alien—a person to be watched, carefully segregated from the citizenry and, to the extent possible, educated in the wonders of Socialist democracy and achievements. *(New York Times)*

3. Though she was stout in build and stood erect, her slow eyes and parted lips gave her the appearance of a woman who did not know where she was or where she was going.   (James Joyce, "The Dead")

4. This nation is even more litigious than religious, and the school prayer issue has prompted more, and more sophisticated, arguments about constitutional law than about the nature of prayer. (George F. Will, *Newsweek*)

5. The first time I ever went naked in mixed company was at the house of a girl whose father had a bad back and had built himself a sauna in the corner of the basement.   (Garrison Keillor, *New Yorker*)

6. I am the son of Mexican-American parents, who speak a blend of Spanish and English, but who read neither language easily. (Richard Rodriguez, *Aria: A Memoir of a Bilingual Childhood*)

7. Winter was always the effort to live; summer was tropical license. (Henry Adams, *The Education of Henry Adams*)

8. Of course, only in extreme cases do graduates become dull immediately.   (Wilfred Sheed, *New York Times*)

9. The most alarming of all man's assaults upon the environment is the contamination of air, earth, rivers, and sea with dangerous and even lethal materials.   (Rachel Carson, *Silent Spring*)

10. At the age of 80, my mother had her last bad fall, and after that her mind wandered free through time.   (Russell Baker, *Growing Up*)

☐   **EXERCISE 9**

Choose one simple, one compound, one complex, and one compound-complex sentence from Exercise 8. Write an original sentence in imitation of each.

Student Writer at Work: Building Sentences ——

A student in a freshman composition class was assigned to interview a grandparent and write a short paper about his or her life. When she set out to turn her grandmother's words into a paper, the student faced a set of choppy notes—words, phrases, and simple sentences—that she had jotted down as her grandmother spoke. She needed to fill out and combine these fragments and short sentences to produce varied, interesting sentences that would establish the relationships among her ideas. Read the notes, turn them into complete sentences when necessary, and combine sentences wherever it seems appropriate. Your goal is to build simple, compound, and complex sentences enriched by modifiers—without adding any information. When you have finished, revise further to strengthen coherence, unity, and style.

**sent
8**

Notes

67 years old. Born in Lykens, PA (old coal-mining town). Got her first paying job at 13. Her parents lied about her age. Working age was 14. Parents couldn't afford all the mouths they had to feed. Before that, she helped with the housework. At work, she was a maid. Got paid only about a dollar a week. Most of that went to her parents. Ate her meals on job. Worked in house where 3 generations of men lived. They all worked in the mines. Had to get up at 4 A.M. First chore was to make lunch for the men. She'd scrub the metal canteens. Then she'd fill them with water. Then she'd make biscuits and broth. Then she'd start breakfast. Mrs. Muller would help. Cooking for 6 hungry men was a real job. Then she did the breakfast dishes. Then she did the chores. The house had 3 stories. She had to scrub floors, dust, and sweep. It wasn't easy. Then Mrs. Muller would need help patching and darning. She had just enough time to get dinner started. Grabbed her meals after the family finished eating. Had no spare time. When not working she had chores to do at home. In spring and summer she would grow vegetables. Canned vegetables for her family. What was left over, she sold. Got married at 16.

9

Writing Emphatic Sentences

When speaking, you add attitude and emphasis to your ideas with facial expressions, gestures, and raising or lowering your voice. When writing, you must find other techniques to highlight important points. Careful sentence construction is one solution to this problem.

9a Achieving Emphasis Through Word Order

Where you place your words, phrases, and clauses within a sentence emphasizes or deemphasizes their importance. For instance, placing a word or word group either at the *beginning* or at the *end* of a sentence tends to focus attention on it. Departures from expected word order also attract attention.

(1) Beginning with important ideas

Readers focus on the *beginning* and the *end* of a sentence, expecting the most important information to appear in these places. To convey emphasis clearly and forcefully, take care to fulfill your readers' expectations. Look at the following sentence.

> In a landmark study of alcoholism, Dr. George Vaillant of Harvard followed 200 Harvard graduates and 400 inner-city, working-class men from the Boston area.

This sentence carries its key idea at the beginning. Greatest emphasis is therefore placed on the study itself, not on those who conducted it or who participated in it. Rephrasing changes the emphasis by focusing attention on the researcher and relegating the information about his work to a parenthetical phrase.

> Dr. George Vaillant of Harvard, in a landmark study of alcoholism, followed 200 Harvard graduates and 400 inner-city, working-class men from the Boston area.

Situations that demand a straightforward presentation— laboratory reports, memos, technical papers, business corre- spondence, and the like—call for sentences that present vital information first and qualify ideas later.

> The possibility of treating cancer with interferon has been the subject of a good deal of research.

> Whether or not dividends will be paid depends on the vote of the stockholders.

The first sentence emphasizes the new treatment, not the re- search; the second sentence stresses the question of dividends, not the vote. For technical and business audiences artificially created suspense is inappropriate—especially if it means read- ers must wade through a series of qualifiers to get the point.

NOTE: Because sentence beginnings are so strategic, the use of unemphatic, empty phrases like *there is* or *there are* in this posi- tion is generally ineffective.

> UNEMPHATIC: There is heavy emphasis placed on the development of computational skills at MIT.

> EMPHATIC: MIT places heavy emphasis on the development of computational skills.

(2)   Ending with important ideas

The close of a sentence can be a very dramatic position for im- portant ideas. Key elements may be placed at the end of a sen- tence in a number of conventional ways. A colon or a dash can add emphasis by isolating an important word or phrase at the end of a sentence.

> Beth had always dreamed of owning one special car: a 1953 Cor- vette.

> The elderly need a good deal of special attention—and they de- serve that attention.

In addition, putting modifiers or other subordinate elements at the beginning of a sentence allows you to place more important elements in the naturally emphatic position at its end.

UNEMPHATIC: The Philadelphia Eagles and the Pittsburgh Steelers became one professional football team, nicknamed the Steagles, during World War II because of the manpower shortage. (modifying phrases at end detract from main idea and weaken sentence)

EMPHATIC: Because of the manpower shortage during World War II, the Philadelphia Eagles and the Pittsburgh Steelers became one professional football team, nicknamed the Steagles. (correctly emphasizes the newly created team)

One special way writers use the emphatic end-of-sentence position is called climactic word order. **Climactic word order** proceeds in a series from the least to the most important point in the sentence. This sentence pattern stresses the key idea—the last point in the sentence—while building suspense and heightening interest.

When the key idea is buried in the middle of a sentence, the sentence will lack emphasis.

Duties of a member of Congress include serving as a district's representative in Washington, making speeches, and answering mail. (Which duty is most important?)

When you use climactic word order, placing the key idea at the end, the momentum of the sentence gives this idea added force.

The nation's most prominent orchestras all boast large annual budgets, locations in important cities, and the most talented musicians and conductors. (Talent is the key idea.)

Foreign cars are capturing the American market because of their styling, performance, and fuel economy. (Fuel economy is the key idea.)

NOTE: Unless you have a good reason to do so, do not waste the end of a sentence on qualifiers such as conjunctive adverbs. In that position a qualifier loses its power as a linking expression that indicates the relationship between ideas. Put transitional phrases earlier, where they can fulfill their functions and add emphasis.

LESS EMPHATIC: Smokers do have rights; they should not try to impose their habits on others, however. (conjunctive adverb at end of clause)

MORE EMPHATIC: Smokers do have rights; however, they should not try to impose their habits on others. (conjunctive adverb at beginning of clause)

LESS EMPHATIC: We wanted the shelves to be water-resistant; we
                 applied three coats of polyurethane for this reason.
                 (transitional expression at end of clause)

       MORE   We wanted the shelves to be water-resistant; for this
   EMPHATIC: reason, we applied three coats of polyurethane.
                 (transitional expression at beginning of clause)

emp
9a

☐   **EXERCISE 1**

Underline the most important word group in each sentence of the following paragraph. Then identify the device the writer used to emphasize those key words. Are the key ideas placed at the beginning or end of
a sentence? Does the writer use climactic order?

Buried in the basement of the computer center, often for hours on
end, the campus computer hackers work. Day after day they sit at their
terminals, working on games, class assignments, research projects, or
schemes to conquer the world. Some computer hackers are totally ab-
sorbed in their terminal keyboards, pausing only for occasional meals or
classes. A few hackers become almost reclusive, spending little time on
recreational activities or social relationships. Sacrificing grades, exercise,
dating, and contact with the outdoors, hackers structure their lives
around their computers. With their own slang, their own habits, and
their own hangouts, computer hackers tend to set themselves apart
from their fellow students. But these computer addicts feel that the
computer experience is worth the sacrifices they must make: Computers have opened up a whole new world for them.

(3)   Departing from expected word order

The word order of most sentences is subject-verb-object (or complement). When you change this order, you call attention to the
word, phrase, or clause that you have inverted. You may even call
attention to the entire sentence.

More modest and less inventive than Turner's paintings are John
Constable's landscapes.

Here the writer calls special attention to the modifying phrase
more modest and less inventive than Turner's paintings by turning the sentence around to stress the comparison with Turner's
work.

This stylistic technique should be used appropriately and
in moderation. Misuse of inverted sentences can distort your
meaning; overuse makes your writing stiff and unnatural. (See
also 11f.1 on sentence variety.)

☐   **EXERCISE 2**

Revise the following sentences to make them more emphatic. For each, decide which ideas should be highlighted, and group key phrases at sentence beginnings or endings, using climactic order or inverted order where appropriate.

1. Out-of-wedlock births among all women rose by over 11 percent in 1980, the last year for which census figures are available.
2. There are increasing numbers of middle-class, well-educated women who are electing to become single mothers.
3. This development is not surprising if we see it as the logical consequence of recent trends toward delayed parenting and increased numbers of women entering the work force and becoming independent.
4. These single women have decided that they do not want to be childless all their lives; they do not necessarily want to marry, however.
5. Still, they worry about what will happen to their children if they should die, about what to tell family and friends about their decisions to have children, and about how to pay for day care.

9b   Achieving Emphasis Through Sentence Structure

Skillful use of subordination can clarify a sentence's emphasis by deemphasizing less important ideas and emphasizing more important ones (see 8b). For instance, supporting details (ideas that are subordinate to the sentence's main idea) may be placed in modifying phrases or dependent clauses. Periodic sentences, in which the modifying phrases or dependent clauses are placed *before* the main clause, are almost always more emphatic than cumulative sentences, in which the supporting details follow the main idea.

(1)   Using cumulative sentences

Most English sentences are classified as cumulative. A **cumulative sentence** begins with a main (independent) clause that is followed by additional words, phrases, or clauses that expand or develop it. Here is a basic sentence.

> She holds me.

It can be expanded with phrases and clauses.

> She holds me in strong arms, arms that have chopped cotton, dismembered trees, scattered corn for chickens, cradled infants,

shaken the daylights out of half-grown upstart teenagers. (Rebecca Hill, *Blue Rise*)

emp
9b

The main clause appears at the beginning of the sentence, and modifiers follow it; therefore the sentence is cumulative. Because it presents its main idea first, a cumulative sentence tends to be clear and straightforward. When you want to communicate an idea in a direct manner, a cumulative sentence is the appropriate choice.

(2) Using periodic sentences

A **periodic sentence** moves from supporting details, expressed in modifying phrases and dependent clauses, to the main idea, usually placed in the main clause.

> Unlike the Pet Rock, which insulted the intelligence, and Rubik's Cube, which defied it, a big new hit on the toy scene tickles the imagination and captivates the eye. *(Time)*

In the preceding sentence, the writer adds emphasis to his main idea not only by placing it in the main clause but also by keeping readers waiting for it to be revealed. As the main clause at the end of the sentence ties the clauses together, the writer emphatically makes his point.

In some periodic sentences the modifying phrase or dependent clause comes between subject and predicate so that only the predicate of the main clause is delayed until the end.

> Columbus, after several discouraging and unsuccessful voyages, finally reached America.

Longer, more complex periodic sentences can be even more forceful. Piling up phrases and clauses, such sentences can gradually build in intensity, and sometimes in suspense, until a climax is reached in the main clause.

> The problems of soiled artificial flowers, soggy undercrust, leaky milk cartons, sour dishrags, girdle stays jabbing, meringue weeping, soda straws sticking out of bag lunches, shower curtains flapping out of the tub, creases in the middle of the tablecloth sticking up, wet boxes in the laundry room, roach eggs in the refrigerator motor, shiny seam marks on the front of recently ironed ties, flyspecks on chandeliers, film on bathroom tiles, steam on bathroom mirrors, rust in Formica drain-boards, road film on windshields—all were acknowledged and certified, probably for the first time ever, in "Hints from Heloise." (Ian Frazier, *New Yorker*)

Here the writer gains force by presenting a long and convincing catalog of details culminating in the statement of the main clause. Again, not only has the writer put the less important details in modifying phrases, he has also located them before the main clause. Thus he places strong emphasis on the main idea.

Periodic sentences are generally more emphatic than cumulative sentences, but the most emphatic sentence is not always the best choice. Because the periodic structure forces readers to wait—or even to search—for the delayed main idea, periodic sentences tend not to be as straightforward as cumulative ones. For this reason they may not be effective when you want to communicate information directly and without subtlety. In addition, a periodic sentence that is just one of an unrelieved string of periodic sentences will lose its impact. Therefore, when deciding whether or not to use a periodic sentence, consider not just the emphasis you wish to achieve but also how directly you wish to communicate your ideas and how all the sentences in a passage work together.

emp
9b

☐   **EXERCISE 3**

A. Bracket the main clause(s) in each sentence, and underline each modifying phrase and dependent clause.
B. Label each sentence cumulative or periodic. Then, relocate the supporting details to make cumulative sentences periodic and periodic sentences cumulative, adding words or rephrasing to make your meaning clear.
C. Be prepared to explain how your revision changes the emphasis of the original sentence.

> EXAMPLE: [Thousands of fans lined the streets], <u>watching the victory parade.</u> (cumulative)
>
> Watching the victory parade, thousands of fans lined the streets. (periodic)

1. The unemployed masses, working stiffs, mechanics, laid-off streetcar conductors, file clerks, shoe salesmen, pants pressers, egg candlers, truck drivers, the residents of huge, drab neighborhoods of "furriners," the greenhorns today described as ethnics—all these swore by him.   (Saul Bellow, "In the Days of Mr. Roosevelt," *Esquire*)
2. Given the constant changes in air fares, any list of travel bargains would almost certainly be out of date even before it was published. *(Consumer Reports)*
3. When people say that a city, or a part of it, is dangerous or is a jungle what they mean primarily is that they do not feel safe on the sidewalks.   (Jane Jacobs, "The Uses of Sidewalks")
4. The English are considered to have enjoyed reasonably benign government during the eighteenth and nineteenth centuries, except for their Irish subjects, debtors, child laborers, and other unfortunates in

various pockets of oppression.   (Barbara Tuchman, "An Inquiry into the Persistence of Unwisdom in Government")

5. [Henry] Moore's personal history is as familiar in outline as are his sculptures: his birth in 1898 as the seventh child of a Yorkshire coal-mining family; his early skill at carving; a conservative artistic education at the Royal College of Art, in London.   (Kay Larson, *New York Magazine*)

☐   **EXERCISE 4**

A. Combine each of the following sentence groups into one cumulative sentence, subordinating supporting details to main ideas.
B. Then combine each group into one periodic sentence. Each group can be combined in a variety of ways, and you will have to add, delete, change, or reorder words.
C. Be prepared to explain how the two versions of the sentence differ in emphasis.

> EXAMPLE: More blacks than ever are registering to vote. They are encouraged by the success of minority candidates.
>
> CUMULATIVE: More blacks than ever are registering to vote, encouraged by the success of minority candidates.
>
> PERIODIC: Encouraged by the success of minority candidates, more blacks than ever are registering to vote.

1. Many politicians oppose the MX missile. They believe it is too expensive. They feel that a smaller, single-warhead missile is preferable.
2. Smoking poses a real danger. It is associated with various cancers. It is linked to heart disease and stroke. It even threatens nonsmokers.
3. Infertile couples who want children sometimes go through a series of difficult processes. They may try adoption. They may also try artificial insemination or in vitro fertilization. They may even seek out surrogate mothers.
4. The Thames is a river that meanders through southern England. It has been the inspiration for literary works like *Alice in Wonderland* and *The Wind in the Willows.* It was also captured in paintings by Constable, Turner, and Whistler.
5. Black-footed ferrets are rare North American mammals. They prey on prairie dogs. They are primarily nocturnal. They have black feet and black-tipped tails. Their faces have racoonlike masks.

☐   **EXERCISE 5**

Combine each of the following sentence groups into one sentence in which you subordinate supporting details to main ideas. In each case, create either a periodic or a cumulative sentence, depending on which structure you think will best convey the sentence's emphasis. Add, delete, change, or reorder words when necessary.

EXAMPLE: The fears of today's college students are based on reality. They are afraid there are too many students and too few jobs.

The fears of today's college students—that there are too many students and too few jobs—are based on reality. (periodic)

1. Today's college students are under a good deal of stress. Job prospects are not very good. Financial aid is not as easy to come by as it was in the past.
2. Education has grown very expensive. The job market has become tighter. Pressure to get into graduate and professional schools has increased.
3. Family ties seem to be weakening. Students aren't always able to count on family support.
4. Students have always had problems. Now college counseling centers report more—and more serious—problems among college students.
5. The term *student shock* has recently been coined. This term describes a syndrome that may include depression, anxiety, headaches, and eating and sleeping disorders.
6. Many students are overwhelmed by the vast array of courses and majors offered at their colleges. They tend to be less decisive. They take longer to choose a major and to complete school.
7. Many drop out of school for brief (or extended) periods or switch majors several times. Many take five years or longer to complete their college education.
8. Some colleges are responding to the pressures students feel. They hold stress-management workshops and suicide-prevention courses. They advertise the services of their counseling centers. They train students as peer counselors. They improve their vocational counseling services.

9c   Achieving Emphasis Through Parallelism and Balance

A **parallel sequence** gives a sentence emphasis and clarity by highlighting corresponding grammatical elements. (For a detailed discussion of parallelism, see 15a.) Parallelism is used in situations where information must be conveyed clearly, quickly, and emphatically.

We seek an individual who is a self-starter, who owns a late-model automobile, and who is willing to work evenings. (classified advertisement)

Do not pass go; do not collect $200. (instructions)

Discuss the role of women in the short stories of Ernest Hemingway and F. Scott Fitzgerald, paying special attention to their relationships with men, to their relationships with other women, and to their roles in their jobs and/or marriages. (examination question)

The Faust legend is central in Benét's *The Devil and Daniel Webster*, in Goethe's *Faust*, and in Marlowe's *Dr. Faustus*. (examination answer)

A **balanced sentence** is neatly divided between two parallel structures. Balanced sentences are typically compound sentences made up of two parallel clauses, but the parallel clauses of a complex sentence can also be balanced. The symmetrical structure of a balanced sentence highlights correspondences or contrasts between clauses.

A balanced sentence can be exactly parallel, matching element for element.

In the fifties, the electronic miracle was the television; in the eighties, the electronic miracle is the computer.

Or, only its major elements may be parallel.

When guns are outlawed, only outlaws will have guns.

Alive, the elephant was worth at least a hundred pounds; dead, he would only be worth the value of his tusks, five pounds, possibly. (George Orwell, "Shooting an Elephant")

Beyond helping you achieve emphasis, parallelism and balance can help you combine ideas and thus write more economically. The judicious use of balanced sentences also helps you achieve sentence variety (see Chapter 11.)

9d   Achieving Emphasis Through Repetition

Ineffective repetition makes sentences dull and monotonous as well as wordy.

He had a good arm and also could field well, and he was also a fast runner.

We got three estimates, and the one we got from the Johnson Brothers seemed more reasonable than the one we got from County Carpenters.

Effective repetition can place emphasis on key words or ideas. Repetition can add emphasis when a word or word group is repeated in a parallel series.

They decided to begin again: to begin hoping, to begin trying to change, to begin working toward a goal.

Repeating a key word or phrase just once can add emphasis.

> During those years when I was just learning to speak, my mother and father addressed me only in Spanish; in Spanish I learned to reply. (Richard Rodriguez, *Aria: A Memoir of a Bilingual Childhood*)
>
> If ever two groups were opposed, surely those two groups are runners and smokers. (Joseph Epstein, *Familiar Territory*)

Repetition may be confined to a sentence, or it may continue throughout a paragraph—or even a paragraph cluster—contributing to coherence (see 4d.3 and 4d.5). In the following group of sentences the parallel structure and repetition of *still* add emphasis, stressing how hard the author's mother worked.

> Still she sewed—dresses and jackets for the children, housedresses and aprons for herself, weekly patching of jeans, overalls, and denim shirts. She still made pillows, using the feathers she had plucked, and quilts every year—intricate patterns as well as patchwork, stitched as well as tied—all necessary bedding for her family. Every scrap of cloth too small to be used in quilts was carefully saved and painstakingly sewed together in strips to make rugs. She still went out in the fields to help with the haying whenever there was a threat of rain. (Donna Smith-Yackel, "My Mother Never Worked")

☐   **EXERCISE 6**

Revise the sentences in this paragraph, using parallelism and balance whenever possible to highlight corresponding elements and using repetition of key words and phrases to add emphasis. (To achieve repetition, you must change some synonyms.) You may combine sentences and add, delete, or reorder words.

> Many readers distrust newspapers. They also distrust what they read in magazines. They do not trust what they hear on the radio and what television shows them either. Of these media, newspapers have been the most responsive to audience criticism. Some newspapers even have ombudsmen. They are supposed to listen to reader complaints. They are also charged with acting on these grievances. One complaint many people have is that newspapers are inaccurate. Newspapers' disregard for people's privacy is another of many readers' criticisms. Reporters are seen as arrogant, and readers feel that journalists can be unfair. They feel reporters tend to glorify criminals, and they believe there is a tendency to place too much emphasis on bizarre or offbeat stories. Finally, readers complain about poor writing and editing. Polls show that despite its efforts to respond to reader criticism, the press continues to face hostility. (Adapted from *Newsweek*)

9e   Achieving Emphasis Through Active Voice

The active voice is generally more emphatic—and frequently more concise—than the passive voice.

PASSIVE: The prediction that oil prices will not rise significantly can now be made by economists.

ACTIVE: Economists can now predict that oil prices will not rise significantly.

The passive voice tends to focus your readers' attention on the action or on its receiver rather than on who is performing it. The subject of the passive sentence receives the action, and the actor tends to fade into the background *(by economists)* or even to be omitted *(The prediction can now be made.)*. This deemphasis of the actor can make a sentence seem off-balance and lacking in force.

Sometimes, of course, you want to present the recipient of the action prominently. If so, it makes sense to use the passive voice (see 23j). To stress the opening of the Western frontier you would write

PASSIVE: The West was opened by Lewis and Clark. (*or* The West was opened.)

To stress the contribution of Lewis and Clark, however, you would write

ACTIVE: Lewis and Clark opened the West.

The passive is also used when the identity of the actor is irrelevant or unknown.

The course was canceled.

Littering is prohibited.

The beaker was filled with a saline solution.

The passive voice occurs frequently in scientific and technical writing, where convention has long dictated that writers avoid the first person singular.

☐   EXERCISE 7

Revise this paragraph to eliminate awkward or excessive use of passive constructions.

Jack Dempsey, the heavyweight champion between 1919 and 1926, had an interesting but uneven career. He was considered one of the greatest boxers of all time. Dempsey began fighting as "Kid Blackie," but his career didn't take off until 1919, when Jack "Doc" Kearns became his manager. Dempsey won the championship when Jess Willard was defeated by him in Toledo, Ohio, in 1919. Dempsey immediately became a popular sports figure; Franklin Delano Roosevelt was one of his biggest fans. Influential friends were made by Jack Dempsey. Boxing lessons were given by him to the actor Rudolph Valentino. He made friends with Douglas Fairbanks, Sr., Damon Runyon, and J. Paul Getty. Hollywood serials were made by Dempsey, but the title was lost by him to Gene Tunney, and Dempsey failed to regain it the following year. Meanwhile, his life was marred by unpleasant developments such as a bitter legal battle with his manager and his 1920 indictment for draft evasion. In subsequent years, after his boxing career declined, a restaurant was opened by Dempsey, and many major sporting events were attended by him. This exposure kept him in the public eye until he lost his restaurant. Jack Dempsey died in 1983.

Student Writer at Work: Writing Emphatic Sentences

Identify the strategies a freshman composition student has used in this draft to add emphasis. Revise the draft to make sentences more emphatic, and then revise again if necessary to strengthen coherence, unity, and style.

Nuclear Power Plants: Threat to the Public

Nuclear power is a relatively new source of energy. Our reliance upon nuclear power increases as conventional sources of energy, such as coal and petroleum, are depleted. There has been much controversy concerning the safety of the reactors currently in use, however. Nuclear power plants are a constant threat to the public and to the environment.

It has been claimed by the nuclear power industry that its plants are safe. The industry points out that safety devices and procedures are rigid and that nuclear plants hold a safety record equal to that of conventional plants using coal or petroleum. These nuclear plants do not use coal or petroleum, however. Instead, they use highly radioactive substances. Safety standards at nuclear power plants should be even more rigidly enforced for this reason.

Many nuclear power plants are poorly built and designed. Some unscrupulous construction firms have been caught altering specifications or using shoddy materials to increase their profit margins. One nuclear reactor in California was designed to withstand massive earthquakes. However, some of the specifications were altered so that the foundation may have to be replaced or modified if it is to withstand an earthquake. Many nuclear plants have been plagued with faulty valves installed by firms that allegedly were aware of the defects.

A large number of poorly trained or inexperienced workers are among those employed as plant operators. The extent of the damage at Three Mile Island would not have been so great if the operators had been more experienced or better trained. Many operators failed their licensing test at Three Mile Island recently. This situation left only the minimum number of personnel required to operate the reactor "safely."

Until more research is done with regard to safety procedures, design, and personnel of nuclear power plants, these plants should be considered a threat to our environment and to our lives. No more plants should be built, and existing ones should be modified or shut down. Nuclear energy should not be used unless facilities are redesigned and thoroughly tested, although it can be a good source of energy. Tighter government controls should be imposed to protect the people and their environment.

10

Writing Concise Sentences

A concise sentence contains just the number of words necessary to achieve its effect: it says what you want to say in as few words as possible. But a sentence is not concise simply because it is short. Conciseness is always related to content: how much you have to say. If you can eliminate words without reducing the amount of information you present, you should do so.

Every word serves a purpose in a concise sentence. Because they are free of unnecessary words and convoluted constructions that come between you and your readers, concise sentences are also clear and emphatic.

10a Eliminating Nonessential Words

One way to find out which words are essential to the meaning of a sentence is to underline the key words. Then, looking carefully at the remaining ones, you can see which are unnecessary or meaningless and delete them.

It seems to me that it doesn't make sense to allow any bail to be granted to anyone who has ever been convicted of a violent crime.

The underlining shows you immediately that none of the words in the long introductory phrase are essential. In revising, you might write

Bail should not be granted to anyone who has ever been convicted of a violent crime.

187

The new sentence includes all the key words and the minimum number of other words needed to give the key ideas coherence.

Dispensable words fall into three loose classifications: *deadwood*, *utility words*, and *circumlocution*.

(1)   Deadwood

Deadwood refers to unnecessary phrases that take up space and add nothing to meaning.

To be can be eliminated in certain contexts.

Kareem Abdul-Jabbar is considered to be a great center.	Kareem Abdul-Jabbar is considered a great center.

Often you can also delete *who are, which are, that is,* and similar phrases that introduce adjective clauses, with no loss of meaning.

WORDY	CONCISE
Shoppers who are looking for bargains often patronize outlets.	Shoppers looking for bargains often patronize outlets.
They played a racquetball game which was exhausting.	They played an exhausting racquetball game.
The box that was in the middle contained a surprise.	The box in the middle contained a surprise.

Removing deadwood from these wordy sentences turns the adjective clauses into simple modifying words or phrases, which in turn helps prevent rambling sentences (see 10c.2).

There is, there are, there were, and *it is* at the beginning of a sentence may also be deadwood. These phrases are frequently unnecessary.

There were many factors that influenced his decision to become a priest.	Many factors influenced his decision to become a priest.
It was lucky that he was able to get his friends to help him move.	He was lucky to get his friends to help him move.

Certain empty self-justifications and pompous sentence extenders too often appear as introductory phrases.

WORDY	CONCISE
With reference to your memo, the points you make are worth considering.	The points in your memo are worth considering.
In my opinion, the characters seem undeveloped.	The characters seem undeveloped.

As far as this course is con- cerned, it looks interesting.	This course looks interesting.
For all intents and purposes, the two brands are alike.	The two brands are alike.
It is important to note that the results were identical in both clinical trials.	The results were identical in both clinical trials.

These and other expressions—*obviously, as the case may be, I feel, it seems to me, all things considered, without a doubt, in conclusion,* and *by way of explanation*—are simply padding. You may think they balance or fill out a sentence or make your writing sound more authoritative, but the reverse is true.

(2)   Utility words

Utility words are vague, all-purpose words that act as fillers and contribute nothing to a sentence. They may be nouns, usually those with vague meanings (*factor, kind, type, quality, aspect, thing, sort, field, area, situation,* and so on); adjectives, usually those with broad meanings (*good, nice, bad, fine, important, significant*); or adverbs, usually common ones concerning degree (*basically, completely, actually, very, definitely, quite*).

WORDY	CONCISE
The field of computer science offers many employment opportunities.	Computer science offers many employment opportunities.
The registration situation was disorganized.	Registration was disorganized.
His offer to share his lunch was a nice gesture.	His offer to share his lunch was a generous gesture.
The scholarship offered Fran a good opportunity to study Spanish.	The scholarship offered Fran an opportunity to study Spanish.
It was actually a worthwhile book, but I didn't completely finish it.	It was a worthwhile book, but I didn't finish it.

When you find yourself using a utility word, try to delete it or to replace it with a more specific word. The result will be a more economical sentence.

(3)   Circumlocution

Taking a roundabout way to say something (using ten words when five will do) is called **circumlocution**. When you use big words, complicated phrases, and rambling constructions instead of short, concrete, commonly used words and phrases, you cannot write concise sentences. Notice how the revised versions of these sentences use fewer words and simpler constructions to say the same thing.

**con
10a**

WORDY	CONCISE
The curriculum was of a unique nature.	The curriculum was unique.
It is not unlikely that the trend toward smaller cars will continue.	The trend toward smaller cars will probably continue.
Joel was in the army during the same time that I was in college.	Joel was in the army while I was in college.
It is entirely possible that the lake is frozen.	The lake may be frozen.

Wordy phrases can almost always be controlled or avoided. Always choose simple, easily understood terms; when you revise, strike out wordy, convoluted constructions.

Commonly Used Wordy Phrases

Instead of	Use
at the present time	now
at this point in time	now
for the purpose of	for
due to the fact that	because
on account of the fact that	because
until such time as	until
in the event that	if
by means of	by
in the vicinity of	near
have the ability to	be able to

Writers use circumlocution for the same reasons they use deadwood and utility words: either they are not paying close attention to what they are writing, or they think that more and longer words make their writing seem polished and substantial. But when you pad a sentence with meaningless words, you interfere with communication.

☐ **EXERCISE 1**

Revise the following paragraph to eliminate deadwood, utility words, and circumlocution. When a word or phrase seems superfluous, delete it or replace it with a more concise expression.

Sally Ride is an astrophysicist who was selected to be the first American woman astronaut. It seems that there were many good reasons why she was chosen. She is a first-rate athlete, and she did graduate work in X-ray astronomy and free-electron lasers. As a result of these and other factors, NASA accepted Ride as a "mission specialist" astronaut in the year 1978. Prior to that time, Ride had been a graduate student at Stanford who knew she had the capability of becoming a specialist in the area of theoretical physics. At NASA she helped to design the remote manipulator arm of the space shuttle, and at a later point she relayed flight instructions to astronauts until such time as she was assigned to a flight crew. Although she is no longer employed by NASA, at this point in time she remains something quite definitely special: America's very first woman in space.

10b   Eliminating Needless Repetition ————

Repetition of words or concepts can add clarity and emphasis to your writing (see 9d), but unnecessary repetition annoys readers and obscures your meaning. Repeated words and **redundant** word groups (words or phrases that say the same thing in different words) are the chief problems. Consider the following sentence.

> Ernest Hemingway, one of the most famous and well-known authors in American literary history, is the author of novels like *The Sun Also Rises* and other novels.

Famous and *well-known* are redundant, while *author* and *novels* are repeated needlessly. The result is a wordy sentence. Compare this sentence.

> Ernest Hemingway, one of the most famous writers in American literary history, is the author of *The Sun Also Rises* and other novels.

In the next sentence careless repetition of *complex* and *political* gives these words undeserved emphasis and makes the sentence tedious.

> Today's complex political climate creates a series of complex challenges for both major political parties.

The following revision is clearer and more economical.

> Today's complex political climate creates a series of challenges for both major parties.

You can correct needless repetition in a number of ways.

**con
10b**

(1)   Deleting unnecessary repetition

The easiest way to correct needless repetition is to delete it.

WORDY	CONCISE
The childhood disease chicken pox occasionally leads to dangerous complications such as the disease known as Reye's Syndrome.	The childhood disease chicken pox occasionally leads to dangerous complications such as Reye's Syndrome.
The speech the president made was the fourth he had made that month.	The speech was the fourth the president had made that month.

(2)   Substituting a pronoun

You can substitute a pronoun for a repeated noun.

WORDY	CONCISE
Agatha Christie's Hercule Poirot solves many difficult cases. *The Murder of Roger Ackroyd* was one of Hercule Poirot's most challenging cases.	Agatha Christie's Hercule Poirot solves many difficult cases. *The Murder of Roger Ackroyd* was one of his most challenging cases.

(3)   Using elliptical clauses

You can use elliptical clauses, substituting commas for omitted words (see 27f.1)

WORDY	CONCISE
The Quincy Market is a popular tourist attraction in Boston; the White House is a popular tourist attraction in Washington, D.C.; and the Statue of Liberty is a popular tourist attraction in New York City.	The Quincy Market is a popular tourist attraction in Boston; the White House, in Washington, D.C.; and the Statue of Liberty, in New York City.

(4)   Using appositives

You can use appositives to eliminate unnecessary repetition.

WORDY	CONCISE
Red Barber was a sportscaster. He was known for his colorful expressions.	Red Barber, a sportscaster, was known for his colorful expressions.

(5)   Creating compounds

You can combine sentences to create compound subjects, compound objects or complements, or compound predicates. In the following sentence pairs the revised sentences are not only more concise but also less choppy.

WORDY

Wendy found the exam difficult, and Karen also found it hard. Ken thought it was tough, too.

Huckleberry Finn is an adventure story. It is also a sad account of an abused, neglected child.

In 1964 Ted Briggs was discharged from the Air Force. He then got a job with Maxwell Data Processing. He married Susan Thompson that same year.

CONCISE

Wendy, Karen, and Ken all found the exam difficult. (compound subject)

Huckleberry Finn is both an adventure story and a sad account of an abused, neglected child. (compound complement)

In 1964 Ted Briggs was discharged from the Air Force, got a job with Maxwell Data Processing, and married Susan Thompson. (compound predicate)

(6)   Using subordination

Finally, you can combine sentences so that one clause is subordinate to the other.

WORDY

One issue in the campaign was police brutality. Police brutality was on many voters' minds.

The first polio vaccine was developed by Jonas Salk. Salk was a physician and a bacteriologist.

CONCISE

One issue in the campaign was police brutality, which was on many voters' minds.

The first polio vaccine was developed by Jonas Salk, who was a physician and bacteriologist.

☐   **EXERCISE 2**

Eliminate any unnecessary repetition of words or ideas in this paragraph. Also revise to eliminate any deadwood, utility words, or circumlocution that you notice.

For a wide variety of different reasons, more and more people today are choosing a vegetarian diet. There are three kinds of vegetarian diets: strict vegetarians eat no animal foods at all; lactovegetarians eat dairy products but they do not eat meat, fish, poultry, or eggs; and ovolactovegetarians eat eggs and dairy products but they do not eat meat, fish, or poultry. Famous vegetarians include such well-known people as George Bernard Shaw, Leonardo da Vinci, Ralph Waldo Emerson, Henry David Thoreau, and Mahatma Gandhi. Like these well-known vegetarians, the vegetarians of today have good reasons for becoming vegetarians. For instance, some religions recommend a vegetarian diet. Some of these religions are Buddhism, Brahmanism, and Hinduism. Other people turn to vegetarianism for reasons of health or for reasons of hygiene. These people feel that meat is a source of potentially harmful chemicals and they believe meat contains infectious organisms. Other people feel meat may cause digestive problems and may lead to other difficulties as well. Other vegetarians adhere to a vegetarian diet because they feel it is ecologically wasteful to kill animals after we feed plants to them. These vegetarians believe *we* should eat the plants. Finally, there are facts and evidence to suggest that a vegetarian diet may possibly help people live longer lives. A vegetarian diet may do this by reducing the incidence of heart disease and lessening the incidence of some cancers. (Adapted from *Jane Brody's Nutrition Book*)

con
10c

10c Tightening Rambling Sentences ─────

Rambling, out-of-control sentences are the inevitable result of using nonessential words, unnecessary repetition, and complicated syntax. Making such sentences concise involves more than simply deleting a word or two. In fact, revising rambling sentences can require ruthless deletion. As you write and revise, the following techniques can help you keep your sentences under control.

(1) Eliminating excessive coordination

Excessive coordination occurs when you string together too many clauses with coordinating conjunctions. Not only does excessive coordination lead to wordiness, it also causes confusion by presenting all your ideas as if they have equal weight when they do not.

> WORDY: Puerto Rico is the fourth largest island in the Caribbean, and it is predominantly mountainous, and it has steep slopes, and they fall to gentle coastal plains.

To revise this sentence, first identify the main idea, and then subordinate the supporting details. The revised sentence emphasizes the mountainous nature of Puerto Rico and recasts the other details as modifiers.

> CONCISE: Fourth largest island in the Caribbean, Puerto Rico is predominantly mountainous, with steep slopes falling to gentle coastal plains. *(National Geographic)*

(2)   Eliminating excessive subordination

When you use a series of adjective clauses instead of concise modifying words or phrases, you are likely to produce a rambling sentence.

WORDY
The *Star Wars* trilogy, which consists of *Star Wars, The Empire Strikes Back,* and *Return of the Jedi,* was conceived by George Lucas, who directed *Star Wars* and who produced all three films, which are popular.

CONCISE
The Star Wars trilogy, consisting of *Star Wars, The Empire Strikes Back,* and *Return of the Jedi,* was conceived by George Lucas, director of *Star Wars* and producer of all three popular films.

Notice how the four subordinate clauses in the first sentence have been turned into more economical modifiers. *Consisting of* gives further information about the trilogy, *director of* and *producer of* are appositives identifying *George Lucas,* and the adjective *popular* is a single-word modifier describing *films.*

(3)   Eliminating passive constructions

The active voice is more economical than the passive. Although some situations call for passive voice (see 9e), the active voice, which communicates the same information in fewer words, is usually more emphatic.

WORDY
"Buy American" rallies are being organized by concerned Americans who hope jobs can be saved by such gatherings.

CONCISE
Concerned Americans are organizing "Buy American" rallies, hoping such gatherings can save jobs.

WORDY
Water rights are being fought for in court by Indian tribes like the Papago in Arizona and the Pyramid Lake Paiute in Nevada.

CONCISE
Indian tribes like the Papago in Arizona and the Pyramid Lake Paiute in Nevada are fighting in court for their water rights.

(4)   Eliminating wordy prepositional phrases

Often you can tighten a rambling sentence by replacing wordy prepositional phrases used as modifiers with single adjectives or adverbs.

WORDY
The trip was one of danger but also one of excitement.

CONCISE
The trip was dangerous but exciting.

The first sentence above uses eleven words to say exactly what the revised sentence says in six. Substituting two adjectives for two prepositional phrases makes the sentence more direct.

WORDY   CONCISE
He spoke in a confident man-   He spoke confidently.
ner.

In the example above one adverb replaces a four-word prepositional phrase. Again, the second sentence is more economical and more direct than the first.

(5)   Eliminating wordy noun constructions

You can also tighten a rambling sentence by substituting strong verbs for convoluted noun phrases.

WORDY   CONCISE
The normalization of commer-   When the United States and
cial relations between the   China normalized commercial
United States and China in   relations in 1979, trade between
1979 led to an increase in trade   the two countries increased.
between the two countries.

In the revision one-word verbs replace long phrases. The result is a much more effective sentence.

WORDY   CONCISE
We have made the decision to   We have decided to postpone
postpone the meeting until   the meeting until all the board
after the appearance of all the   members appear.
board members.

In the example above two noun constructions are replaced by verbs. Again, this substitution produces a more forceful sentence.

☐   EXERCISE 3

Revise the rambling sentences in this paragraph by eliminating excessive coordination and subordination, unnecessary use of the passive voice, and overuse of wordy prepositional phrases and noun constructions. As you revise, make your sentences more concise by deleting nonessential words and superfluous repetition.

Some colleges that have been in support of fraternities for a number of years are at this time in the process of conducting a reevaluation of the position of those fraternities on campus. In opposition to the fraternities are a fair number of students, faculty members, and administrators, who claim fraternities are inherently sexist, which they say makes it impossible for the groups to exist in a coeducational institution, which is supposed to offer equal opportunities for members of both sexes. And, more and more members of the college community see fraternities as elitist as well as sexist and favor their abolition. The situation has already begun to be dealt with at some colleges. For instance, Williams College made a decision in favor of the abolition of fraternities, and Middlebury College got its fraternities to agree to the admittance of women. In some cases, however, students, faculty, and administration remain wholeheartedly in support of fraternities, which they believe are responsible for helping students make the acquaintance of people and learn the leadership skills which they believe will be of assistance to them in their future lives as adults. Supporters of fraternities believe students should retain the right to make their own social decisions and that joining a fraternity is one of those decisions, and they also believe fraternities are responsible for providing valuable services and some of these are tutoring, raising money for charity, and running campus escort services. Therefore, they are not of the opinion that the abolition of fraternities makes sense.

con
10c

Student Writer at Work: Writing Concise Sentences

Revise this excerpt from an essay examination in American literature to make it more concise. After you have done so, revise further if necessary to strengthen coherence, unity, and style.

```
    Oftentimes in the course of a literary work,
characters may find themselves misfits in the sense that
they do not seem to be a real part of the society in which
they find themselves.  This problem often leads to a
series of genuinely serious and severe problems, conflicts
either between the misfits and their own identities or
possibly between them and that society into which they so
poorly fit.
    In "The Minister's Black Veil" Reverend Hooper all of
a sudden gives to the townspeople and members of his
parish a surprise: a piece of black material which he has
wrapped over his face, which causes readers to be as
completely and thoroughly confused as the townspeople
about the possible reason for the minister's decision to
hide his face, until readers learn, in his sermon, that he
is covering his face (from God, his fellow man, and
himself) to atone for the sins of mankind.  As far as
```

con 10

readers can tell, they are never quite sure exactly why he
is in possession of the notion that this act must be
carried out by him, and they are never completely sure
whether Reverend Hooper feels this guilt for some sin that
may exist in his own past or for those sins that may have
been committed by mankind in general, but in any case it
is clear that he feels it is his duty to place himself in
isolation from the world at large around him. To the
Reverend, there is no solution to his problem, and he
lives his whole entire life wearing the veil. Even after
his death he insists that the veil remain covering his
features, for it is said by the Reverend that his face
could not be revealed on earth.

For Reverend Hooper, a terrible conflict exists within
himself, and so Reverend Hooper voluntarily makes himself
a misfit even at the expense of losing everything, even
his true love Elizabeth.

11

Writing Varied Sentences

Varying your sentences helps you to convey emphasis and hold reader interest. To avoid monotonous writing, you can adopt a number of strategies: when you write and revise, you can vary sentence length; combine choppy simple sentences; break up strings of compounds; and vary sentence types, openings, and word order.

11a   Varying Sentence Length

A mixture of long and short sentences not only gives a pleasing texture to your writing, but also keeps readers interested.

(1)   Mixing long and short sentences

A paragraph consisting entirely of short sentences (or entirely of long ones) can be dull.

> Drag racing began in California in the 1940's. It was an alternative to street racing, which was illegal and dangerous. It flourished in the 50's and 60's. Eventually, it became almost a rite of passage. Then, during the 70's, almost one-third of America's racetracks closed. Today, however, drag racing is making a modest comeback.

Although these sentences are varied in structure and have different openings, they are all about the same length. The following revision combines sentences to create units of various lengths.

> Drag racing began in California in the 1940's as an alternative to street racing, which was illegal and dangerous. It flourished

in the 50's and 60's, eventually becoming almost a rite of passage. Then, during the 70's, almost one-third of America's racetracks closed. Today, however, drag racing is making a modest comeback.

(2) Following a long sentence with a short one

Using a short sentence after one or more long ones immediately attracts reader attention. This gear-shifting, illustrated in the following passages, emphasizes the short sentence and its content while adding variety.

> There are two social purposes for family dinners—the regular exchange of news and ideas and the opportunity to teach small children not to eat like pigs. These are by no means mutually exclusive. (Judith Martin, "Miss Manners")

> In arguing the need for [vitamin] supplements, doctors like to point out that the normal diet supplies the RDA (Recommended Dietary Allowance) minimums. Nutritionists counter that the RDA, as established by the National Academy of Sciences, is only the minimum daily dose necessary to prevent the diseases associated with particular vitamin deficiencies. Over the years, vitamin boosters say, a misconception has grown that as long as there are no signs or symptoms of say, scurvy, then we have all of the vitamin C we need. Although we know how much of a particular vitamin or mineral will prevent clinical disease, we have practically no information on how much is necessary for peak health. In short, we know how sick is sick, but we don't know how well is well. (*Philadelphia Magazine*)

☐   **EXERCISE 1**

A. Combine each of the following sentence groups into one long sentence.
B. Then, compose a relatively short sentence to follow each long one.
C. Finally, combine all the sentences into a paragraph, adding a topic sentence and any transitions necessary for coherence. Proofread your paragraph to make sure the sentences are varied in length.

1. Chocolate is composed of over 300 compounds. Phenylethylamine is one such compound. Its presence in the brain may be linked to the emotion of falling in love.
2. Americans now consume a good deal of chocolate. They eat an average of over nine pounds of chocolate per person per year. Belgians, however, consume almost fifteen pounds per year.
3. In recent years, Americans have begun a serious love affair with chocolate. Elegant chocolate boutiques sell exquisite bonbons by the piece. At least one hotel offers a "chocolate binge" vacation. The bimonthly *Chocolate News* for connoisseurs is flourishing. (Adapted from "America's Chocolate Binge," *Newsweek*)

11b Combining Choppy Simple Sentences —

Strings of disconnected simple sentences are nearly always tedious—and sometimes hard to follow as well. Revise such sentences by combining them with adjacent sentences, using coordination, subordination, or embedding.

**var
11b**

(1) Using coordination

Coordination is one way to revise choppy simple sentences, as
illustrated by these notes for part of a short paper on freedom of
the press in America.

> John Peter Zenger was a newspaper editor. He waged and
> won an important battle for freedom of the press in America. He
> criticized the policies of the British governor. He was charged
> with criminal libel as a result. Zenger's lawyers were disbarred by
> the governor. Alexander Hamilton defended him. Hamilton con-
> vinced the jury that Zenger's criticisms were true. Therefore, the
> statements were not libelous.

The information is here, but the presentation is flat and lacks
some of the links necessary for coherence. Coordination can add
interest and clarity.

> John Peter Zenger was a newspaper editor. He waged and
> won an important battle for freedom of the press in America. He
> criticized the policies of the British governor, and as a result, he
> was charged with criminal libel. Zenger's lawyers were disbarred
> by the governor. Alexander Hamilton defended him. Hamilton
> convinced the jury that Zenger's criticisms were true. Therefore,
> the statements were not libelous.

This revision links two of the choppy simple sentences with *and*
to create a compound sentence. The result is a slightly smoother
paragraph.

(2) Using subordination

Subordination can clarify the relationships between ideas. The
following revision changes two simple sentences into dependent
clauses to create two complex sentences.

> John Peter Zenger was a newspaper editor who waged and
> won an important battle for freedom of the press in America. He
> criticized the policies of the British governor, and as a result, he
> was charged with criminal libel. When Zenger's lawyers were dis-
> barred by the governor, Alexander Hamilton defended him. Hamil-
> ton convinced the jury that Zenger's criticisms were true. There-
> fore, the statements were not libelous.

The revised paragraph now includes two complex sentences: one links ideas with a relative pronoun *(who)* and one with a subordinating conjunction *(when)*.

var
11b

(3) Using embedding

Embedding—working phrases, clauses, and sentences into other sentences—is another strategy for varying sentence structure. It is used effectively in the following revision.

> John Peter Zenger was a newspaper editor who waged and won an important battle for freedom of the press in America. He criticized the policies of the British governor, and as a result, he was charged with criminal libel. When Zenger's lawyers were disbarred by the governor, Alexander Hamilton defended him, convincing the jury that Zenger's criticisms were true. Therefore, the statements were not libelous.

In this revision the sentence *Hamilton convinced the jury . . .* has been reworded to create a phrase *(convincing the jury)* that modifies the independent clause *Alexander Hamilton defended him.* Now the sentence has been embedded within another sentence. The result is a varied, readable paragraph that uses coordination, subordination, and embedding to vary sentence length but retains the final short simple sentence for emphasis. This revision, of course, represents only one of the many possible ways to achieve sentence variety.

☐   **EXERCISE 2**

Using coordination, subordination, and embedding, revise this string of choppy simple sentences into a more varied and interesting paragraph.

> The first modern miniature golf course was built in New York in 1925. It was an indoor course with 18 holes. Entrepreneurs Drake Delanoy and John Ledbetter built 150 more indoor and outdoor courses. Garnet Carter made miniature golf a worldwide fad. Carter built an elaborate miniature golf course. He later joined with Delanoy and Ledbetter. Together they built more miniature golf courses. They abbreviated playing distances. They highlighted the game's hazards at the expense of skill. This made the game much more popular. By 1930 there were 25,000 miniature golf courses in the United States. Courses grew more elaborate. Hazards grew more bizarre. The craze spread to London and Hong Kong. The expansion of miniature golf grew out of control. Then interest in the game declined. By 1931 most miniature golf courses were out of business. The game was revived in the early fifties. Today there are between eight and ten thousand miniature golf courses. The architecture of miniature golf remains an enduring form of American folk art. (Adapted from *Games*)

11c   Breaking Up Strings of Compounds ——

An unbroken series of compound sentences can be dull—and unemphatic (see 10c.1). When you connect clauses only with coordinating conjunctions, as in the paragraph that follows, you may fail to indicate emphasis or relationships accurately.

var
11c

> A volcano that is erupting is considered *active*, but one that may erupt is designated *dormant*, and one that has not erupted for a long time is called *extinct*. Most active volcanoes are located in "The Ring of Fire," a belt that circles the Pacific Ocean, and they can be extremely destructive. Italy's Vesuvius erupted in 79 A.D., and it destroyed the town of Pompeii. In 1883 Krakatoa, located between the Indonesian islands of Java and Sumatra, erupted, and it caused a tidal wave, and more than 36,000 people were killed. Martinique's Mont Pelée erupted in 1902, and its lava and ash killed 30,000 people, and this completely wiped out the town of St. Pierre.

> A volcano that is erupting is considered *active;* one that may erupt is designated *dormant;* and one that has not erupted for a long time is called *extinct.* [compound sentence] Most active volcanoes are located in "The Ring of Fire," a belt that circles the Pacific Ocean. [simple sentence with modifier] Active volcanoes can be extremely destructive. [simple sentence] Erupting in 79 A.D., Italy's Vesuvius destroyed the town of Pompeii. [simple sentence with modifier] When Krakatoa, located between the Indonesian islands of Java and Sumatra, erupted in 1883, it caused a tidal wave that killed 36,000 people. [compound-complex sentence with modifier] The eruption of Martinique's Mont Pelée in 1902 produced lava and ash that killed 30,000 people, completely wiping out the town of St. Pierre. [complex sentence with modifier]

☐   **EXERCISE 3**

Revise the compound sentences in this passage so that the sentence structure is varied and the writer's meaning and emphasis are clear.

> Dr. Alice I. Baumgartner and her colleagues at the Institute for Equality in Education at the University of Colorado surveyed 2,000 Colorado schoolchildren, and they found some startling results. They asked, "If you woke up tomorrow and discovered that you were a (boy) (girl), how would your life be different?" and the answers were sad and shocking. The researchers assumed they would find that boys and girls think there are advantages to being either male or female, but instead they found that both boys and girls had a fundamental contempt for females. Many elementary schoolboys titled their answers "The Disaster" or "Doomsday," and they described the terrible lives they would lead as girls, but the girls seemed to feel they would be better off as boys, and they expressed feelings that they would be able to do more and have easier lives.

Boys and girls alike realized that girls are judged by their looks more than boys, and both felt girls had to pay more attention to their looks, so all children perceived boys as having an advantage. In addition, boys and girls both valued boys' activities more highly, and boys and girls agreed that "women's work" is less valuable and less valued than "men's work." Both boys and girls also felt that boys are expected to behave differently, and they felt that boys could get away with more and be more active, but girls did have one advantage and that was that they could express their feelings openly.

Finally, both boys and girls agreed that boys are treated better and respected more than girls, so in other words there is a prejudice against females among both boys and girls, and this sex stereotyping is a psychological handicap for both men and women. (Adapted from *Redbook*)

11d Varying Sentence Types ────────────

You can vary sentence types by mixing **declarative sentences** (statements) with occasional **imperative sentences** (commands or requests), **exclamations,** and **rhetorical questions** (questions that the reader is not expected to answer). The addition of a question, exclamation, or command adds stylistic variety to each of the following paragraphs.

In the following paragraph the humorous rhetorical question at the beginning gives focus and variety.

> Was it any wonder that seven members of the Continental Congress who had seen the draft of the Declaration of Independence had fled to Philadelphia, threatening to defect to King George III? Still, John Hancock had stood firm. Faithful John Hancock. Even now Hancock was scouring Philadelphia chicken coops, searching for a newborn chick with a quill so small that no one would be able to decipher his signature without a microscope. (Russell Baker, *New York Times Magazine*)

Here a pair of exclamations add emphasis.

> Tracks! Tracks! It seemed to the visionaries who wrote for the popular magazines that the future lay at the end of parallel rails. (E. L. Doctorow, *Ragtime*)

In this short paragraph an imperative sentence breaks up the series of declarative sentences.

> Modern dude ranches mix activities found at conventional resorts—golf, swimming, tennis, dances—with elements of the Old West. But some rather elaborate ranches may be quite expensive. Before planning a dude ranch vacation, then, consider your

needs and interests carefully. You may be happier in a more modest (and less costly) setting.

NOTE: Other options for varying sentence types include mixing simple, compound, and complex sentences (see 11c); mixing cumulative and periodic sentences (see 9b); and using balanced sentences where appropriate (see 9c).

var
11e

☐ **EXERCISE 4**

The following paragraph is composed entirely of declarative sentences. To make it more varied, add three sentences—one exclamation, one rhetorical question, and one command—anywhere in the paragraph. Make sure the sentences you create are consistent with the paragraph's purpose and tone.

When the Fourth of July comes around, the nation explodes with patriotism. Everywhere we look we see parades and picnics, firecrackers and fireworks. An outsider might wonder what all the fuss is about. We could explain that this is America's birthday party, and all the candles are being lit at once. There is no reason for us to hold back our enthusiasm—or to limit the noise that celebrates it. The Fourth of July is watermelon and corn on the cob, American flags and sparklers, brass bands and more. Everyone looks forward to this celebration, and everyone has a good time.

11e Varying Sentence Openings ──────────

In addition to varying sentence length and type, you can create variety by choosing different openings for your sentences. Rather than resigning yourself to beginning every sentence with the subject, strengthen your emphasis and clarify the relationship of a sentence to those that surround it by opening some sentences with modifying words, phrases, or clauses.

(1) Adjectives, adverbs, and adverb clauses

You can begin a sentence with one or more *adjectives* or *adverbs* or with an *adverbial clause.*

Proud and relieved, they watched their daughter receive her diploma. (adjectives)

Hungrily, he devoured his lunch. (adverb)

While Woodrow Wilson was incapacitated by a stroke, his wife unofficially performed many presidential duties. (adverb clause)

(2)   Prepositional phrases, participial phrases

You can begin a sentence with a *prepositional phrase* or a *participial phrase.*

> For better or worse, alcohol has been a part of human culture
> through the ages. *(Consumer Reports)* (prepositional phrase)
>
> Located on the west coast of Great Britain, Wales is part of the
> United Kingdom. (participial phrase)

(3)   Coordinating conjunctions, conjunctive adverbs

To clarify the connection between two sentences, you can begin
the second sentence with a *coordinating conjunction* or a *conjunctive adverb.*

> The Big Bang may be the beginning of the universe, or it may be a
> discontinuity in which information about the earlier history of the
> universe was destroyed. But it is certainly the earliest event about
> which we have any record. (Carl Sagan, *The Dragons of Eden*) (co-
> ordinating conjunction)
>
> Pantomime was first performed in ancient Rome. However, it re-
> mains a popular dramatic form today. (conjunctive adverb)

(4)   Inverted appositives, absolute phrases

You can begin a sentence with an *inverted appositive* or with an
absolute phrase.

> A British scientist, Alexander Fleming is famous for having discov-
> ered penicillin. (inverted appositive)
>
> His interests widening, Picasso designed ballet sets and illustrated
> books. (absolute phrase)

☐   **EXERCISE 5**

Each of these sentences begins with the subject. Rewrite each so that it
has a different opening, and then identify the opening strategy you used.

> EXAMPLE: Doug signed up for the ski trip and immediately began
>   taking lessons.
>
>   After he signed up for the ski trip, Doug immediately
>   began taking lessons. (adverb clause)

1. The first lesson taught him how to put on his boots and skis and how
   to hold his poles; it was easy.
2. The second lesson concentrated on finer points, teaching Doug how
   to walk with skis on and how to turn around while wearing them.
3. The third lesson, which was a bit more difficult, focused on such
   minor details as how to start and how to stop.

4. Doug found himself poised on the beginners' slope ready to head downhill at the start of lesson four.
5. Doug decided, when he looked down the slope, to cancel the ski trip and take up backgammon.

11f Varying Standard Word Order

You can use two variations on the usual word order of subject-verb-object (or complement): intentionally inverting this order, or placing words between subject and verb.

(1) Inverting word order

Inverting conventional word order can add emphasis (see 9a.3) as well as variety. You can place the complement or direct object *before* the verb instead of in its conventional position or place the verb *before* the subject instead of after it.

In each of the following sentences, the unusual word order draws attention to what has been inverted.

> *(subject)*
> Nature   I   loved and, next to Nature, Art. (Walter Savage Landor)
> *(object)*   *(verb)*

> *(complement)*
> The book was extremely helpful; especially useful was its index.
> *(verb)   (subject)*

Keep in mind, however, that when it is overused, inversion loses its force and sounds unnatural.

(2) Separating subject from verb

Placing words or phrases between subject and verb is another way to vary standard word order.

> Several states require that infants and young children ride in government-approved car seats because they hope this will reduce needless fatalities. (subject and verb together)

> Several states, hoping to reduce needless fatalities, require that infants and young children ride in government-approved car seats. (subject and verb separated)

If you use this strategy, be very careful to avoid obscuring the relationship between subject and verb (see 14d.3).

var
11f

☐   **EXERCISE 6**

The following sentences use conventional word order. Revise each in
two ways: First, invert the sentence; then, vary the word order by placing
words between subject and verb. After you have completed your revisions, create a varied five-sentence paragraph, choosing one version of
each sentence. Be prepared to explain your choices.

> EXAMPLE: Exam week is invariably hectic and not much fun.
>
>   Invariably hectic and not much fun is exam week.
>
>   Exam week, invariably hectic, is not much fun.

1. The Beach Boys formed a band in 1961, and the group consisted of
   Brian Wilson, his brothers Carl and Dennis, their cousin Mike Love,
   and Alan Jardine, a friend.
2. The group's first single was "Surfin'," which attracted national attention.
3. Capitol Records signed the band to record "Surfin' Safari" because
   the company felt the group had potential.
4. The Beach Boys had many other top-twenty singles during the next
   five years, and most of these hits were written, arranged, and produced by Brian Wilson.
5. Their songs focused on California sun and good times and included
   "I Get Around," "Be True to Your School," "Fun, Fun, Fun," and "Good
   Vibrations."

Student Writer at Work: Writing Varied Sentences

Read this draft of a student essay carefully. Then, revise it to
achieve greater sentence variety by varying the length, type,
openings, and word order of the sentences. After you have done
so, revise further if necessary to strengthen coherence, unity, and
style.

           Advertising: Newspapers versus Television

      Advertising persuades by provoking the senses. It is
big business. It exploits every conceivable method of
enticing consumers to buy. Ads can be straightforward and
informational. Or, they can be filled with intrigue,
hilarity, or sexuality. They can prod the minds of the
hungry, the self-indulgent, the imaginative, and the
gullible. Every conceivable medium is used to advertise.
Each has the same objective: to sell. Television and

newspapers are perhaps the two most influential means of
advertising.   They reach the greatest number and widest
range of people.

Advertisements in local newspapers lace the pages like
a net.   They lure the prospective catch with bait.   This
bait appears in the form of bold lettering and small
dollar signs.   But newspapers are for the serious-minded.
People tend to believe things they read in black and
white.   So newspapers tend to report the facts.   They
announce store hours and liquidation sales.   They support
everything with numerous figures.   Newspaper ads are
concise and informative.   They are also unpretentious and
sensible.   They attract attention to everything from
barbells to diamond rings, using (for the most part) only
facts.

Television is a completely different medium.   It plays
with emotion, fantasy, and impulse.   It seeks to invoke an
immediate response.   Every viewer must remember a time
when he or she got up from the couch to race to the
refrigerator, victim of a commercial that promised
Heavenly Hash satisfaction.   Television uses only two of
the five senses, sound and sight, but with careful
calculation touch, smell, and taste can also be triggered,
and therein lies television's strength.   Viewers feel the
excitement of driving a Pontiac LeMans up a mountain.
They grind their teeth as they prepare to sail in a hang
glider over the craggy California coast (chewing Wrigley's
Spearmint Gum, of course).   Emotionally charged
sensationalism gets the message across.

Television ads roll right into viewers' living rooms.
These advertisements sneak up on viewers.   They play on
their emotions.   The ads appeal to greed, to
competitiveness, to a desire for comfort and luxury.
Newspaper ads finish the job.   They tell where and when to
buy.   Readers already know why.

SECTION III

Solving Common Sentence Problems

12

Sentence Fragments

A **sentence fragment** is an incomplete sentence, a phrase or clause punctuated as if it were a complete sentence.

A sentence may be incomplete because it lacks a subject or a **finite verb,** a verb that changes form to indicate person, tense, and number.

> Many astrophysicists now believe that galaxies are distributed in clusters. And even form supercluster complexes. (subject missing)

> Researchers are engaged in a variety of studies. All suggesting that a predisposition to alcoholism may be inherited. (finite verb missing)

> The streets of many large cities are home to increasing numbers of homeless people. Mentally or physically ill and unable to find shelter. (both subject and finite verb missing)

NOTE: Participles *(suggesting)* and infinitives *(to find)* are verbals. Because they are not finite verbs, they cannot serve as main verbs in a sentence. (For more information about verbals see 21c.)

A sentence may also be incomplete because it is actually a dependent clause, introduced by a subordinating conjunction or by a relative pronoun.

> Bishop Desmond Tutu was awarded the Nobel Peace Prize. Because he struggled to end apartheid. (introduced by subordinating conjunction)

> The pH meter and the spectrophotometer are two scientific instruments. That changed the chemistry laboratory dramatically. (introduced by relative pronoun)

When readers cannot see where sentences begin and end, they cannot understand what you have written. For instance, it is impossible to tell to which independent clause the fragment in the following sequence belongs.

The course requirements were changed last year. Because a new professor was hired at the very end of the spring semester. I was unable to find out about this change until after preregistration.

   Use the following criteria to help you examine any sentence for completeness.

Tests for Sentence Completeness

- A sentence must include a subject.
- A sentence must have a finite verb.
- A sentence cannot consist of a dependent clause alone. (A sentence cannot consist of a single clause that begins with a subordinating conjunction; unless it is a question, it cannot consist of a single clause beginning with *how, who, which, where, when,* or *why.*)

If your sentence does not pass these three tests, it is a fragment and should be revised. Once you determine that a sentence is incomplete, you can use one or more of the following strategies to revise the fragment.

Strategies for Revising Sentence Fragments

- Attach the fragment to an adjacent clause.

   FRAGMENT: According to German legend, Lohengrin is the son of Parzival. And a knight of the Holy Grail.

   REVISED: According to German legend, Lohengrin is the son of Parzival and a knight of the Holy Grail.

- Supply the missing subject and/or finite verb.

   FRAGMENT: Lancaster County, Pennsylvania, is home to many Pennsylvania Dutch. Descended from eighteenth-century settlers from southwest Germany.

   REVISED: Lancaster County, Pennsylvania, is home to many Pennsylvania Dutch. They are descended from eighteenth-century settlers from southwest Germany.

- Delete the subordinating conjunction or relative pronoun.

   FRAGMENT: Property taxes rose sharply. Although city services showed no improvement.

   REVISED: Property taxes rose sharply. City services showed no improvement.

As the preceding summary indicates, supplying the missing subject or verb or deleting a subordinating conjunction or relative pronoun will correct many fragments, but these revision strategies may create choppy, disconnected sentences. Similarly, although attaching a fragment to an adjacent clause will produce the most concise revision, this strategy does not enable you to emphasize information by placing it in a separate independent clause. When you correct sentence fragments, keep in mind that different strategies serve different purposes. Do not hesitate to revise corrected fragments further to achieve clear, concise sentences that convey your emphasis. (For detailed information on revising to create sentences that are emphatic and concise, see Chapter 9 and 10.)

Sentence fragments can take many forms. The following sections identify the grammatical structures most likely to appear as fragments and illustrate the most effective ways of revising each.

12a   Revising Dependent Clauses

A **dependent clause** contains a subject and a verb, but it cannot stand alone as a sentence. Because it needs an independent clause to complete it, a dependent clause (also called a subordinate clause) must always be attached to at least one independent clause. You can recognize a dependent clause because it is always introduced by a subordinating conjunction or a relative pronoun (see 8b).

To correct fragments that result from punctuating dependent clauses incorrectly, you can join the dependent clause to a neighboring independent clause, or you can delete the subordinating conjunction or relative pronoun, creating a complete sentence with a subject and a finite verb. (In many cases, you will have to replace the relative pronoun with another word that can serve as the clause's subject.)

FRAGMENT: The United States declared war. Because the Japanese bombed Pearl Harbor. (Dependent clause is punctuated as a sentence.)

REVISED: The United States declared war because the Japanese bombed Pearl Harbor. (Dependent clause has been attached to an independent clause to create a complete sentence.)

REVISED: The Japanese bombed Pearl Harbor. The United States declared war. (Subordinating conjunction has been deleted; the result is a complete sentence.)

FRAGMENT: The battery is dead. <u>Which means the car won't start.</u>
            (Dependent clause is punctuated as a sentence.)

REVISED: The battery is dead, which means the car won't start.
            (Dependent clause has been attached to an indepen-
            dent clause to create a complete sentence.)

REVISED: The battery is dead. This means the car won't start.
            (Relative pronoun has been deleted; the substitution of
            this creates a complete sentence.)

frag
12a

☐   **EXERCISE 1**

Identify the sentence fragments in the following paragraph, and correct
each, either by attaching the fragment to an independent clause or by
deleting the subordinating conjunction or relative pronoun to create a
sentence that can stand alone. In some cases you will have to replace a
relative pronoun with another word that can serve as the subject of an
independent clause.

The drive-in movie came into being just after World War II. When
both movies and cars were central to the lives of many Americans. Drive-
ins were especially popular with teenagers and young families during
the 1950's. When cars and gas were relatively inexpensive. Theaters
charged by the carload. Which meant that a group of teenagers or a
family with several children could spend an evening at the movies for a
few dollars. In 1958, when the fad peaked, there were over 4,000 drive-ins
in the United States. While today there are fewer than 3,000. Many of
these are in the sunbelt, with most in California. Although many sunbelt
drive-ins continue to thrive because of the year-round warm weather.
Many northern drive-ins are in financial trouble. Because land is so expensive. Some drive-in owners break even only by operating flea markets
or swap meets in daylight hours. While others, unable to attract customers, are selling their theaters to land developers. Soon drive-ins may be a
part of our nostalgic past. Which will be a great loss for many who enjoy
them.

12b   Revising Prepositional Phrases ————

A **prepositional phrase** consists of a preposition, its object, and
any modifiers of the object (see 7f.1). It cannot stand alone as a
sentence.

To correct this kind of fragment most concisely, attach it to
the independent clause that contains the word or word group
modified by the prepositional phrase.

FRAGMENT: President Lyndon Johnson decided not to seek reelec-
            tion. <u>For a number of reasons</u>. (Prepositional phrase is
            punctuated as a sentence.)

REVISED: President Lyndon Johnson decided not to seek reelection for a number of reasons. (Prepositional phrase has
been attached to an independent clause.)

FRAGMENT: He ran sixty yards for a touchdown. In the final minutes of the game. (Prepositional phrase is punctuated as
a sentence.)

**frag
12b**

REVISED: He ran sixty yards for a touchdown in the final minutes
of the game. (Prepositional phrase has been attached to
an independent clause.)

☐   **EXERCISE 2**

Read the following passage and identify the sentence fragments. Then
correct each one by attaching it to the preceding independent clause to
form a sentence.

Most college athletes are caught in a conflict. Between their athletic and academic careers. Sometimes college athletes' responsibilities
on the playing field make it hard for them to be good students. Often
athletes must make a choice. Between sports and a degree. Some athletes would not be able to afford college. Without athletic scholarships.
But, ironically, their commitments to sports (training, exercise, practice,
and travel to out-of-town games, for example) deprive athletes of valuable classroom time. The role of college athletes is constantly being ques-
tioned. Critics suggest athletes exist only to participate in and promote
college athletics. Because of the importance of this role to academic
institutions, scandals occasionally develop. With coaches and even faculty members arranging to inflate athletes' grades to help them remain
eligible. For participation in sports. Some universities even lower admissions standards. To help remedy this inequity, the controversial Proposal 48, passed at the NCAA convention in 1982, establishes minimum
scores on aptitude tests. But many people feel that the NCAA remains
overly concerned. With profits rather than with education. As a result,
college athletic competition is increasingly coming to resemble pro
sports. From the coaches' pressure on the players to win to the network
television exposure to the wagers on the games' outcomes.

12c   Revising Verbal Phrases

A **verbal phrase** consists of a present participle *(walking)*, past
participle *(walked)*, infinitive *(to walk)*, or gerund plus related objects and modifiers *(walking along the lonely beach)*. Because a
verbal phrase does not contain a finite verb, it is not a complete
sentence and should not be punctuated as one.

The most effective ways to correct the fragment that results
when a verbal phrase is punctuated as a sentence are either to

attach the verbal phrase to a related independent clause or to change the verbal to a finite verb and add a subject.

FRAGMENT: In 1948 India became independent. Divided into the nations of India and Pakistan. (Participial phrase is punctuated as a sentence.)

REVISED: Divided into the nations of India and Pakistan, India became independent in 1948. (Participial phrase has been attached to the related independent clause to create a complete sentence.)

REVISED: In 1948 India became independent. It was divided into the nations of India and Pakistan. (Finite verb *was* and subject *it* have been added; the result is a separate independent clause.)

FRAGMENT: The pilot changed course. Realizing the weather was worsening. (Participial phrase is punctuated as a sentence.)

REVISED: The pilot changed course, realizing the weather was worsening. (Participial phrase has been attached to the related independent clause to create a complete sentence.)

REVISED: The pilot changed course. She realized the weather was worsening. (Finite verb *realized* has been substituted for the verbal *realizing* and subject *she* has been added; the result is a separate independent clause.)

frag
12c

☐   **EXERCISE 3**

Identify the sentence fragments in the following paragraph, and correct each. Either attach the fragment to a related independent clause, or add a subject and a finite verb to create a new independent clause.

Many food products have well-known trademarks. Identified by familiar faces on product labels. Some of these symbols have remained the same, while others have changed considerably. Products like Sun-Maid Raisins, Betty Crocker potato mixes, Quaker Oats, and Uncle Ben's Rice use faces. To create a sense of quality and tradition and to encourage shopper recognition of the products. Many of the portraits have been updated several times. To reflect changes in society. Betty Crocker's portrait, for instance, has changed five times since its creation in 1936. Symbolizing women's changing roles. The original Chef Boy-ar-dee has also changed. Turning from the young Italian chef Hector Boiardi into a white-haired senior citizen. Miss Sunbeam, trademark of Sunbeam Bread, has had her hairdo modified several times since her first appearance in 1942; the Blue Bonnet girl, also created in 1942, now has a more modern look, and Aunt Jemima has also been changed. Slimmed down a bit in 1965. Similarly, the Campbell's Soup kids are less chubby

now than in the 1920's when they first appeared. But the Quaker on
Quaker Oats remains as round as he was when he first adorned the
product label in 1877. The Morton Salt girl has evolved gradually. Changing several times from blonde to brunette and from straight- to curly-
haired. But manufacturers are very careful about selecting a trademark
or modifying an existing one. Typically spending a good deal of time and
money on research before a change is made. After all, a trademark of
long standing can help a product's sales. Giving shoppers the sense that
they are using products purchased and preferred by their parents and
grandparents.

12d   Revising Absolute Phrases

An **absolute phrase**—a modifying phrase that is not connected
grammatically to any one word in a sentence—usually consists
of a noun or pronoun plus a participle and any related modifiers.
(Infinitive phrases can also be absolutes; see 7f.3.) An absolute
phrase may contain a subject, but it lacks a finite verb and therefore cannot stand alone as a sentence.

    To correct this kind of fragment, attach the absolute phrase
to the clause it modifies, or substitute a finite verb for the participle or infinitive in the absolute phrase.

> FRAGMENT: India has over 16 million child laborers. Their education
> cut short by the need to earn money. (Absolute phrase
> is punctuated as a sentence.)

> REVISED: India has over 16 million child laborers, their education
> cut short by the need to earn money. (Absolute phrase
> has been attached to the clause it modifies.)

> FRAGMENT: The Vietnam War memorial is a striking landmark. Its
> design featuring two black marble slabs meeting in a V.
> (Absolute phrase is punctuated as a sentence.)

> REVISED: The Vietnam War memorial is a striking landmark. Its
> design features two black marble slabs meeting in a V.
> (Finite verb has been substituted for participle)

☐   **EXERCISE 4**

Identify the sentence fragments in the following passage and correct
each by attaching the absolute phrase to the clause it modifies or by
substituting a finite verb for the participle or infinitive in the absolute
phrase.

    The domestic responsibilities of colonial women were many.
Their fate sealed by the lack of the mechanical devices that have eased
the burdens in recent years. Washing clothes, for instance, was a com-

plicated procedure. The primary problem being the moving of some 50 gallons of water from a pump or well to the stove (for heating) and washtub (for soaking and scrubbing). Home cooking also presented difficulties. The main challenges for the housewife being the danger of inadvertently poisoning her family and the rarity of ovens. Even much later, housework was extremely time-consuming, especially for rural and low-income families. Their access to labor-saving devices remaining relatively limited. (Just before World War II, for instance, only 35 percent of farm residences in the United States had electricity!)

12e   Revising Appositives

An **appositive**—a noun or noun phrase that identifies or renames the person or thing it follows—cannot stand alone as a sentence (see 7f.4). An appositive must directly follow the person or thing it renames, and it must do so within the same sentence.

To correct a fragment created when an appositive is incorrectly punctuated as a sentence, attach the appositive to the independent clause that contains the word or word group the appositive renames.

> FRAGMENT: Piero della Francesca was a leader of the Umbrian school. <u>A school that remained close to the traditions of Gothic art</u>. (Appositive, a fragment that renames *the Umbrian school*, is punctuated as a complete sentence.)

> REVISED: Piero della Francesca was a leader of the Umbrian school, a school that remained close to the traditions of Gothic art. (Appositive has been attached with a comma to the noun it renames.)

Appositives included for clarification are sometimes introduced by a word or phrase like *or, that is, for example, for instance, namely,* or *such as.* These additions do not change anything: appositives still cannot stand alone as sentences. Once again, the easiest way to correct such fragments is to attach the appositive to the preceding independent clause.

> FRAGMENT: Fairy tales are full of damsels in distress. <u>Such as Snow White, Cinderella, and Rapunzel</u>. (Appositive, a phrase that identifies *damsels in distress*, is punctuated as a sentence.)

> REVISED: Fairy tales are full of damsels in distress, such as Snow White, Cinderella, and Rapunzel. (Appositive has been attached with a comma to the noun it renames.)

You can also correct an appositive that is a fragment by embedding the appositive within the related independent clause.

FRAGMENT: Some popular novelists are highly respected by later generations. <u>For example, Mark Twain and Charles Dickens.</u> (Appositive, a phrase that identifies *some popular novelists*, is punctuated as a sentence.)

REVISED: Some popular novelists—for example, Mark Twain and Charles Dickens—are highly respected by later generations. (Appositive has been embedded within the preceding independent clause, directly following the noun it renames.)

**frag
12e**

NOTE: For information on correct punctuation with appositives, see 27d.2.

☐   **EXERCISE 5**

Identify the fragments in this paragraph and correct them by attaching each to the independent clause containing the word or word group the appositive modifies.

The Smithsonian Institution in Washington, D.C., includes fourteen different buildings. Museums and art galleries. These include well-known landmarks. Such as the National Air and Space Museum and the National Gallery of Art. The Smithsonian also includes the National Zoo. Home of the giant pandas Ling-Ling and Hsing-Hsing. The Smithsonian contains many entertaining and educational exhibits. For example, the Wright Brothers' plane, Lindbergh's *Spirit of St. Louis*, and a moon rock. The Smithsonian also includes eleven other museums. The National Museum of American History, the National Museum of Natural History, the Hirshhorn Museum, the Freer Gallery, the Arts and Industries Building, the National Museum of American Art and National Portrait Gallery, the Renwick Gallery, the National Museum of African Art, The Castle, the Arthur M. Sackler Gallery, and the Anacostia Neighborhood Museum. The National Museum of American History contains one especially historic item. Edison's first light bulb. The National Museum of Natural History also includes a spectacular exhibit. A giant squid that washed ashore in Massachusetts in 1980. These and other entertaining and educational exhibits make up the Smithsonian. An attraction that should not be missed.

12f Revising Compounds ───────────────

When detached from its subject, the last part of a **compound predicate** (see 7f.5) cannot stand alone as a sentence.

To correct this kind of fragment, connect the detached part of the compound predicate to the rest of the sentence.

FRAGMENT: People with dyslexia have trouble reading. <u>And may also find it difficult to write.</u> (Fragment, part of the compound predicate *have . . . and may also find,* is punctuated as a sentence.)

REVISED: People with dyslexia have trouble reading and may also find it difficult to write. (Detached part of the compound predicate has been connected to the rest of the sentence.)

The last part of a **compound object** or **compound complement** (see 7f.5) cannot stand alone as a sentence either. Be sure to attach it to the rest of the sentence.

**frag
12f**

FRAGMENT: They took only a compass and a canteen of water. And some trail mix. (Fragment, part of the compound object *compass . . . canteen . . . trail mix,* is punctuated as a sentence.)

REVISED: They took only a compass, a canteen of water, and some trail mix. (Detached part of the compound object has been connected to the rest of the sentence.)

FRAGMENT: When their supplies ran out, they were surprised. And hungry. (Fragment, part of the compound complement *surprised and hungry,* is punctuated as a sentence.)

REVISED: When their supplies ran out, they were surprised and hungry. (Detached part of the compound complement has been connected to the rest of the sentence.)

☐   **EXERCISE 6**

Identify the sentence fragments in this passage, and correct them by attaching each detached compound predicate, object, or complement to the rest of the sentence.

One of the phenomena of the 80's is the number of parents determined to raise "superbabies." Many affluent parents, professionals themselves, seem driven to raise children who are mentally superior. And physically fit as well. To this end they enroll babies as young as a few weeks old in baby gyms. And sign up slightly older preschool children for classes that teach computer skills or violin. Or swimming or Japanese. Such classes are important. But are not the only source of formal education for very young children. Parents themselves try to raise their babies' IQ's. Or learn to teach toddlers to read or to do simple math. Some parents begin teaching with flash cards when their babies are only a few months—or days—old. Others wait until their children are a bit older. And enroll them in day-care programs designed to sharpen their skills. Or spend thousands of dollars on "educational toys." Some psychologists and child-care professionals are favorably impressed by this trend toward earlier and earlier education. But most have serious reservations, feeling the emphasis on academics and pressure to achieve may stunt children's social and emotional growth.

12g Revising Incomplete Clauses ─────────

Not all sentence fragments are short. In the process of adding modifiers it is easy to create a fragment when you lose track of the direction of a long sentence and fail to finish it.

    To correct such a fragment, you must add, delete, or change words to create a complete independent clause.

**frag
12g**

FRAGMENT: *Ancient Evenings,* Norman Mailer's 1983 novel, more than ten years in the making and considered by critics to be a major work, which is set in Egypt before the birth of Christ. (Subject *Ancient Evenings* has no predicate.)

REVISED: *Ancient Evenings,* Norman Mailer's 1983 novel, more than ten years in the making and considered by critics to be a major work, is set in Egypt before the birth of Christ. (Relative pronoun *which* has been deleted; *is set* is now the predicate of a complete independent clause.)

FRAGMENT: Because of Wright Morris's ambition to become a writer, which led him to travel to Paris just as Ernest Hemingway, Gertrude Stein, Samuel Beckett, and Henry Miller had. (Fragment contains no independent clause.)

REVISED: Wright Morris's ambition to become a writer led him to travel to Paris just as Ernest Hemingway, Gertrude Stein, Samuel Beckett, and Henry Miller had. (Subordinating conjunction *because* and relative pronoun *which* have been deleted, leaving one complete independent clause.)

REVISED: Because of Wright Morris's ambition to become a writer, he traveled to Paris just as Ernest Hemingway, Gertrude Stein, Samuel Beckett, and Henry Miller had. (Relative pronoun *which* has been deleted and some words have been changed, leaving a complete independent clause preceded by a dependent clause.)

☐   **EXERCISE 7**

Identify the fragments in the following paragraph and correct each by adding, deleting, or changing words to create a complete independent clause.

    The Brooklyn Bridge, completed in 1883 and the subject of poems, paintings, and films for many years, which helped it to capture the imagination of the public as well as the artist as few other structures have. Because artists like George Bellows, Georgia O'Keeffe, Andy Warhol, and Joseph Stella have used the bridge as a subject, and because it has appeared in the novels of John Dos Passos and Thomas Wolfe and the poems of Hart Crane and Marianne Moore, who have all seen it as a major symbol of America. The Brooklyn Bridge, also making an appearance in essays by writers like Henry James and Lewis Mumford and seen in films from *Tarzan's New York Adventure* and Laurel and Hardy's *Way Out West* to *Annie Hall* and *Sophie's Choice*, which ensured its visibility to the public. Over the years, the bridge has also turned up in songs, in Bugs Bunny cartoons, and on product labels, record jackets, and T-shirts, making it one of the most recognizable structures in America.

frag 12h

12h   Using Fragments Effectively

Some sentence fragments are acceptable and effective. We commonly use fragments in speech and in informal writing.

> See you later.
>
> Back soon.
>
> No sweat.
>
> Could be trouble.
>
> Just a note to let you know I got the loan. Sure will make things a lot easier next semester.

Advertising copywriters also use fragments.

> Be all curls. Not all nerves.
>
> Finally. Vegetables with no salt added.
>
> Lighten up! With low-tar Belair.
>
> Great taste in every bite, and only half the sugar.

Finally, journalists and creative writers frequently use fragments to achieve special effects—for instance, to represent casual conversation or to convey disconnected thinking.

> They tell me that apathy is in this year. Very chic. (Ellen Goodman, *Close to Home*)
>
> Then the curtains breathing out of the dark upon my face, leaving the breathing upon my face. A quarter hour yet. And then I'll not be. The peacefullest words. (William Faulkner, *The Sound and the Fury*)

Keep in mind that you should not use incomplete sentences without carefully considering their suitability for your audience and purpose. In most college writing situations, sentence fragments are not acceptable.

Student Writer at Work: Sentence Fragments ──

Carefully read this excerpt from a draft of a student essay. Identify all the sentence fragments, and determine why each is a fragment. Correct each sentence fragment by adding, deleting, or modifying words to create a sentence or by attaching the fragment to a neighboring independent clause. Finally, go over the draft again and, if necessary, revise further to strengthen coherence, unity, and style.

frag
12

From Ab Snopes: A Trapped Man

Abner (Ab) Snopes, the father in William Faulkner's story "Barn Burning," is trapped in a hopeless situation. Disgusted with his lack of status, yet unable to do much to remedy his dissatisfaction. He has little control over his life, but he still struggles. Fighting his useless battle as best he can.

Ab is a family man. Responsible for a wife, children, and his wife's sister. Unfortunately, he is unable to meet his responsibilities. Such as providing a stable home for his family. Evicted because of Ab's "barn burnings," the family constantly moves from town to town. With all its belongings piled on a wagon. But Ab continues to burn barns. Because he hopes that these acts will give him power as well as revenge.

To the rich landowners he works for, Ab is of little significance. Poor, uneducated, uncultured. There are many men just like him. Who can work the land. Ab understands this situation. But is unwilling to accept his inferior status. Consequently, he approaches new employers with arrogance. His actions and manner soon causing trouble. This behavior, of course, ensures his eventual dismissal. Ab feels that since he can never gain their respect. He should not even bother behaving in a civilized manner. So he insists on playing the role. Of a belligerent, raging man.

Ab's behavior sets in motion a self-fulfilling prophecy. Each time Ab's actions cause an employer to ask him to leave, his prophecy that he will be mistreated is fulfilled. He pretends that the failure is his employer's, not his own. And vents his frustration. By destroying their property with fire. He also feels that such actions will earn him respect. People will be frightened of him, and he will create a name for himself. Only Ab's son, Sarty, sees the truth. That Ab is to his employers "no more . . . than a buzzing wasp."

**frag
12**

13

Comma Splices and Fused Sentences

A **run-on sentence** results when the proper connective or punctuation does not appear between independent clauses. A run-on occurs either as a **comma splice**, two independent clauses joined only by a comma, or as a **fused sentence**, two independent clauses joined with no punctuation.

COMMA SPLICE: Charles Dickens created the character of Mr. Micawber, he also created Uriah Heep.

FUSED SENTENCE: Charles Dickens created the character of Mr. Micawber he also created Uriah Heep.

REVISED: Charles Dickens created the character of Mr. Micawber. He also created Uriah Heep.

Both kinds of run-on sentences confuse readers. Avoid them, and be sure to revise when they occur in your writing.

The Comma Splice

A comma splice is created when two independent clauses are incorrectly joined by a comma. It results from a writer's carelessly omitting a needed coordinating conjunction or wrongly assuming that a conjunctive adverb or other transitional expression can take the place of a coordinating conjunction in a sentence.

You can correct comma splices in one of four ways.

┌──┐
| **Correcting Comma Splices** |
| |
| 1. Substitute a period for the comma. |
| 2. Substitute a semicolon for the comma. |
| 3. Add an appropriate coordinating conjunction. |
| 4. Subordinate one clause to the other. |
└──┘

cs
13b

13a   Substituting a Period for the Comma

Using a period to separate independent clauses creates two separate sentences. A comma splice can be revised in this way when the clauses are of equal importance but are not linked closely enough to be joined in one sentence.

COMMA SPLICE: In the late nineteenth century Alfred Dreyfus, a Jewish captain in the French army, was falsely convicted of treason, his struggle for justice pitted the army and the Catholic establishment against the civil libertarians.

REVISED: In the late nineteenth century Alfred Dreyfus, a Jewish captain in the French army, was falsely convicted of treason. His struggle for justice pitted the army and the Catholic establishment against the civil libertarians.

Substituting a period is the best way to revise a comma splice resulting from the incorrect punctuation of a broken quotation.

COMMA SPLICE: "This is a good course," Eric said, "in fact, I wish I'd taken it sooner."

REVISED: "This is a good course," Eric said. "In fact, I wish I'd taken it sooner."

NOTE: This method of correcting comma splices does have some stylistic limitations (see 11a.1).

13b   Substituting a Semicolon for the Comma

If the two clauses of equal importance are closely related, and if you want to underscore that relationship, use a semicolon.

COMMA SPLICE: In pre-World War II Western Europe only a small elite had access to a university education, this situation changed dramatically after the war.

REVISED: In pre-World War II Western Europe only a small elite had access to a university education; this situation changed dramatically after the war.

You can also use a semicolon to revise a comma splice when the ideas in the joined clauses are presented in parallel terms.

COMMA SPLICE: Chippendale chairs have straight legs, Queen Anne chairs have curved legs.

REVISED: Chippendale chairs have straight legs; Queen Anne chairs have curved legs.

In such cases, the semicolon emphasizes the symmetry between the two clauses (see 15a).

13c Adding a Coordinating Conjunction ——

If two closely related clauses are of equal importance, you can use an appropriate coordinating conjunction to indicate whether the clauses are linked by addition (*and*), contrast (*but, yet*), causality (*for, so*), or a choice of alternatives (*or, nor*).

COMMA SPLICE: Elias Howe invented the sewing machine, Julia Ward Howe was a poet and social reformer.

REVISED: Elias Howe invented the sewing machine, but Julia Ward Howe was a poet and social reformer. (Coordinating conjunction *but* shows emphasis is on contrast.)

Remember that you cannot correct a comma splice simply by adding a conjunctive adverb (*however, nevertheless, therefore,* and so on) or any other transitional expression (*for example, in fact, on the other hand*) between the independent clauses. If you do, you will still have a comma splice.

COMMA SPLICE: The International Date Line is drawn north and south through the Pacific Ocean, largely at the 180th meridian, thus, it separates Wake and Midway Islands.

REVISED: The International Date Line is drawn north and south through the Pacific Ocean, largely at the 180th meridian; thus, it separates Wake and Midway Islands.

REVISED: The International Date Line is drawn north and south through the Pacific Ocean, largely at the 180th meridian. Thus, it separates Wake and Midway Islands.

For information on punctuating conjunctive adverbs or other transitional expressions, see 28c.

13d   Adding a Subordinating Conjunction or Relative Pronoun

When the ideas in two clauses are not of equal importance, correct the comma splice by subordinating the less important idea to the more important one, placing the less important idea in a dependent clause. The subordinating conjunction or relative pronoun establishes the nature of the relationship between the clauses.

cs
13e

COMMA SPLICE: Stravinsky's ballet *The Rite of Spring* shocked Parisians in 1913, its rhythms and the dancers' movements seemed erotic.

REVISED: Because its rhythms and the dancers' movements seemed erotic, Stravinsky's ballet *The Rite of Spring* shocked Parisians in 1913. (Subordinating conjunction *because* has been added to make the original sentence's second clause subordinate to its first; the result is one complex sentence.)

COMMA SPLICE: Lady Mary Wortley Montagu had suffered from smallpox herself, she helped spread the practice of inoculation against the disease in eighteenth-century England.

REVISED: Lady Mary Wortley Montagu, who had suffered from smallpox herself, helped spread the practice of inoculation against the disease in eighteenth-century England. (Relative pronoun *who* has been added to make the original sentence's first clause subordinate to its second; the result is one complex sentence.)

13e   Using Comma Splices Effectively

In rare cases comma splices are acceptable. For instance, a comma is always correct between a statement and a tag question, even though each is a separate independent clause.

This is Ron's house, isn't it?

I'm not late, am I?

In addition, commas may connect two short *balanced* independent clauses, or two or more short parallel independent clauses, especially when one clause contradicts the other.

My nose is stuffed, my throat is sore.

Writers aren't born, they're made.

Commencement isn't the end, it's the beginning.

☐   **EXERCISE 1**

Find the comma splices in the following paragraph. Correct each in *two* of the four possible ways listed on page 227. If a sentence is correct, leave it alone.

EXAMPLE: The fans rose in their seats, the game was almost over.

The fans rose in their seats; the game was almost over.

The fans rose in their seats, for the game was almost over.

Entrepreneurship is the study of small businesses, college students are embracing it enthusiastically. Many schools offer one or more courses in entrepreneurship, these courses teach the theory and practice of starting a small business. Students are signing up for courses, moreover they are starting their own businesses. One student started with a car-waxing business, now he sells condominiums. Other students are setting up catering services, they supply everything from waiters to bartenders. One student has a thriving cake-decorating business, in fact she employs fifteen students to deliver the cakes. All over the country, student businesses are selling everything from tennis balls to bagels, the student owners are making impressive profits. Formal courses at the graduate as well as undergraduate level are attracting more business students than ever, several business schools (such as Baylor University, the University of Southern California, and Babson College) even offer degree programs in entrepreneurship. Many business school students are no longer planning to be corporate executives, instead they plan to become entrepreneurs.

The Fused Sentence

A fused sentence occurs when two independent clauses are joined without suitable punctuation or a coordinating conjunction.

Fused sentences can be corrected in one of four ways.

Correcting Fused Sentences

1. Add a period between clauses.
2. Add a semicolon between clauses.
3. Add a comma and an appropriate coordinating conjunction between clauses.
4. Subordinate one clause to the other.

13f Adding a Period

You may revise a fused sentence by adding a period between clauses to create two separate sentences.

FUSED SENTENCE: Buffalo Bill's Wild West Show was introduced to America in 1883 two years later sharpshooter Annie Oakley joined the show.

REVISED: Buffalo Bill's Wild West Show was introduced to America in 1883. Two years later sharpshooter Annie Oakley joined the show.

fs
13i

13g Adding a Semicolon

Adding a semicolon between clauses can correct a fused sentence.

FUSED SENTENCE: A group of elephants is known as a herd a group of kangaroos is called a mob.

REVISED: A group of elephants is known as a herd; a group of kangaroos is called a mob.

13h Adding a Comma and a Coordinating Conjunction

You may add a comma and an appropriate coordinating conjunction between clauses.

FUSED SENTENCE: The ERA was supported by many Americans the amendment failed to win passage in the allotted time.

REVISED: The ERA was supported by many Americans, but the amendment failed to win passage in the allotted time.

13i Using Subordination

You can correct a fused sentence by subordinating one clause to the other, adding an appropriate subordinating conjunction or relative pronoun.

FUSED SENTENCE: Texas is the largest state in the continental United States Alaska is actually the largest state in the union.

REVISED: Although Texas is the largest state in the continental United States, Alaska is actually the largest state in the union.

□   **EXERCISE 2**

Find the fused sentences in the following paragraph, and correct each in *two* of the possible four ways listed on page 230.

EXAMPLE: Amy applied to four colleges she was accepted at three.

Amy applied to four colleges; she was accepted at three.

Amy applied to four colleges, and she was accepted at three.

Animals are disappearing from the earth about one species a year has become extinct since 1900. Enormous dinosaurs once roamed the earth they became extinct some 65 million years ago. Huge mammals later flourished they included mastodons and mammoths. Over one hundred different species of these large mammals lived on earth some of them were alive only 11,000 years ago. But these animals all vanished no one is quite sure exactly why this happened. Hundreds of other species had developed and eventually died out before humans existed however after man appeared in North America extinction increased dramatically. Hunters killed animals for food therefore some scientists believe it is possible that hunters exterminated the large animals. Other scientists attribute the animals' disappearance to climatic changes during the Ice Age. For instance, marked drops in temperatures ruined grazing lands many animals died from exposure and starvation. Droughts also killed many animals the competition for grasslands was too much for them. Finally, it has been suggested that man did eliminate the animals however many had already been weakened by natural forces like disease and climatic changes.

□   **EXERCISE 3**

Combine each of the following sentence pairs into one sentence without creating comma splices or fused sentences. In each case, either connect the clauses into a compound sentence with a semicolon or with a comma and a coordinating conjunction, or subordinate one clause to the other to create a complex sentence. You may have to add, delete, reorder, or change words or punctuation.

1. It is true that caring for pets can be expensive and time-consuming. They can help their owners in many ways.
2. Dogs and cats are extremely popular pets. Moreover, they can help improve the mental and physical health of their owners.
3. Pets can protect their owners. In addition, they can provide companionship.
4. Pets can also give people something to love. The pet is bound to return the owner's love.

5. Pets can help isolated people to make friends. Thus, they can help fight loneliness and depression.
6. Pets can help people to structure their days. A dog, for instance, needs to be walked and fed at set times.
7. Children who own pets can learn to be more responsible. They can learn loyalty and compassion at the same time.
8. Pets can even help sick and disabled people. Seeing-eye dogs for the blind and "hearing-ear" dogs for the deaf are two examples.
9. Doctors have found pets can be valuable in treating mentally ill people. Pets can coax withdrawn mental patients out of their shells.
10. More than half of all American families own some kind of pet. Considering pets' many benefits, this seems to make sense.

cs/fs
13

Student Writer at Work: Comma Splices and Fused Sentences

Read the following answer to an economics examination question that asked students to discuss the provisions of the 1935 Social Security Act; correct all comma splices and fused sentences. After you have corrected the errors, go over the answer again and, if necessary, revise further to strengthen coherence, unity, and style.

In June of 1934 Franklin D. Roosevelt selected Frances Perkins to head the new Committee on Economic Security, their report was the basis of our current Social Security program. The committee formulated two policies, one dealt with the employable the other with the unemployable. Roosevelt insisted that these programs be self-financing, as a result both employer and employee social insurance were required. In 1935 the Social Security Act was passed it attempted to categorize the poor and provided for federal sharing of the cost, but under local control. (The Social Security Act did not include a public works program, this feature of the New Deal was eliminated.)

Unemployment insurance was one major part of the Act. Funds were to be payable through public employment offices, also the money was to be paid into a trust fund. It was to be used solely for benefits an individual could

not be denied funds even if work were available. The
program provided for payroll taxes, in addition separate
records were to be kept by each state. Old Age Survivor
Insurance, another major provision of the Act, was for
individuals over sixty—five it was amended in 1939 to
cover dependents. A quarter of the total recipients were
disabled. Public Assistance was the third major part of
the Act this program was designed to help children left
alone by the death or absence of the parents and children
with mental or physical disabilities. General assistance
covered everything not included under the Public
Assistance Program this coverage varied from state to
state.

The Social Security Act stressed public administration
of federal emergency relief assistance thus it forced
reorganization of public assistance. These efforts
differed from previous efforts earlier there were no clear
guidelines defining which individuals should get aid and
why. The Social Security Act attempted to eliminate gaps
and overlaps in services.

cs/fs

13

14

Misplaced and Dangling Modifiers

Modifiers add information and show connections between ideas. They also expand and enrich sentences, helping you to communicate meaning accurately and precisely to your readers. Normally, a modifier is placed close to its **headword,** the word or phrase it modifies, and readers expect to find it there. **Faulty modification** is the awkward or confusing placement of modifiers or the modification of nonexistent words.

Faulty modification commonly takes two forms: *misplaced modifiers* and *dangling modifiers.*

Misplaced Modifiers

A **misplaced modifier** is a word or word group whose placement suggests that it modifies one word or phrase when it is intended to modify another. A misplaced modifier has no clear relationship with its headword. Consider the following sentence.

Faster than a speeding bullet, the citizens of Metropolis saw Superman flying overhead.

The placement of the introductory phrase makes it appear to modify *citizens,* yet it should modify *Superman.* Here is a corrected version.

The citizens of Metropolis saw Superman flying overhead, faster than a speeding bullet.

235

When writing and revising, take care to put modifying words, phrases, and clauses in a position that clearly identifies the headword and that does not awkwardly interrupt a sentence.

14a Revising Misplaced Words

mm
14a

Readers expect to find modifiers directly before or directly after their headwords. Conforming to these expectations helps you compose more readable sentences.

Dark and threatening, Wendy watched the storm. (Incorrectly placed adjectives *dark* and *threatening* seem to describe Wendy instead of the storm.)

Wendy watched the storm, dark and threatening. (Correct placement of modifier clarifies meaning.)

Certain modifiers—such as *almost, only, even, hardly, merely, nearly, exactly, scarcely, just,* and *simply*—should always immediately precede the words they modify. Different placements of these modifiers change the meaning of your sentence.

Nick *just* set up camp at the edge of the burned-out town. (He set up camp just now.)

Just Nick set up camp at the edge of the burned-out town. (He set up camp alone.)

Nick set up camp *just* at the edge of the burned-out town. (His camp was precisely at the edge.)

The imprecise placement of modifiers like these sometimes produces a **squinting modifier,** one that seems to modify either a word before it or one after it and to convey different meanings in each case. To avoid ambiguity, be sure to place the modifier so that it clearly modifies its headword.

SQUINTING: The life that everyone thought would fulfill her [totally] bored her. (Was she supposed to be totally fulfilled, or is she totally bored?)

REVISED: The life that everyone thought would totally fulfill her bored her. (Everyone expected her to be totally fulfilled.)

REVISED: The life that everyone thought would fulfill her bored her totally. (She was totally bored.)

☐ **EXERCISE 1**

In the following sentence pairs, the modifier in each sentence points to a different headword. Underline the modifier and draw an arrow to the word it limits. Then paraphrase the meaning of each sentence.

EXAMPLE: She just came in wearing a hat.
          [She just now entered.]
          She came in wearing just a hat.
          [She wore only a hat.]

1. He wore his almost new jeans.
   He almost wore his new jeans.
2. He only had three dollars in his pocket.
   Only he had three dollars in his pocket.
3. I don't even like freshwater fish.
   I don't like even freshwater fish.
4. I go only to the beach on Saturdays.
   I go to the beach only on Saturdays.
5. He simply hated living.
   He hated simply living.

14b   Revising Misplaced Phrases

Placing a modifying phrase illogically can create a sentence that is hard to decipher.

(1) Misplaced verbal phrases

Certain *verbal phrases* act as modifiers (see 7f.2). As a rule, place them directly before or directly after the nouns or pronouns they modify.

[Absorbed in the story], he listened intently.

She watched the car [rolling down the hill].

The incorrect placement of a verbal phrase that acts as a modifier can make a sentence convey an entirely different meaning or make no sense at all.

[Rolling down the hill], she watched the car.

Jane watched the boats [roller skating along the shore].

(2) Misplaced prepositional phrases

When a *prepositional phrase* is used as an adjective (see 7f.1), it nearly always directly follows the word it modifies.

This is a Dresden figurine [from Germany].

Created by a famous artist, Venus de Milo is a statue [with no arms].

Incorrect placement can give rise to confusion or even unintended humor.

Venus de Milo is a statue created by a famous artist [with no arms].

When used as adverbs, prepositional phrases usually follow their headwords.

Cassandra looked [into the future].

As long as the meaning of the sentence is clear, and as long as the headword is clearly identified, you can place an adverbial modifier in any alternative position.

He had been waiting anxiously at the bus stop [for a long time].

However, be careful to avoid ambiguous placement of prepositional phrases serving as adverbs.

MISPLACED: She saw the house she built in her mind.

REVISED: [In her mind], she saw the house she built.

REVISED: She saw [in her mind] the house she built.

☐   **EXERCISE 2**

Underline the modifying verbal or prepositional phrases in each sentence, and draw arrows to their headwords.

EXAMPLE: Calvin is the democrat running for town council.

1. The bridge across the river swayed in the wind.
2. The spectators on the shore were involved in the action.
3. Mesmerized by the spectacle, they watched the drama unfold.
4. The spectators were afraid of a disaster.
5. Within the hour, the state police arrived to save the day.
6. They closed off the area with roadblocks.
7. Drivers approaching the bridge were asked to stop.
8. Meanwhile, on the bridge, the scene was chaos.
9. Motorists in their cars were paralyzed with fear.
10. Struggling against the weather, the police managed to rescue everyone.

☐   **EXERCISE 3**

Use the word or phrase that follows each sentence as a modifier in that sentence. Then draw an arrow to indicate its headword.

EXAMPLE: He approached the lion. (timid)

Timid, he approached the lion.

1. The lion paced up and down in his cage, ignoring the crowd. (watching Jack)
2. Jack stared back at the lion. (fascinated yet curious)
3. The crowd around them grew. (anxious to see what would happen)
4. Suddenly Jack heard a growl from deep in the lion's throat. (terrifying)
5. Jack ran from the zoo, leaving the lion behind. (scared to death)

mm
14c

14c   Revising Misplaced Dependent Clauses

Dependent clauses that serve as modifiers—adjective clauses and adverb clauses—must be clearly related to their headwords. Adjective clauses usually appear immediately after the words they modify.

During the Civil War, Lincoln was the president [who governed the United States].

An adverb clause can appear in any of several positions, as long as the relationship to the clause it modifies is clear and its position conveys the intended emphasis.

During the Civil War Lincoln was president.

Lincoln was president during the Civil War.

To correct misplaced dependent clauses, make the relationship between modifier and headword clear.

MISPLACED: This diet program will limit the consumption of possi-
(adjective ble carcinogens, [which will benefit everyone]. (Will car-
clause) cinogens benefit everyone?)

REVISED: This diet program, [which will benefit everyone], will limit the consumption of possible carcinogens.

MISPLACED: They decided the house was haunted, but they
(adverb changed their minds [when purple grass started grow-
clause) ing out of the fireplace]. (This bizarre phenomenon reassured them?)

REVISED: The decided the house was haunted when purple grass started growing out of the fireplace, but they changed their minds.

REVISED: When purple grass started growing out of the fireplace, they decided the house was haunted, but they changed their minds.

mm
14d

☐   **EXERCISE 4**

Relocate the misplaced verbal or prepositional phrases or dependent clauses so that they clearly point to the words or word groups they modify.

EXAMPLE: *Silent Running* is a film about a scientist left alone in
(misplaced   space with Bruce Dern.
modifier)

Silent Running is a film with Bruce Dern about a scientist left alone in space.

1. She realized she had married the wrong man after the wedding.
2. *The Prince and the Pauper* is about an exchange of identities by Mark Twain.
3. The energy was used up in the ten-kilometer race that he was saving for the marathon.
4. He loaded the bottles and cans into his new Porsche, which he planned to leave at the recycling center.
5. The manager explained the sales figures to the board members using a graph.

14d   Revising Intrusive Modifiers

An **intrusive modifier** interrupts a sentence, making it difficult for readers to see the connections between subjects and their verbs or between verbs and their objects or complements.

(1) Interrupting a verb phrase

Revise when modifiers come between an auxiliary and a main verb.

AWKWARD: She had, without giving it a second thought or considering the consequences, planned to reenlist.

REVISED: Without giving it a second thought or considering the
consequences, she had planned to reenlist.

AWKWARD: He will, if he ever gets his act together, be ready to leave
on Friday.

REVISED: If he ever gets his act together, he <u>will be</u> ready to leave on Friday.

If a modifier is brief, it can usually interrupt a verb phrase.

She <u>had</u> always <u>planned</u> to reenlist.

He <u>will</u>, however, <u>be</u> ready to leave on Friday.

Longer interruptions, however, may obscure your meaning.

(2)   Interrupting an infinitive

Revise when modifiers interrupt an infinitive. As a rule, the parts of an infinitive should be together. When a modifier splits an infinitive—that is, comes between the word *to* and the base form of the verb—the sentence often becomes awkward.

AWKWARD: He hoped <u>to</u> quickly and easily <u>defeat</u> his opponent.

REVISED: He hoped <u>to defeat</u> his opponent quickly and easily.

AWKWARD: He decided <u>to</u> after he considered the possible risks <u>invest</u> all his money in stocks.

REVISED: After he considered the possible risks, he decided <u>to invest</u> all his money in stocks.

Although the general rule in writing is never to split an infinitive, it is occasionally necessary to do so. When the intervening modifier is short, and when the alternative is awkward or ambiguous, a split infinitive is permissible. In the following sentence, for example, a reader would have no trouble connecting the parts of the infinitive.

She expected <u>to not quite beat</u> her previous record.

Moreover, any revision using the same words is awkward or incoherent.

She expected not quite to beat her previous record.

She expected to beat not quite her previous record.

The only way to avoid a split infinitive in this case is to reword the original sentence.

She expected her score to be close to her previous record.

Because a revision often does not have exactly the same meaning as the original, it is sometimes necessary to split an infinitive. Before you decide to do so, however, make sure there is no other reasonable place for the modifier.

(3) Interrupting a subject and its verb or a verb and its object or complement

Revise if you have any doubts about letting a modifier stand between subject and verb or verb and object or complement. It is standard practice to place even a complex or lengthy adjective phrase or clause between a subject and a verb or between a verb and its object or complement. An adverb phrase or clause in this position, however, may not be natural-sounding or clear.

mm

14d

ACCEPTABLE: Major films that were financially successful in the thirties include *Gone with the Wind* and *Citizen Kane*. (Adjective clause between subject and verb does not obscure sentence's meaning.)

CONFUSING: The election, because officials discovered that some people voted twice, was contested. (Adverb clause intrudes between subject and verb.)

REVISED: Because officials discovered that some people voted twice, the election was contested. (Subject and verb are no longer separated.)

CONFUSING: A. A. Milne wrote, when his son Christopher Robin was a child, *Winnie-the-Pooh*. (Adverb clause intrudes between verb and object.)

REVISED: When his son Christopher Robin was a child, A. A. Milne wrote *Winnie-the-Pooh*. (Verb and object are no longer separated.)

☐   EXERCISE 5

Revise these sentences so that the modifying phrases or clauses do not interrupt the parts of a verb phrase or infinitive or separate a subject from a verb or a verb from its object or complement.

EXAMPLE: A play can sometimes be, despite the playwright's best efforts, mystifying to the audience.

Despite the playwright's best efforts, a play can sometimes be mystifying to the audience.

1. The people in the audience, when they saw that the play was about to begin and realized that the orchestra had finished tuning up and had begun the overture, finally quieted down.
2. They settled into their seats, expecting to very much enjoy the first act.
3. However, most people were, even after watching and listening for twenty minutes and paying close attention to the drama, completely baffled.
4. In fact, the play, because it had nameless characters, no scenery, and

a rambling plot that didn't seem to be heading anywhere, puzzled even the drama critics.
5. Finally one of the three major characters explained, speaking directly to the audience, what the play was really about.

Dangling Modifiers

A **dangling modifier** is a word or phrase that cannot logically describe, limit, or restrict any word or word group in the sentence. In fact, its true headword does not appear in the sentence. Consider the following example.

Many undesirable side effects are experienced using this drug.

Using this drug appears to modify *side effects*, but this interpretation makes no sense. Because its true headword does not appear in the sentence, the modifier dangles.

One way to correct the faulty sentence is to add a word or word group that the dangling modifier can logically modify. To do so, you usually must change the subject of the main clause.

<u>Patients</u> using this drug experience many undesirable side effects.

Another way to correct a dangling modifier is to change the modifier into a dependent clause.

Many undesirable side effects are experienced <u>when this drug is used</u>.

The original incorrect sentence, like many sentences that include dangling modifiers, is in the passive voice. The true headword is absent because the passive construction *Many undesirable side effects are experienced* does not tell *who* experiences the side effects. Changing the passive construction to active voice corrects the dangling modifier by changing the subject of the sentence's main clause from *side effects* to *patients*, a word the dangling modifier can logically modify. Sometimes, however, passive voice is a desirable stylistic option (see 9e). In such cases you may correct the dangling modifier by supplying the subject while retaining the passive voice.

Many undesirable side effects are experienced <u>by patients</u> using this drug.

Or, you may change the dangling modifier into a dependent clause.

Many undesirable side effects are experienced <u>when this drug is used</u>.

Correcting Dangling Modifiers

> • Supply a word or word group that the dangling modifier can logically modify.
> • Change the dangling modifier into a dependent clause.

dm 14e

The three most common kinds of dangling modifiers are dangling verbal phrases, dangling prepositional phrases, and dangling elliptical clauses.

14e Revising Dangling Verbal Phrases

Verbal phrases used as modifiers sometimes dangle in a sentence.

DANGLING: Using a pair of forceps, the skin of the rat's abdomen
(participial was lifted, and a small cut was made into the body
phrase) with scissors. (Sentence contains no word the participial phrase can logically modify.)

REVISED: Using a pair of forceps, the technician lifted the skin of the rat's abdomen and made a small cut into the body with scissors. (Subject of main clause has been changed from *the skin* to *the technician*, a headword the participial phrase can logically modify.)

DANGLING: Paid in three installments, Brad's financial situation
(participial seemed stable. (Sentence contains no word the parti-
phrase) cipial phrase can logically modify.)

REVISED: Because the grant was paid in three installments, Brad's financial situation seemed stable. (Modifying phrase is now a dependent clause.)

DANGLING: To make his paper accurate, all references were
(infinitive checked twice. (Sentence contains no word the infini-
phrase) tive phrase can logically modify.)

REVISED: To make his paper accurate, Don checked all references twice. (Subject of main clause has been changed from *references* to *Don*, a headword the infinitive phrase can logically modify.)

DANGLING: Music seemed to carry the children's minds away from
(infinitive reality to dream about the future. (Sentence contains no
phrase) word the infinitive phrase can logically modify.)

REVISED: Music seemed to carry the children's minds away from reality so that they were able to dream about the future. (Infinitive phrase is now a dependent clause.)

DANGLING: The exhibit was very efficiently presented <u>by using dia-</u>
(gerund   <u>grams and photographs.</u> (Sentence contains no word the
phrase)   gerund phrase can logically modify.)

REVISED: <u>By using diagrams and photographs</u>, they presented the
           exhibit very efficiently. (Subject of main clause has been
           changed from *the exhibit* to *they*, a word the gerund
           phrase can logically modify.)

DANGLING: <u>By moving the microscope's mirror</u>, light can be re-
(gerund   flected off its surface up into the viewing apparatus.
phrase)   (Sentence contains no word the gerund phrase can logi-
           cally modify.)

REVISED: <u>When the microscope's mirror is moved</u>, light can be
           reflected off its surface up into the viewing apparatus.
           (Gerund is now a dependent clause.)

dm
14g

14f Revising Dangling Propositional Phrases

Prepositional phrases can also dangle in a sentence.

DANGLING: <u>With fifty pages to read</u>, *War and Peace* was absorbing.
           (Sentence contains no word the prepositional phrase
           can logically modify.)

REVISED: <u>With fifty pages to read</u>, Meg found *War and Peace* ab-
           sorbing. (Subject of main clause has been changed from
           War and Peace to *Meg*, a word the prepositional phrase
           can logically modify.)

DANGLING: <u>On the newsstands only an hour</u>, its sales surprised
           everyone. (Sentence contains no word the prepositional
           phrase can logically modify.)

REVISED: <u>Because the magazine had been on the newsstands only</u>
           <u>an hour</u>, its sales surprised everyone. (Prepositional
           phrase is now a dependent clause.)

14g Revising Dangling Elliptical Clauses

Elliptical clauses are dependent clauses from which part of the
subject or predicate or the entire subject or predicate is missing.
The absent words, therefore, must be inferred from the context
(see 7d.2). When such a clause cannot logically modify the subject of the sentence's main clause, it too dangles.

DANGLING: <u>While still in the Buchner funnel</u>, you should press the
           crystals with a clear stopper to eliminate any residual
           solvent. (Elliptical clause cannot logically modify subject
           or main clause.)

REVISED: <u>While still in the Buchner funnel</u>, the crystals should be pressed with a clear stopper to eliminate any residual solvent. (Subject of main clause has been changed from *you* to *crystals*, a word the elliptical clause can logically modify.)

DANGLING: <u>Though a high-pressure field</u>, I find great personal satisfaction in nursing. (Elliptical clause cannot logically modify subject of main clause.)

dm

14g

REVISED: <u>Though it is a high-pressure field</u>, I find great personal satisfaction in nursing. (Elliptical clause has been expanded into a complete dependent clause.)

☐   **EXERCISE 6**

Eliminate the dangling modifier from each of the following sentences. Either supply a word or word group the dangling modifier can logically modify, or change the dangling modifier into a dependent clause.

EXAMPLE: Medical care will be greatly improved <u>using atomic power to treat disease</u>. (dangling modifier)

<u>Using atomic power to treat disease</u>, physicians will provide greatly improved medical care. (logical headword added)

Medical care will be greatly improved <u>when atomic power is used to treat disease</u>. (dependent clause)

1. As an out-of-state student without a car, it was difficult to get to off-campus cultural events.
2. Some argue that by lowering the drinking age to eighteen, the high schools will be filled with students under the influence of alcohol.
3. When exiting the train, the station will be on your right.
4. Using a piece of filter paper, the ball of sodium is dried as much as possible and placed in a dry test tube.
5. Though a dull movie, the audience applauded anyway.
6. By purchasing only the necessary amounts of food for each member of the family, extra expenses will be eliminated.
7. The enzyme activity of these solutions was immediately stopped by adding the samples to a strong acid solution.
8. To build a house, good blueprints are needed.
9. When voting for president, newspaper polls can be very powerful.
10. Being a freshman, my study habits were not very good.

Student Writer at Work: Misplaced and Dangling Modifiers

Read this draft of a student's technical writing exercise, a description of a 10cc syringe. Correct misplaced and dangling modifiers, and revise again if necessary to strengthen coherence, unity, and style.

Designed to inject liquids into, or withdraw them from, any vessel or cavity, the function of a syringe is often to inject drugs into the body or withdraw blood from it. Syringes are also used to precisely measure amounts of drugs or electrolytes that must be added to intravenous solutions.

There are available on the market today many different types of syringes, but the one most commonly used in hospitals is the 10-cubic-centimeter disposable syringe. Approximately 5 inches long, the primary composition of this particular syringe is transparent polyethylene plastic. The 10cc syringe and the majority of other syringes all share the design of a round plunger or piston within a barrel.

The barrel of a syringe is a round, hollow cylinder about 4½" long with a diameter of ⅜". The bottom end of the barrel has two outward extensions on its opposite sides, which are perpendicular to the cylinder. With a width equal to the diameter of the barrel, the length of these extensions is about ½". The purpose of these extensions is to enable one to hold with the forefinger and middle finger the barrel of the syringe while withdrawing the plunger with the thumb and third finger.

The barrel of the syringe is calibrated on the side in black ink subdivided into gradations of .2cc. At the top of the syringe the barrel abruptly narrows to a very small cylinder, ⅛" in diameter and ¼" in length. This small cylinder is surrounded by another hollow cylinder with a slightly larger diameter. The inside wall of the outer cylinder is threaded like a corkscrew. The purpose of this thread is to secure the needle in place.

The other major part of the syringe is the plunger. The plunger is a solid, round cylinder that fits snugly into the barrel made of plastic. At the bottom of the

plunger is a plastic ring the size of a dime, which
provides something to grasp while withdrawing the
plunger. The body of the plunger connects the bottom rim
with the tip of the plunger, which is made of black
rubber.

15

Faulty Parallelism

Parallelism is the use of similar grammatical elements in sentences or parts of sentences. It ensures that elements sharing the same function also share the same grammatical form—for instance, that verbs match corresponding verbs in tense, mood, and number.

15a Using Parallelism

Effective parallelism adds force, unity, balance, and symmetry to your writing. It makes sentences clear and easy to follow and emphasizes relationships among equivalent ideas. It helps your readers keep track of ideas, and it makes sentences more emphatic, more concise, and more varied. Words, phrases, clauses, or complete sentences may be parallel, and parallel items may be paired or presented in a series.

(1) With items in a series

Coordinate elements—words, phrases, or clauses—in a series should be in parallel form.

> As a vegetarian, he avoided meat, fish, and eggs.
>
> Marijuana use, baby food consumption, and toy production are all starting to decline as the United States population grows older.
>
> Eat, drink, and be merry.
>
> I came; I saw; I conquered.
>
> Three factors influenced him: his desire to relocate; his need for greater responsibility; and his dissatisfaction with his current job.

(2)   With paired items.

Paired points or ideas (words, phrases, or clauses) should be presented in parallel terms. Parallelism conveys their correspondence and connects points to each other.

> Her note was short but sweet.
>
> Roosevelt represented the United States, and Churchill represented Great Britain.
>
> The research focused on muscle tissue and nerve cells.
>
> The more you study, the more you learn.
>
> Ask not what your country can do for you; ask what you can do for your country. (John F. Kennedy, Inaugural Address)

//
15a

Correlative conjunctions (like *not only/but also, both/and, either/or, neither/nor,* and *whether/or*) are frequently used to link paired elements. These phrases convey balance, so the terms they introduce should be parallel.

> The design team paid close attention not only to color but also to texture.
>
> Either repeat physics or take calculus.
>
> Both cable television and videocassette recorders threatened the dominance of the major television networks.

Parallelism can also be used to highlight opposition between paired elements linked by the word *than.*

> Richard Wright and James Baldwin chose to live in Paris rather than to remain in the United States.

(3)   In lists and outlines

Elements in a list should be expressed in parallel terms.

The Irish potato famine had four major causes:
1. The establishment of the landlord-tenant system
2. The failure of the potato crop
3. The reluctance of England to offer adequate financial assistance
4. The passage of the Corn Laws

Elements in an outline should also be parallel (see 2d.3).

☐   **EXERCISE 1**

Identify the parallel elements in these sentences by underlining parallel words and bracketing parallel phrases and clauses.

EXAMPLE: He is 81 now, [a tall man in a dark blue suit], [a smiling man with a nimbus of snowy white hair], and much of

> the world knows him [as the proponent of vitamin C to
> cure colds], [as a quixotic, vaguely ridiculed figure on the
> fringes of medicine]. (Maralyn Lois Polak, *Philadelphia
> Inquirer*)

1. You have lived an American dream when you begin the year setting
pressure gauges for the Caterpillar Tractor Company in Peoria and
end it building rocking chairs for your grandchildren. *(Newsweek)*
2. The public image [of the American woman] in the magazine and television commercials is designed to sell washing machines, cake mixes,
deodorants, detergents, rejuvenating face creams, hair tints. (Betty
Friedan, *The Feminine Mystique*)
3. Surgery restores to function broken limbs and damaged hearts with
amazing safety and little suffering; sanitation removes from our environment many of the germs of disease; new drugs are constantly
being developed to relieve physical pain, to help us sleep if we are
restless, to keep us awake if we feel sleepy, and to make us oblivious
to worries. (René Dubos, *Medical Utopias*)
4. Theoretically—and secretly, of course—I was all for the Burmese and
all against their oppressors, the British. (George Orwell, "Shooting
an Elephant")
5. As nations, we can apply to affairs of state the realism of science:
holding to what works and discarding what does not. (Jacob
Bronowski, *A Sense of the Future*)

☐   **EXERCISE 2**

Combine each of the following sentence pairs or sentence groups into
one sentence that uses parallel structure. Be sure all parallel words,
phrases, and clauses are expressed in parallel terms.

1. Originally, there were five performing Marx Brothers. One was nicknamed Groucho. The others were called Chico, Harpo, Gummo, and
Zeppo.
2. Groucho was very well known. So were Chico and Harpo. Gummo
soon dropped out of the act. And later Zeppo did, too.
3. They began in vaudeville. That was before World War I. Their first
show was called *I'll Say She Is*. It opened in New York in 1924.
4. The Marx Brothers' first movie was *The Coconuts*. The next was *Animal Crackers*. And this was followed by *Monkey Business*, *Horsefeathers*, and *Duck Soup*. Then came *A Night at the Opera*.
5. In each of these movies, the Marx Brothers make people laugh. More
importantly, they establish a unique, zany comic style.
6. In their movies, each man has a set of familiar trademarks. Groucho
has a mustache and a long coat. He wiggles his eyebrows and
smokes a cigar. There is a funny hat that Chico always wears. And he
affects a phony Italian accent. Harpo never speaks.
7. Groucho is always cast as a sly operator. He always tries to cheat
people out of their money. He always tries to charm women.
8. In *The Coconuts* he plays Mr. Hammer, proprietor of the rundown

Coconut Manor, a Florida hotel. In *Horsefeathers* his character is named Professor Quincy Adams Wagstaff. Wagstaff is president of Huxley College. Huxley also has financial problems.

9. In *Duck Soup* Groucho plays Rufus T. Firefly, president of the country of Fredonia. Fredonia was formerly ruled by the late husband of a Mrs. Teasdale. Fredonia is now at war with the country of Sylvania.

10. Margaret Dumont is often Groucho's leading lady. She plays Mrs. Teasdale in *Duck Soup*. In *A Night at the Opera* she plays Mrs. Claypool. Her character in *The Coconuts* is named Mrs. Potter.

15b   Revising Faulty Parallelism

When elements that have the same function in a sentence are not presented in the same terms, the sentence is flawed by **faulty parallelism.** Consider the following sentence.

> FAULTY
> PARALLELISM: Many people in third-world countries suffer because the countries lack sufficient housing to accommodate them, sufficient food to feed them, and their health-care facilities are inadequate.

Because all three reasons have the same weight and are presented in a series connected by the coordinating conjunction *and*, readers expect them to be expressed in parallel terms. The first two elements satisfy this expectation.

> sufficient housing to accommodate them . . .
>
> sufficient food to feed them . . .

The third item in the series, however, breaks this pattern.

> their health-care facilities are inadequate.

To create a clear, emphatic sentence, all three elements should be presented in the same terms.

> Many people in third-world countries suffer because the countries lack sufficient housing to accommodate them, sufficient food to feed them, and sufficient health-care facilities to serve them.

(1)   Repeating parallel elements

Faulty parallelism occurs when a writer does not use parallel elements in a series or in paired points. Nouns must be matched with nouns, verbs with verbs, phrases and clauses with similarly constructed phrases and clauses, and so on, in places where they are expected.

FAULTY PARALLELISM	REVISED
New trends in exercise for women include aerobic dancing, weight lifters, and jogging. (*Dancing* and *jogging* are gerunds; *weight lifters* is a noun phrase.)	New trends in exercise for women include aerobic dancing, weight lifting, and jogging. (three gerunds)
Some of the side effects are skin irritation and eye irritation, and mucous membrane irritation may also develop. (*Skin irritation* and *eye irritation* are noun phrases; *mucous membrane irritation may also develop* is an independent clause.)	Some of the side effects that may develop are skin, eye, and mucous membrane irritation. (three nouns used as modifiers of *irritation*)
I look forward to hearing from you and to have an opportunity to tell you more about myself. (*Hearing from you* is a gerund phrase; *to have an opportunity* is an infinitive phrase.)	I look forward to hearing from you and to having an opportunity to tell you more about myself. (two gerund phrases)

//

15b

(2)   Repeating signals of parallelism

Faulty parallelism also occurs when a writer does not repeat words that signal parallelism: prepositions, articles, the *to* that is part of the infinitive, or the word that introduces a phrase or clause. Although similar grammatical structures (verbs that match verbs, nouns that match nouns, and so on) may sometimes be enough to convey parallelism, sentences are clearer and more emphatic if other key words in parallel constructions are also parallel. Repeating these signals makes the boundaries of each parallel element clear. But be sure to include the same signals with *all* the elements in a series.

FAULTY PARALLELISM	REVISED
Computerization helps industry by not allowing labor costs to skyrocket, increasing the speed of production, and improving efficiency. (Does *not* apply to all three phrases, or only the first?)	Computerization helps industry by not allowing labor costs to skyrocket, by increasing the speed of production, and by improving efficiency. (Preposition *by* is repeated to clarify the boundaries of the three parallel phrases.)

The United States suffered cas-
ualties in the Civil War, French
and Indian War, Spanish-American War and Korean War.
(Without the repeated definite
article, it is hard for readers to
distinguish the four different
wars.)

The United States suffered cas-
ualties in the Civil War, the
French and Indian War, the
Spanish-American War, and the
Korean War. (The article *the* is
repeated for clarity and emphasis.)

// 15b

It may be easier to try remodeling than abandon a house. (Although *try* and *abandon* correspond, the sentence does not
highlight their parallel structure; in fact, *remodeling* and
abandon seem to be the paired
elements.)

It may be easier to try remodeling than to abandon a house.
(The *to* of the infinitive is repeated for clarity and emphasis.)

Koala bears are not as appealing as they look because they
have fleas, they have bad
breath, and a tendency to
scratch. (Are *bad breath* and *a
tendency to scratch* reasons
that Koalas are unappealing, or
are they incidental points?)

Koala bears are not as appealing as they look because they
have fleas, because they have
bad breath, and because they
have a tendency to scratch.
(The introductory words *because they have* are repeated
for clarity and emphasis.)

(3) Repeating relative pronouns

Faulty parallelism occurs when a writer fails to use a clause beginning with the relative pronoun *who, whom,* or *which* before
one beginning with *and who, and whom,* or *and which.*

Like correlative conjunctions, *who . . . and who* and similar
expressions are always paired and always introduce parallel
clauses. When you omit the first part of the expression, you
throw readers off balance.

INCORRECT: *The Thing,* directed by Howard Hawks, and which was
released in 1951, featured James Arness as the monster.

REVISED: *The Thing,* which was directed by Howard Hawks, and
which was released in 1951, featured James Arness as
the monster.

In many cases, however, eliminating the relative pronouns produces a more concise sentence.

REVISED: *The Thing,* directed by Howard Hawks and released in
1951, featured James Arness as the monster.

☐   **EXERCISE 3**

Identify and correct faulty parallelism in these sentences. Then underline the parallel elements—words, phrases, and clauses—in your corrected sentences. If a sentence is already correct, mark it with a C and underline the parallel elements.

> EXAMPLE: Alfred Hitchcock's films include *North by Northwest, Vertigo, Psycho,* and he also directed *Notorious* and *Saboteur.*
>
> REVISED: Films directed by Alfred Hitchcock include *North by Northwest, Vertigo, Psycho, Notorious,* and *Saboteur.*

//
15b

1. The world is divided between those with galoshes on and those who discover continents.
2. Soviet leaders, members of Congress, and the American Catholic bishops all pressed the president to limit the arms race.
3. A national task force on education recommended improving public education by making the school day longer, higher teachers' salaries, and integrating more technology into the curriculum.
4. The fast-food industry is expanding to include many kinds of restaurants: those that serve pizza, fried chicken chains, some offering Mexican-style menus, and hamburger franchises.
5. The consumption of Scotch in the United States is declining because of high prices, tastes are changing, and increased health awareness has led many whiskey drinkers to switch to wine or beer.

Student Writer at Work: Faulty Parallelism ——

In the following section of a draft of a paper written for a class in public health, a student discusses factors that must be taken into account by medical practitioners at the Indian Health Service. Correct the faulty parallelism, and revise again if necessary to strengthen coherence, unity, and style.

      The average life span of Native Americans is
considerably lower than that of the general population.
Not only is their infant mortality rate four times higher
than that of the general population, but they also have a
suicide rate that is twice as high as that of other races.
Moreover, Native Americans both die in homicides more
often than people of other races do and there are more
alcohol-related deaths among Native Americans than among
people of other races. Medical care available for them

does not meet their needs and is presenting a challenge
for the health professionals who serve them.

The Indian Health Service (IHS), a branch of the U.S.
Public Health Service, is responsible for providing
medical care to Native Americans who live on reservations.
The IHS has been criticized for its inability to deal with
cultural differences between health professionals and
Native Americans—cultural differences that interfere with
adequate medical care. In order to diagnose disease
states, for prescribing drug therapy, and to counsel
patients, health professionals need to acquire an
understanding of Native American culture. They must gain a
working knowledge of Native Americans' ideas and feelings
toward health and also God, relationships, and death. Only
then can health professionals communicate their goals,
provide quality medical care, and in addition they will be
able to achieve patient compliance.

There are many obstacles to effective communication:
hostility to white authority and whites' structured,
organized society; language is another obvious barrier to
communication; Native Americans' view of sickness, which
may be different from Anglos'; and some Indian cultures'
concept of time is also different from that of the Anglo
health workers. Other problems are more basic: a physician
cannot expect a patient to refrigerate medication if no
refrigerators are available or dilute dosage forms at home
or be changing wet dressings several times a day if clean
water is not readily available nor quart/pint measuring
devices to dilute stock solutions.

The defects in Native American health care cannot be
completely solved by the improvement of communication
channels or making these channels stronger. But the health
professional's communication with the Native American
patient can be effective enough so that medical staff can
acquire an adequate medical history, monitor drug use, be

alert for possible drug interactions, and to provide
useful discharge counseling. If health professionals can
communicate understanding and respect for Native American
culture and concern for their welfare, they may be able to
meet the needs of their Native American patients more
effectively.

//
15

16

Shifts, Mixed Constructions, and Faulty Predication

Shifts

A **shift** is a change of tense, voice, mood, person, number, or type of discourse within or between sentences. In some cases these shifts are necessary—to indicate changes of time, for example.

> *The Wizard of Oz* is a film that has enchanted audiences since it <u>was made</u> in 1939. (shift from present to past)

When you revise, be careful to eliminate unnecessary or illogical shifts.

16a Shifts in Tense

The verb tenses within a sentence or a related group of sentences should not shift without good reason. The tense of a verb in one clause of a sentence should generally be consistent with the tense of the verbs in the other clauses.

(1) Tense shifts within a sentence

> FAULTY: The judge <u>told</u> the defendant that he would not release him unless he <u>promises</u> to undergo therapy. (unwarranted shift from past to present)

REVISED: The judge told the defendant that he would not release
him unless he promised to undergo therapy. (both verbs
in past tense)

The following sentence is about a work of literature, so its
action should be described in the present (see 42c). The shift to
the past *(drove)* in the subordinate clause is therefore incorrect.

FAULTY: The novel is about two friends who drove across the
United States.

REVISED: The novel is about two friends who drive across the
United States.

shift
16a

Like works of literature, general truths are discussed in the
present tense.

FAULTY: Medical researchers know that asbestos caused cancer.

REVISED: Medical researchers know that asbestos causes cancer.

(2)   Tense shifts in groups of sentences

The verb tenses within a series of related sentences should not
differ unless there is a logical reason for a shift.

ORIGINAL: One night I was driving late at night. Suddenly I see a
dog right in the path of my car. I slam on my brakes and
barely avoid hitting it. (unwarranted shift from past to
present tense)

REVISED: One night I was driving late at night. Suddenly I saw a
dog right in the path of my car. I slammed on my brakes
and barely avoided hitting it. (all verbs in past tense)

The following passage describes an event that occurs regularly (each summer), so the verbs should be in the present tense.
The shift to the past tense throws readers off balance.

ORIGINAL: Each summer I spend a month at the shore. I lie on the
beach and let the sun drive away my troubles. The
breeze blows over the beach and cools the sand. I listened to a radio on a nearby blanket and watched children playing by the water.

REVISED: Each summer I spend a month at the shore. I lie on the
beach and let the sun drive away my troubles. The
breeze blows over the beach and cools the sand. I listen
to a radio on a nearby blanket and watch children playing in the water.

□   **EXERCISE 1**

Revise any of the following sentences and sentence groups that contain unwarranted shifts in tense. Be prepared to explain the changes you make. If a sentence or sentence group is correct, mark it with a *C.*

EXAMPLE: The old man fished and catches a shark.

The old man <u>fished</u> and <u>caught</u> a shark.

shft 16b

1. The Holy Roman Empire was established in 962 and is an attempt to revive the traditions of Rome.
2. The reporter was happy; he has just been awarded a Pulitzer Prize.
3. In his novel *The Grapes of Wrath* Steinbeck creates a portrait of a poor family who left Oklahoma and went to California.
4. The station prefers to present programs that discussed ecology.
5. Hoover resisted giving federal relief funds to the states. He gave aid, however, to financially weak banks. In a speech to bankers, he says that he hopes they will put the money to productive use. Early in 1932 he created the Reconstruction Finance Corporation to make loans to banks, railroads, and insurance companies. None of these tactics, though, are able to help the slumping American economy.

16b   Shifts in Voice

Shifts in voice from active to passive (see 23l) may be necessary to give a sentence proper emphasis.

> Even though consumers protested, controls on the price of natural gas were lifted.

Here the shift from active *(protested)* to passive *(were lifted)* enables the writer to keep the focus on consumer groups and the issue that they protested. To say *Congress lifted the price controls* would change the emphasis of the sentence.

Unwarranted shifts from active to passive, however, can be confusing and misleading.

> F. Scott Fitzgerald <u>wrote</u> *This Side of Paradise*, and later *The Great Gatsby* <u>was written</u>.

The shift from active *(wrote)* to passive *(was written)* makes this sentence ambiguous. Although readers are able to tell that Fitzgerald wrote *This Side of Paradise*, they cannot be certain who wrote *The Great Gatsby*. Consistent use of the active voice makes this sentence clear.

> F. Scott Fitzgerald <u>wrote</u> *This Side of Paradise* and later <u>wrote</u> *The Great Gatsby*.

☐   **EXERCISE 2**

Eliminate any unwarranted shifts in voice in each of the following sentences.

> EXAMPLE: The Etruscans used horses in warfare, and horse races were conducted by them as early as 1500 B.C.
>
> The Etruscans <u>used</u> horses in warfare and <u>conducted</u> horse races as early as 1500 B.C.

1. The ancient Romans loved horse racing, so highly bred strains of horses were developed by them for chariot racing.
2. The first organized horse race was staged in 1780 by the Earl of Derby, and prizes were awarded by him to the winners.
3. Because the American colonists loved horse racing, races were organized at fairs.
4. Gambling was done by many Americans in the nineteenth century. They ignored the opposition of religious reformers.
5. New York instituted the first legalized off-track betting system, and it was hoped that this would increase state revenue.

16c   Shifts in Mood

As with tense and voice, unnecessary shifts in mood (see 23g–23i) can be confusing and annoying.

> INCONSISTENT: It is important that a student <u>buy</u> a dictionary and <u>uses</u> it. (shift from subjunctive to indicative)
>
> REVISED: It is important that a student <u>buy</u> a dictionary and <u>use</u> it. (both verbs in the subjunctive)

> INCONSISTENT: Next, <u>heat</u> the mixture in a test tube and <u>you should make sure</u> it does not boil. (shift from imperative to indicative)
>
> REVISED: Next, <u>heat</u> the mixture in a test tube and <u>be sure</u> it does not boil (both verbs in the imperative)

> INCONSISTENT: The football player demanded that he <u>get</u> a raise and that he <u>wants to play</u> more often. (shift from the subjunctive to the indicative)
>
> REVISED: The football player demanded that he <u>get</u> a raise and that he <u>play</u> more often. (both verbs in the subjunctive)

☐   **EXERCISE 3**

Make the following sentences consistent in mood. If a sentence is correct, mark it with a *C*.

EXAMPLE: To fix a faucet unscrew the handle and you should examine the washer.

To fix a faucet <u>unscrew</u> the handle and <u>examine</u> the
washer.

1. Make an incision along the dorsal axis of the frog, and then you peel
back the skin.
2. First open the hood of the car and then you should examine the
distributor cap.
3. It is necessary that the student fill out the questionnaire and hands
it in.
4. The government wants to eliminate the graduated income tax and
give a fixed rate to all taxpayers.
5. First mail your résumé, and then you call for an interview.

shift
16d

16d   Shifts in Person and Number

Person is the form a pronoun or verb takes to indicate who is
speaking (first person—*I am, we are*), who is spoken to (second
person—*you are*), and who is spoken about (third person—*he,
she, it is;* and *they are*). **Number** indicates one (singular—*novel,
it*) or many (plural—*novels, they, them*).

Faulty shifts between the second- and the third-person
pronouns cause most errors.

INCONSISTENT: When <u>one</u> looks for a loan, <u>you</u> compare the interest
rates from several banks. (shift from third to second
person)

REVISED: When <u>one</u> looks for a loan, <u>one</u> compares the interest
rates from several banks.

REVISED: When <u>you</u> look for a loan, <u>you</u> compare the interest
rates from several banks.

REVISED: When a <u>person</u> looks for a loan, <u>he or she</u> compares
the interest rates from several banks.

Unwarranted shifts in number also create confusion within
sentences. Make sure that singular pronouns refer to singular
antecedents and plural pronouns to plural antecedents
(see 24i–j).

INCONSISTENT: If a <u>person</u> does not study regularly, <u>they</u> will have a
difficult time passing organic chemistry. (shift from
singular to plural)

REVISED: If a <u>person</u> does not study regularly, <u>he or she</u> will
have a difficult time passing organic chemistry.

REVISED: If <u>students</u> do not study regularly, <u>they</u> will have a
difficult time passing organic chemistry.

NOTE: Although college writing follows standard conventions of pronoun-antecedent agreement, use of a plural pronoun referring to a singular antecedent is increasingly common when such use enables the writer to avoid sexist language (see 17g.3).

> Buddy Holly and Janis Joplin each made a significant contribution with their music.

☐ **EXERCISE 4**

Read the following sentences, and eliminate any shifts in tense, voice, mood, person, or number. Some sentences are correct, and some will have more than one possible answer.

1. Gettysburg is a borough of southwestern Pennsylvania where some of the bloodiest fighting of the Civil War occurs in July 1863.
2. Giotto was born near Florence in 1267 and is given credit for the revival of painting in the Renaissance.
3. The early Babylonians divided the circle into 360 parts, and the volume of a pyramid could also be calculated by them.
4. During World War II General Motors expanded its production facilities, and guns, tanks, and ammunition were made.
5. Diamonds, the only gems that are valuable when colorless, were worn to cure disease and to ward off evil spirits.
6. First, clear the area of weeds, and then you should spread the mulch in a six-inch layer.
7. When one visits the Grand Canyon, you should be sure to notice the fractures and faults on the north side of the Kaibab plateau.
8. For a wine grape, cool weather means a higher acid content and a sour taste; hot weather means they will have lower acid content and a sweet taste.
9. Mary Wollstonecraft wrote *Vindication of the Rights of Women,* and then she wrote *Vindication of the Rights of Men.*
10. When one looks at the Angora goat, you should notice it has an abundant undergrowth.

shift
16e

16e Shifts from Direct to Indirect Discourse

Direct discourse reports the exact words of a speaker or writer. It is always enclosed in quotation marks and is usually accompanied by an identifying tag *(he says, she said).*

> Commenting on his play, Eugene O'Neill said, "The script is written in blood and tears."

When a question is reported directly, the identifying tag indicates asking, and the sentence ends with a question mark.

Rousseau asked, "Is it not obvious that where we demand every-thing, we owe nothing?

Indirect discourse summarizes the words of a speaker or writer. No quotation marks are used, and the reported statement is often introduced with the word *that*. As a rule, both pronouns and verb tenses in a reported statement are different from those in a directly quoted statement.

shft
16e

DIRECT DISCOURSE: My instructor said, "I want your paper by this Friday."

INDIRECT DISCOURSE: My instructor said that he wanted my paper by this Friday.

Indirect reporting of a question includes a word like *who, what, why, whether, how,* or *if.* In addition, the pronouns and verb tenses of the original question change, and the question mark at the end of the sentence becomes a period.

DIRECT QUESTION: The mayor asked, "Do you want to work in my reelection campaign?"

INDIRECT QUESTION: The mayor asked if I wanted to work in his re-election campaign.

Shifts from direct to indirect discourse can lead to error because they invite illogical tense shifts.

FAULTY: William Dean Howells said that he felt the equality of things and "I believe in the unity of men." (unwarranted shift from direct to indirect discourse)

REVISED: William Dean Howells said that he felt the equality of things and that he believed in the unity of men. (Past tense indicates indirect discourse)

REVISED: William Dean Howells said, "I feel the equality of things and I believe in the unity of men." (Present tense indi-cates direct discourse.)

☐   **EXERCISE 5**

Transform the direct discourse in the following sentences into indirect discourse. Keep in mind that general truths stay in the present.

EXAMPLE: John F. Kennedy said, "Ask not what your country can do for you—ask what you can do for your country."

John F. Kennedy said that you should not ask what your country can do for you, but what you can do for your country.

1. Thoreau said, "I went to the woods because I wished to live deliber-ately."

2. Martin Luther King, Jr., said, "I would be the first to advocate obeying just laws."
3. Steven Muller said, "I see an American society sadly in need of social services."
4. To the psychologist B. F. Skinner, "Cultures are often judged by the extent to which they encourage self-observation."
5. "Why," asked Freud, "does our memory lag behind all our other psychic activities?"

mix
16f

Mixed Constructions

A **mixed construction** is an error that occurs when you begin a sentence with one grammatical strategy and then shift to another before you have finished the first. Because the two parts of the sentence are at odds with each other, readers have trouble determining your meaning. Mixed constructions can take many forms; some are explained and illustrated in the following sections.

16f Adverbial Phrases as Subjects

An adverbial phrase functions in a sentence as an adverb. Using an adverbial phrase as a sentence's subject creates a mixed construction. To correct this problem, be sure to use a word or phrase that can logically serve as the sentence's subject.

MIXED: By calling for information is the best way to learn more about the benefits of ROTC. (adverbial phrase used as subject)

REVISED: By calling for information you can learn more about the benefits of ROTC.

REVISED: Calling for information is the best way to learn more about the benefits of ROTC.

Often this kind of mixed construction occurs when a clause beginning with *when, why, where,* or *how* is incorrectly used as a subject complement after a form of the verb *be.*

MIXED: By doing research was how she prepared herself to play the role of the empress.

REVISED: By doing research, she prepared herself to play the role of the empress.

16g Adverb Clauses as Subjects ───────────

Using an adverb clause as the subject of a sentence creates a mixed construction. You can avoid this problem by recasting the sentence.

> MIXED: Even though he published a paper on the subject does not mean he should get credit for the discovery. (adverb clause used as subject)

> REVISED: Even though he published a paper on the subject, he should not necessarily get credit for the discovery.

> REVISED: Publishing a paper on the subject does not necessarily give him credit for the discovery.

16h Objects as Apparent Subjects ───────────

Using an object as if it were the subject of a sentence results in another kind of mixed construction. Often you make this error because the object is actually more important to you than the subject. By using the object as the apparent subject, you cause readers to redirect their attention in the middle of the sentence. You can correct this problem by determining your focus and making it the true subject of the sentence.

> MIXED: The book we found in the antique store, we took it to the museum to be appraised. (object used as apparent subject)

> REVISED: We took the book we found in the antique store to the museum to be appraised.

> MIXED: People who had tickets, the ushers told them to line up on the right. (object used as apparent subject)

> REVISED: The ushers told people who had tickets to line up on the right.

16i Independent Clauses as Subjects ───────────

Still another kind of mixed construction results when you use an independent clause as the subject of a sentence. You can correct this error by recasting the independent clause.

> MIXED: The fall of the Roman Empire occurred in the fifth century was what brought the Dark Ages to Europe. (independent clause used as subject)

REVISED: The fall of the Roman Empire in the fifth century brought
the Dark Ages to Europe.

REVISED: Because of the fall of the Roman Empire in the fifth century, the Dark Ages came to Europe.

REVISED: It was the fall of the Roman Empire in the fifth century
that brought the Dark Ages to Europe.

Faulty Predication

**pred
16k**

Faulty predication is an error that occurs when a sentence's subject and predicate are not logically related. Some common types
of faulty predication are explained and illustrated in the following sections.

16j   Faulty Complement

Faulty predication is especially common in sentences that contain a linking verb—a form of the verb *be*, for instance—and a
subject complement. In this situation, faulty predication occurs
when you link the subject with a subject complement with
which it cannot logically be equated. Consider this sentence.

FAULTY: Mounting costs and declining advertising revenue were the
demise of *Look* magazine in 1971.

This sentence states incorrectly that mounting costs and declining advertising *were* the demise of the magazine when, in fact,
they were the *reasons* for its demise. You can correct this problem by substituting a complement with which the subject can
logically be equated.

REVISED: Mounting costs and declining advertising revenue were
the reasons for the demise of *Look* magazine in 1971.

16k   Intervening Words

Faulty predication can occur when intervening words obscure
the connection between the subject and the verb. When you revise, make sure the connection between subject and verb is logical.

FAULTY: The development of telescopes was made in considerable
numbers and was found throughout Europe soon after

their invention. (*Telescopes*, not *development*, were made and found.)

REVISED: Telescopes were made in considerable numbers and were found throughout Europe soon after their invention. (*Telescopes* is now the sentence's subject.)

FAULTY: The purpose of Napoleon's campaign failed because of the Russian winter. (The *campaign*, not the *purpose*, failed.)

**pred
16m**

REVISED: Napoleon's campaign failed because of the Russian winter (*Napoleon's campaign* is now the sentence's subject.)

REVISED: The purpose of Napoleon's campaign was thwarted by the Russian winter (verb changed to correspond with subject.)

16l   *When* or *Where* Clauses

Faulty predication can occur when a clause beginning with *where* or *when* follows *be.* This commonly occurs in definitions that incorrectly equate a *when* or *where* clause with the subject. When you revise, be sure to use a noun or a noun phrase as both the subject and the subject complement.

FAULTY: Taxidermy is where you construct a lifelike representation of an animal using its preserved skin. (In definitions *be* must be preceded and followed by nouns or noun phrases.)

REVISED: Taxidermy is the construction of a lifelike representation of an animal by using its preserved skin. (Subject complement is now a noun phrase.)

16m   Faulty Appositives

A **faulty appositive** is a type of faulty predication in which an appositive is equated with a noun or pronoun which it cannot logically modify.

FAULTY: The salaries are high in professional athletics, such as football players. (*Professional athletics* is not the same as *football players.*)

REVISED: The salaries are high for professional athletes, such as football players. (football players = professional athletes)

☐   **EXERCISE 6**

Revise the following sentences so that their parts fit together grammatically and logically. Keep in mind that each sentence may be revised in more than one way.

EXAMPLE: Radioastronomy is when you use radio wavelengths to study the universe.

Radioastronomy is a branch of astronomy that uses radio wavelengths to study the universe.

pred
16m

1. The war that George III fought, many felt it was a bloody and expensive war.
2. By trying to find a short route to India was how Columbus discovered the New World.
3. Just because Ptolemy said that the world was flat did not make it so.
4. The troops that advanced on Carthage, Scipio Africanus urged them to fight for the glory of Rome.
5. By having movable type was why the first printing press was considered revolutionary.
6. Depression is where a person has a mood of hopelessness and a feeling of inadequacy.
7. A block and tackle attached to the second floor window would be the obvious place to move the piano.
8. Competition is fierce among athletes, such as fencing and water polo.
9. Because of a defect in design made the roof of the stadium collapse.
10. Joseph Lister proved that one of the best germ killers is by coating a wound with carbolic acid.

Student Writer at Work: Shifts, Mixed Constructions, and Faulty Predication

Following is an excerpt from a draft of a student's research paper on immigrant factory workers in New York City in the early twentieth century. In this section of her paper, the student focuses on a fire that contributed to the creation of stricter fire safety codes. Read the paragraphs and correct any mixed constructions, faulty predication, or unwarranted grammatical shifts. If necessary, revise further to strengthen coherence, unity, and style.

In one particularly compelling section of World of Our Fathers, Irving Howe describes the devastating 1911 fire at the Triangle Shirtwaist Company (304–6). In quoting an eyewitness account and contemporary reactions and by reproducing graphic photographs is how he added drama to his account of an already dramatic event. For instance,

Howe quotes labor activist Rose Schneiderman, who said this was not the first time girls had been burned alive in this city, and "The life of men and women is so cheap and property is so sacred" (305)!

shft 16

In his book The Triangle Fire Leon Stein suggests that the fire, in the ten-story Asch Building near Washington Square in New York City, probably began with a cigarette or spark in a rag bin. Some people in the building apparently tried dousing the flames, but because of rotted hoses and rusted water valves made efforts useless (15).

The announcement of the many causes of the fire was obvious. According to the investigating committee, the one fire escape visible from Green Street collapsed after fewer than twenty people escaped. In addition, although sprinkler systems had been invented in 1895 did not mean any were present in the Asch Building. They were considered too expensive. Records show that six months before the fire, the building was cited as a firetrap by the city. The owners failed to make alterations was what the report identified as a cause of the fire. Failure to have regular fire drills and a lack of clearly marked exits also contributed to the high death toll (Stein 117-119).

Because it was 4:30 PM on a Saturday when the fire broke out meant there were 650 workers in the building. The majority of these were young Jewish and Italian women, and there was no common language spoken by them. By not sharing a common language was one reason for the chaos among the workers (Stein 14-15). When those on the ninth floor found the fire exit doors locked, their panic peaked. With their exit blocked, everyone was forced to jump from the windows to avoid the intense fire that swept through the building. Although it took fire fighters only 18 minutes to bring the fire under control, 146 workers died.

SECTION IV

Using Words Effectively

17

Choosing Words

Diction denotes word choice, especially with regard to appropriateness, accuracy, and freshness. But this definition does not reflect the complexity of choosing the right word. Unfortunately, no clear rule exists for distinguishing the right word from the wrong one. The same word may be appropriate in one situation and inappropriate in another.

An added difficulty is that many words in English express the same or almost the same idea. For instance, many English words denote clothing. However, these words do not all mean the same thing. Fine stores sell *apparel*, while most other stores sell *clothing* or *clothes*. Prophets in the Bible wear *raiment*, peasants wear *garb*, bridegrooms wear *attire*, children wear *togs*, priests wear *vestments*, and cowboys wear *duds*.

This chapter will acquaint you with the subtleties of language and help you to express yourself precisely and originally.

17a   Choosing an Appropriate Level of Diction

A word is *appropriate* if it suits the audience, occasion, and purpose for which it is intended. Different audiences and occasions call for different *levels* of diction. You would think it odd, for example, if your history textbook said that Julius Caesar was the *guy* who ruled Rome, even though *man* and *guy* essentially mean the same thing. When you know who your readers are and what they expect, you can determine whether your level of diction should be *formal, informal,* or *popular.*

(1)   Formal diction

When decorum is in order—in eulogies and other addresses, scholarly articles, formal reports, and some essays—readers expect formal diction. **Formal diction** uses words familiar to an educated audience: *impoverished* rather than *poor*, *wealthy* or *affluent* rather than *rich*, *intelligent* rather than *smart*, *automobile* rather than *car*. Contractions, shortened word forms, and utility words like *nice* (see 10a.2) generally do not appear in formal diction.

Formal English is nevertheless often quite simple. Its most apparent characteristic is grammatical accuracy. In addition, the writer often remains a neutral observer, using the impersonal *one* or the collective *we* rather than the more personal *I* and *you*.

wds
17a

The following passage from John F. Kennedy's inaugural address illustrates these characteristics.

> Let the word go forth from this time and place, to friend and foe alike, that the torch has been passed to a new generation of Americans—born in this century, tempered by war, disciplined by a hard and bitter peace, proud of our ancient heritage, and unwilling to witness or permit the slow undoing of those human rights to which this nation has always been committed, and to which we are committed today at home and around the world.

Although formal, the diction is eloquent, graceful, and clear, with parallelism heightening its impact. Word choice suits the occasion, with no shortened forms or colloquialisms.

Academics frequently use formal diction aimed at a learned audience, as the psychologist B. F. Skinner does in the following paragraph.

> We learn to perceive in the sense that we learn to respond to things in particular ways because of the contingencies of which they are a part. We may perceive the sun, for example, simply because it is an extremely powerful stimulus, but it has been a permanent part of the environment of the species throughout its evolution, and more specific behavior with respect to it could have been selected by contingencies of survival (as it has been in many other species). The sun also figures in many current contingencies of reinforcement: we move into or out of sunlight depending on the temperature; we wait for the sun to rise or set to take practical action; we talk about the sun and its effects; and we eventually study the sun with the instruments and methods of science. Our perception of the sun depends on what we do with respect to it. Whatever we do, and hence however we perceive it, the fact remains that it is the environment which acts upon the perceiving person, not the perceiving person who acts upon the environment. (B. F. Skinner, *Beyond Freedom and Dignity*)

Expecting his audience to be familiar with his terminology, Skinner uses such phrases as *powerful stimulus, contingencies of survival,* and *contingencies of reinforcement* for precision. He does not use the personal *I* and *you,* preferring the collective *we* and *our.*

(2) Informal diction

**wds
17a**

Informal diction is the language that people use daily in conversation. It includes *colloquialisms, slang, regionalisms,* and occasionally *nonstandard language.* Much good writing makes use of informal diction. In your college writing, however, limit its use to imitating speech or dialect or to giving an essay a conversational tone.

Colloquialisms   Whereas formal diction is primarily a language of writing and of formal addresses, **colloquial diction** occurs most often in everyday speech. We use it when we are not concentrating on being grammatically correct, and it is perfectly acceptable in informal situations, where formal diction would be out of place.

Contractions—*isn't, won't, I'm,* and *he'd*—are typical colloquialisms, as are shortened word forms—*phone* for *telephone, TV* for *television, dorm* for *dormitory,* and *exam* for *examination,* for instance. Other colloquialisms include the placeholders *you know, sort of, kind of,* and *I mean* and the utility words *nice* for *good* or *acceptable, funny* for *odd,* and *great* meaning almost anything. Colloquial English also includes verb forms like *get across* for *communicate, come up with* for *find,* and *check out* for *investigate.*

In the following passage from J. D. Salinger's novel *The Catcher in the Rye* the narrator, Holden Caulfield, uses colloquial diction.

> The book I was reading was this book I took out of the library by mistake. They gave me the wrong book, and I didn't notice it till I got back to my room. They gave me *Out of Africa,* by Isak Dinesen. I thought it was going to stink, but it didn't. It was a very good book. I'm quite illiterate, but I read a lot. My favorite author is my brother D.B., and my next favorite is Ring Lardner.

Notice that the passage above uses contractions (*didn't, I'm*), shortened word forms (*til* for *until*), and colloquial expressions like *stink.*

Slang   **Slang** words are extremely informal. Whether inventions or existing words redefined, they emerge to meet a need. Words like *high, spaced out, dove, hawk, hippie, uptight, groovy, heavy, be-in, happening,* and *rip off* emerged in the 1960's as part of the counterculture surrounding rock music, drugs, and the protest against the United States involvement in Vietnam. During the 1970's technology, music, politics, and feminism influenced slang, giving us words and phrases like *high tech, hacker, input, feedback, disco, stonewalling, Watergate, nuke, burnout, macho, sexist,* and *male chauvinism.* Other 1970's words that are still with us are *humongous, lifestyle,* and *gentrification.* The 1980's have contributed expressions like *rap music, glasnost, yuppie, chocoholic,* and *crack,* as well as *Valley talk,* a phenomenon that began in California and quickly spread to other parts of the country, yielding words and expressions like *for sure, tubular, awesome,* and *grody.*

wds
17a

Slang varies with time and place, becomes dated quickly, and fades into disuse. (Consider *beatnik, daddy-o,* and *hepcat.*) You should therefore use it in college writing only when imitating speech or dialect.

Regionalisms   **Regionalisms** are words and expressions, commonly used in certain geographical areas, that may not be understood by a general audience. Regionalisms include words like *overshoe, fried cake,* and *angledog* and expressions like *take sick* and *come down with a cold.* In East Tennessee, for example, a paper bag is a *poke* and empty soda bottles are *dope bottles.* Regionalisms also include old forms that have lost their meanings outside a particular area. For example, in Lancaster, Pennsylvania, which has a large Amish population, it is not unusual to hear an elderly person saying *darest* for *dare not* or *daresome* for *adventurous,* expressions that would not be common elsewhere.

In the following passage William Faulkner uses regionalisms of the American South to add authenticity to his writing.

> "It's fixing up to rain," Pa says. "I am a luckless man. I have ever been." He rubs his hands on his knees. "It's that durn doctor, liable to come at any time. I couldn't get word to him till so late. If he was to come tomorrow and tell her the time was nigh, she wouldn't wait." (William Faulkner, *As I Lay Dying*)

Regionalisms can make your writing more vivid. But because they are an informal use of language and often have little meaning to an audience not familiar with a particular region's dialect, use them with care.

Nonstandard Language   **Nonstandard** (or **substandard**) refers to words that are not generally considered a part of standard English, even though many individuals use them when speaking.

Included are words like *ain't, nohow, anywheres, nowheres, hisself, theirselves,* and *wait on* (instead of *wait for*).

Keep in mind that no absolute rules distinguish standard and nonstandard usage. At present this issue is hotly debated by people concerned with language. Dictionaries and handbooks can at best only attempt to define the norms of language (see 18d.9). In the end, you will have to supplement the guidelines that these books provide with your own assessment of your audience and purpose to determine what is appropriate usage in a particular writing situation.

(3)   Popular diction

Popular diction is the language of mass-audience magazines, newspapers, best sellers, and editorials. Conversational in tone, popular diction falls somewhere between formal and informal English. It does not employ words as precisely as formal English, often relying on colloquialisms, contractions, and the first person. Even so, it generally uses correct grammar, avoiding slang and nonstandard language.

This passage from *Esquire* illustrates many of these characteristics.

> Decade after decade of mediocre Disney films triumphed and stoked our sensibilities because the art itself, animation, is such a delight. It has been right from the start. In 1928, when Mickey Mouse as Steamboat Willie joins prototype Minnie to crank up a goat's tail in order to see musical notes leave the beast's mouth and dance to the tune of "Turkey in the Straw," the magic is already in full bloom. When Dumbo's ears flap and the ungainly mass finally soars, nobody cares where he's going. We love this creature; indeed we fall for Disney the way we fall in love: what the eye sees is more important than what the eye judges. (Max Apple, "Uncle Walt")

The contraction *he's* and the colloquial expressions *in full bloom, crank up,* and *fall for* give this piece a relaxed, conversational tone. However, the author also uses relatively formal words like *decade, prototype,* and *indeed* and the collective *we* and *our* instead of the more informal *I* and *you.*

(4)   College writing

The level of diction appropriate for college writing falls somewhere between formal and popular diction, depending on your assignment and your audience. A personal experience essay calls for a natural, informal style, but a research paper, an examination, or a report calls for a more formal vocabulary and a detached tone.

The following passage illustrates the level of diction typical of much college writing.

> Deaf students face many problems. Their needs are greater than those of other students. Often ignored by hearing students, deaf students may develop a severe inferiority complex. Their inability to mix in a large group is another cause of this problem. Because deaf students communicate by sign language or by lip reading, they usually interact on a one-to-one basis. It is not at all unusual for deaf students to be in a classroom and not even realize that someone in the class is speaking. Other problems occur when people in the class first find out that a person has a hearing problem. Often, in an effort to try to help, people begin exaggerating their lip movements. This exaggerated lip movement, called "mouthing," makes it impossible for many deaf students to read lips. For this reason, many deaf students find it better to conceal a hearing impairment than to disclose it.

**wds
17a**

This passage uses no nonstandard language, contractions, or shortened word forms. Despite the occasional use of formal diction, the paragraph moves easily and conversationally.

☐   **EXERCISE 1**

This paragraph, from Sherwood Anderson's short story "I'm a Fool," is characterized by informal diction. As the speech of a young boy, it is laced with slang and grammatical inaccuracies. Underline the words that identify the diction of this paragraph as informal. Then rewrite the paragraph, using popular diction.

> You know how it is. Gee, she was a peach! She had on a soft dress, kind of a blue stuff and it looked carelessly made, but was well sewed and made and everything. I knew that much. I blushed when she looked right at me and so did she. She was the nicest girl I have ever seen in my life. She wasn't stuck on herself and she could talk proper grammar without being a school teacher or something like that. What I mean is, she was O.K. I think maybe her father was well-to-do, but not rich to make her chesty because she was his daughter, as some are. Maybe he owned a drug store or a drygoods store in their hometown or something like that. She never told me and I never asked.

☐   **EXERCISE 2**

After reading the following paragraphs, underline the words and phrases that identify each as formal diction. Then choose one of these paragraphs and rewrite it using a level of diction that you would use in your college writing. Use a dictionary if necessary.

In looking at many small points of difference between species, which, as far as our ignorance permits us to judge, seem quite unimportant, we must not forget that climate, food, etc., have no doubt produced some direct effect. It is also necessary to bear in mind, that owing to the law of correlation, when one part varies and the variations are accumulated through natural selection, other modifications, often of the most unexpected nature, will ensue.   (Charles Darwin, *The Origin of Species*)

I hope you are able to see the distinction I am trying to point out. In no sense do I advocate evading or defying the law, as would the rabid segregationist. That would lead to anarchy. One who breaks an unjust law must do so openly, lovingly, and with a willingness to accept penalty. I submit that an individual who breaks a law that conscience tells him is unjust, and who willingly accepts the penalty of imprisonment in order to arouse the conscience of the community over its injustice, is in reality expressing the highest respect for law.   (Martin Luther King, Jr., "Letter from Birmingham Jail")

17b   Selecting Diction Appropriate to Purpose

Your purpose in writing determines the kinds of words you use. If your purpose is primarily to convey *information*, your words will be predominantly factual and objective. If your purpose is to convey your *personal feelings*, your words will also present opinions and emotional responses. If your purpose is to *persuade*, you will choose words that will help you elicit a specific action or response from a reader.

Naturally, your aims overlap. An informative article in a scientific journal, for example, may contain some persuasive or personal phrases. For the sake of clarity, however, we discuss each type of diction individually.

(1)   Informative writing

Informative writing—the kind that appears in journals, magazines, newspapers, textbooks, expository essays, and examinations—conveys information to its readers. For the most part, it is factual and avoids words with emotional associations. It often relies on third-person pronouns instead of using *I* or *we*. Here is a good example from a student paper.

One method of disposing of nuclear wastes is to store them in air-cooled vaults. Most vaults of this type are large reinforced concrete buildings that are cooled by natural convection. An air-cooled vault requires at least 10,000 square feet of space to hold nuclear waste discharged from an atomic power plant. Spent fuel is packaged in lead containers and stored in compartments within the vault. Air flows through vents that line the inside of the chamber, keeping the vault at a constant temperature. A single air-cooled vault can store approximately 28.2 million pounds of spent fuel. This method of storage has two major drawbacks. First, it requires a large amount of space, and second, it costs $103 for each kilogram of fuel stored.

In this straightforward description of the storage vault, the writer conveys facts about nuclear storage and evaluates the usefulness of the air-cooled vault without expressing his personal feelings.

(2)   Expressive writing

Expressive writing—the kind found in diaries, journals, letters, and personal experience essays—expresses the feelings of the writer. It uses language that is emotive, explicitly or by association; relies on the personal *I* and *we;* and usually contains informal language, although it can also be formal, as in some autobiographies and confessionals. The following paragraph is a good example.

> *March 4.* When will it all end? The idiocy and the tension, the dying of young men, the destruction of homes, of cities, starvation, exhaustion, disease, children parentless and lost, cages full of shivering, staring prisoners, long lines of hopeless civilians plodding through mud, the endless pounding of the battle line. I can scarcely remember what it is like to be where explosions are not going off around me, some hostile, some friendly, all horrible; an exploding shell is a terrible sound. What keeps this war going, now that its end is so clear? What do the Germans think of us, and we of them? I do not think we think of them at all, or much. Do they think of us? I can think of their weapons, their shells, their machine guns, but not of the men behind them. (Donald Pearce, *Journal of War*)

This writer's major concern is to express his frustration about World War II, as indicated by his choice of words: *idiocy, hopeless, endless,* and so on. Many of the words and phrases evoke emotional images, and the use of *I* emphasizes the paragraph's subjectivity.

(3)   Persuasive writing

The purpose of **persuasive writing**—the kind that appears in argumentative essays, political tracts, advertising, editorials, and legal briefs—is to convince someone to do something or to accept something. Words and phrases that convey value judgments and that reinforce the progression of an argument—*further-more, consequently, accordingly,* and *therefore*—often appear. Persuasive essays may use either the first person *I* or *we,* or the more formal third person *he, she, they,* or *one.* Persuasive writing may employ technical or other specialized terms to convince an audience of the validity of an assertion. The following paragraph, from an editorial in a college newspaper, is an example of persuasive writing.

> Students at this college wonder just how long they will have to put up with the dreadful conditions that exist in the cafeteria. The food is often overcooked and tasteless, and the facilities are always cramped and dirty. Even more important, the cafeteria's hours do not correspond to the needs of the students. For the past year the cafeteria has served lunch from eleven to one-thirty. A recent study conducted by this paper revealed that almost 37 percent of all students have classes straight through this time period. As a result, these students must miss lunch entirely or eat "on the run." Accordingly, most students interviewed voiced the hope that the cafeteria would serve light snacks and sandwiches all afternoon. So far, neither the management of the cafeteria nor the administration has responded to these concerns.

This persuasive paragraph uses words and phrases that emphasize the structure of the argument (*Even more important, As a result,* etc.), and it also employs words that clearly indicate value judgments (*dreadful, cramped and dirty,* etc.).

☐ **EXERCISE 3**

Identify the major purpose of each of the following paragraphs. Underline the words and phrases that help you make your determination.

> There also was more than a hint of unseen mass in the finding last year by the High Energy Astronomical Observatory that an invisible ring of superheated gas circled the constellation Northern Cross like a halo. The halo extends 72 quadrillion miles. Its temperature is 3.5 million degrees, hot enough to create out of the gas in the halo as many as 10,000 new stars. Carrying powerful X-ray telescopes, HEAO was able to map 90 percent of the halo, which is invisible in space to any but an X-ray telescope. The halo is so hot that its light is paler than the sun's corona; surrounding bright stars and the background light of the galaxy are sufficient to wash out its light by the time it reaches Earth. (Thomas O'Toole, "Will the Universe Die by Fire or Ice?")

> Why did I write it down? In order to remember, of course, but exactly what was it I wanted to remember? How much of it actually happened? Did any of it? Why do I keep a notebook at all? It is easy to deceive oneself on all those scores. The impulse to write things down is a peculiarly compulsive one, inexplicable to those who do not share it,

useful only accidentally, only secondarily, in the way that any compulsion tries to justify itself. I suppose that it begins or does not begin in the cradle. Although I have felt compelled to write things down since I was five years old, I doubt that my daughter ever will, for she is a singularly blessed and accepting child, delighted with life exactly as life presents itself to her, unafraid to go to sleep and unafraid to wake up.   (Joan Didion, *Slouching Toward Bethlehem*)

College, then, may be a good place for those few young people who are really drawn to academic work, who would rather read than eat, but it has become too expensive, in money, time, and intellectual effort, to serve as a holding pen for large numbers of our young. We ought to make it possible for those reluctant, unhappy students to find alternative ways of growing up, and more realistic preparation for the years ahead.   (Caroline Bird, *The Case Against College*)

**wds
17c**

17c   Using Accurate Words ────────────

According to Mark Twain, the difference between the right word and almost the right word is the difference between the lightning and the lightning bug. If you use the wrong words—or even *almost* the right ones—you will confuse your readers.

(1)   Denotations and connotations

A word's **denotation** is its explicit meaning, what it stands for without any emotional associations. Denotative language is informative language, devoid of judgments or opinions. Often a word's denotative meaning is referred to as its dictionary meaning. Naturally, no dictionary definition of a word can be completely objective. At best, all a dictionary can present is the socially agreed upon neutral meaning of a term.

You would think that determining the denotative meaning of a word would present few problems, but this is not always so. Words can have different denotations for different people. The linguist S. I. Hayakawa points out that in England and in America *robin* refers to entirely different species of birds and that the English sparrow is not really a sparrow but a weaver finch. In addition, words can have similar but not identical meanings, and this too can cause confusion. For example, you make an error in denotation when you say *molecule* when you mean *atom* or *compound* when you mean *mixture*.

A word's **connotations** are the emotional, social, and political associations that it has in addition to its denotations. Connotations suggest *feelings*, *attitudes*, *opinions*, and *desires*. The word *group*, for instance, is neutral; *gathering* suggests orderliness; and *mob* brings to mind unruliness, even danger. To say "The mob stood before the mayor" suggests that the mayor faced an angry group of people. Some words can have different connotations for different people. *Communism*, for example, will have a negative connotation for a conservative member of the United States Senate and a positive connotation for a member of the Russian politburo.

Selecting a word with the appropriate connotation is not always easy. Slang and colloquialisms sometimes give ideas unintended connotations. For instance, the sentence "In school we *mess around* with computers" gives the impression that your involvement with computers is not serious or important. If indeed your involvement is serious, it would be far better to say that in school you *work* with computers. Words that contain built-in judgments are another possible source of unintended connotations. For example, *mentally ill, insane, neurotic, nuts, crazy, psychopathic,* and *disturbed* have different social and political connotations that color the way people will respond. If you use these terms without considering their connotations, you run the risk of undercutting your credibility, to say nothing of confusing and possibly angering your readers.

You rely on denotative language when you want to describe things as they are. In laboratory reports, technical writing, examinations, and case studies, you use language that reinforces your objectivity and detachment. Opinion papers, arguments, and analyses, however, require words that reinforce your critical judgments and therefore call for connotative language as well. Fiction and personal essays rely on the connotations conveyed by imaginative comparisons and figurative language (see 17e).

Most of the writing that you do, however, uses a combination of connotative and denotative language. Technical reports will sometimes use an analogy to explain an unfamiliar concept or situation and fiction routinely employs precise denotative language to describe a scene or character. Used appropriately, both connotative and denotative language enable you to express your ideas and emotions clearly and effectively.

Errors in denotation and connotation sometimes result from carelessness, but often they are caused by a lack of sensitivity to the subtlety of language. As you read and speak, pay attention to the shades of meaning that words have in different contexts. When you write, take the time to think about a word's emotional associations. Revise carefully, making sure that the words you have used convey the feelings and judgments that you intend. Keep in mind that a dictionary can suggest some of the connotations of a word, but only experience and familiarity with language can give you the ability to use words effectively. If you are not sure about the connotations of a word, ask your instructor or use a word whose connotations you understand.

☐   **EXERCISE 4**

The following words have negative connotations. For each, list one word with a similar meaning whose connotation is neutral and another whose connotation is favorable.

> EXAMPLE: *Negative*   skinny
> *Neutral*   thin
> *Favorable*   slender

**wds
17c**

1. deceive   6. blunder
2. antiquated   7. argumentative
3. egghead   8. politician
4. pathetic   9. shack
5. cheap   10. stench

☐   **EXERCISE 5**

Think of a trip you took. First, write a one-paragraph description that would discourage anyone from taking the same trip. Next, rewrite this paragraph, describing your trip favorably. Finally, rewrite your paragraph using neutral words that convey no judgments. In all three versions of your paragraph, underline the words that helped you to convey your impressions to your readers.

(2)   Euphemisms

A **euphemism** is a positive or neutral word or phrase used in place of a word or phrase that describes a subject that society considers unmentionable. According to William Safire, who writes a column on language for the *New York Times*, a euphemism should be used only when it "lessens pain and does not deny truth."

In the Victorian era, direct reference to the body and its functions was disdained. Consequently, table supports were delicately referred to as *limbs*, and to avoid saying *leg* and *breast*, people referred to the meat of a turkey as *dark* or *light*.

People still avoid discussing certain subjects, such as bodily functions, death, and certain social problems. Therefore, toilets are *lounges, bathrooms,* or *powder rooms*. (The word *toilet* itself is a euphemism for *dressing* or *shaving*.) We say that the dead have *passed on, gone to their reward,* or *departed,* and we call we call graveyards *resting places* or *memorial parks*. We refer to divorce as *marital dissolution*, adultery as an *affair*, the poor as *deprived*, and retarded children as *exceptional*.

Euphemisms are even more prevalent in business and government. Used cars are *preowned automobiles*, and corporate takeovers are *mergers* or *marriages*. Garbage collectors are called *sanitation engineers* and barbers, *hair stylists*. Government facilities are *relocated*, not closed, and budget deficits are called *negative growth*.

College writing is no place for such coyness. Say what you mean—*pregnant*, not *expecting; died*, not *passed away*; and *strike*, not *work stoppage*.

**wds
17c**

(3)   Specific or general words

Specific words refer to particular persons, items, or events, while **general** words signify an entire class or group. *Queen Elizabeth II*, for example, is more specific than *monarch; topcoat* is more specific than *clothing*; and *Corvette* is more specific than *automobile*. General words are, of course, useful. Statements that use general words to describe entire classes of items or events are often necessary to convey a point. But such statements must also include specific words for support and clarity. The more specific your choice of words, the more vivid your writing will be.

Whether a word is general or specific is relative, determined by its relationship to other words. The following word chains illustrate increasing specificity, with the word farthest to the left denoting a general category or class and the one farthest to the right, a specific, tangible member of that class.

> History—American history—Civil War history—History 263
> Apparel—accessory—tie—bow tie—my blue bow tie
> Human being—official—president—Thomas Jefferson
> Reading matter—book—nonfiction book—*The Fate of the Earth*
> Machine—vehicle—train—*Orient Express*

Using general words when specific words are needed results in vagueness. If you want your readers to visualize a certain building—say, the new wing of the National Gallery in Washington, D.C.—it is not enough to say that it has an angular shape. If you want your audience to "see" Picasso's *Guernica*, you must do more than note its mythic imagery. What specific images? What else can you say about it? You must use specific words to convey information to your readers whenever you can.

(4)   Concrete or abstract words

Abstract words—*beauty, truth, justice,* and so on—refer to ideas, qualities, or conditions that cannot be perceived by the senses. **Concrete** words, on the other hand, convey a vivid picture by naming things that readers can *see, hear, taste, smell,* or *touch.* Concrete words are specific: they get your point across. Abstract words are often too general to communicate much about real things.

ABSTRACT	CONCRETE
The night I stayed too late I was spellbound by the beautiful sights.	The night I stayed too late I was hunched on the log staring spellbound at spreading, reflected stains of lilac on the water. A cloud in the sky suddenly lighted as if turned on by a switch; its reflection just as suddenly materialized on the water upstream, flat and floating, so that I couldn't see the creek bottom, or life in the water under the cloud. Downstream, away from the cloud on the water, water turtles smooth as beans were gliding down with the current in a series of easy, weightless push-offs, as men bound on the moon. (Annie Dillard, *Pilgrim at Tinker Creek*)

wds 17c

Of course, as with general and specific words, whether a word is abstract or concrete is relative. The more concrete your words and phrases, the more vivid the image you evoke in the reader.

We need abstract words to discuss concepts. The works of many great writers concentrate on abstractions such as *truth, faith,* and *beauty.* But because such terms provide no tangible details, they can create problems for beginning writers, who may use them—without concrete supporting detail—as a cover for fuzzy, inexact thinking.

Good writing usually describes the abstract with concrete details. In the following paragraph the overuse of abstract words does not conceal the lack of concrete detail.

Too ABSTRACT:	*The Balzac Monument* is Rodin's most daring creation. The figure is unusual. Balzac is wrapped in a cloak in an interesting way. He has an unusual expression on his face.

Why is the figure of Balzac unusual? What is interesting about the way the cloak wraps the figure? What is the unusual expression on Balzac's face? When concrete words replace abstract words, the passage is much more informative.

> MORE   *The Balzac Monument* is Rodin's most daring cre-
> CONCRETE: ation. The figure is large and resembles a ghost or spec-
>   ter. Balzac seems to tower above us so that from a dis-
>   tance we see only his great size. Upon closer inspection
>   we see that Balzac is wrapped in a cloak. From the in-
>   distinct lines of the cloak, Balzac's head emerges god-
>   like, with eyes that stare off into the distance.

wds
17c

Imprecise diction often results when you use abstract terms like *nice, great,* and *terrific* that say nothing and could be used in almost any sentence (see 10a.2). These **utility words** indicate only enthusiasm. Replace them with more specific words.

> VAGUE: The movie was nice.

> BETTER: The movie was entertaining.

☐   **EXERCISE 6**

Good writing usually mixes specific and general words and abstract and concrete words. Read the following passage and underline words that are specific and concrete. How do they make the paragraph more effective? Are any general and abstract words used? How do they function? What impression does the writer want to convey?

> Near the end of March, 1845, I borrowed an axe and went down to the woods by Walden Pond, nearest to where I intended to build my house, and began to cut down some tall arrowy white pines, still in their youth, for timber. It is difficult to begin without borrowing, but perhaps it is the most generous course thus to permit your fellowmen to have an interest in your enterprise. The owner of the axe, as he released his hold on it, said that it was the apple of his eye; but I returned it sharper than I received it. It was a pleasant hillside where I worked, covered with pine woods, through which I looked out on the pond, and a small open field in the woods where pines and hickories were springing up. The ice in the pond was not yet dissolved, though there were some open spaces, and it was all dark colored and saturated with water. There were some slight flurries of snow during the days that I worked there; but for the most part when I came out on to the railroad, on my way home, its yellow sand heap stretched away gleaming in the hazy atmosphere, and the rails shone in the spring sun, and I heard the lark and pewee and other birds already come to commence another year with us. They were pleasant spring days, in which the winter of man's discontent was thawing as well as the earth, and the life that had lain torpid began to stretch itself. (Henry David Thoreau, *Walden*)

☐   **EXERCISE 7**

Revise this paragraph from a job application letter by substituting specific, concrete language for general or abstract words and phrases.

> I have had several part-time jobs lately. Some of them would qual-
> ify me for the position you advertised. In my most recent job, I sold
> products in a store. My supervisor said I was a good worker who pos-
> sessed a number of valuable qualities. I am used to dealing with different
> types of people in different types of settings. I feel that my qualifications
> would make me a good candidate for your job.

17d   Using Original Language ——————

Whenever possible, choose words that are original, vivid, and interesting, and avoid *jargon, neologisms, clichés,* and *pretentious
diction,* which deaden writing and leave your meaning unclear.

(1)   Jargon

Jargon refers to the specialized or technical vocabulary of a
trade, profession, or academic discipline. Jargon is useful in the
field for which it was developed. Outside that field, however, it is
imprecise and confusing. Medical doctors tell patients that a
procedure is *contraindicated* or that they are going to carry out a
differential diagnosis of the symptoms that patients *present with*.
Business executives ask for *feedback* or *input* and want departments to *interface* effectively. On a recent television talk show, a
sociologist spoke about the need for *perspectivistic thinking* to
achieve organizational goals. Is it any wonder that the befuddled
host asked his guest to explain this term to the audience?

Jargon is often accompanied by overly formal diction, the
passive voice, and wordy constructions. The following sentence
is typical.

> ORIGINAL: Procedures were instituted to implement changes in the
> parameters used to evaluate all aspects of the process.

Here is what this sentence means.

> TRANSLATION: We used different criteria to judge the process.

Many people deliberately use jargon to impress their audience. Its effect is usually just the opposite. When writing, avoid
jargon and concentrate on a vocabulary that is appropriate for
your audience and purpose.

(2) Neologisms

Neologisms are newly coined words that are not part of standard English. New situations call for new words, and frequently such words become a part of the language. The recent explosion of scientific knowledge, for example, has brought about literally thousands of new words whose use is acceptable.

quark	A hypothetical subatomic particle
synthesizer	An electronic apparatus for the production of sound
microelectronics	A branch of electronics that deals with the miniaturization of electronic circuits and components

**wds
17d**

Other coined words, however, have not yet crossed into standard English; some of these may never be accepted. Many of these questionable neologisms are created when the suffixes *-wise* and *-ize* are added to existing words. Police officers say that a criminal must be *Mirandized*. Business people *prioritize* before they *finalize* things *investmentwise*. Popular journalists and news commentators seem to attach these suffixes to many words—creating new words like *weatherwise*, *sportswise*, *timewise*, *productwise*, and so on.

If you are not sure whether to use a term, look it up in your college dictionary. If it is not there, it is probably not standard usage.

(3) Pretentious diction

In an effort to impress readers, beginning writers sometimes use **pretentious diction**: they elevate their style, overusing adjectives and adverbs, learned words, and poetic devices. Good writing is clear writing, and pompous or flowery language is no substitute for thought.

PRETENTIOUS DICTION: The expectations of offspring may be appreciably different from their parents'.

REVISED: Children's goals may be different from their parents'.

PRETENTIOUS DICTION: As I fell into slumber, I cogitated about my day ambling through the splendor of the Appalachian Mountains.

REVISED: As I fell asleep, I thought about my day hiking through the Appalachian Mountains.

Pretentious diction is always out of place. By calling attention to itself, it draws readers away from the point you are making. Consider the inappropriate use of imagery in the following paragraph.

> The Tammany Society [a political association] was an all-engulfing weed that rapidly overran and choked New York City's political gardens. Times were filled with danger for those who dared protest this corruption. Even the champion of the people—*The Sun*—refused to encourage the few flowers that dared to rear their heads in that field of briars. Although the situation improved somewhat in the hands of skillful gardeners, much corruption existed for years to come.

This overblown diction obscures the writer's meaning. Comparing Tammany to a weed is certainly valid, but here it is the imagery that has grown like one. Compare this paragraph, revised for clarity and consistency.

**wds
17d**

> The Tammany Society was a weed that quickly overran New York City. Times were hard for those who dared to speak against its spread; even *The Sun* did not encourage reformers. Although the situation improved somewhat in the hands of reform-minded politicians, much corruption existed for years to come.

Pretentious diction is not formal diction used in the wrong situation; it is overwritten, inappropriately elevated, and out of control. Good writing—whether formal or popular—relies on the choice of appropriate words. Whenever you discover pretentious diction in your essays, delete it.

(4)   Clichés

Clichés are expressions that have lost all interest and meaning through overuse. Writers use them to paper over holes in their sentences, cluttering their work with useless phrases that hamper communication. Sayings like "This isn't my cup of tea," "We're in the same boat," "That's the last straw," and "Let's get down to brass tacks" once had the power to call forth vivid mental images. But they have long since lost their concrete associations and are now ineffective.

Familiar sayings are not the only clichés. In many pat phrases, words have become bound—*inextricably bound*, no doubt—to other words. For example, political, social, or economic situations are often described as *rapidly deteriorating. Root causes* need to be uncovered, so *options are explored, Herculean efforts* are made, and sometimes *mutually agreeable solutions* are found. If not, *viable alternatives* may allow the two sides to *peacefully coexist.*

The purpose of academic writing is always to convey information clearly; clichés only damage that effort.

☐   **EXERCISE 8**

Rewrite the following passage, eliminating jargon, neologisms, pretentious diction, and clichés. Feel free to add words and phrases and to reorganize sentences to make their meaning clear. If you are not certain about the meaning or status of a word, consult a dictionary.

At a given point in time there coexisted a hare and a tortoise. The aforementioned rabbit was overheard by the tortoise to be blowing his horn about the degree of speed he could attain. The latter quadruped thereupon put forth a challenge to the former by advancing the suggestion that they interact in a running competition. The hare acquiesced, laughing to himself. The animals concurred in the decision to acquire the services of a certain fox to act in the capacity of judicial referee. This particular fox was in agreement, and consequently implementation of the plan was facilitated. In a relatively small amount of time the hare had considerably outdistanced the tortoise and, after ascertaining that he himself was in a more optimized position distancewise than the tortoise, he arrived at the unilateral decision to avail himself of a respite. He made the implicit assumption in so doing that he would anticipate no difficulty in overtaking the tortoise when his suspension of activity ceased. An unfortunate development racewise occurred when the hare's somnolent state endured for a longer-than-anticipated time frame, facilitating the tortoise's victory in the contest and affirming the concept of unhurriedness and firmness triumphing in competitive situations. Thus the hare was unable to snatch victory out of the jaws of defeat. Years later he was still ruminating about the exigencies of the situation.

☐   **EXERCISE 9**

Go through a newspaper or magazine and list the jargon, neologisms, pretentious diction, or clichés that you find. Then substitute more original words for the ones you identified. Be prepared to discuss your interpretation of each word and the word you chose to put in its place.

17e   Using Figurative Language

Language that adheres to fact is called **literal language.** But when writers want to express their personal reactions, they often must go beyond literal meanings. They do so by using **figurative language**—language that uses imaginative comparisons called **figures of speech.** A writer who wanted to express his or her reaction upon seeing the moon could say, "The moon was big and beautiful." Figurative language is more expressive: "The moon rose quickly and hung in the sky like a papier-maché ball." Here the comparison conveys the writer's feelings vividly.

Figurative language is not just for literary writing; it has its place in journalism, in academic writing, and even in scientific and technical writing. Although you should not overuse figurative language, do not be afraid to use it when you think it will help you to communicate with a reader.

The five most commonly used figures of speech are *simile, metaphor, analogy, personification,* and *allusion.*

(1)   Similes

A **simile** is a comparison between two essentially unlike items on the basis of a shared quality. Similes are introduced by a term such as *like* or *as.*

> SIMILE: <u>Like</u> travelers with exotic destinations on their minds, the graduates were remarkably forceful. (Maya Angelou, *I Know Why The Caged Bird Sings*)

> SIMILE: He stared at his hands while I thought about my father who has been opened and closed on the operating table <u>like</u> a book whose first page proves too difficult. (Lee Zacharias, *Lessons*)

> SIMILE: We live in a single-wide trailer shaped <u>like</u> a Velveeta cheese box and made of white metal. (Holley Ballard, *Redbook*)

> SIMILE: A cloud in the sky suddenly lighted <u>as if</u> turned on by a switch. (Annie Dillard, *Pilgrim at Tinker Creek*)

NOTE: A simile must compare two *dissimilar* things. The first sentence below is not a simile, but t'ıe second one is.

My dog is <u>like</u> your dog.

My dog is <u>as</u> sleek <u>as</u> a seashell.

(2)   Metaphors

A **metaphor** also compares two essentially dissimilar things, but instead of saying that one thing is *like* another, it *equates* them.

Metaphors are compressed similes. By omitting the comparative term, metaphors equate the two dissimilar items. Because of their economy of expression, they can convey ideas with considerable power. Notice the use of metaphors in the following sentences.

> The high grey-flannel fog of winter closed off the Salinas Valley from the sky and all the rest of the world. (John Steinbeck, "The Chrysanthemums")

> In its first days of operation, a new telescope orbiting the earth has returned infrared images showing previously unobserved features of distant galaxies and revealing cosmic "maternity wards"

where clouds of interstellar gas appear at various stages of giving birth to stars. (John Noble Wilford, *New York Times*)

Perhaps it is easy for those who have never felt the stinging darts of segregation to say, "Wait." (Martin Luther King, Jr., "Letter from Birmingham Jail")

Science and technology like all creations of the human spirit are unpredictable. If we had a reliable way to label our toys good and bad, it would be easy to regulate technology wisely. (Freeman Dyson, *Disturbing the Universe*)

wds
17e

NOTE: For a metaphor to work, it has to employ images with which readers are familiar. If the comparison is too remote, readers will miss the point entirely. If it is too common, it will become a cliché (see 17d.4).

(3) Analogies

An **analogy** explains an unfamiliar object or idea by comparing it to a more familiar one.

An atom is like a miniature solar system.

Robert Frost said that writing free verse is like playing tennis without a net.

The circulatory system runs through the body like a network of rivers and streams.

Analogies can extend over several sentences or even several paragraphs. Extended analogies resemble comparison-and-contrast paragraphs (see 4f.6) with one important difference: whereas comparisons give equal weight to both things being compared, extended analogies use one part of the comparison for the *sole* purpose of shedding light on the other. Here is how one author uses the behavior of people to explain the behavior of ants.

Ants are so much like human beings as to be an embarrassment. They farm fungi, raise aphids as livestock, launch armies into wars, use chemical sprays to alarm and confuse enemies, capture slaves. The families of weaver ants engage in child labor, holding their larvae like shuttles to spin out the thread that sews the leaves together for their fungus gardens. They exchange information ceaselessly. They do everything but watch television. (Lewis Thomas, "On Societies as Organisms")

NOTE: Analogies work only when the subjects you are comparing have something in common. If you compare things that are too dissimilar, your analogy will not work. Drawing an analogy between tables and ants would be a problem. But explaining ants by comparing them to people—both social animals—makes good sense.

(4)   Personification

Personification gives an idea or inanimate object human attributes, feelings, or powers. We use personification every day in expressions like *The engine coughed.*

Personification can make an entity that is abstract or hard to describe more concrete and familiar. By doing so, it also makes your writing more precise and more interesting.

> Wit is a lean creature with a sharp inquiring nose. (Charles Brooks, *Wit and Humor*)

> Truth strikes us from behind, and in the dark, as well as from before in broad daylight. (Henry David Thoreau, *The Journals*)

> One night I was allowed to stay up until the stars were in full command of the sky. (Russell Baker, "Summer beyond Wish")

> Institutions, no longer able to grasp firmly what is expected of them and what they are, grow slovenly and misshapen and wander away from their appointed tasks in the Constitutional scheme. (Jonathan Schell, *The Time of Illusion*)

(5)   Allusion

An **allusion** is an indirect reference to a well-known historical, biblical or literary person or event, which readers are expected to recognize. Allusion enriches your readers' understanding by suggesting a relationship between your writing and something outside it. For example, suppose that you title an essay you have written about your personal goals "Miles to Go Before I Sleep." By reminding your readers of the concluding lines of Robert Frost's poem "Stopping by Woods on a Snowy Evening," you suggest your determination and self-discipline.

Literary allusions such as the one above enrich your expression of feelings. *Biblical* allusions allow you to express a moral attitude ("Eyes have they, but they see not"). *Historical* allusions, such as "The Iran-Contra affair of 1987 had the potential to become another Watergate," elucidate current events by drawing parallels between a recent event (Iran-Contra) and an event of historical importance (the political scandal that brought down the Nixon presidency.)

Once again, for an allusion to work, readers must know what you are alluding to. Family jokes, expressions that your friends use, and esoteric references mean nothing to a general audience.

17f Avoiding Ineffective Figures of Speech

Effective figures of speech enrich your diction; ineffective figures of speech weaken it.

(1) Dead Metaphors and Similes

Metaphors and similes stimulate thought by calling up vivid images in a reader's mind. A **dead metaphor** or **simile** has been so overused that it calls up no image. It has become a pat, meaningless cliché. Here are some examples.

beyond a shadow of a doubt	off the beaten path
crying shame	a shot in the arm
sit on the fence	smooth sailing
green with envy	blind as a bat
pull up stakes	dead as a doornail
off the track	up in arms
the last straw	sink or swim

Avoid dead metaphors and similes by taking the time to think of images that make your writing fresher and more vivid.

(2) Mixed metaphors

A **mixed metaphor** results when you combine two or more incompatible images in a single figure of speech. Mixed images leave readers wondering what you are trying to say—or leave them laughing. When you revise mixed metaphors, make your imagery consistent. Notice that in the revised versions of the following sentences the message is clear.

MIXED: The German army advanced ravenously and swept away all opposition. (ravenously sweeping?)

REVISED: The German army advanced ravenously and devoured all opposition.

MIXED: The president extended an olive branch in an attempt to break some of the ice between the United States and the Soviet Union. (break the ice with an olive branch?)

REVISED: The president extended an <u>olive branch</u> with the hope
that the leaders of the Soviet Union <u>would pick it up</u>.

(3)   Strained metaphors

A **strained metaphor** compares two things that do not have
enough in common to justify the comparison.

STRAINED: The wind rose in the morning like a giant getting out of
bed.

STRAINED: The plane was a fragment of candy falling through the
sky.

How is the wind like a giant? And in what sense is a plane comparable to a piece of candy? By comparing items that have a
strong basis of comparison, the following revisions create effective metaphors.

REVISED: The wind rose in the morning like a great wave.

REVISED: The plane was a wounded bird falling through the sky.

**wds
17f**

☐   **EXERCISE 10**

Read the following paragraph from Mark Twain's *Life on the Mississippi*,
and identify as many figures of speech as you can.

Now when I had mastered the language of this water, and had
come to know every trifling feature that bordered the great river as famil-
iarly as I knew the letters of the alphabet, I had made a valuable acquisi-
tion. But I had lost something, too. I had lost something which could
never be restored to me while I lived. All the grace, the beauty, the poetry, had gone out of the majestic river! I still keep in mind a certain
wonderful sunset which I witnessed when steamboating was new to me.
A broad expanse of the river was turned to blood; in the middle distance
the red hue brightened into gold, through which a solitary log came
floating black and conspicuous; in one place a long, slanting mark lay
sparkling upon the water; in another the surface was broken by boiling,
tumbling rings, that were as many-tinted as an opal; where the ruddy
flush was faintest, was a smooth spot that was covered with graceful
circles and radiating lines, ever so delicately traced; the shore on our left
was densely wooded, and the somber shadow that fell from this forest
was broken in one place by a long, ruffled trail that shone like silver; and
high above the forest wall a clean-stemmed dead tree waved a single
leafy bough that glowed like a flame in the unobstructed splendor that
was flowing from the sun. There were graceful curves, reflected images,
woody heights, soft distances; and over the whole scene, far and near,
the dissolving lights drifted steadily, enriching it every passing moment
with new marvels of coloring.

☐   **EXERCISE 11**

Rewrite the following sentences, adding one of the figures of speech discussed above to each sentence to make the ideas more vivid and exciting. Make sure that you identify the technique you use and that you use each of the five figures of speech at least once.

EXAMPLE: The night was cool and still.

The night was cool and still like the inside of a cathedral. (simile)

1. The child was small and carelessly groomed.
2. I wanted to live life to its fullest.
3. The December morning was bright and cloudy.
4. As I walked I saw a cloud floating in the sky.
5. House cats can be a lot like tigers.
6. The sunset turned the lake red.
7. The street was quiet except at the hour when the school at the corner let out.
8. A shopping mall is a place where teenagers like to gather.
9. The president faced an angry Senate.
10. Education is a long process that takes much hard work.

**wds
17g**

17g Avoiding Offensive Language

Racial and ethnic slurs, obscenities, and sexist language are offensive. Avoid the use of such language in your writing.

(1) Racial, ethnic, and religious slurs

When referring to any racial, ethnic, or religious group, use words with neutral connotations or words that the groups use *formally* to refer to themselves. The derogatory terms with which we are all too familiar are unacceptable in your writing.

Racial, ethnic, and religious stereotypes are also offensive. Avoid biased generalizations that brand certain groups as stupid, pushy, or tight with money, for instance. Such generalizations are rooted in prejudice and are always inaccurate.

(2) Obscenities

The freedom to use obscene language when writing is *not* one of the characteristics that distinguishes college students from high school students. An X-rated paper does not establish your sophistication. It does reveal an eagerness to shock and a lack of respect for your audience.

(3) Sexist language

Sexist language is insulting to both men and women. It entails much more than the use of derogatory words like *broads* and *chicks*. Assuming that some professions are exclusive to one sex—that, for instance, *nurse* denotes only women and *doctor* denotes only men—is also sexist. So is the use of job titles like *postman* for letter carrier, *fireman* for firefighter, and *policeman* for police officer. Habits of thought and language change slowly, but they do change.

Sexist language also results when a writer fails to use the same terminology when referring to men and women. For example, you should not refer to two scientists with Ph.D's as Dr. Sagan and Mrs. Yallow, but as Dr. Sagan and Dr. Yallow. You should refer to two writers as James and Wharton, not Henry James and Mrs. Wharton.

In your writing, always use *women*—not *girls*—when referring to adult females. Similarly, use *Ms.* as the form of address when a woman's marital status is unknown or irrelevant. If the woman you are addressing refers to herself as Mrs. or Miss, however, then you should use the form of address she prefers. Finally, avoid using the generic *he* or *him* when your subject could be either male or female. Use the third-person plural or the phrase *he or she* when possible (not *he/she*).

wds
17g

> TRADITIONAL: Before boarding, each passenger should make certain that he has his ticket.
>
> REVISED: Before boarding, passengers should make certain that they have their tickets.
>
> REVISED: Before boarding, each passenger should make certain that he or she has a ticket.

Be careful, however, not to overuse *his or her* or *he or she* constructions, which can make your writing repetitious and wordy.

Also be careful not to create ungrammatical constructions like the following.

> UNGRAMMATICAL: Before boarding, each passenger should be certain that they have their tickets.

Although many educated speakers do use *they* and *their* in cases like the preceding sentence, where doing so avoids an awkward alternative (*he or she* has *his or her* ticket) or a sexist construction (*he* has *his*), you should avoid using a singular noun along with a plural pronoun in your college writing. Instead, use a plural noun.

The following table suggests some alternatives for many common usage problems involving sexist language.

**wds
17g**

Sexist Usage	Possible Revisions
1. The student should choose his courses carefully.	Students should choose their courses carefully. The student should choose his or her courses carefully.
2. Equality is a desirable goal for all men.	Equality is a desirable goal for everyone.
3. Mankind Man's accomplishments Man-made	people, human beings human accomplishments synthetic
4. The manager . . . he The nurse . . . she The librarian . . . she The lawyer . . . he	The manager . . . he or she; the managers . . . they The nurse . . . he or she; the nurses . . . they. The librarian . . . he or she; the librarians . . . they The lawyer . . . he or she; the lawyers . . . they.
5. Female doctor Woman lawyer Lady painter	doctor lawyer painter
6. Mailman Fireman Policeman/woman Salesman/woman/girl Businessman/woman	letter carrier firefighter police officer salesperson businessperson
7. The girl at the desk answered the phone.	the person, the receptionist, the secretary.
8. Women's libber Women's lib	feminist women's movement
9. Spinster Old maid	single woman; no mention of marital status
10. Stewardess Steward	flight attendant
11. Phyllis Knable, wife of Dr. Peter Knable, was given the Benjamin Rush Award for her outstanding work as a surgeon.	Dr. Phyllis Knable was given the Benjamin Rush award for her outstanding work as a surgeon.
12. Linda Richards, mother of three, was the first woman to be inducted into the Leola branch of the International Association of Lions Clubs.	Linda Richards was the first woman to be inducted into the Leola branch of the International Association of Lions Clubs.
13. A professor works hard to get tenure. As a result, his wife and children must be supportive.	As a result, his or her spouse and children must be supportive; Professors work hard to get tenure. As a result, their spouses and children must be supportive.

14. Everyone should complete his   Everyone should complete his or
     application by Tuesday.   her application by Tuesday; All
                                                students should complete their
                                                applications by Tuesday.

☐   **EXERCISE 12**

Suggest possible alternative forms for any of the following which you consider sexist. In each case, comment on the advantages and disadvantages of the alternative you recommend. If you feel that a particular term is not sexist, explain why.

wds
17g

forefathers	longshoreman
man-eating shark	committeeman
manpower	(to) man the battle stations
workman's compensation	Girl Friday
men at work	Board of Selectmen
copy boy	stock boy
bus boy	cowboy
first baseman	man overboard
corpsman	fisherman
congressman	foreman

☐   **EXERCISE 13**

These terms denote professions which have traditionally been linked with a particular gender. Now that the professions are open to both sexes, are any new terms needed? If so, suggest possible terms. If not, explain why not.

miner	beautician
mechanic	barber
soldier	rabbi
sailor	minister
rancher	ballet dancer
farmer	bartender

☐   **EXERCISE 14**

The following terms have emerged in the last few years as possible alternatives for older gender-specific words. Which do you believe are likely to become part of the English language? Which do you expect to disappear? Explain.

Coinage	*Older form*
a. waiter waitperson server	waiter or waitress
b. househusband homemaker	housewife
c. weatherperson	weatherman, weathergirl

d. chair   chairman
    chairwoman
    chairperson
e. spokesperson   spokesman

☐   **EXERCISE 15**

wds

17g

Each of the following pairs of terms includes a feminine form which was at one time in wide use; all are still used to some extent. Which do you think are likely to remain in our language for some time, and which do you think will disappear? Explain your reasoning.

heir/heiress   author/authoress
benefactor/benefactress   poet/poetess
murderer/murderess   tailor/seamstress
actor/actress   comedian/comedienne
hero/heroine   villain/villainess
host/hostess   prince/princess
aviator/aviatrix   widow/widower
executor/executrix

☐   **EXERCISE 16**

In recent years the word *parenting* has been introduced as a gender-free equivalent of *mothering*. How do the connotations of *parenting* differ from those associated with *mothering*? with *fathering*? Given those differences, what is your opinion about the continued use of *parenting* in years to come?

Student Writer at Work: Choosing Words

The following draft was written for a freshman composition class. Revise it for appropriateness, accuracy, and freshness. Change words and rewrite sentences as you see fit. If necessary, revise further to strengthen coherence, unity, and style.

```
                    Computers and Society

    Computers are presently addressing many thorny
problems that are just begging to be solved. In fact,
their widespread use is making advances possible in many
fields. At the present time computers are a major part of
our environment, cutting down time-consuming chores and
making our lives easier.
```

A computer is a device engineered to make computation easier and faster. Today the computer has taken the image of a highly sophisticated electronic complex. By transforming Base 10 into Base 2, the computer's binary coded hexadecimal system allows it to distinguish numbers through the use of electronic switches. An open switch represents an 0 state and a closed switch represents a 1 state. By the use of programming, you can accomplish a desired result in a matter of milliseconds.

wds 17

The computer's applications have spread like wildfire to almost every field of endeavor. In the fields of mathematics and science, the computer has been used in activities as diverse as studying the structure of the atom and sending satellites into space. Another recent application is the use of computers in hospitals to detect drugs and toxins in human blood. Doctors will be cognizant of poisoning immediately and can embark upon an appropriate course of action and resuscitate the victim. This technique is a vast improvement over conventional laboratory analysis methods.

Computers can also be used at a person's residence to make his daily life easier. For example, a computer can turn on and off lights even though a person is not home. Thus a thief can be thwarted in his attempt to violate a home. Likewise, a computer can direct a remote-controlled vacuum cleaner to make a house super-clean, and it can do laundry and dishes through the use of more automatic devices. Taking care of everyday financial matters can also be easy as pie. In addition, alarm clocks can be programmed so members of the household could be awakened at different times.

In conclusion, the computer is a useful tool for society. It can be used beneficially in business and industry as well as in the home. And just as the automatic dishwasher has replaced doing dishes by hand, the computer

will alter the way we do many things. The computer is an
idea whose time has come and an idea that will open the
door to the future.

wds
17

18

Using the Dictionary

When asked what three books he would want with him if he were marooned on a desert island, the poet W. H. Auden chose the complete works of Shakespeare, the Bible, and the Oxford English Dictionary. Most experienced writers agree that a dictionary is one of the most valuable books they own. It contains considerable information about many subjects, and it is extremely useful when you revise your writing.

18a Exploring the Contents of a Dictionary

A dictionary is usually divided into three parts: the *front matter*, the *alphabetical listing*, and the *back matter.*

The **front matter** differs in each dictionary but generally contains a preface explaining how the dictionary is set up and guides for pronunciation and abbreviations. Some dictionaries contain special material in the front matter. *The American Heritage Dictionary,* a standard reference dictionary, has articles focusing on the history of the language, dialects, usage and acceptability, and computers and language analysis.

The **alphabetical listing** is the largest section of every dictionary. Entries tell how a word is spelled, pronounced, and used, and some dictionaries also include information on stress, grammatical function, and *etymology* (history and origin of the word). On the basis of hundreds of examples of usage, lexicographers also classify word usage into categories such as *regional, slang,* and *preferred.* Dictionaries may disagree regarding these designations, however.

Meanings under each entry may also be arranged differently from one dictionary to another. Some dictionaries list meanings in historical order, with the oldest usage coming first; others list meanings in order of most frequent usage. Therefore, you cannot assume that the first definition under an entry is the preferred usage. You must look in the front matter to find out what principle of arrangement the lexicographers used.

The **back matter** also differs in each dictionary. Some dictionaries contain a list of weights and measures; others, an essay on punctuation; and still others, a glossary of foreign words. To get the most out of your dictionary, acquaint yourself with its back matter so that you can refer to it when the need arises.

**dict
18b**

18b Choosing a Dictionary

Many people think that the meanings listed in dictionaries are the only correct meanings of a word, but in fact dictionaries suggest only the *possible* meanings of a word. They provide guidance, especially on disputed usage, but in no way do they legislate meaning or cover every use of a word. In addition, because of rapid growth in the communications industry and in scientific research, new words are coming into our language at an unprecedented rate. Twenty years ago, who had heard of *quarks, software, microchips, interferon,* or *CAT scans?* Because new words enter the language so rapidly, you should choose a dictionary that is the most current available—especially if you frequently look up specialized terms. When you buy a dictionary, check the date of its edition, *not* its printing, to make certain that you have the most recent one.

Many people also think that all dictionaries are essentially alike. This too is a misconception. Like tools, different dictionaries are designed for different tasks. The most widely used type of dictionary, the one-volume abridged dictionary (called a **desk dictionary** or a **college dictionary**), is ideal for daily use. Other types of dictionaries—including multivolume, unabridged dictionaries, which give a great deal of specialized data, and the many special-purpose dictionaries—have their own special uses.

18c Surveying Abridged Dictionaries

An **abridged dictionary** is one that is condensed from a more complete collection of words and meanings. A good hardback abridged dictionary will contain about 1,500 pages and about 150,000 entries. Paperback dictionaries usually contain fewer entries, treated in less detail. A paperback dictionary is adequate as a spelling reference that you can easily carry to class, but for home reference, any of the following hardback abridged dictionaries does a better job.

The American Heritage Dictionary of the English Language. 2d Coll. ed. Boston: Houghton Mifflin, 1982.

This extensively illustrated dictionary was first published in 1969. In an effort to create a readable dictionary, the editors keep technical terms and abbreviations to a minimum. The front matter of the dictionary discusses etymology, the history of language, usage and acceptability, dialects, and computers and language analysis. Within the alphabetical listing the principal and most current meaning appears first, with other meanings branching out from it. Throughout the dictionary, the editors have provided *usage notes* based on the responses of a panel of one hundred experts. Synonyms and sometimes antonyms are also listed.

dict 18c

In general, this dictionary gives more guidance than any of the other abridged dictionaries listed here. Its back matter contains biographical and geographical entries, abbreviations, and a list of two-year and four-year colleges.

The Concise Oxford Dictionary of Current English, 7th ed. New York: Oxford University Press, 1982.

This no-nonsense dictionary contains no illustrations and gives little guidance on usage. It lists meanings according to the most common usage, includes illustrative quotations, and gives British as well as American spellings. Front and back matter is sparse: there is a short preface, and the back matter includes a table of weights and measures, the Greek and Russian alphabets, and a compendium of the principal monetary units of the world.

The Random House College Dictionary, rev. ed. New York: Random House, 1984.

This is an abridged version of the larger unabridged *Random House Dictionary of the English Language.* It lists meanings according to frequency of use and indicates informal and slang usage. It also gives synonyms and antonyms as well as geographical and biographical names. Illustrations are helpful but less extensive than those in *The American Heritage Dictionary.* Back matter includes a manual of style.

Webster's Ninth New Collegiate Dictionary. Springfield, MA.: Merriam, 1987.

Like *The Random House College Dictionary*, this dictionary is an abridged version of a larger unabridged dictionary. The first Merriam Webster collegiate dictionary appeared in 1898, and the ninth edition incorporates many of the features of its predecessors. Information is derived from the more than 13 million citations gathered by the G. & C. Merriam Company. Meanings are listed chronologically rather than according to frequency of usage, and historical information precedes each definition. *Webster's Collegiate* contains fewer illustrations than *The American Heritage Dictionary*.

dict
18d

    Two new features characterize the ninth edition. First, entries are accompanied by dates showing how old a word is and when a definition came into use. Second, many entries are now followed by usage notes that discuss problems of usage and diction.

    The front matter of this dictionary contains a detailed essay on the English language commissioned for this edition. Foreign words and phrases as well as biographical and geographical names appear in separate sections in the back matter. This dictionary also contains a list of American and Canadian colleges and universities, a handbook of style, and an index.

Webster's New World Dictionary. 2d Coll. ed. Englewood Cliffs: Prentice-Hall, 1983.

This good basic dictionary presents meanings in historical order and indicates frequent usage. Foreign terms and geographical and biographical names are included in the alphabetical listing. Back matter includes information on mechanics, manuscript form, and punctuation.

NOTE: The name *Webster*, referring to the great lexicographer Noah Webster, is in the public domain. Because it cannot be copyrighted, it appears in the titles of many dictionaries of varying quality.

18d   Using a Dictionary

To fit a lot of information into a small space, abridged dictionaries use a system of symbols, abbreviations, and different typefaces. Each dictionary uses a slightly different system, so you should consult the front matter of your dictionary to determine how its system operates.

    Two labeled entries, from *The American Heritage Dictionary*

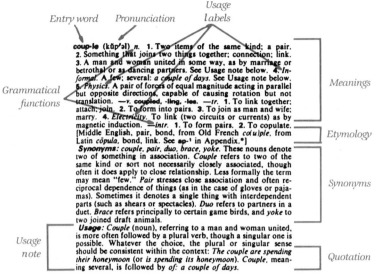

Entry word   *Pronunciation*   *Usage labels*

Grammatical functions

Meanings

Etymology

Synonyms

Usage note

Quotation

dict
18d

FIGURE 3

2nd College Edition and *Webster's Ninth New Collegiate Diction-ary*, respectively, are shown in Figures 3 and 4.

(1)   Using guide words

To help you locate words all dictionaries include a pair of guide words at the top corner of each page.

Couperin/court-martial
shriek · shut

The **guide words** indicate the first and last entries appearing on that page. The word on the left shows the first entry on the page,

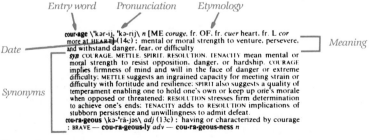

Entry word   *Pronunciation*   *Etymology*

Date

Synonyms

Meaning

FIGURE 4

and the word on the right shows the last. All entries on the páge fall alphabetically between these words.

(2) Understanding the entry word

The **entry word,** which appears in boldface at the beginning of the entry, gives the spelling of a word and also its variant forms.

>   col · or n. Also chiefly British col · our

An entry word is divided into syllables by small, centered dots.

>   cour · age

An entry of more than one word will appear as such on the page.

>   county seat

If a word is hyphenated, the hyphen will appear as part of the entry.

>   **vacuum-packed**

Dictionaries differ in their treatment of word division and compound words. *The American Heritage Dictionary*, for example, has *crossfire, The Concise Oxford Dictionary* has *cross-fire,* and *Webster's Ninth New Collegiate Dictionary* has *cross fire.*

☐   **EXERCISE 1**

Use your college dictionary to help you divide the following words into syllables and list all variant spellings. Consult a second college dictionary to see if both dictionaries agree.

1. cross reference   6. lovable
2. dexterous   7. theater
3. aesthetic   8. judgment
4. although   9. counselor
5. austerity   10. flavor

(3) Understanding the pronunciation guide

The pronunciation of a word appears in parentheses after the main entry (or between slashes [/ /] in *Webster's Ninth New Collegiate Dictionary*). Dictionaries use symbols to represent sounds, and an explanation of these symbols usually appears at the bottom of each page or across the bottom of facing pages throughout the alphabetical listing. (A full guide to pronunciation appears as part of the front matter of the dictionary.) The stressed syllable of a word is indicated by an accent mark (′). A secondary stress is indicated with a similar but lighter mark (′). In *The American Heritage Dictionary*, the accent mark follows the stressed syllable.

(kûr′ ij)
(dĭ-prē′shē-āt′)

In *Webster's Ninth New Collegiate Dictionary*, the accent precedes the stressed syllable.

/′kar-ij,`ka-rij/

Dictionaries often include more than one pronunciation of a word, but they rarely include all its regional variations. Therefore, they are not perfect guides to pronunciation. They are most reliable for the pronunciation of unusual words that are used more in writing than in speech and therefore have no colloquial variants.

**dict
18d**

☐   **EXERCISE 2**

Determine the pronunciation of the following words by looking up each in your college dictionary. Write out the symbols that the dictionary uses, and include variant pronunciations.

1. Cartesian   6. sangfroid
2. entablement   7. tiara
3. narwhal   8. malamute
4. insouciance   9. cavil
5. chimera   10. envoi

(4)   Using grammatical function labels

Dictionaries use part-of-speech labels to indicate grammatical categories. These are the labels for the eight traditional parts of speech.

de · cep · tive	adj [adjective]
hap · pi · ly	adv [adverb]
be · cause	conj [conjunction]
hey	interj [interjection]
cour · age	n [noun]
of	prep [preposition]
they	pron [pronoun]
re · lax	vb [verb]

If a verb is regular, the entry provides only the base form of the verb.

help . . . vb

If a verb is irregular, the entry lists the principal parts of the verb.

with · draw . . . vb -drew . . . ; -drawn . . . ; -drawing . . .

In addition, the entry indicates whether a verb is transitive, intransitive, or both.

in · fect . . . vt
va · ca · tion . . . vi
pen · e · trate . . . vb . . . vt . . . vi

dict
18d

Part-of-speech labels also indicate the plural form of irregular nouns.

fly . . . n pl flies

to · ma · to . . . n pl -toes

a · lum · nus . . . n pl -ni

moth · er-in-law . . . n pl moth · ers-in-law

When the plural form is regular, it is not shown.

Dictionaries usually show the comparative and superlative forms of both regular and irregular adjectives and adverbs.

red . . . adj redder; reddest

bad . . . adv worse; worst

Most entries for regular adjectives and adverbs show the comparative and superlative forms with -er and -est. The fact that the entry shows -er and -est does not preclude your using *more* and *most* as an alternate way to form the comparative and the superlative, however. An entry without -er and -est, however, always uses *more* and *most* to form the comparative and the superlative.

☐   **EXERCISE 3**

Use your college dictionary to answer the following questions about grammatical function.

1. What are the principal parts of the following verbs; *drink, deify, carol, draw,* and *ring?*
2. Which of the following nouns can be used as verbs: *canter, aesthetic, minister, council, command, magistrate, mother,* and *lord?*
3. What are the plural forms of these nouns: *silo, sheep, seed, dry, scissors, genetics,* and *alchemy?*
4. What are the comparative and superlative forms of the following adverbs and adjectives: *fast, airy, good, mere, homey,* and *unlucky?*

5. Are the following verbs transitive, intransitive, or both? Copy the
phrase or sentence from the dictionary that illustrates the use of each
verb: *bias, halt, dissatisfy, die,* and *turn.*

(5)   Understanding etymology

The **etymology** of a word is its history, its evolution over the
years. This information appears in brackets—[   ]—either before
or after the list of meanings. The etymology traces a word back to
its roots and shows its form when it entered English. For instance, *The American Heritage Dictionary* shows that *couple*
came into Middle English (1150–1475) from Old French and into
Old French from Latin. *Webster's Ninth New Collegiate Dictionary*
shows *cup* to have the same form, *cuppe,* in both Old and Middle
English and to have come into English from the Latin *cuppa.*

dict
18d

Here are the most common abbreviations used in etymologies.

OE	Old English	OF	Old French
ME	Middle English	G	German
AS	Anglo Saxon	ON	Old Norse or
	(or Old English)		Early Scandinavian
F	French	L	Latin
MF	Middle French		

☐   **EXERCISE 4**

Using your college dictionary, trace the etymologies of two of the following words. Write a paragraph on each explaining how their definitions
have changed or remained the same over the years.

1. atom   6. car
2. rampart   7. capitol
3. liquor   8. silly
4. poll   9. populace
5. assassin   10. custard

(6)   Understanding meanings

Some dictionaries, like *The American Heritage Dictionary,* give
the most common usage first and then list less common ones.
Others, like *Webster's Ninth New Collegiate Dictionary,* begin with
the oldest meaning and move to the most current ones. Regardless of the method your dictionary uses, you should remember
certain points when looking up a word's meaning.

First, remember that a dictionary records the meanings that
appear most regularly in speech and in writing. If a word is in the

process of acquiring new meanings, the dictionary may not yet include them.

Also remember that a dictionary meaning is primarily a record of the **denotations,** or exact meanings, of a word. Its emotional associations, or **connotations,** are not usually among the meanings listed, although some dictionaries do attempt to suggest them. *Webster's New World Dictionary,* for example, says that *scheme* "often connotes either an impractical, visionary plan or an underhanded intrigue." As a rule, however, a word is richer in everyday speech and writing than its dictionary definition suggests.

(7)   Understanding synonyms and antonyms

A dictionary entry often lists synonyms and occasionally antonyms in addition to definitions. **Synonyms** are words that have similar meanings, like *well* and *healthy.* **Antonyms** are words that have opposite meanings, like *courage* and *cowardice.* Dictionaries present synonyms—and sometimes antonyms—because they clarify the meanings of a word and are also useful to writers who want to vary their choice of words. However, no two words are exactly equivalent, so you must use synonyms carefully, making certain that the connotation of the synonym is as close as possible to that of the original word.

□   **EXERCISE 5**

Using your dictionary, as well as your own knowledge, write a paragraph explaining the differences in the connotations of the words in one of the groups below.

1. car, automobile, limousine   4. portly, heavy, fat
2. cabin, shack, hovel   5. slumber, sleep, snooze
3. cry, weep, sob

(8)   Understanding idioms

Dictionary entries often show how certain words are used with other words in set expressions called **idioms.** Such phrases present problems for some native speakers and especially for non-native speakers, as you may know from your own study of other languages. For example, what are we to make of the expression *from the shoulder?* That it means "in a direct or outspoken manner of telling" is not at all apparent. Such idiomatic phrases do not follow any rules; they have become fixed through custom and must be memorized.

Dictionaries also indicate the idiomatic use of prepositions. Under a usage note for the word *acquiesce,* for instance, *The American Heritage Dictionary* says that *acquiesce* is used with *in* when it takes a preposition. Similarly, we do not say that we *abide with* a decision or that we *interfere on* a performance. We say *abide by* and *interfere with.* The idiomatic use of prepositions is a matter of custom.

Most dictionaries list common idiomatic phrases under an individual entry. For example, *The Random House College Dictionary* lists the following idiomatic phrases under the entry *hat.*

Pass the hat

Take one's hat off to

Talk through one's hat

Throw one's hat into the ring

Under one's hat

**dict
18d**

(9)   Understanding usage labels

Dictionaries use special labels to indicate restrictions on word meanings. The most common labels are *nonstandard* or *substandard; informal* or *colloquial; slang; dialect* or *regional; vulgar; obsolete; archaic* or *rare; poetic;* and *foreign language* and *field* labels. Where such labels involve value judgments, dictionaries differ.

Nonstandard or Substandard Nonstandard or substandard means that a word is in wide use but is not considered part of standard usage. **Nonstandard** refers to words that have existed side by side with standard forms but have never been accepted as standard usage. **Substandard** refers to words even more removed from the mainstream than those designated nonstandard. Some linguists object to the designation *substandard* because it suggests inferiority, and dictionaries disagree about which words are nonstandard or substandard. For instance, *The American Heritage Dictionary* says that nonstandard usage includes forms such as *ain't. Webster's Ninth New Collegiate Dictionary,* however, labels *ain't* substandard.

Informal or Colloquial **Informal** or **colloquial** discourse is the language of conversation, and it is acceptable in informal situations. Its use does not imply ignorance of more formal forms. Rather, it occurs when people concentrate more on what they are saying than on how they are saying it. Most words may be used in either formal or informal situations, but some words usually appear only in speech or informal writing—contractions such as *I've* for *I have* and the word *sure* for the more formal *surely*, for example. (For more information on levels of usage, see 17a.)

Slang Words labeled **slang** by the dictionary are appropriate only in extremely informal situations but, unlike regionalisms, are widely used. *Clip joint* and *prof* (for professor) are good examples. Certain words are acceptable in some usages but are considered slang in others. "The pig squeals," for example, is standard usage of the word *squeals*. But when it is used to mean informing on someone, *squeal* is slang. Use of slang does not imply that one is illiterate. In writing it can be used intentionally to produce an irreverent or exaggerated effect or to record dialect.

dict
18d

Dialect or Regional These labels indicate that a word or meaning of a word is limited to a certain geographical region. The term *hero sandwich* is a good example: its many names include *hoagie, grinder, submarine, zeppelin,* and *poor boy*. Although some dictionaries label those words *slang*, others consider them regionalisms; *grinder*, for instance, is used almost exclusively in New England. Other regionalisms include *arroyo*, a word used in the Southwest to mean "deep gully," and *potlatch*, a word used in the Northwest to mean "celebration."

Vulgar Words so labeled are offensive. Vulgar words differ from slang in that some social taboo is usually attached to them. This category includes words labeled **obscene,** which are extremely offensive, and words labeled **profane,** which show disrespect for the Diety.

Obsolete This label indicates that a word is no longer in use. The word *egal*, meaning equal, is **obsolete.** Note, however, that just because the thing a word refers to is obsolete does not mean that the word itself is obsolete. A *ruff*, for example, is a stiff collar worn by men and women in the late sixteenth century. Ruffs are no longer in fashion, but their name still exists. The label *obsolete* applies only to words that have disappeared from the language.

Archaic or Rare The label **archaic** indicates that a word or meaning of a word was once common but now is seldom used. Archaic differs from **rare,** which means that a word was never in common usage. For example, the archaic word *affright*, meaning "to arouse fear or terror," was once widely used but now is no longer in general use. On the other hand, the rare word *nocent*, meaning "guilty" or "harmful," has not been used since the Middle English period and was not in common usage then.

Poetic This label refers to words that are or were used commonly only in poetry. These words include shortened forms such as *eve* for *evening* and *o'er* for *over*.

Foreign Language Labels These labels identify expressions or words from other languages that are commonly used by English-speaking people but are not considered part of English. Examples are *adios*, Spanish for "goodbye," and *sine qua non*, Latin for "something that is essential."

**dict
18d**

Field Labels These labels (*Mathematics, Chemistry, Biology, Military,* etc.) indicate that a word or meaning of a word is limited to a certain field or discipline. For example, *The American Heritage Dictionary* uses the labels *Physics* and *Electricity* to indicate special meanings of the word *couple.*

☐   **EXERCISE 6**

Use your college dictionary to find the restrictions on the use of the following words.

1. irregardless   6. ope
2. apse   7. whilst
3. flunk   8. integer
4. lorry   9. bannock
5. kirk   10. blowhard

(10)   Finding general information

In addition to containing information about words, your abridged dictionary is an excellent source of general information. Most abridged dictionaries contain lists of geographical and biographical names as well as references to topics of general interest. If you wanted to find out the year in which John Glenn orbited the earth, you might look up the entry *Glenn, John* in the biographical listing. If you needed to find out after whom the Davis Cup is named, you would look up *Davis Cup* in the alphabetical listing. Thus, when no other references are handy, your abridged dictionary can serve as a valuable source of information.

☐   **EXERCISE 7**

To test the research capability of your dictionary, use it to answer the following questions.

1. Where is Kitty Hawk, the site of Wilbur and Orville Wright's first heavier-than-air powered flight?
2. How many satellites does the planet Uranus have?
3. What is the population of Los Angeles?
4. In what year did Martin Luther King, Jr., win the Nobel Peace Prize?
5. In what year did Edward VII of England abdicate?
6. Who was Grandma Moses?
7. After whom was the ferris wheel named?
8. What is the atomic weight of sulfur?
9. What was Joseph Conrad's original name?
10. What is surrealism?

dict
18e

18e   Using Unabridged Dictionaries ─────

In some situations you may need more information than your college dictionary offers. When you are looking for a detailed history of a word or when you want to look up an especially rare usage, you need to consult an unabridged dictionary. An **unabridged dictionary** attempts to present a comprehensive survey of all words in a language. Consequently, it gives a wider and more detailed treatment of entries than an abridged dictionary, with comprehensive listings that may extend over several volumes. The following unabridged dictionaries are excellent sources of information available at many college libraries.

The Random House Dictionary of the English Language. 2nd edition, unabridged. New York: Random House, 1987.

This short unabridged dictionary—the shortest listed here—contains about 315,000 entries. In the process of updating the first (1966) edition, the editors have added 50,000 new words and 75,000 new definitions of old words.

Webster's Third New International Dictionary of the English Language. Springfield, MA: Merriam, 1986.

This unabridged dictionary contains over 450,000 entries along with illustrations, some in color. Meanings appear in chronological order and are extensively illustrated with quotations. This dictionary does not, however, give much guidance on usage.

The Oxford English Dictionary. New York: Oxford University Press, 1933; 1986.

Consisting of twelve volumes plus four supplements, *The Oxford English Dictionary* offers over 500,000 definitions, historically arranged, and 2 million supporting quotations. The quotations begin with the earliest recorded use of a word and progress through each century either until the word becomes obsolete or until its latest meaning is listed. For this reason, many scholars consider *The Oxford English Dictionary* the best place to find the history of a word or to locate illustrations of its usage. However, *The Oxford English Dictionary* emphasizes British usage and does not treat American usage fully.

Also available is the compact edition, a photographic reduction of the entire thirteen-volume edition into two volumes. The one drawback of the compact edition is that it must be read with a magnifying glass.

The entry from *The Oxford English Dictionary* shown in Figure 5 illustrates the in-depth coverage offered by an unabridged dictionary. Compare this entry on *courage* to the one on page 307.

dict
18e

Courage (kʋ rǝdʒ), *sb.* Forms : 4-7 corage, curage, (4 6 corrage, 5 curag, coreage, 6 currage, courra(d)ge, 7 corege). 5- courage. [ME. *corage*, a. OF. *corage*, *curage*. later *courage* Pr. and Cat. *coratge*, Sp. *corage*, It. *coraggio*, a Common Romanic word, answering to a L. type **corāticum*, f. *cor* heart. Cf. the parallel *ætáticum* from *ætāt-em* (AGE) ; and see -AGE.]

† **1.** The heart as the seat of feeling, thought, etc. ; spirit, mind, disposition, nature. *Obs.*

c 1300 *K. Alis.* 3559 Archelaus, of proud corage. *c* 1386 CHAUCER *Prol.* 11 Smale fowles maken melodie. .So priketh hem nature in here corages. *c* 1430 *Pilgr. Lyf Manhode* 1. xxxiii. 186) 20 What thinke·t in thi corage? *c* 1430 *Stans Puer* 5 To all norture thi corage to enclyne. *c* 1500 *Knt. Cur'esy* 407 in Ritson *Met. Rom.* III. 213 In his corage he was full sad. **1593** SHAKS. 3 *Hen. VI,* 11. ii. 57 This soft courage makes your Followers faint. **1638** DRUMM. OF HAWTH. *Irene* Wks. (1711) 163 Men's courages were growing hot, their hatred kindled. **1659** B. HARRIS *Parival's Iron Age* 41 The Spaniards .. attacked it with all the force and maistry the greatest courages were able to invent.

† **b.** *transf.* Of a plant. *Obs.* (Cf. ' To bring a thing into *good heart*.')

c 1420 *Palladius on Husb.* XI. 90 In this courage Hem forto graffe is goode.

† **c.** Applied to a person : cf. *spirit. Obs.*

1561 T. HOBY tr. *Castiglione's Courtyer* (1577) V j b, The prowes of those diuine courages [viz. Marquesse of Mantua, etc.]. **1647** W. BROWNE *Polex.* 11. 197 These two great courages being met, and followed by a small companie of the most resolute pirates.

† **2.** What is in one's mind or thoughts, what one is thinking of or intending ; intention, purpose ; desire or inclination. *Obs.* (Cf. ' To speak one's *mind*', ' to tell all one's *heart*'.)

c 1320 *Seuyn Sag.* (W.) 2446 Lo her, sire, a litel page! That schal sai the thi corage. *c* 1386 CHAUCER *Merch. T.* 10 Swich a greet corage Hadde this knyght to been a wedded man. **1484** CAXTON *Chivalry* 7 Fayr frend what is

your corage or entent. *c* 1530 LD. BERNERS *Arth Lyt. Bryt.* (1814) 277 Ye mayster dyscouered to her all his courage, how that he loued her. **1567** NORTH tr. *Gueuara's Diall Pr.* 93 b/1 The romaines had a great corage to conquere straunge realmes. **1568** GRAFTON *Chron.* II. 289 Many were taken of their owne courage, which might have scaped if they had list. **1607** SHAKS. *Timon* III. iii. 24 I'de such a coura„e to do him good. *a* 1626 BACON *Max.* 4 *Uses Com. Law* xxii. 81 The law..shall..make construction that my minde and courage is not to enter into the greater bond for any menace.

† **3.** Spirit, liveliness, lustiness, vigour, vital force or energy ; also *fig. Obs.*

a 1498 WARKW. *Chron.* (Camden) 2 Thei.. were greved with colde and rayne, that thei hade no coreage to feg. t. **1565** JEWEL *Def. Apol.* (1611) 505 In the Cardinals of Rome, Pride, Auarice, and Lechery are in their greatest Courage. **1630** R. *Johnson's Kingd. & Commw.* 247 They have horses of excellent courage. **1705** *Lond. Gaz.* No. 4182/4 A Chesnut Mare. .of great Courage.

† **b.** Anger, wrath ; **c.** Haughtiness, pride ; **d.** Confidence, boldness. *Obs.*

c 1386 CHAUCER *Knt.'s T.* (Harl.) 1154 The hunt[e] strangled with wilde bores corage. **1483** CAXTON *G. de la Tour* F iij b, [She] became. .so grete of courage that also to the kynge her lord she bare not so grete reuerence as she ought. **1568** GRAFTON *Chron.* II.285 Every man cryed and besought the king to have mercy. .for Gods sake refraine your courage, ye have the name of sovereigne nobles esse. **1590** SPENSER *F. Q.* III. x. 30 Trompart.. Besought him his great courage to appease, And pardon simple man. **1608** MIDDLETON *Trick to catch* I. i, I will. . set so good a courage on my state, That I will be believed.

† **e.** Sexual vigour and inclination ; lust. *Obs.*

1541 BARNES *Wks.* (1573) 329/1 By the reason that priestes are so hoate of courage, and can not keepe theyr chastitie. **1577** B. GOOGE *Heresbach's Husb.* III. 1586) 129 If the Bull be not lusty enough about his businesse. .his courage is also stirred up by the like odours. **1606** G. W[OODCOCKE] tr. *Justin* 56 Darius horse. .by reason of the courage had to the Mare, forthwith neighed alowde. **1615** CROOKE *Body of Man* 45 If they be taken away, the iollity and courage of the Creature is extinguished.

FIGURE 5

18f Using Special-Purpose Dictionaries ———

Special-purpose dictionaries focus on particular fields of interest
or endeavor, providing more information on these topics than
standard dictionaries do. The following dictionaries may be of
help.

Dictionaries of Usage

> Evans, Bergen, and Cornelia Evans. *Dictionary of Contemporary
> American Usage*, 1957.
> Fowler, H. W. *A Dictionary of Modern English Usage*, 2nd ed. rev., 1983
> (paperback).
> Nicholson, Margaret. *Dictionary of American-English Usage*, 1957.

Dictionaries of Synonyms

> *Roget's International Thesaurus*, 4th ed. Revised by Robert Chapman,
> 1984.
> *Webster's Dictionary of Synonyms*, 1951.

NOTE: *Thesaurus*, from the Greek word *treasure*, and *Roget*, the
name of a man who published a well-known thesaurus, are not
copyrighted names and can be attached to any dictionary of synonyms.

Dictionaries of Slang and Idioms

> Chapman, Robert. *The New Dictionary of American Slang*, 1986.
> Partridge, Eric. *Dictionary of Slang and Unconventional English*, 8th
> ed., 1985.

Dictionaries of Etymologies

> Morris, William, and Mary Morris. *Dictionary of Word and Phrase Ori-
> gins*, 1977.
> Onions, C. T. *The Oxford Dictionary of English Etymology*, 1966.
> Partridge, Eric. *Origins: A Short Etymological Dictionary of Modern
> English*, 1966.

Dictionaries of Foreign Terms

> Guinagh, Kevin. *Dictionary of Foreign Phrases and Abbreviations*, 3rd
> ed., 1983.
> Mawson, C. O. Sylvester, and Charles Berlitz. *Dictionary of Foreign
> Terms*, 2nd ed., 1979.
> Pei, Mario, and Salvatore Ramondino. *Dictionary of Foreign Terms*,
> 1974.

☐   **EXERCISE 8**

Use special-purpose dictionaries to answer the following.

1. Find as many synonyms as you can for these words: *navigator, fra-grance, boast, memory,* and *zigzag.*
2. Find the origins of the following slang terms: *vamoose, highbrow, clip joint,* and *humongous.*
3. Give the etymologies of these words: *gargantuan, amazon, doily, galvanize, hygiene, fathom,* and *maverick.*
4. Find the meaning of the following foreign phrases: *quid pro quo, tout passe, todo el mundo, idée fixe, con brio,* and *dos-à-dos.*

**dict
18f**

19

Building a Vocabulary

19a Analyzing Your Vocabulary

In a sense, your vocabulary comprises all the words you know. But this definition oversimplifies the situation. Actually you have four overlapping vocabularies that you use in various situations. First, you have a **speaking vocabulary,** the words you use in general conversation. For most people this vocabulary consists of the few hundred words they use when talking with friends. Next, you have a **writing vocabulary,** the words you use when writing. This vocabulary is considerably larger than your speaking vocabulary, consisting of about 10,000 to 45,000 words. Many of the words in your spoken vocabulary are also part of your written vocabulary. But certain words—like *satire, analogy, positron,* and *logarithm*—belong almost exclusively to your writing vocabulary. The colloquialisms and slang that are part of your spoken vocabulary are usually excluded from your writing vocabulary.

You also have a **reading vocabulary,** the words whose meanings you know but which you do not necessarily use in writing or in conversation. Words like *plutocrat, elucidate,* and *equivocate* might fall into this category. Most college students have a reading vocabulary of between 50,000 and 100,000 words. Finally, there is your **guess vocabulary,** words whose meanings you do not know exactly but can infer because the words are similar to ones you already know or because their context gives clues to their meanings.

Beyond these are words that you do not know and that you cannot figure out. These words you must look up in a dictionary.

19b   Why Build a Vocabulary?

Why should you spend time increasing your vocabulary? One reason is that in college a good vocabulary not only strengthens your performance on written examinations, papers, and oral reports, but it also increases your ability to comprehend reading material and your instructors' comments in class. Without an extensive vocabulary, your ability to learn is limited. Broadly speaking, then, education is the learning of a new vocabulary, the words with which you express new ideas.

Think for a moment about how much time your instructors spend explaining the basic vocabulary of any discipline. You cannot study psychology without knowing the meaning of *neurosis*, *psychosis*, and *conditioning* or understand sociology without knowing the meaning of *class*, *ethnocentrism*, and *culture.*

voc
19c

Many of the new terms you learn will go into your writing and reading vocabularies, and some will even become a part of your speaking vocabulary. Many words whose popular meanings you know will acquire new, specialized meanings in an academic setting. The word *set*, for example, means one thing in everyday conversation and another thing in a mathematics class. Certain words that are specific to a subject simply have to be memorized. In biology, for example, your previous experience has probably not prepared you to guess the meaning of *mitosis, mitochondria,* or *pineal body.* You must also cope with a general group of "learned" words—*aesthetic, concomitant,* and *penultimate,* for example—that occur often enough in an academic setting to cause trouble if you cannot understand them readily.

19c   Avoiding Ineffective Vocabulary Building

When trying to increase their vocabularies, many people overlook the distinctions between their speaking, writing, reading, and guess vocabularies. Books that claim to build "word power" often make the same mistake. They list complicated words that you are to memorize and practice using every day. If you do this, you put words into your speaking vocabulary that belong in your reading or writing vocabularies. Imagine how your friends would react, for example, if you made the following statement.

> After I admonished him about his table manners, my brother masticated his food more thoroughly.

Memorizing lists of words has other limitations as well.

Words that are not regularly used are quickly forgotten. Furthermore, people are not usually motivated to memorize someone else's vocabulary list. If you do not need to learn a new word, the chances are that you will rapidly forget it.

Reading will not automatically increase your vocabulary either. It does so only if you constantly look up and study new words. But students who must read extensively, especially while studying for examinations, often do not take the time to do this. Nor will your vocabulary somehow increase as you get older. Unless you work at it, your vocabulary actually *decreases.* As you can see, building a vocabulary takes conscious effort and considerable work.

19d   Building a Better Vocabulary: Preliminaries

Learning new words takes work and, at first, a good deal of time. But as you proceed, your vocabulary increases and your task gets easier. Here are some ideas for beginning a program of vocabulary development.

(1)   Becoming a reader

One way to build your vocabulary is to make a habit of reading. Set aside a certain amount of time each day—say, an hour—and do your private reading. Having to read for your courses will occasionally throw off your schedule, but whenever you can, read.

Reading in itself will not increase your vocabulary. But focusing on words as you read is one of the best ways of learning new words. Seeing words in context, remembering the sentences in which they appear and the ideas with which they are associated, helps you recall them later. Get into the routine of looking up new words as you encounter them and then writing them down along with their meanings. As your vocabulary grows, you will have to do this less often.

(2)   Keeping a vocabulary journal

A **vocabulary journal** is a systematic record of the words you look up as you read. In the following sample the student not only includes the definition of a word but also an example of its usage.

Word	Meaning	Example
satire	a work in which wit is used to expose folly or wickedness	"A Modest Proposal" by Jonathan Swift is a <u>satire</u> that attacks Britain's oppression of Ireland.
nadir	the lowest point	By 1868 Andrew Johnson had reached the <u>nadir</u> of his political career.
acrid	harsh in taste or smell	The fertilizer plant covered the town with <u>acrid</u> smoke.

voc
19e

By regularly reviewing the words in your journal, you will gradually build your reading vocabulary. Once you acquire a good working vocabulary, you can move on to more advanced methods of vocabulary building.

☐   **EXERCISE 1**

Keep a vocabulary journal for a week. Enter in it words you encounter in your academic and personal reading. Bring your journal to class and compare its entries with those of your classmates. Do certain words appear regularly? Why? What words do you expect to be of little use to you? Explain.

19e   Building a Better Vocabulary: Continuing the Program

Surrounding a word with associations helps you remember it. You can use a number of techniques to create such associations.

(1)   Learning the histories of words

Many of the words you encounter have interesting histories, or **etymologies**. Knowing the etymology of a word will help you remember its definition. For example, *cliché*, meaning a worn-out expression, is a French word that refers to a plate used for printing. It thus suggests the idea of being cast in metal from a mold. Hence a *cliché* is a fixed form of expression.

The word *vandal* is another interesting example. An ancient Germanic tribe, the Vandals, destroyed temples, buildings, books, and works of art as they overran Rome in the fifth century A.D.

Eventually, *vandal* became synonomous with anyone who willfully destroys or defaces property.

You can find the history of a word in any good college dictionary, or you can consult a specialized dictionary of etymology (see 18f). As you build your vocabulary, see if the history of a word provides associations that help you remember it.

☐ **EXERCISE 2**

Using your college dictionary, look up the histories of the following words. How does the history of each word help you remember its definition?

voc
19e

1. mountebank	6. cicerone
2. pyrrhic	7. fathom
3. pittance	8. gossamer
4. protean	9. rigmarole
5. gargantuan	10. maudlin

(2) Learning roots, prefixes, and suffixes

The words you encounter in your college studies are sometimes long and complex. Usually, however, these words can be broken down into smaller units that give you clues to their meanings. For instance, *bigamy* can be divided into the Greek prefix *bi*, meaning "two," and the root *gamos*, meaning "marriage," thus revealing *bigamy* to mean being married to two people at once. Over half the words in English come from Latin and Greek sources, so knowing something about Latin and Greek roots, prefixes, and suffixes can help you to determine what these words mean and to remember their definitions once you learn them. Once you see how roots, prefixes, and suffixes work in the words you already know, you can discover the meaning of new words based on these forms. Thus, once you know the derivation of *bigamy*, you can probably guess the meaning of *bicolor*, *biconvex*, and *polygamy*.

Roots   A **root** is a word from which other words are formed. Both *hypodermic* and *dermatologist*, for example, come from the Greek root *derma*, meaning "skin." *Manual* means working by hand, *manuscript* refers to a handwritten draft of a book, and *manufacture* literally means making a product by hand. All these words derive from the Latin root *manus*, meaning "hand."

Many scientific words are based on Latin and Greek roots. *Biography* contains the Greek root *graph*, meaning "to write," and *vacuum* contains the Latin root *vac*, meaning "empty." *Biology* contains the Greek root *bios*, meaning "life," as do *biosphere*, *biophysics*, *bionics*, and *biopsy*. When you come across words that contain *bio*, you already know half their meaning.

NOTE: Be careful when making generalizations based on roots, prefixes, and suffixes. Some words appear to have the same root but do not—for instance, *homosexual* (from the Greek *homos*, meaning "same"), *homo sapiens* (from the Latin *homo*, meaning "man").

Here are some common Latin and Greek roots whose meanings can help you identify and remember new words.

voc
19e

Latin Roots

1. aequus	equal	equivocal, equinox
2. amare, amatum	to love	amiable
3. annus	year	annual
4. audire	to hear	audible
5. capere, captum	to take	capture
6. caput	head	caption, capital
7. dicere, dictum	to say, to speak	edict, diction
8. duco, ductum	to lead	aqueduct
9. facere, factum	to make, to do	manufacture
10. loqui, locutum	to speak	eloquence
11. lucere	to be light	elucidate, translucent
12. manus	hand	manual, manuscript
13. medius	middle	mediate
14. mittere, missum	to send	admit, permission
15. omnis	all	omnipotent
16. plicare, plicatum	to fold	implicate
17. ponere, positum	to place	post, depose
18. portare, portatum	to carry	porter
19. quarere, quaesitum	to ask, to question	inquire
20. rogare, ragatum	to ask	interrogate
21. scribere, scriptum	to write	scribble
22. sentire, sensum	to feel	consent, sense
23. specere, spectrum	to look at	inspect
24. spirare, spiratum	to breathe	inspire, conspire
25. tendere, tentum	to stretch	extend, attend
26. verbum	word	verb, verbiage

Greek Roots

1. bios (bio-)	life	biology, biography
2. chronos (chrono-)	time	chronology
3. derma (derma-, -dermic)	skin	dermatologist, hypodermic
4. ethos (ethno-)	race, tribe	ethnic

5. gamos (-gamy, -gamous)	marriage, union	bigamy, bigamous
6. genos (gene-)	race, kind, sex	genetics, genealogy
7. geo-	earth	geology, geography
8. graphein (-graph)	to write	paragraph
9. helios (helio-)	sun, light	heliotrope
10. krates (-crat)	member of a group	plutocrat, democrat
11. kryptos (crypto-)	hidden, secret	cryptic, cryptogram
12. metron (-meter, metro-)	to measure	barometer, metronome
13. morphe (morph)	form	morphology
14. osteon (osteo-)	bone	osteopath, osteomyelitis
15. pathos (patho-, -pathy)	suffering, feeling	sympathy
16. phagein (phag)	to feed, to consume	bacteriophage
17. philos (philo-, -phile)	loving	bibliophile, philosophy
18. phobos (-phobe, phobia)	fear	Anglophobe, claustrophobia
19. photos (photo-)	light	photograph
20. pneuma	wind, air	pneumatic
21. podos (-pod, -poda)	foot	tripod, hexapoda
22. pseudein (pseudo-)	to deceive	pseudonym
23. pyr (pyro-)	fire	pyrotechnical
24. soma	body	psychosomatic
25. tele-	distant	telephone
26. therme (thermo-, -therm)	heat	thermometer

voc
19e

☐ **EXERCISE 3**

Using the above list of roots, speculate on the meaning of the following words. If you cannot determine the exact meaning of a word, make the best guess you can. Check your definition against one that you find in your college dictionary.

1. amateur
   amative
2. pathology
   pathetic
3. photosensitive
   photoengraver
   photoelectric

4. audio
   audiometer
5. verbalize
   verbose
   verbalist

Prefixes A **prefix** is a letter or group of letters put before a root or word that adds to or modifies it. The prefix *anti*, for example, means "against." When combined with other words, it forms new words.

antiaircraft	A weapon used against aircraft
antibiotic	A substance used to combat microorganisms
anticoagulant	A substance that suppresses the clotting of the blood
antidote	A remedy that counteracts poison
antifreeze	A substance used to stop a liquid from freezing

Knowing even a few prefixes can help you to deduce the meanings of a great many words. Here is a list of prefixes that, combined with different roots, form thousands of words.

Prefixes Indicating Number

Prefix	Meaning	Example	Definition
uni-	one	unify	To make into a unit
bi-	two	bimonthly	Every two months
duo-	two	duotone	Printed in two tones of the same color
tri-	three	triad	A group of three
quadri-	four	quadruped	A four-footed animal
tetra-	four	tetrachloride	A chemical with four chlorine atoms
quint-	five	quintuplets	Five offspring born in a single birth
pent-	five	pentagon	A five-sided figure
multi-	many	multilateral	Having many sides
mono-	one	monogamy	Having one spouse
poly-	many	polygamy	Having many spouses
omni-	all	omnivore	Eating all kinds of food

Prefixes Indicating Smallness

Prefix	Meaning	Example	Definition
micro-	small	microscope	An instrument for observing small things
mini-	small	minibus	A small bus

Prefixes Indicating Sequence and Space

Prefix	Meaning	Example	Definition
ante-	before	antebellum	Before the war
pre-	before	prehistory	Before history
intro-	within	introspective	Looking into oneself
post-	after	postscript	A message written after the body of the letter
re-	back, again	review	To look at again
sub-	under	submarine	An underwater ship
super-	above	supervise	To look over the performance of others
inter-	between	international	Between nations

intra-	within	intramural	Within the bounds of an institution
in-	in, into	incorporate	To form into a body
ex-	out, from	exhale	To breathe out
circum-	around	circumnavigate	To sail or fly around (the earth, an island, etc.)
con-	with, together	congregate	To come or bring together

Prefixes Indicating Negation

Prefix	Meaning	Example	Definition
non-	not	nonpartisan	Not affiliated
in-	not	inactive	Not active
un-	not, the opposite of, against	unequal	Not equal
anti-	against	antiseptic	Free from germs
counter-	opposing	countermand	To revoke an order with another order
contra-	against	contradict	To speak against
dis-	not, the opposite of	dislike	To not like
mis-	wrong, ill	mislead	To give bad advice
mal-	bad, wrong, ill	malformed	Incorrectly shaped
pseudo-	false	pseudonym	A false name

voc 19e

☐   **EXERCISE 4**

Review the preceding list of prefixes and list one additional word and definition for each prefix.

Suffixes   **Suffixes** are syllables added to the end of a word or root that change its part of speech. For example, suffixes added to the verb *believe* form two nouns, an adjective, and an adverb.

believe	(verb)
believer	(noun)
believability	(noun)
believable	(adjective)
believably	(adverb)

English has relatively few suffixes that form verbs and adverbs. A large number of suffixes, however, form nouns and adjectives. Knowing the most common ones helps you to identify several words from a single base word.

Verb Suffixes

Suffix	Meaning	Example
-en	to cause to or become	cheapen, redden
-ate	to cause to be	activate, animate

| -ify, -fy | to make or cause to be | fortify, magnify |
| -ize | to make, to give, to practice | memorize, modernize |

Adverb Suffixes

The only regular suffix for adverbs is -ly, as in *slowly*, *wisely*, and *energetically*.

Adjective Suffixes

Suffix	Meaning	Example
-al	capable of, suitable for	comical
-ial	pertaining to	managerial
-ic	pertaining to	democratic
-ly	a resemblance	sisterly
-ly	at specific intervals	hourly
-ful	abounding in	colorful
-ous, -ose	full of	porous, verbose
-ive	quality of	creative, adaptive
-less	lack of, free of	toothless
-ish	having the qualities of, preoccupied with	childish, bookish

voc
19e

Noun Suffixes

Suffix	Meaning	Example
-ance, -ence	quality or state of	insurance, competence
-acy	quality or state of	piracy, privacy
-or	one who performs an action	doctor
-arium, orium	place for	aquarium, auditorium
-ary	place for, pertaining to	dictionary
-cide	kill	suicide, homicide
-icle, -cle	a diminutive ending	icicle, corpuscle
-hood	state or condition of	childhood
-ism	quality or doctrine of	Marxism, conservatism
-ity	quality or state of	acidity
-itis	inflammation of	appendicitis
-ics	the science or art of	economics
-ment	act or condition of	resentment
-mony	resulting condition	testimony
-ology	the study of	biology, psychology

(3) Learning words according to a system

Learning related words according to a system is far more effective than memorizing words at random. Consider the following pair of words.

duct   a tubular passage
aqueduct   a conduit designed to transport water

Both words share the Latin root *ducere* (to lead). Because you are already familiar with the word *duct,* you have a clue to the meaning of *aqueduct.* If you know that *aqua* is a Latin word meaning "water," you can easily remember the definition of the word.
Other words also share the root *ducere.*

conduct	to direct the course of
induct	to install, to admit as a member
viaduct	a series of spans used to carry a railroad over a valley or other roads
abduct	to carry off
deduct	to take away
ductile	capable of being fashioned into a new form

VOC
19e

Learning these related words together would clearly be easier than learning them at random.
Other word groupings also facilitate learning. You can, for example, study together words that are confusing because they sound so much alike.

imminent	about to occur
eminent	prominent
ascent	a rise
assent	agreement
capital	a seat of government
capitol	the building where the legislative body meets
principal	the most important; the head of a school
principle	a basic law or truth

You can also study together words that are confusing because they look somewhat alike.

marital	referring to marriage
martial	referring to war
descent	a downward movement
decent	characterized by good taste or morality

Finally, you can study together words that are confusing because their meanings are so closely associated with each other.

imply	to suggest
infer	to conclude
explicit	stated outright
implicit	implied, unsaid

See the Glossary of Usage for additional examples of confusing word pairs.

(4)   Keeping a vocabulary file

Get in the habit of writing new words down on $3'' \times 5''$ cards and grouping together cards that you associate with one another. One section of your vocabulary file might consist of words whose roots are the same; another might contain look-alike or sound-alike words. On each card list synonyms, antonyms, roots, and any other associations that will help you to remember the definition.

Side 1
1. The word
2. A sentence in which the word appears
3. The word, divided into syllables, along with its pronunciation

Side 2
1. Prefix, root, and suffix (if applicable)
2. Definitions
3. Synonyms, antonyms, root words, or other related words.

voc
19e

Carry a packet of these cards around with you and look at them whenever you have a spare moment. When you feel that you have learned the words in the stack, return them to your card file and take out another stack. Review the cards periodically so you do not forget what you have learned.

Be on the lookout for ways to categorize a series of words for easy recall. After learning a word, look up its synonyms and antonyms, and learn them, too. Find other words that contain the same prefix, suffix, or root. After a while you will find that you have a surprisingly large number of words and cross-references in your card file and an expanded vocabulary at your command.

☐   **EXERCISE 5**

Select word pairs from your vocabulary journal that fall into the categories mentioned above: (1) words that have the same root, (2) words that sound alike, (3) words that look alike, and (4) words that are closely associated with each other. Make out $3'' \times 5''$ cards for each pair and begin your own vocabulary file.

20

Improving Spelling

Contrary to popular opinion, spelling usually *does* count on examinations, essays, and reports, and many instructors do not hesitate to lower the grade of a paper that contains poor spelling. Spelling errors distract readers and make it difficult for them to understand what you are trying to say. In some cases, incorrectly spelled words actually misrepresent your meanings, as when you use *equivalents* for *equivalence*, for example, or *benzene* for *benzoin.*

If spelling has always given you trouble, you will probably not become a champion speller overnight. But the situation is not hopeless. Most people can spell even difficult words "almost" correctly; usually just a letter or two is wrong. For this reason, memorizing a few simple rules and their exceptions and learning the correct spelling of the most commonly misspelled words can make a big difference.

20a Spelling and Pronouncing Words ————

Because many words in English are not spelled as they are pronounced, sound alone does not necessarily indicate a word's spelling. For instance, *gh* is silent in *light* but pronounced *f* in *cough;* the ō sound is spelled differently in *mow, toe, though, sew,* and *beau.* These and other inconsistencies between English spelling and pronunciation create a number of problem areas to watch for.

(1) Vowels in unstressed positions

Many unstressed vowels sound exactly alike when we say them. For instance, it is hard to tell from pronunciation alone that the *i* in *terrible* is not an *a*. In general, the vowels *a*, *e*, and *i* are impossible to distinguish in the suffixes *-able* and *-ible*, *-ance* and *-ence*, and *-ant* and *-ent*.

comfortable	compatible
brilliance	excellence
servant	independent

This blurring of sounds is problematic for both native and nonnative speakers of English.

(2)   Silent letters in words

A number of words in English contain silent letters. The *b* in *climb* and *dumb* is silent, as is the *t* in *mortgage*. Silent letters at the beginning of a word are especially bothersome because they make its proper spelling difficult to look up in a dictionary. You cannot look up *gnu* (pronounced *new*) if you do not already know that it begins with a *g*. The spelling of words with silent letters follows no rules, so you have to memorize words as you encounter them. Here are some examples.

aisle	knight
condemn	pneumonia
climb	silhouette
depot	sovereign

(3)   Words that contain letters or syllables not pronounced in informal speech

Most people pronounce words rather carelessly in everyday speech. If they then use pronunciation as a guide to spelling, they leave out, add, or misplace letters. The following words are often misspelled because they are pronounced incorrectly.

literature	nuclear
February	environment
candidate	disastrous
library	hundred
government	lightning
perform	probably
quantity	specific
recognize	surprise

(4)   Variant forms of the same word

Some spelling problems occur because different forms of a word have different spellings, with the root of the word changing spelling as it changes form.

Spelling problems can occur when the spellings of the verb and noun forms of a word are different.

advise (v)	advice (n)
renounce (v)	renunciation (n)
announce (v)	annunciation (n)
describe (v)	description (n)
omit (v)	omission (n)

Spelling differences also occur among the principal parts of irregular verbs.

**sp
20a**

arise, arose, arisen	ride, rode, ridden
drive, drove, driven	spring, sprang, sprung
grow, grew, grown	throw, threw, thrown

Irregular nouns change spelling when the plural is formed.

man, men	goose, geese
calf, calves	wife, wives
child, children	woman, women

Some words (such as *rime/rhyme*) have more than one accepted spelling. In addition, some words are spelled one way in America and another way in Great Britain. You should always consult a dictionary to determine the preferred American spelling.

American	*British*
check	cheque
color	colour
judgment	judgement

(5) Words that sound alike but are spelled differently

Many words in English are pronounced alike but spelled differently. Such words, called **homonyms,** can cause spelling problems. The following is a partial list of the homonyms that are misspelled most often. For other examples see the Glossary of Usage.

accept/except	principal/principle
affect/effect	stationary/stationery
cite/site/sight	there/their/they're
complement/compliment	theirs/there's
its/it's	weather/whether

☐   **EXERCISE 1**

Use your dictionary to determine the proper word for each sentence.

1. In the short story "Araby," James Joyce makes an allusion/illusion to Sir Walter Scott's *The Abbott*.
2. The gangster John Dillinger alluded/eluded capture for years.
3. The scientists warned of eminent/imminent disaster from the volcano.
4. A fine wine is a perfect complement/compliment to dinner.
5. Because its rotation matched the earth's, the satellite appeared stationary/stationery.

20b   Learning Spelling Rules

The few reliable rules that govern English spelling can help you overcome the general inconsistency between pronunciation and spelling. These rules have exceptions, but they are still useful guides.

(1)   The *ie/ei* combinations

The old rule still stands: use *i* before *e* except after *c* or when pronounced *ay* as in *neighbor*.

i before *e*		*ei* after *c*	*ei* pronounced *ay*
belief	niece	ceiling	neighbor
chief	piece	conceit	weigh
field	friend	deceit	freight
		receive	eight
		perceive	

There are a few exceptions to this rule: *either, neither, foreign, leisure, weird,* and *seize*. In addition, if the *ie* combination is not pronounced as a unit, the rule does not apply: *atheist, science*.

☐   EXERCISE 2

Fill in the blanks with the proper *ie* or *ei* combination. After completing the exercise, use your dictionary to check your answers.

> EXAMPLE: conc __ei__ ve

1. rec _____ pt
2. var _____ ty
3. caff _____ ne
4. ach _____ ve
5. kal _____ doscope
6. misch _____ f
7. effic _____ nt
8. v _____ n
9. spec _____ s
10. suffic _____ nt

(2)   Doubling consonants

Some words double their final consonants before a suffix that begins with a vowel (*-ed, -ing*); others do not. Fortunately, there is a rule to distinguish them. The only words that double their consonants in this situation are those that meet the following criteria.

1. They have one syllable or are stressed on the last syllable.
2. They contain only one vowel in the last syllable.
3. They end in a single consonant.

   The word *tap* satisfies all three conditions: it has only one syllable, it contains only one vowel *(a)*, and it ends in a single consonant *(p)*. Therefore, the final consonant doubles before a suffix beginning with a vowel *(tapped, tapping)*. The word *relent* meets two of the above criteria (it has one vowel in the last syllable and it is stressed on the last syllable), but it does not end in a single consonant. Therefore, its final consonant is not doubled *(relented, relenting)*.

(3)   Prefixes

The addition of a prefix never affects the spelling of the root.

   un + acceptable = unacceptable
   dis + agree = disagree
   mis + spell = misspell
   dis + joint = disjoint

(For a more complete list of prefixes, see 19e.2.)
   Some prefixes can cause spelling problems because they are easily confused or because they are pronounced alike although they are not spelled alike. Be especially careful of the prefixes *ante-/anti-, en-/in-, per-/pre-,* and *de-/di-.*

   antebellum   antiaircraft
   encircle   integrate
   perceive   prescribe
   deduct   direct

(4)   Suffixes: silent *e*

When a suffix that starts with a consonant is added to a word ending in silent *e,* the *e* is generally kept: *hope/hopeful; lame/lamely; bore/boredom.*
   Familiar exceptions include *argument, truly, ninth, wholly, judgment,* and *abridgment.*
   When a suffix that starts with a vowel is added to a word ending in silent *e,* the *e* is generally dropped: *hope/hoping; trace/traced; grieve/grievance; love/lovable.*

Familiar exceptions include *changeable, noticeable,* and *courageous.* In these cases the *e* is kept so that the *c* or *g* will be pronounced like the initial consonants in *cease* or *gem* and not like the initial consonants in *come* or *game.*

sp
20b

☐   **EXERCISE 3**

Combine the following words with the suffixes in parentheses. Determine whether you keep or drop the silent *e,* and be prepared to explain your choice.

    EXAMPLE: fate (al)
                 fatal

1. surprise (ing)	6. outrage (ous)
2. sure (ly)	7. service (able)
3. force (ible)	8. awe (ful)
4. manage (able)	9. shame (ing)
5. due (ly)	10. shame (less)

(5)   Suffixes: words ending in *y*

When a word ends in *y* (*beauty, bounty*), the *y* often changes when a suffix is added. The *y* changes to an *i* when a suffix begins with a consonant (*beautiful, bountiful*). The *y* is retained, however, when the ending begins with *a vowel* (*-ed, -ing*), or when the *y* ends a proper name (*play/played; tally/tallying; Levy/Levys*).

Familiar exceptions include some one-syllable words.

day/daily but days

pay/paid but payment

say/said but says

☐   **EXERCISE 4**

Add the endings in parentheses to the following words. Change or keep the final *y* as you see fit, and be prepared to explain your choice.

    EXAMPLE: valley (s)
                 valleys

1. journey (ing)	6. study (es)
2. toy (ed)	7. bury (ed)
3. carry (ing)	8. likely (hood)
4. deputy (ize)	9. plenty (ful)
5. study (ing)	10. supply (er)

(6)   Suffixes: *seed* endings

Endings with the sound *seed* are nearly always spelled *cede,* as in *precede, intercede, concede,* and so on. The only exceptions are *supersede, exceed, proceed,* and *succeed.*

(7) Suffixes: *-able, -ible*

These endings sound alike, and they often cause spelling problems. Fortunately, there is a rule that can help you distinguish them. If the stem of a word is itself an independent word, the suffix *-able* is most commonly used. If the stem of a word is not an independent word, the suffix *-ible* is most often used.

*comfort*able	compatible
*agree*able	incredible
*dry*able	plausible

(8) Forming plurals

Most nouns form plurals by adding *-s*. This applies to words ending with consonants or with the vowels *a, e, i,* and *u.*

savage/savages	tortilla/tortillas
girl/girls	gnu/gnus
boat/boats	taxi/taxis

There are, however, a number of exceptions.

Words Ending in *f* or *fe* Words ending in *f* or *fe* can form plurals in several ways. Some words ending in *f* or *fe* form plurals by changing the *f* to *v* and adding *-es* or *-s.*

knife/knives	wife/wives
life/lives	self/selves

Some words ending in *f* or *fe* just add *-s.*

belief/beliefs	proof/proofs

A few such words can form plurals either by adding *-s* or by substituting *-ves* for *f.*

scarf/scarfs/scarves	hoof/hoofs/hooves

Words ending in double *f* take *-s* to form plurals *(tariff/tariffs).*

Words Ending in *y* Most words that end in a consonant followed by *y* form plurals by changing the *y* to *i* and adding *-es.*

baby/babies	blueberry/blueberries
seventy/seventies	worry/worries

Proper nouns, however, are exceptions: the *Kennedys* (never the *Kennedies*).

Words that end in a vowel followed by a *y* form plurals by adding *-s.*

monkey/monkeys	key/keys
turkey/turkeys	day/days

Words Ending in *o*   Most words that end in a consonant followed by *o* add *-es* to form the plural.

tomato/tomatoes   hero/heroes

Some, however, add *-s.*

silo/silos	piano/pianos
memo/memos	soprano/sopranos

Still other words that end in *o* add either *-s* or *-es* to form plurals.

memento/mementos/mementoes
mosquito/mosquitos/mosquitoes

Words that end in a vowel followed by *o* form the plural by adding *-s.*

radio/radios   stereo/stereos   zoo/zoos

Words Ending in *s, ss, sh, ch, x,* and *z*   These words form plurals by adding *-es.*

Jones/Joneses	lunch/lunches	tax/taxes
mass/masses	box/boxes	latch/latches
rash/rashes	buzz/buzzes	ax/axes

NOTE: Some one-syllable words that end in *s* or *z* double their final consonants when forming plurals *(quiz/quizzes).*

Compound Nouns   Compound nouns—nouns formed from two or more words—usually conform to the rules governing the last word in the compound construction.

welfare state/welfare states   snowball/snowballs

However, in compound nouns where the first element of the construction is more important than the others, the plural is formed with the first element *(sister-in-law/sisters-in-law).*

Irregular Plurals   Some words in English have irregular plural endings. No rules govern these plurals, so you have to memorize them.

child/children	ox/oxen
woman/women	louse/lice
man/men	mouse/mice
goose/geese	

**sp
20b**

Foreign Plurals Some words, especially those borrowed from Latin or Greek, keep their foreign plurals. When you use these words, you must look up their plural forms in your college dictionary if you do not know them. Here are some of the more common Latin and Greek words and their plurals.

Singular	*Plural*
criterion	criteria
datum	data
larva	larvae
memorandum	memoranda
stimulus	stimuli

sp
20c

Some foreign words have a regular English plural as well as the one from their language of origin.

Singular	*Plural*
hippopotamus	hippopotami, hippopotamuses
antenna	antennae, antennas

No Plural Forms A few words use the same form for both the singular and the plural.

Singular	*Plural*
apparatus	apparatus
deer	deer
fish	fish (*also* fishes)
sheep	sheep
species	species

20c   Developing Spelling Skills ─────────

To form good spelling habits, you must invest time and effort. In addition to studying the rules outlined in 20b, you can do a number of things to help yourself become a better speller.

(1)   Learning commonly misspelled words

Following is a list of some of the most commonly misspelled words. It is a good idea to take a group of these words—say, twenty each day—and learn them. Copy them on 3″ × 5″ cards and review them whenever you have a few extra minutes. Or ask a friend to quiz you on them. After isolating the words you chronically misspell, you can concentrate on learning them.

When you master the following list, you can study the look-alike words in the Glossary of Usage.

A

absence	acquaintance	analysis/analyze
absorption	across	angel/angle
abundance	address	annual
accessible	advice/advise	apparent
accidentally	aggravate	appearance
acclaim	allotted	argument
accommodate	a lot	atheist
accomplish	all right	attendance
accumulate	already	auxiliary
achievement	amateur	

B

balloon	believe	breathe
barbiturate	benefited	Britain
bargain	biscuit	buoyant
basically	bouillon	bureaucracy
beggar	boundary	business
beginning	breadth/breath	

C

calendar	colossal	consciousness
camouflage	column	consensus
cantaloupe	coming	consistent
capital/capitol	committee	continuous
cemetery	commitment	controlled
chagrined	comparative	coolly
challenge/challengeable	competent	corollary
characteristic	completely	correlate
changing	concede	correspondence
chief	conceive	council/counsel
choose/chose	condemn	counselor
cigarette	condescend	courteous
climbed	conscience	courtesy
colonel	conscientious	criticize

D

deceive	desperate	disappoint
defendant	develop	disastrous
deferred	developed	discipline
definitely	development	disease
dependent/dependant	dilemma	dissatisfied
descend	dining	dominant
desirable	disappearance	drunkenness
despair		

E

easily	environment	exhaust
ecstasy	equipped	exhilarate
efficiency	equivalent	existence

eighth   especially   expense
eligible   exaggerate   experiment
embarrass   exceed   explanation
eminent   excellence   extremely
enemy   exuberance
entirely

F
fallacious   fiery   forfeit
fallacy   finally   formerly
familiar   financially   forty
fascinate   forcibly   fourth
February   foreign   fulfill
fictitious   foresee   fundamentally

G
gauge   governor   guard
generally   grammar   guerrilla
genius   grievous   guidance
government   guarantee

H
handkerchief   hemorrhage   hoping
happily   heroes   humorous
harass   hesitancy   hypocrisy
height   hindrance   hypocrite
heinous   hoarse

I
ideally   independent   interference
idiosyncrasy   indicted   interpret
ignorance   indispensable   interrupt
imaginary   inevitable   introduce
immediately   inoculate   irrelevant
implement   insurance   irresistible
incidentally   intelligence   island
incredible   intercede

J
jealousy   judicial   judgment
jewelry

K
knowledge

L
laboratory   license   literally
legitimate   lieutenant   loneliness
leisure   lightning   loose
length   likelihood   lose
lenient   likely   luxury

sp
20c

M

magazine
maintain
maintenance
manageable
maneuver
marriage
mathematics
medicine

medieval
millionaire
miniature
minor
minutes
mischievous
missile

misspelled
mortgage
mosquito
mosquitoes
murmur
muscle
mysterious

N

narrative
naturally
necessity
neighbor
neither

neutron
niece
ninety
ninth

noticeable
nowadays
nuclear
nuisance

sp
20c

O

obedience
obstacle
occasionally
occurred
occurrence
official

omission
omit
omitted
opinion
opponent
opportunity

oppression
optimism
ordinarily
origin
outrageous
overrun

P

panicky
parallel
parliament
particularly
peaceable
peculiar
penetrate
perceive
performance
permanent
permissible
permitted
perseverance
persistent
physical
physician
picnicked

piece
pitiful
planning
playwright
possessive
potato
potatoes
practically
prairie
precede
preceding
predominant
preference
preferred
prejudice
preparation
prescription

prevalent
primitive
principle
privilege
probably
procedure
proceed
process
professor
prominent
pronounce
pronunciation
propaganda
prophecy/prophesy
psychology
publicly
pursue

Q

quandary
quarantine

questionnaire

quizzes

R

realistically
realize

really
recede

receipt
receive

recognize   religious   reservoir
recommend   remembrance   resistance
reference   reminiscence   restaurant
referred   repetition   rheumatism
relevant   representative   rhythmical
relieving   resemblance   roommate

S

sacrifice   skeptical   subtle
safety   skiing   succeed
salary   soliloquy   succession
satellite   sophomore   sufficient
scenery   souvenir   summary
schedule   specifically   supersede
secede   specimen   suppress
secretary   sponsor   surprise
seize   spontaneous   surround
separate   statistics   susceptible
sergeant   stopped   suspicious
several   strategy   syllable
shining   strength   symbol
simile   strenuous   symmetrical
simply   stubbornness   synonymous
sincerely   subordinate

T

tangible   themselves   tournament
technical   theories   tourniquet
technique   therefore   tragedy
temperature   thorough   transferred
tenant   though   truly
tendency   through   twelfth
than/then   till   tyranny
their/there/they're tomorrow

U

unanimous   unnecessary   usage
unconscious   until   usually
undoubtedly

V

vacuum   vengeance   villain
valuable   vigilant   violence
varies   village   visible

W

warrant   wherever   women
weather/whether   wholly   writing
Wednesday   whose/who's   written
weird   woman

XYZ

yacht   your/you're   zoology
yield

(2)   Making your own spelling list

Each of us has individual spelling problems, so you should compile a list of your own problem words. When you write a first
draft, circle any words whose spelling you are unsure of. Then
look them up in your dictionary as you revise, and add them all
(even those you have guessed correctly) to your list. When your
instructor returns a paper, you should record on your list any
words you have misspelled. In addition, record words that you
encounter when reading, including those from class notes and
textbooks. It is especially important that you master words that
are basic to a course or given field of study.

> Review your list periodically so that the correct spelling of
your problem words becomes a part of your long-term memory.

**sp
20c**

(3)   Uncovering patterns of misspelling

In addition to studying individual words, review your list as a
whole to see whether any patterns of misspelling emerge. Do you
consistently have a problem with plurals, or with *-ible/-able* endings? If so, review the spelling rules that apply to these particular
problems. By using this strategy to get at the source of your spelling difficulties, you can eliminate the need to memorize single
words.

(4)   Fixing each word in your mind

Once you isolate the words that you consistently misspell, take
the time to think of associations that will help fix the correct
spellings in your mind. For example, you can arrive at the correct
spelling of *definite* (often misspelled *definate*) by remembering
that it contains the word *finite*, which suggests the concept of
limit, as does *definite.* You can recall the *a* in *brilliance* (often
misspelled *brillience*) by remembering that brilliant people often
get *A*'s in their classes. You can master the spelling of *criticism* by
remembering that it contains the word *critic.*

> Another way of fixing words in your mind is to write them
down. When you review your spelling list, do not just *read* the
words on it; *write* them. This repeated copying will help you
remember the correct spellings.

☐   **EXERCISE 5**

Begin your own spelling list by selecting thirty words from the list of
commonly misspelled words on pages 341–344. Choose ten especially
troublesome words from your list, and think of associations to help you
remember them.

SECTION V

Understanding Grammar

21

Identifying the Parts of Speech

The eight basic parts of speech—the building blocks for all English sentences—are *nouns, pronouns, verbs, adjectives, adverbs, prepositions, conjunctions,* and *interjections.* The part of speech to which a word belongs depends on its function in a sentence.

21a Nouns

Nouns name people, places, things, ideas, actions, or qualities.

A **common noun** names any of a class of people, places, or things: *artist, judge, building, event, city.*

A **proper noun,** always capitalized, refers to a particular person, place, or thing: *Mary Cassatt, Learned Hand, World Trade Center, Crimean War, St. Louis.*

A **mass noun** names a quantity that is not countable: *time, dust, work, gold.* Mass nouns are generally treated as singular.

A **collective noun** designates a group of people, places, or things thought of as a unit: *committee, class, navy, band, family.* Collective nouns are generally treated as singular unless the sentence clearly refers to the members of the group as individuals.

An **abstract noun** refers to an intangible idea or quality: *love, hate, justice, anger, fear, prejudice.*

21b Pronouns

Pronouns are words that may be used in place of nouns in a sentence. The noun for which a pronoun stands is called its antecedent. There are eight different types of pronouns. Note that different types of pronouns may have the same forms but are distinguished by *their functions in the sentence.*

A **personal pronoun** stands for a person or thing: *I, me, we, us, my, mine, our, ours, you, your, yours, he, she, it, its, one, one's, him, his, her, hers, they, them, their, theirs.*

They made her an offer she couldn't refuse.

An **indefinite pronoun** functions in a sentence as a noun but does not refer to any particular person or thing. For this reason, indefinite pronouns do not require antecedents. Indefinite pronouns include *another, any, each, few, many, some, nothing, anyone, everyone, everybody, everything, someone, something, either,* and *neither.*

Many are called, but few are chosen.

A **reflexive pronoun** is one that ends with *-self* and refers back to the sentence's or clause's subject: *myself, yourself, himself, herself, itself, oneself, themselves, ourselves, yourselves.*

They found themselves in downtown Pittsburgh.

An **intensive pronoun** ends with *-self* and emphasizes a noun or pronoun in the sentence.

Darrow himself was sure his client was innocent.

A **relative pronoun** introduces an adjective or noun clause in a sentence: *which, who, whom, that, what, whose, whatever, whoever, whomever, whichever.*

Gandhi was the charismatic man who helped lead India to independence. (introduces adjective clause)

Whatever happens will be a surprise. (introduces noun clause)

An **interrogative pronoun** introduces a question: *who, which, what, whom, whose, whoever, whatever, whichever.*

Who was that masked man?

A **demonstrative pronoun** points to a particular thing or group of things: *this, that, these, those.*

This is one of Shakespeare's early plays.

A **reciprocal pronoun** denotes a mutual relationship: *each other, one another.*

Ah, love, let us be true/to one another! (Matthew Arnold, "Dover Beach")

gr
21b

21c Verbs

A **verb** may either express action or a state of being.

> He <u>ran</u> for the train. (action)
>
> Elizabeth II <u>became</u> queen after the death of her father, George VI. (state of being)

Verbs can be classified into two groups: main verbs and auxiliary verbs (sometimes called helping verbs).

Main verbs carry most of the meaning in the sentence or clause in which they appear.

> Bulfinch's *Mythology* <u>contains</u> a discussion of Greek mythology.
>
> Emily Dickinson <u>anticipated</u> much of twentieth-century poetry.

A main verb is a **linking verb** when it is followed by a **subject complement,** a word or phrase that defines or describes the subject. Linking verbs include forms of the verb *be;* the verbs *become, seem, appear, believe, grow, turn, remain,* and *prove;* and verbs that denote the five senses.

> Kevin <u>is</u> bright.
>
> Carbon disulfide <u>smells</u> bad.

Auxiliary verbs such as *be* and *have* combine with main verbs to form **verb phrases.** The auxiliary verbs indicate tense, voice, mood, and so on.

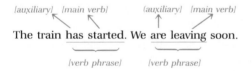

Certain auxiliary verbs, known as **modal auxiliaries** *(must, will, would, shall, should, may, might, can, could, need [to],* and *ought [to]),* indicate necessity, possibility, willingness, obligation, or ability.

> In the near future farmers <u>might</u> cultivate seaweed as a food crop.
>
> Coal mining <u>would</u> be safer if dust were controlled in the mines.

Verbals, such as *known* or *running* or *to go,* are **nonfinite verbs.** That is, they do not change form to indicate person, tense, and number. They cannot serve as a sentence's main verb unless used with an auxiliary. Verbals include *participles, infinitives,* and *gerunds.*

Virtually every verb has a **present participle,** which ends in
-ing (loving, learning, going, writing), and a **past participle,** which
usually ends in *-d* or *-ed (agreed, learned).* Some verbs have irregular past participles *(gone, begun, written).* Participles may function in a sentence as adjectives or as nouns.

Twenty brands of running shoes were displayed at the exhibition.
(Present participle *running* serves as adjective modifying noun
shoes.)

The crowded bus went right by those waiting at the corner. (Past
participle *crowded* serves as adjective modifying noun *bus.*)

The wounded were given emergency first aid. (Past participle
wounded serves as sentence's subject.)

An **infinitive**—the base form of the verb preceded by *to*—
may serve as an adjective, an adverb, or a noun.

gr
21d

Ann Arbor was clearly the place to be. (Infinitive *to be* serves as
adjective modifying noun *place.*)

They say that breaking up is hard to do. (Infinitive *to do* serves as
adverb modifying adjective *hard.*)

Carla went outside to think. (Infinitive *to think* serves as adverb
modifying verb *went.*)

To win was everything. (Infinitive *to win* serves as sentence's subject.)

Gerunds, special forms of verbs ending in *-ing,* are always
used as nouns.

Seeing is believing. (Gerund *seeing* serves as sentence's subject;
gerund *believing* serves as subject complement.)

He worried about interrupting. (Gerund *interrupting* is object of
preposition *about.*)

Andrew loves skiing. (Gerund *skiing is* direct object of verb *loves.*)

NOTE: When the *-ing* form of a verb is used as a noun, as it is here,
it is considered a *gerund;* when it is used as a modifier, it is a
present participle.

21d Adjectives

Adjectives are words that describe, limit, qualify, or in any other
way modify nouns or pronouns.

Descriptive adjectives, the largest class of adjectives, name
a quality of the noun or pronoun they modify.

Strike while the iron is <u>hot</u>.

They ordered a <u>chocolate</u> soda and a <u>butterscotch</u> sundae.

The <u>little</u> one is the runt of the litter.

Some descriptive adjectives are formed from common nouns or from verbs *(friend/friendly, agree/agreeable).* Others, called **proper adjectives,** are formed from proper nouns.

Eubie Blake was a talented <u>American</u> musician who died in 1983.

The <u>Shakespearean</u> or <u>English</u> sonnet consists of an octave and a sestet.

Two or more words may be joined, with or without a hyphen, to form a **compound adjective** *(foreign born, well-read).* (See 34b.1)

Another class of adjectives is composed of words like articles, pronouns, and numbers. When these words are used to limit or qualify nouns they are considered adjectives.

gr 21e

Articles *(a, an, the).*

<u>The</u> boy found <u>a</u> four-leaf clover.

Possessive adjectives (the personal pronouns *my, your, his, her, its, our, their, one's).*

<u>Their</u> lives depended on <u>my</u> skill.

Demonstrative adjectives *(this, these, that, those).*

<u>This</u> song reminds me of <u>that</u> song we heard yesterday.

Interrogative adjectives *(what, which, whose).*

<u>Whose</u> book is this?

Indefinite adjectives *(another, each, both, many, any, some,* and so on).

<u>Both</u> candidates agreed to return <u>another</u> day.

Relative adjectives *(what, whatever, which, whichever, whose, whosever).*

I forgot <u>whatever</u> reasons I had for leaving.

Numerical adjectives *(one, two, first, second,* and so on).

The <u>first</u> time I played I only got <u>one</u> hit.

21e   Adverbs

Adverbs are words that describe the action of verbs or modify adjectives, other adverbs, or complete phrases, clauses, or sentences. They answer the questions "How?" "Why?" "Where?" "When?" "To what extent?" and "To what degree?"

> He walked <u>rather hesitantly</u> toward the front of the room.
>
> It seems <u>so</u> long since we met <u>here yesterday</u>.
>
> <u>Unfortunately</u>, the program didn't run.
>
> Cody's brother and sister were <u>staggeringly</u> unobservant. (Anne Tyler, *Dinner at the Homesick Restaurant)*

Interrogative adverbs—the words *how, why,* and *where*—introduce questions. (*Why* did the compound darken?)

Conjunctive adverbs join and relate independent clauses.

Commonly Used Conjunctive Adverbs

accordingly	furthermore	meanwhile	similarly
also	hence	moreover	still
anyway	however	nevertheless	then
besides	incidentally	next	thereafter
certainly	indeed	nonetheless	therefore
consequently	instead	now	thus
finally	likewise	otherwise	undoubtedly

Conjunctive adverbs may appear in any of several positions in a sentence.

> Jason forgot to register for chemistry. However, he managed to sign up during the drop/add period. (conjunctive adverb placed at beginning of sentence)
>
> Jason forgot to register for chemistry; however, he managed to sign up during the drop/add period. (conjunctive adverb placed at beginning of clause)
>
> Jason forgot to register for chemistry. He managed, however, to sign up during the drop/add period. (conjunctive adverb set within sentence)
>
> Jason forgot to register for chemistry. He managed to sign up during the drop/add period, however. (conjunctive adverb placed at end of sentence)

21f Prepositions ——————————————

A **preposition** introduces a word or word group consisting of one or more nouns or pronouns or of a phrase or clause functioning in the sentence as a noun. The word or word group the preposition introduces is called its **object**.

prep   *obj*   *prep*   *obj*

They received a postcard from Bobby which told them about his trip

prep   *obj*

to the Soviet Union.

gr
21g

Frequently Used Prepositions

about	beneath	inside	since
above	beside	into	through
across	between	like	throughout
after	beyond	near	to
against	by	of	toward
along	concerning	off	under
among	despite	on	underneath
around	down	onto	until
as	during	out	up
at	except	outside	upon
before	for	over	with
behind	from	past	within
below	in	regarding	without

21g Conjunctions

Conjunctions are words used to connect single words, phrases, clauses, or sentences.

    Coordinating conjunctions *(and, or, but, nor, for, so, yet)* connect words, phrases, or clauses of equal weight.

> He had to choose pheasant or venison. (Coordinating conjunction links two nouns.)

> . . . of the people, by the people, and for the people (Coordinating conjunction links three prepositional phrases.)

> Thoreau wrote *Walden* in 1854, and he died in 1862. (Coordinating conjunction connects two independent clauses.)

    Correlative conjunctions, always used in pairs, also link items of equal weight (see 8a.3).

Frequently Used Correlative Conjunctions

both . . . and	not only . . . but also
either . . . or	whether . . . or
neither . . . nor	just as . . . so

<u>Both</u> Hancock <u>and</u> Jefferson signed the Declaration of Independence. (Pair of correlative conjunctions connects two nouns.)

<u>Either</u> I will renew my lease, <u>or</u> I will move. (Pair of correlative conjunctions links two independent clauses.)

Subordinating conjunctions (*since, because, although, if, after, when, while, before, unless,* and so on) introduce adverb clauses. Thus, a subordinating conjunction connects the sentence's main (independent) clause with a subordinate (dependent) clause (see 8b).

<u>Although</u> drug use is a serious concern for parents, many parents are afraid to discuss it with their children.

It is best to draw a diagram of your garden <u>before</u> you start to plant it.

For a list of the most commonly used subordinating conjunctions, see 8b.

Conjunctive adverbs, also known as adverbial conjunctions, are discussed in 21e.

gr
21h

21h Interjections

Interjections are words used as exclamations: *Oh! Ouch! Wow! Alas! Hey!* These words, which express emotion, are grammatically independent; that is, they do not have a grammatical function in a sentence. Interjections may be set off in a sentence by commas.

The message, alas, arrived too late.

Or, for greater emphasis, they can be punctuated as independent units, set off with an exclamation point.

Alas! The message arrived too late.

Other words besides interjections are also sometimes used in isolation. These include words like *yes, no, hello, good-bye, please,* and *thank you.* All such words, including interjections, may be collectively referred to as **isolates.**

22

Nouns and Pronouns

Case

Case is the form a noun or pronoun takes to indicate how it functions in a sentence. English has three cases: objective, subjective, and possessive.

As the English language developed, nouns generally lost their case distinctions and now change form only in the possessive case: the *cat's* eyes, *Bradley's* book (see 29a). Therefore, discussions of case usually focus on pronouns.

In English, only the pronouns *I, we, he, she, they,* and *who* change forms in all cases.

Pronoun Case Forms

Subjective

I	he, she	it	we	you	they	who	whoever

Objective

me	him, her	it	us	you	them	whom	whomever

Possessive

my	his, her	its	our	your	their	whose
(mine)	(hers)		(ours)	(yours)	(theirs)	

22a   Using the Subjective Case

A pronoun takes the **subjective case** when it acts as the *subject of a verb;* when it serves as a *subject complement;* when it is the *subject of a clause;* and when it is an *appositive identifying the subject.*

> David and I bought the same kind of ten-speed bicycle. (*I* is the subject of a verb.)

> It was he the men were looking for. (*He* is the subject complement.)

> The sergeant asked whoever wanted to volunteer to step forward. (*Whoever* is the subject of the noun clause *whoever wanted to step forward.*)

> Both scientists, Oppenheimer and he, worked on the atomic bomb. (*Oppenheimer and he* is an appositive identifying the subject *Both scientists.*)

NOTE: Using the proper case for subject complements sometimes creates forced-sounding constructions. Most people feel silly saying "It is I" or "It is he," and they use the more natural colloquial constructions "It's me" or "It's him" in speech or informal writing.

ca
22b

22b   Using the Objective Case

A pronoun takes the **objective case** when it acts as a *direct object,* an *indirect object,* an *object of a preposition,* an *object of an infinitive,* an *object of a gerund,* a *subject of an infinitive,* or an *appositive identifying an object.*

> Our sociology teacher likes Adam and me. (*Me* is a direct object of the verb *likes.*)

> During the 1950's the *Kinsey Report* gave them quite a shock. (*Them* is the indirect object of the verb *gave.*)

> In 1502 Leonardo da Vinci designed the fortifications of the city for him. (*Him* is the object of the preposition *for.*)

> Hoover did not want to anger Alfred E. Smith or him. (*Him* is the object of the infinitive *to anger.*)

> Finding her was not easy for Marlow. (*Her* is the object of the gerund *finding.*)

> They told him to defend his flank against the French cavalry. (*Him* is the subject of the infinitive *to defend.*)

> Rachel discussed both authors, Hannah Arendt and her. (*Hannah Arendt and her* is an appositive identifying the object *authors.*)

NOTE: Discard the mistaken idea that *I* is somehow always more appropriate than *me.* This impulse to overcorrect is often expressed in compound constructions.

He told Jason and me [not I] to run our computer program. (*Me* is the object of the verb *told*.)

Between you and me [not I] we own ten shares of stock. (*Me* is the object of the preposition *between*.)

Let's you and me [not I] go to the art museum. (*Me* is an appositive identifying *us*, direct object of the verb *let*.)

22c   Using the Possessive Case

A pronoun takes the **possessive case** when it indicates ownership (*our* car, *your* book). Some possessive forms—*his, hers, mine, ours, yours,* and *theirs*—may be used alone in a noun position in place of a noun.

**ca
22c**

The blue Volvo is mine.

Last year we all decided to plant gardens; theirs grew vegetables, and ours grew weeds.

In your sentences be sure to distinguish gerunds, which always function as nouns, from present participles functioning as adjectives (see 21c). Keep in mind that in college writing you should use the possessive, not the objective, before the gerund.

Napoleon approved of their ruling Naples. (*Ruling* is a gerund.)

You should not, however, use the possessive case with a participle.

The astronaut orbiting the earth saw flecks of white crystals. (*Orbiting* is a participle that serves as an adjective.)

NOTE: Remember the distinction between the possessive pronoun *its* and the contraction *it's*. *Its* designates possession (*its* leg) while *it's* is the contraction of *it is* ("*It's* a nice day") or *it has* ("*It's* faded in the sunlight").

☐   **EXERCISE 1**

Choose the correct form of the pronoun within the parentheses. Be prepared to explain why you chose each form.

EXAMPLE: Traveling down the Columbia River, Balboa and (he, him) sighted the Pacific Ocean.

1. Rodin and (he, him) participated in the Paris exhibit.
2. It was (they, them) who fought in the revolution of 1848.
3. Milton Friedman says it is (us, we) who are responsible for the declining dollar.
4. Both writers, Conrad and (he, him), wrote books about the sea.

5. My father gave Brian and (I, me) advice.
6. The heat along with the humidity made (he, him) sick.
7. The foreman agreed to (me, my) working there.
8. Hester was disturbed by (his, him) ignoring her.
9. (Us, We) students deserve better food.
10. Marat, Robespierre, and (he, him) were the most radical members of the cabinet.

22d Correcting Common Errors: Case

(1) Omitted words

In constructions where words are left out but definitely under-stood, the case of a pronoun depends on the missing words. Implied comparisons using *than* or *as* are especially trouble-some. When a sentence that has implied elements ends with a pronoun, your meaning dictates your choice of pronoun.

ca
22d

Darcy likes John more than I. *(more than I like John)*
Darcy likes John more than me. *(more than she likes me)*
Alex helps Dr. Elliott as much as I. *(as much as I help)*
Alex helps Dr. Elliott as much as me. *(as much as he helps me)*

(2) *Who* and *whom*

The case of the pronouns *who* and *whom* depends on their func-tion within their own clause. When a pronoun serves as the sub-ject, use *who* or *whoever;* when it functions as an object, use *whom* or *whomever.*

The Salvation Army gives food and shelter to whoever is in need. (*Whoever* is the subject of the verb *is* in the dependent clause; the entire clause *whoever is in need* serves as the object of the prepo-sition *to.*)

Shortly after leaving Oklahoma the Joads were reminded who they were and where they came from. (*Who* is the subject complement of the verb *were* even though the entire clause serves as the ob-ject of the verb *reminded.*)

I wonder whom Rousseau influenced. (*Whom* is the object of *in-fluenced;* the entire clause *whom Rousseau influenced* is the object of the verb *wonder.*)

Whomever Stieglitz photographed, he revealed. (*Whomever* is the object of *photographed;* the entire clause is the direct object of the verb *revealed.*)

Watch out for intervening phrases such as *I think, we know, or she or he says.* The choice of *who* or *whom* depends upon how the pronoun functions in its own clause. If intervening phrases cause problems, read the sentence without the intervening phrase.

> Isaac Newton is the man who [we know] revolutionized the science of physics. (*Who* is the subject of the clause *who we know revolutionized the science of physics.*)

To determine the case of *who* at the beginning of a question, answer the question using a personal pronoun.

> <u>Who</u> wrote *Gone with the Wind*? <u>She</u> wrote it. (Subject)
>
> <u>Whom</u> do you want for mayor? I want <u>her</u>. (Object)
>
> For <u>whom</u> is the letter? It is for <u>him</u>. (Object of a preposition)

**ca
22d**

NOTE: Although formal writing requires that *whom* be used for all objects, strict adherence to this rule can result in stilted constructions. In all but the most formal situations, current usage accepts *who* at the beginning of questions.

> <u>Who</u> do you want for Mayor?
>
> <u>Who</u> is the letter for?

☐   **EXERCISE 2**

Using the word in parentheses, combine each pair of sentences into a single sentence. You may change word order and add or delete words.

> EXAMPLE: Lee is a carpenter. Many people employ him. (whom)
>
>   Lee is a carpenter whom many people employ.

1. Henry Ford was a famous automobile manufacturer.
   He introduced his Model T in 1908. (who)
2. Christopher Columbus interested the king and queen.
   He met them in Madrid in 1486. (whom)
3. Does anyone know the author?
   He wrote *Catch 22*. (who)
4. He mourned for his friend.
   He last saw him in October. (whom)
5. Wyndham Lewis was a writer.
   He was cofounder and editor of *Blast* magazine in 1914. (who)

Pronoun Reference

An **antecedent** is the word or word group to which a pronoun refers. In the sentence "Melville knew he had written more than a whaling book," *he* refers to the antecedent *Melville*.

Indefinite pronouns, such as *everyone, someone, no one, each,* and *some,* refer to unspecified persons or things; therefore they require no antecedents (see 21b). But most pronouns do have antecedents. Just as pronouns must be in the proper case, they must also refer clearly to their antecedents.

22e   Making Pronoun References Clear ———

A pronoun reference is clear when readers can correctly identify the noun or pronoun whose place it takes. In the following passage, notice how the underscored pronouns point clearly to a definite word.

> Warts are wonderful structures. They can appear overnight on any part of the skin, like mushrooms on a damp lawn, full grown and splendid in the complexity of their architecture. Viewed in stained sections under a microscope, they are the most specialized of cellular arrangements, constructed as though for a purpose. They sit there like turreted mounds of dense impenetrable horn, impregnable, designed for defense against the world outside. (Lewis Thomas, *The Medusa and the Snail)*

Although the pronouns *they* and *their* carry through several sentences, Thomas has made their references to *warts* in the first first sentence quite clear.

☐   **EXERCISE 3**

Supply the proper pronoun for the underlined antecedent.

> EXAMPLE: Indians occupied North America before the arrival of Europeans. They are called Indians because Columbus thought he had reached the Indies.

1. Indians probably migrated into North America from Asia via the Bering Strait. When _____ arrived in Alaska, _____ spread south.
2. Evidence of Indians in America goes back 25,000 years. Consisting of pottery, cave drawings, and artifacts, _____ placed Indians in every part of the continent.
3. Many Indians occupied the Northwest Coast area. According to geological records, _____ was thickly wooded and temperate.
4. The Plains Indians gave other Indians the horse, the tepee, and deerskin clothes. _____ caused great cultural changes.
5. The Plateau Indians occupied the area above the Canadian border. _____ winter villages had subterranean lodges with cone-shaped roofs.

22f Revising Unclear Pronoun References —

When a pronoun refers to more than one antecedent, its reference is ambiguous. Vague pronoun references occur when a pronoun is too far from its antecedent for the reference to be obvious or when it refers to a nonexistent antecedent.

(1) Ambiguous antecedents

The meaning of a pronoun is **ambiguous** if the pronoun appears to refer to more than one antecedent. The pronouns *this, that, which,* and *it* are most likely to invite this kind of confusion. To ensure clarity make sure that each pronoun points to a specific antecedent. Here is an example of an ambiguous reference.

ref 22f

> The accountant took out his calculator and completed the tax return. Then, he put <u>it</u> in his briefcase.

The pronoun *it* can refer either to *calculator* or to *tax return*. The ambiguity can be eliminated if a noun is substituted for the pronoun.

> The accountant took out his calculator and completed the tax return. Then, he put <u>the calculator</u> in his briefcase.

In the following example, the pronoun *this* is the problem.

> Some one-celled organisms contain chlorophyll and are considered animals. <u>This</u> is one reason one-celled organisms are difficult to classify.

This can refer either to the fact that some one-celled organisms are animals or to the fact that they contain chlorophyll. It could also refer to the implied idea that some one-celled organisms are not easily classified as plants or animals. Recasting the sentence and repeating the antecedent eliminates this ambiguous reference.

> Some one-celled organisms that contain chlorophyll are considered animals. <u>This fact</u> points out the difficulty of classifying single-celled organisms as either animals or plants.

If you are certain that no misunderstanding will occur, you can use *this, that, which,* or *it* to refer to a previous clause.

> Visitors would constantly interrupt Edison. <u>This</u> made him angry.

Be careful, however. General references often invite confusion.

(2)   Remote antecedents

The farther a pronoun is from its antecedent, the more difficult it is for readers to make a connection between them. As a result, readers lose track of meaning and must reread a passage to determine the connection. Here is an example.

> Rumors of gold, letters from friends and relatives, and newspaper articles praising democracy persuaded many Czechs to come to America. By 1860 about 23,000 Czechs had left their country. Many immigrants were children under the age of twelve. By 1900, 13,000 Czech immigrants were coming to <u>its</u> shores each year.

The pronoun *its* in the last sentence is so far removed from its antecedent, *America,* that the reference cannot easily be understood. For clarity, the antecedent should be restated in the final sentence.

> By 1900, 13,000 Czech immigrants were coming to <u>America's</u> shores each year.

ref
22f

(3)   Unidentified antecedents

An unclear pronoun reference also occurs when a pronoun refers to a nonexistent antecedent.

> Our township has decided to build a computer lab in the elementary school. <u>They</u> feel that children should learn to use computers in fourth grade.

In the second sentence *they* seems to refer to *township* as a collective noun. Actually *they* refers to an antecedent that the writer has neglected to mention. Supplying the noun *teachers* eliminates the confusion.

> Our township has decided to build a computer lab in the elementary school. <u>Teachers</u> feel that children should learn to use computers in fourth grade.

References such as "*It* says in the paper" and "*They* said on the news" refer to unidentified antecedents and therefore are incorrect. To correct this problem, substitute the noun for the unclear pronoun: "*The article* in the paper says. . . ." and "In his commentary, *Ted Koppel* said. . . ."

☐   **EXERCISE 4**

Analyze the pronoun errors in each of the following sentences about the Lewis and Clark expedition. After doing so revise each sentence by substituting an appropriate noun or noun phrase for the underlined pronoun.

> EXAMPLE: Jefferson asked Lewis to head the expedition, and Lewis selected him as his associate.
>
> ANALYSIS: *Him* refers to a nonexistent antecedent.
>
> REVISION: Jefferson asked Lewis to head the expedition, and Lewis selected Clark as his associate.

ref
22f

1. The purpose of the expedition was to search out a land route to the Pacific and to gather information about the West. The Louisiana Purchase increased the need for it.
2. The expedition was going to be difficult. They trained the men in Illinois, the starting point.
3. Clark and most of the men descended the Yellowstone River and camped on the bank. It was beautiful and wild.
4. Both Jefferson and Lewis had faith he would be successful in his transcontinental journey.
5. The expedition was efficient, and only one man was lost. This was extraordinary.

Student Writer at Work: Nouns and Pronouns

Following is part of a draft of an essay about John Updike. This section of the essay gives a plot summary of Updike's short story "A & P." Read the draft and revise it to correct errors in case and to eliminate inexact pronoun reference. After you have corrected the errors, go over the draft again and, if necessary, revise further to strengthen coherence, unity, and style.

> John Updike's "A & P" is the fourteenth short story in the book Pigeon Feathers. It takes place in a small town similar to Updike's hometown. The character who has the significant role in "A & P" is Sammy, a cashier at the supermarket. Sammy is a nineteen-year-old boy whom is just out of high school. He analyzes everyone who comes to the A & P to shop. It is him who is the narrator of the story.
>
> The story takes place on a Thursday afternoon when three girls in bathing suits walk into the store. They are different from the other shoppers. Their manner and the way they walk make them different from them. Sammy

notices that one of the girls, who he calls Queenie, leads
the other girls. This appeals to him. He identifies with
her because he feels that he too is a leader.

When the girls come to his check—out counter, he rings
up their purchase. Suddenly the store manager, Lengel,
begins scolding the girls for coming into the store in
bathing suits. Sammy feels sorry for them, and in a
gesture of defiance he quits. Sammy feels that him
quitting is a rejection of him and all that he stands
for. To Sammy, Lengel is a drab person who represents the
narrow morality of the town.

Sammy quitting is the climax of the story. Sammy
chooses to follow his conscience and in doing so pays the
price. He feels that not following his ideals would be
bad. Because he is young, however, he does not realize
the significance of his act. For a moment Lengel and
Sammy face each other, but he does not change his mind.
Sammy feels that he has won his freedom. His confidence
is short—lived though. When he walks out into the parking
lot, the girls are gone, and he is alone. It is then he
realizes that the world is going to be hard for him from
this point on.

**ref
22**

23

Verbs

Verb Forms

All verbs have four **principal parts** from which their tenses are derived: a **base form** (the form of the verb used with *I, we, you,* and *they* in the present tense),* a **present participle,** a **past tense form,** and a **past participle.** Most verbs in English are **regular** and form their principal parts with *-ing* and *-ed* or *-d* added to the base form.

Base Form	Present Participle	Past	Past Participle
smile	smiling	smiled	smiled
talk	talking	talked	talked
jump	jumping	jumped	jumped

Irregular verbs, however, do not follow this pattern.

23a Identifying the Principal Parts of Irregular Verbs

Many irregular verbs change an internal vowel in the past tense and past participle.

Base Form	Present Participle	Past	Past Participle
begin	beginning	began	begun
come	coming	came	come
fly	flying	flew	flown

Other irregular verbs not only change an internal vowel in the past tense but also add *-n* or *-en* to the past participle.

---

* NOTE: The verb *be* is so irregular that it is the one exception to this definition; its base form is *be.*

Base Form	*Present Participle*	*Past*	*Past Participle*
fall	falling	fell	fallen
rise	rising	rose	risen
write	writing	wrote	written

Still other irregular verbs take the same form in both the past and the past participle forms.

Base Form	*Present Participle*	*Past*	*Past Participle*
bet	betting	bet (betted)	bet
have	having	had	had
spin	spinning	spun	spun

23b   Using Standard Verb Forms

Consult a dictionary whenever you are uncertain about the form of a verb. If only the base form is listed, the verb is regular and forms both its past tense and past participle by adding -*d* or -*ed*. If the verb is irregular, the dictionary lists its forms, three if the past tense and past participle are different and two if the past tense and the past participle are the same.

hide, v (past hid, pp hidden)

fall, v (past fell, pp fallen)

make, v (made)

spin, v (spun)

The following list presents the irregular verbs that can cause trouble. If you have problems with some of these verbs, familiarize yourself with their principal parts, and refer to this list when you edit your writing.

Base Form	*Present Participle*	*Past*	*Past Participle*
arise	arising	arose	arisen
awake	awaking	awoke, awaked	awoke, awaked
be	being	was/were	been
bear (carry)	bearing	bore	borne
beat	beating	beat	beaten
begin	beginning	began	begun
bend	bending	bent	bent
bet	betting	bet, betted	bet
bid	bidding	bid	bid
bind	binding	bound	bound
bite	biting	bit	bitten

Base Form	Present Participle	Past	Past Participle
bleed	bleeding	bled	bled
blow	blowing	blew	blown
break	breaking	broke	broken
bring	bringing	brought	brought
build	building	built	built
burn	burning	burned, burnt	burned, burnt
burst	bursting	burst	burst
buy	buying	bought	bought
catch	catching	caught	caught
choose	choosing	chose	chosen
cling	clinging	clung	clung
come	coming	came	come
creep	creeping	crept	crept
cut	cutting	cut	cut
deal	dealing	dealt	dealt
dig	digging	dug	dug
dive	diving	dived, dove	dived
do	doing	did	done
drag	dragging	dragged	dragged
draw	drawing	drew	drawn
drink	drinking	drank	drunk
drive	driving	drove	driven
eat	eating	ate	eaten
fall	falling	fell	fallen
feed	feeding	fed	fed
feel	feeling	felt	felt
fight	fighting	fought	fought
find	finding	found	found
fling	flinging	flung	flung
fly	flying	flew	flown
forbid	forbidding	forbade, forbad	forbidden, forbid
forget	forgetting	forgot	forgotten, forgot
forsake	forsaking	forsook	forsaken
freeze	freezing	froze	frozen
get	getting	got	got, gotten
give	giving	gave	given
go	going	went	gone
grind	grinding	ground	ground
grow	growing	grew	grown
hang (suspend)	hanging	hung	hung
hang (execute)	hanging	hanged	hanged
have	having	had	had
hear	hearing	heard	heard

vbs 23b

Base Form	Present Participle	Past	Past Participle
hit	hitting	hit	hit
keep	keeping	kept	kept
know	knowing	knew	known
lay	laying	laid	laid
lead	leading	led	led
leap	leaping	leaped, leapt	leaped, leapt
learn	learning	learned, learnt	learned, learnt
lend	lending	lent	lent
let	letting	let	let
lie (recline)	lying	lay	lain
lie (tell an untruth)	lying	lied	lied
light	lighting	lighted, lit	lighted, lit
mow	mowing	mowed	mowed, mown
plead	pleading	pleaded, pled	pleaded, pled
prove	proving	proved	proved, proven
put	putting	put	put
read	reading	read	read
rid	ridding	rid, ridded	rid, ridded
ride	riding	rode	ridden
ring	ringing	rang	rung
rise	rising	rose	risen
run	running	ran	run
see	seeing	saw	seen
seek	seeking	sought	sought
set	setting	set	set
shake	shaking	shook	shaken
shed	shedding	shed	shed
shine	shining	shone	shone
shoe	shoeing	shod, shoed	shod, shoed
shrink	shrinking	shrank, shrunk	shrunk, shrunken
sing	singing	sang	sung
sink	sinking	sank	sunk
sit	sitting	sat	sat
slay	slaying	slew	slain
sneak	sneaking	sneaked	sneaked
sow	sowing	sowed	sowed, sown
speak	speaking	spoke	spoken
speed	speeding	sped, speeded	sped, speeded
spin	spinning	spun	spun
spring	springing	sprang	sprung
stand	standing	stood	stood
steal	stealing	stole	stolen
stick	sticking	stuck	stuck
strike	striking	struck	struck, stricken
strive	striving	strove	striven

vbs
23b

Base Form	Present Participle	Past	Past Participle
swear	swearing	swore	sworn
swim	swimming	swam	swum
swing	swinging	swung	swung
take	taking	took	taken
teach	teaching	taught	taught
tear	tearing	tore	torn
think	thinking	thought	thought
throw	throwing	threw	thrown
tread	treading	trod	trodden, trod
wake	waking	woke	waked, woke, wakened
wear	wearing	wore	worn
weave	weaving	wove	woven
wed	wedding	wed, wedded	wed, wedded
weep	weeping	wept	wept
win	winning	won	won
wind	winding	wound	wound
wring	wringing	wrung	wrung
write	writing	wrote	written

**vbs
23b**

☐   **EXERCISE 1**

Complete the following sentences with an appropriate form of the verbs in parentheses.

> EXAMPLE: The inhabitants of Easter Island _____ Polynesian. (be)
>
> The inhabitants of Easter Island __are__ Polynesian.

1. John Hancock _____ to write his name first on the Declaration of Independence. (choose)
2. In *The Scarlet Letter* Hester Prynne _____ the consequences of her guilt. (bear)
3. Before mechanization workers _____ the water out of the fabric by hand. (wring)
4. Daedalus warned his son what would happen if he _____ too close to the sun. (fly)
5. John Brown was _____ for his attack on Harpers Ferry, Virginia. (hang)

Tense

Tense is the form of a verb that indicates when an action occurred or when a condition existed. Tense, however, is not the same as time. The present tense, for example, indicates present time, but it can also indicate future time or a generally held belief.

English has three tenses. The **simple tenses** consist of the present, past, and future. The **perfect tenses,** formed with the auxiliaries *have* and *had* plus the past participle, include the present perfect, the past perfect, and the future perfect. The **progressive tenses** are formed with the appropriate tense of the verb *be* plus the present participle.

23c   Using the Simple Tenses

(1)   The present tense (*I finish, she* or *he finishes*)

The **present tense** usually indicates that an action is taking place when you are speaking or writing. With subjects other than singular nouns or third-person singular pronouns, the present tense uses just the base form of the verb.

> I smile when I am nervous.
> They wear wool in the winter.

With singular nouns or third-person singular pronouns, *-s* or *-es* is added to the base form.

> She smiles when she is nervous.
> He wears wool in the winter.

In addition to expressing action in the present, the present tense has some special uses.

> The rector opens the chapel every morning at six o'clock. (indicates that something occurs regularly)
> The grades arrive next Thursday. (indicates future time)
> Studying pays off. (states a generally held belief)
> An object at rest tends to stay at rest. (states a scientific truth)
> In *The Catcher in the Rye* Holden Caulfield spends a weekend wandering through New York City. (discusses the plot, characters, or meaning of literary works)

Notice that in some cases the words *every* and *next* help to indicate time.

(2)   The past tense (*I finished*)

The **past tense** is the form of the verb that indicates that an action has taken place. It is formed by adding *-d* or *-ed* to the base form or, for irregular verbs, by changing the form of the verb. The past tense has two uses.

Charles Lindbergh <u>flew</u> across the Atlantic Ocean on May 20, 1927. (indicates an action completed in the past)

When he <u>was</u> young, Mark Twain <u>traveled</u> across the mining towns of the Southwest. (indicates actions that recurred in the past but did not extend into the present)

(3)   The future tense *(I will finish)*

The **future tense** indicates that an action will take place. A number of constructions can be used to indicate future action, including the present tense (see 23c.1), but here we discuss future tense verb forms. These verb forms consist of the auxiliaries *will* or *shall* plus the present tense. The future tense has the following uses.

**vbs
23d**

Halley's Comet will <u>reappear</u> in 2061. (indicates a future action that will definitely occur)

The college has announced it will <u>require</u> all freshmen to buy microprocessors. (indicates intention)

If you expose white phosphorous to oxygen, a violent reaction <u>will occur</u>. (indicates what will happen if certain conditions occur)

The land boom in Florida <u>will</u> most likely <u>continue</u>. (indicates probability)

NOTE: At one time *will* was used exclusively for the second- and third-person future of a verb, and *shall* was used for the first person. Except in formal usage, however, *shall* is now rare.

23d   Using the Perfect Tenses   ——————

The perfect tenses designate actions that were or will be completed before other actions or conditions. The perfect tenses are formed with the appropriate tense form of the auxiliary verb *have* plus the past participle.

(1)   Forming the present perfect tense *(I have finished, she* or *he has finished)*

The **present perfect** can indicate three types of continuing action that begin in the past.

Dr. Kim <u>has finished</u> studying the effects of BHA on rats. (indicates an action that begins in the past and is finished when you are speaking or writing)

My father <u>has invested</u> his money wisely. (indicates an action that begins in the past and extends into the present)

I have read all the books in the *Dune* series by Frank Herbert. (indicates an action that occurred at an unspecified past time)

(2)   Forming the past perfect tense *(I had finished)*

The **past perfect** has three uses.

By 1946 engineers had built the first electronic digital computer. (indicates an action occurring before a certain time in the past)

By the time Alfred Wallace wrote his paper, Darwin had already published *The Origin of Species*. (indicates that one action was finished before another one started)

We had hoped to visit the Kennedy Space Center on our trip to Florida. (indicates an unfulfilled desire in the past)

(3)   Forming the future perfect tense *(I will have finished)*

The **future perfect** has two uses.

By Tuesday the transit authority will have run out of money. (indicates that an action will be finished by a certain future time)

By the time a commercial fusion reactor is developed, the government will have spent billions of dollars in research. (indicates that one action will be finished before another occurs in the future)

vbs
23e

23e   Using the Progressive Tense Forms   ———

The tenses discussed so far, the simple tenses and the perfect tenses, are called **common forms.** They indicate a completed, momentary, or habitual action.

English also has **progressive forms** that express continuing action. The progressive forms consist of the appropriate tense of the verb *be* plus the present participle.

(1)   Present progressive tense *(I am finishing, she or he is finishing)*

The **present progressive** has two specific uses.

The volcano is erupting and lava is flowing toward the town. (indicates that something is happening when you are speaking or writing)

Law is becoming an overcrowded profession. (indicates that an action is happening even though it may not be taking place when you are speaking or writing)

(2) Past progressive tense *(I was finishing)*

The **past progressive** has two uses.

> Roderick Usher's actions were becoming increasingly bizarre. (indicates an action continuing in the past)

> The French revolutionary Marat was stabbed to death while he was bathing. (indicates an action occurring at the same time in the past as another action)

(3) Future progressive tense *(I will be finishing)*

The **future progressive** has two uses.

> The Secretary of the Treasury will be carefully monitoring the money supply. (indicates a continuing action in the future)

> Next month NATO forces will be holding military exercises. (indicates a continuing action at a specific future time)

**vbs
23e**

(4) Present perfect progressive tense *(I have been finishing)*

The **present perfect progressive** has only one use.

> The number of women getting lung cancer has been increasing dramatically. (indicates action continuing from the past into the present and possibly into the future)

(5) Past perfect progressive tense *(I had been finishing)*

The **past perfect progressive** has only one use.

> Before Julius Caesar was assassinated, he had been increasing his power. (indicates that one past action went on until a second occurred)

(6) Future perfect progressive tense *(I will have been finishing)*

The **future perfect progressive** has only one use.

> By eleven o'clock we will have been driving for seven hours. (indicates that an action will continue until a certain future time)

☐ **EXERCISE 2**

A verb is missing from each of the following sentences. Fill in the form of the verb indicated in parentheses after each sentence.

EXAMPLE: The full moon _____ now. (rise: present progressive)

The full moon is rising now. (the action is happening when you are writing or speaking)

1. April showers _____ May flowers. (bring: present)
2. Before he sailed through the Straits of Magellan, Sir Francis Drake _____ Robert Dudley. (execute: past)
3. The movie *E.T.* _____ the contact between a traveler from outer space and an earth boy. (examine: present)
4. The Securities and Exchange Commission always _____ the interests of the public regarding the sale of securities. (protect: present perfect)
5. The Hindenburg _____ and people _____ to the ground. (burn, jump: present progressive)
6. Four engineers _____ on this system since March. (work: present perfect progressive)
7. The Environmental Protection Agency _____ cleaning up a chemical dump in North Jersey. (finish: present perfect)
8. Columbus _____ when the man on watch sighted land. (rest: past progressive)
9. By 1895 Sigmund Freud _____ the science of psychoanalysis. (develop: past perfect)
10. To Rutherford current models of the atom _____ questionable. (become: past progressive)

vbs
23f

23f Using the Correct Sequence of Tenses —

The relationship among the verb tenses in a sentence is called the **sequence of tenses.** If the actions of all the verbs in a sentence occur at approximately the same time, the tenses should be the same.

When Katherine Hepburn walked on stage, the audience rose and applauded.

Often, however, a sentence contains several verbs describing actions that occur at different times. The tenses of the verbs must therefore shift. Which tense to use depends both on meaning and on the nature of the clauses in which the verbs occur.

The tense of verbs that appear in adjacent independent clauses can shift as long as their relationships to their subjects and to each other are clear.

The debate was not impressive, but the election will determine the winner.

(1) Verbs in dependent clauses

When a verb appears in a dependent clause, its tense depends on the tense of the main verb in the independent clause. When the main verb in the independent clause is in any tense except the past or past perfect, the verb in the dependent clause may be in any tense needed for meaning.

MAIN VERB	VERB IN DEPENDENT CLAUSE
Ryan <u>knows</u>	that Herman Melville <u>wrote</u> *The Confidence Man.*
The mayor <u>will explain</u>	why she <u>changed</u> her position.

When the main verb is in the past tense, the verb in the dependent clause is usually in the past or past perfect tense. When the main verb is in the past perfect, the verb in the dependent clause is usually in the past tense.

MAIN VERB	VERB IN DEPENDENT CLAUSE
George Hepplewhite <u>was</u> an English cabinetmaker	who <u>designed</u> distinctive chair backs.
The battle <u>had ended</u>	by the time reinforcements <u>arrived</u>.

vbs
23i

(2)   Infinitives in verbal phrases

When an infinitive appears in a verbal phrase, the tense it expresses depends on the tense of the main verb in the independent clause. The *present infinitive* (*to* plus the base form of the verb) indicates an action happening at the same time as or later than the main verb. The *perfect infinitive* (*to have* plus the past participle) indicates action happening earlier than the main verb.

MAIN VERB	INFINITIVE
I <u>went</u>	to <u>hear</u> Carlos Fuentes last week. (The going and hearing occurred at the same time.)
I <u>want</u>	to <u>hear</u> Carlos Fuentes tomorrow. (Wanting is in the present, and hearing is in the future.)
I would have <u>liked</u>	to <u>hear</u> Carlos Fuentes last week. (Both liking and hearing occur at the same time.)
I would <u>like</u>	to <u>have heard</u> Carlos Fuentes lecture. (Liking occurs in the present, and hearing would have occurred in the past.)

(3)   Participles in verbal phrases

When a participle appears in a verbal phrase, its tense depends on the tense of the main verb in the independent clause. The *present participle* indicates action happening at the same time as the action of the main verb. The *past participle* or the *present perfect participle* indicates action occurring before the action of the main verb.

PARTICIPLE	MAIN VERB
Addressing the 1896 Democratic Convention,	William Jennings Bryan delivered his Cross of Gold speech. (The addressing and the delivery occurred at the same time.)
Having published his General Theory of Relativity,	Einstein worked on a Unified Field Theory. (The publishing occurred before the work on the Unified Field Theory.)

☐ EXERCISE 3

**vbs
23f**

From inside each pair of parentheses, choose the correct verb form. Make certain you check the sequence of the verb forms and are able to explain your choices.

> EXAMPLE: When the instructor _____ (speaks, spoke), the class listened.
>
> When the instructor spoke, the class listened. (The action occurred at same time as the action of the main verb.)

1. Alexandre Dumas was a French novelist who (wrote, writes) *The Three Musketeers.*
2. When the war ends, the peasants _____ (will go, will have gone) home.
3. I have stopped writing letters of application because I _____ (have heard, heard) all the jobs are filled.
4. The disgruntled fans left the stadium before the game _____ (had ended, ended).
5. Having studied all night, she _____ (had felt, felt) a sense of accomplishment.
6. Playing poker in a saloon, Wild Bill Hickok _____ (had been shot, was shot) in the back.
7. When the temperature _____ (drops, dropped) below freezing, rain turns to snow.
8. Scientists have studied quasars ever since they _____ (discovered, had discovered) them.

Mood

Mood is the verb form that indicates a writer's basic attitude toward what he or she is saying. For a statement or a question, use the indicative mood; for a command, use the imperative mood; and for a wish or a hypothetical condition, use the subjunctive mood.

23g Using the Indicative Mood

The **indicative** is the mood used to express an opinion, state a fact, or ask a question. It may be used along with a form of *do* for emphasis.

> Jackie Robinson <u>had</u> an impact on American professional baseball.
>
> <u>Did</u> Margaret Mead <u>say</u> that behavioral differences are rooted in culture?

23h Using the Imperative Mood

The **imperative** is the mood used in commands and direct requests. Usually the imperative includes only the base form of the verb without a subject.

> (You) <u>Use</u> a dictionary.
>
> (You) Please <u>vote</u> today.

When you include yourself in a command, use *let's* or *let us* before the base form of the verb.

> <u>Let us examine</u> Machiavelli's view of human nature.
>
> <u>Let's go</u> to the movies.

23i Using the Subjunctive Mood

The **subjunctive mood** is used to state wishes, conditions, and contrary-to-fact statements. It is also used in *that* clauses and in certain idiomatic phrases.

The *present subjunctive* uses the base form of the verb, regardless of the subject. The *past subjunctive* has the same form as the past tense of the verb. (The auxiliary verb *be*, however, takes the form *were* regardless of the number or person of the subject.) The *past perfect subjunctive* has the same form as the past perfect.

> Dr. Gorman suggested that I <u>study</u> the Cambrian period. (present subjunctive)
>
> I wish I <u>were</u> going to Europe. (past subjunctive)
>
> I wish I <u>had gone</u> to the review session. (past perfect subjunctive)

The subjunctive is used in the following cases.

(1)   *That* clauses

The subjunctive is used in *that* clauses after words such as *ask, suggest, require, recommend,* and *demand.*

> The report <u>recommended</u> that juveniles <u>be</u> given mandatory counseling.
>
> During the 1930's Huey Long <u>suggested</u> that personal fortunes above a certain amount <u>be</u> liquidated.
>
> Captain Ahab <u>insisted</u> that his crew <u>hunt</u> the white whale.

(2)   Contrary-to-fact statements

The subjunctive is used in conditional statements that are contrary to fact and in statements that express a wish. A **conditional statement** begins with a dependent *if* clause that presents a condition and concludes with an independent clause that presents the effect of that condition. If the effect is even slightly possible, use the indicative mood for the verb in the *if* clause.

vbs 23i

> If a nuclear treaty <u>is</u> signed, the world will be safer. (A nuclear treaty is possible.)

If the condition is impossible or **contrary to fact,** use the subjunctive mood for the verb in the *if* clause.

> If Teller <u>were</u> there, he would have seen Oppenheimer. (Teller was not there.)

NOTE: A conditional clause beginning with *as if* is contrary to fact and should be in the subjunctive mood.

> The father acted as if he <u>were</u> having the baby. (The father couldn't be having the baby.)

A **wish** is a condition that does not exist and so should be expressed in the subjunctive mood.

> I wish I <u>were</u> more organized.

(3)   Idiomatic expressions

The subjunctive is used in some special expressions.

> If need <u>be</u>, we will stay up all night to finish the report.
>
> <u>Come</u> what may, they will increase their steel production.
>
> Far <u>be</u> it for me to correct an expert.
>
> Special interest groups have, as it <u>were</u>, shifted the balance of power.

☐   **EXERCISE 4**

Complete the sentences in the following paragraph by inserting the appropriate form (indicative, imperative, or subjunctive) of the verb in parentheses. Be prepared to explain your choices.

    Harry Houdini was a famous escape artist. He _____ (perform) escapes from every type of bond imaginable: handcuffs, locks, straitjackets, ropes, sacks, and sealed chests underwater. In Germany workers _____ (challenge) Houdini to escape from a packing box. If he _____ (be) to escape, they would admit that he _____ (be) the best escape artist in the world. Houdini accepted. Before getting into the box he asked that the observers _____ (give) it a thorough examination. He then asked that a worker _____ (nail) him in the box. " _____ (place) a screen around the box," he ordered after he had been sealed inside. In a few minutes Houdini _____ (step) from behind the screen. When the workers demanded that they _____ (see) the box, Houdini pulled down the screen. To their surprise they saw the box with the lid still nailed tightly in place.

vbs

23j

Voice

Voice indicates whether the subject of a verb acts or is acted upon. When the subject of a verb does something—that is, acts—the verb is in the **active voice.**

    ACTIVE VOICE: <u>Hart Crane</u> <u>wrote</u> *The Bridge.*

    When the subject of a verb receives the action—that is, is acted upon—the verb is in the **passive voice.**

    PASSIVE VOICE: <u>The Bridge</u> <u>was written</u> by Hart Crane.

    The active voice is usually briefer, clearer, and more emphatic than the passive voice (see 9e). Some situations, however, require the passive voice for clarity or emphasis.

23j   Using the Passive Voice

The passive voice enables you to emphasize what happened when the person or thing acting is unknown or unimportant.

    DDT <u>was found</u> in local soil samples. (Passive emphasizes finding of DDT, not who found it.)

    We <u>were required</u> to embroider and I had trunkfuls of colorful dish towels, pillowcases, runners, and handkerchiefs to my credit. (Maya Angelou, *I Know Why the Caged Bird Sings*) (Passive emphasizes what they had to do, not who made them do it.)

The passive voice also enables you to emphasize whatever logically receives, or is the logical object of, the action.

> Darwin's faith in fixed species <u>was destroyed</u> on his five-year trip on the *Beagle*. (Emphasis is on fact that Darwin's faith was destroyed, not on who or what destroyed it.)

> The art of the Greek sculptors of the great age <u>is known</u> to us by long familiarity. (Edith Hamilton, *The Greek Way*) (The passive emphasizes the art, not what we know about it.)

> Numerical superiority <u>was achieved</u> by the Allies at the Battle of the Marne. (The passive enables the sentence to focus on superiority.)

NOTE: Because constructions involving passive voice can be awkward or wordy, you should use the passive voice only when you have a good reason (see 10c.3).

vbs
23k

☐   **EXERCISE 5**

Read the following paragraph, and determine which verbs are active and which are passive. Comment if you can on why the author used the passive voice in each case.

> The human species is now undertaking a great venture that if successful will be as important as the colonization of the land or the descent from the trees. We are haltingly, tentatively breaking the shackles of Earth—metaphorically, in confronting and taming the admonitions of those more primitive brains within us; physically, in voyaging to the planets and listening for the messages from the stars. These two enterprises are linked indissolubly. Each, I believe, is a necessary condition for the other. But our energies are directed far more toward war. Hypnotized by mutual mistrust, almost never concerned for the species or the planet, the nations prepare for death. And because what we are doing is so horrifying, we tend not to think of it much. But what we do not consider we are unlikely to put right.   (Carl Sagan, *Cosmos*)

23k   Changing from Passive to Active Voice

You can change a verb from passive to active voice by making the subject of the passive verb the object of the active verb. The person or thing performing the action then becomes the subject of the new sentence.

> PASSIVE: The novel *Frankenstein* <u>was written</u> by Mary Shelley.

In this sentence the subject, *Frankenstein*, receives the action and the object of the preposition, *Mary Shelley*, initiates it. To put this verb into the active voice, you must reorganize the sentence.

ACTIVE: Mary Shelley <u>wrote</u> the novel *Frankenstein.*

Now *Mary Shelley* is the subject, and the novel *Frankenstein* is the object. The emphasis therefore shifts from the recipient of the action to the person initiating it.

You can easily change a verb from passive to active if the sentence contains an *agent* that performs the action. Often the word *by* follows the passive verb *(written by Mary Shelley)*, indicating the agent that can become the subject of an active verb.

If a passive verb has no agent, supply a subject for the active verb; if you cannot, keep the passive construction.

PASSIVE: Baby elephants are taught to avoid humans. (By whom are baby elephants taught?)

ACTIVE: <u>Adult elephants</u> teach baby elephants to avoid humans.

**vbs
23l**

☐   **EXERCISE 6**

Determine which verbs in the following paragraph should be changed from the passive to the active voice. Rewrite the sentences containing these verbs, and be prepared to explain your changes.

Rockets were invented by the Chinese about A.D. 1000. Gunpowder was packed into bamboo tubes and ignited by means of a fuse. These rockets were fired by soldiers at enemy armies and usually caused panic. In thirteenth-century England an improved form of gunpowder was introduced by Roger Bacon. As a result rockets were used in battles and were a common—although unreliable—weapon. In the early eighteenth century a twenty-pound rocket that traveled almost two miles was constructed by William Congreve, an English artillery expert. By the late nineteenth century thought was given to supersonic speeds by the physicist Ernst Mach. The sonic boom was predicted by him. The first liquid fuel rocket was launched by the American Robert Goddard in 1926. A pamphlet written by him anticipated almost all future rocket developments. As a result of his pioneering work, he is called the father of modern rocketry.

23l   Changing from Active to Passive Voice

You can change verbs from active to passive voice by making the object of the active verb the subject of the passive verb. The subject of the active verb then becomes the object of the passive verb.

ACTIVE: Sir James Murray <u>compiled</u> the *Oxford English Dictionary.*

PASSIVE: *The Oxford English Dictionary* <u>was compiled</u> by Sir James Murray.

Remember that an active verb must have an object or it cannot be put into the passive voice. If an active verb has no object, supply a subject or keep the active construction.

ACTIVE: Shakespeare wrote.
          _____?_____ was written by Shakespeare.

PASSIVE: *Twelfth Night* was written by Shakespeare.

☐   **EXERCISE 7**

Determine which sentences in the following paragraphs would be more effective in the passive voice. Rewrite these sentences, making sure that you can explain the reasons for your choices.

Thomas Eakins was a painter and sculptor who was born in Philadelphia in 1844. Many people consider Eakins one of America's best nineteenth-century artists. Eakins, an innovative artist who knew anatomy and who insisted on working with nude models, led the move toward American realism. As a result, some people forced his resignation from the Pennsylvania Academy in 1886.

Eakins never flattered his subjects. He painted what he saw and relied on photographs to help him paint accurately and to study motion. Many people recognized Eakins as a major painter by the time of his death in 1916. Some people considered *The Surgical Clinic of Professor Gross* (1875) and *The Swimming Hole* (1883) to be his best paintings. Eakins was unusual in a period when most artists concerned themselves with painting the ideal or the exotic.

Student Writer at Work: Verbs ————————

Revise this background section of a draft of a short paper on the writing of Samuel Pepys, the famous seventeenth-century English diarist. Look for inconsistencies in tense and mood and ineffective use of both passive and active voice. You may add words and phrases and rearrange sentences. After you have corrected the errors, go over the draft again and, if necessary, revise further to strengthen coherence, unity, and style.

Samuel Pepys was born on February 23, 1633, in a house in Shaftsbury Court, where the business of tailoring was carried out by his father. Samuel Pepys was the fifth child and second son of his family. A primary education was secured for Pepys with the aid of his father's cousin, Sir Edward Montagu. In 1650 Pepys enters Trinity College, Cambridge, and after transferring to Magdalene College a

vbs
23l

Bachelor of Arts Degree and a Master's Degree were
eventually secured. In 1665 Pepys began a career in the
navy. Between 1672 and 1679 various important offices
were held by Pepys. He eventually rised to be secretary
of the Admiralty, and many important duties were given to
him. The revolution of 1688 terminated King James's
reign, and also the career of Pepys was ended. On May
25,1703, Pepys died and was buried beside his wife.

     Throughout his life Pepys's true character was
probably not known to those around him. Between 1660 and
1669, however, Pepys recorded his personal observations in
his diary. This document was written in shorthand,
French, Spanish, Latin, Greek, and invented ciphers. More
than one hundred years after Pepys's death six volumes had
been discovered by the Reverend John Smith, and in 1825
the first edition of *The Diary* was published. In the nine
years he kept his diary, a brilliant and candid picture of
Restoration life was given by Pepys. Today Pepys is
regarded by most scholars as the most insightful of the
English diarists.

**vbs
23**

24

Agreement

Agreement is the correspondence between words in number, gender, or person. Subjects and verbs agree in **number** (singular or plural) and **person** (first, second, or third); pronouns and their antecedents agree in number, person, and **gender** (masculine, feminine, or neuter).

Subject-Verb Agreement

Verbs should agree in number and person with their subjects: singular subjects have singular verbs, and plural subjects have plural verbs.

SINGULAR: Hydrogen peroxide is an unstable compound.

PLURAL: The characters are not well developed in most of O. Henry's short stories.

Present tense verbs, except *be* and *have*, add -*s* or -*es* when the subject is third-person singular. Third-person singular subjects include nouns; the personal pronouns *he*, *she*, *it*, and *one*; and many indefinite pronouns.

The president has the power to veto congressional legislation.

She frequently cites statistics to support her assertions.

In every group somebody emerges as a natural leader.

Present tense verbs do not add -*s* or -*es* when the subject is first-person singular (*I*), first-person plural (*we*), second-person singular or plural (*you*), or third-person plural (*they*).

I recommend that dieters avoid processed meat because of its high salt content.

In our Bill of Rights, we guarantee all defendants the right to a speedy trial.

At this stratum, you see rocks dating back fifteen million years.

They say that some wealthy people default on their student loans.

Subject-verb agreement is generally straightforward, but some situations can be troublesome. You can achieve proper agreement if you are familiar with the following conventions.

24a Intervening Phrases

Even if a modifying phrase comes between subject and verb, the verb should agree with the subject, not with a word in the intervening phrase. For example, consider the following sentence.

agr
24b

> The sound of the drumbeats builds in intensity in *The Emperor Jones.*

Here the subject, *sound,* is singular and takes a singular verb, *builds.* Even though the plural *drumbeats* immediately precedes the verb, it is not the subject. Now consider this sentence.

> The games won by the intramural team are usually few and far between.

Here the plural subject, *games,* takes the plural verb form, *are.* *Team* is not the subject.

When phrases introduced by *along with, as well as, in addition to, including,* and *together with* come between subject and verb, the intervening phrases do not change the subject's number.

> Heavy rain, together with high winds, causes hazardous driving conditions along the Santa Monica Freeway.

24b Compound Subjects

(1) Compound subjects joined by *and*

Compound subjects joined by *and* take plural verbs.

> Air conditioning and power steering are two of the available options on most domestic automobiles.

There are, however, two exceptions to this rule.

- Some compound subjects joined by *and* stand for a single idea or person. These should be treated as a unit and given singular verbs.

Rhythm and blues is a forerunner of rock and roll.

The chairman of the board and chief executive officer of Todd and Honeywell is Andrew Eastwood, widely known for his innovations in publishing.

- When *each* or *every* precedes a compound subject joined by *and,* the subject also takes a singular verb.

Each complaint and contract violation passes through the grievance committee.

Every nook and cranny was searched before the purloined letter was found in plain sight on the mantel.

(2)   Compound subjects linked by *or*

Compound subjects linked by *or* or by the correlative conjunctions *either . . . or* or *neither . . . nor* may take singular or plural verbs. If both subjects are singular, use a singular verb; if both subjects are plural, use a plural verb.

Either radiation or chemotherapy is combined with surgery for the most effective results. (Both parts of the compound subject, *radiation* and *chemotherapy,* are singular, so the verb is singular.)

Either radiation treatments or chemotherapy sessions are combined with surgery for the most effective results. (Both parts of the compound subject, *treatments* and *sessions,* are plural, so the verb is plural.)

When a singular and a plural subject are linked by *or,* or by the correlative conjunctions *either . . . or, neither . . . nor,* or *not only . . . but also,* the verb should agree with the subject that is nearer to it.

Either radiation treatments or chemotherapy is combined with surgery for the most effective results. (Singular verb agrees with *chemotherapy,* the part of the compound subject closer to it.)

Either chemotherapy or radiation treatments are combined with surgery for the most effective results. (Plural verb agrees with *treatments,* the part of the compound subject closer to it.)

Sometimes a compound subject is made up of nouns and pronouns that differ in person and therefore require different verb forms. In such cases, the verb should agree in person as well as in number with the element of the compound subject to which it is closer.

Neither my running mate nor I wish to contest the election.

Neither I nor my running mate wishes to contest the election.

24c Indefinite Pronouns ————————————————

In most cases, you should use a singular verb when using an indefinite pronoun as a subject. Although some indefinite pronouns—*both, many, few, several, others*—are always plural, most—*another, anyone, everyone, one, each, either, neither, anything, everything, something,* and *somebody*—are singular.

> <u>Anyone</u> <u>is</u> welcome to apply for a grant, providing certain financial qualifications are met.
>
> <u>Something</u> <u>was</u> wrong with the way the results were tabulated.
>
> <u>Each</u> of the chapters <u>includes</u> a review exercise.
>
> <u>Everyone</u> on the team <u>likes</u> to win.

**agr
24d**

Some indefinite pronouns—*some, all, any, more, most,* and *none*—can be singular or plural. In these cases the noun to which the pronoun refers determines whether the verb form should be singular or plural.

> Of course, <u>some</u> of this trouble <u>is</u> to be expected. (*Some* refers to *trouble;* therefore, the verb is singular.)
>
> <u>Some</u> of the spectators <u>are</u> getting restless. (*Some* refers to *spectators;* therefore, the verb is plural.)

24d Collective Nouns ————————————————

A **collective noun** is a word that is singular in form but denotes a group of persons or things—for instance, *navy, union, association, group.* Collective nouns, like indefinite pronouns, may take either singular or plural verbs, depending on how they are used. When a collective noun refers to a group as a unit, it takes a singular verb; when it refers to the individuals or items that make up the group, it takes a plural verb.

> To many people the <u>royal family</u> <u>symbolizes</u> Great Britain. (The family, as a unit, is the symbol.)
>
> After years of living together, the nuclear <u>family</u> <u>begin</u> to go their separate ways. (Each member leaves separately.)

Sometimes, however, even when usage is correct, a plural verb sounds awkward with a collective noun. If this is the case, rewrite the sentence to eliminate the awkwardness.

> After years of living together, <u>the members of the nuclear family</u> <u>begin</u> to go their separate ways.

Phrases that name a fixed amount—*three-quarters, twenty dollars, the majority*—are treated like collective nouns. When the amount is considered as a unit, it takes a singular verb; when it denotes parts of the whole, it takes a plural verb.

Three-quarters of those taking the math anxiety workshop improve dramatically. (All individuals in this group improve.)

Three-quarters of his usual Social Security check is not enough. (Three-quarters denotes a unit.)

NOTE: *The number* is always singular and *a number* is always plural.

The number of voters has declined.

A number of students have missed the opportunity to preregister.

24e   Singular Subjects with Plural Forms ——

Be sure to use a singular verb with a singular subject, even if the form of the subject is plural.

Statistics deals with the collection, classification, analysis, and interpretation of data.

Politics makes strange bedfellows.

The subjects of these sentences might seem at first glance to be plural because of their *-s* endings. But in fact, each is singular and must take a singular verb. In certain contexts, however, some of these words may actually have plural meanings. In these cases, a plural verb should be used.

Her politics are too radical for her parents. (*Politics* refers not to the science of political government but to political principles or opinions.)

The statistics prove him wrong. (*Statistics* denotes not a body of knowledge but the numerical facts or data themselves.)

Be sure that titles of individual works take singular verbs, even if their form is plural.

The Grapes of Wrath describes the journey of migrant workers and their families from the Dust Bowl to California.

This convention also applies to words referred to as words, even if they are plural.

Good vibes is a 60's slang term meaning positive feelings.

24f Inverted Subject-Verb Order

Be sure a verb agrees with its subject, even when the verb precedes the subject.

> Is either answer correct?
>
> There but for fortune go you and I.
>
> There are currently twelve circuit courts of appeals in the federal court system.

Note that the usual word order of a sentence is inverted with constructions involving *there is* or *there are*.

24g Linking Verbs

Be sure linking verbs agree with their subjects, not with the subject complement.

> The problem was termites.

Here the verb *was* agrees with the subject *problem*, not with the subject complement *termites*. If *termites* were the subject, the verb would be plural.

> Termites were the problem.

24h Relative Pronouns

When you use a relative pronoun (*who, which, that*) to begin a dependent clause, the verb in that clause should agree in number with the pronoun's antecedent. Because these pronouns have the same form for singular and plural, they provide no clues to subject-verb agreement.

> The farmer is one of the ones who suffer during a grain embargo.

Here the verb *suffer* agrees with the antecedent *ones* of the relative pronoun *who*. Compare this sentence.

> The farmer is the only one who suffers during the grain embargo.

Now the verb agrees with the antecedent *one*, which is singular.

☐   **EXERCISE 1**

Each of these ten correct sentences illustrates one of the eight conventions just explained. Read the sentences carefully, and explain why each verb form is used in each case.

EXAMPLE: "Frankie and Johnny" is a ballad about a woman's revenge against her unfaithful lover. (The verb *is* is singular
because the subject *"Frankie and Johnny"* is the title of
an individual work even though it is plural in form.)

1. Sugar and spice is what little girls are supposedly made of.
2. All is quiet.
3. Weight Watchers was founded by Jean Nidetch.
4. An army marches on its stomach.
5. *Typee,* like *Omoo* and *White-Jacket,* is an early Melville novel.
6. Neither famine nor wars destroy a strong nation.
7. Sir Laurence Olivier is one of the actors who are considered great.
8. *Star Wars* was directed by George Lucas.
9. The time-consuming part of the job is all these credit checks.
10. There is no reason for this kind of delay, and I would appreciate
your giving this matter your prompt attention.

□   **EXERCISE 2**

agr
24h

Some of these sentences are correct, but others illustrate common errors in subject-verb agreement. If a sentence is correct, mark it with a *C;*
if it has an error, correct it.

1. Margaret Farrar is one of the people who is considered important in
the history of the crossword puzzle.
2. Mme. Dionne's surprise was quintuplets.
3. The bargaining team always prepared their initial demands before
meeting with management.
4. Neither Pac Man nor Space Invaders are a substitute for chess.
5. Some say gentrification is destroying our neighborhoods by driving
out long-term residents.
6. There is currently specific laws, grants, and tax credits designed to
help low-income elderly people.
7. Canada is the country that is directly north of the United States.
8. Dungeons and Dragons are popular with those who like fantasy
role-playing games.
9. The *Dune* novels, which revolve around efforts to survive on a desert
planet, emphasizes the relationship between people and their environment.
10. Martha's Vineyard, Hilton Head Island, and Mackinac Island continues to attract numerous tourists.

Pronoun-Antecedent Agreement

Pronouns must agree with their **antecedents** in number, person,
and gender. Singular pronouns—such as *he, him, she, her, it, me,
myself,* and *oneself*—should refer to singular antecedents. Plural
pronouns—such as *we, us, they, them,* and *their*—should refer to

plural antecedents. (See 21b for a complete list of pronouns.) Pronouns must also agree with their antecedents in person (first, second, third) and gender (masculine, feminine, neuter). Several conventions govern pronoun-antecedent agreement.

24i More than One Antecedent

In most cases use a plural pronoun to refer to two or more antecedents connected by *and,* even if one or more of the antecedents is singular.

> Mormonism and Christian Science were influenced in their beginnings by Shaker doctrines.

However, if the compound antecedent denotes a single unit—one person or thing or idea—use a singular pronoun to refer to the compound antecedent.

> In 1904 the husband and father brought his family from Poland to America.

The same convention applies when the compound antecedent is preceded by *each* or *every*: here, too, a singular pronoun should be used.

> Every programming language and software package has its limitations.

Use a singular pronoun to refer to two or more singular antecedents linked by *or* or *nor.*

> Neither Thoreau nor Whitman lived to see his work read widely.

When one antecedent is singular and one is plural, however, you should be sure the pronoun agrees in person and number with the closer antecedent.

> Neither Great Britain nor the Benelux nations have experienced changes in their borders in recent years.

24j Collective Noun Antecedents

Consider the context and meaning of collective nouns carefully. Collective noun antecedents usually call for singular pronouns, but occasionally they may require plural pronouns. If the meaning of the collective noun antecedent is singular, use a singular pronoun. If its meaning is plural, use a plural pronoun.

> The teachers' union was ready to strike for the new contract its members had been promised. (All the members act as one.)

> When the whistle blew, the team left their seats and moved toward the court. (Each member acts individually.)

Within any one sentence a collective noun should be treated consistently as either singular or plural. When one collective noun serves as both the subject of a verb and the antecedent of a pronoun, both verb and pronoun must agree with the noun. In this sentence, verb and pronoun are not consistent.

> The teachers' union, ready to strike for the new contract its members had been promised, were still willing to negotiate.

Here the collective noun *union* is singular; the verb *were* is plural and, therefore, incorrect.

agr
24k

24k   Antecedent Indefinite Pronouns ─────

In most cases use singular pronouns when your antecedent is an indefinite pronoun. Most indefinite pronouns—*each, either, neither, one, anyone,* and the like—are singular in meaning and should take singular pronouns. (Others may be plural—see 24c—and require plural pronouns.)

> Neither of these men is likely to have his proposal ready by the application deadline.

> Each of these neighborhoods is like a separate nation, with its own traditions and values.

> Everyone will get basic instruction in the modern foreign language of his choice.

NOTE: *Everyone* presents some special problems for writers. Because *everyone* is singular in meaning and does not specify gender, convention says that it should be referred to by the singular pronoun *his.* But indefinite pronouns really denote members of both sexes, so many writers feel that using *his* is inaccurate. In speech, it is common to use the plural pronouns *they* or *their* to refer to *everyone.* In college writing, this is not acceptable.

Though it can be somewhat cumbersome if overused, one solution to this problem is to use *both* the masculine and feminine pronouns.

Everyone will get basic instruction in the modern foreign language of his or her choice.

Another solution is to change the subject and use a plural pronoun.

All students will get basic instruction in the modern foreign language of their choice.

For more information on avoiding sexist language, see 17g.3.

agr
24k

☐   **EXERCISE 3**

Find and correct any errors in subject-verb and/or pronoun-antecedent agreement.

1. Either the Boy Scouts or the 4-H Program are offering special courses and publications to help latchkey children take care of themselves.
2. Gilbert and Sullivan's classic *The Pirates of Penzance* were revived in the early 80's in stage and screen versions.
3. None of the lower forty-eight states is able to match Alaska's coal reserves.
4. A creole is a kind of language that comes into being when several different languages are spoken in an area. To make communication easier, speakers of each of these different languages tend to borrow from all the area's languages.
5. Although many students now enrolled in U.S. dental schools are female, in 1979 there was only one oral pathologist, four endodontists, and six oral surgeons who were women.
6. A number of drugs currently banned in America is still routinely sold to "underdeveloped" countries by American manufacturers.
7. Alcohol use among college students, frequently associated with campus vandalism and traffic fatalities, are on the rise.
8. Since the 1960's, vegetarianism has moved apart from any particular religious, political, or ethical philosophy; now they have become a legitimate nutritional movement instead of a fad.
9. Neither paralegals, systems analysts, radiation therapy technologists, nor physician's assistants was in existence a generation ago.
10. Groups as diverse as the Moral Majority, Phyllis Schlafly's Eagle Forum, NOW, People for the American Way, and the DAR seeks to influence textbook selection committees.

☐   **EXERCISE 4**

The ten sentences below illustrate correct subject-verb and pronoun-antecedent agreement. After following the instructions in parentheses after each sentence, revise each so that its verbs and pronouns agree with the newly created subject.

EXAMPLE: One child in ten suffers from a learning disability.
(Change *one child in ten* to *ten percent of all children.*)

Ten percent of all children suffer from a learning disability.

1. The governess is seemingly pursued by evil as she tries to protect Miles and Flora from those she feels seek to possess the children's souls. (Change *The governess* to *The governess and the cook.*)
2. Insulin-dependent diabetics are now able to take advantage of new technology that can help alleviate their symptoms. (Change *diabetics* to *the diabetic.*)
3. All homeowners in shore regions worry about the possible effects of a hurricane on their property. (Change *All homeowners* to *Every homeowner.*)
4. Federally funded job-training programs offer unskilled workers an opportunity to acquire skills they can use to secure employment. (Change *workers* to *the worker.*)
5. Foreign imports pose a major challenge to the American automobile market. (Change *Foreign imports* to *The foreign import.*)
6. *Brideshead Revisited* tells how one family and its devotion to its Catholic faith affect Charles Ryder. (Delete *and its devotion to its Catholic faith.*)
7. *Writer's Digest* and *The Writer* are designed to aid novice and experienced writers as they seek markets for their work. (Change *writers* to *the writer.*)
8. Most American families have access to television; in fact, more have televisions than have indoor plumbing. (Change *Most American families* to *Almost every American family.*)
9. In Montana it seems as though every town's elevation is higher than its population. (Change *Every town's elevation* to *All the towns' elevations.*)
10. A woman without a man is like a fish without a bicycle. (Change *A woman/a man* to *Women/men.*)

agr
24k

Student Writer at Work: Agreement

Read the following draft of an English composition essay carefully, correcting all errors in subject-verb and pronoun-antecedent agreement. After you have corrected the errors, go over the draft again and, if necessary, revise further to strengthen coherence, unity, and style.

                    Marriage in the Ashanti Tribe

     The Ashanti tribe is the largest in the small West
African country of Ghana. The language of the Ashantis,

Akan, is the most widely spoken in the country. The unity in the Ashanti tribe is derived from a golden stool which the Ashantis believe descended from the skies at the command of their chief priest. This unity has encouraged the Ashantis to create a system in which the family is so strong that the tribe has little need for formal support services. For instance, the tribe need few institutions to care for their orphans or homeless people. Among the Ashanti people, home and family means plenty of relatives, living and working and playing and worrying as well-knit units who live in single or neighboring households. Marriage among members of the Ashanti tribe is therefore a union of two families as well as two individuals.

In Ashanti, marriage is less an agreement entered into by two individuals before God or the justice of the peace than it is a social contract between two families, each of whom are represented by a partner to the marriage. Because a marriage binds two families together, it is not to be entered into hurriedly. In fact, everyone in the tribe fear the social consequences of an ill-conceived union. The families of both of the young people are active counselors during the courtship, and its wholehearted approval and endorsement is essential to the success of the marriage. The family seek the answers to many questions. For instance, are the bride and bridegroom of similar age? Have either been married before? If so, why did the previous marriage fail? What is the history of the family? Is the family in debt? Most important, of what clan is the family?

When all the questions have been answered satisfactorily, the man and the woman are married. The respective troths, for bride and groom, for bride's family and groom's family, are plighted in a quiet ceremony without benefit of either clergy or justice of the peace. The crucial part of the ceremony is the giving of a small

sum of money and various gifts and drinks by the family of
the groom to that of the bride. The actual value of such
payments are often small, amounting to about fifty
dollars. A royal family gives more and receives more.
This money is sometimes referred to as "bridewealth." It
constitutes only a token of the agreement reached between
bride and groom and between their families. In the giving
and receiving of the gifts the young people and their
families mutually pledge their faithfulness and support.
When this transaction has been witnessed by both families,
the man and woman are joined together as husband and
wife. For better or for worse, they are married.

agr
24

25

Adjectives and Adverbs

Adjectives and adverbs are modifiers used alone or in combination to enrich sentences. **Adjectives** modify nouns and pronouns; **adverbs** modify verbs, adjectives, other adverbs, or entire phrases, clauses, or sentences. Both adjectives and adverbs describe, limit, or qualify other words, phrases, or clauses. But they have different functions, forms, and positions in a sentence.

The *function* of a word, not its *form*, determines whether it is classified as an adjective or an adverb. Although many adverbs (like *immediately* and *hopelessly*) end in -*ly*, others (like *almost* and *very*) do not. Moreover, some adjectives (like *lively*) end in -*ly*. Only by locating the modified word and determining its part of speech can you identify a modifier as an adjective or adverb.

Adjectives are commonly placed close to the nouns or pronouns they modify. They most often appear immediately *before* nouns and directly *after* linking verbs, direct objects, and indefinite pronouns.

They bought two shrubs for the yard. (before noun)

The name seemed familiar. (after linking verb)

The coach ran them ragged. (after direct object)

Anything sad makes me cry. (after indefinite pronoun)

Two or more adjectives can be placed *after* the noun or pronoun they modify.

The expedition, long and arduous, ended in triumph.

Adverbs are also usually located close to the words they modify. However, because they modify more kinds of words and word groups than adjectives do, they may occur in a greater variety of positions. In a given sentence an adverb can be located in more than one position.

He walked slowly across the room.

Slowly he walked across the room.

He slowly walked across the room.

He walked across the room slowly.

ad
25a

25a Using Adjectives

Be sure to use an adjective—not an adverb—as a subject complement or an object complement (see 21d).

A **subject complement** is a word that follows a linking verb and that modifies the sentence's subject, not its verb. **Linking verbs** show no action; their function is to connect a sentence's subject and complement. Words that are or can be used as linking verbs include *seem, appear, believe, become, grow, turn, remain, prove, look, sound, smell, taste, feel,* and forms of the verb *be.* Because a subject complement modifies the subject—a noun or pronoun—it must be an adjective.

Melissa seemed brave.

Here *seemed* shows no action and is therefore a linking verb. Because *brave* is a subject complement that modifies the noun *Melissa,* the adjective form is used. Compare the following sentence.

Melissa smiled bravely.

Here *smiled* shows action, so it is not a linking verb. *Bravely* modifies *smiled,* so it takes the adverb form.

Sometimes the same verb can either serve as a linking verb or convey action. Compare these two sentences.

He remained stubborn. (He was still stubborn.)
He remained stubbornly. (He remained, in a stubborn manner.)

In the first sentence, *remained* is a linking verb, and *stubborn,* a subject complement, modifies the pronoun *he.* In the second sentence, however, *remained* is used to convey action. *Stubbornly* modifies *remained,* so the adverb form is used.

When a word following a sentence's direct object modifies that object and not the verb, it is an **object complement.** Objects are nouns or pronouns, so their modifiers must be adjectives.

Most people called him <u>shy</u>. (Most people thought he was shy.)

Shy modifies the sentence's direct object (*him*), so the adjective form is correct. But in the following sentence *shyly* modifies the verb (*called*)—not the object—so the adverb form is used.

Most people called him <u>shyly</u>. (Most people were shy when they called him.)

<table>
<tr><td>ad
25b</td><td>

25b   Using Adverbs

</td></tr>
</table>

Be sure to use an adverb—not an adjective—to modify verbs, adjectives, other adverbs, or entire phrases, clauses, or sentences (see 21e).

> FAULTY: The majority of the class did <u>great</u> on the midterm. (adjective form used to modify verb)
> My parents dress a lot more <u>conservative</u> than my friends do. (adjective form used to modify verb)

> REVISED: The majority of the class did <u>well</u> (or <u>very</u> <u>well</u>) on the midterm.
> My parents dress a lot more <u>conservatively</u> than my friends do.

In informal speech adjective forms like *good, bad, sure, real, slow, quick,* and *loud* are often incorrectly used to modify verbs, adjectives, and adverbs.

> FAULTY: The program ran <u>good</u> the first time we tried it.
> The new system performed <u>bad</u>.
> The tutoring project <u>sure</u> needs volunteers.
> Be <u>real</u> careful when you proofread the bibliography.
> Go <u>slow</u> or you might miss the turnoff.
> Speak <u>loud</u> so they can hear your answer.

In college writing, however, be sure to avoid these informal modifiers and to use adverbs to modify verbs, adjectives, and other adverbs.

> REVISED: The program ran <u>well</u> the first time we tried it.
> The new system performed <u>badly</u>.
> The tutoring project <u>surely</u> (or <u>certainly</u>) needs volunteers.
> Be <u>really</u> (or <u>extremely</u>) careful when you proofread the bibliography.

Go slowly or you might miss the turnoff.
Speak loudly so they can hear your answer.

☐   **EXERCISE 1**

Revise each of the incorrect sentences in this paragraph so that only
adjectives modify nouns and pronouns and only adverbs modify verbs,
adjectives, or other adverbs. Be sure to eliminate informal forms. Put a
check mark before any sentence that is correct.

Although cruises have become extremely popular, steamship lines
are still trying real hard to promote their cruises, and their upbeat message comes through loud and clear. Most advertisements emphasize the
unlimited quantities of gourmet food, the good value, the varied activities, the sense of luxury, and the possibility of romance. As a result,
people who sign up for cruises believe they will be able to travel quite
cheap—after all, almost everything is included in the prepaid price.
They also believe that it is possible to fall in love fairly quick, all the while
cruising along slow and easy under the stars. Enjoying a cruise is not
hard, and it sure helps if people allow themselves to believe their fanta-
sies can come true.

☐   **EXERCISE 2**

Being careful to use adjectives—not adverbs—as subject complements
and object complements, write five sentences in imitation of each of the
following. Be sure to use five different linking verbs in your imitations of
each sentence.

1. Julie looked worried.
2. Dan considers his collection valuable.

25c   Distinguishing Between Comparative and Superlative Forms

Adjectives and adverbs change their forms to indicate an increase or decrease in the quality described. The **positive** degree
(big) simply describes a quality. It indicates no comparisons. The
comparative (bigger) and **superlative** (biggest) degrees indicate
comparisons—between two qualities (greater or lesser) or
among many qualities (greatest or least), respectively. The comparative degree compares two persons or things, and the superlative compares one person or thing with all the others in the
class. (John's house is *bigger* than Hal's; Randy's house is the
biggest one on the block.)
NOTE: Some adverbs, particularly those indicating time, place,

and degree (*almost, very, here, yesterday,* and *immediately*), do not have comparative or superlative forms.

(1) The comparative degree

Adjectives To indicate a *greater* degree, all one-syllable adjectives and many two-syllable adjectives (particularly those that end in *-y, -ly, -le, -er,* and *-ow*) add *-er* to form the comparative.

slow	slower
funny	funnier
lovely	lovelier

(Note that a final *y* becomes *i* before *-er* is added.)

ad 25c

Other two-syllable adjectives and all long adjectives form the comparative with *more.*

| famous | more famous |
| incredible | more incredible |

NOTE: Many two-syllable adjectives can form the comparative with either *more* or *-er*—for example, *more lovely* or *lovelier.*
All adjectives indicate a lesser degree with the word *less.*

| lovely | less lovely |
| famous | less famous |

Adverbs Adverbs ending in *-ly* indicate a greater degree with *more.*

| slowly | more slowly |

Other adverbs use the *-er* ending to indicate a greater degree.

| soon | sooner |

Adverbs always indicate a lesser degree with the word *less.*

less slowly
less soon

NOTE: Never use both *more* and *-er* to form the comparative degree.

FAULTY: Nothing could have been more easier.

REVISED: Nothing could have been easier.

(2) The superlative degree

Adjectives Adjectives that indicate the comparative with *-er* add *-est* to indicate the superlative (the *greatest* degree).

nicer   nicest
funnier   funniest

Adjectives that indicate the comparative with *more* use *most* to indicate the superlative.

more famous   most famous
more challenging   most challenging

All adjectives indicate the least degree with the word *least*.

least interesting
least enjoyable

Adverbs The majority of adverbs are preceded by *most* to indicate the greatest degree.

most quickly
most helpfully
most efficiently

Others use the *-est* ending to indicate the greatest degree.

soonest

All adverbs use *least* to indicate the least degree.

least willingly
least fashionably

NOTE: Never use both *most* and *-est* to form the superlative degree.

FAULTY: Jack is the most meanest person in town.

REVISED: Jack is the meanest person in town.

(3)   Irregular comparatives and superlatives

Some adjectives and adverbs do not conform to the rules stated above. Instead of adding a word or an ending to the positive form, they use different words to indicate each degree.

Irregular Comparatives and Superlatives

	Positive	Comparative	Superlative
ADJECTIVES:	good	better	best
	bad	worse	worst
	a little	less	least
	many, some, much	more	most
ADVERBS:	well	better	best
	badly	worse	worst

(4) Illogical comparisons

Many adjectives and adverbs have absolute meanings—that is, they can logically exist only in the positive degree. Good sense suggests that words like *perfect, unique, excellent, impossible,* and *dead* can never be used in the comparative or superlative degree: How can one thing be more excellent or less impossible than another?

Consider the word *unique,* which means one of a kind. It can *never* be used in the comparative or superlative degree.

FAULTY: The vase is the <u>most unique</u> piece in her collection.

REVISED: The vase in her collection is <u>unique</u>.

Although comparative and superlative forms of absolutes should be avoided in college writing, they may, however, be used in informal contexts.

> He revised eight times, always looking for the <u>most perfect</u> draft.
> It was the <u>most impossible</u> course I ever took.

**ad
25d**

NOTE: Absolutes can be modified by words that suggest approaching the absolute state—*nearly* or *almost,* for example.

> He revised until his draft was <u>almost perfect</u>.

☐   **EXERCISE 3**

Supply the correct comparative and superlative forms for each of the adjectives or adverbs listed below. Then use each form in a sentence.

EXAMPLE: strange   stranger   strangest

> The story had a *strange* ending. The explanation sounded *stranger* each time I heard it. This is the *strangest* gadget I have ever seen.

1. many   6. softly
2. eccentric   7. tremendous
3. confusing   8. well
4. bad   9. often
5. mysterious   10. tiny

25d Using Nouns as Adjectives

Many nouns can function as modifiers in a sentence.

> He made a sandwich of <u>turkey</u> bologna, <u>egg</u> salad, and <u>tomato</u> slices on <u>wheat</u> bread.

Many familiar phrases, such as *space station, art history,* and *amusement park,* consist of a noun modifying another noun. In such cases using a noun as a modifier saves words. But overusing nouns as modifiers can create cluttered, clumsy, and even incoherent sentences.

> Confusing: The Chestnut Hill Fathers' Club Pony League beginners spring baseball clinic will be held Saturday.

To revise cluttered sentences like the one above, restructure to break up long series of nouns. You can also substitute equivalent adjective forms, where such forms exist, or possessives for some of the nouns used as modifiers.

> Improved: The Chestnut Hill Fathers' Club's spring baseball clinic for beginning Pony League players will be held Saturday.

ad
25d

Of course, eliminating the passive voice could make this sentence even clearer.

> On Saturday, the Chestnut Hill Fathers' Club will hold its spring baseball clinic for beginning Pony League players.

☐   **EXERCISE 4**

Identify every noun used as a modifier in the following passage. Then revise where necessary to eliminate clumsy or unclear phrasing resulting from overuse of nouns as modifiers. Try substituting adjective or possessive forms, and rearrange word order where you feel it is indicated.

The student government business management trainee program is extremely popular on campus. The student government donated some of the seed money to begin this management trainee program, which is one of the most successful the university business school has ever offered to undergraduate students. Three core courses must be taken before the student intern can actually begin work. First, there is a management theory course given every spring semester in conjunction with the business school. Then, the following fall semester, students in the trainee program are required to take a course in personnel practices, including employee benefits. Finally, they take a business elective.

During the summer, the student interns are placed in junior management positions in large electronics, manufacturing, or public utility companies. This job experience is considered the most valuable part of the program because it gives students a taste of the work world.

Student Writer at Work: Adjectives and Adverbs

Read carefully this draft of an essay, and correct errors in the use of adjectives and adverbs. Check to make sure adjectives modify nouns or pronouns and adverbs modify verbs, adjectives, or other adverbs; make sure the correct comparative and superlative forms are used; and eliminate any overuse of nouns as modifiers. After you have corrected the errors, go over the draft again and, if necessary, revise further to strengthen coherence, unity, and style.

                          Save the Harp Seals

        What do rabbits, minks, foxes, and seals all have in
common? Each is a victim of fashion. Many people want to
own a fur coat real bad, and for those who can afford it,
buying one seems to be a simple decision. This is all
fine for the fur coat showroom salesperson who earns a
commission on the sale, but what about the original owner
of the fur? What about the animal who lost its life so
its fur could sit on someone's shoulders? Too many animals
have been slaughtered for just this reason, and in some
cases the animals are skinned quick before they are even
completely dead. Something sure must be done to stop the
slaughter of these animals before they become extinct.
The harp seal is an example of an animal in grave danger.

        The harp seal has suffered a very large reduction in
numbers during recent times because hunters have subjected
these seals to mass slaughter. The issue is not only that
the harp seals are butchered, but also that they are
killed in the inhumanest manner possible.

        The traditional method uses a gaff, which is a length
of wood with a hook at one end and a spike at the other.
Using this device, the hunter strikes the seal in the head
with the hook. Some people consider this method
painlessly; however, sometimes the spike misses the vital
spot and the seal, still alive, is skinned by the hunter.

Thus the gaff can prove painful indeed. The second method used is clubbing. Hunters who favor this technique use wooden clubs or great iron hooks. Seals often pull in their heads in alarm, covering their skulls with a thick layer of fat. It takes many powerful blows to penetrate the fat and kill the seal.

The seals are being killed in more greater numbers each year, and being killed savagely. Even the existing laws, which are supposed to help save the seals, have no effect. One such law limits the size and weight of the club, but if the clubs are made more lightly the only thing that will change is that more blows will be required to kill the seal. This law does not prevent the killings. Many other regulations are constantly being broken, and the problem of enforcement remains seriously. Meanwhile, the harp seals are the unwilling victims of brutal killings.

When will this mass slaughter end? If strong, immediate action is not taken, it will be too late for the animals. Something must be done quick before the harp seal becomes extinct.

ad
25

SECTION VI

Understanding Punctuation and Mechanics

26

The Period, the Question Mark, and the Exclamation Point

26a

Use a period. . .
- To end a sentence (26a.1)
- To mark an abbreviation (26a.2)
- To mark divisions in dramatic and poetic references (26a.3)

Use a question mark. . .
- To mark the end of a direct question (26b.1)
- To mark questionable dates and numbers (26b.2)

Use an exclamation point. . .
- To mark emphasis (26c.1)

26a   Using Periods

Periods are used to end declarative sentences (statements), mild commands, polite requests, and indirect questions. They are also used in most familiar abbreviations and in dramatic and poetic references.

(1)   Ending a Sentence

Periods signal the end of a statement, a mild command or polite request, or an indirect question.

410

Something is rotten in the state of Denmark. (statement)

Be sure to have the oil checked before you start out. (mild command)

When the bell rings, please exit in an orderly fashion. (polite request)

They wondered whether it was safe to go back in the water. (indirect question)

NOTE: An indirect question tells what has been asked, but because it does not use the speaker's exact words, it does not take a question mark.

DIRECT QUESTION: How much is that doggie in the window?

INDIRECT QUESTION: He asked the price of the dog in the window.

(2)   Marking an abbreviation

Periods appear in most abbreviations.

Mrs. Robinson	Captain Newman, M.D.	25 B.C.
Mr. Spock	George McGovern, Ph.D.	N.Y., N.Y., U.S.A.
Ms. J. R. Jones	Sue Barton, R.N.	221b Baker St.
Dr. Kildare	9 P.M.	etc.

Punctuating with Abbreviations That Take Periods

At the End of a Sentence

If the abbreviation ends the sentence, do not add another period.

FAULTY: He promised to be there at 6 A.M..

REVISED: He promised to be there at 6 A.M.

However, do add a question mark after the abbreviation's final period if the sentence is a question.

Did he arrive at 6 P.M.?

Within a Sentence

If the abbreviation falls within a sentence, use normal punctuation after the abbreviation's final period.

FAULTY: He promised to be there at 6 P.M. but he forgot his promise.

REVISED: He promised to be there at 6 P.M., but he forgot his promise.

Some abbreviations do not require periods (see 35b). These include **acronyms,** new words formed from the first letters of a groups of words or abbreviations made from the first few letters of a series of words.

NATO	radar	OSHA	scuba
NOW	VISTA	SALT	CAT scan

Fannie Mae (Federal National Mortgage Association)

Gestapo (Geheime Staats Polizei)

Modem (modulator demodulator)

The periods are also usually dropped from frequently used capital-letter abbreviations of names of corporations, government agencies, and scientific and technical terms.

CIA	NYU	IBM	FBI	WCAU-FM
EPA	CCC	DNA	IRA	AFT
MGM	RCA	HBO	UCLA	UFO

26a

Do not use a period after commonly accepted shortened forms of words (gym, dorm, math, and so on) or after abbreviations that do not require them. If you are unsure whether or not to use a period with a particular abbreviation, consult a good college dictionary.

(3) Marking divisions in dramatic and poetic references

Periods separate act, scene, and line references in plays, and book and line references in long poems.

DRAMATIC REFERENCE: *Long Day's Journey into Night* II.ii.1–5.

POETIC REFERENCE: *Paradise Lost* VII.163–67.

☐   **EXERCISE 1**

Correct these sentences by adding missing periods and deleting superfluous ones. If a sentence is correct, mark it with a *C*.

EXAMPLE: I wonder who's kissing her now?
I wonder who's kissing her now.

1. Julius Caesar was killed in 44 B.C.
2. Please begin speaking when you hear the beep!
3. Carmen was supposed to be at A.F.L.-C.I.O. headquarters by 2 P.M.; however, she didn't get there until 10 P.M.
4. He asked whether anyone had change for a dollar?
5. Representatives from the U.M.W. began collective bargaining after an unsuccessful meeting with Mr. L Pritchard, the coal company's representative.

26b   Using Question Marks

Question marks appear at the end of direct questions. They are also used to indicate questionable dates or numbers.

(1)   Marking the end of a direct question

Use a question mark to signal the end of a direct question.

> Who was that masked man? (direct question)
>
> Who was it who asked, "Who was that masked man?" (question within a question)
>
> Did he say where he came from, who his companion was, or where they were headed? (series of direct questions)
>
> Did he say where he came from? Who his companion was? Where they were headed? (series of direct questions with each question asked separately)
>
> Did he say where he came from? who his companion was? where they were headed? (series of direct questions; informal usage does not require capitalization of first word of each question)
>
> "Is this a silver bullet?" they asked. (declarative sentence opening with a direct question)
>
> They asked, "Could he have been the Lone Ranger?" (declarative sentence closing with a direct question)

NOTE: A pair of dashes or a pair of parentheses is used around a direct question within a declarative sentence.

> Someone—a disgruntled office seeker?—is sabotaging the campaign.
>
> Part of the shipment (three dozen cases?) was delayed.

(2)   Marking questionable dates or numbers

Use a question mark in parentheses to indicate that a date or number is uncertain.

> Aristophanes, the Greek author of satirical comic dramas, was born in 448 (?) B.C. and died in 380 (?) B.C.
>
> The clock struck five (?) and stopped.

(3)   Editing to eliminate misuse or overuse of question marks

The use of question marks can be redundant or incorrect. Question marks are not used in the following situations.

?
26b

After an indirect question

An indirect question calls for a period only.

> FAULTY: The personnel officer asked if he knew how to type?
>
> REVISED: The personnel officer asked if he knew how to type.

With other punctuation

A question mark is not used along with an exclamation point, comma, semicolon, or period.

> FAULTY: "Can it be true?," he asked.
>
> REVISED: "Can it be true?" he asked.

> FAULTY: Can you believe this run of good luck?!
>
> REVISED: Can you believe this run of good luck?

With another question mark

?
26b

It is incorrect to end a sentence with more than one question mark.

> FAULTY: You did what?? Are you crazy??
>
> REVISED: You did what? Are you crazy?

As an indication of attitude

Question marks are not used to convey sarcasm. Instead, suggest your attitude through word choice.

> FAULTY: I refused his generous (?) offer.
>
> REVISED: I refused his not-very-generous offer.

In an exclamation

A question mark is not used after an exclamation phrased as a question.

> FAULTY: Will you please stop that at once?
>
> REVISED: Will you please stop that at once!

☐   **EXERCISE 2**

Correct the use of question marks and other punctuation in the following sentences.

> EXAMPLE:
>
> ORIGINAL: She asked whether Freud's theories were accepted during his lifetime?
>
> REVISED: She asked whether Freud's theories were accepted during his lifetime.

1. He wondered whether he should take a nine o'clock class? Or would that be too early?
2. The instructor asked, "Was the Spanish-American War a victory for America?"?
3. Are they really going to China??!!
4. He took a modest (?) portion of dessert—half a pie.
5. "Is *data* the plural of *datum*?," he inquired.

26c   Using Exclamation Points ─────────────

An **exclamation point** is used to convey strong feeling—astonishment, drama, shock, and the like—at the end of an emphatic statement, interjection, or command.

(1)   Marking emphasis

Use an exclamation point to signal the end of an emotional or emphatic statement, an emphatic interjection, or a forceful command.

> Remember the Maine!
>
> No! Don't leave!
>
> Finish this job at once!

NOTE: An exclamation point can follow a complete sentence ("What big teeth you have!") or a phrase ("What big teeth!")

(2)   Editing to eliminate misuse or overuse of the exclamation point

Except for recording dialogue, exclamation points are almost never appropriate in college writing. Use exclamation points sparingly, even in informal writing. Too many exclamation points give readers the impression that you are overwrought, even hysterical. Exclamation points should **not** be used in the following situations.

With mild statements

Exclamation points are not used with mildly emphatic statements or with mild interjections or commands.

> Please close the door behind you.
>
> Stand by your man.

!
26c

With another exclamation point

It is incorrect to end a sentence with more than one exclamation point.

> FAULTY: I could hardly believe my eyes!!!
>
> REVISED: I could hardly believe my eyes!

With other punctuation

An exclamation point is not used with a comma, period, semicolon, or question mark.

> FAULTY: "Fire!," he shouted.
>
> REVISED: "Fire!" he shouted.

> FAULTY: You can't be serious?!
>
> REVISED: You can't be serious!

As an indication of attitude

!
26c

Do not use an exclamation point to suggest sarcasm or humor. Use word choice and sentence structure instead.

> FAULTY: The team's record was a near-perfect (!) 0 and 12.
>
> REVISED: The team's record was a far-from-perfect 0 and 12.

☐   **EXERCISE 3**

Correct the use of exclamation points and other punctuation in these sentences.

> EXAMPLE: "Don't touch that dial!," he cried.
>
>   "Don't touch that dial!" he cried.

1. When the cell divided, each of the daughter cells had an extra chromosome!
2. Wow. Just what I always wanted. A chocolate-brown Mercedes.
3. He stared in amazement and gasped, "That's incredible!!!"
4. Please don't forget to leave your key in the ignition!
5. "Eureka!," cried Archimedes as he sprang from his bathtub.

☐   **EXERCISE 4**

Add appropriate punctuation to this passage.

Dr Craig and his group of divers paused at the shore, staring respectfully at the enormous lake Who could imagine what terrors lay beneath its surface Which of them might not emerge alive from this adventure Would it be Col Cathcart Capt Wilks, the MD from the naval base Her husband, P L Fox Or would they all survive the task ahead Dr Craig decided some encouraging remarks were in order

"Attention divers" he said in a loud, forceful voice "May I please have your attention The project which we are about to undertake—"

"Oh, no" screamed Mr Fox suddenly "Look out It's the Loch Ness Monster"

"Quick" shouted Dr Craig "Move away from the shore" But his warning came too late

!
26

27

The Comma

27a

The **comma** is essential for clarifying relationships among words, phrases, and clauses; indicating separations between word groups; and sorting out elements in a series.

> Use Commas . . .
> - To set off independent clauses (27a)
> - To set off items in a series (27b)
> - To set off introductory elements (27c)
> - To set off nonessential elements (27d)
> - In other conventional contexts (27e)
> - To prevent misreading (27f)

27a Setting Off Independent Clauses

(1) Comma plus coordinating conjunction

Use a comma before the conjunction when you form a compound sentence by linking two independent clauses with a **coordinating conjunction** (*and, but, or, nor, for, yet, so*).

The year was 2081, and everybody was finally equal. (Kurt Vonnegut, Jr., "Harrison Bergeron")

It was what I had longed for, but I can't reconstruct our reunion scene. (Geoffrey Wolfe, *The Duke of Deception*)

The bride was not young, nor was she very pretty. (Stephen Crane, "The Bride Comes to Yellow Sky")

The fires next door we extinguish without question, yet who among us would snuff out a star? (Dennis Smith, *New York Times Book Review*)

No matter how many independent clauses a compound sentence has, a comma precedes each coordinating conjunction.

She had bonny children, yet she felt they had been thrust upon her, and she could not love them. (D.H. Lawrence, "The Rocking Horse Winner")

Use a comma after the first clause when correlative conjunctions link two independent clauses.

Just as it's fascinating to find out where your barber gets his hair cut or what the top chef eats, so it can be worthwhile to find out how top brokers invest their own money. *(Money)*

(2)   Omitting the comma

You may omit the comma if two clauses connected by a coordinating conjunction are very short.

Seek and ye shall find.

Love it or leave it.

Some writers omit the comma when no possibility exists that the sentence will be misread without it.

He began to feel thirsty again and he longed to be back in the hot reeking public-house. (James Joyce, "Counterparts")

In most cases, however, use a comma before any coordinating conjunction that separates two independent clauses.

(3)   Substituting a semicolon

Use a semicolon—not a comma—to separate two clauses linked by a coordinating conjunction when one or more of the independent clauses already contains commas (see 28b).

The tour visited Melbourne, the capital of Australia; and it continued on to Wellington, New Zealand.

You may also use a semicolon when one or more clauses are especially complex, or when the second clause stands in sharp contrast to the first.

Helena wanted to marry her sister's brother-in-law in an elaborate outdoor wedding on June 24; but her parents thought she should wait until she turned 21 in September. (complex clauses)

The advent of T.V. has increased the false values ascribed to reading, since T.V. provides a vulgar alternative. But this piety is silly;
and most reading is no more cultural nor intellectual nor imaginative than shooting pool or watching *What's My Line?* (Donald
Hall, "Four Kinds of Reading") (contrasting clauses)

In the sentences above you could delete the coordinating conjunctions that follow the semicolons; however, using both makes
the separation between the clauses more emphatic.

☐   **EXERCISE 1**

Combine each of the following sentence pairs into one compound sentence, adding commas where necessary.

> EXAMPLE: Emergency medicine became an approved medical spe-
> cialty in 1979. Now pediatric emergency medicine is be-
> coming increasingly important. (and)
>
> Emergency medicine became an approved medical spe-
> cialty in 1979, and now pediatric emergency medicine is
> becoming increasingly important.

1. The Pope did not hesitate to visit his native Poland. He did not hesitate to meet with Solidarity leader Lech Walesa. (nor)
2. Agents place brand name products in prominent positions in films.
   The products will be seen and recognized by large audiences. (so)
3. Unisex insurance rates may have some drawbacks for women. They
   may be very beneficial. (or)
4. Cigarette advertising no longer appears on television. It does appear
   in print media. (but)
5. Dorothy Day founded the Catholic Worker movement over fifty years
   ago. Today her followers still dispense free food, medical care, and
   legal advice to the needy. (and)

27b Setting Off Items in a Series ————

(1) Coordinate elements

Use commas with three or more coordinate elements (words,
phrases, or clauses in a series).

> *Chipmunk, raccoon,* and *Mugwump* are words of Indian origin. (se-
> ries of words)
>
> She is a child of her age, of depression, of war, of fear. (Tillie
> Olsen, "I Stand Here Ironing") (series of phrases)
>
> Brazilians speak Portugese, Colombians speak Spanish, and
> Haitians speak French and Creole. (series of clauses)

In journalistic and technical writing, the final comma is
usually omitted. To avoid ambiguity, however, always use a

comma between the last two items in a series—before the coordinating conjunction if the series includes one.

AMBIGUOUS: The party was made special by the company, the light from the hundreds of twinkling candles and the excellent hors d'oeuvres.

REVISED: The party was made special by the company, the light from the hundreds of twinkling candles, and the excellent hors d'oeuvres.

Do not, however, use a comma to introduce or to close a series, unless the context requires it.

FAULTY: The evaluators felt the most important criteria were, fat content, presence of artificial ingredients, and taste.

REVISED: The evaluators felt the most important criteria were fat content, presence of artificial ingredients, and taste.

FAULTY: Quebec, Ontario, and Saskatchewan, are three Canadian provinces.

REVISED: Quebec, Ontario, and Saskatchewan are three Canadian provinces.

NOTE: If phrases or clauses in a series already contain commas, separate the items with semicolons (see 28d).

(2)   Coordinate adjectives

Use a comma between two or more **coordinate adjectives**—adjectives that modify the same word or word group—unless they are joined by a conjunction.

She brushed her long, shining hair.

The fruit was crisp, tart, mellow—in short, good enough to eat.

The baby was tired and cranky and wet. (adjectives joined by conjunctions; no commas needed)

Sometimes several adjectives will all seem to modify one noun, pronoun, or noun phrase when in fact one or more of them modifies another word or word group. In the following sentence, for instance, the adjective *red* modifies the noun *balloons*, but the adjective *ten* modifies the word group *red balloons*.

Ten red balloons fell from the ceiling.

In this case, only one adjective modifies the noun; the adjectives are not coordinate, so no comma is needed.

NOTE: Numbers—such as *ten* in the example above—are not coordinate with other adjectives.

Tests for Comma Use with Series of Adjectives

1. If you can reverse the order of the adjectives ("She
   brushed her shining, long hair"), you need a comma. If
   you cannot ("Red ten balloons fell from the ceiling"), the
   adjectives are not coordinate, and you do not need a
   comma.
2. If you can insert *and* between the adjectives without
   changing the meaning of the sentence ("She brushed her
   long and shining hair"), use a comma. If you cannot
   ("Ten and red balloons fell from the ceiling"), the adjectives are not coordinate, and you should not use a
   comma.

☐   **EXERCISE 2**

27b

Correct the use of commas in the following sentences, adding or deleting commas where necessary. If a sentence is punctuated correctly,
mark it with a C.

EXAMPLE: Neither dogs snakes bees nor dragons frighten her.

Neither dogs, snakes, bees, nor dragons frighten her.

1. Seals, whales, dogs, lions, and horses, are all mammals.
2. Mammals are warm-blooded vertebrates that bear live young, nurse
   them, and usually have fur.
3. Seals are mammals but lizards, and snakes, and iguanas are reptiles,
   and newts and salamanders are amphibians.
4. Amphibians also include frogs, and toads.
5. Eagles and geese and ostriches and turkeys chickens and ducks are
   classified as birds.

☐   **EXERCISE 3**

Add two coordinate adjectives to modify each of the following combinations, inserting commas where required.

EXAMPLE: classical music

strong, beautiful classical music

1. distant thunder	6. loving couple
2. silver spoon	7. computer science
3. New York Yankees	8. wheat bread
4. doll house	9. art museum
5. Rolling Stones	10. new math

27c   Setting Off Introductory Elements

Use a comma to separate introductory elements from the rest of the sentence.

(1)   Introductory adverb clauses

Introductory adverb clauses, including elliptical adverb clauses (see 7d.2), are generally set off from the rest of the sentence by commas.

> Although the CIA used to call undercover agents *penetration agents*, they now routinely refer to them as *moles*.

> When war came to Beirut and Londonderry and Saigon, the victims were the children.

> While [he was] working in the mines, Paul longed for a better life.

If the adverb clause is short, you may omit the comma, *provided the sentence will be clear without it.*

> When I exercise I drink plenty of water.

NOTE: When an adverb clause falls at the *end* of a sentence, no comma separates it from the main clause.

> FAULTY: Jane Addams founded Hull House, because she wanted to help Chicago's poor.

> REVISED: Jane Addams founded Hull House because she wanted to help Chicago's poor.

27c

(2)   Introductory phrases

Introductory phrases are usually set off from the rest of the sentence by commas. Such phrases include participial phrases, infinitive phrases, and prepositional phrases.

> Thinking that this might be his last chance, Scott struggled toward the Pole. (introductory participial phrase)

> To succeed in a male-dominated field, women engineers must work extremely hard. (introductory infinitive phrase)

> During the worst days of the Depression, movie attendance rose dramatically. (introductory prepositional phrase)

NOTE: Commas do not follow gerunds and gerund phrases that serve as subjects rather than modifiers.

> FAULTY: Laughing out loud, can release tension.

> REVISED: Laughing out loud can release tension.

If the introductory phrase is short and no ambiguity is possible, you may omit the comma.

> For the first time Clint felt truly happy.
>
> After the exam I took a four-hour nap.

(3)   Introductory transitional expressions

When they begin a sentence, conjunctive adverbs or other transitional expressions are usually set off from the rest of the sentence with commas.

> Originally, the pleats in the cummerbunds worn with tuxedos were designed to conceal theater tickets.
>
> Fortunately, Ralph got up the nerve to propose. Unfortunately, Alice turned him down.

NOTE: Various *nonessential elements*—mild interjections, for instance—may appear at the beginning of a sentence, and when they do, they are usually set off by commas (see 27d).

27d

☐   **EXERCISE 4**

Add commas in this paragraph where they are needed to set off an introductory element from the rest of the sentence.

> Once upon a time European "welfare states" supported ambitious social welfare programs. However these same governments today are having economic problems that are forcing them to seriously limit their social-welfare spending. In countries like Holland, Great Britain, and Germany unexpected economic and demographic conditions have forced governments to spend less. For instance longer life expectancies have made health care and old-age pensions more costly. In addition the declining birthrate has left fewer people to support the programs with tax revenues. Finally unemployed workers are placing a strain on unemployment insurance and disability insurance funds. Burdened by the increasing costs but unwilling to abandon social programs the nations of Western Europe are unable to invest in new businesses or industry. Because the governments cannot generate sufficient revenue to support them many programs are in serious trouble.   (Adapted from "The Welfare Crisis," *Newsweek*)

27d   Setting Off Nonessential Elements from the Rest of the Sentence

Certain elements at the beginning, middle, or end of a sentence are considered nonessential, or parenthetical. Although these words, phrases, or clauses do contribute to the meaning of the sentence, they are not essential to its meaning.

> Designer jeans are a contradiction in terms, like educational television. (Fran Lebowitz)

> There is no place I know of, other than the bathtub, where people should not have to worry about manners. (Judith Martin)

Commas should mark the boundaries of nonessential elements to keep them from blending into the rest of the sentence. (If the nonessential element falls at the beginning or end of a sentence, only one comma sets it off.)

(1) Nonrestrictive modifiers

Modifying phrases or clauses may be restrictive or nonrestrictive.

Restrictive modifiers limit the meaning of the word or word group they modify, and they should not be separated from it by commas.

> Men who were drafted when war was declared found themselves at a disadvantage.

Who were drafted when war was declared limits the noun *men* to just those who were drafted, and it is therefore *restrictive.* The modifying clause is essential to the meaning of *men*, the noun it modifies. Without the modifying clause, the meaning of the sentence would change.

Nonrestrictive modifiers do not limit or particularize the words they modify; they merely supply additional information about them. Therefore, they should be set off by commas.

> Men, who were drafted when war was declared, found themselves at a disadvantage.

In this sentence, the modifying clause *who were drafted when war was declared,* set off by commas, is nonrestrictive. The modifying clause in this case describes *all* the men, and therefore it is not essential to the meaning of the noun it modifies. Without the modifying clause, the sentence would still be about all the men.

As the following examples illustrate, commas set off nonrestrictive modifiers *only*—never restrictive modifiers.

> The counterculture hero who created Zap Comix during the 1960's has also had artwork displayed at the Whitney Museum of American Art. (restrictive clause)

> Robert Crumb, who created Zap Comix during the 1960's, is credited with popularizing the slogan "Keep on Truckin'." (nonrestrictive clause)

Environmental groups have become much more militant in recent years; now the sincere and passionate demands that such groups make are inspiring recreational campers and the logging industry to mobilize against them. (restrictive clause)

Environmental groups have become much more militant in recent years; now their sincere and passionate demands, which groups like recreational campers and the logging industry oppose, are inspiring controversy. (nonrestrictive clause)

The president hoping to encourage Americans to become more physically fit was Dwight D. Eisenhower. (restrictive phrase)

President Eisenhower, hoping to encourage Americans to become more physically fit, created the President's Council on Youth Fitness. (nonrestrictive phrase)

or

Hoping to encourage Americans to become more physically fit, President Eisenhower created the President's Council on Youth Fitness. (nonrestrictive phrase)

27d To determine whether a particular modifier is restrictive or nonrestrictive, ask yourself the following questions.

Tests for Determining Whether Modifier Is Restrictive or Nonrestrictive

1. Is the modifier essential to the meaning of the noun it modifies (*The counterculture hero who created Zap Comix*—not just any counterculture hero)? If so, it is restrictive and does not take commas. If not, commas should set off the modifier.
2. Is the modifier introduced by *that* (*the sincere and passionate demands that such groups make*)? If so, it is restrictive. *That* cannot introduce a nonrestrictive clause.
3. Can you delete the relative pronoun without causing ambiguity or confusion (*the sincere and passionate demands [that] such groups make*)? If so, the clause is restrictive and requires no commas. (A relative pronoun that is not the subject of the relative clause can be deleted if the clause is restrictive. Relative pronouns that introduce nonrestrictive clauses, however, cannot be deleted.)
4. Can you rearrange the sentence so that the modifying phrase or clause precedes the word or word group it modifies (*Hoping to encourage Americans to become more physically fit, President Eisenhower . . .*)? If so, the modifier is nonrestrictive and requires a comma. Restrictive phrases and clauses, on the other hand, nearly always *follow* the words they modify.

☐ **EXERCISE 5**

Insert commas where necessary to set off nonrestrictive phrases and clauses.

   The Statue of Liberty which was dedicated in 1886 has undergone extensive renovation. Its supporting structure whose designer was the French engineer Alexandre Gustave Eiffel is made of iron. The Statue of Liberty created over a period of nine years by sculptor Frédéric-Auguste Bartholdi stands 151 feet tall. The people of France who were grateful for American help in the French revolution raised the money to pay the sculptor who created the statue. The people of the United States contributing over $100,000 raised the money for the pedestal on which the statue stands.

(2) Nonrestrictive appositives

An **appositive** is a noun or noun phrase that identifies or describes a noun, pronoun, or noun phrase (see 7f.4). A **nonrestrictive appositive,** one that provides nonessential information about the word or words it modifies, is set off by commas.

> Steve Howe, relief pitcher for the Los Angeles Dodgers, struggled with a cocaine habit. (Appositive *relief pitcher for the Los Angeles Dodgers* further identifies Howe but is not essential to the meaning of *Steve Howe.*)

An appositive that is essential to the meaning of the word or word group it modifies is, however, **restrictive** and takes no commas. Normally, an appositive is restrictive if it is more specific than the noun that precedes it.

> Orson Welles's film *Citizen Kane* has received great critical acclaim. (Without the appositive *Citizen Kane*, the sentence would imply that Welles directed only one film; therefore, the appositive is essential to the meaning of *Orson Welles's film* and to the sentence.)

(3) Conjunctive adverbs and other transitional expressions

Conjunctive adverbs—words like *however, therefore, thus,* and *nevertheless*—and **transitional expressions** like *for example* and *on the other hand* qualify, clarify, and make connections explicit, but they are not essential to meaning. (For a complete list of such expressions, see 4d.4.)

   When a conjunctive adverb or transitional expression interrupts a clause, it is set off by commas.

The House Ethics Committee recommended reprimanding two members of Congress. The House, <u>however</u>, overruled the recommendation and voted to censure them.

The Outward Bound program, <u>according to its staff</u>, is extremely safe.

A conjunctive adverb or similar expression at the end of a clause is still parenthetical, and it is separated from the rest of the sentence by a single comma.

Some things were easier after school started. Other things were a lot harder, <u>however</u>.

These transitional expressions are also usually set off by commas when they introduce a sentence (see 27c.3).

NOTE: When a conjunctive adverb or transitional expression separates two independent clauses, it must be preceded by a semicolon or a period and followed by a comma (see 28c).

Laughter is the best medicine; <u>of course</u>, penicillin also comes in handy sometimes.

(4) Contradictory phrases

A parenthetical phrase that expresses contrast is usually set off from the rest of the sentence by commas.

This medication should be taken after a meal, <u>never on an empty stomach</u>.

It was Roger Maris, <u>not Mickey Mantle</u>, who broke Babe Ruth's home run record.

(5) Absolute phrases

An **absolute phrase** usually consists of a noun plus a participle. If the verb is a form of *to be*, however, the participle may be omitted (see 7f.3). An absolute phrase is always set off by commas from the sentence it modifies.

<u>His fear increasing</u>, he waited to enter the haunted house.

A number of soldiers have vanished in Southeast Asia, <u>their bodies never recovered</u>.

(6) Miscellaneous nonessential elements

Wherever they appear, the following nonessential elements are usually separated from the rest of the sentence by commas.

Tag questions (auxiliary verb + pronoun added to a statement)

This is your first day on the job, isn't it?

It seems possible, does it not, that carrots may provide some protection against cancer?

Names in direct address

I wonder, Mr. Honeywell, whether Mr. Albright deserves a raise.

Freddie, what's your opinion?

What do you think, Margie?

Mild interjections

Well, it's about time.

NOTE: Stronger interjections may be set off by dashes or exclamation points (see 31d and 26c.1).

Yes and No

Yes, we have no bananas.

No, we're all out of lemons.

☐   **EXERCISE 6**

Set off the nonessential elements in these sentences with commas. If a
sentence is correct, mark it with a C.

> EXAMPLE: Piranhas like sharks will attack and eat almost anything if
> the opportunity arises.
>
> Piranhas, like sharks, will attack and eat almost anything
> if the opportunity arises.

1. Kermit the frog is a muppet a cross between a marionette and a
   puppet.
2. The common cold a virus is frequently spread by hand contact not
   by mouth.
3. The account in the Bible of Noah's Ark and the forty-day flood may
   be based on an actual deluge.
4. More than two-thirds of U.S. welfare recipients, such as children, the
   aged, the severely disabled, and mothers of children under six, are
   people with legitimate reasons for not working.
5. The submarine *Nautilus* was the first to cross under the North Pole
   wasn't it?
6. The 1958 Ford Edsel was advertised with the slogan "Once you've
   seen it, you'll never forget it."
7. Superman was called Kal-El on the planet Krypton; on earth however he was known as Clark Kent not Kal-El.
8. Its sales topping any of his previous singles Elvis Presley's "Heart-
   break Hotel" was his first million seller.

9. Two companies Nash and Hudson joined in 1954 to form American Motors.
10. A firefly is a beetle not a fly and a prairie dog is a rodent not a dog.

27e   Using Commas in Other Conventional Contexts

(1)   Around direct quotations

In most cases, use commas to set off a direct quotation from the **identifying tag**—the phrase that identifies the speaker *(he said, she answered)*.

> Emerson said to Thoreau, "I greet you at the beginning of a great career."

> "I greet you at the beginning of a great career," Emerson said to Thoreau.

> "I greet you," Emerson said to Thoreau, "at the beginning of a great career."

When the identifying tag comes between two complete sentences, however, the tag is introduced by a comma but followed by a period.

> "Winning isn't everything," Vince Lombardi said. "It's the only thing."

If the first sentence of an interrupted quotation ends with a question mark or exclamation point, no commas are used.

> "Should we hold the front page?" she asked. "After all, nothing much has happened this week."

> "Hold the front page!" he cried. "This is the biggest story of the decade."

(For further information on punctuation with quotation marks, see 30f.)

(2)   Between names and titles or degrees

Use a comma to set off a person's name from his or her title or degree.

> Alice Vaselli, D.D.S.
>
> Henry Kissinger, Ph.D.
>
> Charles, Prince of Wales
>
> Perry White, Editor-in-Chief
>
> Martin Luther King, Jr.

If the title or degree precedes the name, however, no comma is required.

Dr. Kissinger

Prince Charles

No comma is used between a name and II, III, and so on.

Queen Elizabeth II

Andrew Bott III

(3)   In dates and addresses

Use commas to separate items in dates and addresses.

August 9, 1975 (9 August 1975—no commas—also acceptable)
600 West End Avenue, New York, N.Y. 10024

With hundreds watching, the space shuttle *Challenger* was launched on August 30, 1983, from Cape Canaveral, Florida.

NOTE: Commas are not used to separate the day from the month; when only the month and year are given, no commas are used (May 1968). No comma separates the street number from the street or the state name from the zip code. When a date or address punctuated with commas appears within a sentence, a comma follows its last element.

(4)   In salutations and closings

Use commas in informal correspondence following salutations and closings and following the complimentary close in personal or business correspondence.

Dear John,

Dear Aunt Sophie,

Love,

Sincerely,

NOTE: Keep in mind that in business correspondence a colon, not a comma, always follows the salutation (see 43a.4).

(5)   In long numbers

Use commas with long numbers.

When writing a number of four digits or more, separate the numbers by placing a comma every three digits, counting from the right.

1,200   (comma optional with four digits)
12,000
120,000
1,200,000

Commas are not required in long numbers used in addresses, telephone numbers, zip codes, or years.

☐   **EXERCISE 7**

Add commas where necessary to set off quotations, names, dates, addresses, and numbers in the following sentences.

1. India became independent on August 15 1947.
2. The UAW has over 1500000 dues-paying members.
3. Nikita Krushchev, former Soviet premier, said "We will bury you!"
4. Mount St. Helens, northeast of Portland Oregon, began erupting on March 27 1980 and eventually killed at least thirty people.
5. Located at 1600 Pennsylvania Avenue Washington D.C., the White House is a major tourist attraction.
6. In 1956, playing before a crowd of 64519 fans in Yankee Stadium in New York New York, Don Larsen pitched the first perfect game in World Series history.
7. Lewis Thomas M.D. was born in Flushing N.Y. and attended Harvard Medical School in Cambridge Massachusetts.
8. In 1967 2000000 people worldwide died of smallpox, but in 1977 only about twenty died.
9. "The reports of my death" Mark Twain remarked "have been greatly exaggerated."
10. The French explorer Jean Nicolet landed at Green Bay Wisconsin in 1634, and in 1848 Wisconsin became the thirtieth state; it has 10355 lakes and a population of over 4700000.

, 27f

27f Using Commas to Prevent Misreading

Commas may be needed simply for clarity. Consider the following sentence.

Those who can, sprint the final lap.

Without the comma, *can* appears to be an auxiliary verb ("Those who can sprint. . . .") and the sentence seems incomplete.

Commas that tell readers to pause prevent confusion and ambiguity. To facilitate reading, commas are used in two situations.

(1)   To indicate an omission

Use a comma to acknowledge the omission of a repeated word, usually a verb.

> Pam carried the box; Tim, the suitcase.
>
> Edwina went first; Marco, second.

(2)   To separate repeated words

Use a comma to separate words repeated consecutively within a sentence.

> Those of you who know me well, know well that I hate to get up in the morning.
>
> Everything bad that could have happened, happened.

☐   **EXERCISE 8**

Add commas where necessary to prevent misreading.

> EXAMPLE: Whatever will be will be.
>
> Whatever will be, will be.

1. According to Bob Frank's computer has three disk drives.
2. Da Gama explored Florida; Pizarro Peru.
3. By Monday evening students must begin preregistration for fall classes.
4. Whatever they built they built with care.
5. When batting practice carefully.
6. Brunch includes warm muffins topped with whipped butter and freshly brewed coffee.

☐   **EXERCISE 9**

Commas have been intentionally deleted from some of the following sentences. Add commas where needed, and be prepared to explain why each is necessary. If a sentence is correct, mark it with a C.

1. The world is before you and you need not take it or leave it as it was when you came in.   (James Baldwin, *Nobody Knows My Name)*
2. The great secret known to internists but still hidden from the general public is that most things get better by themselves. Most things in fact are better by morning.   (Lewis Thomas, *Lives of a Cell*)
3. Her face was young and smooth and fresh-looking.   (Katherine Anne Porter, "Rope")
4. He was wearing his cape and had his cap on and he came directly toward my machine and put his arm on my shoulder.   (Ernest Hemingway, "In Another Country")

27f

5. That she was in some way related to the girl though not of an age to be her mother was evident from their manner together.   (Shirley Hazzard, *The Transit of Venus*)

6. Every family is its own country and happy families are no more alike than peaceful nations.   (Frances Taliaferro, *Harper's*)

7. The downtown square is a brisk trading area its broad avenue resolving into a central square which framed by three-story buildings seems as though it is entirely walled.   (Joan Chase, *During the Reign of the Queen of Persia*)

8. It had rained long and hard during the night and an early morning mist drifted over Lake Placid. Tumbling low clouds covered the tops of the mountains that ringed the lake totally obscuring Whiteface highest of the peaks.   (Bernard F. Conners, *Dancehall*)

9. Dandelions crabgrass Queen Anne's lace lamb's quarters sheep sorrel and even bluegrass are but a small sample of a large constellation of alien plant species that have been assimilated into the ecology of North America.   (John C. Kricher, *Natural History*)

10. Oh I know intellectually that people have been circling the earth for centuries and there's nothing to it.   (Russell Baker, *New York Times Magazine*)

27g

27g Editing to Eliminate Misuse or Overuse of Commas

As you revise, be careful not to use commas in the following situations.

(1) Between two independent clauses

Using a comma alone to connect two independent clauses creates a comma splice (see 13a–e).

FAULTY: The season was unusually cool, nevertheless the orange crop was not seriously harmed.

REVISED: The season was unusually cool; nevertheless, the orange crop was not seriously harmed.

REVISED: The season was unusually cool. Nevertheless, the orange crop was not seriously harmed.

REVISED: The season was unusually cool, but the orange crop was not seriously harmed.

REVISED: Although the season was unusually cool, the orange crop was not seriously harmed.

(2) Around restrictive elements

Commas are not used to set off restrictive elements (see 27d).

FAULTY: Women, who seek to be equal to men, lack ambition.

REVISED: Women who seek to be equal to men lack ambition.

FAULTY: The film, *American Graffiti*, was directed by George Lucas.

REVISED: The film *American Graffiti* was directed by George Lucas.

FAULTY: They planned a picnic, in the park.

REVISED: They planned a picnic in the park.

FAULTY: The word, *snafu*, is an acronym for "situation normal—all fouled up."

REVISED: The word *snafu* is an acronym for "situation normal—all fouled up."

(3) Between inseparable grammatical constructions

A comma should not be placed between a subject and its predicate; a verb and its complement or direct object; a preposition and its object; or an adjective and the noun, pronoun, or noun phrase it modifies. Placing a comma between such constructions interrupts the logical flow of a sentence.

FAULTY: We think that anyone who can walk a straight line out of the office before lunch, ought to be able to travel the same route on the way back. (Advertisement, Spirits Council of the United States) (comma between subject and predicate)

REVISED: We think that anyone who can walk a straight line out of the office before lunch ought to be able to travel the same route on the way back.

FAULTY: Louis Braille developed, an alphabet of raised dots for the blind. (comma between verb and object)

REVISED: Louis Braille developed an alphabet of raised dots for the blind.

FAULTY: They relaxed somewhat during, the last part of the obstacle course. (comma between preposition and object)

REVISED: They relaxed somewhat during the last part of the obstacle course.

FAULTY: Wind-dispersed weeds include the well-known and plentiful, dandelions, milkweed, and thistle. (comma between adjective and words it modifies)

REVISED: Wind-dispersed weeds include the well-known and plentiful dandelions, milkweed, and thistle.

(4) Between a verb and a dependent clause to set off indirect quotations or indirect questions

Commas are not used between verb and dependent clause to set off indirect quotations or indirect questions.

FAULTY: Art Buchwald once said, that the problem with television news is that it has no second page.

REVISED: Art Buchwald once said that the problem with television news is that it has no second page.

FAULTY: The landlord asked, whether we would be willing to sign a two-year lease.

REVISED: The landlord asked whether we would be willing to sign a two-year lease.

27g

(5) Between coordinate phrases that contain correlative conjunctions

Commas are not used between coordinate phrases that contain correlative conjunctions.

FAULTY: As a rule, college students of twenty years ago had access to neither photocopiers, nor pocket calculators.

REVISED: As a rule, college students twenty years ago had access to neither photocopiers nor pocket calculators.

FAULTY: Both typewriters, and tape recorders were generally available, however.

REVISED: Both typewriters and tape recorders were generally available, however.

(6) Between certain paired elements

Commas are not used between two elements of a compound subject, predicate, object, complement, or auxiliary verb.

FAULTY: During the Middle Ages plagues, and pestilence were not uncommon. (Comma interrupts compound subject.)

REVISED: During the Middle Ages plagues and pestilence were not uncommon.

FAULTY: Women students age thirty-five and older are returning to college in large numbers, and tend to be very good students. (Comma interrupts compound predicate.)

REVISED: Women students age thirty-five and older are returning to college in large numbers and tend to be very good students.

FAULTY: Mattel has marketed a doctor's uniform, and an astronaut suit for its Barbie doll. (Comma interrupts compound object.)

REVISED: Mattel has marketed a doctor's uniform and an astronaut suit for its Barbie doll.

FAULTY: Bottled water appeals to many who believe it is pure, and fashionable. (Comma interrupts compound complement.)

REVISED: Bottled water appeals to many who believe it is pure and fashionable.

FAULTY: She can, and will be ready to run in the primary. (Comma interrupts compound auxiliary verb.)

REVISED: She can and will be ready to run in the primary.

REVISED: She can, and will, be ready to run in the primary.

,
27g

☐ **EXERCISE 10**

Unneeded commas have been intentionally added to some of the sentences that follow. Delete any unnecessary commas. If a sentence is correct, mark it with a C.

EXAMPLE: Spring fever, is a common ailment.

Spring fever is a common ailment.

1. A book is like a garden, carried in the pocket. (Arab proverb)
2. Like the iodine content of kelp, air freight, is something most Americans have never pondered. (*Time*)
3. Charles Rolls, and Frederick Royce manufactured the first Rolls Royce Silver Ghost, in 1907.
4. The hills ahead of him were rounded domes of grey granite, smooth as a bald man's pate, and completely free of vegetation. (Wilbur Smith, *Flight of the Falcon*)
5. Food here is scarce, and cafeteria food is vile, but the great advantage to Russian raw materials, when one can get hold of them, is that they are always fresh and untampered with. (Andrea Lee, *Russian Journal*)

In the following passage, punctuation errors have been deliberately made. Delete excess commas, and add any necessary ones. Be prepared to justify your revisions.

The most famous wild elephant in the world, lived in the mountain forest of Marsabit, in Kenya, and was called Ahmed. He was remarkable, for the beauty of his tusks. They descended, almost to the ground, in a graceful curve and their slender points were sharp, at the tip, and slightly raised. Ahmed was protected, from danger by special presidential decree. He was a symbol, of all the remaining animals running wild in Kenya and as such he was of some importance to both the science, and the business of supervising elephants. It would have been a very serious matter, if the president's wishes had been ignored, and Ahmed had been poached. Everywhere he went through the forest of Marsabit he was followed, by two armed forest rangers. When he left the safety of the mountain reserve, and wandered off into the surrounding desolation, his guards went, too. Because of this his position was always known, to the local authorities, and he became accustomed to people. He was very easy to photograph and every tourist, who came to Marsabit, wanted to see him. Thousands of visitors even made the uncomfortable trek, hundreds of miles away from their usual haunts, in order to view this singular beast.

But one night, in 1974, Ahmed died. (Adapted from Patrick Marnham, *Harper's*)

27g

28

The Semicolon

The **semicolon** is weaker than the period and stronger than the comma. It signals a shorter pause than the period, but a longer pause than the comma. The semicolon is used only between items of equal grammatical rank: two independent clauses, two phrases, and so on. The two principal uses of the semicolon are to separate independent clauses and, in certain situations, to separate elements in a series.

;
28a

Use Semicolons . . .
* To separate independent clauses (28a)
* To separate complex, internally punctuated clauses (28b)
* To separate clauses containing conjunctive adverbs (28c)
* To separate items in a series (28d)

28a Separating Independent Clauses

Use a semicolon rather than a coordinating conjunction or a period between independent clauses that are closely related in meaning.

> Paul Revere's *The Boston Massacre* is an early example of traditional American protest art; Edward Hicks's later "primitive" paintings are socially conscious art with a religious strain. (clauses related by contrast)

> The U.S. auto industry has been left in the dust of foreign competition; the automobile as we know it is doomed by dwindling fuel supplies; the American love affair with the automobile is dead. (Noel Grove, *National Geographic*) (clauses related by causality)

439

Separate sentences marked by periods would be correct but would fail to convey the close relationships between the clauses.

> Paul Revere's *The Boston Massacre* is an early example of traditional American protest art. Edward Hicks's later "primitive" paintings are socially conscious art with a religious strain.

Periods would also produce short, choppy sentences.

> The U.S. auto industry has been left in the dust of foreign competition. The automobile as we know it is doomed by dwindling fuel supplies. The American love affair with the automobile is dead.

Coordinating conjunctions, although also grammatically correct, would produce rambling sentences that lack focus.

> Paul Revere's *The Boston Massacre* is an early example of traditional American protest art, but Edward Hicks's later "primitive" paintings are socially conscious art with a religious strain.

> The U.S. auto industry has been left in the dust of foreign competition, and the automobile as we know it is doomed by dwindling fuel supplies, and the American love affair with the automobile is dead.

NOTE: Using only a comma or no punctuation at all between independent clauses will produce a comma splice or a fused sentence (see Chapter 13).

28b Separating Complex, Internally Punctuated Clauses

Even when two clauses are already joined by a coordinating conjunction, use a semicolon instead of a comma before the coordinating conjunction if one clause contains internal punctuation or is long or complex.

The semicolon in the following sentence not only distinguishes the two clauses but also emphasizes the warning at the end by isolating it.

> If such a world government is not established by a process of agreement among nations, I believe it will come anyway, and in a much more dangerous form; for war or wars can only result in one power being supreme and dominating the rest of the world by its overwhelming military supremacy. (Albert Einstein, *Einstein on Peace*)

Using a semicolon to separate clauses linked by a coordinating conjunction does more than clarify your meaning. It also conveys strong contrasts or firm distinctions between ideas.

☐   **EXERCISE 1**

Add semicolons, periods, or commas plus coordinating conjunctions where necessary to separate independent clauses. Reread the paragraph when you have finished to make certain no comma splices or fused sentences remain.

EXAMPLE: *Birth of a Nation* was one of the earliest epic movies it was based on the book *The Klansman.*

Birth of a Nation was one of the earliest epic movies; it was based on the book *The Klansman.*

During the 1950's movie attendance declined because of the increasing popularity of television. As a result, numerous gimmicks were introduced to draw audiences into theaters. One of the first of these was Cinerama, in this technique three pictures were shot side by side and projected on a curved screen. Next came 3-D, complete with special glasses, *Bwana Devil* and *The Creature from the Black Lagoon* were two early 3-D ventures. *The Robe* was the first picture filmed in Cinemascope in this technique a shrunken image was projected on a screen twice as wide as it was tall. Smell-O-Vision (or Aroma-rama) was a short-lived gimmick that enabled audiences to smell what they were viewing problems developed when it became impossible to get one odor out of the theater in time for the next smell to be introduced. William Castle's *Thirteen Ghosts* introduced special glasses for cowardly viewers who wanted to be able to control what they saw, the red part of the glasses was the "ghost viewer" and the green part was the "ghost remover." Perhaps the ultimate in movie gimmicks accompanied the film *The Tingler* when this film was shown seats in the theater were wired to generate mild electric shocks. Unfortunately, the shocks set off a chain reaction that led to hysteria in the theater. During the 1960's such gimmicks all but disappeared, viewers were able once again to simply sit back and enjoy a movie.

;
28b

☐   **EXERCISE 2**

Combine each of the following sentence groups into one sentence that contains only two independent clauses. Use a semicolon to join the two clauses. You will need to add, delete, relocate, or change some words; keep experimenting until you find the arrangement that best conveys the sentence's meaning.

EXAMPLE: The Congo River Rapids is a ride at the Dark Continent in Tampa, Florida. Riders raft down the river. They glide alongside jungle plants and animals.

The Congo River Rapids is a ride at the Dark Continent in Tampa, Florida; riders raft down the river, gliding alongside jungle plants and animals.

1. Amusement parks offer exciting rides. They are thrill packed. They flirt with danger.

2. Free Fall is located in Atlanta's Six Flags over Georgia. In this ride, riders travel up a 128-foot-tall tower. They plunge down at 55 miles per hour.
3. In the Sky Whirl riders go 115 feet up in the air and circle about 75 times. This ride is located in Great America. Great America parks are in Gurnee, Illinois, and Santa Clara, California.
4. The Kamikaze Slide can be found at the Wet 'n Wild parks in Arlington, Texas, and Orlando, Florida. This ride is a slide 300 feet long. It extends 60 feet in the air.
5. Parachuter's Perch is another exciting ride. It is found at Great Adventure in Jackson, New Jersey. Its chutes fall at 25 feet per second.
6. Astroworld in Houston, Texas, boasts Greezed Lightnin'. This ride is an 80-foot-high loop. The ride goes from 0 to 60 miles per hour in four seconds and moves forward and backward.
7. The Beast is at Kings Island near Cincinnati, Ohio. The Beast is a wooden roller coaster. It has a 7400-foot track and goes 70 miles per hour.   (Adapted from *Seventeen*)

28c   Separating Clauses Containing Conjunctive Adverbs

Use a semicolon between two closely related independent clauses when the second clause is introduced by a conjunctive adverb or other transitional expression. (For a complete list of such expressions, see 4d.4.)

> Thomas Jefferson brought 200 vanilla beans and a recipe for vanilla ice cream back from France; <u>thus</u>, he gave America its all-time favorite ice-cream flavor.

Within a clause, the position of a conjunctive adverb or other transitional expression may vary, and so will the punctuation (see 21e).

☐   **EXERCISE 3**

Combine each of the following sentence groups into one sentence that contains only two independent clauses. Use a semicolon and the conjunctive adverb or transitional phrase in parentheses to join the two clauses, adding commas within clauses where necessary. You will need to add, delete, relocate, or change some words. There is no one correct version; keep experimenting until you find the arrangement you feel is most effective.

EXAMPLE: The Aleutian Islands are located off the west coast of Alaska. They are an extremely remote chain of islands. They are sometimes called America's Siberia. (in fact)

The Aleutian Islands, located off the west coast of Alaska, are an extremely remote chain of islands; in fact, they are sometimes called America's Siberia.

1. The Aleutians lie between the North Pacific Ocean and the Bering Sea. The weather there is harsh. Dense fog, 100-mile-per-hour winds, and even tidal waves and earthquakes are not uncommon. (for example)
2. These islands constitute North America's largest network of active volcanoes. The Aleutians boast some beautiful scenery. The islands are relatively unexplored. (still)
3. The Aleutians are home to a wide variety of birds. Numerous animals, such as fur seals and whales, are found there. These islands may house the largest concentration of marine animals in the world. (in fact)
4. During World War II, thousands of American soldiers were stationed on Attu Island. They were stationed on Adak Island. The Japanese eventually occupied both Attu and Kiska Islands. (however)
5. The islands' original population of native Aleuts was drastically reduced in the eighteenth century by Russian fur traders. Today the total population is only about 8500. The U.S. military and its employees comprise more than half of this. (consequently)   (Adapted from Lael Morgan, *National Geographic*)

;
28d

28d   Separating Items in a Series

Use semicolons between items in a series when one or more of these items are sufficiently complex to require commas. Without semicolons it may be difficult to distinguish the individual elements in the series.

Three papers are posted on the bulletin board outside the building: a description of the exams; a list of appeal procedures for students who fail; and an employment ad from an automobile factory, addressed specifically to candidates whose appeals are turned down. (Andrea Lee, *Russian Journal*)

As ballooning became established, a series of firsts ensued: the first balloonist in the United States was 13-year-old Edward Warren, 1784; the first woman aeronaut was a Madame Thible who, depending on your source, either recited poetry or sang as she lifted off; the first airmail letter, written by Ben Franklin's grandson, was carried by balloon; and the first bird's-eye photograph of Paris was taken by a balloon. (Elaine B. Steiner, *Games*)

Each of the sentences above calls for strong punctuation. Even when the items in a series are brief, however, semicolons are required if any element in the series contains commas or other internal punctuation.

Laramie, Wyoming; Wyoming, Delaware; and Delaware, Ohio were the first three places they visited.

☐   EXERCISE 4

Replace commas with semicolons where necessary to separate lengthy, complex, or internally punctuated items in a series.

> EXAMPLE: Luxury automobiles have some strong selling points: they are status symbols, some, such as the Corvette, appreciate in value, and they are usually comfortable and well appointed.
>
> Luxury automobiles have some strong selling points: they are status symbols; some, such as the Corvette, appreciate in value; and they are usually comfortable and well appointed.

1. A quarter of a million Americans marched on Washington in 1983 to commemorate the twentieth anniversary of Dr. King's "I Have a Dream" speech, to remind the government that many Americans, even those who attended the 1963 march, are still without jobs and full equality, and to demonstrate for peace.
2. Steroids, used by some athletes, can be dangerous because they can affect the pituitary gland, causing a lowered sperm count, because they have been linked to the development of liver tumors, and because they can stimulate the growth of some cancers.
3. Tennessee Williams wrote *The Glass Menagerie*, which is about a handicapped young woman and her family, *A Streetcar Named Desire*, which starred Marlon Brando, and *Cat on a Hot Tin Roof*, which won a Pulitzer Prize.
4. New expressions like *outro*, used to designate the segment of a broadcast where the announcer signs off, *heavy breather*, used to describe a popular romance novel, *commuter marriage*, a union in which the partners live and work in different places, and *dentophobe*, a person who is afraid of dentists, are terms which have not yet appeared in most dictionaries.
5. Carl Yastrzemski is the former Red Sox star who replaced Ted Williams in 1961, joining Boston to play left field, who was chosen an all-star eighteen times, and who hit over 450 home runs in his career and was inducted into the Hall of Fame.

;
28d

☐   EXERCISE 5

Combine each of the following sentence groups into one sentence that includes a series of items separated by semicolons. You will need to add, delete, relocate, or change words. Try several versions of each sentence until you find the most effective arrangement.

> EXAMPLE: Collecting baseball cards is a worthwhile hobby. It helps children learn how to bargain and trade. It also encour-

ages them to assimilate, evaluate, and compare data about major league ball players. Perhaps most important, it encourages them to find role models in the athletes whose cards they collect.

Collecting baseball cards is a worthwhile hobby because it helps children learn how to bargain and trade; encourages them to assimilate, evaluate, and compare data about major league ball players; and, perhaps most important, encourages them to find role models in the athletes whose cards they collect.

1. A good dictionary offers definitions of words, including some obsolete and nonstandard words. It provides information about synonyms, usage, and word origins. It also offers information on pronunciation and syllabication.
2. The flags of the Scandinavian countries all depict a cross on a solid background. Denmark's flag is red with a white cross. Norway's flag is also red, but its cross is blue, outlined in white. Sweden's flag is blue with a yellow cross.
3. Over one hundred international collectors' clubs are thriving today. One of these associations is the Cola Clan, whose members buy, sell, and trade Coca-Cola memorabilia. Another is the Citrus Label Society. There is also a Cookie Cutter Collectors' Club.
4. Listening to the radio special, we heard "Shuffle Off to Buffalo" and "Moon Over Miami," both of which are about eastern cities. We heard "By the Time I Get to Phoenix" and "I Left My Heart in San Francisco," which mention western cities. Finally, we heard "The Star Spangled Banner," which seemed to be an appropriate finale.
5. There are three principal types of contact lenses. Hard contact lenses, also called conventional lenses, are easy to clean and handle and quite sturdy. Soft lenses, which are easily contaminated and must be cleaned and disinfected daily, are less durable. Gas-permeable lenses, sometimes advertised as semihard or semisoft lenses, look and feel like hard lenses but are more easily contaminated and less durable.

28e   Editing to Eliminate Misuse of Semicolons

Some writers use semicolons just because they feel that they are characteristic of a mature style. Others use them to break up the monotony of standard punctuation. But semicolons are only called for in the contexts outlined in this chapter. In the following situations a semicolon is not used.

Between items of unequal grammatical rank

A semicolon is not used between a dependent and an independent clause or between a phrase and a clause.

FAULTY: Because new drugs can now suppress the body's immune reaction; fewer organ transplants are rejected by the body. (Semicolon incorrectly used between dependent and independent clause.)

REVISED: Because new drugs can now suppress the body's immune reaction, fewer organ transplants are rejected by the body.

FAULTY: Increasing rapidly; computer crime poses a challenge for government, financial, and military agencies. (Semicolon incorrectly used between phrase and clause.)

REVISED: Increasing rapidly, computer crime poses a challenge for government, financial, and military agencies.

In introducing a list

Use a colon, not a semicolon, to introduce a list.

FAULTY: The evening news is a battleground for the three major television networks; CBS, NBC, and ABC.

REVISED: The evening news is a battleground for the three major television networks: CBS, NBC, and ABC.

With direct quotations

A semicolon is not used to introduce a direct quotation. (See 30a for information on punctuation with direct quotations.)

FAULTY: Marie Antoinette said; "Let them eat cake."

REVISED: Marie Antoinette said, "Let them eat cake."

28f Editing to Eliminate Overuse of Semicolons

Semicolons should be used selectively. A string of clauses connected by semicolons can be extremely tedious. Consider the following paragraph.

Art deco was a reflection of the jazz age of the roaring 1920's and more sober 1930's; at that time it was the dominant style, particularly in the United States. This was an art glorifying the machine; it was inspired by the speed of the automobile and airplane. It found expression in soaring skyscrapers and luxury ocean liners; streamlined statuettes, overstuffed furniture, and jukebox designs; and radio cabinets, toasters, and other kitchen gadgetry. Art deco was motivated by the vibrant energy released at the end of World War I; it was motivated by a faith in mechanized modernity; and it was also inspired by a joy in such new materials as glass, aluminum, polished steel, and shiny chrome.

Although semicolon use in the preceding paragraph is grammatically correct, the string of clauses connected by semicolons creates a monotonous passage. Compare the following paragraph.

> Art deco was a reflection of the jazz age of the roaring 1920's and more sober 1930's when it was the dominant style, particularly in the United States. This was an art glorifying the machine and inspired by the speed of the automobile and airplane. It found expression in everything from soaring skyscrapers and luxury ocean liners to streamlined statuettes, overstuffed furniture, jukebox designs, radio cabinets, toasters, and other kitchen gadgetry. Art deco was motivated by the vibrant energy released at the end of World War I, a faith in mechanized modernity, and a joy in such new materials as glass, aluminum, polished steel, and shiny chrome. (William Fleming, *Arts & Ideas*)

☐   **EXERCISE 6**

Read this paragraph carefully. Then add semicolons where necessary and delete excess or incorrectly used ones, substituting other punctuations where necessary.

> Barnstormers were aviators; who toured the country after World War I, giving people short airplane rides and exhibitions of stunt flying, the name *barnstormer* was derived from the use of barns as airplane hangars. Americans' interest in airplanes had all but disappeared after the war; planes had served their function in battle, but when the war ended, most people saw no future in aviation. The barnstormers helped popularize flying; especially in rural areas. Some of them were pilots who had flown in the war; others were just young men with a thirst for adventure. They gave people rides in airplanes, sometimes they charged a dollar a minute. For most passengers, this was their first ride in an airplane, in fact, sometimes it was their first sight of one. In the early 1920's, people grew bored with what the barnstormers had to offer; so groups of pilots began to stage spectacular—but often dangerous—stunt shows. Then, after Lindbergh's 1927 flight across the Atlantic; Americans suddenly needed no encouragement to embrace aviation. The barnstormers had outlived their usefulness; and an era ended. (Adapted from William Goldman, *Adventures in the Screen Trade*)

;
28f

29

The Apostrophe

Use an apostrophe. . .
- To form the possessive case (29a)
- To indicate omissions in contractions (29c)
- To form plurals (29d)

29a

29a Forming the Possessive Case

The possessive case indicates ownership, specifically or generally. In English the possessive case of nouns and indefinite pronouns is indicated in two ways: either with a phrase that includes the word *of* (the hands *of* the clock) or with an apostrophe and, in most cases, an -s (the clock's hands). Special forms are used to indicate the possessive case of personal pronouns (see 29b).

With singular nouns and indefinite pronouns

To form the possessive case of singular nouns and indefinite pronouns, add -'s.

"The Monk's Tale" is one of Chaucer's *Canterbury Tales*.

When we would arrive at Dan's house was anyone's guess.

With singular nouns ending in -s

To form the possessive case of singular nouns that end in -s, add -'s in most cases.

Reading Henry James's *The Ambassadors* was not Maris's idea of fun.

The class**'s** time was changed to 8 A.M.

However, a few singular nouns that end with an *s* or *z* sound require only an apostrophe in the possessive case. This is because pronouncing the possessive ending as a separate syllable would create an awkward-sounding phrase.

For goodness' sake—are we really required to read both Aristrophanes' *Lysistrata* and Thucydides' *History of the Peloponesian War?*

An apostrophe is not used to form the possessive case of a title that already contains an -*'s* ending; use a phrase instead.

NOT *Logan's Run's* star   BUT the star of *Logan's Run*

With plural nouns ending in -*s*

To form the possessive case of regular plural nouns (those that end in -*s* or -*es*), add only an apostrophe.

The Readers' Guide to Periodical Literature is located in the reference section.

Two weeks' severance pay and three months' medical benefits were available to some workers.

The Lopezes' three children are identical triplets.

With irregular plural nouns

To form the possessive case of nouns that have irregular plurals, add -*'s*.

Long after they were gone, the geese**'s** honking could still be heard.

The Children's Hour is a play by Lillian Hellman; *The Women's Room* is a novel by Marilyn French.

The two oxen**'s** yokes were securely attached to the cart.

NOTE: Noun plurals that are not possessive do not use apostrophes (see 29b).

With compound nouns or groups of words

To form the possessive case of compound words or of word groups, add -*'s* to the last word.

The editor-in-chief's position is open.

He accepted the Secretary of State's resignation under protest.

This is someone else's responsibility.

29a

With two or more items

To indicate individual ownership of two or more items, add -'s to each item. To indicate joint ownership, add -'s only to the last item.

INDIVIDUAL OWNERSHIP: Ernest Hemingway's and Gertrude Stein's writing styles have some similarities. (Hemingway and Stein have two separate writing styles.)

JOINT OWNERSHIP: Gilbert and Sullivan's operettas include *The Pirates of Penzance* and *H.M.S. Pinafore.* (Gilbert and Sullivan collaborated on both operettas.)

☐   EXERCISE 1

In these examples change the modifying phrases that follow the nouns to possessive forms that precede the nouns.

EXAMPLE: the pen belonging to my aunt
          my aunt's pen

1. the songs recorded by Ray Charles
2. the red glare of the rockets
3. the idea Warren had
4. the housekeeper Leslie and Rick hired
5. the first choice of everyone
6. the dinner given by Harris
7. furniture designed by William Morris
8. the climate of Bermuda
9. the sport the Russells play
10. the role created by the French actress

☐   EXERCISE 2

Wherever possible change each word or phrase in parentheses to its possessive form. In some cases you may have to use a phrase to indicate possession.

EXAMPLE: The (children) toys were scattered all over their (parents) bedroom.

The children**'s** toys were scattered all over their parents' bedroom.

1. Jane (Addams) settlement house was called Hull House.
2. (*A Room of One's Own*) popularity increased with the rise of feminism.
3. The (chief petty officer) responsibilities are varied.
4. Vietnamese (restaurants) numbers have grown dramatically in ten (years) time.
5. (Harold Robbins) and (Jacqueline Susann) popular novels have sold millions of copies.

29a

29b   Omitting the Apostrophe

An apostrophe is not used with plural nouns that are not posses-sive or in the possessive case of personal pronouns.

With plural nouns

Noun plurals that are not possessive never include apostro-phes.

FAULTY	REVISED
The Thompson's aren't at home.	The Thompsons aren't at home.
The down vest's were very warm.	The down vests were very warm.
The Philadelphia Seventy Sixer's played well.	The Philadelphia Seventy Sixers played well.

With personal pronouns

Personal pronouns never use apostrophes to form the pos-sessive case. Rather, they have special, possessive forms—*his, hers, its, ours, yours, theirs,* and *whose*—none of which include apostrophes.

FAULTY	REVISED
This ticket must be your's or her's.	This ticket must be yours or hers.
The next turn is their's.	The next turn is theirs.
The doll had lost it's right eye.	The doll had lost its right eye.
The next great moment in his-tory is our's.	The next great moment in his-tory is ours.

NOTE: Do not confuse these possessive forms of personal pro-nouns with contractions (see 29c.1).

☐   **EXERCISE 3**

In the following sentences, correct any errors in the use of apostrophes to form noun plurals or the possessive case of personal pronouns. If a sentence is correct, mark it with a *C*.

EXAMPLE: Dr. Sampson's lecture's were more interesting than her's.

Dr. Sampson's lectures were more interesting than hers.

1. The Schaefer's seats are right next to our's.
2. Most of the college's in the area offer computer courses open to outsider's as well as to their own students.
3. The network completely revamped its daytime programming.
4. Is the responsibility for the hot dog concession Cynthia's or your's?

5. Romantic poets are his favorite's.
6. Debbie returned the books to the library, forgetting they were her's.
7. Cultural revolution's do not occur very often, but when they do they bring sweeping change's.
8. Roll-top desk's are eagerly sought by antique dealer's.
9. A flexible schedule is one of their priority's, but it isn't one of our's.
10. Is yours the red house or the brown one?

29c Indicating Omissions in Contractions —

Apostrophes are used to mark the omission of letters or numbers in contractions.

(1) Omitted letters

Apostrophes replace omitted letters in frequently used contractions that combine a pronoun and a verb *(he+will = he'll)* or the elements of a verb phrase *(do + not = don't)*.

29c

Commonly Used Contractions

it's (it is)	let's (let us)
he's (he is)	we've (we have)
who's (who is)	they're (they are)
isn't (is not)	we'll (we will)
wouldn't (would not)	I'm (I am)
couldn't (could not)	we're (we are)
don't (do not)	you'd (you would)
won't (will not)	

Although acceptable in speech and informal writing, contractions are not generally used in college writing except to reproduce dialogue or to create an informal tone deliberately.

Be especially careful not to confuse contractions with the possessive forms of personal pronouns (see 22c and 29b).

Contractions versus Possessive Forms

Contractions	*Possessive Forms*
Who's on first?	Whose book is this?
They're playing our song.	Their team is winning.
It's raining.	Its paws were muddy.
You're a real pal.	Your résumé is very impressive.

(2)   Omitted numbers

In informal writing an apostrophe may be used to represent the century in a year.

Crash of '29   Class of '90   '57 Chevy

In college writing, however, write out the year in full: *the Crash of 1929, the class of 1990, a 1957 Chevrolet.*

☐   **EXERCISE 4**

In the following sentences correct any errors in the use of standard contractions or personal pronouns. If a sentence is correct, mark it with a C.

 EXAMPLE: Who's troops were sent to Korea?

           Whose troops were sent to Korea?

 1. Its never easy to choose a major; whatever you decide, your bound to have second thoughts.
 2. Olive Oyl asked, "Whose that knocking at my door?"
 3. Their watching too much television; in fact, they're eyes are glazed.
 4. Whose coming along on the backpacking trip?
 5. The horse had been badly treated; it's spirit was broken.
 6. Your correct in assuming its a challenging course.
 7. Sometimes even you're best friends won't tell you your boring.
 8. They're training had not prepared them for the hardships they faced.
 9. It's too early to make a positive diagnosis.
10. Robert Frost wrote the poem that begins, "Who's woods these are, I think I know."

29d   Forming Plurals ─────────────

The apostrophe plus -*s* is used to form plurals in some special cases. In these cases adding an -*'s* avoids a confusing combination that might obscure the fact that the word is plural.

With plurals of letters

The Italian language has no *j*'**s** or *k*'**s**.

Mind your *p*'**s** and *q*'**s**.

Sesame Street helps children learn their ABC'**s**.

With plurals of numbers

Dick Button could make outstanding figure 8'**s**.

Styles of the 1950'**s** are back in fashion.

Some writers prefer to omit the apostrophe with plurals of numbers.

The 1920s are sometimes called the roaring twenties.

With plurals of symbols

The +'s and −'s indicate positive and negative numbers, respectively.

The entire paper used &'s instead of *and*'s.

With plurals of abbreviations followed by periods

Only two R.N.'s worked the 7-to-11 shift.

Four Ph.D.'s and seven M.D.'s attended the high school reunion.

With plurals of words referred to as words

The supervisor would accept no *if*'s, *and*'s, or *but*'s.

His first sentence contained three *therefore*'s.

29d

NOTE: Letters, numerals, and words spoken of as themselves are always set in italic type (see 33c); the plural ending is further distinguished by being set in Roman type. When you write or type, indicate italics by underlining. If no confusion is possible, you may omit the apostrophe, but you should still use italics where they are required.

The editor deleted all the *4*s in the report.

☐ **EXERCISE 5**

In the following sentences, form correct plurals for the letters, numbers, and words in parentheses. Underline to indicate italics where necessary.

EXAMPLE: The word *bubbles* contains three (b).

The word *bubbles* contains three *b*'s.

1. She closed her letter with a row of (x) and (o) to indicate kisses and hugs.
2. The three (R) are reading, writing, and 'rithmetic.
3. The report included far too many (maybe) and too few (definitely).
4. His (4) and (9) were almost identical, and his (5) looked exactly like (s).
5. Her two (M.A.) were in sociology and history.

30

Quotation Marks

" "

30a

Use quotation marks. . .
- To set off direct quotations (30a)
- To set off titles (30b)
- To set off words used in a special sense (30c)
- To set off dialogue, long prose passages, and poetry (30e)

A **direct quotation** is a passage reproduced word for word from another source. A pair of quotation marks (" ") establishes the boundaries of a direct quotation.

30a Setting Off Direct Quotations

When you reproduce exactly a word, phrase, or brief passage from someone else's speech or writing, you must enclose the borrowed material in a pair of quotation marks.

> Gloria Steinem observed, "We are becoming the men we once hoped to marry."

Do not use quotation marks with **indirect quotations**—that is, when you report someone else's written or spoken words without quoting them exactly.

> Gloria Steinem observed that many women are now becoming the men they once hoped to marry.

Use single quotation marks to enclose a quotation within a quotation.

> Claire said, "It was Liberace who first said, 'I cried all the way to the bank.'"

455

Special punctuation problems occur when quoted material must be set off from phrases (like *he said*) that identify its source. The following guidelines cover the most common problems.

With an identifying tag in the middle of a passage

Use a pair of commas to set off the identifying phrase that interrupts a passage.

"In the future," pop artist Andy Warhol once said, "everyone will be world-famous for 15 minutes."

If the identifying tag follows a completed sentence but the quoted passage continues, use a period after the tag. Begin the new sentence with a capital letter, and place it within quotation marks.

"Be careful," Erin warned. "Reptiles can be tricky."

With an introductory identifying tag

Use a comma after the tag that introduces quoted speech or writing.

The Raven repeated, "Nevermore."

When you quote just a word or phrase, however, you may also introduce it without any punctuation.

The weatherman said he expected March to be "unpredictable."

Use a colon instead of a comma before a long or formal quotation.

The Secretary of State announced: "All American citizens are asked to leave the area immediately. The instability of the military government and the acts of hostility toward Americans make this action necessary."

Use a colon before any quotation, even a brief one, if the introductory tag is an independent clause.

She gave her final answer: "No."

With an identifying tag at the end

Use a comma to set off the end of a quotation from the identifying tag that follows.

"Be careful out there," the sergeant warned.

If the quotation ends with a question mark or an exclamation point, however, that punctuation mark replaces the comma. The tag begins with a lower-case letter even though it follows end punctuation.

"Is Ankara the capital of Turkey?" she asked.
"Oh boy!" he cried.

If no identifying tag follows a quotation, use a period or other
appropriate end punctuation after the quotation.

The principal said, "Education is serious business."

☐   **EXERCISE 1**

Add single and double quotation marks to these sentences where necessary to set off direct quotations. Then add appropriate punctuation to
set off direct quotations from identifying tags. If a sentence is correct,
mark it with a C.

EXAMPLE: Wordsworth's phrase splendour in the grass was used as
             the title of a movie about young lovers.

             Wordsworth's phrase "splendour in the grass" was used
             as the title of a movie about young lovers.

1. Mr. Fox noted Few people can explain what Descartes' words I think,
   therefore I am actually mean.
2. Gertrude Stein said You are all a lost generation.
3. Freedom of speech does not guarantee anyone the right to yell fire in
   a crowded theater she explained.
4. Dorothy kept insisting there was no place quite like home.
5. If everyone will sit down the teacher announced the exam will begin.

" "

30b

30b   Setting Off Titles

Titles of short works and titles of parts of long works are enclosed
in quotation marks (other titles are set in italics; see 33a). Use
quotation marks for titles of the following.

Articles in magazines, newspapers, and professional journals

   "To Live in Harlem" *(Reader's Digest)*

   "A Doll for All Seasons" *(Philadelphia Inquirer)*

   "The Case for Syntactic Imagery" *(College English)*

Essays

   "Fenimore Cooper's Literary Offenses"

   "Once More to the Lake"

Short stories

   "Barn Burning"

   "I Stand Here Ironing"

Short poems (those not divided into numbered sections)

"Daddy"

"The Emperor of Ice Cream"

Songs

"The Star-Spangled Banner"

"Stairway to Heaven"

Chapters or sections of books

"The Poles of Violence: Ambrose Bierce and Richard Harding Davis" (Chapter 8 of *The American 1890's*)

"Miss Sharp Begins to Make Friends" (Chapter 10 of *Vanity Fair*)

"Franklin D. Roosevelt: The Politician as Opportunist" (Chapter 12 of *The American Political Tradition*)

Speeches

"I Have a Dream"

"How to Tell a Story"

Descriptive titles of speeches, such as Kennedy's Inaugural Address, are not enclosed in quotation marks.

Episodes of radio or television series

"Lucy Goes to the Hospital" *(I Love Lucy)*

"Do Civil Rights Equal Affirmative Action?" *(Firing Line)*

Single quotation marks indicate a title in a quotation already enclosed in double quotation marks.

I think what she said was, "Play it, Sam. Play 'As Time Goes By.'"

30c Setting Off Words Used in a Special Sense

Words used in a special sense are enclosed in quotation marks.

It was clear that adults approved of children who were "readers," but it was not at all clear why this was so. (Annie Dillard, *New York Times Magazine*)

It is often remarked that words are tricky—and that we are all prone to be deceived by "fast talkers," such as high-pressure salesmen, skillful propagandists, politicians or lawyers. (S. I. Hayakawa, "How Words Change Our Lives")

Coinages—that is, invented words—also take quotation marks.

> After the twins were born, Martha's station wagon became a "babymobile."

When a word is referred to as a word, however, it is italicized (see 33c).

> How do you pronounce *trough*?
>
> Is their name spelled *Smith* or *Smythe*?

When you quote a dictionary definition, put the word you are defining in italics and the definition in quotation marks.

> To *infer* means "to draw a conclusion"; to *imply* means "to suggest."

☐   **EXERCISE 2**

Add quotation marks to the following sentences where necessary to set off titles and words. If italics are incorrectly used, substitute quotation marks.

> EXAMPLE: To Tim, social security means a date for Saturday night.
>
>   To Tim, "social security" means a date for Saturday night.

1. *First Fig* and *Second Fig* are two of the poems in Edna St. Vincent Millay's *Collected Poems.*
2. In the article Feminism Takes a New Turn, Betty Friedan reconsiders some of the issues first raised in her 1964 book *The Feminine Mystique.*
3. Edwin Arlington Robinson's poem Richard Cory was the basis for the song Richard Cory written by Paul Simon.
4. *Beside* means next to, but *besides* means except.
5. In an essay on *An American Tragedy* published in *The Yale Review*, Robert Penn Warren noted, Theodore Dreiser once said that his philosophy of love might be called Varietism.

30d   Editing to Eliminate Misuse or Overuse of Quotation Marks

Misusing or overusing quotation marks weakens your writing by distracting readers.

Quotation marks should not be used in the following situations.

(1)   To convey special emphasis or sarcasm

FAULTY: William Randolph Hearst's "modest" home is a castle
called San Simeon.

REVISED: William Randolph Hearst's far-from-modest home is a castle called San Simeon.

(2)   To set off nicknames or slang

FAULTY: The former "Lady Di" became the Princess of Wales when
she married Prince Charles.

REVISED: The former Lady Diana Spencer became the Princess of
Wales when she married Prince Charles.

FAULTY: Dawn is "into" running.

REVISED: Dawn is very involved in running.

" "

30d

In formal writing situations, do not make the mistake of thinking
that quotation marks will make nonstandard or slang terms acceptable. Avoid substituting nicknames for full names or slang for
standard diction.

(3)   To enclose titles of long works

FAULTY: "War and Peace" is even longer than "Paradise Lost."

REVISED: *War and Peace* is even longer than *Paradise Lost.*

NOTE: Titles of long works are set in italics (see 33a).

(4)   To set off terms being defined

FAULTY: The word "tintinnabulation," meaning the ringing sound
of bells, was used by Poe in his poem "The Bells."

REVISED: The word *tintinnabulation*, meaning the ringing sound of
bells, was used by Poe in his poem "The Bells."

NOTE: Words that are defined should be italicized (see 33c).

(5)   To set off technical terms

FAULTY: "Biofeedback" is sometimes used to treat migraine headaches.

REVISED: Biofeedback is sometimes used to treat migraine headaches.

(6)   To set off the title on the title page of a student essay

FAULTY: "Images of Light and Darkness in George Eliot's *Adam Bede*"

REVISED: Images of Light and Darkness in George Eliot's *Adam Bede*

(7)   To set off indirect quotations

FAULTY: Freud wondered "what a woman wanted."

REVISED: Freud wondered what a woman wanted.

REVISED: Freud wondered, "What does a woman want?"

☐   **EXERCISE 3**

In the following paragraph, correct the use of single and double quotation marks to set off direct quotations (including dialogue), titles, and words used in a special sense. Supply the appropriate quotation marks where required, and delete those not required. Be careful not to use quotation marks where they are not necessary.

> In her essay 'The Obligation to Endure' from the book "Silent Spring," Rachel Carson writes: As Albert Schweitzer has said, 'Man can hardly even recognize the devils of his own creation.' Carson goes on to point out that many chemicals have been used to kill insects and other organisms which, she writes, are "described in the modern vernacular as pests." Carson believes such "advanced" chemicals, by contaminating our environment, do more harm than good. In addition to "Silent Spring," Carson is also the author of the book "The Sea Around Us." This work, divided into three sections (Mother Sea, The Restless Sea, and Man and the Sea About Him) was published in 1951.

30e   Setting Off Dialogue, Long Prose Passages, and Poetry

(1)   Dialogue

When you record dialogue, begin a new paragraph for each new speaker. Be sure to enclose the quoted words in quotation marks.

> "Sharp on time as usual," Davis said with his habitual guilty grin.
> "My watch is always a little fast," Castle said, apologizing for the criticism which he had not expressed. "An anxiety complex, I suppose." (Graham Greene, *The Human Factor*)

Notice that the phrases identifying the speaker (*Davis said, Castle said*) appear in the same paragraph as the speaker's words.

When you are quoting several paragraphs of dialogue by one speaker, begin each new paragraph with quotation marks. However, use closing quotation marks only at the end of the entire quoted passage, not at the end of each paragraph.

☐   **EXERCISE 4**

Add appropriate quotation marks to the dialogue in this passage, beginning a new paragraph whenever a new speaker is introduced.

The next time, the priest steered me into the confession box himself and left the shutter back [so] I could see him get in and sit down at the further side of the grille from me. Well, now, he said, what do they call you? Jackie, father, said I. And what's a-trouble to you, Jackie? Father, I said, feeling I might as well get it over while I had him in good humor, I had it all arranged to kill my grandmother.

He seemed a bit shaken by that, all right, because he said nothing for quite a while. My goodness, he said at last, that'd be a shocking thing to do. What put that into your head? Father, I said, feeling very sorry for myself, she's an awful woman. Is she? he asked. What way is she awful? She takes porter, father, I said, knowing well from the way Mother talked of it that this was a mortal sin, and hoping it would make the priest take a more favorable view of my case. Oh, my! he said, and I could see that he was impressed. And snuff, father, said I. That's a bad case, sure enough, Jackie, he said.   (Frank O'Connor, "First Confession")

(2) Long prose passages

A prose passage of more than four lines is set off from the body of your paper. Omit quotation marks and indent the text ten spaces from the left-hand margin, with double-spacing above and below the quotation and double-spacing between lines within it. A long prose passage is introduced by a colon.

```
     A portrait of Aunt Juley illustrates several of the
devices Galsworthy uses throughout The Forsyte Saga, such
as a journalistic detachment that is almost cruel in its
scrutiny, a subtle sense of the grotesque, and an ironic
stance:
               Aunt Juley stayed in her room, prostrated by the
          blow.  Her face, discoloured by tears, was
          divided into compartments by the little ridges
          of pouting flesh which had swollen with emotion
```

```
    . . . .  At fixed intervals she went to her
    drawer, and took from beneath the lavender bags
    a fresh pocket-handkerchief.  Her warm heart
    could not bear the thought that Ann was lying
    there so cold. (329)
Similar characterizations appear throughout the book. . . .
```

NOTE: When a quoted passage is a single paragraph or less, do not indent the first line. When quoting two or more paragraphs, indent each new paragraph three additional spaces.

If the long passage you are quoting already includes material quoted by the author, enclose those words in double quotation marks.

(3) Poetry

Three or fewer lines of poetry are treated like a short prose passage—enclosed in quotation marks and run into the text.

One of John Donne's best-known poems begins with the line, "Go and catch a falling star."

Two or more lines of poetry should be separated by a slash (/) (see 31m).

Alexander Pope writes, "True Ease in Writing comes from Art, not Chance, / As those move easiest who have learned to dance."

Four or more lines of poetry should be set off like a long prose passage (see 30e.2). For special emphasis, fewer lines may also be set off in this manner. Punctuation, spelling, capitalization, and indentation are reproduced *exactly*.

```
    Wilfred Owen, a poet who was killed in action in World
War I, expressed the horrors of war with vivid imagery:
            Bent double, like old beggars under sacks,
            Knock-kneed, coughing like hags, we cursed
              through sludge,
            Till on the haunting flares we turned our backs
            And towards our distant rest began to trudge. (22)
```

30f Using Quotation Marks with Other Punctuation

Quotation marks frequently occur along with other punctuation marks. Sometimes the quotation marks are placed inside other punctuation, and sometimes they are placed outside.

With final commas or periods

Quotation marks belong *outside* the comma or period at the end of a quotation.

Many, like Frost, think about "the road not taken," but not many really consider where it might have led them.

Janis Joplin sang, "Freedom's just another word for nothing left to lose."

With final semicolons or colons

Quotation marks belong *inside* a semicolon or colon at the end of a quotation.

Students who do not pass the functional-literacy test receive "certificates of completion"; those who pass are awarded diplomas.

Taxpayers were pleased with the first of the candidate's promised "sweeping new reforms": a balanced budget.

With question marks, exclamation points, and dashes

Quotation marks may be placed inside or outside a question mark, exclamation point, or dash at the end of a quotation, depending on the sentence's meaning.

If the question mark, exclamation point, or dash is part of the quotation, place the quotation marks *outside* the punctuation.

"Who's there?" she demanded.

"Stop!" he cried.

"Should we leave now, or—" Vicki paused, waiting for a sign from Joe.

If the question mark, exclamation point, or dash is not part of the quotation, place the quotation marks *inside* the punctuation.

Did you finish reading "The Black Cat"?

Whatever you do, don't yell "Uncle"!

The first essay—George Orwell's "Politics and the English language"—made quite an impression on the class.

" "
30f

If both the quotation and the tag are questions or exclamations, place the quotation marks *inside* the punctuation.

Who asked, "Is Paris Burning"**?**

☐   **EXERCISE 5**

Correct the use of quotation marks in the following sentences, making sure that the use and placement of any accompanying punctuation marks are consistent with accepted conventions. If a sentence is correct, mark it with a C.

EXAMPLE: The "Watergate" incident brought many new terms into the English language.

The Watergate incident brought many new terms into the English language.

1. Kilroy was here and Women and children first are two expressions *Bartlett's Familiar Quotations* attributes to "Anon."
2. Neil Armstrong said he was making a small step for man but a giant leap for mankind.
3. "The answer, my friend", Bob Dylan sang, "is blowin' in the wind".
4. The novel was a real "thriller," complete with spies and counter-spies, mysterious women, and exotic international chases.
5. The sign said, Road liable to subsidence; it meant that we should look out for potholes.
6. One of William Blake's best-known lines—To see a world in a grain of sand—opens his poem Auguries of Innocence.
7. In James Thurber's short story The Catbird Seat, Mrs. Barrows annoys Mr. Martin by asking him silly questions like Are you tearing up the pea patch? Are you scraping around the bottom of the pickle barrel? and Are you lifting the oxcart out of the ditch?
8. I'll make him an offer he can't refuse, promised "the godfather" in Mario Puzo's novel.
9. What did Timothy Leary mean by "Turn on, tune in, drop out?"
10. George, the protagonist of Bernard Malamud's short story, A Summer's Reading, is something of an "underachiever."

" "

30f

31

Other Punctuation Marks

The Colon

The **colon** is a strong punctuation mark that points ahead to the remainder of the sentence, linking the words that follow it to the words that precede it.

31a Using a Colon to Introduce Material

(1)   Lists or series

Colons set off lists or series, including those introduced by phrases like *the following* or *as follows.*

> He looked like whatever his beholder imagined him to be: a bank clerk, a high school teacher, a public employee, a librarian, a fussy custodian, an office manager. (Norman Katkov, *Blood and Orchids*)

> Like croup and whooping cough, it was treated with remedies Ida Rebecca compounded from ancient folk-medicine recipes: reeking mustard plasters, herbal broths, dosings of onion syrup mixed with sugar. (Russell Baker, *Growing Up*)

> Each camper should bring the following: a sleeping bag, a mess kit, a flashlight, and plenty of insect repellent.

NOTE: A colon introduces a list or series *only* when an independent clause precedes the colon.

> FAULTY: Each camper should be equipped with: a sleeping bag, a mess kit, a flashlight, and plenty of insect repellent. (*Each camper should be equipped with* is not a grammatically complete clause; colon is incorrectly used between preposition and object.)

:
31a

(2)   Explanatory material

Colons often precede the introduction of material that explains, details, exemplifies, clarifies, or summarizes. They frequently introduce **appositives,** constructions that identify or describe nouns, pronouns, or noun phrases. In such cases, the colon substitutes for a phrase like *for example, namely,* or *that is.*

> For dancers, the call to the dance begins with the body: an accident of birth which, nurtured and sculpted through years of rigorous training, culminates in the coveted invitation to join a professional ballet company. (Diane Solway, *New York Times*)

> Her hair was the longest and strangest Mrs. Miller had ever seen: absolutely silver-white, like an albino's. (Truman Capote, "Miriam")

Sometimes a colon separates two independent clauses: one general clause and a subsequent, more specific one that illustrates or clarifies the first.

> A *U.S. News and World Report* survey has revealed a surprising fact: Americans spend more time at shopping malls than anywhere else except at home and at work.

NOTE: When a complete sentence follows the colon, that sentence may or may not begin with a capital letter. However, if the sentence introduced by a colon is a quotation, its first word is always capitalized, unless it was not capitalized in the source.

(3)   Quotations

Colons are used to set off quotations that are introduced by a complete independent clause.

> The French Declaration of the Rights of Man includes these words: "Liberty consists in being able to do anything that does not harm another person."
>
> With great dignity, Bartleby repeated the words once again: "I prefer not to."

A long quotation is introduced by a colon whether or not the introductory tag is a complete clause (see 30e.2).

(4)   Business letters

Use a colon after the salutation to introduce the body of a business letter (see 43a.4).

> Dear Dr. Evans:
>
> Thank you for your letter of April 12, in which you commented favorably on our plan to reclassify certain controlled substances . . . .

31b   Using a Colon Where Convention Requires It

Use colons in the following contexts where convention dictates their use.

To separate titles from subtitles

> *Family Installments: Memories of Growing Up Hispanic*
> *Tennyson: The Unquiet Heart*

To separate chapter from verse in Biblical citations

> Judges 4:14
> I Kings 11:8

To separate minutes from hours in numerical expressions of time

6:15 A.M.

3:03 P.M.

To separate place of publication from name of publisher in a list of works cited (see 39c.2).

New York**:** Holt

31c   Editing to Eliminate Misuse or Overuse of Colons

(1)   After *such as, for example,* and the like

Colons are not used after expressions like *such as, namely, for example,* or *that is.* These words serve the same purpose as the colon. Remember that a colon introduces a list or series only after an independent clause.

:
31c

FAULTY: The Eye Institute treats patients with a wide variety of conditions, such as: myopia, glaucoma, cataracts, and oculomotor dysfunction.

REVISED: The Eye Institute treats patients with a wide variety of conditions, such as myopia, glaucoma, cataracts, and oculomotor dysfunction.

REVISED: The Eye Institute treats patients with a wide variety of conditions: myopia, glaucoma, cataracts, and oculomotor dysfunction.

(2)   In verb and prepositional constructions

Colons should not be placed between verbs and their objects or complements or between prepositions and their objects.

FAULTY: James A. Michener wrote: *Hawaii, Centennial, Space,* and *Poland.*

REVISED: James A. Michener wrote *Hawaii, Centennial, Space,* and *Poland.*

FAULTY: Hitler's armies marched through: the Netherlands, Belgium, and France.

REVISED: Hitler's armies marched through the Netherlands, Belgium, and France.

☐ **EXERCISE 1**

Add colons where required in the following sentences. If necessary, delete superfluous colons.

> EXAMPLE: There was one thing he really hated getting up at 700 every morning.
>
>   There was one thing he really hated: getting up at 7:00 every morning.

1. Books about the late John F. Kennedy include the following *A Hero For Our Time; Johnny, We Hardly Knew Ye;* and *One Brief Shining Moment.*
2. Only one task remained to tell his boss he was quitting.
3. The story closed with a familiar phrase "And they all lived happily ever after."
4. The sergeant requested: reinforcements, medical supplies, and more ammunition.
5. She kept only four souvenirs a photograph, a matchbook, a theater program, and a daisy pressed between the pages *of William Shakespeare The Complete Works.*

31d

The Dash

Commas are the mark of punctuation most often used to set off nonessential elements (see 27d), but dashes and parentheses also serve this function. While parentheses deemphasize the enclosed words, **dashes** tend to call attention to the material they set off.

31d Setting Off Nonessential Material ⸺

Explanations, qualifications, and appositives may be set off by dashes for emphasis or clarity. When you are typing, indicate a dash with two unspaced hyphens; when writing, form a dash with an unbroken line about as long as two hyphens.

Around parenthetical material

Use a pair of dashes to set off parenthetical material within a sentence.

> Although we are by all odds the most social of all social animals—more interdependent, more attached to each other, more inseparable in our behavior than bees—we do not often feel our conjoined intelligence. (Lewis Thomas, *Lives of a Cell*)

Before afterthoughts.

Use a single dash to set off material at the end of a sentence.

They could not afford to jump to conclusions—any conclusions. (Michael Crichton, *The Andromeda Strain*)

Most of the best-sellers are cookbooks and diet books—how not to eat it after you've cooked it. (Andy Rooney, *The New Yorker*)

31e   Introducing a Summary

A dash is used to introduce a statement that summarizes a list or series before it.

Walking to school by myself, losing my first tooth, getting my ears pierced, and starting to wear makeup—these were some of the milestones of my life.

"Study hard," "Respect your elders," "Don't talk with your mouth full"—Sharon had heard her parents say these things hundreds of times.

31f   Indicating an Interruption

A dash is sometimes used in dialogue to mark a sudden interruption—for example, a correction, a hesitation, a sudden shift in tone, or an unfinished thought.

Groucho told the steward, "I'll have three hard-boiled eggs—make that four hard-boiled eggs."

"I think—no, I know—this is the worst day of my life," Julie sighed.

31g   Editing to Eliminate Misuse and Overuse of Dashes

Dashes give a loose, casual tone to a piece of writing; too many of them make a passage seem disorganized and out of control. Do not overuse dashes in academic writing, and do not use them carelessly in place of periods or commas or in any context that calls for other marks of punctuation. Compare these two paragraphs.

FAULTY: (overuse of dashes)   Registration was a nightmare—most of the courses I wanted to take—geology and conversational Spanish, for instance—met at inconvenient times—or were closed by the time I tried to sign up for them—it was really depressing—even for registration.

REVISED: Registration was a nightmare. Most of the courses I
(moderate wanted to take—geology and conversational Spanish,
use of for instance—met at inconvenient times or were closed
dashes) by the time I tried to sign up for them. It was really
depressing—even for registration.

☐   **EXERCISE 2**

Add dashes where needed in the following sentences. If a sentence is
correct, mark it with a *C*.

EXAMPLE: World War I called "the war to end all wars" was, unfortunately, no such thing.

World War I—called "the war to end all wars"—was, unfortunately, no such thing.

1. Tulips, daffodils, hyacinths, lilies all of these flowers grow from bulbs.
2. St. Kitts and Nevis two tiny island nations are now independent after
   360 years of British rule.
3. "But it's not" She paused and reconsidered her next words.
4. He considered several different majors history, English, political science, and business before deciding on journalism.
5. The two words added to the Pledge of Allegiance in the 1950's "under
   God" remain part of the Pledge today.

Parentheses

Like commas and dashes, parentheses may be used to set off
interruptions within a sentence.

31h Setting Off Nonessential Material   ————

Parentheses may be used to set off nonessential material that
expands, clarifies, defines, illustrates, or supplements an idea.

A compound may be used in any grammatical function: as noun
(*wishbone*), adjective (*foolproof*), adverb (*overhead*), verb (*gainsay*),
or preposition (*without*). (Thomas Pyles, *The Origin and Development of the English Language*)

It took Gilbert Fairchild two years at Harvard College (two academic years, from September, 1955, to June, 1957) to learn everything he needed to know. (Judith Martin, *Gilbert: A Comedy of
Manners*)

Parentheses may also enclose a complete sentence, as in the
example that follows. When a sentence set off by parentheses

( )
31h

falls within another sentence, it should not begin with a capital
letter or end with a period.

> Born in 1893, four years before Queen Victoria's Diamond Jubilee,
> at Cathedral Choir School, Oxford, where her father was head-
> master, Sayers became a first-rate medievalist (she translated
> Dante) and a theologian (her miracle play, *The Man Born To Be
> King*, outsold her mystery novels in her lifetime); she died in
> 1957. (Barbara Grizzuti Harrison, *Off Center*)

If the parenthetical sentence does not interrupt another sentence, it must begin with a capital letter and end with a period,
question mark, or exclamation point that falls within the closing
parenthesis.

> A few days later he called and asked me to come in and bring
> anything else I had written. (The only thing I had was a notebook
> full of isolated sentences like "She walked across the room wear-
> ing her wedding ring like a shield.") (Jeremy Bernstein, *New York
> Times Book Review*)

When a parenthetical element falls within a sentence,
punctuation never precedes the opening parenthesis. Punctuation may follow the closing parenthesis, however.

( )
31i

31i In Other Conventional Situations ————

Parentheses are used to set off letters and numbers that identify
points on a list and around dates, cross-references, documentation, and the like.

> All reports must include the following components: (1) an opening
> summary; (2) a background statement; and (3) a list of conclusions
> and recommendations.

> Russia was finally victorious in the Great Northern War with Swe-
> den (1700–1721).

> For detailed information on cell division, see Chapter 6 (pp. 145–
> 72).

> Arvin believes that the novel has autobiographical elements (72).

> The teachers' contract specifies that class size be limited to thirty-
> three (33) children.

NOTE: The last example illustrates a convention often used in
legal and technical writing.

☐   **EXERCISE 3**

Add parentheses where necessary in the following sentences. If a sentence is correct, mark it with a C.

EXAMPLE: The greatest battle of the War of 1812 the Battle New Orleans was fought after the war was declared over.

The greatest battle of the War of 1812 (the Battle of New
Orleans) was fought after the war was declared over.

1. George Orwell's *1984* 1949 focuses on the dangers of a totalitarian society.
2. The final score 45–0 was a devastating blow for the Eagles.
3. Belize formerly British Honduras is a country in Central America.
4. The first phonics book *Phonics is Fun* has a light blue cover.
5. Some high school students have so many extracurricular activities band, sports, drama club, and school newspaper, for instance that they have little time to study.

Brackets

Brackets are used in two special situations.

[ ]
31k

31j   Setting Off Comments Within Quotations

Brackets are used within quotations to tell readers that the words enclosed are yours and not those of your source. Bracketed material may be a correction, an opinion, or a clarification.

"Dues are being raised $1.00 per week [to $5.00]," the treasurer announced.

"The use of caricature by Dickens is reminiscent of the satiric sketches done by [Joseph] Addison and [Richard] Steele [in *The Spectator*]."

"Even as a student at Princeton he [F. Scott Fitzgerald] felt like an outsider."

"The miles of excellent trails are perfect for [cross-country] skiing."

If a quotation contains an error, indicate that the error is not yours by following the error with the italicized Latin word *sic* ("thus") in brackets.

"The octopuss [*sic*] is a cephalopod mollusk with eight arms."

31k   In Place of Parentheses Within Parentheses

When one set of parentheses falls within another, substitute brackets for the inner set.

In her narrative history of American education between 1945 and 1960 (*The Troubled Crusade* [New York: Basic Books, 1963]), Diane Ravitch addresses issues like progressive education, race, educational reforms, and campus unrest.

The Slash

The **slash** is used as a punctuation mark in three instances.

31l   Separating One Option from Another

The either/or fallacy assumes that a given question has only two possible answers.

Will pass/fail courses be accepted for transfer credit?

The producer/director attracted more attention at the film festival than the actors.

In this usage, do not leave space before or after the slash.

Unless you are really presenting three alternatives (Bring a pencil or pen or both to the exam), the construction *and/or* (Bring a pencil and/or a pen to the exam) should be avoided. Instead use *and* or *or*.

Bring a pencil and pen to the exam.

Bring a pencil or pen to the exam.

31m   Separating Lines of Poetry Run into the Text

The poet James Schevill writes, "I study my defects / And learn how to perfect them."

When you use the slash to separate lines of poetry, leave a space both before and after the slash.

31n   Separating the Numerator from the Denominator in Fractions

7/8

1 4/5

If your typewriter or computer has a special key for a particular fraction ($\frac{1}{2}$, $\frac{1}{4}$), use that instead of the slash.

The Ellipsis Mark

The **ellipsis mark** (three spaced periods) indicates the omission of words from a quotation. When deleting material before inserting ellipses, be careful not to change the meaning of the original passage.

310 Indicating an Omission in a Quotation

The ellipsis mark is used to indicate words omitted from a quotation.

. . .
310

> ORIGINAL: When I was a young man, being anxious to distinguish myself, I was perpetually starting new propositions. But I soon gave this over; for I found that generally what was new was false. (Samuel Johnson)

> WITH OMISSION: When I was a young man, being anxious to distinguish myself, I was perpetually starting new propositions. But I soon . . . found that generally what was new was false. (three spaced periods indicate omission)

If a punctuation mark occurs in the original text before the words that are deleted, include it in the quoted sentence ("If we give up now, . . . we will answer to history.").

When deleting *words at the beginning of a sentence* within a quoted passage, retain the period of the previous sentence before the ellipsis mark, leaving a space between the period and the ellipses that follow.

> ORIGINAL: And Dickens tells of long mornings when he forced himself to stay at the desk making false starts, lest by giving up he should give up forever. For all his books already in print, he might just as well have been the common schoolboy who is told to write of his visit to Aunt Julia and who honestly finds nothing to say except that he arrived on Friday and left on Sunday. (Jacques Barzun, *Writing, Editing, and Publishing*)

> WITH OMISSION: And Dickens tells of long mornings when he forced himself to stay at the desk making false starts, lest by giving up he should give up forever. . . . he might just as well have been the common school-

> boy who is told to write of his visit to Aunt Julia
> and who honestly finds nothing to say except that
> he arrived on Friday and left on Sunday. (period
> retained; three equally spaced periods indicate
> omission)

Note: Do not begin a quoted passage with an ellipsis mark.

FAULTY: Barzun notes that Dickens " . . . might just as well have
          been the common schoolboy. . . . "

REVISED: Barzun notes that Dickens "might just as well have been
          the common schoolboy. . . . "

In deleting *words at the end of a sentence* within a quoted
passage, retain the sentence period or other end punctuation,
leaving a space between it and the ellipsis mark.

ORIGINAL: We hold these truths to be self-evident, that all men
               are created equal, that they are endowed by their
               Creator with certain unalienable rights, that among
               these are life, liberty and the pursuit of happiness.
               (The Declaration of Independence)

WITH OMISSION: We hold these truths to be self-evident, that all men
               are created equal, that they are endowed by their
               Creator with certain unalienable rights. . . . (period
               retained; three equally spaced periods indicate
               omission)

In omitting *one or more complete sentences from a quoted
passage,* follow any end punctuation with a space and the ellipsis mark.

ORIGINAL: Everywhere one meets the idea that reading is an
               activity desirable in itself. It is understandable that
               publishers and librarians—and even writers—
               should promote this assumption, but it is strange
               that the idea should have general currency. People
               surround the idea of reading with piety, and do not
               take into account the purpose of reading or the
               value of what is being read. (Donald Hall)

WITH OMISSION: Everywhere one meets the idea that reading is an
               activity desirable in itself. . . . People surround the
               idea of reading with piety, and do not take into
               account the purpose of reading or the value of
               what is being read. (period retained; three equally
               spaced periods indicate omission)

Note that complete sentences must precede and follow the period plus ellipsis mark.

. . .
31o

Guidelines for Punctuating and Placing Ellipsis Marks

- Countries were . . . not willing to compromise.
- It was, . . . as if they wanted war.
- Peace was to last only six months; . . . France would then attack.
- During the summer ambassadors negotiated feverishly. . . .
- Self-interest would divert the German armies . . . " (147).
- Who were the victors? . . .

31p Indicating an Omission Within Verse

When you omit one or more lines of poetry (or a paragraph or more of prose), use a complete line of spaced periods.

> ORIGINAL: Stitch! Stitch! Stitch!
> In poverty, hunger, and dirt,
> And still with a voice of dolorous pitch,
> Would that its tone could reach the Rich,
> She sang this "Song of the Shirt!"
> (Thomas Hood)

> WITH OMISSION: Stitch! Stitch! Stitch!
> In poverty, hunger, and dirt,
> . . . .
> She sang this "Song of the Shirt!"

31q Indicating Unfinished Statements

An ellipsis mark can also be used to indicate an interrupted statement.

"If only. . . . " He sighed and turned away.

This use is generally not appropriate in academic writing.

☐ **EXERCISE 4**

Read this paragraph and follow the instructions below it, taking care in each case not to delete essential information.

The most important thing about research is to know when to stop. How does one recognize the moment? When I was eighteen or thereabouts, my mother told me that when out with a young man I should always leave a half-hour before I wanted to. Although I was not sure how this might be accomplished, I recognized the advice as sound, and exactly the same rule applies to research. One must stop *before* one has finished; otherwise, one will never stop and never finish.   (Barbara Tuchman, *Practicing History*)

1. Delete a phrase from the middle of one sentence and mark the omission with ellipses.
2. Delete words at the beginning of any sentence and mark the omission with ellipses.
3. Delete words at the end of any sentence and mark the omission with ellipses.
4. Delete one complete sentence from the middle of the passage and mark the omission with ellipses.

☐   **EXERCISE 5**

Add appropriate punctuation—colons, dashes, parentheses, brackets, or slashes—to the following sentences. Be prepared to explain why you chose the punctuation marks you did. If a sentence is correct, mark it with a *C*.

> EXAMPLE: There was one thing she was sure of if she did well at the interview, the job would be hers.
>
> There was one thing she was sure of: if she did well at the interview, the job would be hers.

1. Mark Twain Samuel L. Clemens made the following statement "I can live for two months on a good compliment."
2. Liza Minnelli, the actress singer who starred in several films, is the daughter of Judy Garland.
3. Saudi Arabia, Oman, Yemen, Qatar, and the United Arab Emirates all these are located on the Arabian peninsula.
4. John Adams 1735–1826 was the second president of the United States; John Quincy Adams 1767–1848 was the sixth.
5. The sign said "No tresspassing *sic*."
6. *Checkmate* a term derived from the Persian phrase meaning "the King is dead" announces victory in chess.
7. The following people were present at the meeting the president of the board of trustees, three trustees, and twenty reporters.
8. Before the introduction of the potato in Europe, the parsnip was a major source of carbohydrates in fact, it was a dietary staple.
9. In this well-researched book (*Crime Movies* New York Norton, 1980), Carlos Clarens studies the gangster genre in film.
10. I remember reading though I can't remember where that Upton Sinclair sold plots to Jack London.

Student Writer at Work: Punctuation

Review Chapters 26–31; then read this student essay. Commas, semicolons, quotation marks, apostrophes, parentheses, and dashes have been intentionally deleted; only the end punctuation has been retained. When you have read the essay carefully, add all appropriate punctuation marks.

The dry pine needles crunched like eggshells under our thick boots.

Wont the noise scare them away Dad?

He smiled knowingly and said No deer rely mostly on smell and sight.

I thought That must be why were wearing fluorescent orange jumpsuits but I didn't feel like arguing the point.

It was a perfect day for my first hunting experience. The biting winds were caught by the thick bushy arms of the tall pines and I could feel a numbing redness in my face. Now I realized why Dad always grew that ugly gray beard which made him look ten years older. A few sunbeams managed to carve their way through the layers of branches and leaves creating pools of white light on the dark earth.

How far have we come? I asked. Oh only a couple of miles. We should be meeting Joe up ahead.

Joe was one of Dads hunting buddies. He always managed to go off on his own for a few hours and come back with at least a four-pointer. Dad was envious of Joe and liked to tell people what he called the real story.

You know Joe paid a fortune for that buck at the checking station hed tell his friends. Dad was sure that this would be his lucky year.

We trudged up a densely wooded hill for what seemed like hours. The sharp needled branches whipped my bare face as I followed close behind my father occasionally I wiped my cheeks to discover a new cut in my frozen flesh.

All this for a lousy deer I thought.

The still pine air was suddenly shattered by four rapid gunshots echoing across the vast green valley below us.

Joes got another one. Come on! Dad yelled. It seemed as if I were following a young kid as I watched my father take leaping strides down the path we had just ascended. I had never seen him so enthusiastic before. I plodded breathlessly along trying to keep up with my father.

Suddenly out of the corner of my eye I caught sight of an object that didn't fit in with the monotony of trunks and branches and leaves and needles. I froze and observed the largest most majestic buck I had ever seen. It too stood motionless apparently grazing on some leaves or berries. Its coloring was beautiful with alternating patches of tan brown and snow white fur. The massive antlers towered proudly above its head as it looked up and took notice of me. What struck me most were the tearful brown eyes almost feminine in their gaze.

Once again the silence was smashed this time by my fathers thundering call and I watched as the huge deer scampered gracefully off through the trees. I turned and scurried down the path after my father. I decided not to mention a word of my encounter to him. I hoped the deer was far away by now.

Finally, I reached the clearing from where the shots had rung out. There stood Dad and Joe smiling over a fallen six-point buck. The purple-red blood dripped from the wounds to form a puddle in the dirt. The bucks sad brown eyes gleamed in the sun but no longer smiled and blinked.

Where have you been? asked Dad. Before I could answer he continued Do you believe this guy? Every year he bags the biggest deer in the whole state!

While they laughed and talked I sat on a tree stump

31

to rest my aching legs. Maybe now we can go home I
thought. But before long I heard Dad say Come on Bob I
know theres one out there for us.

We headed right back up that same path and sure enough
that same big beautiful buck was grazing in that same spot
on that same berry bush. The only difference was this
time Dad saw him.

This is our lucky day he whispered.

I froze as Dad lifted the barrel of his rifle and
took careful aim at the silently grazing deer. I closed
my eyes as he squeezed the trigger but instead of the
deadly gun blast I heard only a harmless click. His rifle
had jammed.

Use your rifle quick he whispered.

As I took aim through my scope the deer looked up at
me. Its soulful brown eyes were magnified in my sight
like two glassy bullseyes. My finger froze on the
trigger.

Shoot him! Shoot him!

But instead I aimed for the clouds and fired. The
deer vanished along with my fathers dreams. Dad never
understood why it was the proudest moment of my life.

31

32

Capitalization

Familiarizing yourself with the conventions of capitalization is important. Conventions change, however, and if you are not certain whether a word should be capitalized, consult a recent dictionary.

32a Capitalizing the First Word of a Sentence or of a Line of Poetry

The first word of a sentence, including a sentence of directly quoted speech or writing, should start with a capital letter.

> The square of the hypotenuse is equal to the sum of the squares of the other two sides.

> Shakespeare wrote, "Who steals my purse steals trash."

NOTE: Do not capitalize a sentence set off within another sentence by dashes or parentheses.

> FAULTY: Finding the store closed—It was a holiday—they went home.

> REVISED: Finding the store closed—it was a holiday—they went home.

> FAULTY: The candidates are Frank Lester and Jane Lester (They are not related).

> REVISED: The candidates are Frank Lester and Jane Lester (they are not related).

When a complete sentence is introduced by a colon, capitalization is optional (see 31a.2).

The first word of a line of poetry is also capitalized.

> Tyger! Tyger! burning bright
> In the forests of the night,
> What immortal hand or eye
> Could frame thy fearful symmetry? (William Blake, "The Tyger")

If the poet uses a lowercase letter to begin a line, however, that style should be followed in any quotation.

> Old age is
> a flight of small
> cheeping birds
> skimming
> bare trees
> above a snowglaze. (William Carlos Williams, "To Waken an Old
>   Lady")

32b Capitalizing Proper Nouns, Titles Accompanying Them, and Adjectives Formed from Them

Proper nouns—the names of specific persons, places, or things (Diana Ross, Madras, the Enoch Pratt Free Library)—are capitalized.

Specific people's names

Clark Gable	Elvis Presley
Jackie Robinson	William the Conqueror

When a title precedes a person's name, or is used instead of the name, it too is capitalized.

Dad	Princess Diana
Count Dracula	Justice Marshall

Titles that *follow* names, or those that refer to the general position, not the particular person who holds it, are usually not capitalized. A title denoting a family relationship is never capitalized when it follows an article or a possessive pronoun.

CAPITALIZE	DO NOT CAPITALIZE
Grandma	my grandmother
Private Hargrove	Mr. Hargrove, a private in the army
Queen Mother Elizabeth	a popular queen mother
Senator John Glenn; the Senator (referring to a particular senator)	John Glenn, the senator from Ohio

Uncle Harry   my uncle

General Patton; the General (re-   a four-star general
ferring to a particular general)

    Titles or abbreviations of academic degrees are always capitalized, even when they follow a name.

Perry Mason, Attorney at Law
Benjamin Spock, M.D.

Titles that indicate high-ranking positions may be capitalized even when they are used alone or when they follow a name.

the Secretary of Defense
the Speaker of the House
the President of the United States

Specific things

    Capitalize names of particular structures, special events, monuments, vehicles, and so on.

Hoover Dam	the Taj Mahal
the *Titanic*	Mount Rushmore
the Brooklyn Bridge	the Eiffel Tower
the World Series	Independence Hall

**cap
32b**

NOTE: When a common noun such as *bridge, river,* or *lake* is part of a proper noun, it too is capitalized. Do not, however, capitalize such words when they complete the names of more than one thing (as in Kings and Queens counties).

Places, regions, and directions

    Capitalize names of particular places or geographical regions.

Chicago	the Straits of Magellan
Saturn	the Western Hemisphere
Budapest	Venice
Walden Pond	the Fiji Islands

    The points of the compass are also capitalized when they denote particular geographical regions, but designations of directions are not.

The Middle West seemed like a wasteland to F. Scott Fitzgerald's Nick Carroway, so he decided to come East. (Capital letters necessary because *Middle West* and *East* refer to specific regions.)

Turn west at the corner of Broad Street and continue north until you reach Market. (No capitals needed because *west* and *north* refer to directions, not specific regions.)

Days of the week, months of the year, and holidays

Saturday	Ash Wednesday
January	Rosh Hashanah
Veterans Day	Labor Day

Historical periods, events, and documents; names of legal cases and awards

the Battle of Gettysburg	the Treaty of Versailles
the Industrial Revolution	the Voting Rights Act
the Reformation	*Brown v. Board of Education*

Philosophic, literary, and artistic movements

Naturalism	Dadaism
Romanticism	Fauvism
Neoclassicism	Expressionism

NOTE: Dictionaries vary in their advice on capitalizing these nouns, but current usage tends toward capitalization.

Races, ethnic groups, nationalities, and languages

Asian	French
Negro, Afro-American	Danish
Chicano, Chicana	Dutch
Caucasian	Turkish

NOTE: When the words *black* and *white* refer to races, they have traditionally not been capitalized. Current usage is divided on whether or not to capitalize *Black*.

Religions and their followers; sacred books and figures

Muslim	the Talmud	Buddha
Jewish	the Koran	the Virgin Mary
Christianity	God	the Messiah
Buddhism	the Lord	the Scriptures

NOTE: It is not necessary to capitalize pronouns referring to God unless the pronoun might also refer to another antecedent in the sentence.

CONFUSING: Alex's grandfather taught him to trust in God and to love all his creatures.

REVISED: Alex's grandfather taught him to trust in God and to love all His creatures.

Political, social, athletic, civic, and other groups and their members

New York Yankees
Democratic Party
International Brotherhood of Electrical Workers

cap 32b

National Organization for Women
National Council of Teachers of English
The Who

Businesses; government agencies; and medical, educational, and
other institutions

Congress
Environmental Protection Agency
Lincoln High School
Brookings Institute
University of Maryland

NOTE: When the name of a group or institution is abbreviated, the
abbreviation uses capital letters in place of the capitalized words.

IBEW
NOW
NCTE

Trade names and words formed from them

Pontiac	Coke
Sanka	Pampers
Kleenex	Xerox

NOTE: Trade names that have been used so often and for so long
that they have become synonymous with the product are no
longer capitalized. (Consult the dictionary on whether or not to
capitalize a familiar trade name.)

frisbee	victrola
jello	aspirin

Specific academic courses

Sociology 201
English 101

But do not capitalize a subject area unless it is the name of a
language.

Although his major was engineering, he registered for courses in
sociology, English, and zoology.

Adjectives formed from proper nouns are usually capitalized.

Keynesian economics	Elizabethan era
Freudian slip	Shakespearean sonnet
Platonic ideal	Marxist ideology
Aristotelian logic	Shavian wit

However, when words derived from proper nouns have lost their
specialized meanings, do not capitalize them.

The china pattern was very elaborate.

We need a 40-watt bulb.

32c   Capitalizing Important Words in Titles   —

In general, all words in titles of books, articles, essays, films, and the like, including your own papers, are capitalized, with the exception of articles (*a*, *an*, and *the*), prepositions, conjunctions, and the *to* in infinitives. If an article, preposition, or conjunction is the *first* or *last* word in the title, however, it too is capitalized.

"Dover Beach"	*On the Waterfront*
The Declaration of Independence	*The Skin of Our Teeth*
Across the River and into the Trees	*Of Human Bondage*
	"Politics and the English Language"
Two Years before the Mast	

32d   Capitalizing the Pronoun *I* and the Interjection *O* ————————

Even if the pronoun *I* is part of a contraction (*I'm, I'll, I've*), it is always capitalized.

Sam and I finally went to the Grand Canyon, and I'm glad we did.

The interjection *O* is also always capitalized.

Give us peace in our time, O Lord.

The interjection *oh*, however, is capitalized only when it begins a sentence.

NOTE: Many other single letters are also capitalized in certain usages. Check your dictionary if you are unsure whether to use a capital letter.

U-boat	Vitamin B
D-Day	an A in history
Model T	C major

32e   Capitalizing Salutations and Closings of Letters ————————

In salutations of business or personal letters, always capitalize the first word.

Dear Mr. Reynolds:
Dear Fred,

The first word of the complimentary close is also always capitalized.

Sincerely,   Very truly yours,

(See also 43a.3.)

32f   Editing to Eliminate Misuse and Overuse of Capitals

Capital letters should not be used for emphasis or as an attention-getting device. If you are not certain whether a word should be capitalized, consult your dictionary.

Seasons

Do not capitalize the names of the seasons—summer, fall, winter, spring—unless they are strongly personified, as in Old Man Winter.

cap
32f

Centuries and loosely defined historical periods

Do not capitalize the names of centuries or general historical periods.

seventeenth-century poetry
the automobile age

But do capitalize names of specific historical, anthropological, and geological periods.

Iron Age
Paleozoic Era

Diseases and other medical terms

Do not capitalize names of diseases or medical tests or conditions unless a proper noun is part of the name.

polio   Apgar test
Reye's syndrome   mumps

☐   **EXERCISE**

Capitalize words where necessary in these sentences.

EXAMPLE: John F. Kennedy won the pulitzer prize for his book *profiles in courage.*

John F. Kennedy won the Pulitzer Prize for his book *Profiles in Courage.*

1. The brontë sisters wrote *jane eyre* and *wuthering heights,* two nineteenth-century novels that are required reading in many english classes that study victorian literature.

2. It was a beautiful day in the spring—it was april 15, to be exact—but all Ted could think about was the check he had to write to the internal revenue service and the bills he had to pay by friday.

3. Traveling north, they hiked through british columbia, planning a leisurely return on the cruise ship *canadian princess.*

4. Alice liked her mom's apple pie better than aunt nellie's rhubarb pie; but she liked grandpa's punch best of all.

5. A new elective, political science 30, covers the vietnam war from the gulf of tonkin to the fall of saigon, including the roles of ho chi minh, the communists, and the buddhist monks; the position of presidents johnson and nixon; and the influence of groups like the student mobilization committee and vietnam veterans against the war.

6. When the central high school drama club put on a production of shaw's *pygmalion,* the director xeroxed extra copies of the parts for eliza doolittle and professor henry higgins so he could give them to the understudies.

7. Shaking all over, Bill admitted, "driving on the los angeles freeway is a frightening experience for a kid from the bronx, even in a bmw."

8. The new united federation of teachers contract guarantees teachers many paid holidays, including columbus day, veterans day, and washington's birthday; a week each at christmas and easter; and two full months (july and august) in the summer.

9. The sociology syllabus included the books *beyond the best interests of the child, regulating the poor,* and *a welfare mother;* in anthropology we were to begin by studying the stone age, and in geology we were to focus on the mesozoic era.

10. Winners of the nobel peace prize include lech walesa, leader of the polish trade union solidarity; the reverend dr. martin luther king, jr., founder of the southern christian leadership conference; and bishop desmond tutu of south africa.

33

Italics

In an italic typeface, the characters slant upward to the right: *Moby-Dick*. Indicate **italics** in written or typed text by underlining: <u>Moby-Dick</u>. As with other punctuation marks, a number of conventions govern the use of italics.

33a Setting Off Titles and Names

Italicize the titles of books, newspapers, magazines, and journals; pamphlets; films; television and radio programs; long poems; plays; long musical works; paintings and sculpture; and names of ships, trains, aircraft, and spacecraft. All other titles are set off with quotation marks (see 30b).

NOTE: Titles of your own essays, typed at the top of the first page or on a title page, are neither italicized nor placed within quotation marks. Names of sacred books, such as the Bible, and well-known documents, such as the Constitution and the Declaration of Independence, are also neither italicized nor placed within quotation marks.

Books

David Copperfield	*The Other America*
Cujo	*A Connecticut Yankee in King Arthur's Court*

Newspapers

the *Washington Post*	*The Philadelphia Inquirer*
the *New York Times*	*St. Louis Post-Dispatch*

Articles and names of cities are italicized only when they are a part of a title.

Magazines

People   *Scientific American*
The Atlantic   *Psychology Today*

Journals

Columbia Journalism Review   *New England Journal of Medicine*
College English   *American Sociological Review*

Pamphlets

Paine's *Common Sense*
Milton's *Tetrachordon*

Films

Psycho   *Casablanca*
Citizen Kane   *Gone with the Wind*

Punctuation is italicized when it is part of a title.

Television programs

Face the Nation   *Dallas*
Sesame Street   *Leave It to Beaver*

Radio programs

All Things Considered   *Prairie Home Companion*
CBS Mystery Theater   *Fibber McGee and Molly*

Long poems

Paradise Lost   *The Faerie Queen*
John Brown's Body   *Evangeline*

Plays

The Glass Menagerie   *Awake and Sing*
Macbeth   *A Raisin in the Sun*

Long musical works

Rigoletto   *Lohengrin*
Eroica   *Messiah*

Paintings and sculpture

Rembrandt's *The Night Watch*   Wyeth's *Christina's World*
Michelangelo's *Pietà*   Picasso's *Guernica*

Ships

Queen Elizabeth II   U.S.S. *Saratoga*
Lusitania   *The Delta Queen*

S.S. and U.S.S. are not italicized when they precede the name of a ship.

Trains

Silver Meteor	*The Patriot*
City of New Orleans	*The Orient Express*

Aircraft

the *Spruce Goose*	the *Hindenburg*
Air Force One	*Enola Gay*

Only particular aircraft, not makes or types like Piper Cub or Boeing 707, are italicized.

Spacecraft

Sputnik	*Apollo II*
Challenger	*Enterprise*

33b   Setting Off Foreign Words and Phrases

ital
33c

Thousands of foreign words and phrases are now considered part of the English language. These words—*naive, lasso, chaperon,* and *catharsis,* for example—receive no special treatment. Foreign words and phrases not yet fully assimilated into the language, however, should be set in italics. All such foreign words, with the exception of foreign proper nouns, must be italicized.

> The *carpe diem* theme is expressed in Andrew Marvell's poem "To His Coy Mistress."

> *Spirochaeta plicatilis, Treponema pallidum,* and *Spirilbum minus* are all bacteria with corkscrew-like shapes.

If you are not sure whether a foreign word has been assimilated into English, consult a dictionary.

33c   Setting Off Elements Spoken of as Themselves and Terms Being Defined

Italicize letters, numerals, words, and phrases when they refer to the letters, numerals, words, and phrases themselves.

> Is that a *p* or a *g*?

> I forget the exact address, but I know it has a *3* in it.

> Does *through* rhyme with *cough*?

> His pronunciation of the phrase *Mary was contrary* told us he was from the Midwest.

Italicize to set off words and phrases that you go on to define.

A *closet drama* is a play meant to be read, not performed.

33d Using Italics for Emphasis

Italics lend unusually strong weight to a word or phrase and should therefore be used in moderation. Overuse of italics interferes with the tone and even the meaning of what you write. Whenever possible, emphasis should emerge from word choice and sentence structure. The following sentences illustrate acceptable use of italics for emphasis.

As for protecting the children from exploitation, the chief and indeed only exploiters of children these days *are* schools. (John Holt, "School Is Bad for Children")

Initially, poetry might be defined as a kind of language that says *more* and says it *more intensely* than does ordinary language. (Lawrence Perrine, *Sound and Sense*)

ital
33e

33e Using Italics for Clarity

Occasionally, it is necessary to italicize a word to avoid confusion or ambiguity when a sentence may have more than one meaning.

This time Jill forgot the *key*. (Last time Jill forgot something else.)

This time *Jill* forgot the key. (Last time someone else forgot the key.)

☐ **EXERCISE**

Underline to indicate italics where necessary, and delete any italics that are incorrectly used. If a sentence is correct, mark it with a *C*.

EXAMPLE: However is a conjunctive adverb, not a coordinating conjunction.

However is a conjunctive adverb, not a coordinating conjunction.

1. I said Carol, not Darryl.
2. A *deus ex machina*, an improbable device used to resolve the plot of a fictional work, is used in Charles Dickens's novel Oliver Twist.
3. He dotted every i and crossed every t.
4. The Metropolitan Opera's production of Carmen was a real tour de force for the principal performers.
5. *Laissez-faire* is a doctrine that holds that government should not interfere with trade.

6. Antidote and anecdote are often confused because their pronunciations are similar.
7. Hawthorne's novels include Fanshawe, The House of the Seven Gables, The Blithedale Romance, and The Scarlet Letter.
8. Words like mailman, policeman, and fireman are rapidly being replaced by nonsexist terms like letter carrier, police officer, and firefighter.
9. A classic black tuxedo was considered de rigueur at the charity ball, but Jason preferred to wear his *dashiki.*
10. Thomas Mann's novel Buddenbrooks is a Bildungsroman.

ital

33

34

Hyphens

Hyphens have two conventional uses: to break words at the end of a typed or handwritten line and to link words in certain compounds.

34a Breaking Words at the End of a Line

Whenever possible, avoid breaking a word at the end of a line; if you must do so, divide words only between syllables. Consult a dictionary to determine correct syllabication. Whenever you can, divide a word between prefix and root (sus · pending) or between root and suffix (develop · ment). Divide words that contain doubled consonants between the doubled letters (let · ter) unless the doubled letters are part of the root (cross · ing) or unless the doubled letters do not break into two syllables (ex · pelled). Do not end two consecutive lines with hyphens, and never divide a word at the end of a page.

Here are additional guidelines for determining how a word should be divided.

(1) One-syllable words

Never hyphenate one-syllable words. Keep a one-syllable word intact even if it is relatively long (*thought, blocked, French, laughed*). If you cannot fit the whole word at the end of the line, move it to the next line.

> FAULTY: Mark Twain's novel *The Prin-
> ce and the Pauper* considers the effects of environment on
> personality.

496

REVISED: Mark Twain's novel *The Prince and the Pauper* considers the effects of environment on personality.

(2)   Short syllables

Never leave a single letter at the end of a line or carry one or two letters to the beginning of a line. One-letter prefixes (like the *a-* in *away*) or short suffixes (like *-y, -ly, -er,* and *-ed*) should not be separated from the rest of the word. The suffixes *-able* and *-ible* cannot be broken into two syllables.

FAULTY: Nadia walked very slowly a-
long the balance beam.

REVISED: Nadia walked very slowly along
the balance beam.

FAULTY: Amy's parents wondered whether the terrible twos would ever end.

REVISED: Amy's parents wondered whether the terrible twos would ever end.

34a

(3)   Compounds

If you must hyphenate a compound word, put the hyphen between the elements of the compound. (For correct use of hyphens in compound words, see 34b.)

FAULTY: Environmentalists believe snowmo-
biles produce air and noise pollution.

REVISED: Environmentalists believe snow-
mobiles produce air and noise pollution.

If the compound already contains a hyphen, divide it at the existing hyphen.

FAULTY: She met her ex-hus-
band on a blind date.

REVISED: She met her ex-
husband on a blind date.

(4)   Illogical or confusing hyphenation

Some words contain letter combinations that look like other words. If a word break leaves a fragment that reads as a word not related to the divided word, the reader will be confused.

CONFUSING: The supervisor did not appreciate the face-
tious remark.

REVISED: The supervisor did not appreciate the
          facetious remark.

(5)   Numerals, contractions, and abbreviations

Contractions, numerals, acronyms, and abbreviations should not
be divided. A hyphen is not used between a numeral and an
abbreviation.

FAULTY: Whether or not the meeting began on time was-
         n't important.

REVISED: Whether or not the meeting began on time
          wasn't important.

FAULTY: The special on child abuse was watched by over 23,-
         000,000 Americans.

REVISED: The special on child abuse was watched by over
          23,000,000 Americans.

34a

FAULTY: During the sixties, participation in RO-
         TC declined on many college campuses.

REVISED: During the sixties, participation in ROTC declined
          on many college campuses.

FAULTY: The balloon was launched at precisely 8-
         P.M.

REVISED: The balloon was launched at precisely 8 P.M.

☐   **EXERCISE 1**

Divide each of these words into syllables, consulting a dictionary if necessary; then, indicate with a hyphen where you would divide each word
at the end of a line.

EXAMPLE: underground

          un · der · ground

          under-ground

1. transcendentalism   6. side-splitting
2. calliope   7. markedly
3. martyr   8. amazing
4. longitude   9. unlikely
5. bookkeeper   10. thorough

34b Dividing Compound Words ———————

A **compound word** is composed of two or more words. Some familiar compound words are always hyphenated.

no-hitter	two-step
play-off	helter-skelter
run-down	topsy-turvy

Other compounds are always written as one word.

fireplace	peacetime
lighthouse	ninepin
sunset	nearsighted

Finally, some compounds are always written as two separate words.

cherry tomato	bunk bed
salt lick	labor relations
medical doctor	chocolate pudding

Your dictionary can tell you whether a particular compound requires a hyphen: *snow job*, for instance, is two unhyphenated words: *snowsuit* is one word; and *snow-white* is hyphenated. Usage changes, however, so it is important to have a dictionary that is up-to-date.

Although hyphenization of compound words is not uniform, a few reliable rules do apply.

(1) In compound adjectives

A **compound adjective** is two or more words combined into a single grammatical unit that modifies a noun. When a compound adjective *precedes* the noun it modifies, its elements must be joined by hyphens.

He stayed tuned to his favorite listener-supported radio station, waiting for a hard-hitting editorial.

The research team tried to use nineteenth-century technology to design a space-age project.

However, when a compound adjective *follows* the noun it modifies, it does not require a hyphen.

The three government-operated programs were run smoothly, but the one that was not government operated was short of funds.

Compound adjectives that contain words ending in *-ly* are not hyphenated, even when they precede the noun.

34b

Many upwardly mobile families consider items like home computers, microwave ovens, and videocassette recorders to be necessi-
ties.

Use **suspended hyphens**—hyphens followed by space or by the
appropriate punctuation and space—in a series of compounds
that have the same principal elements.

The seventh- and eighth-grade students were noisy.

The three-, four-, and five-year-old children were assigned to the
same group.

(2)   With certain prefixes or suffixes

Use a hyphen between a prefix and a proper noun or an adjective
formed from a proper noun.

mid-July	trans-Siberian
non-Catholic	un-American
anti-Christ	pre-Columbian

34b

Use a hyphen to connect the prefixes *all-, ex-, half-, quarter-,
quasi-,* and *self-* and the suffixes *-elect* and *-odd* to a noun.

all-pro	quasi-serious
ex-senator	self-centered
half-pint	president-elect
quarter-moon	thirty-odd

NOTE: The words *selfhood, selfish,* and *selfless* do not include
hyphens. In these cases *self* is the root, not a prefix.

(3)   For clarity

Hyphenate to prevent misreading one word for another.

co-op	coop
re-form	reform
re-creation	recreation

Hyphenate to avoid hard-to-read combinations, like two *i*'s
(*semi-illiterate*) or more than two of the same consonant (*shell-
less*) in a row.

Hyphenate in most cases between a capital initial and a
word when the two combine to form a compound.

A-frame   T-shirt

But check your dictionary; some letter- or numeral-plus-word
compounds do not require hyphens.

B flat   F major

(4)   In compound numerals and fractions

Hyphenate compounds that represent numbers below one hundred, even if they are part of a larger number.

   the twenty-first century   three hundred sixty-five days

Compounds that represent numbers over ninety-nine *(two thousand, thirty million, two hundred fifty)* are not hyphenated. Therefore, in the expression *three hundred sixty-five days* the compound *sixty-five* is hyphenated because it represents a number below one hundred, but no hyphens connect *three* to *hundred*.

     Hyphenate fractions when they serve as compound modifiers.

   a two-thirds share of the business
   a three-fourths majority

Hyphens are not required in other cases, but most writers do use them.

    PREFERRED: seven-eighths of the circle

    ACCEPTABLE: seven eighths of the circle

    –
    34b

(5)   In newly created compounds

A coined compound, using a new combination of words as a unit, uses hyphens.

   He looked up with a <u>who-do-you-think-you-are</u> expression on his face.

☐   **EXERCISE 2**

Form compound adjectives from the following word groups, inserting hyphens where necessary.

    EXAMPLE: a contract for three years

              a three-year contract

1. a relative who has long been lost
2. someone who is addicted to video games
3. a salesperson who goes from door to door
4. a display calculated to catch the eye
5. friends who are dearly beloved
6. a household that is centered on a child
7. a line of reasoning that is hard to follow
8. the border between New York and New Jersey
9. a candidate who is thirty-two years old
10. a computer that is friendly to its users

☐ **EXERCISE 3**

Add hyphens to the compounds in these sentences wherever they are required. Consult a dictionary if necessary.

> EXAMPLE: Alaska was the forty ninth state to join the United States.
>
> Alaska was the forty-ninth state to join the United States.

1. One of the restaurant's blue plate specials is chicken fried steak.
2. Virginia and Texas are both right to work states.
3. He stood on tiptoe to see the near perfect statue, which was well hidden by the security fence.
4. The five and ten cent store had a self service makeup counter and stocked many up to the minute gadgets.
5. The so called Saturday night special is opposed by pro gun control groups.
6. He ordered two all beef patties with special sauce, lettuce, onions, cheese, and pickle on a sesame seed bun.
7. The material was extremely thought provoking, but it hardly presented any earth shattering conclusions.
8. The Dodgers Phillies game was rained out, so the long suffering fans left for home.
9. Bone marrow transplants carry the risk of what is known as a graft versus host reaction.
10. The state funded child care program was considered a highly desirable alternative to family day care.

—
34b

35

Abbreviations

Abbreviations save time and space. They also communicate meaning quickly and efficiently, but only when they are familiar to your readers.

Many abbreviations are acceptable only in informal writing and are not appropriate in college writing. Others are acceptable in scientific, technical, or business writing, or only in a particular discipline. If you are unsure whether to use a particular abbreviation, check a style manual in your field.

(For information on use of punctuation with abbreviations, see 26a.2; for a list of abbreviations used in footnotes and bibliographies, see 39g.)

35a Abbreviating Titles

Titles before and after proper names are usually abbreviated.

Mr. Walter Cronkite Dr. Helen Zweizig
Henry Kissinger, Ph.D. St. Jude

But military, religious, academic, and government titles are not abbreviated.

General George Patton
the Reverend William Gray
Professor Kenneth G. Schaefer
Senator Daniel Moynihan

In informal writing, abbreviations like Gen., Rev., Sen., and the like are acceptable if they precede a complete name (Rep. Patricia Schroeder, for example). Abbreviated forms of these titles

are not acceptable before a surname alone or when they do not
precede a proper name.

FAULTY: Rep. Schroeder is a member of Congress from Colorado.

FAULTY: Patricia Schroeder is a congressional rep. from Colorado.

REVISED: Representative Patricia Schroeder is a member of Congress
          from Colorado.

35b Abbreviating Technical Terms and Agency Names

Certain abbreviations are used in speech and in college writing
to designate groups, institutions, people, substances, and so on.
For example, businesses and government, social, and civic organizations are commonly referred to by initials. These abbreviations fall into two categories: abbreviations formed from capitalized initials (CIA) and those that are acronyms (CORE). (See 26a.2
for additional examples and explanation.)

abbr
35c

    Accepted abbreviations for terms that are not well known
may also be used, but only if you have cited the abbreviation in
parentheses directly after your first mention of the full term.

> Citrus farmers have been injecting ethylene dibromide (EDB), a
> chemical pesticide, into the soil for over twenty years. Now, how-
> ever, EDB has seeped into wells and contaminated water supplies,
> and it is a suspected carcinogen.

NOTE: The extent to which abbreviations are used varies from
discipline to discipline. Regardless of discipline, however, excessive use of abbreviations can be confusing to your readers, so use
them sparingly.

35c Abbreviating Designations of Specific Dates, Times of Day, Temperatures, and Numbers

50 B.C. (B.C. follows the date)
A.D. 432 (A.D. precedes the date)
6 A.M.
3:03 P.M.
20° C (Centigrade or Celsius)
180° F (Fahrenheit)

Always capitalize B.C. and A.D. You may, however, use either
uppercase or lowercase letters for a.m. and p.m. (A.M., a.m., P.M.,

p.m.). Printers conventionally set A.M., P.M., B.C., and A.D. in small capital letters (A.M., P.M., B.C., A.D.). These abbreviations are used only when they are accompanied by numbers.

FAULTY: We will see you in the A.M.

REVISED: We will see you in the morning.

REVISED: We will see you at 8 A.M.

In technical writing you may use the abbreviation *no.* (number), but only before a specific number. This abbreviation may be written either *no.* or *No.*

FAULTY: The no. on the label of the unidentified substance was 52.

REVISED: The unidentified substance was labeled no. 52.

REVISED: The number on the label of the unidentified substance was 52.

In nontechnical writing *no.* is acceptable only in certain documentation formats (see 39c–e).

CORRECT: *The Journal of the Institute for Socioeconomic Studies,* Vol. 11, No. 2, Spring 1977.

FAULTY: The no. 1 consumer of electricity in many households is a frost-free refrigerator.

REVISED: The number one consumer of electricity in many households is a frost-free refrigerator.

abbr
35d

35d Editing to Eliminate Misuse and Overuse of Abbreviations

Abbreviations are not used in the following cases.

For certain familiar Latin expressions

Abbreviations of the common Latin phrases *i.e.* ("that is"), *e.g.* ("for example"), and *etc.* ("and so forth") are sometimes appropriate for informal writing, and they may occasionally be acceptable in a parenthetical note. In most college writing, however, an equivalent phrase should be written out in full.

INFORMAL: Poe wrote "The Gold Bug," "The Masque of the Red Death," etc.

PREFERABLE: Poe wrote "The Gold Bug," "The Masque of the Red Death," and other stories.

INFORMAL: Other musicians (e.g., Bruce Springsteen) have been influenced by Dylan.

PREFERABLE: Other musicians (for example, Bruce Springsteen) have
been influenced by Dylan.

The Latin abbreviations *et al.* ("and others") and *cf.* ("compare")
are used only in bibliographic entries.

Davidson, Harley, et al. *You and Your Motorcycle.* New York: Ten
Speed Press, 1968.

For the names of days, months, or holidays

FAULTY: Sat., Aug. 9, was the hottest day of the year.

REVISED: Saturday, August 9, was the hottest day of the year.

FAULTY: Only twenty-three shopping days remain until Xmas.

REVISED: Only twenty-three shopping days remain until Christmas.

For units of measurement

abbr 35d

In informal and technical writing some units of measurement are abbreviated when preceded by a numeral.

The hurricane had winds of 35 m.p.h.

The new Honda gets over 50 m.p.g.

In general, however, write out such expressions, and spell out
words such as *inches, feet, years, miles, pints, quarts,* and *gallons.*

NOTE: Abbreviations for units of measurement are not used in the
absence of a numeral.

FAULTY: The laboratory equipment included pt. and qt. measures
and a beaker that could hold a gal. of liquid.

REVISED: The laboratory equipment included pint and quart measures and a beaker that could hold a gallon of liquid.

For names of places, streets, and the like

Abbreviations of names of streets, cities, states, countries,
and geographical regions are common in informal writing. For
college assignments these words should be spelled out.

FAULTY	REVISED
B'way	Broadway
Riverside Dr.	Riverside Drive
Phila.	Philadelphia
Calif. or CA	California
Catskill Mts.	Catskill Mountains

EXCEPTIONS: The abbreviations *U.S.A.,* or *USA,* and *U.S.S.R.,* or
USSR are often acceptable, as is *D.C.* (for District of Columbia) in
the phrase *Washington, D.C.* It is also permissible to use the abbreviation *Mt.* before the name of a mountain *(Mt. Etna)* and *St.* in
a place name *(St. Albans).*

For names of academic subjects

Names of academic subjects are not abbreviated.

FAULTY: Psych., soc., and English lit. are all required for graduation.

REVISED: Psychology, sociology, and English literature are all required for graduation.

For parts of books

Abbreviations that designate parts of written works *(Pt. II, Ch. 3, Vol. IV)* should not be used within the text of a paper. Such abbreviations are acceptable only in documentation and bibliographic entries.

For people's names

FAULTY: Mr. Harris's five children were named Robt., Eliz., Jas., Chas., and Wm.

REVISED: Mr. Harris's five children were named Robert, Elizabeth, James, Charles, and William.

**abbr
35d**

In company names

The abbreviations *Inc., Bros., Co.,* or *Corp.* and the ampersand (&) are not used unless they are part of a firm's official name.

Company names are written exactly as the firms themselves write them.

Holt, Rinehart and Winston
Western Union Telegraph Company
Santini Bros.
Rohm & Haas
AT&T
Charles Schwab & Co., Inc.

EXCEPTION: Shortened forms of publishers' names are preferred in bibliographic citations (see 39c.2).

Abbreviations for *company, corporation,* and the like are not used in the absence of a company name.

FAULTY: The corp. merged with a small co. in Pittsburgh.

REVISED: The corporation merged with a small company in Pittsburgh.

The ampersand (&) is used in college writing only in the name of a company that requires it.

FAULTY: "Frankie & Johnny" is a ballad about a woman who shoots her unfaithful lover.

REVISED: "Frankie and Johnny" is a ballad about a woman who shoots her unfaithful lover.

Symbols

The symbols %, =, +, #, and ¢ are acceptable in technical and scientific writing but not in nontechnical college writing.

FAULTY: The 90¢ cost of admission represents a 50% increase over last year's price.

REVISED: The ninety-cent cost of admission represents a 50 percent increase over last year's price.

The symbol $ is acceptable in all types of writing, but only before specific numbers. It is not used as a substitute for the words *money* or *dollars.*

CORRECT: The first of her books of poetry cost $4.25 per copy.

FAULTY: The value of the $ has declined steadily in the last two decades.

REVISED: The value of the dollar has declined steadily in the last two decades.

abbr
35d

☐   **EXERCISE**

Correct any incorrectly used abbreviations in the following sentences, assuming that all are intended for an academic audience. If a sentence is correct, mark it with a C.

EXAMPLE: *Romeo & Juliet* is a play by Wm. Shakespeare.

Romeo and Juliet is a play by William Shakespeare.

1. The committee meeting, attended by representatives from Action for Children's Television (ACT) and NOW, Sen. Putnam, & the pres. of ABC, convened at 8 A.M. on Mon. Feb. 24 at the YWCA on Germantown Ave.
2. An econ. prof. was suspended after he encouraged his students to speculate on securities issued by corps. under investigation by the SEC.
3. Benjamin Spock, the M.D. who wrote *Baby and Child Care,* is a respected dr. known throughout the USA.
4. The FDA has banned the use of Red Dye no. 2 in food, but BHT and other food additives are still in use.
5. The Rev. Dr. Martin Luther King, Jr., leader of the S.C.L.C., led the famous Selma, Ala., march.
6. Wm. Golding, a novelist from the U.K., won the Nobel Prize for lit.
7. The adult education center, financed by a major computer corp., offers courses in basic subjects like introductory bio. and tech. writing as well as teaching programming languages like COBOL and FORTRAN.

8. All the bros. in the fraternity ageed to write to Pres. Dexter appealing their disciplinary probation under Ch. 4, Sec. 3, of the IFC constitution.
9. A 4 qt. (i.e., 1 gal.) container is needed to hold the salt solution.
10. According to Prof. Morrison, all those taking the MCAT's should bring two sharpened no. 2 pencils to the St. Joseph's University auditorium on Sat.

**abbr
35**

36

Numbers

Convention determines when to use a number (22) and when to spell out a number (twenty-two). Numerals are generally more common in scientific and technical writing, in journalism, and in informal writing, while numbers are more often spelled out in formal or literary writing. In certain contexts one option is preferred over the other.

Common sense and a knowledge of the conventions of a particular discipline should guide your final decision. If spelling out numbers is cumbersome, use figures. Whatever your choice, usage should be consistent, and numerals and spelled-out forms should generally not be mixed in the same passage.

36a Spelling Out Numbers That Begin Sentences

Never begin a sentence with a numeral. If a number begins a sentence, express it in words.

> FAULTY: 200 students are currently enrolled in freshman English.

> REVISED: Two hundred students are currently enrolled in freshman English.

Or reword the sentence, especially when the opening number is more than two words long.

> CORRECT: Current enrollment in freshman English is 200 students.

510

36b   Spelling Out Numbers That Can Be Expressed in One or Two Words ———

Unless a number falls into one of the categories listed in 36d, spell it out if you can do so in one or two words.

The Hawaiian alphabet has only twelve letters.

Class size stabilized at twenty-eight students.

Approximate numbers can often be expressed in one or two words.

Guards turned away over ten thousand disappointed fans.

The subsidies are expected to total about two million dollars.

NOTE: In some disciplines, such as the social sciences and engineering, the rule is to spell out all numbers below ten and to use numerals for ten and above.

**num
36d**

36c   Using Numerals for Numbers That Cannot Be Expressed in One or Two Words ———

Numbers more than two words long are expressed in figures.

The pollster interviewed 3,250 voters before the election.

The dietitian prepared 125 sample menus.

When Levittown, Pennsylvania, was built in the early 1950's, the builder's purchases included 300,000 doorknobs, 153,000 faucets, 53,600 ice cube trays, and 4,000 manhole covers.

Note that to be consistent with the spelled-out forms used in the last sentence above, the number 4,000 is expressed in figures even though it could be written in just two words.

36d   Using Numerals Where Convention Requires Their Use ———

Numerals are used for addresses; dates; exact times; exact sums of money; pages and divisions of written works; measurements accompanied by symbols or figures; numbers that include percentages, decimals, or fractions; ratios, scores, and statistics; and identification numbers.

Addresses

1600 Pennsylvania Avenue
10 Downing Street
111 Fifth Avenue, New York, New York 10003

Dates

January 15, 1929   62 B.C.
November 22, 1963   1914–1919

Exact times

9:16   10 A.M. (or 10:00 A.M.)   6:50

EXCEPTIONS: Spell out times of day when they are used with *o'clock: eleven o'clock*, not *11 o'clock*. Also spell out times expressed as round numbers: *They were in bed by ten.*

Exact sums of money

$25.11
$6752.00 (or $6,752.00)
$25.5 million (or $25,500,000)

num
36d

EXCEPTION: You may write out a round sum of money if the number can be expressed in fewer than three words.

five dollars   two thousand dollars
fifty-three cents   six hundred dollars

Pages and divisions of written works

Numerals are used for chapter numbers; volume numbers; acts, scenes, and lines of plays; books of the Bible; and line numbers of long poems.

The "Out, out brief candle" speech appears in Act 5, scene 5, of *Macbeth* (lines 17–28); in Kittredge's *Complete Works of Shakespeare* it appears on page 1142.

Measurements

When a measurement is expressed by a number accompanied by a symbol or an abbreviation, use figures.

55 mph   12″
32°   15 cc

Numbers containing percentages, decimals, or fractions

80% (or 80 percent)   6 3/4
98.6   3.14

Ratios, scores, and statistics

Children preferred Crispy Crunchies over Total Bran by a ratio of 20 to 1.

The Orioles defeated the Phillies 6 to 0.

The median age of the voters was 42; the mean age was 40.

Identification numbers

Route 66   Track 8
Channel 12   Social Security number 146–07–3846

36e   Using Numerals with Spelled-out Numbers

Even when all the numbers in a particular passage are short enough to be spelled out, figures are sometimes used along with spelled-out numbers to distinguish one number from another.

CONFUSING: The team was divided into twenty two-person squads.

CLEAR: The team was divided into twenty 2-person squads.

CONFUSING: They lived at 500 5th Avenue.

CLEAR: They lived at 500 Fifth Avenue.

num
36e

☐   **EXERCISE**

Revise the use of numbers in these sentences, making sure usage is correct and consistent. If a sentence uses numbers correctly, mark it with a C.

EXAMPLE: The Empire State Building is one hundred and two stories high.

The Empire State Building is 102 stories high.

1. *1984*, a novel by George Orwell, is set in a totalitarian society.
2. The English placement examination included a 30-minute personal-experience essay, a 45-minute expository essay, and a 100-item objective test of grammar and usage.
3. In a control group of two hundred forty-seven patients, almost three out of four suffered serious adverse reactions to the new drug.
4. Before the thirteenth amendment to the Constitution, slaves were counted as 3/5 of a person.
5. The intensive membership drive netted 2,608 new members and additional dues of over 5 thousand dollars.
6. They had only 2 choices: either they could take the yacht at Pier Fourteen, or they could return home to the penthouse at Twenty-seven Harbor View Drive.
7. The atomic number of lithium is three.

8. Approximately 3 hundred thousand school children in District 6 were given hearing and vision examinations between May third and June 26.

9. The United States was drawn into the war by the Japanese attack on Pearl Harbor on December seventh, 1941.

10. An upper-middle-class family can spend over two hundred fifty thousand dollars to raise each child up to age 18.

SECTION VII

Writing with Sources

37

Research for Writing

We all engage in **research** from time to time. Before we make any major purchase—a car, personal computer, stereo, or television, for instance—we gather information to guide our choice. We ask friends for advice, we study advertisements and brochures, we look at magazines such as *Consumer Reports.* Government agencies, investment firms, advertising agencies, corporations, universities, professional organizations, political parties, and special-interest groups of all sorts also spend a lot of time—and money— doing research. In an age of proliferating information, it sometimes seems as if nothing is done without the recommendations of a research staff.

Using methods designed to locate information as quickly as possible, experienced researchers look for accurate, current, and relevant material. They do not immediately undertake an exhaustive library search. Usually they call people who can advise them, asking them which experts or which books and articles to consult. They take advantage of computerized search facilities: five minutes at a terminal can eliminate hours of poring through print indexes. In the library, they use research tools suited to their field of inquiry—indexes that summarize important work done in an area or that list works with bibliographies, for example. These techniques help them to assemble a preliminary bibliography quickly and efficiently. Because book-length studies and even articles can be out of date by the time they appear in print, researchers often contact experts directly.

Experienced researchers also recognize the difference between **primary** and **secondary sources**—that is, between original documents and commentaries on those documents. Whenever they can, researchers go back to primary sources to avoid being misled by the biases or errors of others.

When you are preparing a college assignment, your topic and your time determine how much research you do. But knowing the techniques used by experienced researchers can streamline your task and give you more time for writing.

37a   Setting Up a Search Strategy ─────────

The most important thing you can do to make your research efficient and productive is to avoid a haphazard, hit-or-miss search for material. Instead, begin your research by meeting with both your instructor and your reference librarian, two knowledgeable people who can direct you to the most useful and reliable sources of information for your paper and help you to plan your search strategy. A **search strategy** is a systematic process of collecting and evaluating source material, moving in a logical, orderly progression from general sources of information to more and more specific ones. It stands to reason that before you can actively gather information for a paper, you need to gain a general understanding of your topic. A search strategy reflects the way research works: as your research becomes more focused, so do your ideas. One effective search strategy is outlined below.

**res
37a**

Search Strategy ─────────

- Set up conferences with instructor and librarian to plan search strategy and get names of helpful sources of information (books, organizations, experts, and so on).
- Visit reference area: survey encyclopedias, basic textbooks, and other general reference works to get an overview of your topic; pay particular attention to bibliographies.
- Plan and set up interviews; draft letters of inquiry; consider possibilities for field research.
- Consult periodical catalog: locate articles recommended by experts or noted in basic reference works or their bibliographies.
- Consult author-title section of card catalog: locate books recommended by experts or noted in basic reference works or their bibliographies.
- Search periodical indexes.
- Do database search if necessary.
- Search subject section of card catalog.
- Use special library services if necessary.
- Consult experts if necessary.
- Do field research if necessary.
- Return to reference area: consult specialized reference works as needed to fill in details.

This outline represents just one way to map out your progress, and many variations are possible. For example, you may decide to consult experts or write letters requesting information at more than one point in your research. When you are just beginning your work, the information you are seeking may be fairly basic—names of additional people or organizations to contact, titles of useful print sources about your subject, and so on. Later in your research, when your goal is to find answers to specific questions, you may need to turn again to various people or organizations.

Although you map out your search strategy in advance, your plan should be flexible. Your search strategy is a general structure for your research activity; you fill in and arrange the specific tasks pertinent to your research as you go along. Remember that you should modify your search strategy as your objectives become more specific and your research becomes more focused.

37b Doing Library Research

res 37b

The library is central to many research projects. To make appropriate use of the materials in your college library, you should know how the library is organized and what specialized reference tools it contains. Even before you begin your research, familiarize yourself with your library: its physical layout, its holdings, its personnel, its hours. Later, as you do library research, be sure to copy down the *complete* publication information—author, title, volume number, date of publication, and so on—that you will need to locate a particular source. In addition, remember how to distinguish between a book and a periodical citation: a citation for a book includes a publisher's name and a place of publication; one for a periodical includes an article title set in quotation marks.

To find material in the library you will use the following reference tools:

- reference books
- periodical indexes
- database searches
- card catalogs
- special library services

(1) Consulting reference books

You will consult reference books at at least two stages: during exploratory research and later when you do focused research.

Reference Sources for Exploratory Research

At this early stage you want to get acquainted with your topic, so you want to find works that give useful overviews but that are not too technical. The exploration you do here can help you to familiarize yourself with key terms, people, and events relevant to your topic. The reference works you consult now in your library's reference room—general encyclopedias; encyclopedias, dictionaries, and bibliographies in special subjects; general bibliographies; biographical dictionaries and encyclopedias; and even introductory textbooks in the area of your topic—can also offer useful bibliographies.

General Encyclopedias General multivolume encyclopedias such as *Encyclopedia Americana* and *Collier's Encyclopedia* contain information about many different subjects. Articles, often written by experts on the topic, are arranged alphabetically. Although general encyclopedias give you a good overview, they do not replace in-depth research.

Perhaps the most respected multivolume encyclopedia is the *Encyclopaedia Britannica*, now in its fifteenth edition. The newest edition is divided into three sections: the *Propaedia*, a one-volume general subject index; the *Micropaedia*, a twelve-volume index containing brief articles; and the *Macropaedia*, a nineteen-volume detailed discussion of selected subjects listed in the *Micropaedia*. The information in the *Britannica* is invaluable, but this encyclopedia takes some getting used to. You can begin by searching the *Propaedia* for subject categories and then reading the brief articles in the *Micropaedia*. The longer discussions in the *Macropaedia* frequently contain brief bibliographies.

To get a sense of your topic in less time, use a one-volume general encyclopedia. Two of the best are *The New Columbia Encyclopedia* and *The Random House Encyclopedia*. Both contain many short entries listed in alphabetical order by subject. The cross-references and in-depth bibliographical information provided by the multivolume encyclopedias, however, do not appear in these short volumes. You may still have to consult a multivolume encyclopedia if you need more general information.

Encyclopedias, Dictionaries, and Bibliographies in Special Subjects These specialized reference works contain in-depth articles on single subjects and greater detail than do general encyclopedias, and articles sometimes include annotated bibliographies and cross-references. Specialized reference works are listed in Eugene P. Sheehy's *Guide to Reference Works*, available at the reference desk in most libraries. The following list suggests the variety of sources available.

res
37b

Art
>   *McGraw-Hill Encyclopedia of World Art*, 15 volumes. Scholarly arti-
>   cles, detailed bibliographies, and many plates. Covers art of all
>   periods and countries.
>   *Oxford Companion to Art*. A one-volume encyclopedia devoted to the
>   visual arts.

Biology
>   *Encyclopedia of Bioethics*, 4 volumes. Three hundred scholarly essays
>   dealing with human life and ethical issues such as euthanasia and
>   abortion.
>   Gray, Peter, ed. *The Encyclopedia of the Biological Sciences*. Directed
>   at students and experts reading outside their fields. Includes bib-
>   liographies, biographical articles, and illustrations.
>   *A Dictionary of Genetics*. Comprehensive information about genetic
>   research, including definitions of terms.

Business and Economics
>   *The McGraw-Hill Dictionary of Modern Economics*. Extended defini-
>   tions of terms. Also includes bibliographies.
>   Heyel, Carl, ed. *The Encyclopedia of Management*. Definitions and
>   explanations. Includes references for further reading.
>   Munn, Glenn Gaywaine. *Encyclopedia of Banking and Finance*. De-
>   fines and explains pertinent terms.

**res
37b**

Chemistry
>   *Encyclopedia of Chemistry*. Articles about distinguished chemists,
>   various chemical associations, and chemicals themselves.
>   *Chemical Technology: An Encyclopedic Treatment*. Focuses on the
>   applied uses of chemical technology.

Drama
>   *The Oxford Companion to the Theatre*. A one-volume encyclopedia of
>   the theater.
>   *McGraw-Hill Encyclopedia of World Drama*, 4 volumes. Comprehen-
>   sive coverage of all aspects of drama from ancient to present times.

Education
>   *Dictionary of Education*. A scholarly dictionary with extended defini-
>   tions of terms.
>   *The Encyclopedia of Educational Research*. A four-volume set that
>   summarizes various aspects of educational research.

Engineering
>   *Engineering Encyclopedia*. A concise encyclopedia and mechanical
>   dictionary. Includes definitions of engineering terms and some
>   historical material.
>   *McGraw-Hill Encyclopedia of Science and Technology*. Not specifically
>   geared to engineering, but includes articles of related interest.

History

Cambridge Ancient History. Egypt to the fall of Rome. Each chapter is
written by a specialist; each volume includes a full bibliography.

Cambridge Medieval History. Reference history of the Middle Ages
prepared by experts in the field.

New Cambridge Modern History. Authoritative and comprehensive
general modern history, covering the Renaissance through World
War II, with an emphasis on Europe.

Dictionary of American History. Brief articles on many topics on
American history and life. Does not include biography.

Great Events in History. A series of books summarizing important
events. Excellent bibliographies.

Literature

Oxford Companion to American Literature. Short articles dealing with
the literature of Canada and the United States. Entries cover a
wide range of subjects: authors, specific works, historical figures.

Oxford Companion to English Literature. Concise articles on English
authors and on characters and allusions encountered in English
literature.

Oxford Companion to Classical Literature. Handbook of information
on classical Greek and Roman literary works, authors, history, institutions, and religion.

Spiller, Robert E., and others. Literary History of the United States, 2
volumes. A detailed literary history of the United States from colonial times to the present. Volume I concentrates on specific periods; Volume II has bibliographical essays and a detailed index.

Cassell's Encyclopedia of World Literature, 3 volumes. Volume I includes brief definitions of literary terms and essays on literary history. Volumes II and III contain biographical sketches.

Contemporary Authors. A good source of biographical and critical
information on twentieth-century writers.

Mathematics

The Universal Encyclopedia of Mathematics. Alphabetically arranged
articles on topics from arithmetic to calculus. Over two hundred
pages of formulas and tables.

The International Dictionary of Applied Mathematics. Defines terms
and describes methods of applying math to various fields of physical science and engineering.

Music

Grove's Dictionary of Music and Musicians, 9 volumes. Covers the field
from 1450 to the present. Includes biographies; musical history,
theory, and practice; definitions of terms; and analyses of songs
and operas. Emphasis on English subjects.

Apel, Willi. Harvard Dictionary of Music. A one-volume dictionary
with articles based on scholarship; numerous definitions; no biographies. Emphasizes historical point of view.

Physics

    Encyclopedic Dictionary of Physics, 9 volumes. A scholarly dictionary of physics, also dealing with astronomy, geophysics, biophysics, and related subjects. Articles are signed; many have bibliographical references.

    Encyclopedia of Physics, 54 volumes. Covers the field comprehensively.

Political Science

    The American Political Dictionary. Includes definitions and explanations of terms, laws, and cases pertaining to civil liberties, the Constitution, and the legislative process.

    Dunner, Joseph, ed. *Dictionary of Political Science.* Compact encyclopedia treats important people, places, terms, and events.

    Encyclopedia of the Third World. Three-volume set that provides political, economic, and social data for third-world countries.

    Theimer, Walter. *Encyclopedia of Modern World Politics.* Brief articles on current political issues and figures of all periods and countries; also covers current political terms.

Psychology

    Encyclopedia of Psychology, 4 volumes. Contains both short and long entries. Good bibliographies.

    International Encyclopedia of Psychiatry, Psychology, Psychoanalysis and Neurology, 12 volumes. Readable articles on many topics dealing with psychology or psychiatry.

    Contemporary Psychology. Collection of current reviews in the field.

Religion and Philosophy

    Concise Encyclopedia of Living Faiths. In-depth articles on the world's religions.

    Encyclopedia Judaica, 16 volumes. Gives a comprehensive view of Jewish life, customs, religion, history, and literature.

    New Catholic Encyclopedia, 15 volumes. Examines in detail the teachings, history, organization, and activities of the Catholic Church.

    Oxford Dictionary of the Christian Church. A collection of historical and biographical articles and definitions of ecclesiastical terms and customs.

    Burr, Nelson R. *A Critical Bibliography of Religion in America.* Bibliography of books, articles, and reviews. Includes social and cultural aspects of religion.

    The Concise Encyclopedia of Western Philosophy and Philosophers. A one-volume work including brief articles on thinkers and ideas of all time periods.

    Encyclopedia of Philosophy, 8 volumes. Lengthy articles on all aspects of philosophy.

Social Sciences

    International Encyclopedia of Social Sciences, 17 volumes. Covers anthropology, economics, geography, history, law, political science,

res
37b

psychiatry, psychology, sociology, and statistics. Good biographical supplement.

Sociology, Social Work, and Anthropology
Encyclopedia of Social Work. Articles on social work history, theory,
practice, and policy.
Encyclopedia of Sociology. Very brief articles by experts, covering a
wide variety of subjects.
Winick, Charles. *Dictionary of Anthropology.* Brief articles identifying
prominent early (pre-1900) anthropologists and their contributions.

Women and Minorities
Encyclopedia of Black America. Many lengthy entries on various aspects of black culture—history, literature, education, and so forth.
Handbook of North American Indians. Planned as a twenty-volume
set, of which only a few have been completed. Scholarly articles,
extensive bibliographies, valuable illustrations.
Harvard Encyclopedia of American Ethnic Groups. Information on all
ethnic groups with sizable populations in the United States. Includes bibliographies and thematic essays.
The Negro Almanac: A Reference Work on the Afro-American. Historical, political, economic, social, and biographical information.
Stineman, Esther. *Women's Studies: A Recommended Core Bibliography.* Lists and annotates major works on women in various disciplines—for example, women in sports, women in education.
Trejo, Arnulfo, *Bibliografía Chicana: A Guide to Information Sources.*
Guide to studies of Latin American populations in the United
States. Useful annotations.

res
37b

General Bibliographies General bibliographies list books available in a wide variety of fields.

Books in Print. A helpful index of authors and titles of every book in
print in the United States. *The Subject Guide to Books in Print*
indexes books according to subject area. *Paperbound Books in
Print* is an index to all currently available paperbacks.
The Bibliographic Index. A tool for locating bibliographies, this index
is particularly useful for researching a subject which is not well
covered in other indexes. Provides references to long bibliographies in books and brief ones in periodical articles.

Biographical References Specialized biographical reference
books provide valuable information about people's lives and
times. Bibliographic listings are often included.

Living Persons
Who's Who in America. Published every other year, this dictionary
gives very brief biographical data and addresses of prominent living Americans.

Who's Who. Concise biographical facts about notable living English
men and women.

Current Biography. Informal articles on living people of many nationalities; articles often include portraits.

American Men and Women of Science. Information about prominent
Americans in the physical, biological, social, and behavioral sciences.

Twentieth Century Authors. Informal biographies of contemporary
authors of many nationalities. Portraits and lists of authors' writ-
ings included.

Deceased Persons

Dictionary of American Biography. Considered the best of American
biographical dictionaries. Offers articles on over thirteen thousand
deceased Americans who have made contributions in all fields.

Dictionary of National Biography. The most important reference work
for English biography.

Webster's Biographical Dictionary. Perhaps the most widely used biographical reference work. Includes people from all periods and
places.

*American Authors 1600–1900; European Authors 1000–1900; British
Authors Before 1800.* These works provide biographical data on
authors who wrote before the twentieth century.

Who Was When? A Dictionary of Contemporaries. A reference source
for historical biography; covers 500 B.C. through the early 1970's.

Who Was Who in America 1607–1896. Entries on deceased Americans;
supplemented by *Who Was Who in America 1897–1960.* These volumes, though useful, do contain some inaccuracies.

res
37b

Reference Sources for Focused Research

When you have moved beyond the exploratory stage of your
research, you return to the library's reference area with more
narrowly focused objectives. With your paper well underway,
you use reference works to fill in specific details—facts, examples, statistics, definitions, quotations—to support your ideas.
For this purpose, you consult different reference works: unabridged dictionaries, special dictionaries, yearbooks and almanacs, atlases, and quotation books.

Unabridged Dictionaries **Unabridged dictionaries** are comprehensive works that give detailed information about words. For a
list of unabridged dictionaries see 18e.

Special Dictionaries These dictionaries focus on topics like
usage, synonyms, slang and idioms, etymologies, and foreign
terms. For a list of special-purpose dictionaries see 18f.

Yearbooks and Almanacs Yearbooks and almanacs are useful places to find facts or statistics. A **yearbook** is an annual publication that brings information on a subject up to date. An **almanac** provides lists, charts, and statistics about a number of subjects.

> *World Almanac.* Includes statistics about government, population, sports, and many other subjects. Includes a chronology of events of the previous year. Published annually since 1868.
>
> *Information Please Almanac.* Supplements the *World Almanac* (each work includes information unavailable in the other) and is somewhat easier to read. Published annually since 1947.
>
> *Facts on File.* A news digest with index. Covering 1940 to the present, this work offers digests of important news stories from metropolitan dailies. Published weekly, *Facts on File* serves as a kind of current encyclopedia.
>
> *Editorials on File.* Reprints important editorials from American and Canadian newspapers. Editorials represent both sides of controversial issues and are preceded by a summary of the principles involved.
>
> *Statistical Abstracts.* Summarizes the innumerable statistics gathered by the U.S. government.

Atlases An **atlas** contains maps and charts and often a wealth of historical, cultural, political, and economic information.

> *Rand McNally Cosmopolitan World Atlas.* A modern and extremely legible medium-sized atlas.
>
> *Encyclopaedia Britannica World Atlas.* Uses *Rand McNally Cosmopolitan* maps and includes geographical summaries and information on world distribution.
>
> *Times*, London. *The Times Atlas of the World*, 5 volumes, John Bartholomew, ed. Considered one of the best large world atlases. Includes inset maps for many cities. Very accurate and attractive maps throughout.
>
> Shepherd, William Robert. *Historical Atlas*, 9th ed. Covers period from 2000 B.C. to 1955. Excellent maps showing war campaigns and development of commerce.

Quotation Books A **quotation book** contains numerous quotations, on a wide variety of subjects, often by well-known persons. Such quotations can be especially useful for your paper's introductory and concluding paragraphs.

> *Bartlett's Familiar Quotations.* Quotations are arranged chronologically by author. The volume also includes an index of authors and a key word index which can help you to find a quotation on a specific subject.
>
> *The Home Book of Quotations.* Quotations are arranged by subject. An author index and a key word index are also included.

```
        GV              Modern Language Journal
         3                  St. Louis, MO
        L7

                Monthly
                Bound 1–62, 1916 – 78
                Microfilm 63, 1979 –

                Current Issues unbound
```

FIGURE 6

(2) Using periodical indexes

In the early stages of your research, you may come across references to useful journal articles. After you copy down the necessary bibliographic information, you can proceed to your library's **periodical catalog,** which lists the journal, newspaper, and magazine holdings of your library. The periodical catalog can tell you whether or not your library has the issues of the journals in which the articles you are looking for appear and where in the library those journals are housed.

As the card in Figure 6 indicates, libraries house periodicals in yearly bound volumes or in current issues located in the periodical section of your library. The words *microfiche, microprint,* or *microfilm* tell you that the periodicals have been stored photographically.

Later in your research, you consult specific periodical indexes as you search for additional articles to support your thesis. A **periodical index** lists, by subject, articles from a selected group of magazines, newspapers, or scholarly journals. In most indexes entries are arranged according to subject. The key to the abbreviations at the front of the volume enables you to use the index and gives all the information you need to compile your documentation and list of works cited. The entry in Figure 7 from the *Humanities Index* illustrates information contained in a citation from a periodical index. Once you locate potentially useful articles in the periodical index, you return to the periodical catalog to locate the appropriate journals.

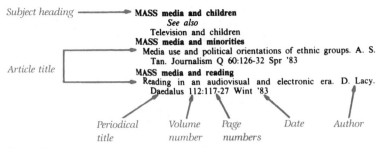

FIGURE 7

Many periodicals are indexed in databases (see 37b.3), and their number is growing. But not all libraries subscribe to a wide variety of information services, and not all students have access to electronic search facilities. Moreover, many articles in newspapers, magazines, and scholarly journals are indexed only in bound volumes or paperbound supplements kept in your library's reference section.

Not all indexes are useful to you as a beginning researcher, and not all will prove useful for every kind of topic. There are three levels of periodical indexes: general indexes, specialized indexes, and abstracting services.

**res
37b**

General Indexes   General indexes lead you to articles in newspapers and popular magazines. Three of the most frequently used are the *Readers' Guide to Periodical Literature*, the *Magazine Index*, and the *New York Times Index*.

Readers' Guide to Periodical Literature

The *Readers' Guide* lists articles that appear in over 150 magazines for general readers. You have probably used this index before, and the fact that you are familiar with it may encourage you to consult it first. However, you should be aware of its limitations. First, the *Readers' Guide* indexes only popular periodicals, whose articles may oversimplify complex issues. As a result, you must supplement information derived from such sources with material from more scholarly works. Second, even for popular periodicals, the *Readers' Guide* is neither as comprehensive nor as accessible as the *Magazine Index*.

Appearing in yearly volumes and paperbound supplements, articles in the *Readers' Guide* are listed and cross-referenced under subject headings.

Magazine Index

The *Magazine Index*, now widely used in college libraries, is an automated microfilm reader that indexes popular periodicals. It covers more periodicals (over 400) than the *Readers' Guide* and is more up to date. In addition, it is easier to use. With the *Magazine Index* you can look at more than four years' worth of periodicals at a time; if you were using the *Readers' Guide,* you might have to look through many different volumes—bound volumes and supplements—to scan the same period.

The *New York Times Index*

The *New York Times* is an excellent and reliable record of current events. In addition to news, it contains feature-length articles on issues of general interest. The *New York Times Index* lists major articles and features of the *Times* since 1851 by year or years. To find articles on a subject, locate the volume for the appropriate year. Articles are listed alphabetically by subject with short summaries. Supplements are published every two weeks. If your library subscribes to the *New York Times* microfilm service, you have access to every issue of the *Times* back to 1851. Articles give a contemporary view of a wide variety of subjects—everything from business and politics to literature and the arts.

NOTE: Some college libraries have a CD-ROM system called InfoTrac, which also indexes periodicals for general readers. Consult a reference librarian for information on this service.

res 37b

Specialized Indexes Specialized indexes lead you to articles in professional journals. The most commonly used of these volumes, listed here, index scholarly periodicals that are largely American and fairly easy to obtain. Many of the articles listed in such indexes assume expert knowledge, but some are accessible to general readers.

Applied Science and Technology Index

A monthly publication that lists articles from over three hundred periodicals.

Art Index

Indexes periodicals dealing with fine art, design, architecture, and art history.

Biography Index

Indexes books and periodicals about people.

Biological and Agricultural Index

Lists articles on all aspects of the life sciences.

Business Periodicals Index

A monthly publication covering business and related topics from 1958 to the present. Lists under subject or company name.

Education Index

Contains listings for articles in 230 journals. Coverage extends beyond education; in fact, this index is a good source of information on any topic dealing with children or adolescents.

Environment Index
Indexes both scholarly and popular articles on all aspects of the environment.

Essay and General Literature Index
Indexes essays and articles in books by author, subject, and sometimes by title. (Strictly speaking, this is not a periodical index but an index to parts of books.) Emphasis is on the social sciences.

General Science Index
Lists articles pertaining to all scientific subjects; a basic tool for general information on the sciences.

Humanities Index
The *Humanities Index* lists articles from 259 scholarly journals in areas such as archeology, history, language, literary criticism, philosophy, and religion.

Music Index
Indexes periodicals focusing on popular as well as classical music.

Public Affairs Information Service
Indexes periodicals dealing with political science, foreign affairs, and public policy.

Social Sciences Index
The *Social Sciences Index* lists articles from 265 scholarly journals that focus on economics, political science, criminology, sociology, psychology, and sociology, for example.

Abstracting Services Abstracting services have a wider scope than general or specialized indexes, with comprehensive, often international, listings of literature in a discipline. In addition to providing citations for journal articles, abstracting services also include **abstracts,** brief summaries of the articles' major points. As a beginning researcher you may find these indexes difficult to use. Still, abstracting services might be of some value to you now, enabling you to preview an article before you go to the trouble of searching for it, and they will be useful to you later in your academic career, as you do more serious research in your field of specialization. The most commonly used abstracting services include *Biological Abstracts, Chemical Abstracts, MLA International Bibliography of Articles on the Modern Languages and Literature, Psychological Abstracts, Historical Abstracts* (focuses on Europe), *America: History and Life* (focuses on the United States), *Sociological Abstracts, Journal of Economic Literature,* and *Personnel Management Abstracts.* Even if your library does not receive copies of these publications, you will be able to search most of them if your library has online searching. For information about which abstracting services might be of value to you—and how to use them—consult a reference librarian.

(3)   Doing a database search

Perhaps the fastest way to locate relevant information is to do a database search. Such a search enables you to use a computer to scan various **databases**—electronic indexes that list thousands of bibliographic sources. All databases contain bibliographic citations, and some contain abstracts that summarize entire books and articles. Not all databases are equally useful. Social science and natural science databases, for example, are currently more extensive than those in the humanities. Ask your librarian which databases would be appropriate for your subject matter and which journals and periodicals the relevant databases contain. If certain important journals are not included, you will have to limit your search to periodical indexes (see 37b.2).

In many college libraries the librarian carries out the search. However, many libraries have or will soon have equipment that enables students to do their own searches. Whatever system applies in your library, understanding the following general guidelines for carrying out a database search should make retrieving information easier.

res
37b

Choosing Appropriate Databases The first step in doing a computer search is determining which databases include the information you need. Many colleges subscribe to information services that have access to hundreds of databases. By reviewing the databases available, you and your librarian can decide which ones are appropriate to your research. Among the useful databases most commonly available in college libraries are ERIC, PSYCINFO, and MLA BIBLIOGRAPHY. In addition, most indexes (like the *Humanities Index*, the *Social Sciences Index*, the *Business Index*, the *Education Index*, the *Art Index*, and many others) can be searched by computer in many libraries.

Narrowing Your Topic to Key Words Before you begin a database search, you must define your topic in one or more **key words** (sometimes called *descriptors*). These words are your entry into the database, for they enable the computer to call up articles that contain your key words in their titles or abstracts. For this reason, the more precise your key words are, the more specific the information you get. For example, if your topic were "teaching science fiction," general key words like *science* or *teaching* would not be helpful to you, for they would yield thousands of references, most of them irrelevant. *Science fiction*, although narrower, would yield several hundred—still too many to be helpful. *Teaching and science fiction*, however, would yield about thirty references—a manageable number.

A list of key words and phrases accompanies each database. Some information services issue a printed book, called a **thesaurus,** that lists these words. Other databases contain a **dictionary** that can be called up on the video terminal. By consulting the thesaurus or the dictionary, you can determine which key words best describe your topic. If the first key word or words you have chosen do not yield enough information, you will have to try different ones or different combinations to search your topic.

Entering Key Words into the Computer   Once you have entered your key words, the computer will indicate how many citations they elicit. You can then decide if you want a printout of these citations or if you want to narrow your search. Keep in mind that you can search each key word individually, or you can examine key words in combination. By entering the combination *science fiction* AND *teaching*, for instance, you get only citations that contain *both* key words (e.g., "Teaching Children Reading Using Science Fiction"). By entering the combination *science fiction* OR *teaching*, you get citations that contain *either* key word (e.g., "Children Create Using Science Fiction" or "Science Fiction and History").

**res
37b**

Selecting the Format You Want for Each Citation   Before you print out the citations, you must select the format you prefer. You can command the computer to print just the bibliographic citation, which gives the author, title, and journal reference, or you can command the fullest format, which gives you, in addition to the above, an abstract, publishing information, reprint costs, and other key words. Between these two extremes a few other formats are usually available. Because computer time is costly, select the format that gives you only the information you need.

Making a Printout   You can print out all the citations, but if there are too many you may choose to print out only certain years—all entries between 1988 and 1989, for example. In the printout for a paper on teaching science fiction (see Figure 8), the student requested abstracts of all citations containing the key words *science fiction* AND *teaching*.

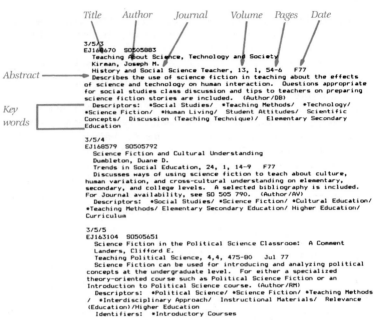

res
37b

Figure 8

☐   **EXERCISE 1**

If you have access to database-search facilities, answer the following questions.

1. Which database would you use to search the topic "architectural innovations of the Brooklyn Bridge"?
2. Which key words would you use to search this topic? Use a thesaurus or dictionary to help you decide.
3. In what form would you enter the words into the computer?
4. How many citations are there under each key word or key word combination?

(4)   Finding books in the card catalog

All the books in your college library are listed in the **card catalog**. Many libraries have installed computerized systems that allow students to call up catalog entries on video terminals. Other have transferred catalog cards to **microfiche**—a sheet of microfilm, containing rows of microimages of catalog cards, that you can scan on a viewing device. For the near future, however, most college libraries will continue to list their holdings in print form in the drawers of the card catalog.

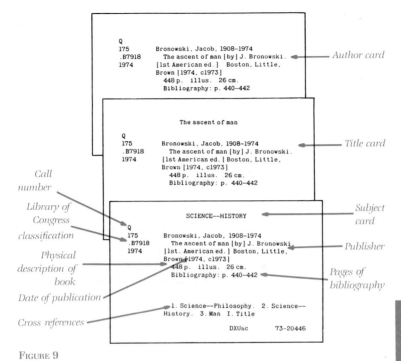

Author card

Title card

Call
number

Library of
Congress

classification

Physical
description of
book

Date of publication

Cross references

Subject
card

Publisher

Pages of
bibliography

FIGURE 9

Libraries have either a single catalog that interfiles author, title, and subject cards or two separate catalogs, one for author-title cards and another for subject cards. (See Figure 9 for examples of author, title, and subject cards.) Books in the author-title file are alphabetized by author or by title; books in the subject catalog are alphabetized by subject.

Early in your research, you go to the author-title section of the card catalog to see whether your library owns books mentioned in bibliographies or texts you have skimmed in the reference room, and to see where those books are located. Later, when you have narrowed the focus of your research and know more precisely what kind of information you are looking for, you consult the subject catalog for further information to support your tentative thesis.

If you have trouble thinking of subject headings or if you want to be thorough, you can consult the index volume called *Library of Congress Subject Headings,* which is kept at the reference desk. Also keep in mind that the card catalog itself contains cross-reference cards (see Figure 10) that refer you to related

```
        Science--History, see also


        1. Science--Philosophy
        2. Science--History   3. Man
```

FIGURE 10

subject headings. By using them, you can find more material related to your subject.

To locate a book in the stacks, you need its **call number**, which appears in the upper left of its catalog card (Figure 9). College libraries use the Dewey Decimal System, the Library of Congress System, or both to classify books. The **Dewey Decimal System** uses a number code to classify books according to subject. It is being replaced in most libraries, however, by the more flexible **Library of Congress System**, which uses a combination of numbers and letters to identify subject areas.

The call number refers you to the general area of the library that houses books on your subject. The same call number that appears on the catalog card is written on the spine of the book. When you find a book you need, look through the books shelved nearby. Browsing is not in itself an effective research technique, but as part of a focused search strategy it can sometimes yield good results.

If you cannot find a book, go to the circulation desk for help. The book may be out, on reserve, or held in a different section of the library. If it has been checked out, the person at the desk will tell you when it is due back and, in many cases, will notify the borrower that someone else needs it.

(5) Using special library services

Your most valuable resource is your librarian, a trained professional whose business it is to know how to locate information.

Before you begin any complicated research project, you should ask your librarian about any of the following special services you may plan to use.

Interlibrary Loans   If you need a book or article that the library does not own, you can ask your librarian to arrange an interlibrary loan. Libraries can arrange to borrow books or acquire copies of articles from other college libraries or from the holdings of municipal and state libraries. However, because interlibrary loans may take several weeks, you may not be able to take advantage of this service unless you initiate the loan early in your research.

Special Collections   Your librarian can also help you locate special collections of books, manuscripts, or documents housed in your college library or nearby in the community. Churches, specialized libraries, government agencies, ethnic societies, historical trusts, and museums sometimes have books and articles that you cannot find anywhere else. Your librarian may be able to get you permission to see them.

Government Documents   Federal, state, and local governments publish a wide variety of print materials, ranging from consumer information to detailed technical reports. These documents vary widely in quality and complexity as well as in subject matter. Although some government documents may be overly technical—or overly simplistic—for your research needs, others can be valuable. Government documents are particularly useful sources of statistics.

res
37b

Some government documents, such as *Statistical Abstracts of the United States*, may be housed in your library's reference room. A large university library may have a separate government documents room or section with its own catalog or index; in smaller libraries, government documents may be shelved along with books and indexed in the main subject catalog. The *Monthly Catalog of U.S. Government Publications*, which may be located either among the indexes in the reference room or in a special government documents area, indexes many, but not all, publications of the federal government.

Vertical File   The **vertical file** is the place where libraries keep miscellaneous source materials that may or may not be suitable for research. This file includes pamphlets from a variety of organizations and interest groups, some requested by your library and others unsolicited. The file may also include newspaper clippings and other material collected by your librarians because of its relevance to the needs and interests of your college's population. Much of the material contained in the vertical file's pamphlets is consumer oriented, designed for lay readers, and therefore not appropriate for research. In addition, materials in the file may not be up to date, and the date of publication of some sources may be hard to determine. Some sources, however, may be acceptable and useful for research. Consult a reference librarian for help in evaluating the materials in your library's vertical file.

☐   **EXERCISE 2**

What library research sources would you consult to find the following information?

1. A book review of Maxine Hong Kingston's *China Men* (1980)
2. Biographical information about the American anthropologist Margaret Mead
3. Books about Margaret Mead and her work
4. Information about the theories of Albert Einstein
5. Whether your college library has *The Human Use of Human Beings* by Norbert Wiener
6. How many pages there are in *On Death and Dying* by Elisabeth Kübler-Ross and how long the bibliography is
7. Where you could find other books on death and dying
8. Where you could find other books by Elisabeth Kübler-Ross
9. Articles about Walt Whitman's *Leaves of Grass*
10. Whether *Leaves of Grass* is presently available in a Norton Critical Edition
11. An article describing work done in particle physics in 1985
12. Whether your library has *Yale Review* 35 (September 1945)
13. The reaction of the country to Charles Lindbergh's flight across the Atlantic Ocean
14. Information about the New York clothing industry in the late nineteenth century
15. All the articles that cited the article "A Structure for Deoxyribonucleic Acid" by J. D. Watson and F. H. C. Crick in 1953

**res
37c**

37c   Gathering Information Outside the Library

By relying exclusively on the library for research materials, you may ignore important sources of more current information. Public service organizations, lobbies, and government agencies have available a wealth of current data. People who work in a field or who have a unique view of a situation are also excellent sources. Your problem as a researcher is finding these sources and obtaining information from them.

(1)   Finding organizations

Numerous organizations offer literature, often free of charge, to interested parties. Your instructor or reference librarian may suggest appropriate organizations for you to contact, and local businesses, chambers of commerce, and corporate public information departments may also direct you to potentially helpful groups. The most useful source of information, however, is the *Encyclopedia of Associations*. This valuable resource lists thousands of organizations by subject area. It also has a key word index, which enables you to discover whether or not an organization in a particular subject area exists. For example, to find out whether there is an association of people with an interest in research on twins, you would simply look up the key word "twins" in the encyclopedia's index. All organizations that include the word *twins* in their titles will be listed.

**res
37c**

(2)   Finding people

An important step in your research is locating people who can suggest reliable and up-to-date sources of information. A meeting with your instructor may be all that you need to get started, or your instructor may refer you to someone else more familiar with your topic. Just one or two good contacts can help you to establish a research network: your first contact might suggest another, who in turn might suggest two more.

Many excellent guides to people who are experts in various fields are available in the reference section of your library. Most of these guides focus on people in a particular area of endeavor.

Who's Who Among Black Americans
Who's Who and Where in Women's Studies
Who's Who in American Art
Who's Who in American Education
Who's Who in American Politics
American Men and Women of Science
Biographical Directory of the American Psychological Association
Contemporary Authors
Directory of The Modern Language Association

Once you have identified someone who can help you, you may want to write to that person requesting the information you want. If you have enough time to wait for an answer and if, after consulting your instructor, you feel that writing for information is both necessary and appropriate, write a letter explaining why you need this person's help. (The guidelines for this type of letter appear in 43f.)

☐   **EXERCISE 3**

You are beginning to gather information for the research projects outlined below. Whom in your college or your community might you approach to establish a research network? Write five exploratory questions that you would ask each person.

1. A paper for a biology course examining new developments in DNA recombinant research
2. A short paper for a history course in which you examine the validity of slave narratives for historical research
3. A research paper for a composition course in which you explore the possibility of scientists' developing artificial intelligence
4. A paper for a political science course about the issues in a local election.

res
37c

(3)   Conducting an interview

Interviews allow you to ask well-prepared questions and to follow up on the answers if necessary. You might ask for biographical information, a firsthand account of an event, or the views of an expert on a particular subject. Interviews often give you material that you cannot get by any other means.

When you call on anyone for advice, be sure to observe certain courtesies. Always make an appointment to discuss your initial plans. Prepare for your interview: have ready a clear description of your topic, along with a list of specific questions. Before you meet with someone, make sure you know something about your topic. Most people will be glad to help you, but they will not have the time to determine what it is you want to know or to do your work for you. Asking for a starting point, a piece of obscure information, or a subjective reaction is fine; asking someone else to think of a topic for you or to give you information that you could easily find yourself is not.

Your interview questions must elicit detailed, useful responses, and therefore you must design them carefully. *Leading questions*, for instance, make some people defensive, and *vague questions* can confuse them. *Dead-end questions*—questions that call for yes/no answers, for example—yield limited information. As the following examples illustrate, the way you phrase a question determines the response to it.

The city intends to spend 2 billion dollars over the next ten years to rehabilitate the port area. Do you support this plan? Why or why not? (good question)

Are you against the city's innovative plans to rehabilitate the port area? (leading question)

What are your feelings about the port area? (vague question)

Do you think the port area should be developed? (dead-end question; likely to elicit a yes/no answer)

The success or failure of an interview often depends on how you prepare for it. First, learn something about your topic and about the person you are interviewing. Before interviewing the author of a new book, for example, you should have read it yourself.

Next, prepare a list of questions tailored to the subject matter and time limit of your interview. It is better to have a few questions that can be answered in depth than many that can be answered only superficially.

The kinds of questions you ask depend on the kind of information you are after. **Open-ended** questions elicit general information and allow a respondent great flexibility in answering.

How was this neighborhood's population different forty years ago?

Do you think that students today are motivated? Why or why not?

If you could change something in your life, what would it be?

Closed-ended questions elicit specific information. They enable you to zero in on a subject and flush out specific details.

Has your family become more or less religious over the past ten years? How do you account for this?

What is the most important health benefit of your findings concerning Vitamin C?

How much money did the government's cost-cutting programs actually save?

Have a pencil and paper with you for the interview. Allow the person you are interviewing to complete an answer before you ask another question. Take notes, but continue to pay attention to your respondent while you do so. If you want to use a tape recorder, get the person's permission first. The reactions of the person you are interviewing can lead you to further questions, so pay attention to them. Do not hesitate to deviate from your prepared list of questions to follow up a particularly interesting response. Finally, after the interview, send a brief note thanking your subject for his or her time and cooperation.

☐   **EXERCISE 4**

Assume you could interview one of the following four singers on the
current status of popular music in America. Make a list of ten questions
that you would ask the singer, and indicate whether the questions are
open or closed. Before making your list, read an article about the singer
in a periodical.

1. Stevie Wonder   3. Bruce Springsteen
2. Charlie Daniels   4. Whitney Houston

☐   **EXERCISE 5**

Use the resources of your library to help you answer the following questions. Cite the source or sources of your answers.

1. What government publication could give you information about how
   to solar heat your home?
2. What government agency could you contact to find out what is
   being done to help the aging get proper nutrition?
3. At what address could you contact Bruce Evans, a young American
   artist?
4. At what university does the astronomer Carl Sagan teach?
5. What organizations could you contact to find out what is being done
   to prevent the killing of wolves in North America?
6. How could you get current information about the tobacco lobby?
7. What government agency could tell you what government services
   are available to resident aliens?
8. At what address could you contact Harold Bloom, a scholar who
   does work on nineteenth-century English literature?
9. Is there a government pamphlet that gives information about buying
   a new car?
10. How could you get current information about the Peace Corps?

**res
37c**

38

Working with Source Material

Once you have located sources of information for your paper, your next step is to read and evaluate them and to take notes on 3″ × 5″ cards (see 40e.2). When you write your paper, you will use the information you have collected on these cards to support your points and to help you evaluate the work of others.

38a   Reading Sources

Like writing, reading is an active process. When you read a source actively, you interact with the text: you read and reread, highlight key ideas, make marginal annotations, and eventually take notes. In the process you ask questions, identify the author's key assumptions, react to them, make connections, and arrive at your own conclusions. This interaction between you and your source generates the ideas you will go on to develop in your paper.

Three activities can help you to become a better reader: *previewing, highlighting,* and *annotating.*

(1)   Previewing

The first time you encounter a text, skim it to gain a sense of the author's meaning and emphasis. When previewing a book, begin by looking at its table of contents, especially at the sections that pertain to the topic you plan to write about. A quick look at the index will reveal the kind and amount of coverage the book gives to subjects that may be important to you. As you leaf through the chapters, notice any pictures, graphs, or tables, reading the captions that appear under them. When previewing magazine articles, look at headlines or boxed excerpts that may appear throughout the text. Also scan the introductory and concluding paragraphs for summaries of the author's main points. Journal articles in the sciences and social sciences often begin with summaries called **abstracts**. Read these as part of your previewing process.

Writers of both books and articles rely on a variety of visual cues to stress ideas. For example, a key idea may be emphasized by being set prominently in capital letters. Textbooks and periodical articles frequently isolate important points by using underlining, boxing, *italics*, **boldface**, or color. Concepts may be set off as indented lists that can be further emphasized with numbers or bullets (●). Headings can indicate the basic organization of a discussion and signal the author's major points. In addition to these visual cues, stylistic elements like thesis statements, topic sentences, repeated key terms, transitional words and phrases, and transitional paragraphs can also help you gain an overview of a text.

In the following excerpt from a music and art textbook, the authors use various visual signals and stylistic devices to help readers follow their discussion.

source 38a

Baroque Music

There were two main lines of musical development during the Baroque. One was the development of dramatic vocal music, both secular and religious, such as the opera, oratorio, and the cantata. The other was the emancipation of instrumental music from its nearly exclusive use of vocal forms, leading it to a position of dominance by the end of the period. Moreover, for the first time in musical history, two styles were purposely used side by side, the older style of the Renaissance and the modern style of the Baroque. During this time composers became even more conscious of musical conventions. However, certain characteristics of style were developed in this period that tied together such seemingly disparate composers as Peri, Monteverdi, and Frescobaldi of the early seventeenth century with Bach, Handel, and Domenico Scarlatti of the first half of the eighteenth century.

In spite of stylistic differences, there were four unifying elements: (1) the establishment of tonality as the basic concept of musical organization, (2) the use of basso continuo, (3) the development of the recitative, and (4) the development of true vocal and instrumental idioms.

The first of these, the establishment of tonality as the basis for harmonic organization, puts Baroque music. . . . (Milo Wald et al., *Music and Art in the Western World*)

Notice that the heading "Baroque Music" is set in boldface type and that the discussion is introduced by a sentence that clearly sets forth the period's "two main lines of musical development." Transitional elements *(One was, The other was)* link these types of musical development to each other and to the paragraph's unifying idea. In paragraph 2 the Baroque style's "four unifying elements" are set off as a numbered list preceded by a colon. The transitional phrase *The first of these* and the repeated key phrase *The establishment of tonality* establish the logical progression of the discussion to follow. Other transitions *(Moreover, However, In spite of)* also add coherence and help readers to understand the writer's meaning. By recognizing such signals, you can gain valuable insight into a text before you actually begin to read it closely.

(2) Highlighting

When you preview a selection, you skim it to get a general idea of its meaning and emphasis. When you **highlight,** you read a selection carefully, marking it to identify the key points and the relationship of one point to another. As you highlight, use a system of symbols and underlining to identify ideas and to reflect your understanding of a selection. (Never mark up books and articles that are not yours, however. If you are working with library material, photocopy the pages you need and then highlight them.) What symbols you use is up to you; the idea is to develop symbols that will clearly identify the visual and stylistic cues of a selection and that you will be able to understand when you re-read them at a later time. As you practice highlighting, you will discover the symbols that work best for you. The following suggestions can help you get started.

source
38a

Highlighting Symbols

- Underline to indicate information that you should read again.
- Box or circle key words or important phrases.
- Put a question mark (?) next to confusing passages, unclear points, or words you have to look up.
- Draw lines or arrows to show connections between ideas.
- Number points that appear in sequence.
- Draw a vertical line in the margin to set off an important section of text.
- Place a star (★) next to an especially important idea.

The following selection has been highlighted by a student preparing to write a paper on the topic of animal rights. Notice how the student uses a system of symbols to help her isolate the author's key ideas and to emphasize the progression of ideas in the passage.

Public zoos came into existence at the beginning of the period which was to see the disappearance of animals from daily life. The zoo to which people go to meet animals, to observe them, to see them, is, in fact, a monument to the impossibility of such encounters. Modern zoos are an epitaph to a relationship which was as old as man. They are not seen as such because the wrong questions have been addressed to zoos.

When they were founded—the London Zoo in 1828, the Jardin des Plantes in 1793, the Berlin Zoo in 1844—they brought considerable prestige to the national capitals. The prestige was not so different from that which had accrued to the private royal menageries. These menageries, along with gold plate, architecture, orchestras, players, furnishings, dwarfs, acrobats, uniforms, horses, art and food had been demonstrations of an emperor's or king's power and wealth. Likewise in the 19th century, public zoos were an endorsement of modern colonial power. The capturing of the animals was a symbolic representation of the conquest of all distant and exotic lands. "Explorers" proved their patriotism by sending home a tiger or an elephant. The gift of an exotic animal to the metropolitan zoo became a token in subservient diplomatic relations.

Yet, like every other 19th century public institution, the zoo, however supportive of the ideology of imperialism, had to claim an independent and civic function. The claim was that it was another kind of museum, whose purpose was to further knowledge and public enlightenment. And so the first questions asked of zoos belonged to natural history; it was then thought possible to study the natural life of animals even in such unnatural conditions. A century later, more sophisticated zoologists such as Konrad Lorenz asked behavioristic and ethological questions, the claimed purpose of which was to discover more about the springs of human action through the study of animals under experimental conditions. (John Berger, *About Looking*)

Notice how symbols help the student understand the passage. For example, she underlines and stars the main idea of the passage and uses arrows to show the relationship of one point to another. In addition, she circles and puts a question mark next to unfamiliar words, phrases, and names—*ideology of imperialism, ethological, behavioristic,* and *Konrad Lorenz*—that she will have to look up. Finally, she numbers the two reasons why imperial governments established public zoos.

source
38a

(3)   Annotating

As you are highlighting a selection, you react to what you read—
you question the author's assumptions, develop your own
thoughts, isolate points of agreement, and identify areas of faulty
reasoning. You record these reactions as **annotations** in the margins or between the lines of the text.

With your annotations you define new words and unfamiliar references, write brief summaries, clarify points, point out
areas of disagreement, voice approval, show relationships among
key points, make connections with other sources, and note possibilities for future research. This interaction between you and
the text leads you to the critical insights that are necessary for
your paper. In a sense, annotating is a form of focused brainstorming that you do as you read.

As you review your annotations you will find that some are
dead ends or are not useful. Some of your notes, however, will
suggest interesting connections or unusual perspectives that
could well become a key idea or even the thesis of your paper.
The important thing to remember is to keep the subject and
purpose of your paper in mind as you make your annotations.

Following is the preceding highlighted passage along with
annotations.

Interesting point— could use in introduction.

   Public zoos came into existence at the
beginning of the period which was to see the
disappearance of animals from daily life. The
zoo to which people go to meet animals, to
observe them, to see them, is, in fact, a monument to the impossibility of such encounters. Modern zoos are an epitaph to a relationship which was as old as man. They are
not seen as such because the wrong questions have been addressed to zoos.

*Possibly could focus on
zoos – their purpose –
their history. Could
tie in with Desmond
Morris's The Naked Ape
and The Human Zoo.*
✳
why "impossible"?

   When they were founded—the London
Zoo in 1828, the Jardin des Plantes in 1793,
the Berlin Zoo in 1844—they brought considerable prestige to the national capitals. The
prestige was not so different from that which
had accrued to the private royal menageries.
These menageries, along with gold plate, architecture, orchestras, players, furnishings,
dwarfs, acrobats, uniforms, horses, art and
food had been demonstrations of an emper-
or's or king's power and wealth. Likewise in
the 19th century, public zoos were an endorsement of modern colonial power. The
capturing of the animals was a symbolic rep-

*Reasons why 19th century
zoos brought prestige
to governments*
①

② *i.e. The zoo showed
how powerful the
country was. The animals
were from the countries
that the imperialist
power dominated*

resentation of the conquest of all distant and exotic lands. "Explorers" proved their patriotism by sending home a tiger or an elephant. The gift of an exotic animal to the metropolitan zoo became a token in subservient diplomatic relations.

Policy of extending power + domination of a nation by territorial aquisition—eg. European countries in Africa—England in India, etc.

Yet, like every other 19th century public institution, the zoo, however supportive of the ~~ideology of imperialism~~, had to claim an independent and civic function. <u>The claim was that it was another kind of <u>museum</u>, whose purpose was to further knowledge and public enlightenment. And so the first questions asked of zoos belonged to natural history; it was then thought possible to study the natural life of animals even in such unnatural conditions.</u> A century later, more sophisticated zoologists such as ~~Konrad Lorenz~~ asked ~~behavioristic~~ and ~~ethological~~ questions, <u>the claimed purpose of which was to discover more about the springs of human action through the study of animals under experimental conditions.</u>

?

Awarded the 1973 Nobel Prize

ethology = science of animal behavior

Animal behavior is a product of evolution ??

behaviorism = school of psychology that focuses on behavior rather than mind.

source 38b

Because this student has already chosen a topic, her annotations are quite specific. She comments on the author's main idea, explores its relevance for her paper, and includes definitions of unfamiliar terms and a brief identification of Konrad Lorenz. The questions she writes in the margin suggest possible directions for her research.

38b   Evaluating Sources

Whenever you read, you should evaluate the potential usefulness of a source as soon as possible, so you will not waste time on irrelevant reading. Keep in mind that no matter how good a single source is, you cannot rely exclusively on it for your ideas. Your reading should include a wide variety of sources that reflect a number of possible viewpoints.

One efficient way to evaluate a source and its author is to ask your librarian or your instructor for an opinion. But even if a source is highly recommended, it may not suit your needs. The following guidelines can help you learn to evaluate sources on your own.

Guidelines for Evaluating Sources

- Is your source comprehensive?
- Is your source current?
- Is your source reliable?

(1)   Evaluating print sources

To measure the usefulness of a print source, look at its *scope.* How comprehensively does it treat your subject? Skim a book's table of contents and index for references to your topic. To be of any real help, a book should devote a section or chapter to your topic, not simply a footnote or a brief mention. For articles, read the entire abstract, or skim the entire article for key facts, looking closely at section headings, boldface type, and topic sentences. An article should have your topic as its central subject.

The *date of publication* tells you whether the information in a book or article is current. A discussion of computer languages written in 1966, for instance, is probably obsolete. Scientific and technological subjects usually demand state-of-the-art treatment. Even in the humanities new discoveries and new ways of thinking lead scholars to reevaluate and modify their ideas over time.

Some classic works, however, never lose their usefulness. Although Edward Gibbon wrote *The History of the Decline and Fall of the Roman Empire* in the eighteenth century, the book still offers a valuable overview of the events it describes. Contemporary historians may interpret events differently, but Gibbon's information is sound, and the book is required reading for anyone studying Roman history. If a number of your sources cite certain earlier works, you should consult those works, regardless of their publication dates. Do, however, check such sources for information that may be obsolete.

Another factor to consider is the *reliability* of your source. Is a piece of writing intended to inform or to persuade? Does the author have an ulterior motive? One way to judge the objectivity of a source is to find out something about its author. The source itself may contain biographical information, sometimes in a separate section, or you can consult a biographical dictionary. Skim the preface to see what the author says about his or her purpose. What do other sources say about the author: Is he or she well known and respected, or unknown? reliable or unreliable? fair or biased? Compare a few statements with another source—a textbook or an encyclopedia, for instance—to see whether an author is slanting facts.

A contemporary review of a source is another way of judging the source's reliability. *Book Review Digest*, available in the reference section of your library, lists popular books that have been reviewed in at least three newspapers or magazines and includes excerpts from representative reviews. Scholarly books are indexed in *Book Review Index*. Although this book contains no excerpts, it does include citations that refer you to the periodicals in which books were reviewed.

You can also find out about the standing of a source in the scholarly community by consulting a special class of indexes called **citation indexes**. These books list all scholarly articles published in a given year that mention a particular source. Information is listed under the original article, the author of the article in which the original article is mentioned, or the subject. Seeing how often an article is mentioned and how it is regarded by others in the field, can help you evaluate its usefulness. Citation indexes are available for the humanities, the sciences, and the social sciences.

source
38b
Note: Be sure to examine carefully articles found in popular periodicals. You may consult popular sources for background or for leads, but remember that such sources are commercial. Because their aim is to sell copies to many people, their treatment may be biased, superficial, or sensational. For this reason, you should not rely on such material for your research.

(2) Evaluating nonprint sources

Nonprint sources—interviews, telephone calls, films, and so on—must also be evaluated. Here too you must consider the *scope* of the source—the extent to which it covers your topic. An interview with an expert on family planning who knows little about sex education may be an excellent source if your paper will focus on changing trends in birth control methods, but such an interview may not be worthwhile if your paper is about teenage pregnancy.

The *currency* of a nonprint source is also a factor. A 1970 television documentary on the topography of a Pacific island may still be accurate, but a documentary on the lives of its people may not reflect today's conditions at all.

Reliability is important, too. Is a radio feature on energy conservation part of a balanced news program or a thinly veiled commercial sponsored by a public utility? Is the material presented by experts in the field or by actors? Check the credits and acknowledgments and read reviews to see which sources were consulted. Do the participants in a panel discussion on nuclear weapons all agree on how they should be deployed, or do they represent different points of view? Find out who they are and try to check their credentials. Is a person you plan to interview fair and impartial or biased on some issues?

☐ EXERCISE 1

Read the following paragraphs. When you have finished, reread them, highlighting and annotating them. As you read, pay close attention to the information provided about their sources and authors as well as to their content. Decide which sources would be most useful and reliable in supporting the thesis "Winning the right to vote has (or has not) significantly changed the role of women in national politics." Which sources, if any, should be disregarded? Which would you examine first? Be prepared to discuss your decisions.

1. Almost forty years after the adoption of the Nineteenth Amendment, a number of promised or threatened events have failed to materialize. The millennium has not arrived, but neither has the country's social fabric been destroyed. Nor have women organized a political party to elect only women candidates to public office. . . . Instead, women have shown the same tendency to divide along orthodox party lines as male voters. (Eleanor Flexner, *Century of Struggle*, Atheneum 1968. *A scholarly treatment of women's role in America since the Mayflower, this book was well reviewed by historians.*)

2. In Kentucky a woman breezed to victory in the state's gubernatorial election. San Francisco's Mayor Dianne Feinstein won re-election with an overwhelming 80 percent of the vote—then grew irritable at questions about whether she is available for the vice presidency. Houston's Mayor Kathy Whitmire fought off an oilman's spirited challenge and won re-election with more than 63 percent of the vote. ("Lessons from the Off-Off Year Vote," *Newsweek*, 1984)

3. Woman has been the great unpaid laborer of the world, and although within the last two decades a vast number of new employments have been opened to her, statistics prove that in the great majority of these, she is not paid according to the value of the work done, but according to sex. The opening of all industries to women, and the wage question as connected with her, are the most subtle and profound questions of political economy, closely interwoven with the rights of self-government.   (Susan B. Anthony; first appeared in Vol. I of *The History of Woman Suffrage*; reprinted in *Voices from Women's Liberation*, ed. Leslie B. Tanner, NAL 1970. *An important figure in the battle for women's suffrage, Susan B. Anthony [1820–1906] also lectured and wrote on abolition and temperance.*)

4. Women . . . have never been prepared to assume responsibility; we have never been prepared to make demands upon ourselves; we have

never been taught to expect the development of what is best in our-selves because no one has ever expected *anything* of us—or for us. Because no one has ever had any intention of turning over any seri-ous work to us.   (Vivian Gornick, "The Next Great Moment in History is Ours," *Village Voice* 1969. *The* Voice *is a liberal New York City weekly.)*

5. With women as half the country's elected representatives, and a woman President once in a while, the country's *machismo* problems would be greatly reduced. The old-fashioned idea that manhood depends on violence and victory is, after all, an important part of our troubles. . . . I'm not saying that women leaders would eliminate vio-lence. We are not more moral than men; we are only uncorrupted by power so far. When we do acquire power, we might turn out to have an equal impulse toward aggression.   (Gloria Steinem, "What It Would Be Like If Women Win," *Time* 1970. *Steinem, a well-known fem-inist and journalist, was one of the founders of* Ms. *magazine.)*

6. 1982 was the year that time ran out for the proposed equal rights amendment. Eleanor Smeal, president of the National Organization for Women, the group that headed the intense 10-year struggle for the ERA, conceded defeat on June 24. Only 24 words in all, the ERA read simply: "Equality of rights under the law shall not be denied or abridged by the United States or by any state on account of sex." Two major opinion polls had reported just weeks before the ERA's defeat that a majority of Americans continued to favor the amendment. (June Foley, "Women 1982: The Year that Time Ran Out," *The World Almanac & Book of Facts*, 1983)

38c   Taking Notes

When taking notes, experienced researchers do not simply copy a source word for word. They combine direct *quotation* with *para-phrase* and *summary*, refining and interpreting material from the very beginning. A good paper uses each of these techniques and blends them skillfully.

(1)   Writing a summary

You summarize when you want to capture the general idea of a source. A **summary,** sometimes called a précis, is a brief restate-ment in your own words of the main idea of a passage, article, or entire book. A summary omits the examples, asides, and analo-gies that authors use to illustrate their points and to interest their readers. When you write a summary, you should be careful not to leave out important points or to misrepresent an author's intention. And, because you want to remain faithful to the meaning and spirit of the original, your summary should include none of your own ideas or observations.

Before you write your summary, make sure that you thoroughly understand your source. As you reread a source, pay careful attention to your highlighting and annotations, especially those that identify topic sentences, headings, or key words that will help clarify the source's meaning. After you have finished reading, write down the main idea, including all key concepts, in a sentence. Next, write your summary using your one-sentence restatement as your guide. Your summary should present the important ideas of the original without using the exact language or phrasing.

Following is an original source and a summary of the source that appeared in a student research paper. Notice that the summary is much shorter than the original and gives just the main idea of the passage.

ORIGINAL SOURCE: Barasch, Moshe. "The City." *Dictionary of the History of Ideas.* Ed. Philip P. Wiener. 4 vols. New York: Scribner's, 1973. 1: 427.

The religious and cosmic symbolism of the city reaches back to the early stages of human culture. It seems that in none of the great archaic cultures have cities been understood simply as settlements, arbitrarily established at a certain place and in a given form; both the placing and the shape of the cities were conceived as related, in a hidden or manifested form, to the structure of the universe. The most common form of this symbolism is the belief that the cities have astral or divine prototypes, or even descended from heaven; sometimes they were believed to have a relationship to the underworld. In both cases, however, they refer to an extraterrestrial reality.

source 38c

SUMMARY: In ancient times cities had symbolic significance. They were seen, in part, as having a divine form—perhaps related to a heavenly or, less commonly, underworld counterpart (Barasch 1:427).

After you have written your summary, check to make sure that it conveys both the meaning and the spirit of the original. Make certain that you have not missed any important points or inadvertently used any of the author's exact words. (Of course you can use *some* words from a source. As a rule, you can use the same proper nouns, simple words, or technical terms as your source without documentation.) Reread your summary to see if you can condense it further, and make sure that you have included documentation to identify the source you have summarized. If you have done a careful job, your summary will include only the most important points of your source.

Checklist for Writing a Summary

1. Reread your source until you understand it.
2. Write a one-sentence restatement of the main idea.
3. Write the summary using the one-sentence restatement as your guide. Focus on what the text says, not on your own ideas or opinions.
4. Revise your summary, making sure that you have adequately condensed the original and included its most important ideas.
5. Add appropriate documentation.

(2) Writing a paraphrase

source
38c

You paraphrase when you need detailed information from specific passages in a source, but not the exact language of the original. A **paraphrase** is a detailed restatement in your own words of the content of a passage. It not only indicates its main points, but also follows its order, tone, and emphasis. Often a paraphrase will quote brief phrases from the original to convey the flavor of the source. Usually, but not always, a paraphrase is briefer than the original. Keep in mind that when paraphrasing you convey the *author's* ideas, not your own. Keep your own analyses, interpretations, and evaluations separate.

A good paraphrase will capture a fairly complete sense of an author's ideas without using the author's syntax or phrasing. For this reason, paraphrase is especially useful in a paper in which you want to explain technical material to a general audience. Paraphrase is also useful when you want to convey the essence of dialogue or for reporting complex material in easily understood terms. Moreover, the very act of putting someone else's ideas into your own words helps you to gain a better understanding of what has been said. It is therefore a good idea to develop your skill in this area by paraphrasing important material as soon as you finish reading it.

Begin your paraphrase by reading your source until you understand it. For long passages, make an outline to clarify the progression of ideas. This approach may be time consuming, but in the long run it can help you write a clear and accurate paraphrase. Next, write your paraphrase, following the order, tone, and emphasis of the original source. Finally, add appropriate documentation.

Below is a paraphrase of a passage that discusses a player's state of mind during a video game. Notice that although the paraphrase follows the order and emphasis of the original, and even quotes a key phrase from the source, its wording and sentence structure are very different.

ORIGINAL SOURCE:
Turkle, Sherry.
The Second Self:
Computers and
the Human
Spirit. New York:
Simon & Schuster, 1984: 83–84.

When you play a video game you enter into the world of the programmers who made it. You have to do more than identify with a character on the screen. You must act for it. Identification through action has a special kind of hold. Like playing a sport, it puts people into a highly focused, and highly charged, state of mind. For many people, what is being pursued in the video game is not just a score, but an altered state.

The pilot of a race car does not dare to take . . . attention off the road. The imperative of total concentration is part of the high. Video games demand this same level of attention. They can give people the feeling of being close to the edge because, as in a dangerous situation, there is no time for rest and the consequences of wandering attention feel dire. With pinball, a false move can be recuperated. The machine can be shaken, the ball repositioned. In a video game, the program has no tolerance for error, no margin of safety. Players experience their every movement as instantly translated into game action. The game is relentless in its demand that all other time stop and in its demand that the player take full responsibility for every act, a point that players often sum up by the phrase "One false move and you're dead."

Executives, accountants, and surgeons stand behind the junior-high-schoolers in games arcades. For people under pressure total concentration is a form of relaxation.

PARAPHRASE:
As Sherry Turkle says, the programmer controls the world of video games. Video games enable a player to merge with a character or object that is part of the game. This identification draws a player into the game. Like sports, video games put a player into an emotionally charged "altered state" that is a central part of the game.

Because video games demand a high degree of involvement, they can simulate the thrill of participating in a dangerous activity without the risks.

source
38c

> Unlike pinball machines, video games provide no time to rest and no opportunity to correct errors in judgment. Every move a player makes appears at once on the screen. The game forces a player to adapt to its rules and to act carefully.
>
> Many people with high-pressure jobs use video games as a way to unwind (83–84).

After you have written your paraphrase, make certain that you have avoided the phrasing of the original and that you have put quotation marks around any terms taken from your source. Remember to document the paraphrase itself, as well any quotations. Make sure that your paraphrase contains all the important points of the original. Finally, insert any transitional words or phrases that are needed to make your paraphrase flow smoothly.

Checklist for Writing a Paraphrase

1. Reread your source until you understand it.
2. If necessary make an outline of long passages.
3. Write your paraphrase, following the order, tone, and emphasis of the original.
4. Revise your paraphrase, making sure that it conveys the sense of the original and that you have not accidentally used the words or phrasing of the original.
5. Add appropriate documentation.

source 38c

(3) Recording quotations

You quote when you feel that an author's exact words will enhance your paper. When you **quote,** you copy an author's remarks just as they appear, word for word and punctuation mark for punctuation mark. Pay particular attention to spelling and capitalization. When recording quotations, be sure that you do not inadvertently leave out quotation marks. You may even want to circle them to be sure you notice them when you transfer them from your notes to your paper. If a quotation continues onto the back of your note card, clearly mark "over" on the front of the card, so that you do not overlook the rest of the quotation later on.

As a rule, avoid including numerous direct quotations in your papers. When used indiscriminately, they break the flow of your discussion and give the impression that your paper is nothing more than a collection of other people's words. Quote only when something vital would be lost otherwise, and use only those quotations that support your points and provide a perspective that contributes to the effectiveness of your presentation. Before you include any quotation, ask yourself if your purpose would be better served by using your own words.

Guidelines for Using Quotations

- Quote when a source's wording or phrasing is so distinctive that to summarize or paraphrase would diminish its impact. In such cases it is best to let the source speak for itself.
- Quote when a source's words lend authority to your presentation. If an author is a recognized expert on your subject, his or her words are as convincing as expert testimony at a trial.
- Quote when an author's words are so concise that a paraphrase would create a long, clumsy, or incoherent phrase or would change the meaning of the original.

38d   Integrating Your Notes into Your Writing

source
38d

Once you have gathered material from your sources, you cannot just drop it into your paper. You have to weave quotations into the fabric of your discussion and use paraphrases and summaries to support your points as you interpret the ideas of others.

(1)   Integrating quotations

Quotations should be introduced by identifying phrases and smoothly embedded into sentences. In other words, they must be placed in context. Consider this passage.

> For the Amish, the public school system represents a problem. "A serious problem confronting Amish society from the viewpoint of the Amish themselves is the threat of absorption into mass society through the values promoted in the public school system" (Hostetler 193).

The direct quotation is awkwardly dropped into the passage above. It could be worked into the sentence this way.

> For the Amish the public school system represents "the threat of absorption into mass society" (Hostetler 193).

Or you could use a **running acknowledgment,** in which you introduce the source of the quotation into the text.

> As John A. Hostetler points out, the Amish feel the public school system threatens them with "absorption into the mass society . . . " (193).

You could also combine quotation and paraphrase, quoting only a significant word or two and paraphrasing the rest.

> According to John A. Hostetler one of the most serious problems that the Amish face is a "threat of absorption" posed by the public schools (193).

To avoid monotonous sentence structure, experiment with different methods of integrating quoted material into your paper. As a rule, the running acknowledgment is most effective when you want to call attention to the author's name because his or her expertise in the area you are researching strengthens your paper's credibility. You should vary the verbs you use for attribution; for example, you can use *suggests, observes, notes, concludes, believes,* or any of several other more precise alternatives to *says.* You can also vary the placement of the identifying phrase, putting it at the beginning or at the end of the quoted material, or even in the middle.

> "A serious problem confronting Amish society from the viewpoint of the Amish themselves," observes Hostetler, "is the threat of absorption into mass society through the values promoted in the public school system" (193).

Changes Within Quotations If the verb tense of the quotation is not consistent with the tense of your sentence, you may need to change it somewhat. If you alter words, *you must acknowledge your changes* by enclosing them in brackets.

AWKWARD: The Amish were traditionally opposed to the modern industrialized society around them. "They are a slow-changing, distinctive cultural group who place a premium on cultural stability rather than change" (Hostetler vii).

REVISED: The Amish were traditionally opposed to the modern industrialized society around them and tended toward "cultural stability rather than change" (Hostetler vii). (only a few words taken from the original quotation)

REVISED: The Amish were traditionally opposed to the modern industrialized society around them: "They [were] a slow-changing, distinctive cultural group who [placed] a premium on cultural stability rather than change" (Hostetler vii). (verb tense changed to match the paper's tense)

source 38d

Omissions Within Quotations You can reduce the length of quotations by substituting an ellipsis mark (three spaced periods) for the deleted words (see 31o).

ORIGINAL: "Not only have the Amish built and staffed their own elementary and vocational schools, but they have gradually organized on local, state, and national levels to cope with the task of educating their children" (Hostetler 206).

REVISED: "Not only have the Amish built and staffed their own elementary and vocational schools, but they have gradually organized . . . to cope with the task of educating their children" (Hostetler 206).

When you omit a word or phrase at the beginning of a quoted passage, you do not use ellipsis points to indicate the omission.

FAULTY: Josephine Baker danced in La Revue Nègre in 1923 in Paris and ". . . was instrumental in introducing the French to Jazz" (David 126).

REVISED: Josephine Baker danced in La Revue Nègre in 1923 in Paris and "was instrumental in introducing the French to Jazz" (David 126).

Long Quotations Occasionally, you may want to use a quotation consisting of more than four lines of text. Set off this quotation from the text by indenting it ten spaces from the margin. Double-space, do not use quotation marks, and introduce the long quotation with a colon. If you are quoting a single paragraph, do not indent the first line (see 30e.2).

**source
38d**

According to Hostetler, the Amish were not always hostile to public education:

> The one-room rural elementary school served the Amish community well in a number of ways. As long as it was a public school, it stood midway between the Amish community and the world. Its influence was tolerable, depending upon the degree of influence the Amish were able to bring to the situation. As long as it was small, rural, and near the community, a reasonable influence could be maintained over its worldly character. (196)

Use long quotations when you want to convey a sense of an author's style or thought process. Keep in mind, however, that long quotations can be distracting. They interrupt your argument and, when used excessively, give the impression that you have relied too heavily on the words of others.

☐ **EXERCISE 2**

Assume that in preparation for a paper on the topic "The effects of the rise of suburbia," you read the following passage from the book *Great Expectations: America and the Baby Boom Generation* by Landon Y. Jones. Reread the passage, highlighting and annotating it to aid your comprehension. Then, write a one-paragraph summary of the passage. Next, paraphrase one paragraph. Finally, make a note that combines paraphrase with quotation, making certain to quote only when appropriate.

source 38d

As an internal migration, the settling of the suburbs was phenomenal. In the twenty years from 1950 to 1970, the population of the suburbs doubled from 36 million to 72 million. No less than 83 percent of the total population growth in the United States during the 1950's was in the suburbs, which were growing fifteen times faster than any other segment of the country. As people packed and moved, the national mobility rate leaped by 50 percent. The only other comparable influx was the wave of European immigrants to the United States around the turn of the century. But as *Fortune* pointed out, more people moved to the suburbs every year than had ever arrived on Ellis Island.

By now, bulldozers were churning up dust storms as they cleared the land for housing developments. More than a million acres of farmland were plowed under every year during the 1950's. Millions of apartment-dwelling parents with two children were suddenly realizing that two children could be doubled up in a spare bedroom, but a third child cried loudly for something more. The proportion of new houses with three or more bedrooms, in fact, rose from one-third in 1947 to three-quarters in 1954. The necessary *Lebensraum* could only be found in the suburbs. There was a housing shortage, but young couples armed with VA and FHA loans built their dream homes with easy credit and free spending habits that were unthinkable to the baby-boom grandparents, who shook their heads with the Depression still fresh in their memories. Of the 13 million homes built in the decade before 1958, 11 million of them—or 85 percent—were built in the suburbs. Home ownership rose 50 percent between 1940 and 1950, and another 50 percent by 1960. By then, one-fourth of *all* housing in the United States had been built in the fifties. For the first time, more Americans owned homes than rented them.

We were becoming a land of gigantic nurseries. The biggest were built by Abraham Levitt, the son of poor Russian-Jewish immigrants, who had originally built houses for the Navy during the war. The first of three East Coast Levittowns went up on the potato fields of Long Island. Exactly $7900—or $60 a month and no money down—bought you a Monopoly-board bungalow with four rooms, attic, washing machine, outdoor barbecue, and a television set built into the wall. The 17,447 units eventually became home to 82,000 people, many of whom were pregnant or wanted to be. In a typical story on the suburban explosion, one magazine breathlessly described a volleyball game of nine couples in which no less than five of the women were expecting.

(2)   Integrating ideas: Writing an interpretation

A paper that uses sources usually does more than present summaries and paraphrases of your sources. It also contains passages of interpretation in which you present your conclusions and support them with your own ideas and with the ideas of others, which you have recorded in your notes (see 40e.2).

An **interpretation,** sometimes called a critique, is a systematic evaluation of a source. When interpreting source material, you put it into perspective, comment on its usefulness, or explain what it means. An interpretation involves more than saying that an article is "interesting" or that a discussion "sheds light on a subject"; to be effective, it must clearly present the standards by which you judge your material. When they read your interpretation, your readers must be able to understand the thought processes that led you to your conclusions.

Sometimes you are able to make critical judgments based on personal knowledge of a subject. More often, however, your research yields the information on which you base your interpretation. As you highlight and annotate a source, you begin to develop basic assumptions about your subject. Perhaps several of the authors whose works you read share a set of ideas. Or perhaps several authors disagree. You will find, however, that there are no ready-made criteria by which you can judge your sources. Writing a good interpretation takes time and practice, and it also involves taking some risks. After all, it requires you to judge other people's ideas. To do so you must read widely and consider a variety of points of view; you must then isolate specific points in your source and decide how valid you think they are. Having arrived at your conclusions, you must support your judgments with references to the author's words, with personal insights, or with material that others have written about your subject.

Begin your interpretation by presenting your evaluation of your source and the criteria you will use to judge it. Next, give readers the background they will need to understand your interpretation. You may want to paraphrase relevant sections of your source or summarize articles that you have read about your source. Then, present and discuss the criteria you will use to judge your source. For example, you could disagree with the source's basic assumptions or say that you feel that its treatment of the subject is slanted. After establishing your criteria, go through your source's points one by one, supporting your judgments with your own ideas or with material you have gathered from your research. Conclude by restating your judgments and the criteria you used. Make sure that all your points relate to your criteria and that you have differentiated your ideas from those of your source. Finally, add appropriate documentation.

Following is an interpretation of a short passage about the movie director John Ford. In it the student isolates important points from his source and counters them with his own judgments.

ORIGINAL SOURCE:
Bogdanovich, Peter. "The Cowboy and the American West . . . as Directed by John Ford." *Esquire* Dec. 1983: 423.

In his later years, nevertheless, Ford came to be considered close to a reactionary, because throughout the Sixties, while the chic American cultural fashion became increasingly . . . antimilitarist, antipolice, and antifamily, Ford continued to make pictures with men in uniform, fighting the chivalrous fight, honoring the women and the way of life they protected and cherished.

source 38d

INTERPRETATION:
In a recent article in *Esquire* Peter Bogdanovich evaluates the career of the famous director, John Ford. Although Bogdanovich is correct in saying that Ford was seen by some in the 1960's as reactionary (423), he simplifies the situation by ignoring the fact that Ford has always enjoyed great popularity, and in recent years has become something of a cult figure. Bogdanovich seems to accept the critical position that Ford glorifies the military and uses violence as a ready solution to complex problems (423). But when these themes occur in Ford's films—and they do not occur in all of them—they are usually in service of a much larger theme: the ability of the individual to affect events. Films like *The Informer* (1935), *The Grapes of Wrath* (1940), *The Quiet Man* (1952), and *Mister Roberts* (1962) demonstrate the versatility of Ford's vision and his ability to move beyond the narrow limits that Bogdanovich discusses.

The student who wrote the preceding interpretation evaluated his source using his own knowledge. But as already indicated, you will often have to use research to help you analyze and evaluate the ideas of others—when you are writing about works of literature or about controversial subjects, for example. If you do use the ideas of others, remember to clearly identify ideas that are not your own (see 38e).

Below is an interpretation of Mark Twain's novel *Huckleberry Finn*. The student who wrote this interpretation begins by establishing the context of her discussion and then goes on to define her subject. Notice how she uses her research and several references to the novel to bolster her argument.

When we consider the novel *Huckleberry Finn*, one question should be asked. Does *Huckleberry Finn* reflect the social attitudes prevalent at the time Twain wrote it? Apparently a number of schools think so because they have removed the book from their reading lists.

Although well meaning, these detractors focus on only one part of *Huckleberry Finn*. When the character of Jim is considered in the context of the whole novel, we see that Twain's portrayal of Jim is sympathetic. On the raft, Jim and Huck achieve understanding and, eventually, mutual respect. Perhaps no other sequence in the book more accurately and clearly reflects Twain's feelings about the subject of slavery. According to Leslie Fiedler, the raft floating in the river is a symbol of freedom. It is cut loose from the land and, by implication, from the land's constraints and prejudices (48). On the raft, Huck comes to see Jim not as a slave but as a human being, a friend, and eventually as a person who wants to return to his wife and children. According to Daniel Hoffman, when Jim emerges from slavery, he is transformed into a man. This view, says Hoffman, coincides with Twain's own growth as a novelist (433).

By showing the Grangerford-Shepherdson feud to be a senseless waste of life, Twain characterizes as cruel and without honor the society that upholds the values of slavery. To Judith Fetterly, the Duke and the King seem to be portrayed as two confidence men who degrade Huck and Jim and treat them as if they were objects (447). Tom Sawyer, who enters the book near the end, is shown to be a self-righteous and hypocritical representative of the larger society. By the end of the book Huck, as well as the reader, is brought to the realization that any society that can accept the buying and selling of human beings like Jim is hopelessly corrupt (Fetterley 450).

In this light *Huckleberry Finn* can be seen as a story about Huck's spiritual maturation. Those who claim that the novel is unsuitable for students can be criticized on two grounds: (1) that they oversimplify the book; and (2) that by removing it from schools, they take away from students the opportunity to read one of America's great literary works.

source
38d

Remember that interpretations are as varied as the people who write them. Different people might have opposing opinions on the same topic or focus on entirely different issues. No matter what your point of view, however, your interpretation should clearly distinguish between your ideas and the ideas of the author you are interpreting.

Checklist for Writing an Interpretation

1. Present your evaluation of your source and define the criteria you will use to judge it.
2. Give readers the background they need to understand your judgment.
3. Present and discuss your criteria.
4. Go through your source's points, making judgments as you proceed.
5. Conclude by restating your judgments.
6. Revise, making sure that your points apply to your criteria.
7. Add documentation to differentiate your ideas from those of your source.

☐ **EXERCISE 3**

Look back at Exercise 2 and write an interpretation of the passage, discussing what you believe to be the author's attitude toward his subject. Use material from the source to support your assertions, and document all material that is not your own.

38e Avoiding Plagiarism

Plagiarism is presenting another person's words or ideas as if they were your own. By not acknowledging a source, you mislead readers into thinking that the material you are presenting is yours when, in fact, it is the result of someone else's time and effort.

Some writers plagiarize deliberately, copying passages word for word or even going so far as to present another person's entire work as their own. Students who do so are doing themselves and their classmates a great disservice. They are undercutting the learning process, thereby sacrificing the education that they are in college to obtain. If found out, they are usually punished severely. Some students have failed courses and even had degrees withheld because of plagiarism.

Most plagiarism, however, is accidental. It results when students are not aware of what constitutes plagiarism, or when they forget that a note they jotted down is really a direct quotation or that an idea they are using is really someone else's. Sometimes students just forget to document a paraphrase or summary, or forget to include quotation marks when they write their paper. Even so, accidental plagiarism is often dealt with just as harshly as intentional plagiarism. Plagiarism is not taken lightly in education, business, or anyplace else. Plagiarism is theft.

One way to avoid plagiarism is to use documentation wherever it is required. In general, document all direct quotations, opinions, judgments, and insights of others that you summarize or paraphrase. You must also document facts that are not open to dispute or are not commonly accepted. Finally, document tables, graphs, charts, and statistics taken from any source.

Common knowledge, information that you would expect most educated readers to know, need not be documented. You can safely use facts that are widely available in encyclopedias, textbooks, newspapers, and magazines without citing their source. Even if the information is new to you, if it is generally known you need not indicate a source. You can usually assume that information which appears in several of your sources is generally known. Information that is in dispute, however, or that a particular person has discovered or theorized about, must be acknowledged. You need not, for example, document the fact that John F. Kennedy graduated from Harvard in 1940 or that he was elected president in 1960. You must, however, document a historian's analysis of Kennedy's performance as president or a researcher's recent discoveries about his private life.

source
38e

Material from a Source Not Acknowledged

ORIGINAL: The person with Type B Behavior Pattern is the exact
Friedman, opposite of the Type A subject. He, unlike the Type A
Meyer, person, is rarely harried by desires to obtain a wildly
and R. H. increasing number of things or participate in an end-
Rosen- lessly growing series of events in an ever-decreasing
man. *Type* amount of time. His intelligence may be as good as or
A Behavior even better than that of the Type A subject. <u>Similarly,</u>
and Your <u>his ambition may be as great as or even greater than</u>
Heart. <u>that of his Type A counterpart.</u> He may also have a
New York: considerable amount of "drive," but its character is
Knopf: such that it seems to steady him, give confidence and
1974. 87. security to him, rather than to goad, irritate, and infuri-
ate, as with the Type A man.

PLAGIARISM: The Type B person, unlike the Type A person, is not
bothered by a need to acquire things or to participate
in a great number of activities. The Type B may be as
bright as the Type A, and <u>his ambition may be as great</u>
<u>as or greater than that of his Type A counterpart.</u> In
addition, although he may be just as motivated, his
motivation gives him balance and confidence and does

> not drive him the way a Type A person's does
> (Friedman and Rosenman 87).

The student who wrote this passage is guilty of plagiarism. Even though he documents the entire paragraph, he neglects to acknowledge that he borrows a specific phrase. To correct this problem, the student should reword the questionable phrase or use quotation marks to indicate his borrowing.

CORRECT
(phrase reworded):
The Type B person is not the same as the Type A person. Unlike the Type A, the Type B is not bothered by a need to acquire things or to participate in a great number of activities. The Type B may be as bright as the Type A and be just as ambitious. He may also be just as motivated, but his motivation gives him balance and confidence and does not drive him the way a Type A person's does (Friedman and Rosenman 87).

CORRECT
(phrase in quotation marks):
The Type B person is not the same as the Type A person. Unlike the Type A, the Type B is not bothered by a need to acquire things or to participate in a great number of activities. The Type B may be as bright as the Type A, and, according to Friedman and Rosenman, "his ambition may be as great as or greater than that of his Type A counterpart" (87). He may also be just as motivated, but his motivation gives him balance and confidence and does not drive him the way a Type A person's does (Friedman and Rosenman 87).

source 38e

Summary Too Close to Its Source

ORIGINAL:
Sheils, Merrill, et al. "And Man Created the Chip." *Newsweek* 30 June 1980: 92.
The next giant step in the small-is-beautiful revolution was the simultaneous announcement in 1959 by Texas Instruments Company and Fairchild Semiconductor that both had successfully produced integrated circuits—single semiconductor chips containing several complete electronic circuits. Once again, the breakthrough enabled manufacturers to pack more computing power into less space.

PLAGIARISM:
After transistors came semiconductors, pioneered by Texas Instruments Company and Fairchild Semiconductor. This advancement enabled companies to build smaller and more powerful computers (Sheils et al., 92).

Although this student documents the passage and does not use the exact words of her source, she borrows the author's main points, order, emphasis, and sentence structure. She could have avoided this plagiarism by substantially changing the author's words and syntax.

CORRECT: The development of integrated circuits by Texas Instru-
(para- ments and Fairchild Semiconductor made possible
phrased) computers that were not only smaller but more powerful (Sheils et al. 92).

Statistics Not Attributed to a Source

ORIGINAL: From the time they [male drivers between 16 and 24]
Schuman, started to drive, 187 of these drivers (almost two thirds)
Stanley, et reported one or more accidents, with an average of 1.6
al. "Young per involved driver. Features of 303 accidents are tabu-
Male Driv- lated in Table 2. Almost half of all first accidents oc-
ers: Acci- curred before the legal driving age of 18, and the me-
dents and dian age of all accidents was 19. One resulted in a
Viola- fatality. Crashes involving death or injury were in the
tions." minority (14 percent); the large majority resulted in
JAMA 50 property damage only. The picture for this group of
(1983): "normal" drivers was thus one of accidents of relatively
1027. mild character occurring well before adulthood. The
emotional immaturity of this group is the most important factor related to the high frequency of accidents in
this age group.

PLAGIARISM: By and large male drivers between the ages of 16 and
24 accounted for the majority of accidents. Of 303 accidents recorded in Michigan, almost one half took place
before the drivers were legally allowed to drive at 18.
Most of these accidents resulted in property damage
and not in injury or loss of life. It seems likely that the
immaturity of these drivers had a lot to do with their
many accidents.

The student who used this information assumed that it was common knowledge—that it could be found in many sources and is accepted as accurate by many experts in the field. These statistics, however, appeared in a journal article and were the result of a study carried out by the authors. Because both the statistics and the conclusion concerning the emotional immaturity of male drivers are the original contributions of the authors, they must be documented.

CORRECT: According to one study, male drivers between the ages of
16 and 24 accounted for the majority of accidents. Of 303
accidents recorded almost one half took place before the
drivers were legally allowed to drive at 18. Most of these
accidents resulted in property damage and not injury or

source
38e

loss of life. It seems likely that the immaturity of this group of drivers has a lot to do with their many accidents (Schuman et al., 1027).

A Writer's Words and Ideas Not Kept Separate from Those of the Source

ORIGINAL: Anderson, Charles R. *Emily Dickinson's Poetry: Stairway of Surprise*. New York: Holt, 1960: 145–46.

[Emily Dickinson's] debt to Shakespeare was just as pervasive and even less visible. Poetic language in mid-nineteenth-century America had been reduced to a relatively flat and nerveless state, but he furnished her with clues for its resurrection. The major writers of the preceding generation had not only finished their careers but had brought the older way to a dead end. For a poet to come of age at such a time, as she did, may have been a handicap in that it deprived her of a living tradition within which or against which to work.

PLAGIARISM: A careful reading of her poetry shows that Emily Dickinson was deeply concerned with language and the function of words. Although her style seems derivative, she actually creates a distinctive idiom all her own. Even so, many of her images show that she owed much to Shakespeare. Although she read many of the writers that had preceded her, they were of no use to her. She was in many respects "deprived . . . of a living tradition within which or against which to work" (Anderson 145–46).

Because the student who wrote this passage did not differentiate his ideas from those of his source, it appears that he borrowed only the quotation in the last sentence. Actually, the student used source material in the last three sentences of the passage. As a result, the student passes off some of his source's ideas as his own and unwittingly commits plagiarism. He could have clearly defined the boundaries of the borrowed material by placing an introductory phrase *before* and documentation *after* the borrowed material. In the following example, notice that both the summary and the quotation are documented. (Keep in mind that every quotation requires its own documentation.)

CORRECT: A careful reading of her poetry shows that Emily Dickinson was deeply concerned with language and the function of words. Although her style seems derivative, she actually creates a distinctive idiom all her own. According to Charles R. Anderson, many of her images show that she owed much to Shakespeare. Although she read many of the writers that had preceded her, they were of no use to her (145). She was in many respects "deprived . . . of a living tradition within which or against which to work" (145–46).

In general, you can avoid plagiarism by following these guidelines.

Guidelines for Avoiding Plagiarism

- Take careful notes. Make certain that you have recorded information from your sources carefully and accurately.
- Make sure that on your note cards all words taken from sources are put inside circled quotation marks and that your ideas are enclosed within brackets.
- In your paper differentiate your ideas from those of your sources by clearly introducing borrowed material with the author's name and by ending with documentation.
- Make sure that all direct quotations used in your paper are enclosed within quotation marks.
- Review paraphrases and summaries in your paper to make certain that they are in your own words and that any words and phrases from the original are quoted.
- Document all direct quotations and all paraphrases and summaries of your sources. (See Chapter 39 for a full discussion of documentation.)
- Document all facts that are open to dispute or that are not common knowledge.
- Document all opinions, conclusions, figures, tables, graphs, and charts taken from a source.

Student Writer at Work: Working with Source Material

This student paragraph uses material from three sources, but its author has neglected to cite them. After reading the paragraph and the three sources that follow it, identify material that has been quoted directly from one of the sources. Compare the wording against the original for accuracy, and insert quotation marks where necessary, making sure that the quoted passages fit smoothly into the text. Next, paraphrase passages that the student did not need to quote, and, after consulting Chapter 39, document each piece of information that requires it.

Student Paragraph: Oral History

Oral history became a legitimate field of study in 1948,
when the Oral History Research Office was established by
Allan Nevins. Like recordings of presidents' fireside
chats and declarations of war, oral history is both oral
and historical. But it is more: oral history is the
creation of new historical documentation, not the
recording or preserving of documentation that already
exists. Oral history also tends to be more spontaneous
and personal and less formal than ordinary tape
recordings. Nevins's purpose was to collect and prepare
materials to help future historians to better understand
the past. Oral history has enormous potential to do just
this, for it draws on people's memories of their own lives
and deeds and of their associations with particular
people, periods, or events. The result, when it is
recorded and transcribed, is a valuable new source.

**source
38e**

Source 1

When Allan Nevins set up the Oral History Research Office
in 1948, he looked upon it as an organization that in a
systematic way could obtain from the lips and papers of
living Americans who had led significant lives a full
record of their participation in the political, economic,
and cultural affairs of the nation. His purpose was to
prepare such material for the use of future historians.
It was his conviction that the individual played an
important role in history and that an individual's
autobiography might in the future serve as a key to an
understanding of contemporary historical movements.
(Excerpted from Benison, Saul. "Reflections on Oral
History." The American Archivist 28.1 [January 1965]:71.)

Source 2

Typically, an oral history project comprises an organized
series of interviews with selected individuals or groups
in order to create new source materials from the
reminiscences of their own life and acts or from their
association with a particular person, period, or event.
These recollections are recorded on tape and transcribed
on a typewriter into sheets of transcript. . . . Such
oral history may be distinguished from more conventional
tape recordings of speeches, lectures, symposia, etc., by
the fact that the former creates new sources through the
more spontaneous, personal, multitopical, extended
narrative, while the latter utilizes sources in a more
formal mode for a specific occasion. (Excerpted from
Rumics, Elizabeth. "Oral History: Defining the Term."
Wilson Library Bulletin 40 [1966]: 602.)

**source
38e**

Source 3

Oral history, as the term came to be used, is the creation
of new historical documentation, not the recording or
preserving of documentation--even oral documentation--that
already exists. Its purpose is not, like that of the
National Voice Library at Michigan State University, to
preserve the recordings of fireside chats or presidential
declarations of war or James Whitcomb Riley reciting
"Little Orphan Annie." These are surely oral and just as
surely the stuff of history; but they are not oral
history. For this there must be the creation of a new
historical document by means of a personal interview.
(Excerpted from Hoyle, Norman. "Oral History." Library
Trends July 1972: 61.)

39

Documentation

Documentation is the formal acknowledgment of the sources you use for your paper. Your documentation enables your readers to judge the quality and originality of your work and to determine how authoritative and relevant each work you cite is.

39a Knowing What to Document

In general, you should document any information that is not yours, except information that is common knowledge (see 38c). In addition to printed material, sources may include interviews, conversations, films, records, or radio or television programs. As a beginning researcher, you should document any material you think might need it. By doing so, you avoid any possibility of plagiarism (see 38c).

Your documentation should clearly indicate the sources of all your information. Readers should not have to guess what passages you attribute to your readers and what statements you claim as your own. For this reason you should avoid "blanket" documentation—single references meant to cover several unrelated borrowings throughout a passage. Instead, place documentation after each quotation and at the end of each paraphrase and summary passage. Be sure to place documentation so that it will not interrupt your ideas—ideally at the end of a sentence. Make sure to differentiate your ideas from those of your sources by placing introductory phrases before, and documentation after, all borrowed material.

39b   Using Documentary Forms

Different fields of study use different forms of documentation. Three of the most widely used formats are those recommended by the Modern Language Association (MLA), the American Psychological Assocation (APA), and the Council of Biology Editors (CBE). Instructors in the humanities usually prefer MLA style, which uses parenthetical references within the text to refer to sources listed at the end of the paper. Instructors in the social sciences and in education prefer the APA style, which uses parenthetical references that differ slightly from MLA style. Other disciplines—the physical and biological sciences and medicine, for example—prefer a number-reference format, similar to CBE style, which uses numbers in parentheses in the text that refer to a list of works at the end of the paper.

Before you begin any paper, find out what form your in-

Overview of Documentation Styles

MLA Documentation Style

Note in the text

```
. . . Thoreau's reference to Abraham Lincoln
(Miller 308).
```

doc
39b

Work listed at the end of the paper

```
Miller, Perry. The American Transcendentalists:
    Their Prose and Poetry. New York: Doubleday, 1983.
```

APA Documentation Style

Note in the text

```
. . . a psychological profile of Adolph Hitler
(Langer, 1972).
```

Work listed at the end of the paper

```
Langer, W. C. (1972). The mind of Adolph Hitler.
    New York: Basic.
```

CBE Documentation Style

Note in the text

```
. . . the pigment's relation to photosynthesis (1).
```

Work listed at the end of the paper

```
1. Cotton, F. A. Photooxidation and photosynthetic
    pigments. J. Cell. Biol. 87:32–43; 1987.
```

structor requires. Then consult the appropriate guide and follow it to the letter (see 39f for a list of style manuals).

39c   Using MLA Format[*]

MLA format is recommended by the Modern Language Association of America, a professional organization of more than 25,000 teachers of English and other languages. It is required by teachers in the humanities at colleges throughout the United States and Canada. This method of documentation has three parts: parenthetical references in the text, a list of works cited, and explanatory notes.

(1)   Providing parenthetical references in the text

MLA documentation uses references inserted in parentheses within the text and keyed to a list of works cited at the end of the paper. A typical reference consists of the author's last name and a page number.

doc/
MLA
39c

        The colony's religious and political freedom appealed

        to many idealists in Europe (Ripley 132).

If you use more than one source by the same author, shorten the title of each work to one or two key words and include the appropriate shortened title in the parenthetical reference.

        Penn emphasized his religious motivation (Kelley,

        William Penn 116).

If the author's name or the title of the work is stated in the text, do not include it in the parenthetical reference.

        Penn's political motivation is discussed by Joseph P.

        Kelley in Pennsylvania, The Colonial Years, 1681—1776

        (44).   (Because the author's name is mentioned in the text,
        only a page reference is necessary.)

    Keep in mind that you punctuate differently with paraphrases and summaries, direct quotations run in with the text, and quotations that are set off from the text.

    Parenthetical documentation for *paraphrases and summaries* should appear *before* terminal punctuation marks.

---

[*] MLA documentation format follows the guidelines set in the *MLA Handbook for Writers of Research Papers*. 2d ed. New York: MLA, 1984.

```
Penn's writings epitomize seventeenth-century
religious thought (Degler and Curtis 72).
```

Parenthetical documentation for *direct quotations run in with the text* should appear *after* the quotation marks but *before* the terminal punctuation.

```
As Ross says, "Penn followed his conscience in all
matters" (127).

We must now ask, as Ross does, "Did Penn follow Quaker
dictates in his dealings with the Indians" (128)?

According to Williams, "Penn's utopian vision was
informed by his Quaker beliefs . . ." (72).
```

Parenthetical documentation for *quotations that are set off from the text* should appear two spaces *after* the final punctuation.

```
. . . a commonwealth in which all individuals can
follow God's truth and develop according to God's
will. (Smith 314)
```

Sample References

Parenthetical references are a straightforward and easy way to provide documentation. Here are the forms required in some special situations.

Works by more than one author

```
One group of physicists questioned many of the
assumptions of relativity (Harbeck and Johnson 31).
```

For books with three authors, list the authors in the order in which they appear on the title page, with *and* before the last name.

```
With the advent of behaviorism psychology began a new
phase of inquiry (Cowen, Barbo, and Crum 31–34).
```

For books with more than three authors, list the first author followed by *et al.* ("and others") in place of the rest.

```
A number of important discoveries were made off the
coast of Crete in 1960 (Dugan et al. 63).
```

Works with a volume and page number

A colon separates volume and page numbers of books. The number before the colon is the volume number; the number after the colon is the page number.

```
In 1912 Virginia Stephen married Leonard Woolf, with
whom she founded the Hogarth Press (Woolf 1: 17).
```

Works without a listed author

For works without a listed author, use a shortened version of the title in the parenthetical reference.

```
Television ratings wars have escalated during the past
ten years ("Leaving the Cellar" 102).
```

Omit the page reference if you are citing a one-page article.

```
It is a curious fact that the introduction of
Christianity at the end of the Roman Empire "had no
effect on the abolition of slavery" ("Slavery").
```

**doc/
MLA
39c**

Indirect sources

You should always try to get material from the original source, but sometimes you will have to use an indirect source. Indicate the material is from an indirect source by using the abbreviation *qtd. in* ("quoted in") as part of the parenthetical reference.

```
Wagner said that myth and history stood before him
"with opposing claims" (qtd. in Winkler 10).
```

More than one work within a parenthesis

You may cite more than one work within a single parenthesis. Cite each work as you normally would, separating one from another with semicolons.

```
The Brooklyn Bridge has been used as a subject by many
American artists (McCullough 144; Tshjian 58).
```

Keep these citations short, however, since long parenthetical references will distract readers. Whenever possible, present long references as explanatory notes (see 39c.3).

Literary works

In citations to prose works it is often helpful to include more than just author and page number. For example, the chapter number of a novel enables readers to locate your reference in any edition of the work to which you are referring. In parenthetical references to prose works, begin with the page number, include a semicolon, and add any additional information that might be necessary.

```
In Moby—Dick Melville refers to a whaling expedition

funded by Louis XIV of France (151; ch. 24).
```

In parenthetical references to poems, separate the divisions and line numbers with periods. Titles of books in the Bible are often abbreviated (Gen. 5.12).

```
Virgil describes the ships as cleaving the "green

woods reflected in the calm water" (The Aeneid 8.
```
124).   (In this citation the reference is to book 8 page 194 of The Aeneid.)

An entire work

When citing an entire work rather than part of a work, all you need to do is include the author's last name in your text. If you wish, you may mention the author's name in a parenthetical reference.

```
Northrup Frye's Fearful Symmetry presents a complex

critical interpretation of Blake's poetry.
```

```
Fearful Symmetry presents a complex critical

interpretation of Blake's poetry (Frye).
```

Tables and illustrations

When citing tables and illustrations, include the documentation below the illustrative material. (See Appendix B for the format for tables and illustrations.)

```
Miscues which alter meaning       51%

Overall loss of comprehension     40%

Retelling score                   20%
```

Source: Alice S. Horning, "The Trouble with Writing Is
the Trouble with Reading," Journal of Basic Writing 6
(1987): 46.

(2) Listing works cited

The *Works Cited* section appears at the end of your paper and
lists all the research materials that you have used. If your instructor tells you to list all the sources you read, whether you actually
cite them or not, use the title *Works Consulted.*

If you have no explanatory notes, the list of works cited
begins on a new page after the last page of text. Number the page
on which the list of works cited begins as the next page of text—
for example, if your paper ends on page 8, the *Works Cited* section begins on page 9. The items should appear in alphabetical
order according to the authors' last names. If one of your sources
is unsigned, as is the case with many magazine and newspaper
articles, alphabetize by the first main word of the title (excluding
a, an, or *the*).

doc/
MLA
39c
The first line of each entry should be flush with the left-
hand margin, and subsequent lines of the entry should be indented five spaces from the left. The list of works cited is double-
spaced within and between items.

An item in a list of works cited has three divisions, each
separated by a period and two spaces.

Works Cited Format

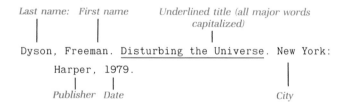

Last name: First name   Underlined title (all major words
                                          capitalized)

Dyson, Freeman. Disturbing the Universe. New York:
      Harper, 1979.
      Publisher Date   City

List of Works Cited Entries
---

1. A book by one author
2. A book by two or three authors
3. A book by more than three authors
4. Two or more books by the same author
5. An edited book
6. An essay that has *not* been published previously that is
   cited in an anthology

7. An essay that *has* been published previously that is cited in an anthology
8. A cross-reference
9. A multivolume work
10. A multivolume work in which each volume has an individual title
11. The foreword, preface, or afterword of a book
12. A short story in an anthology
13. A short story in a collection
14. A short poem in a collection
15. A book-length poem
16. A play in an anthology
17. A book whose title contains a title that is normally enclosed within quotation marks
18. A book whose title contains a title that is normally underlined
19. A translation
20. A reprint of an older edition
21. A published dissertation
22. An unpublished dissertation
23. An unsigned article in an encyclopedia
24. A signed article in an encyclopedia
25. A pamphlet
26. A government publication
27. An article in a journal with continuous pagination through an annual volume
28. An article in a journal that has separate pagination in each issue
29. A signed article in a weekly magazine
30. An unsigned article in a weekly magazine
31. An article in a monthly magazine
32. An article that does not appear on consecutive pages
33. A signed article in a daily newspaper
34. An unsigned article in a daily newspaper
35. An editorial
36. A letter to the editor
37. A titled book review
38. An untitled book review
39. An article whose title includes a title that is underlined
40. An article whose title includes a quotation or a title within quotation marks
41. Computer software
42. Material from a computer information service
43. A lecture

44. A personal interview
45. A personal letter
46. A letter in a library's archives
47. A film
48. A videocassette
49. A radio or television program

Citations for Books

1. A book by one author

Enter the full title of the book. To conserve space use a short form of the publisher's name; do not include *Incorporated, Publishers,* or *Company* after the name of the publisher. *Alfred A. Knopf, Inc.,* for example, is shortened to *Knopf,* and *Oxford University Press* becomes *Oxford UP.*

```
Bettelheim, Bruno.  The Uses of Enchantment: The
        Meaning and Importance of Fairy Tales.  New
        York: Knopf, 1976.
```

When citing an edition other than the first, indicate the edition number in the form used on the work's title page.

```
Gans, Herbert J.  The Urban Villagers, 2nd ed.  New
        York: Free, 1982.
```

2. A book by two or three authors

Only the first author's name is reversed, with last name first. Subsequent authors' names should be listed in the order in which they appear on the book's title page.

```
Davidson, James West, and Mark Hamilton Lytle.  After
        the Fact: The Art of Historical Detection.  New
        York: Knopf, 1982.
```

3. A book by more than three authors

For more than three authors, list only the first author followed by *et al.* ("and others").

```
Spiller, Robert E., et al., eds.  Literary History of
        the United States.  New York: Macmillan, 1974.
```

4. Two or more books by the same author

Books by the same author are listed in alphabetical order by title. Three hyphens followed by a period take the place of the author's name after the first entry.

```
Thomas, Lewis.  The Lives of a Cell: Notes of a
        Biology Watcher.  New York: Viking, 1974.

---. The Medusa and the Snail: More Notes of a
        Biology Watcher.  New York: Viking, 1979.
```

5. An edited book

An edited book is a work that has been prepared for publication by a person other than the author. When citing a work, if you are referring to the work itself, begin your citation with the author's name. If you are referring to a particular edition, begin your citation with the editor's name.

```
Bartram, William.  The Travels of William Bartram.
        Ed. Mark Van Doren. New York: Dover, 1955.

Van Doren, Mark, ed.  The Travels of William Bartram.
        By William Bartram.  New York: Dover, 1955.
```

**doc/
MLA
39c**

6. An essay that has *not* been published previously that is cited in an anthology

When citing an essay appearing in an anthology, include the *full* span of pages on which the whole essay appears, even though you may cite only one page in your paper.

```
Lloyd, G. E. R.  "Science and Mathematics."  The
        Legacy of Greece.  Ed. M. I. Finley.  New York:
        Oxford UP, 1981.  256-300.
```

7. An essay that *has* been published previously that is cited in an anthology

If the essay you cite has been published previously, include publishing data for the first publication followed by the current information along with the abbreviation *Rpt. in* ("Reprinted in").

```
Warren, Austin.  "Emily Dickinson."  The Sewanee
        Review 17 (1957):162-77. Rpt. in Emily
```

>Dickinson: A Collection of Critical Essays. Ed.
>Richard B. Sewall. Englewood Cliffs: Prentice,
>1963. 101–116.

8. A cross-reference

If you use more than one essay from a collection, list each essay separately, including a cross-reference to the collection. In addition, list complete publication information for the collection itself.

>Bolgar, R. R.   "The Greek Legacy." Finley 429–72.
>Davies, A. M.   "Lyric and Other Poetry." Finley
>   93–119.
>Finley, M. I., ed.   The Legacy of Greece. New York:
>   Oxford UP, 1981.

9. A multivolume work

>Raine, Kathleen.   Vol. 1 of Blake and Tradition.
>   2 vols. Princeton: Princeton UP, 1968.

**doc/
MLA
39c**

10. A multivolume work in which each volume has an individual title

If the volume you are using has an individual title, give the title after the author's name. Next, include the number of the volume that you are using followed by the title of the entire work.

>Durant, Will, and Ariel Durant.   The Age of Napoleon:
>   A History of European Civilization from 1789 to
>   1815. Vol. 11 of The Story of Civilization.   11
>   vols. New York: Simon, 1975.

11. The foreword, preface, or afterword of a book

>Taylor, Telford.   Preface. Less Than Slaves. By
>   Benjamin B. Ferencz. Cambridge: Harvard UP,
>   1979. xiii–xxii.

12. A short story in an anthology

>Singer, Isaac Bashevis.   "The Spinoza of Market
>   Street." The Norton Anthology of Short
>   Fiction. Ed. R. V. Cassill. 3rd ed. New York:
>   Norton, 1986. 1210–1224.

13. A short story in a collection

> Singer, Isaac Bashevis.   "The Spinoza of Market
>   Street."   The Collected Stories of Isaac
>   Bashevis Singer.   New York: Farrar, 1983.

14. A short poem in a collection

Enclose the title of a short poem in quotation marks.

> Pound, Ezra.   "A Virginal."   Selected Poems of Ezra
>   Pound.   New York: New Directions, 1957. 23.

15. A book-length poem

Underline the title of a book-length poem.

> Eliot, T. S.   The Waste Land.   T. S. Eliot: Collected
>   Poems 1909—1962.   New York: Harcourt, 1963.
>   51—70.

16. A play in an anthology

> Shakespeare, William.   Othello, The Moor of Venice.
>   Shakespeare: Six Plays and The Sonnets.   Eds.
>   Thomas Marc Parrott and Edward Hubler. New York:
>   Scribner's, 1956.

17. A book whose title contains a title that is normally enclosed within quotation marks

If the book you are citing contains a title enclosed in quotation marks, keep the quotation marks.

> Herzog, Alan, ed.   Twentieth Century Interpretations
>   of "To a Skylark."   Englewood Cliffs: Prentice,
>   1975.

18. A book whose title contains a title that is normally underlined

If the book you are citing contains a title that is normally underlined, do not underline it.

> Knoll, Robert E, ed.   Storm Over The Waste Land.
>   Chicago: Scott, 1964.

19. A translation

> García Marquez, Gábriel.   <u>One Hundred Years of
> Solitude</u>.   Trans. Gregory Rabassa. New York:
> Avon, 1971.

20. A reprint of an older edition

> Wharton, Edith.   <u>The House of Mirth</u>.   1905. New York:
> Scribner's, 1975.

21. A published dissertation

Enter a published dissertation the way you would a book. Most American dissertations are published by University Microfilms International (UMI), so include the order number in your citation.

> Spann, Marcella Joyce.   <u>An Analytical and Descriptive
> Catalogue of the Manuscripts and Letters in the
> Louis Zukofsky Collection at the University of
> Texas at Austin</u>.   Diss. U of Texas at Austin,
> 1969.   Ann Arbor: UMI, 1970. 7010867.

**doc/
MLA
39c**

22. An unpublished dissertation

Enclose the title of an unpublished dissertation within quotation marks.

> Gainor, Charles Michael.   "Cultural and Philosophical
> Determinants of Modern Economic Theory."   Diss.
> Columbia U, 1984.

23. An unsigned article in an encyclopedia

Enter the title of an unsigned article just as it is listed in the encyclopedia.

> "Cubism."   <u>Encyclopaedia Britannica: Micropaedia</u>.
> 1974 ed.

24. A signed article in an encyclopedia

For a signed article, enter the author's name, and then cite the article. Because encyclopedia entries appear in alphabetical order, no volume number is needed.

> Monro, D. H.   "Humor."   <u>The Encyclopedia of
> Philosophy</u>.   1974 ed.

25. A pamphlet

Enter pamphlets as if they were books. If no author is listed, enter the underlined title first, and follow with publishing information.

Existing Light Photography.   Rochester: Kodak, 1982.

26. A government publication

If the publication has no author, state the name of the government first, followed by the name of the agency and then the title of the pamphlet or bulletin.

United States.   President's Commission for the Study
        of Ethical Problems in Medicine and Biomedical
        and Behavioral Research.   Deciding to Forgo
        Life—Sustaining Treatment: Ethical, Medical, and
        Legal Issues in Treatment Issues in Treatment
        Decisions.   Washington: GPO, 1983.

**doc/
MLA
39c**

Citations for Articles

Article citations contain the author's name; the title of the article, in quotation marks; and the underlined name of the journal. They also give the pages on which the full article appears. The abbreviations *p.* and *pp.* are not included.

27. An article in a scholarly journal with continuous pagination through an annual volume

For an article in a journal with continuous pagination—for example, one issue ends on page 172 and the next issue begins with page 173—include the volume number followed by the date of publication in parentheses.

Huntington, John.   "Science Fiction and the Future."
        College English 37 (1975):340—58.

28. An article in a scholarly journal that has separate pagination in each issue

For a journal with separate pagination in each issue—each issue begins with page 1—add a period and the issue number after the volume number.

Sipes, R. G.   "War, Sports, and Aggression: An

Empirical Test of Two Rival Theories." American

Anthropologist 4.2 (1973):65—84.

29. A signed article in a weekly magazine

Dates for articles follow military format with the day preceding
the month. Notice that the date is not set in parentheses unless a
volume number is mentioned.

Bergley, Sharon. "Redefining Intelligence.." Newsweek

14 Nov. 1983:123—24.

30. An unsigned article in a weekly magazine

"Solzhenitsyn: A Candle in the Wind." Time 23 March

1970:70.

31. An article in a monthly magazine

Roll, Lori. "Careers in Engineering." Working Woman

Nov. 1982:62.

32. An article that does not appear on consecutive pages

When an article does not appear on consecutive pages—that is,
it begins on page 15, continues on page 16, and then skips to
page 86—include only the first page and a (+) sign.

Rodman, Selden. "Where Art Is Joy." Caribbean Travel

and Life. Oct. 1987:58 + .

33. A signed article in a daily newspaper

Stipp, David. "Japanese Firms Find Little Success in

the U.S. Small Computer Market." Wall Street

Journal 11 Sept. 1983, late ed.:6.

34. An unsigned article in a daily newspaper

"The Summit on Soviet Television." Los Angeles Times

13 Dec. 1987, sec. 2:3 + .

35. An editorial

"We Hear You, Mr. President." Editorial. New York

Times 11 Sept. 1983, late ed.:C11.

36. A letter to the editor

Bishop, Jennifer. Letter. Philadelphia Inquirer. 10

Dec. 1987:A26.

37. A titled book review

A review begins with the reviewer's name and is followed by the title of the review (if any), the title and author of the book reviewed, and the date on which the review appeared. An unsigned review begins with the name of the review, if any, or the title of the book being reviewed.

> Prescott, Peter S.   "A Movable Feast on Fiction."
>   Rev. of The Assassination of Jessie James by the
>   Coward, by Ron Hansen.   Newsweek 14 Nov. 1983:
>   112.

38. An untitled book review

> Harris, Joseph.   Rev. of Perspectives on Research and
>   Scholarship in Composition, eds. Ben W.
>   McLelland and Timothy R. Dononan.   College
>   Composition and Communication 38(1987):101—02.

**doc/
MLA
39c**

39. An article whose title includes a title that is underlined

> Leicester, H. Marshall, Jr.   "The Art of
>   Impersonation: A General Prologue to The
>   Canterbury Tales."   PMLA 95(1980):213—224.

40. An article whose title includes a quotation or a title within quotation marks

If a title contains material that is normally enclosed within quotation marks, use single quotation marks.

> Nash, Robert.   "About 'The Emperor of Ice—Cream.'"
>   Perspectives 7(1954):122—24.

Citations for Nonprint Sources

41. Computer software

Citations for computer software include the writer of the program, the title of the program, a descriptive label (*computer software*), the distributor, and the date of publication.

> Atkinson, Bill.   Macpaint.   Computer software.   Apple,
>   1983.

42. Material from a computer information service

Enter material from a computer information service—BRS or DIALOG, for example—just as you would printed material. In addition, mention the information service and the identification numbers of the material at the end of the entry.

> Baer, Walter S. "Telecommunications Technology in the
>   1980's." Computer Science June 1984:137 + .
>   DIALOG file 102, item 0346142.

43. A lecture

> Sandman, Peter. "Communicating Scientific
>   Information." Communications Seminar, Dept. of
>   Humanities and Communications. Drexel U, 26
>   Oct. 1984.

44. A personal interview

> Cavett, Dick. Personal interview. 28 Dec. 1987.
>
> Sagan, Carl. Telephone interview. 8 June 1988.

45. A personal letter

> Kingston, Maxine Hong. Letter to the author. 7 April
>   1985.

46. A letter in a library's archives

> Stieglitz, Alfred. Letter to Paul Rosenberg. 5 Sept.
>   1923. Stieglitz Archive. Yale, New Haven.

47. A film

A citation for a film includes the title of the film (underlined), the distributor, and the date. You may also include other information such as the performers, the director, and the writer if this information would be of use to a reader.

> The Big Chill. Dir. Lawrence Kasdan. With Kevin
>   Kline, William Hurt, Jeff Goldblum, Tom
>   Berenger, Glenn Close, Mary Kay Place, Jobeth
>   Williams, and Meg Tilly. Columbia Pictures,
>   1983.

If you are focusing on the contribution of a particular person, begin with that person's name (Kasdan, Lawrence, dir. <u>The Big Chill</u> . . .).

48. A videocassette

> <u>Arthur Miller:</u> The Crucible.   Videocassette.   Dir.
>
>   William Schiff.   The Mosaic Group, 1987.   20
>
>   min.

49. A radio or television program

> <u>Kennedy</u>.   Writ. Reg Gadney.   With Martin Sheen, John
>
>   Shea, and Blair Brown.   NBC. KNBC, Los Angeles.
>
>   20 Nov. 1983.

(3)   Using explanatory notes

Explanatory notes—commentary on sources or additional information on content that does not fit smoothly into the text—may be used along with parenthetical documentation and are indicated by a raised number in the text. The full text of these notes appears on the first full numbered page, entitled *Notes*, following the last page of the paper and before the list of works cited.

doc/
MLA
39c

For more than one source

Use explanatory notes for references to numerous citations in a single reference. Many references within a single pair of parentheses will distract readers.

In the paper

> Many researchers emphasize the necessity of
> having dying patients share their experiences.[1]

In the note

> [1]Kübler—Ross 27; Stinnette 43; Poston 70; Cohen
> and Cohen 31—34; Burke 1: 91—95.

For explanations

Use notes to provide comments or explanations that are needed to clarify a point in the text.

In the paper

> The massacre of the Armenians by the Turks during

```
World War I is an event that the survivors cannot
forget.²
```

In the note

```
    ²For a firsthand account of these events, see
Bedoukian 17–81.
```

39d   Using APA Format*

APA format, which is used extensively in the social sciences, relies on short references—consisting of the last name of the author and the year of publication—inserted within the text. These
references are keyed to an alphabetical list of references that
follows the paper.

(1)   Providing parenthetical references in the text

One author

APA style calls for a comma between the name and the date,
whereas MLA style does not.

```
One study of stress in the workplace (Weisberg, 1983)
shows a correlation between. . . .
```

As with MLA style, you do not include in the parenthetical reference information that appears in the text.

```
In his study Weisberg (1983) shows a correlation. . . .
(author's name in text)
```

```
In Weisberg's 1983 study of stress in the work-
place. . . . (author's name and date in text)
```

Two publications by same author(s), same year

If you cite two or more publications by the same author that
appeared the same year, the first is designated *a*, the second *b*
(e.g., Weisberg 1983a and Weisberg 1983b), and so on. These letter
designations also appear in the reference list that follows the text
of your paper.

```
He completed his next study of stress (Weisberg,
1983b). . . .
```

---

*APA documentation format follows the guidelines set in the *Publication Manual
of the American Psychological Association*. 3rd ed. Washington, DC: APA, 1983.

A publication by two or more authors

When a work has two authors, both names are cited.

> There is a current and growing concern over the use of
> psychological testing in elementary schools (Albright
> & Glennon, 1982).

If a work has more than two authors but fewer than six authors, mention all names in the first reference, and in subsequent references cite the first author followed by *et al.* and the year (Sparks et al. 1984). When a work has six or more authors, cite the name of the first author followed by *et al.* and the year.

When citing multiple authors in your text, join the names of the last two with *and* (According to Rosen, Wolfe, and Ziff [1988]. . .). In parenthetical documentation, however, use an ampersand to join multiple authors (Rosen, Wolfe, & Ziff, 1988).

Specific parts of a source

When citing a specific part of a source, identify that part in your reference. APA documentation includes abbreviations for the words *page* ("p"), *chapter* ("ch."), and *section* ("sec."), whereas MLA format does not.

doc/
APA
39d

> These theories have an interesting history (Lee, 1966,
> p. 53).

Two or more works within the same parenthetical reference

Identify works by different authors in alphabetical order.

> . . . among several studies (Barson & Roth, 1985;
> Rose, 1987; Tedesco, 1982).

Identify works by the same author in order of date of publication.

> . . . among several studies (Weiss & Elliot, 1982,
> 1984, 1985).

Identify works by the same author that appeared in the same year by designating the first *a,* the second *b,* and so on.

> . . . among several studies (Hossack, 1985a, 1985b,
> 1985c, in press). (*In press* designates a work about to
> be published.)

(2) Listing the references

The list of all the sources cited in your paper falls at the end on a
new numbered page with the heading *References*.

Items are arranged in alphabetical order, with the author's
last name spelled out in full and initials only for the author's first
and second names. Next comes the date of publication, title, and,
for journal entries, volume number and pages. For books, the
date of publication, city of publication, and publisher are included.

When determining the order of works in the reference list,
keep the following guidelines in mind.

- Single-author entries are arranged before multiple-author entries
  that begin with the same name.

      Field, S. (1987). . . .

      Field, S., & Levitt, M. P. (1984). . . .

- Entries by the same author are arranged according to date of
  publication, starting with the earliest date.

      Ruthenberg, H., & Rubin, R. (1985). . . .

      Ruthenberg, H., & Rubin, R. (1987). . . .

- Entries by the same author and having the same date of publication are arranged alphabetically according to title. They include lower-case letters after the year.

      Wolk, E. M. (1986a). Analysis. . . .

      Wolk, E. M. (1986b). Hormonal. . . .

Like MLA entries, APA citations have three divisions separated by periods. Notice, however, that significant differences
exist between the two formats.

Reference List Format

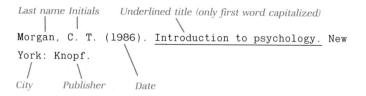

**doc/
APA
39d**

Citations for Books

Capitalize only the first word of the title and the first word of the subtitle of books. Be sure to underline the title and to enclose in parentheses the date, volume number, and edition number.

A book with one author

> Maslow, A. H. (1974).   Toward a psychology of being.
>   Princeton: Van Nostrand.

A book with more than one author

Notice that both authors are cited with last names first.

> Blood, R. O., & Wolf, D. M. (1960).   Husbands and
>   wives: The dynamics of married living.   Glencoe:
>   Free Press.

An edited book

> Lewin, K., Lippitt, R., & White, R. K. (Eds.).
>   (1985).   Social learning and imitation.   New
>   York: Basic Books.

doc/
APA
39d

Citations for Articles

Capitalize only the first word of the title and the first word of the subtitle of articles. Do not underline the article or enclose it in quotation marks. Give the journal title in full; underline the title and capitalize all major words. Underline the volume number and include the issue number in parentheses. Give inclusive page numbers.

An article in a scholarly journal with continuous pagination through an annual volume

> Miller, W. (1969).   Violent crimes in city gangs.
>   Journal of Social Issues, 27, 581—593.

An article in a scholarly journal that has separate pagination in each issue

> Williams, S., & Cohen, L. R. (1984).   Child stress in
>   early learning situations.   American
>   Psychologist, 21, (10), 1—28.

A magazine article

Use *pp.* when referring to page numbers in magazines, but omit this abbreviation when referring to page numbers in journals.

McCurdy, H. G. (1983, June). Brain mechanisms and
    intelligence. Psychology Today, pp. 61–63.

A newspaper article, no author

Study finds many street people mentally ill. (1984,
    June). New York Times, p. 7.

A newspaper article, author

James, W. R. (1985, January 3). The unemployed and
    the flat tax. The Wall Street Journal, pp. 1, 12.

    (article appears on two separate pages)

An article in an edited book

Tappan, P. W. (1980). Who is a criminal? In M. E.
    Wolfgang, L. Savitz, & N. Johnston (Eds.),
    The sociology of crime and delinquency
    (pp. 41–48). New York: Wiley.

**doc/
CBE
39e**

A government report

National Institute of Mental Health. (1987). Motion
    pictures and violence: A summary report of
    research (DHHS Publication No. ADM 91–22187).
    Washington, DC: U.S. Government Printing Office.

39e   Using CBE Format[*] ————————————

CBE format is the documentation format recommended by the Council of Biology Editors and distributed by the American Institute of Biological Sciences. It is used by authors, editors, and publishers in biology, botany, zoology, physiology, anatomy, and genetics. The number-reference format recommended by the *CBE Style Manual* is similar to the formats used in the applied and medical sciences. Numbers inserted parenthetically in the text correspond to a reference list at the end of the paper. Works are arranged in the order in which they are mentioned in the text

[*] CBE documentation format follows the guidelines set in the *CBE Style Manual*. 5th ed. Bethesda: Council of Biology Editors, 1983.

and then numbered consecutively. When the list of references is typed, all lines begin at the left margin.

In the paper

```
One study (1) has demonstrated the effect of low
dissolved oxygen.  Cell walls of. . . .
```

In the reference list

```
1. White, R. P. An introduction to biochemistry.
    Philadelphia: W. B. Saunders, 1974.
```

Name   Initials   Title not underlined   City   Publisher
Date   (only first word capitalized)

Citations for Books

For book entries, list the author(s), the title (with only the first word capitalized), the city of publication followed by a colon, the name of the publisher followed by a semicolon, and the year followed by a period. Do not underline book titles.

A book with one author

doc/
CBE
39e

```
1. Rathmil, P. D.  The synthesis of milk and related
    products.  Madison, WI: Hugo Summer; 1985.
```

A book with more than one author

```
2. Krause, K. F.; Paterson, M. K., Jr.  Tissue
    culture: methods and application.  New York:
    Academic Press, Inc; 1973.
```

An edited book

```
3. Marzacco, M. P., A survey of biochemistry.  New
    York: R. R. Bowker Co.; 1985.
```

A specific section of a book

```
4. Baldwin, L. D.; Rigby, C. V.  A study of animal
    virology.  2nd ed. John Wiley & Sons; 1984:121–
    133.
```

Citations for Articles

For journal articles list the author(s), the title of the article (with only the first word capitalized), the title of the journal (capitalized), the volume number followed by a colon, the inclusive page numbers of the article, and the year followed by a period.

An article in a scholarly journal with continuous pagination in each issue

> 1. Bensley, L. Profiling women physicians. Medica
>   1:140–145; 1985.

An article in a scholarly journal that has separate pagination in each issue

> 2. Wilen, W. W. The biological clock of insects. Sci.
>   Amer. 234(2):114–121; 1976.

An article with a subtitle

> 3. Schindler, A; Donner, K. B. On DNA: the evolution
>   of an amino acid sequence. J. Mol. Evol. 8:94–101;
>   1980.

An article with no author

doc
39f

> 4. Anonymous. Developments in microbiology. Int. J.
>   Microbiol. 6:234–248; 1987.

An article with discontinuous pages

> 5. Williams, S.; Heller, G. A.; Special dietary foods
>   and their importance for diabetics. Food Prod.
>   Dev. 44:54–62, 68–73; 1984.

39f Using Other Documentary Forms ———

Here are some style manuals that describe documentation formats different from the ones already mentioned. When the need arises, consult them in your college library.

Chemistry

> American Chemical Society. Handbook for Authors of
>   Papers in American Chemical Society
>   Publications. Washington: American Chemical
>   Soc., 1978.

Geology

> United States Geological Survey. <u>Suggestions to</u>
> <u>Authors of the Reports of the United States</u>
> <u>Geological Survey</u>. 6th ed. Washington DC: Dept.
> of the Interior, 1978.

Linguistics

> Linguistic Society of America. <u>LSA Bulletin</u>, Dec.
> issue, annually.

Mathematics

> American Mathematical Society. <u>A Manual for Authors</u>
> <u>of Mathematical Papers</u>. 7th ed. Providence:
> American Mathematical Soc., 1980.

Medical Sciences

> American Medical Association. <u>Style Book</u>: <u>Editorial</u>
> <u>Manual</u>. 6th ed. Acton, MA: Publishing Sciences
> Group, 1976.

doc
39g

Physics

> American Institute of Physics. Publications Board.
> <u>Style Manual for Guidance in the Preparation of</u>
> <u>Papers</u>. 3rd ed. New York: American Inst. of
> Physics, 1978.

Other disciplines

> <u>The Chicago Manual of Style</u>. 13th ed. Chicago: U of
> Chicago P, 1982.

See John Bruce Howell, *Style Manuals for the English-Speaking World* (Phoenix: Oryx, 1983) for other guides to style.

39g   Using Abbreviations ────────────

Although many of the abbreviations that made documentation so tedious have been eliminated from the latest style manuals, you should be familiar with certain abbreviations that you may encounter in your research. Remember that your audience determines whether or not you abbreviate. If you suspect that an abbreviation will confuse your readers, write out the word in full.

anon.	anonymous
bk., bks.	*book*(s)
c., ca.	*circa* ("about"). Used with dates that are approximate, as in c. 1920 (approximately 1920).
cf.	*confer* ("compare")
ch., chs.	chapter(s)
col., cols.	column(s)
comp., comps.	compiled by, compiler(s)
diss.	dissertation
ed., eds.	edition(s), editor(s)
et al.	*et alia* ("and others")
ff.	and the following pages, as in pp. 88 ff.
illus.	illustrated by, illustration(s)
l., ll.	line(s)
ms., mss.	manuscript(s)
n., nn.	note(s), as in p. 12, n. 1
n.d.	no date (of publication)
n.p.	no place (of publication), no publisher
n. pag.	no pagination
p., pp.	page(s)
passim	throughout
q.v.	*quod vide* ("which see")
rev.	revision, revised by
rpt.	reprint, reprinted
sec.	section
supp., supps.	supplement(s)
trans.	translated by

doc
39g

☐   **EXERCISE**

The following are the notes for a paper on approaches to teaching composition. Put them in the proper format for MLA parenthetical documentation, and then arrange them in the proper format for the list of works cited. (If your instructor requires a different method of documentation, use it instead.)

1. Page 2 in a book called Teaching Expository Writing by William F. Irmscher. The book has 188 pages and was published by Holt, Rinehart and Winston, which has offices in New York, in 1979. (author's name mentioned in the text of your paper)
2. Something Erika Lindemann said in a lecture on November 9, 1982. She called the talk Some Approaches to Teaching. (no name mentioned in text)
3. Irmscher's book again, this time pages 34, 35, and 36. (author's name mentioned in the text)
4. The Search for Intelligible Structure, an essay written by Frank J.

D'Angelo in a book by Gary Tate and Edward P. J. Corbett that is a collection of essays. Oxford University Press in New York published the book, and its copyright date is 1981. Your quotation is from the first page of the essay, which runs from page 80 to page 88. The book is called The Writing Teacher's Sourcebook. (no name mentioned in the text)

5. Page vii of the introduction to a book called Teaching Composition: 10 Bibliographical Essays, which Texas Christian University Press published in 1976 in Fort Worth. It was edited by Gary Tate. (no name mentioned in the text)

6. An article in *Time* on October 25, 1980, called Teaching Johnny to Write. You paraphrased a paragraph on page 73. The article ran from page 72 to page 79, and the last page was signed M. Hardy Jones. (no name mentioned in the text)

7. Page 61 in Teaching Expository Writing. (author's name mentioned in the text)

8. Using a Newspaper in the Classroom, which appeared in the Durham Morning Herald on page 1 of section D in the Sunday paper on November 14, 1982. It was written by Kim Best. (no name mentioned in the text)

9. Lee Odell's article in the February 1979 issue of College Composition and Communication. The article, called Teachers of Composition and Needed Research in Discourse Theory, ran from page 39 to page 45, and you got your information from page 41. That was volume 30 of the journal. (author's name mentioned in the text)

doc
39g

10. You found a book written by Erika Lindemann that you want to quote. You use material on pages 236 and 237 of the book, titled A Rhetoric for Writing Teachers, which was published in 1982 by the New York office of Oxford University Press. (no name mentioned in the text)

11. You decide you need to talk to someone with some experience at the University of North Carolina, so you interview English professor Robert Bain. You talked to him on November 5 and now you are quoting something he said. (no name mentioned in the text)

12. This material is from page 78 of that *Time* article. (no name mentioned in the text)

13. You summarize pages 179–185 of Irmscher. (author's name mentioned in the text)

14. You find the perfect conclusion on page 635 of volume 33 of College English in Richard Larson's article Problem-Solving, Composing and Liberal Education. This is the March 1972 issue and the article begins on page 628 and ends on page 635. (no name mentioned in the text)

40

Writing a Research Paper

Doing research involves more than absorbing the ideas of others: it requires you to evaluate and interpret the ideas presented in your sources and to develop ideas of your own. As you prepare your paper, you are involved in a constant process of decision-making. You weigh alternatives, deciding which material to keep and which to discard as you come to see the connections among the ideas in your sources. You also decide how to arrange and juxtapose material and whether you need to do more research. These decisions lead you to the conclusions that give focus and direction to your paper.

Searching out resources involves considerably more than looking in the card catalog and consulting a few indexes. Conducting research requires planning. As you plan your paper, leave enough time to formulate and reformulate ideas. The final shape of your paper should emerge gradually as your ideas and your understanding of your subject become clearer.

The sample schedule on page 599 will help you to manage your time as you write a research paper.

Planning

40a Moving from Assignment to Topic

(1) Understanding your assignment

Your research paper begins with an assignment. Your first step is to find a direction for your research within the guidelines of this assignment. Even before you can do this, however, you must make sure that you understand your assignment.

The Research Process

Activity	Date Due	Date Completed
Moving from assignment to topic		
—understanding your assignment	_____	_____
—choosing a topic	_____	_____
—starting a research notebook	_____	_____
Doing Exploratory Research and Focusing on a Research Question		
—doing exploratory research	_____	_____
—focusing on a research question	_____	_____
Assembling a Working Bibliography and Making Note Cards		
—assembling a working bibliography	_____	_____
—making note cards	_____	_____
Developing a Tentative Thesis		
Doing Focused Research and Taking Notes		
—reading sources	_____	_____
—making note cards	_____	_____
Deciding on a Thesis	_____	_____
Making an Outline	_____	_____
Writing Your First Draft	_____	_____
Revising Your Drafts	_____	_____
Preparing Your Final Draft	_____	_____

res pap 40a

First, determine how much the assignment asks you to do. Are you to choose a topic from among a list of possible topics provided by your instructor? Have you been given a general subject area and asked to focus on one aspect of it? Or are you being asked to select a topic on your own?

Next, consider the assignment's specific, practical requirements. When is the completed research paper due? About how long should it be? Will you be given a specific research schedule to follow, or are you expected to set your own schedule? Are you to do research only in the library, or should you also use nonprint sources? Does your instructor require you to keep a research notebook? What format is required? Should the paper include an outline and a separate title page? What documentation style are you to use? Does your instructor expect to review your note cards, outline, or drafts with you at regular intervals? What help is available to you—from your instructor, your fellow students, experts in the field your paper will explore, your library? Before you can proceed, you will need to know the answers to these questions.

(2) Choosing a topic

Once you understand your assignment, you can look for a direction for your research. You begin this task by narrowing your focus to a topic you can explore within the limits of your assignment.

In most cases, your instructor will help you choose a topic, either by providing a list of suitable topics or by assigning a general subject area—a famous trial, an event that happened on the day you were born, an ethnic group. Even in these instances your work is not complete: you will need to choose one of the topics or narrow the subject area: decide on one trial, one event, one ethnic group. And even when you have made your choice, you will still have to decide exactly how to approach that topic.

If your instructor prefers that you select a topic on your own, your task is somewhat more difficult: you must consider various topics and weigh both their suitability for research and your interest in researching them. You find a focus for your paper in much the same way you decide on a topic for a short essay: you brainstorm, ask questions, talk to people, and read widely. With a research paper, however, you know from the start that you will examine not just your own ideas on a topic, but also the ideas of others.

A good research topic has four characteristics. First, the topic you choose must be manageable enough to enable you to do productive research. For instance, the subject areas on the list below are too general for research. The narrowed topics are more suitable starting points.

Subject Area	Topic
Computers	The possible negative effects of computer games on adolescents

Feminism	The relationship between the feminist movement and the use of sexist language
Mood-altering drugs	The use of mood-altering drugs in state mental hospitals

A topic must fit within the boundaries of your assignment; it can be neither too broad nor too narrow. "Julius and Ethel Rosenberg: Atomic Spies or FBI Scapegoats?" is far too broad for a ten-page—or even a hundred-page—treatment. But how one newspaper reported the Rosenbergs' trial or how college students reacted at the time to the couple's 1953 execution for espionage might work. On the other hand, "One piece of evidence that played a decisive role in establishing the Rosenbergs' guilt" would probably be too narrow for a ten-page research paper— even if you could gain access to significant information.

Second, the topic you choose must be suitable for research. Topics based exclusively on personal experience or on value judgments are therefore ruled out. "How attending an integrated high school has made me a more tolerant person" is a topic that can be supported only by self-analysis. "The immorality of the Vietnam War" or "The superiority of J. R. R. Tolkein's work to that of Frank Herbert" are issues that might interest you, but neither research nor expert testimony can ever resolve them.

Third, your topic must be one that can be researched in the library to which you have access. If your instructor gives you a specific topic or subject area to write about, he or she will probably have made sure that your library has the resources you need. If you choose your own topic, you will have to learn what your library has to offer and what its limitations are before you select a topic. For instance, the library of an engineering or business college may not have a large collection of journals about literature; most small liberal arts college libraries will not have extensive resources for technical or medical topics.

Finally, the topic you select should be one in which you are genuinely interested. You will be deeply involved with this topic for many weeks—perhaps even for an entire semester—and your research will be most productive if you are able to see your paper as more than just an exercise in collecting and assimilating information and drawing conclusions. If you are interested in your topic, you are more likely to see the research paper as an opportunity to discover new ideas, and new connections among ideas.

res
pap
40a

(3)   Starting a research notebook

As soon as you have your assignment, you should start a **research notebook,** a combination journal of your reactions and log of your progress. A research notebook maps out your direction and keeps you on track; throughout the research process it defines and redefines the boundaries of your assignment.

In this notebook you can record lists of things to do, sources to check, leads to follow up on, appointments, possible community contacts, questions to which you would like to find answers, stray ideas, possible thesis statements or titles, and so on. Be sure to date your entries and to check off and date work completed; this will save you from repeating steps.

Some students use a spiral notebook that includes pockets to hold note and bibliography cards. Others use a small assignment book. Whatever kind of book you use, the research notebook can serve as a useful record of what has been done and what is left to do.

■   A Student Does Research:
Moving from Assignment to Topic

Michael Schrader, a student in a freshman composition class, was given this research assignment: "Write an eight- to ten-page research paper on some aspect of the immigrant experience in America, choosing *one* ethnic group and exploring *one* issue." This was a full-semester project, so Michael had fourteen weeks to research and write the paper.

Michael's instructor told the class that she would require regular conferences at which she would review each student's progress; a segment of the assignment would be due at each meeting. She also would require each student to keep a research notebook, and she expected them to research their topic in nonprint sources as well as in the library. With these general guidelines in mind, Michael began to think about his assignment.

Michael's mother's family was Italian, so he decided to do his paper on Italian-Americans. His maternal grandparents lived in an Italian neighborhood and subscribed to ethnic newspapers and magazines. They had many friends among the political, religious, and social leaders of the community who could be of great assistance to him. Narrowing down the subject to one aspect of the Italian immigrant experience took more time, but Michael eventually decided to research family life. Exploring this area would be interesting and fruitful, and his own family, with whom he was close, could be of help. With these decisions, Michael had found a topic.

Assignment	*Topic*
Discuss one aspect of one ethnic group's immigrant experience	Family life of Italian immigrants

Michael began his research notebook by listing his assignment and pasting the instructor's research schedule on the inside front cover. This would enable him to check off each part of the project as he completed it. Next he jotted down the assignment's other requirements and the time of his first conference with his instructor. Then he recorded his topic and listed a few family members he thought might be able to help him. Now he was ready to move on to the next stage of his assignment: exploratory research.

☐   **EXERCISE 1**

Using your own instructor's guidelines for selecting a research topic, choose a topic for your paper. Begin your research notebook by entering information about your assignment, schedule, and topic.

40b   Doing Exploratory Research and Focusing on a Research Question

Research is a process of questioning, and the key to successful research lies in finding out what questions to ask. Your research should be guided by a **search strategy,** a systematic process of gathering and evaluating potential source material, moving from general to specific sources (see 37a). Your first meeting with your instructor can help you to map out such a search strategy for the project you have in mind. At this meeting your instructor can give you valuable suggestions and direct you to appropriate sources. As you continue your research, you will modify your search strategy, tailoring it to fit your changing priorities and recording your progress in your research notebook.

res
pap
40b

(1)   Doing exploratory research

Once you have a topic, you work to focus more specifically on what you want to discover about it. **Exploratory research** helps you to get an overview of your topic and an understanding of its possibilities.

Do your exploratory research with an open mind, allowing the results to determine your conclusions. Look at a wide range of material. Accidents, wrong turns, and unconventional sources sometimes yield the most exciting results. As you explore possible sources, be alert for material that will shed light on your topic and help you to focus on a research question.

One productive way to explore your topic is by asking questions to probe various aspects of it (see 1b.2). As you look through general sources and search your mind for ideas, a variety of questions will suggest themselves to you. Your exploratory research will help you decide whether any of these questions suggests a promising direction for your research: whether enough material is available to enable you to answer the question, whether your question's focus is narrow enough, and whether you are interested in finding an answer to it.

Another way of exploring your topic is to look at those sources that are likely to yield the most helpful material—in the library and outside it. At this early stage, you want to explore the boundaries of your topic, checking to make sure that you can find enough information about it. You do this by looking at the general reference works in your college library. Read quickly and note bibliographical information. Your notes should record potential sources and their locations, not the specific information each source contains. Evaluate each briefly, perhaps rating its importance or noting promising areas. This work can lead you to a research question.

(2)   Focusing on a research question

res pap 40b

As you do exploratory research, your goal is to find a **research question**, the question you want your research paper to answer. This question will guide your exploratory research and your assembly of a working bibliography. By suggesting ideas to look for, it helps you decide which sources to seek out, which to examine first, and which to skip. The answer to your research question will be expressed as your paper's **thesis**, the statement the body of your paper will support.

▌ A Student Does Research: Doing Exploratory Research and Focusing on a Research Question

Planning a Search Strategy

Michael Schrader approached his topic in an orderly, systematic way. He began his work on the topic "Family life of Italian immigrants" by conferring with his instructor, who helped him to outline a search strategy. She suggested that he start by consulting the *Harvard Encyclopedia of American Ethnic Groups,* which has listings for each ethnic group, and perhaps a general encyclopedia, which would provide an overview of his topic. Then she referred him to a colleague in the sociology department, Dr. Harold Kramer, who had recently done some research on Italians in America. To prepare for a meeting with Dr. Kramer, Michael visited the library's reference room. There he looked at the *Harvard Encyclopedia of*

American Ethnic Groups, photocopying the helpful bibliography that followed the entry on Italians, and read the entry "Migration" in the *Encyclopaedia Britannica.*

Consulting an Expert

Michael then met with Dr. Kramer and spent about twenty minutes with him reviewing potential sources. Dr. Kramer directed Michael to two classic works: Herbert Gans's *The Urban Villagers,* a 1962 study of Italian immigrants in Boston, and Nathan Glazer and Daniel F. Moynihan's *Beyond the Melting Pot,* a 1963 study of ethnic groups in New York City. Dr. Kramer strongly suggested that Michael look at the relevant sections of the most recent edition of each.

Next he thought Michael should look for journal articles on his topic, perhaps starting with the *Social Sciences Index,* which lists articles appearing in specialized journals such as the *American Sociological Review* and the *American Journal of Sociology.* He also suggested two specialized indexes, *Public Affairs Information Services* and *Sociological Abstracts,* pointing out that the library subscribes to information services whose databases include these two publications. Dr. Kramer also recommended that Michael read a 1983 *New York Times* article about a major conference on Italian-Americans that Dr. Kramer had attended.

In addition, Dr. Kramer strongly urged Michael to do some field work. Specifically, he felt Michael should interview members of his own family, his grandparents' parish priest, and his grandfather's barber (the barber shop is the center of social life in Italian communities in Italy). He might observe his grandparents' neighborhood firsthand, and he might also ask the Sons of Italy, the largest Italian fraternal order, for material that could help him.

Dr. Kramer had many other suggestions. For instance, he thought Michael could try examining church records, census data, and other primary sources. Michael listened politely and took careful notes in his research notebook, but privately he knew that he did not have time to do everything Dr. Kramer suggested. As Michael took notes, he asked Dr. Kramer to spell unfamiliar names and to clarify his instructions. He listened especially carefully to Dr. Kramer's advice about what his priorities should be. When he got home, he sent a note to Dr. Kramer thanking him for his time.

Asking Questions

Michael's preliminary reading and his meeting with Dr. Kramer suggested many questions he could explore. He listed all these questions in his research notebook.

Why did Italian families come to the United States?
Where did they settle when they came here?
How are families in America different from those who remained in
    Italy?
How did World War II affect the Italian family in Italy?

res
pap
40b

What was the role of the church in maintaining stability in
Italian-American families?
What role does the church play in family life of Italian-Americans
today?
What other institutions contribute to family stability?
What factors threaten family stability?

Establishing Research Priorities
During the next few days, Michael planned his research. He
checked the Gans and the Glazer and Moynihan books out of the library,
noting the titles of other books on his topic in the stacks nearby. He found
the listing for the article Dr. Kramer had suggested—"Scholars Find Bad
Image Still Plagues U.S. Italians," by Walter Goodman—in the *New York
Times Index* and noted the date it appeared. But he decided not to read
the article yet, or to look for any other specific information, until he knew
exactly what he wanted.

He did call his grandparents, asking them for their help in setting up
interviews with the parish priest and the neighborhood barber. In a brief
letter to the local Sons of Italy chapter, he explained the purpose of his
paper and asked these questions: What activities does your group offer?
What services do you provide, and how have they changed in the last fifty
years? Do you collect statistics on family situations? Has your membership increased or decreased in the past fifty years? Finally, he asked for
permission to attend an upcoming Sons of Italy meeting, and he promised
to send a copy of his finished paper to the organization for its files.

Next Michael went back to the library to get assistance with a database search. However, the librarian he consulted told him that such a
search would be more productive later in his research, when he had
focused on a specific research question. This advice led Michael to postpone his search of the indexes Dr. Kramer had suggested.

Michael had a few additional directions to pursue. He remembered
seeing a film on educational television of director Martin Scorsese interviewing his Italian immigrant parents. He thought he might try to locate a
copy of it, and perhaps look at some back issues of *Attenzione,* a popular
magazine for Italian-Americans to which his grandfather subscribed. Perhaps, too, informal telephone surveys of his Italian friends and relatives
might yield information. He kept all these possibilities in mind as he continued his research, recording his ideas—and his progress—in his research notebook.

Focusing on a Research Question
When Michael reviewed his notes on his preliminary reading and
discussion, he was able to decide on the research question he would
pursue in his paper.

How did the Italian family change when Italians
emigrated to the United States?

This question guided the balance of his exploratory research and the
assembly of his working bibliography.

40c   Assembling a Working Bibliography and Making Bibliography Cards

(1)   Assembling a working bibliography

Whenever you encounter a promising source, jot down its complete bibliographic information on a 3″ × 5″ card. As you narrow your focus to one research question and become reasonably sure that you have access to enough good sources to answer that question, you can begin to construct a **working bibliography,** a collection of index cards representing all the sources (print and nonprint) that you will examine later when you do your concentrated research and take notes. This preliminary bibliography is neither permanent nor complete: you may eventually discard some of the sources, and you may add others. Even so, record full and accurate bibliographical data for each source so that you can find it if you do need it.

Because your objective is to evaluate the potential usefulness of a source quickly, you should not waste time on irrelevant reading. One efficient way to assess a work's usefulness is to consult an expert, in person or in print. Even if a book is highly recommended, however, it may not suit your particular needs. You will have to evaluate most sources on your own (see 38b).

res
pap
40c

(2)   Making bibliography cards

When you make up a 3″ × 5″ bibliography card for a source that looks promising, include the following information.

Book	Article
Author(s)	Author(s)
Title (underlined)	Title of article (in quotation
Call number (for future refer-	marks)
ence)	Title of journal (underlined)
City of publication	Volume
Publisher	Date
Date of publication	Inclusive page numbers
Brief evaluation	Brief evaluation

You should also make up cards for interviews (including telephone interviews), meetings, lectures, films, and other nonprint sources of information. Here too you should include all essential information.

Your cards need not follow the format of your final bibliography, but bibliographic information must be *full* and *accurate*. If it is not, you may be unable to find sources later. Include a brief evaluation of each source as you prepare each card, noting the kind of information the source contains, how much information is offered, its relevance to your topic, and its limitations—whether it is biased or outdated, for instance.

As you compile your bibliography cards, continue to review them to see which research question they can best answer. Once you have confirmed your research question, look over your cards again to reevaluate the usefulness of your sources. Select the cards that seem essential, and make them the basis of your working bibliography. Retain *all* the cards you have made, however, even those for sources that do not seem very promising. You may decide to use a rejected source later on when you have a definite thesis for your paper.

Once your exploratory research is finished, check your cards again for completeness. Consider your research question one last time to see that your sources support it sufficiently. If you still have doubts, or if you notice gaps, note where further research is needed.

■ A Student Does Research: Assembling a Working Bibliography and Making Bibliography Cards

During his exploratory research, Michael Schrader recorded evaluations of his sources as well as bibliographical data on his 3″ × 5″ cards. Michael's first advisers had directed him to many of his most important sources and had given him good information about them. He knew, for instance, that the books by Gans and by Glazer and Moynihan, although not recently published, were still considered important works. The participants in the conference on Italian-Americans described in the *New York Times* article represented a variety of viewpoints that, if pursued, would give him a balanced picture. After consulting with his grandparents, Michael was reassured that his personal interviews with the elderly barber and the parish priest would give him a view of changes in various aspects of Italian family life, at least in one community. He also decided that information from his grandparents, though limited to their own experience, would dramatize many points in his paper. He was able to evaluate the usefulness of print sources he found on his own by reading abstracts of articles or skimming the prefaces or indexes of books. One 1948 article in the *American Journal of Sociology*, for instance, still seemed worth reading because, he noticed, it was included in bibliographies in Gans's book and in the *Harvard Encyclopedia of American Ethnic Groups*. By the time he had completed his exploratory research, Michael had a good idea what help his sources would give him, and he had a good start on his working bibliography.

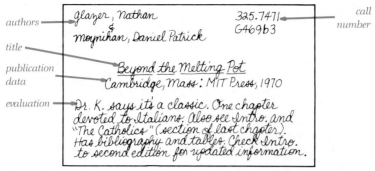

authors

title

publication
data

evaluation

call
number

Glazer, Nathan
&
Moynihan, Daniel Patrick

325.7471
G469b3

Beyond the Melting Pot
Cambridge, Mass: MIT Press, 1970

Dr. K. says it's a classic. One chapter
devoted to Italians. Also see Intro. and
"The Catholics" (section of last chapter).
Has bibliography and tables. Check Intro.
to second edition for updated information.

FIGURE 11

Two of Michael Schrader's bibliography cards are illustrated in Figures 11 and 12.

During his exploratory research, Michael noticed that many of his most promising sources suggested that Italian family life, while still strong, had deteriorated somewhat in this country. On this basis, he decided that he was well on his way to finding an answer to his research question.

**res
pap
40c**

☐   **EXERCISE 2**

Do exploratory research to find a research question for your paper, carefully evaluating the relevance and usefulness of each source. Make a bibliography card for each source, and compile a working bibliography for your research paper in progress. When you have finished, reevaluate your research question to make sure that your sources can answer it, and revise your question—or plan additional research—as you think necessary.

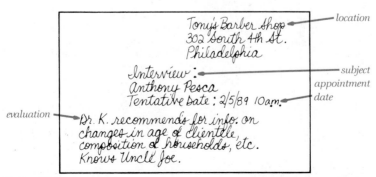

evaluation

location

subject
appointment
date

Tony's Barber Shop
302 South 4th St.
Philadelphia

Interview:
Anthony Pesca
Tentative Date: 2/5/89 10am.

Dr. K. recommends for info. on
changes in age of clientele,
composition of households, etc.
Knows Uncle Joe.

FIGURE 12

40d Developing a Tentative Thesis

Your **tentative thesis** is a preliminary statement of what you think
your research will demonstrate. This statement, which you will
eventually refine into a thesis, is the answer to your research
question.

Your tentative thesis draws a preliminary conclusion about
your topic; further research will lead you to accept, modify, or
reject this assumption. At this point, the tentative thesis provides
a direction for your focused research.

The following table illustrates the progress from subject
area to topic to research question to tentative thesis.

res
pap
40d

Subject Area	Topic	Research Question	Tentative Thesis
Computers	The possible negative effects of computer games on adolescents	Do computer games have any negative effects on adolescents?	Computer games interfere with adolescents' ability to learn.
Feminism	The relationship between the feminist movement and the use of sexist language	What is the relationship between the feminist movement and the use of sexist language?	The feminist movement is largely responsible for the decline of sexist language.
Mood-altering drugs	The use of mood-altering drugs in state mental hospitals	How has the use of mood-altering drugs affected patients in state mental hospitals?	The use of mood-altering drugs has changed the population of state mental hospitals.

As you move through the research process, your tentative thesis and even your research question may change considerably. A line of inquiry may lead to a dead end, a key source may not be available, or a lead you uncover in your research may encourage you to branch out in a new direction. But whether or not you make major adjustments to your tentative thesis, it should grow increasingly more precise, eventually leading you to a thesis your research can support. (For a full discussion of the thesis statement, see 2b.)

■ A Student Does Research: Developing a Tentative Thesis

Michael Schrader's exploratory research led him not just to a clearly focused research question ("How did the Italian family change when Italians emigrated to the United States?"), but also to a possible answer to that question: that, despite his initial assumptions, the family did not in fact change very much at all. The answer to his research question, which he recorded in his research notebook, was the tentative thesis which would guide his focused research.

In the United States, as in Italy, the family is the Italian immigrant's most important resource.   ■

res
pap
40e

☐ EXERCISE 3

Following your own instructor's guidelines, develop a tentative thesis for your research paper.

40e Doing Focused Research and Taking Notes

Once you have located your print sources and mapped out a plan for acquiring firsthand information from other sources, you are ready to begin your focused research and note taking.

(1) Reading sources

As you read, follow the active reading strategies explained in 38a: preview each source, skimming it quickly; read it carefully, highlighting potentially useful material; annotate the source; and take notes.

Your time limit makes it impossible for you to read all your print sources thoroughly, so you must read only those sections of a work that pertain to your topic. Before you begin, survey the work carefully, checking a book's index, and also the headings and subheadings in the table of contents, to determine which pages to read thoroughly and which to skim. Look carefully at abstracts and headings of articles. As you read, respond in writing to your sources, directly on the text where possible, and take additional notes on index cards. You will use this information as you plan and write your paper.

By focusing on sources that are directly relevant to your research question, you narrow your topic further. As you begin to grasp your subject and to develop ideas about it, continue taking careful notes. This whole process is what moves you toward your thesis.

(2)   Making note cards

The advantages of using index cards become obvious when you start arranging and rearranging your material. You seldom know where a particular piece of information belongs at first—or even whether you will use it. You will rearrange your ideas many times, and index cards make it easy for you to add and delete information and to experiment with different sequences. You cannot do that with notes on a tablet or on loose sheets of paper.

As you do library research, take notes on 4″ × 6″ index cards. Transfer the information you have acquired from nonprint sources—interviews, lectures, films, observation, and so on—onto cards, too. Duplicating important sources that do not circulate can save you a lot of time, but do not get carried away at the copying machine. Duplicating every source is expensive and inefficient. And remember, if you encounter a promising new source while you are taking notes, make up a bibliography card for the new source immediately.

At the top of each note card, *include a short heading* that links the information on your card to some aspect of your topic. This heading will help you to make your outline and organize your notes.

Each card should accurately *identify the source* of the information you are recording. You need not include the complete citation, but you must include enough information to identify your source. "Gallo 53" would be enough to send you back to the bibliography card carrying the complete documentation for Patrick Gallo's *Old Bread, New Wine.* For a book with more than one author or one of two books by the same author, you need a more complete reference. "Glazer and Moynihan 16" would suffice for Nathan Glazer and Daniel Moynihan's *Beyond the Melting Pot.*

"Gallo, *Old Bread* 53" would be necessary if you were using more than one book by Patrick Gallo. Be sure to identify each nonprint source with a brief descriptive heading. The rest of the card should carry the information you may decide to include in your paper.

Taking certain precautions at this stage will make the actual writing of your paper easier.

Put only one note on each 4" × 6" card. If you do not do this, you lose the flexibility that is the whole point of this method of note taking.

Include everything now that you will need later to understand your note. After a few weeks you will not remember the meaning of any but the most explicit notes.

Indicate what kind of information appears on your note card. If you copy a source's words, use quotation marks. If you use a source's ideas but not its words, do not use quotation marks. If you write down your own ideas, enclose them in brackets. This system will help you to avoid mixups—and plagiarism (see 38e).

Put an author's comments into your own words whenever possible. Word-for-word copying is probably the most inefficient way to take notes. You may use quotations in your final paper, but for the most part you will summarize and paraphrase your source material (see 38c), adding your own observations and judgments. Putting information into your own words initially prevents you from producing a paper that is a patchwork of other people's words. If you do need to use an author's words, be sure to copy them accurately, transferring the author's exact words, spelling, punctuation marks, and capitalization to your note card.

Figure 13 illustrates two good note-card formats, the first for a print source, the second for a nonprint source.

res
pap
40e

A Student Does Research:
Doing Focused Research and
Taking Notes

Library Work

At the library, Michael now felt ready to do a database search. He had a specific research question in mind, and he thought he was close to deciding on a thesis. This time, the librarian agreed with him. She consulted the **thesaurus,** a printed index listing key words (see 37b.3) and advised him to begin by requesting all citations that included in their titles the phrases *Italian family* and *United States* or *Italian family* and *assimila-*

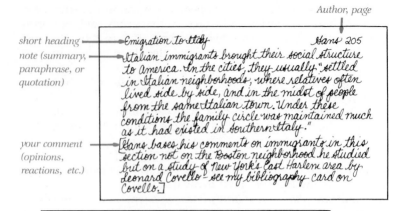

Author, page

short heading

note (summary, paraphrase, or quotation)

Emigration To Italy   Hans 205

Italian immigrants brought their social structure to America. In the cities, they usually "settled in Italian neighborhoods, where relatives often lived side by side, and in the midst of people from the same Italian town. Under these conditions the family circle was maintained much as it had existed in southern Italy."

your comment (opinions, reactions, etc.)

[Hans bases his comments on immigrants in this section not on the Boston neighborhood he studied but on a study of New York's East Harlem area by Leonard Covello – see my bibliography card on Covello.]

Family responsibilities   Sons of Italy meeting

One man responded angrily to Congressman Flavio's suggestion that the 4th ward welcome federal scatter-site housing, insisting the family and the community––not the federal government–– should be responsible for its poor. His statement was applauded.

FIGURE 13

tion. If these key words proved to be too specific to yield enough sources, he could widen his scope somewhat, requesting all citations that included the words *Italy, Italian,* or *Italians* and *family* or *families.*

When Michael received his printout, which included abstracts of articles, he read it carefully to identify the most promising articles. He also found an additional journal article in the *Social Sciences Index.* He took careful notes on most of the articles (periodicals do not circulate), but he duplicated two especially useful pieces so that he would have them at home for reference.

In the card catalog he found the call numbers of several books he had seen mentioned in other sources and then went to the stacks to find these and other books in his working bibliography. He skimmed each source and decided which to check out and what to photocopy. When he could not find a book, he tried to determine whether or not it had been checked out. If it had, he put a hold on it. When the librarian told him that one book on his list that the library did not have could be acquired through an interlibrary loan—but that this would take several weeks—Michael decided to look in another library, but he asked her to request the book anyway.

Fieldwork

With his library research well underway, Michael set out for his grandparents' neighborhood to begin his fieldwork.

Walking Tour. He started by making observations during a walk around the neighborhood. He noticed, for instance, an unusual number of elderly people in the community and a good many more children than in his own suburban neighborhood. He also saw four men in the barber shop, only one of whom was getting a haircut. He made notes on everything he saw and planned to follow up by asking his grandparents for their observations.

Interviews. Michael did not want to conduct a formal interview with his grandparents. He told them at the outset that he needed to find out the differences between family life in Italy and in America. He did not ask prepared questions because he knew from experience that his gregarious subjects would willingly describe their vivid memories. The problem would be to keep them focused on his topic. Michael's primary role as interviewer, then, would be to guide them tactfully back to the topic whenever they digressed. As he expected, his grandparents were extremely generous with their reminiscences. In fact, his grandmother even produced a letter his uncle had written to her in 1980 while he was in the army. Michael thought he might quote a section of it in his paper.

res
pap
40e

Before Michael set out to interview the barber and the priest, he first learned something about them from his grandfather. His grandfather's introductions lent a positive tone to the interviews. Michael assured both men of confidentiality, asking their permission for him to take notes and use a tape recorder. He had also prepared in advance several questions arising from his reading. Michael asked Father D'Ancona about changes in the parish's marriage and divorce rates, in family size, in church attendance, and in sources of family tension. He also asked about general differences between family life in Italy and in the United States and about where the children of the parish settle when they marry, and why.

Michael was able to get a good deal of valuable information from Father D'Ancona, and he planned to transfer his notes to note cards quickly. His interview with Anthony Pesca, the barber, did not go as smoothly. People kept dropping into the barber shop to say hello and trade bits of news and gossip, so Michael finally arranged to continue the interview by telephone. When he reached Mr. Pesca, he had time to ask only a few general questions about the differences between Pesca's American-born and Italian-born customers and about the most obvious value conflicts between parents and children. Mr. Pesca did recommend, however, that Michael look at the community newspaper and the church bulletin board if he wanted to know what was going on in the neighborhood.

Follow-up. Michael felt he had accumulated some significant firsthand information to supplement his reading. He reviewed his notes, transferred portions of them onto 4″ × 6″ index cards, and recorded in his research notebook follow-up questions he wanted to ask and inconsistencies he needed to check. He wrote thank-you notes to Mr. Pesca and Father D'Ancona, taking the opportunity to ask Father D'Ancona another question: whether those who move out of the neighborhood bring their children back to be christened.

Observation. The Sons of Italy had answered Michael's letter and invited him to attend the next meeting. At the meeting, Michael took notes on the proceedings. He noticed that the average age of the members was about fifty and that the questions they asked the speaker revealed a conservative approach to social issues like welfare, taxes, and public housing. Toward the end of the meeting, Michael got some useful information: one particularly vocal person drew applause when he said that family and community—not public tax revenues—should be responsible for supporting and housing indigent persons. Michael jotted down these remarks and the audience reaction. When he got home, he put this one note on an index card (see Figure 13) and also made a bibliography card for the meeting. Then he wrote a brief note thanking the chapter president. ■

res pap 40f

☐ **EXERCISE 4**

Begin focused research for your paper, taking notes from your sources on 4″ × 6″ cards. Remember that your notes should include paraphrase, summary, and your own observations and reactions as well as direct quotations.

Shaping Your Material

40f Deciding on a Thesis ————————————

Even after you have finished your focused research and note taking, your thesis is still not definite. Your focus has been narrowed and modified, but it remains tentative. Now you must refine this tentative thesis so that it accurately reflects your research. You must decide on a **thesis,** a carefully worded statement that draws a conclusion that your research can support. This thesis will give your paper a clear focus and direction and will help you shape your material.

Your thesis should be consistent with the ideas you have formed and the source material you have explored. It should be considerably more focused and detailed than your tentative thesis, presenting an overview of the main points your paper will make.

Tentative Thesis	*Thesis*
Computer games interfere with adolescents' ability to learn.	Because they interfere with concentration and teach players to expect immediate gratification, computer games interfere with adolescents' ability to learn.
The feminist movement is responsible for the decline of sexist language.	By raising public awareness of careless language habits and changing the image of women, the feminist movement has helped to bring about a decline of sexist language.
The development of mood-altering drugs has changed the population of state mental hospitals.	It is the development of psychotropic (mood-altering) drugs, not advances in psychotherapy, that has made possible the release of large numbers of mental patients from state hospitals into the community.

res
pap
40f

If your thesis still does not convey the point you want to make, you may need to do more than just reword it. Sometimes rereading your note cards and grouping ideas in different ways will help you to arrive at an accurate thesis. Sometimes making a scratch outline will help you see what it is your notes can demonstrate (see 40g). Or you may try other techniques—for instance, brainstorming or freewriting with your research question as a starting point, or asking questions about your topic. The thesis you finally decide on depends on the kind and amount of source material you have collected and the ideas you have developed in response to that material.

A Student Does Research: Deciding on a Thesis

As Michael Schrader did his research, he revised his tentative thesis several times. He had begun with "In the United States, as in Italy, the family is the Italian immigrant's most important resource" because this was what he had expected his research to support. As he read, however, he found that, in fact, family ties eroded to some extent after emigration from Italy. He therefore modified his tentative thesis to reflect this realiza-

tion: "Family life while still the Italian immigrant's most important resource, is not as mportant in America as it was in Italy."

Throughout his research, Michael vacillated between these two
statements. He had to decide which stand to take, but he had to take the
stand his research would support, not the one he preferred. When he
reread his note cards, he understood the reason for his indecision: to
some extent his notes supported both thesis statements. His final thesis
represented a compromise between the two.

```
Although emigration from Italy led to assimilation,
which weakened the family system to some extent, the
Italian family in the United States remains
unusually close and stable.
```

This thesis combines the idea of the erosion of family ties with the idea of
continued strength in the family unit. It also indicates that Michael considers the latter more significant and that this is the point his paper will
make.   ▪

□   **EXERCISE 5**

**res
pap
40f**

Read these three passages from various sources. Assume that you are
writing a research paper on the influences that shaped young writers in
the 1920's. What possible thesis statements could be supported by the
information in these passages?

1. Yet in spite of their opportunities and their achievements the genera-
    tion deserved for a long time the adjective that Gertrude Stein had
    applied to it. The reasons aren't hard to find. It was lost, first of all,
    because it was uprooted, schooled away and almost wrenched away
    from its attachment to any region or tradition. It was lost because its
    training had prepared it for another world that existed after the war
    (and because the war prepared it only for travel and excitement). It
    was lost because it tried to live in exile. It was lost because it accepted
    no older guides to conduct and because it formed a false picture of
    society and the writer's place in it. The generation belonged to a
    period of transition from values already fixed to values that had to be
    created.   (Malcolm Cowley, *Exile's Return*)

2. The 1920's were a time least likely to produce substantial support
    among intellectuals for any sound, rational, and logical program. Pre-
    war stability and convention were condemned because all evidences
    of stability seemed illusory and artificial. The very lively and active
    interest in science was perhaps the decade's most substantial contri-
    bution to modern civilization. Yet in this case as well, achievement
    became a symbol of disorder and a source for disenchantment.
    (Frederick J. Hoffman, *The 20's*)

3. Societies do not give up old ideals and attitudes easily; the conflicts
    between the representatives of the older elements of traditional
    American culture and the prophets of the new day were at times as
    bitter as they were extensive. Such matters as religion, marriage, and

moral standards, as well as the issues over race, prohibition, and immigration were at the heart of the conflict.   (Introduction to *The Twenties,* ed. George E. Mowry)

☐   **EXERCISE 6**

Carefully read over all the notes you have collected during your focused research, and develop a thesis for your paper.

40g   Making an Outline

Once you have a thesis, you can plan a structure for your paper. Making an outline helps you to put your research into focus. Once you see how different aspects of your research are connected, you can isolate gaps or inconsistencies in your material.

At some stage of your focused research, you should draw up a **scratch outline,** a list of the major points you will present in the order in which you think you will present them. This informal outline serves as a general guide, and its divisions enable you to sort and categorize your note cards. Before you arrange your cards, however, check each card carefully to make sure it contains only one general idea or one brief related group of facts. If it does not, distribute the information among two or more cards. If the information on two cards overlaps, combine it on one card. Then make sure the headings on all your cards are accurate.

Lay out your note cards on a big table—or on the floor— and sort them into piles, one for each division of your scratch outline. (Keep a miscellaneous pile for notes that do not seem to fit anyplace. You may discard these notes later, or you may find— or make—a place for them in your paper when you construct your formal outline.) With your piles assembled, you can see how well your categories are balanced. What if, for example, most of your notes support only three divisions of a four-division outline? You have two options: (1) do more research to fill out the fourth point; or (2) drop it, narrow the scope of your paper, and revise your thesis. A review of your notes should tell you which course to take.

Guided by the headings in the upper left-hand corner of each card, sort and organize the cards *within* each group. Within each group, put related information together in an order that highlights the most important ideas and subordinates lesser ones. Once again, do some discarding, setting aside note cards that do not fit into your emerging scheme. (And remember to retain these cards. They may fit a new line of inquiry as you

**res
pap
40g**

experiment with different arrangements.) When you have organized the notes in each pile, review the order of the major divisions of your scratch outline to make sure the sequence is right.

When you are satisfied with the arrangement, make a **formal outline,** with subdivisions corresponding to those of your
note cards. This outline can be either a **topic outline,** which uses
short phrases or single words, or a **sentence outline,** which uses
complete sentences. Reviewing your completed outline can reveal potential problems—for instance, whether you lack supporting information in a particular area or have placed too much
emphasis on a relatively unimportant idea. Because an outline is
a skeleton version of your note cards, it can also tell you at a
glance if ideas are illogically or ineffectively placed or if similar
concepts turn up in different parts of your plan. Remember that
this outline is just a guide, and that it very likely will change as
you write your paper. The final outline, produced after your
paper is complete, will serve as a guide for your readers. (For full
information on constructing outlines, see 2d.)

**res
pap
40g**

A Student Does Research: Making an Outline

Michael's scratch outline reflected the four major divisions that emerged
as he did his focused research.

Thesis: Although emigration from Italy led to
assimilation, which weakened the family system to
some extent, the Italian family in the United States
remains unusually close and stable.

    I. Family relationships in Italy
   II. Changes resulting from emigration
  III. Current status of Italian family
   IV. Projections for future of Italian family

Following this outline, Michael sorted his note cards into four groups.
When he was satisfied with his arrangement, he went on to organize the
cards *within* each group, making changes in his outline as he went along.
This process forced him to consider the relevance of each piece of information carefully and to discard material that seemed irrelevant to his
paper. For example, Michael found that the interview with his grandparents seemed too personal, and that much of their conversation was not
relevant to his thesis. As he tried different arrangements of his note cards,
he found himself changing his outline somewhat so that it accurately reflected his material. When he had finished sorting his note cards, he
constructed the topic outline that follows. (A sentence outline appears
with his paper on pp. 631–33.)

Thesis: Although emigration from Italy led to
assimilation, which weakened the family system to some
extent, the Italian family in the United States remains
unusually close and stable.

I. Immigrants from southern Italian villages
    A. In Italy
        1. Separate customs maintained
        2. Identification with family and village
    B. In America
        1. Italian customs recreated
        2. Identification with Italy
II. Italian villagers' reliance on extended family
    A. Patriarchal structure
        1. Mother's responsibilities
        2. Father's responsibilities
    B. Children's roles
        1. Sons
        2. Daughters
III. Italians' insulation from outside world
    A. Family as refuge
    B. Distrust of outsiders
IV. Italian-Americans' aloofness
    A. "Little Italys"
        1. Remain in northeastern United States
        2. Improve neighborhoods
        3. Often make two-generational moves
        4. Live near parents and siblings
    B. Family-oriented society
V. Changes experienced in United States
    A. Employment for women
    B. Parent-child conflicts
    C. Changes in family system
        1. Family less patriarchal
        2. Sex roles less rigid

       3. Friends preferred over relatives
VI. Family closeness and stability
    A. Family closeness
        1. Extended family more important
        2. Elderly relatives welcomed
        3. Emotional and social support provided
    B. Family stability
        1. Low divorce, separation, and desertion rates
        2. Low intermarriage rate

☐   **EXERCISE 7**

Review your notes and your thesis carefully. If you have not already done so, make a scratch outline for your paper. Sort and group your note cards accordingly, and construct a formal outline for your paper.

Writing and Revising

**res
pap
40h**

40h   Writing Your First Draft ────────────

When you are ready to write your first draft, lay out your note cards in the order in which you intend to use them. Follow your outline as you write, moving from one entry to the next and using your note cards as you need them. (It is important to keep referring to the outline because it reminds you of the hierarchy of your ideas and the connections among them.)

    Your paragraphs will probably correspond to subdivisions of your outline, at least in this draft. As you write, make an effort to supply transitions between sentences and paragraphs. These transitions need not be polished; you will refine them in subsequent drafts. But if you leave them out entirely at this stage, you may forget what they are, which will make revising much more difficult.

    The purpose of the first draft is to get ideas down on paper. You will not be able to write the whole draft in a single sitting, but do plan to write in segments that you can complete without interruption. One major heading from your outline, for instance, is a realistic goal for a morning or afternoon of writing. Once you get started, you will find that the time you spent taking careful, accurate notes and preparing a formal outline will pay off.

    If you have trouble, freewriting for a short period can get

you started. Sometimes leaving your paper for only five or ten minutes gives you a fresh view of your material. Another good strategy for overcoming writer's block is beginning your drafting with the section for which you have the most material. This technique allows you to get moving and sometimes even enables you to expand a single section into the entire body of your paper.

As you write, concentrate on getting out your ideas. You should *expect* to revise (see 3b), so postpone precise word choices and refinements of style. As you write, jot down questions to yourself or points that need further checking; leave space for material you plan to add; and bracket phrases or whole sections that you may move or delete—in other words, lay the groundwork for a major revision. Remember that even though you are working from an outline and note cards, you are not bound to follow their content or sequence exactly. As you get your words on paper, new ideas or new connections between ideas may occur to you. Jot them down as they come to mind, and plan to incorporate them in your next draft. If you find yourself deviating from your thesis or outline, reexamine them to see whether the departure is justified. (For information about drafting your essay on a computer, see Appendix A.)

**res
pap
40h**

(1)   The parts of the paper

Like most essays the research paper has an introduction, a body, and a conclusion.

Introduction You open the introduction by identifying your topic and establishing those aspects you will discuss. You can, for example, survey previous research in a field or provide background for a problem. Next, state your thesis—the position you will support in the rest of the paper. You might then go on to summarize briefly your major supporting points (the major divisions of your outline) in the order in which you will present them. This overview of your thesis and support provides a smooth transition into the body of your paper.

You should not spend much time planning an introduction for a rough draft. Your ideas will take shape as you write, and you will want to refine your introduction later to reflect these revisions.

Body As you draft the body of your paper, indicate its direction with strong topic sentences that correspond to the divisions of your outline.

> The immigrants maintained their Old World family
> system in the United States.

You can also use section headings if they are a convention of the discipline in which you are writing.

> Family Solidarity
>
> Family solidarity gave the southern Italian
> family its essential unity and cohesiveness.

Even in your first draft, descriptive headings and topic sentences will help you keep your discussion under control.

Use the patterns of development discussed in 4f to construct the individual sections of your paper, and be sure to connect ideas with transitional words and phrases. The same principles that apply to writing good paragraphs and essays also apply to writing research papers.

Conclusion Restate your thesis in your conclusion. This is especially important in a long paper because by the time your readers get to the end, they may have lost sight of your thesis. After this restatement, you can end your paper with a summary of your major points, a call for action, or perhaps an apt quotation. Just remember that your conclusion must be based on your supporting data and that it should help persuade your readers to accept your thesis.

res pap 40h

(2)   Working source material into your paper

One of the biggest problems students have is taking control of their source material. A good research paper evaluates and interprets its sources, comparing different ideas and synthesizing conflicting points of view. As a writer, your job is to consolidate information from various sources into a paper that presents a coherent view of your topic to your readers. To this end, you should use your sources effectively, paraphrasing and summarizing accurately, smoothly blending your direct quotations into your text, and drawing your own conclusions to create an original paper (see 38d).

Your source material must be truly integrated into your paper. Blend the opinions of one source with those of another so that the relationship between them is apparent. This is easy to do when one source supports another. If, however, two sources present conflicting interpretations, use precise language and accurate transitions to make the contrast readily apparent. (For instance, "Although Gans suggests the situation has changed, a later study reveals. . . .") You will then have a context for making your own comments and drawing conclusions. If different sources present partial pictures of a subject, blend details from each source *carefully*, providing an accurate account of which details come from which source, to reveal the complete picture.

As you write your rough draft, *be sure to keep track of your sources.* You will find it difficult to fill in source information later, so even if you are not sure that a piece of information needs documentation, supply the source anyway and make a final decision when you revise. *Include every source and page number in the text*, as Michael Schrader does in the paragraphs from his draft on pages 626 and 627.

☐   **EXERCISE 8**

Write a draft of your paper, being careful to incorporate source material smoothly and to record source information accurately. Begin with the section for which you have the most material.

40i   Revising Your Drafts

A good way to start revising is to make sure that your thesis still suits your paper. Make an outline of your draft, and compare it with the outline you made before you began the draft. If you find significant differences, you will have to refine your thesis or rewrite sections of your paper. Valuable new ideas do occur to you as you write, so changes are to be expected. Make sure, though, that the rest of your paper and your thesis are consistent with any revisions you make.

When reconsidering your draft, follow the revision procedures that apply to any paper (see 3c–e). Make sure that your introduction and conclusion are effective, and read the body of your paper paragraph by paragraph, asking yourself if thesis and topic sentences are supported with enough material. Should you do more research to find support for certain points? Do you need to reorder the major divisions of your discussion? Should you rearrange the order in which you present your points within those divisions? Do you need section headings? Clearer topic sentences or transitions? Stylistic changes in sentences or individual words?

Next, look at how you have integrated your sources into your paper. Are direct quotations blended with paraphrase, summary, and your own observations and reactions? Are they woven smoothly into the text? Do you introduce your sources and draw original conclusions from your research?

If your instructor allows peer criticism, take advantage of it. The first draft is primarily for you. As you move toward a final draft, however, you should think more and more about your readers' reactions. Testing out your draft at this point can be extremely helpful.

■ A Student Does Research: Writing and Revising

When Michael Schrader revised his first draft, he made changes in structure and style. Using his note cards as a guide, Michael had drafted the paragraphs illustrated in Figure 14. When Michael reviewed this section of his first draft, he saw that he had simply copied material from his note cards without introducing it, adding proper transitions, or drawing his own conclusions. In his next draft (see Figure 15) he tried to incorporate his source material more smoothly, reworking three skimpy paragraphs into one unified whole that blended material from three sources with his own observations and conclusions. By reworking his material, Michael gave it new shape and eliminated the impression that he was parroting other people's ideas.   ■

You will probably take your paper through several drafts, changing different parts of it each time or working on one part over and over again. After editing your original draft thoroughly, you should write or type out a corrected version and make additional corrections on that draft before typing your final version.

> Italian americans, even gangsters, typically maintain very close and highly stable family relationships (Glazer and Moynihan 196).
> In addition, Italians are more likely to have relatives over 60 living with them (Goodman). In a walking tour of a typical Italian-american neighborhood, I noticed a large proportion of elderly residents often accompanied by children and grandchildren as they conducted routine errands and shopping. This convinced me that generations remain close.
> Even though households may not include members of the extended family, the family relationships are close; the family provides close emotional support and serves as a social network (Gans 46).

FIGURE 14

Clear topic sentence
reflects main idea

After they emigrated from Italy to America, the Italian-American family continued to be extremely close. Today Italians remain more likely than most other ethnic groups to have relatives over 60 living with them (Goodman). A walking tour of a typical urban Italian-American neighborhood confirmed this, revealing a large proportion of elderly residents, often accompanied by children and grandchildren as they

Support: examples from
reading and firsthand
observation

conducted routine errands and shopping. Even when members of the extended family are not actually part of the household, the relationships among family members are close; the family provides close emotional support and also serves as a social network (Gans 46). In fact, even Italian-American gangsters typically maintain very close and highly stable family relationships (Glazer and Moynihan 196).

FIGURE 15

To facilitate the revision process, be sure to follow the guidelines recommended in 3b: double-space, write on only one side of your paper, and so on. Be careful to recopy your source information accurately *on each draft*, placing the documentation as close as possible to the material it identifies. (For information on revising with a computer, see Appendix A.)

**res
pap
40j**

☐   **EXERCISE 9**

Following the guidelines in 40i and in 3d and e, revise your research paper until you feel you are ready to prepare your final draft.

40j   Preparing Your Final Draft

With your revision complete, you are ready to prepare the final version of your formal outline (usually a sentence outline) that you will hand in with your paper. Also, you can prepare your documentation and your list of works cited. When you have finished these tasks, edit your draft and all related material—outline, documentation, works cited list, and so on (see 3e.3).

Before you begin typing your paper, stop for a moment to consider its title. Your title should be descriptive enough to tell your readers what your paper is about, but it need not be dull. The following titles are interesting as well as descriptive.

"Is the Welfare State Replacing the Family?" Mary Jo Bane, *The Public Interest*

"The Limited American, the Great Loneliness, and the Singing Fire: Carl Sandburg's 'Chicago Poems.'" William Alexander, *American Literature*

Of course, you would hardly want a witty title for a paper about the death penalty or world hunger. Still, your titles can be engaging and to the point and sometimes even provocative. Often a quotation from one of your sources suggests a likely title. Michael Schrader used "The Italian Family" as the working title for his paper, but "The Italian Family: 'Stronghold in a Hostile Land,'" which included a quotation from one of his sources, conveyed his paper's thesis more dramatically.

Now you can proceed to type your final draft. (See Appendix B for full information on manuscript preparation.) Before you hand in your manuscript, read it through one last time to look for grammar, spelling, or typing errors you may have missed. Pay particular attention to notes and bibliographic references. Remember that every error takes away from the credibility of your whole paper. If your instructor gives you permission, you may make *minor* corrections on your final draft with correction fluid or by neatly crossing out a word or two and writing or typing the correct word or phrase above the line. If you find a mistake that you cannot correct neatly, however, retype the page. Once you are satisfied that your manuscript is as accurate as you can make it, you are ready to hand it in.

☐   **EXERCISE 10**

Edit your research paper, including notes and list of works cited, and then type it according to the format your instructor requires. Proofread your typed copy carefully before you hand it in.

▌ A Student Does Research: The Completed Paper

Michael Schrader's completed research paper, "The Italian Family: 'Stronghold in a Hostile Land,'" appears on the pages that follow. The paper uses MLA documentation. It is accompanied by a sentence outline, explanatory notes, and a list of works cited. Annotations opposite each page of the manuscript comment on stylistic and structural aspects of the paper; explain the format for proper documentation; illustrate various methods of incorporating source material into the paper; and highlight some of the choices Michael made as he moved from note cards to first draft to completed paper.

If your instructor does not require a title page, include all identifying information—your name, the name of the course, your instructor's name, and the date—in the upper left-hand corner of your paper's first page, one inch from the top and flush with the left-hand margin. The title should be centered two spaces below the last line of this heading. Type the number *1* in the upper right-hand corner, one-half inch from the top.

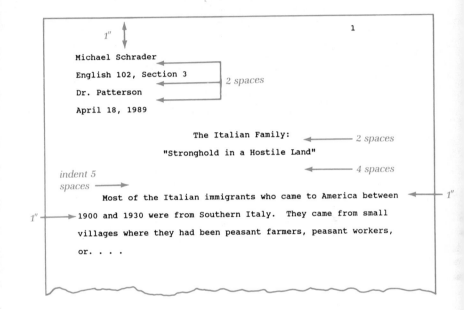

1"   1

Michael Schrader

English 102, Section 3   *2 spaces*

Dr. Patterson

April 18, 1989

The Italian Family: *2 spaces*

"Stronghold in a Hostile Land"

4 spaces

indent 5
spaces

Most of the Italian immigrants who came to America between   *1"*

1"   1900 and 1930 were from Southern Italy. They came from small

villages where they had been peasant farmers, peasant workers,

or. . . .

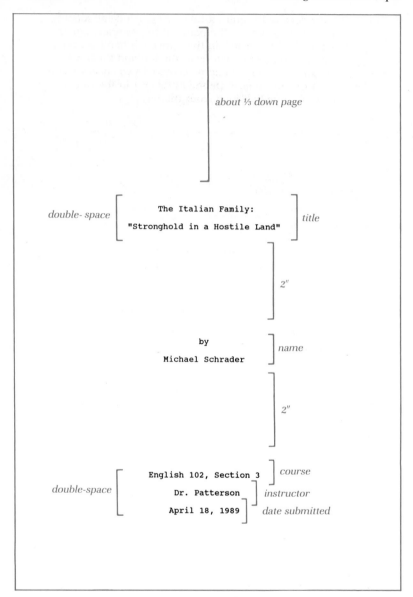

about ⅓ down page

double-space The Italian Family:
"Stronghold in a Hostile Land" *title*

2″

by
Michael Schrader *name*

2″

double-space English 102, Section 3 *course*
Dr. Patterson *instructor*
April 18, 1989 *date submitted*

name, page number ⟶ **Schrader   i**
on every page

center ⟶   **Outline**

double-space ⟶

<u>Thesis</u>: Although emigration from Italy led to assimilation,
which weakened the family system to some extent, the
Italian family in the United States remains unusually
close and stable.

I. Most Italian immigrants came to America from the
Mezzogiorno.

    A. In Italy, each village was separate and unique.

        1. Each village had its own customs.

        2. Villagers identified with family and village.

    B. In America, Italians recreated their Italian villages.

        1. Italians in America established customs and living
conditions like those in Italy.

        2. In America, Italians began to identify with other
Italians.

II. Most Italians from the Mezzogiorno were of the <u>contadini</u>
or <u>giornalieri</u> classes, which relied heavily on the
extended family.

    A. The southern Italian family was usually patriarchal.

        1. The mother maintained the home and managed the
finances.

        2. The father earned the money and made all major
decisions.

    B. Children's roles mirrored adult roles.

        1. Parents prepared their sons to be heads of
households.

      2.   Parents prepared their daughters to love and obey

         their husbands.

III. Family solidarity insulated the <u>contadino</u> family from the

    hostile outside world.

    A.   Barzini sees the family as a "stronghold" and a

      "refuge."

    B.   Italians did not trust outsiders.

IV.   Italians in America have remained somewhat aloof.

    A.   Immigrants often joined fellow villagers in urban

      "Little Italys."

      1.   Most Italians remain in northeastern United

         States.

      2.   Italians are more likely to improve old

         neighborhoods than to relocate.

      3.   Two generations often move to suburbs together.

      4.   Italians are more likely to live near parents and

         siblings than are other ethnic groups.

    B.   Immigrants maintain a family-oriented society in

      America.

V.   The Italian family in America has undergone many changes.

    A.   Some women have sought employment.

    B.   Conflicts have occurred between parents and children.

    C.   The family system has changed.

      1.   The family has become less patriarchal and more

         democratic.

      2.   Third-generation Italian-Americans have relaxed

         the rigid sex roles of Old World society to some

extent.

    3.   Third-generation Italian-Americans often prefer to associate with friends rather than relatives.

VI.   Despite changes, the family remains close and stable.

    A.   The Italian family remains close.

       1.   The extended family has become more important.

       2.   Italians are more likely than other ethnic groups to open their homes to elderly relatives.

       3.   The family provides emotional and social support.

    B.   The Italian family remains stable.

       1.   Italians have low rates of divorce, separation, and desertion.

       2.   Italians have a low intermarriage rate.

Beginning with the first page of your paper, type your last name
and the page number one-half inch from the top in the upper
right-hand corner. Do not use punctuation before or after the
page number. Leave one-inch margins.

Title typed 2″ from top of page

Four spaces between title and first line of paper

¶1: Introduction, presenting background information

Information is available in several sources and is therefore considered general knowledge. For this reason, no documentation is
required.

¶2: Introduces discussion of outline point IA [Each village was self-
contained and unique.]

First two sentences of ¶2 present information available in several
sources; therefore, it does not require documentation.

"Francis Femminella and Jill Quadagno note. . . ." introduces material from source.

The Italian Family:

"Stronghold in a Hostile Land"

¶1   Most of the Italian immigrants who came to America between
1900 and 1930 were from Southern Italy. They came from small
villages where they had been peasant farmers, peasant workers,
or artisans. When they emigrated to America, these southern
Italians brought with them their close family system and their
enormous respect for the family unit. Even with all of the
demands and pressures of adjusting to life in a foreign country,
the family remained the number-one priority for the Italians.
Today, this is still true among Italian-Americans. Some
assimilation did occur after migration, but it did not take
place to the same degree as it did with other ethnic groups.
Although emigration from Italy led to assimilation, which
weakened the family system to some extent, the Italian family in
the United States remains unusually close and stable.

¶2   The southern peasant Italians came to America from a region
known as the Mezzogiorno, which consisted of six provinces south
and east of Rome. Each village in this region was
self-contained, with its own local church and bell tower, and
the language, manners, and mores differed from village to
village. Francis Femminella and Jill Quadagno note that in
Italy, the people did not see themselves as Italians; instead,

<u>61–64</u> refers to four pages of source material, summarized here to convey general ideas rather than specific detail.

¶3: Transitional paragraph. Introduces outline point II [Most Italians from the Mezzogiorno were of the *contadini* or *giornalieri* classes, which relied heavily on the extended family.]

¶4: Outline point IIA [The southern Italian family was usually patriarchal.]

<u>65–66</u> indicates that preceding material summarizes two pages in the source.

Schrader   2

they identified with their families, villages, and towns. When
the Italian villagers migrated to America, they naturally sought
out their **paisani**, their fellow villagers, who had already come
to the United States. There they tried to establish customs and
living conditions similar to those they had left behind. In
fact, Italian immigrants did not really take on an Italian
ethnic identity until after they arrived in America (61-64).

¶3   As Herbert Gans notes, most southern Italians belonged to
the peasant class of farmers called the **contadini** or to the
class of day laborers known as **giornalieri**. Both these groups
were very poor (199-200). Femminella and Quadagno believe that
it was because of this poverty, and because they were exploited
by landowners, that these classes rejected the social
institutions of the rest of the country and came to rely almost
exclusively on the family (65). For the southern Italian,
however, family meant not only husband, wife, and children, but
also grandparents, uncles, aunts, and cousins--in fact, all
blood relatives--and even godparents.

¶4   According to Femminella and Quadagno, the southern Italian
family is usually seen as patriarchal, but although the father
was the head of the family, the mother had a great deal of
power. For example, the mother was responsible for maintaining
the home, the true center of the family; for arranging her
children's marriages; and for managing financial affairs. The
father made all major decisions that involved the family's
relationship with the world at large and, of course, was
responsible for earning a living (65-66). In short, as Virginia

Quotation woven into last sentence of paragraph.

¶5: Outline point IIB [Children's roles mirrored adult roles.]

Old Bread 152 indicates that information is a paraphrase of source
material. A short title is included because two books by Gallo are
used in this paper.

¶6: Outline point IIIA [Barzini sees the family as a "stronghold" and
a "refuge."]

Both references in ¶6 cite the same source; two separate references
are needed because a direct quotation requires its own reference.

Long quotation is introduced by a running acknowledgment.

Over four lines long, this quotation is typed as a block, indented ten
spaces from the left margin, double-spaced, with two spaces
above and below. No quotation marks are used. Because the quotation is a single paragraph, no further paragraph indentation is
needed. Note that in a long quotation, final punctuation is placed
before the parenthetical reference.

The reference qtd. in Gallo, *Old Bread* 152 indicates that the Barzini
quotation was cited in Gallo's *Old Bread, New Wine.*

Schrader   3

Yans-McLaughlin points out, the Italian family was "father-
dominated but mother-centered" (84).

¶5   Children were a very important part of the family, and the
roles defined for them by their parents mirrored traditional
adult roles. For instance, Patrick Gallo observes that although
parents of the peasant class wanted their children to be well
educated in proper behavior, their expectations were very
different for their sons and their daughters. Male children
were taught to be patient, to have inner control over their
emotions, and to show respect for their elders and acknowledge
their wisdom. The females were taught household skills and
encouraged to develop qualities that would enable them to take
their place as the center of the family (Old Bread 152).

¶6   Family solidarity gave the southern Italians a sense of
unity and cohesiveness (Gallo, Old Bread 152). Within the
family, a strong value system protected each individual from a
hostile environment. Luigi Barzini describes the role of the
family in Italian society in this way:

> The Italian family is a stronghold in a hostile land;
> within its walls and among its members, the individual
> finds consolation, help, advice, provision, loans,
> weapons, allies, and accomplices to aid in his
> pursuits. No Italian who has a family is ever alone.
> He finds in it a refuge in which to lick his wounds
> after a defeat, or an arsenal and a staff for his
> victorious drives. (qtd. in Gallo, Old Bread 152)

¶7: Outline point IIIB [Italians did not trust outsiders.]

Quotation is blended into last sentence of paragraph. Direct quotation is used here because wording of original is distinctive and hard to paraphrase.

¶8: Transitional paragraph. Introduces outline point IV [Italians in America have remained somewhat aloof.]

Two references indicate that the paragraph's information comes from two different sources.

Schrader   4

The Italian family was so strongly bonded that it became the most powerful single unit to the individual. Since Southern Italy was perceived as threatening and lawless, the family was the only unit the individual could rely on.

¶7   The southern Italian family rarely became entangled in conflicts outside its own close-knit unit. If individuals placed any type of trust outside the family, they were considered by members of their own family to be taking risks that in the end could cause them to lose everything. To go outside the family for help was just not done since by so doing Italians would be placing themselves in a situation where "the form was alien, the access unequal, the rules unknown, and the justice pernicious" (Gallo, <u>Old Bread</u> 156).

¶8   As Yans-McLaughlin points out, the Italians came to America with a culture that was in many ways different from a rapidly developing industrial society, a society that needed their labor but rejected their "unusual" customs. The extent to which they were successful in staying apart from the larger society can be seen through an examination of the characteristics of Italian-Americans today. Although assimilation has occurred, cultural traditions, maintained by strong family ties, have affected the relationship of the Italians to American society (79). In addition, Yancy, Ericksen, and Juliani believe that the Italians have become increasingly aware that their ethnic identity has been maintained by the stability and isolation of their communities and by their reliance on the services and institutions offered by their communities (399).

¶9: Outline point IVA [Immigrants often joined fellow villagers in urban "Little Italys."]

Paragraph 9 uses paraphrase, summary, and direct quotation from four sources. See page 614 for Michael's note card for Gans 205 (his own comments appear in brackets).

Three references indicate paraphrase of source material.

Original source for Femminella and Quadagno 77: "According to the 1960 census, nearly 70 percent of Italian-Americans are concentrated in the northeastern portion of America."

Original source for Glazer and Moynihan 187: "Even the trek to the suburbs, when it does occur among Italians, is very often a trek of families of two generations, rather than simply of the young. And it is striking how the old neighborhoods have been artfully adapted to a higher standard of living rather than simply deserted, as they would have been by other groups, in more American style."

Original source for Femminella and Quadagno 77: "of all the ethnic groups, Italians most often live in the same neighborhood as their parents and siblings and visit them every week."

See page 614 for Michael's note card for the Sons of Italy meeting.

The last sentence of paragraph 9 sums up main idea of paragraph and clarifies connections among sources' ideas.

¶10: Outline point IVB [Immigrants maintain a family-oriented society in America.]

¶9   Many Italian families migrated to America to join relatives
or friends from their villages. At the beginning of the
immigration, many Italians settled into areas known as "Little
Italys," urban neighborhoods "where relatives often lived side
by side, and in the midst of people from the same Italian town.
Under these conditions, the family circle was maintained much as
it had existed in Southern Italy" (Gans 205). To a great
extent, these "Little Italys" have been maintained, becoming
extended families for their residents. The 1960 census showed
that almost 70 percent of Italian-Americans were still clustered
in the northeastern region of the United States (Femminella and
Quadagno 77). Glazer and Moynihan note that second- and third-
generation Italian-Americans are more likely to work to improve
old neighborhoods than to move. When they do leave the old
neighborhoods, children and parents often move together (187).
National Opinion Research Center surveys have found that
Italians are more likely than other ethnic groups to live in the
same neighborhood as their closest family members and to visit
them regularly (Femminella and Quadagno 77). Italian-Americans
also exhibit a strong sense of loyalty to and responsibility for
their paisani, insisting, for instance, that family and
community should house and support their own indigents rather
than relying on government agencies (Sons of Italy). It is
clear that many Italian-Americans value their ethnic solidarity
and their independence from the larger society.
¶10   Italian immigrants have by and large maintained their

61 indicates paraphrase of a source. The original reads: "The society which these peasants left behind is frequently termed 'familistic' because the nuclear and extended family, rather than the individual or the community, dominated social life to such an extent that an individual's primary social role was his or her role in the family."

¶11: Outline points VA and B [Some women have sought employment. Conflicts have occurred between parents and children.]

Paragraph 11 opens with a transitional phrase ("Despite this cohesiveness. . . .") introducing a discussion of the changes the family experienced in America and relating them to the preceding discussion. The paragraph combines paraphrase, summary, and direct quotation from two print sources and two interviews.

71 indicates paraphrase of a source.

Comments of interview subjects, summarized, are introduced by running acknowledgments. Interview subjects are listed in the Works Cited section at the end of the paper.

The Completed Paper

Schrader   6

Old World family system in the United States. As
Yans-McLaughlin observes, the type of society they left behind
is frequently referred to as "familistic" because the
individual's social role was defined primarily by the family
(61). In the United States as in Italy, the importance of the
family over the community or the individual was maintained, and
this too kept Italians somewhat aloof from outsiders.

¶11   Despite this cohesiveness, the first-generation Italian
family in America was in transition. It was torn between the
Italian culture transmitted by the family and the American
culture transmitted by American institutions. As Femminella and
Quadagno point out, many changes occurred when the family came
to America. When the Italian immigrants arrived in America,
many were faced with difficulties in finding work. It was often
necessary for the mother to go out and find a job. In Southern
Italy, the mother rarely left the house to go out and work, but
in America her employment was often necessary for the family's
survival. Some researchers view this as a breakdown of the
Italian-American family, but others disagree, believing women
took only those jobs that they felt were in line with the family
value system--for instance, work in a factory that employed
other Italian-American women (71). Father Vincent P. D'Ancona,
a parish priest in the heavily Italian South Philadelphia area,
reports that even today a wife's or mother's need to seek
employment remains one of the primary sources of family tension,
whether the need is economic or emotional. Conflicts also
occurred among parents and their children--even though many

Note that even though the quotation begins in the middle of a sentence, an ellipsis mark (. . .) is not used.

Source for <u>Gallo</u>, *Old Bread* 159 uses present tense. To tailor the quotation to the sentence, the verb *are* was dropped.

Notice the reference to the explanatory note at the end of paragraph 11. Michael includes material in this note that would distract readers if it were included in the text. The note itself does not present information that is necessary to the discussion, but it does shed light on Michael's research.

¶12: Outline point VC [The family system has changed.]

Paragraph 12 opens with a transitional phrase ("Although some patterns did remain the same. . . .") to signal movement from discussion of adherence to Old World family system to focus on changes within the family. The topic sentence is supported by information from two sources.

Summary of main points of Campisi article is introduced by a running acknowledgment citing author, date, and title of this important study.

443–49 cites the entire article, indicating that the material represents a summary of the article. Because the author's name appears in the text, only the page numbers are noted parenthetically.

Three references are made to Herbert Gans's book-length study, which is the source of the paraphrase and quotation in this paragraph. Running acknowledgments clearly distinguish information in Gans's original 1962 study from material added in the second edition (1982) and points made by Gans himself from conclusions drawn by Crispino and only cited by Gans.

children agreed that their parents were "too good to fight with"
(Gallo, <u>Old Bread</u> 159). Both Father D'Ancona and barber Anthony
Pesca, long-time residents of South Philadelphia, observe that
today parents and children (despite their love and respect for
each other) regularly engage in heated quarrels over issues like
dating and curfews, use of drugs and alcohol, and church
attendance. The most sensitive issue, Father D'Ancona believes,
is the desire of a child to live outside the community or to
marry a non-Italian.[1]

¶12 Although some patterns did remain the same, the Old World
family system changed as time went on. Paul J. Campisi's often-
cited 1948 study, "Ethnic Family Patterns: The Italian Family
in the United States," examines the changes between the southern
Italians and first- and second-generation Italian-Americans.
One of the major changes this study found was that although the
peasant family was primarily ruled by the father, by the second
generation the family had become democratic, with the father's
position more equal to that of the mother and children. Campisi
also found that the influence of Italian culture was growing
weaker, with more and more cultural values shaped by the larger
society rather than by the family (443-49). As recently as
1962, however, Herbert Gans noted that the husband was still the
breadwinner and the wife's primary responsibilities were still
her home and children. In fact, in Gans's working-class
population, the roles of husband and wife were clearly
differentiated (50-52). But in the 1982 update of his study,
when he considers the third generation of Italian-Americans,

Michael's discussion of the Crispino study cited by Gans blends a
direct quotation smoothly into the sentence. Because it is clear
that Crispino is quoted by Gans, there is no need to include the
abbreviation *qtd. in* as part of the citation. Ellipses indicate the
omission of an unnecessary word. The original source reads: "Increasingly, friends replaced family members as preferred associates, however, and many were not Italian-American or peers they
had known since childhood." The last sentence sums up the paragraph's main point and ends with a reference to an explanatory
note. Again, the information in this note would have interrupted
the flow of the discussion, so the decision to put it in a note was
a sensible one.

¶13: Outline point VIA [The Italian family remains close.]

Paragraph 13 begins with a transitional phrase ("Despite these
changes. . . ."), which introduces information directly supporting
the paper's thesis.

The paragraph includes summary, paraphrase, and direct quotation
from five different sources—four print sources and Michael's
own observations. See page 636 for an earlier draft of part of this
paragraph.

Palisi 49–50 indicates that the preceding sentences summarize information from two pages of a source.

Goodman's article is one page long; therefore, no page number is
included in the citation.

Gans finds that even in Italian urban neighborhoods, "the
traditional social segregation of husbands and wives has been
reduced considerably, although some men remain reluctant to help
with childrearing and housework" (231).   In his study, Gans
cites an unpublished study of Bridgeport, Connecticut, by James
Crispino.   As Gans notes, Crispino reports that while his third-
generation Italian-Americans felt very close to their relatives,
more and more often "friends replaced family members as
preferred associates. . .and many were not Italian-American or
peers they had known since childhood" (230).   It is clear, then,
that some aspects of the traditional family systems are
changing.[2]

¶13   Despite these changes, however, the Italian-American family
has remained close-knit and stable.   After coming to America,
the Italian-American family continued to be extremely close.   In
fact, in one study, which involved fifty first-generation and
ninety second-generation Italian-American adults from an ethnic
neighborhood in New York City, researchers found that the
extended family was more important to second-generation than to
first-generation Italian-Americans.   Although the second-
generation family had generally become larger, relatives tended
to live in closer physical proximity and to have closer and more
extensive social ties with one another (Palisi 49-50).   Today,
Italians remain more likely than members of most other ethnic
groups to have relatives over sixty living with them (Goodman).
A walking tour of a typical urban Italian-American neighborhood
seems to support this conclusion, showing a large proportion of

¶14: Outline point VIB [The Italian family remains stable.]

Paragraph 14 combines paraphrase, summary, and direct quotation from three sources.

Ellipsis mark indicates that nonessential material has been deleted from the end of a sentence.

¶15: Conclusion

Topic sentence of paragraph 15 indicates paragraph will draw paper's ideas together.

Schrader   9

elderly residents,often accompanied by children and
grandchildren as they go about routine errands and shopping.
Even when members of the extended family are not actually part
of the household, the relationships among family members are
close; the family provides emotional support and also serves as
a social network (Gans 46). In fact, even Italian-American
gangsters typically maintain very close and highly stable family
relationships (Glazer and Moynihan 196).

¶14   The stability of the Italian family is reflected in the low
rates of divorce and intermarriage. The 1970 census showed that
only about 3 percent of all Italian-Americans were divorced and
that the divorce rate was not significantly higher for younger
Italians. Alfred J. Tella, special adviser to the Director of
the Census Bureau, notes that despite increasing affluence,
Italian-Americans retain closer family ties than other groups.
Tella sees the fact that Italians as a group get fewer divorces
as one indication of this continued closeness (Goodman). Glazer
and Moynihan support this view. They say: "That the family is
'strong' is clear. Divorce, separation, and desertion are
relatively rare. Family life is considered the norm for
everyone. . ." (197). Moreover, two separate studies show
Italians to have one of the lowest intermarriage rates;
therefore, it can be concluded that they retain a high degree of
ethnic identity (Femminella and Quadagno 74).

¶15   Several conclusions may be drawn about the Italian-American
family today. Assimilation has occurred, but the notion of the
importance of family has been passed down from generation to

Direct quotations from a personal letter and a scholarly source both stress the continuing importance of family to Italian-Americans, reinforcing the paper's thesis.

generation and has remained an important characteristic of the
Italian-American family. As Frank Mucci, a third-generation
Italian-American says, "You can't do without your family, and
they can't do without you. Your family has to stay your first
responsibility, no matter what happens." So far, the stable
Italian family system has survived through the years, and it
seems likely to continue to do so. As Patrick Gallo notes, "The
family for the southern Italian remains the supreme societal
organization" (Ethnic 87).

This page receives a number.

Notes 1 and 2 are explanatory notes that provide supplementary information to the reader.

Schrader   11

center   ━━━━━━━━━━━━▶   Notes
double-space ━━━━━━━━━━━▶

[1]Because of the many interruptions in the interview with Mr. Pesca, I was unable to determine which issue he views as most likely to produce serious conflict between parents and children.

[2]The nomination of Congresswoman Geraldine Ferraro, an Italian-American wife and mother, as the Democratic vice-presidential candidate in 1984 seems to support the impression that the role of women in the Italian family is changing.

Every page of the Works Cited section receives a number.

The first entry illustrates the correct form for a signed journal article by a single author. Note that it provides inclusive pagination.

Use alphabetical order

Indent 5 spaces

Double-space
between and
within entries

Entry illustrates form for a book with more than one author.

Entry identifies the subject of a personal interview.

Entry refers to an article by Femminella and Quadagno in a book edited by Mindel and Habenstein.

The List of Works Cited contains two works by Patrick Gallo. Note that the author's name is not repeated; instead, three unspaced hyphens, followed by a period, are used.

Entry identifies a book with a single author.

Entry refers to a signed newspaper article, giving section and page number of the article.

Entry refers to a personal letter.

Entry identifies the subject of a telephone interview.

Entry refers to a meeting the author attended.

Entry refers to a neighborhood walking tour taken by the author.

1"   Schrader   12

center ⟶   Works Cited
double-space ⟶

Campisi, Paul J. "Ethnic Family Patterns: The Italian
    Family in the United States." <u>American Journal of Sociology</u>
    53 (1948): 443-49.

D'Ancona, Father Vincent P. Personal interview. 10 Feb. 1989.

Femminella, Francis X., and Jill S. Quadagno. "The Italian
    American Family." <u>Ethnic Families in America</u>. Ed. Charles
    H. Mindel and Robert W. Habenstein. New York: Elsevier,
    1976. 61-88.

Gallo, Patrick J. <u>Ethnic Alienation</u>. Cranbury, N.J.:
    Fairleigh Dickinson UP, 1974.

---. <u>Old Bread, New Wine</u>. Chicago: Nelson-Hall, 1981.

Gans, Herbert J. <u>The Urban Villagers</u>. 2nd ed. New York: Free,
    1982.

Glazer, Nathan, and Daniel Patrick Moynihan. <u>Beyond the Melting
    Pot</u>. 2nd ed. Cambridge, Mass.: MIT P, 1970.

Goodman, Walter. "Scholars Find Bad Image Still Plagues U.S.
    Italians." <u>New York Times</u> 15 Oct. 1983, late ed.: B25.

Mucci, Frank. Letter to author's grandmother. 17 Nov. 1980.

Palisi, Bartolomeo S. "Ethnic Generation and Family Structure."
    <u>Journal of Marriage and Family</u> 28 (1966): 49-50.

Pesca, Anthony. Telephone interview. 10 Feb. 1989.

Sons of Italy Meeting. Philadelphia, Pa. 30 March 1989.

Walking Tour. South Philadelphia. 10 Feb. 1989.

Entry refers to a signed journal article with more than one author.

Yancy, William L., Eugene Ericksen, and Richard N. Juliani.
    "Emergent Ethnicity: A Review and Reformulation." <u>American</u>
    <u>Sociological Review</u> 41.3 (1976): 391-403.

Yans-McLaughlin, Virginia. <u>Family and Community: Italian</u>
    <u>Immigrants in Buffalo</u>. Ithaca: Cornell UP, 1977.

SECTION VIII

Writing
Special
Assignments

41

Writing Essay Examinations

Taking examinations is a skill, one you have been practicing throughout your life as a student. Although both short-answer and essay examinations require you to study, to recall what you know, and to budget your time carefully as you write your answers, only essay questions ask you to synthesize information and to arrange ideas in a series of clear, logically connected sentences. To write an essay examination, you must do more than memorize facts; you must see the relationships among many facts and be able to infer from them a meaning that is greater than the sum of its parts.

41a Planning an Essay Examination ────────

Because you write quickly and under pressure during an examination, you may be tempted to skip the planning and revision stages. But if you write in a frenzy and hand in your examination without a second glance, you are likely to produce a disorganized or even incoherent answer. With advance planning and sensible editing, you can write an answer that clearly demonstrates your understanding of the material. Following the strategies listed below will help you to write effective answers.

(1) Review your material

Be sure you know beforehand the scope and format of the examination. How much of your text and class notes will the examination cover—the entire semester's work or just the material covered since the last test? Will you have to answer every question, or will you be able to choose among alternatives? Will the examination be composed entirely of short-answer questions, or will it include one-sentence, one-paragraph, or essay-length answers? Will the examination emphasize your recall of specific facts or your ability to demonstrate your understanding of the course material by drawing conclusions?

Examinations challenge you to recall and express in writing what you already know—what you have read, what you have heard in class, what you have reviewed in your notes. Before you even begin your examination, then, you will have studied for it: rereading your text and class notes, underlining key points, and perhaps outlining key sections of your notes. If you are preparing for a short-answer examination, you may memorize facts—the definition of pointillism, the date of Queen Victoria's death, the formula for a quadratic equation, three reasons for the fall of Rome, two examples of conditioned reflexes, four features of a feudal economy, six steps in the process of synthesizing vitamin C—without analyzing their relationship to one another or to a body of knowledge as a whole. When preparing for an essay examination, however, you must do more than remember information; you must also make connections among ideas and relate them to the question you are considering.

When you are certain that you know what to expect, you can prepare by carefully reviewing the appropriate material. You should also try to anticipate the essay questions your instructor might ask. As you study, note key concepts and the connections among them, and practice answering likely essay questions. Try out potential questions on classmates, and see whether you can brainstorm together on a few of them.

**exam
41a**

(2)   Consider your audience and purpose

The *audience* for any examination is almost always the instructor who prepared it. He or she already knows the answers to the questions and a great deal more about the subject. As you read the questions, think about what your instructor has emphasized in class. Although you want to respond to your instructor's question, you may certainly arrange material in a new way or use it to make your own point. Do keep in mind, however, that your *purpose* is to demonstrate that you understand the material, not to make clever remarks or bring up irrelevant information. Instructors read a lot of examinations, and anything you can do to ease their task will be appreciated.

(3)   Read through the entire examination

Your time is usually limited when you take an examination, so you must plan carefully. How long should a "short-answer" or "one-paragraph" or "essay-length" answer be? How much time should you devote to answering each question? The question itself may specify the length of your answer, so look for that information. More often the point value of each question or the number of questions on the examination will determine how much time to spend on each answer. If an essay question is worth 50 out of 100 points, for example, you will probably have to spend at least half and perhaps more of your time planning, writing, and proofreading your answer.

Before you begin to write, read the entire examination carefully to determine your priorities and your strategy. First, make sure that your copy of the test is complete and that you understand the format each question requires. If you need clarification, ask your instructor or proctor for help. Then decide where to start. Responding first to short answers (or to essay questions whose answers you are sure of) is usually a good strategy because it ensures that you will not get bogged down in a question that baffles you, leaving too little time to write a strong answer to a question you understand well. Moreover, starting with the questions you are sure of can help build your confidence.

**exam
41a**

(4)   Read each question very carefully

To answer correctly, you need to know exactly what the question asks. As you read any essay question, you may find it helpful to underline key words.

> Sociology: Distinguish among Social Darwinism, instinct theory , and sociobiology, giving examples of each.

> Music: Explain how Milton Babbitt used the computer to expand Schoenberg's twelve-tone method.

> Philosophy: Define existentialism and name three influential existentialist works, explaining why they are important.

Look at the verbs contained in the instructions: explain, compare, contrast, trace, evaluate, discuss, interpret, analyze, summarize, describe, classify, or give examples. Then look at the other words. If the question calls for a *comparison and contrast* of *two* styles of management, a *description* or *analysis* of *one* style, no matter how well done, will not be acceptable. If the question asks for causes *and* effects, a comprehensive discussion of causes alone will not do. The wording of the question suggests what you should emphasize. For instance, an American history instructor would expect very different answers to these two examination questions.

1. Give a detailed explanation of the major *causes* of the Great Depression, noting briefly some of the effects of the economic collapse on the United States. (1 hour)
2. Give a detailed summary of the *effects* of the Great Depression on the United States, briefly discussing the major causes of the economic collapse. (1 hour)

Although these questions look somewhat alike, the first calls for an essay that focuses on *causes*, whereas the second asks you to stress the *effects*.

(5)   Brainstorm to find ideas

Once you understand the question, begin brainstorming. The brainstorming process will help reveal the scope of your knowledge. If you know your material well, you may be able to brainstorm mentally. Otherwise, write down your ideas. Quickly list all the relevant points you can remember; then select key points and delete less promising ones. You might even tentatively arrange the key points you have arrived at. A quick review of your ideas should lead you toward a workable thesis for your essay answer. (Sometimes, particularly if you are very familiar with your material and have a thesis firmly in mind, you may find it more practical to brainstorm as you prepare your scratch outline.)

exam
41b

41b   Shaping an Examination Answer ────

(1)   Finding a thesis

Often you can expand the examination question into a thesis statement. For example, the second American history examination question above suggests this thesis.

> EFFECTIVE THESIS: The Great Depression, caused by the American government's economic policies, had major political, economic, and social effects on the United States.

A good thesis addresses all aspects of the question but highlights only relevant concerns. The following thesis statements are not effective.

VAGUE: The Great Depression, caused largely by profligate spending patterns, had a number of very important results.

INCOMPLETE: The Great Depression caused major upheaval in the United States.

IRRELEVANT: The Great Depression, caused largely by America's poor response to the 1929 crash, had more important consequences than World War II.

(2) Making a scratch outline

Because time is limited, you should plan your answer before you write it. Therefore, once you have a suitable thesis, you should make a scratch outline of your major points.

Write on the inside cover of your exam book or on its last sheet. Use the pattern of development suggested by the question—process, classification, or cause and effect, for instance—to shape your outline, and list your supporting points in their approximate order. Once you have an outline, check it against the question to make certain it covers everything the question requires and only what the question requires.

A scratch outline for an answer to the American history question might look like this.

exam
41b

QUESTION: Give a detailed summary of the effects of the Great Depression on the United States, briefly discussing the major causes of the economic collapse.

THESIS: The Great Depression, caused by the American government's economic policies, had major political, economic, and social effects on the United States.

SUPPORTING POINTS: *Causes* American economic policies: income poorly distributed, factories expanded too much, more goods produced than could be purchased.

Effects
1. Economic situation worsened—farmers, businesses, workers, and stock market all affected.
2. Roosevelt elected—closed banks, worked with Congress to enact emergency measures.
3. Reform—TVA, AAA, NIRA, etc.
4. Social Security Act, W.P.A., P.W.A.

An answer based on this outline will correctly follow a *cause-and-effect* pattern (see 4f.5), with an emphasis on effects, not causes.

41C   Writing and Revising an Examination Answer

Referring to both thesis and outline, you can now write your answer. A simple statement of your thesis that summarizes your answer is your best introduction, for it shows the reader that you are addressing the question directly. Do not bother crafting an elaborate or unusual introduction; your time is precious, and so is your reader's.

To develop the body of the essay, follow your outline point by point, using clear topic sentences and transitions to indicate your progression and to help the reader see that you are answering the question in full. Such signals, along with parallel sentence structure and repeated key words, make your answer easy to follow.

The most effective conclusion for an essay examination is a clear, simple restatement of the thesis or a summary of the essay's main points.

Essay answers should be complete and detailed, but they should not contain irrelevant material. Every unnecessary fact or opinion only increases your chance of error. Do not repeat yourself or volunteer unrequested information. Padding is instantly recognized. Do not express your own feelings or opinions (unless such information is specifically called for). Use objective evidence, and be sure to support all your general statements with specific facts or examples.

Finally, leave enough time to reread and revise what you have written. Try to view your answer from a fresh perspective. Have you left out words or written illegibly? Is your thesis clearly worded? Does your answer support your thesis and answer the question? Are your facts correct, and are your ideas presented in logical order? Review your topic sentences and transitions. Check sentence structure and word choice, spelling and punctuation. If a sentence—or even a whole paragraph—seems irrelevant, cross it out. If you suddenly remember something you want to add, you can insert a few additional words using a caret (∧). Neatly insert a longer addition at the end of your answer, box it, and write a brief note telling your instructor where it belongs.

In the following essay answer, written in response to a single-question one-hour examination, notice how the student restates the question in her thesis and keeps the question in focus by using words like *cause, effect, result, response,* and *impact.*

exam
41c

Introduc-
tion—
Thesis
rephrases
exam
question

1   The Great Depression, caused by the American government's economic policies, had major political, economic, and social effects on the United States.

Summa-
rizes
policies
leading to
Depression
(causes)

2   The Depression was precipitated by the stock market crash of October 1929. But its actual causes were more subtle; they lay in the U.S. government's economic policies. First, personal income was not well distributed. Although production rose during the 1920's, the farmers and other workers got too little of the profits; instead, a disproportionate amount of income went to the richest 5 percent of the population. The tax policies at this time made inequalities in income even worse. A good deal of income also went into development of new manufacturing plants. This expansion stimulated the economy but encouraged the production of more goods than consumers could purchase. Finally, during the economic boom of the 1920's the government did not attempt to limit speculation or impose regulations on the securities market; it also did little to help build up farmers' buying power. Even after the crash began, the government made mistakes: instead of trying to counter the country's deflationary economy, the government focused on keeping the budget balanced and making sure the United States adhered to the gold standard.

exam
41c

Transition
from
causes to
effects

3   The Depression, devastating to millions of individuals, had a tremendous impact on the nation as a whole. Its political, economic, and social consequences were great.

Early
effects

4   Between October 1929 and Roosevelt's inauguration on March 4, 1932, the economic

Paragraphs 4-8 summarize important results in chrono- logical order

situation grew worse. Businesses were going bankrupt, banks were failing, and stock prices were falling. Farm prices fell drastically, and hungry farmers were forced to burn their corn to heat their homes. There was massive unemployment, with millions of workers jobless and humiliated, losing skills and self-respect. President Hoover's Reconstruction Finance Corporation made loans available to banks, railroads, and businesses, but he felt state and local funds (not the federal government) should finance public works programs and relief. Confidence in the president declined as the country's economic situation worsened.

More effects: Roosevelt's emergency measures

5   One result of the Depression, then, was the election of Franklin Delano Roosevelt. By the time of his inauguration, most American banks had closed, 13 million workers were unemployed, and millions of farmers were threatened by foreclosure. Roosevelt's response was immediate: two days after he took office, he closed all banks and took steps to support the stronger ones with loans and prevent weak ones from reopening. During the first hundred days of his administration, he kept Congress in special session. Under his leadership, Congress enacted emergency measures designed to provide "Relief, Recovery, and Reform."

More effects: Roosevelt's reform measures

6   In response to the problems caused by the Depression, Roosevelt set up agencies to reform some of the conditions that had helped to cause the Depression in the first place. The Tennessee Valley Authority, created in May of 1933, was one of these. Its purposes were to control floods by building new dams and improving old ones and to

provide cheap, plentiful electricity. The TVA
improved the standard of living of area farmers
and drove down the price of power all over the
country. The Agricultural Adjustment
Administration, created the same month as the
TVA, provided for taxes on basic commodities,
with the tax revenues used to subsidize farmers
to produce less. This reform measure caused
prices to rise.

More effects: NIRA, etc.

7   Another response to the problems of the
Depression was the National Industrial Recovery
Act. This act established the National Recovery
Administration, an agency that set minimum wages
and maximum hours for workers and set limits on
production and prices. Other laws passed by
Congress between 1935 and 1940 strengthened
federal regulation of power, interstate commerce,
and air traffic. Roosevelt also changed the
federal tax structure to redistribute American
income.

**exam
41c**

More effects: Social Security, etc.

8   One of the most important results of the
Depression was the Social Security Act of 1935,
which established unemployment insurance and
provided financial aid for the blind and disabled
and for dependent children and their mothers.
The Works Progress Administration (W.P.A.) gave
jobs to over 2 million workers, who built public
buildings, roads, streets, bridges, and sewers.
The W.P.A. also employed artists, musicians,
actors, and writers. The Public Works
Administration (P.W.A.) cleared slums and created
public housing. In the National Labor Relations
Act (1935), workers received a guarantee of
government protection for their unions against
unfair labor practices by management.

Conclusion   9   As a result of the economic collapse known
as the Great Depression, Americans saw their
government take responsibility for providing
immediate relief, for helping the economy
recover, and for taking steps to ensure that the
situation would not be repeated. The economic,
political, and social impact of the laws passed
during the 30's are still with us today, helping
to keep our government and our economy stable.

Notice that the student does not digress by describing the conditions of people's lives in detail, blame anyone in particular, discuss the president's friends and enemies, or consider parallel events in other countries. She covers only what the question asks for. Notice, too, how topic sentences—like "One result of the Depression. . . ."; "In response to the problems caused by the Depression. . . ."; and "One of the most important results of the Depression. . . ." —keep the primary purpose of the essay in focus and serve as a guide for the reader.

A well-planned essay like this one is not easy to write. Consider the following answer to the same question.

**exam
41c**

*No clear
thesis
Vague,
subjective
impressions
of the
Depression*   1   The Great Depression is generally considered
to have begun with the Stock Market Crash of
October 1929 and to have lasted until the defense
build-up for World War II. It was a terrible
time for millions of Americans, who were not used
to being hungry or out of work. Perhaps the
worst economic disaster in our history, the
Depression left its scars on millions of
once-proud workers and farmers who found
themselves reduced to poverty. We have all heard
stories of businessmen committing suicide when
their investments failed, of people selling
apples on the street, and of farmers and their

families leaving the dust bowl in desperate search of work. My own grandfather, laid off from his job, had to support my grandmother and their four children on what he could make from odd carpentry jobs. This was the Depression at its worst.

2   What else did the Depression produce? One result of the Depression was the election of Franklin Delano Roosevelt. Roosevelt immediately closed all banks. Then Congress set up the Federal Emergency Relief Administration, the Civilian Conservation Corps, the Farm Credit Administration, and the Home Owners' Loan Corporation. The Reconstruction Finance Corporation and the Civil Works Administration were two other agencies designed to provide *Gratuitous* Relief, Recovery, and Reform. All these agencies *summary* helped Roosevelt in his efforts to lead the nation to recovery while providing relief and reform.

3   Along with these emergency measures, Roosevelt set out to reform some of the conditions he felt were responsible for the economic collapse. Accordingly, he created the Tennessee Valley Authority (TVA) to control floods and provide electricity in the Tennessee Valley. The Agricultural Adjustment Agency levied taxes and got the farmers to grow less, *Unsup-* causing prices to rise. Thus these agencies, the *ported* TVA and the AAA, helped to ease things for the *generali-* *zation* farmers.

4   The National Industrial Recovery Act established the National Recovery Administration, which was designed to help workers. It established minimum wages and maximum hours, both of which made conditions better for workers.

exam 41c

Why were these agencies important? What did they do?

Other important agencies included the Federal Power Commission, the Interstate Commerce Commission, the Maritime Commission, and the Civil Aeronautics Authority. Changes in the tax structure at about this time made the tax system fairer and eliminated some inequities. Roosevelt, working smoothly with his cabinet and with Congress, took many important steps to ease the nation's economic burden.

Discussion of Roosevelt irrelevant to topic

5   Roosevelt, despite the fact that he was handicapped by polio, was a dynamic president. His fireside chats, which millions of Americans heard on the radio every week, helped to reassure Americans that things would be fine. This increased his popularity. But he had problems, too. Not everyone agreed with him. Private electric companies opposed the TVA, big business disagreed with his support of labor unions, the rich did not like the way he restructured the tax system, and many people saw him as dangerously radical. Still, he was one of our most popular presidents ever, and he was elected to four terms.

exam
41c

Undeveloped information

6   Social Security Act——unemployment insurance, aid to blind and disabled and children

WPA——built public projects

PWA——public housing

National Labor Relations Act——strengthened labor unions

This essay only partly answers the examination question. It devotes too much space to unnecessary elements—an emotional introduction, repetition of words and phrases, gratuitous summaries, and unsupported generalizations. Without a thesis to guide her, the writer easily slips into a discussion that considers only the immediate impact of the Depression and never discusses its causes or long-term effects. Although the body paragraphs do provide the names of many agencies created by the Roosevelt administration, they do not explain the purpose of most of them. It appears that the student considers the mere formation of the agencies, not their contributions, to be the Depression's most significant result.

Because the student took a time-consuming detour, she ends up having to list points at the end of the essay without discussing them fully. Although it is better to include undeveloped information than to skip it altogether, an undeveloped list has shortcomings. Essay answers are by definition made up of full paragraphs, and many teachers will not give credit if you do not write out your answer in full. More important, you cannot effectively show logical or causal relationships in a list. This student's digression also left her no time to sum up her main points, even in a one-sentence conclusion.

41d Writing Paragraph-length Examination Answers

Some essay questions ask for a paragraph-length answer, not a full essay. A paragraph should be just that: not one or two sentences, not a list of points, not more than one paragraph.

A paragraph-length answer should be *unified* by a clear topic sentence. Just as an essay answer begins with a thesis statement, a paragraph answer opens with a topic sentence that summarizes what the paragraph says. You should generally phrase this sentence to echo the examination question. The paragraph should also be *coherent*—that is, its statements should be linked by transitions that move the reader along. And the paragraph should be as *well developed* as possible, with enough relevant detail to convince your reader that you know what you are talking about. (See Chapter 4 for a full discussion of paragraphs.)

A typical paragraph-length answer to a question on a business examination might look like this.

QUESTION: In one paragraph, define the term *management by objectives,* give an example of how it works, and briefly discuss an advantage of this approach.

ANSWER: As defined by Horngren, management by

Definition   objectives is an approach in which a manager and

his or her superior together formulate goals, and

plans by which they can achieve these goals, for

Example   a forthcoming period. For example, a manager and

a superior can formulate a responsibility

accounting budget, and the manager's performance can then be measured according to how well he or she meets the objectives defined by the budget.

Advantage The advantage of this approach is that the goals set are attainable because they are not formulated in a vacuum. Rather, the objectives are based on what the entire team, with knowledge of the constraints on its task, reasonably expects to accomplish. As a result, the burden of responsibility is shifted from the superior to the team: the goal itself defines all the steps needed for its completion.

In this answer, key phrases ("As *defined* by. . . ."; "For *example* . . . ."; "The *advantage* of this approach. . . .") point to the various aspects of the question being covered. The writer volunteers no more than the question asks for, and his use of the wording of the question helps make the paragraph orderly, coherent, and emphatic.

The following paragraph is less successful.

Sketchy, casual definition Management by objectives is when managers and their bosses get together to formulate their goals. This is a good system of management

No example given because it cuts down on hard feelings between managers and their superiors. Since they set the goals together, they can make sure they're attainable by considering all possible influences, constraints, etc., that might occur.

Vague This way neither the manager nor the superior gets all the blame when things go wrong.

exam 41d

This student may know what *management by objectives* is, but his paragraph sounds more like a casual explanation to a friend than an answer to an examination question. Just as with an essay-length answer, a paragraph answer will not be effective unless you take the time to read the question carefully, plan your response, and outline your answer before you begin to write. It is always a good idea to echo the wording of the question early in your answer and to reread your answer to make sure it explicitly addresses the question.

Student Writer at Work: Writing Essay Examinations

The long student paragraph below was written in response to the following question on an American literature examination.

QUESTION: In one paragraph, explain the thematic relationship between the vignettes and the short stories in Hemingway's *In Our Time*, giving a few brief examples to illustrate the parallels.

Edit this rambling answer to eliminate irrelevancies, redundancies, and superfluous information. Your revision should be a tightly organized paragraph introduced by a topic sentence that explicitly addresses the question.

ANSWER:

Hemingway's short—story collection <u>In Our Time</u> consists of fifteen short stories and sixteen brief vignettes. The vignettes originally appeared as a separate collection, published in 1924 as <u>in our time</u>. Later they were interspersed with short stories to form <u>In Our Time</u> (1925). In both the stories and the vignettes there is an undercurrent of brutality and emptiness and tragedy. In "On the Quai at Smyrna," the introduction, the narrator talks about women and their dead babies, and about mules with broken legs being pushed off the dock into the water. In the first short story, "Indian Camp," a boy, Nick Adams (who appears in several of the stories and vignettes), accompanies his father, a physician, to an Indian camp to deliver a baby. There he not only sees the woman's suffering but also the Indian father who has slashed his own throat. A thread of senseless violence runs through the vignettes. Some depict women suffering through childbirth and people in pain. Many treat the senseless brutality of war in grim, matter—of—fact accounts of bombings and shootings, descriptions of dead bodies lying about, and even a sketch of Nick himself wounded and paralyzed. Five vignettes are about bullfighting, with vivid images of dead and wounded bulls

and matadors. The short stories, some of which are about
Nick Adams, deal with unpleasant things like lies, bitter
arguments, lack of communication, and drinking. One
depicts deserted land where a thriving lumber mill once
stood; another describes an encounter with a washed-up
former champion fighter. "My Old Man" is about a jockey
who is killed in an accident; his son witnesses his
death. In "Big Two-Hearted River" Nick Adams, apparently
recovering from terrible war experiences, takes refuge in
a deserted, burned-out setting and takes comfort in the
rituals of setting up camp. The collection takes its
title from a prayer: "Give us peace in our time, O Lord."

exam
41

42

Writing About Literature

42a Approaching Literature

Literature is different from other kinds of writing. First, it uses certain special forms and is more likely than other kinds of writing to use particular kinds of language. Second, literature has the power to stimulate the imagination. Third, literature is open to interpretation. Understanding the special qualities of literature is the first step toward appreciating its possibilities.

Writing with Special Features When writers create literary works, they work within certain categories called **genres:** short stories, novels, plays, poems, and the like. Each of these types of literature has its own special characteristics, and all rely for their effect on special kinds of language. If you recognize these special forms and features, literary works will be more accessible to you because you will be able to approach literature with some basic assumptions about what it will and will not be.

Imaginative Writing Literature is imaginative writing, and to create a mood it depends on experiments with language and form. The effect of a literary work is determined not just by its ideas but also by the artful arrangement of words and images and events. Literature has nearly limitless possibilities. In experimental modern fiction a short story can consist entirely of an alumni magazine's class notes or a short series of diary-like entries moving backward in time to the narrator's birth; it can even consist of just a single paragraph. A poem may sound like prose, and may be just a few lines—or just a few words—long. It may be written entirely in lower-case letters, or its lines may be arranged in the shape of an animal. A play may have only a single character, or it may have a narrator who speaks directly to the audience. A novel may switch narrators with each section or chapter, and it can skip from one time period to another. In other words, literature has the power to surprise readers by doing what they do not expect it to do: by breaking the rules.

Writing That Is Open to Interpretation When you read a work of literature, you do not read to magically discover the one correct meaning the writer had in mind. In fact, you will appreciate a literary work most fully if you approach it with the assumption that it has no single, carved-in-stone meaning but that it can be interpreted in a variety of ways. Writers do not necessarily set out to convey one particular message. Sometimes a story starts out with one purpose and develops another, different one. Sometimes it has *no* set purpose but is simply an experiment in form or style. Sometimes a work means one thing to a writer when the work is written and means something quite different years (or even hours) later.

Similarly, readers do not see only one meaning: a poem may seem to have one meaning to you when you first read it and another meaning or meanings when you read it more carefully. And of course the same work can have markedly different meanings to different readers, who bring to it a variety of assumptions and experiences. These experiences color their responses, leading them to notice certain details and overlook others, to find special significance in some objects and events and not in others, and to respond positively or negatively to an image or idea or character.

The "meaning" of a literary work is created by the interaction among a writer, a text, and its readers. This should not suggest that a work can mean whatever a reader wants it to mean; ultimately, your interpretation of a work must be consistent with the stylistic signals or thematic suggestions or patterns of imagery in the text. These elements may be subject to interpretation, but they cannot be ignored. Remembering that each writer is part of a community of writers, part of a discipline with its own history, context, and conventions, will also aid your understanding. For instance, the knowledge that a writer is influenced by a particular literary movement, alluding to another work, using a conventional figure of speech or a familiar plot, paying homage to another writer, or experimenting with an unusual poetic form may help bring a work to life. Ideally, your writing about works of literature will represent a balance between what you know or can learn about the special qualities of literature and the unique reactions you bring to a work.

lit
42a

42b Reading Literature ———————————————

When you read a literary work about which you plan to write, you use the same active reading strategies you apply to other works you read: you *preview* the work, *highlight* it to identify key ideas and cues to meaning, and *annotate* it carefully (see 38a).

As you read and take notes, you focus on the special concerns of literary analysis, considering elements like a short story's plot, a poem's rhyme or meter, or a play's characters. You look for *patterns*, related groups of words, images, or ideas that run through a work. You look for *anomalies*, unusual forms, unique uses of language, unexpected actions by characters, or unusual treatments of topics. And you look for *connections*, links with other literary works, with historical events, or with biographical information.

Then, you *list* to organize into a useful order the material you have identified in your notes. As you arrange related material into lists, a structure for your paper may emerge.

These active reading strategies, tailored to the special demands of writing about literature, help you to detect relationships among ideas, to uncover links to other works, and to find material to write about and a shape and central focus for your essay.

**lit
42c**

42c Writing About Literature ———————————————

Just as literature is different from other kinds of writing, the writing you do *about* literature is also different. When you write about literature, you respond to the possibilities created by experiments in form, content, and style. As you write, you observe the conventions of literary criticism, which has its own discipline-specific vocabulary and forms. When you write about literature, you also respond to certain typical assignments. For instance, you may be asked to *analyze* a work, taking it apart to consider one or more of its elements—perhaps the plot or characters in a story, or the use of language in a poem. Or, you may be asked to *interpret* a work, trying to discover its possible meanings. Less often, you may be called upon to *evaluate* a work, to judge its merits and consider whether or not its author has been successful. More specifically, you may be asked to trace the critical or popular reception to a work; to compare two works by a single writer (or by two different writers); to consider the relationship between a work of literature and a historical context or literary movement. You may be asked to consider the effect on a literary work of certain circumstances or events in a writer's life, or the relationship between a work and its author's writing process. You may be asked to analyze a character's motives or the relationship between two characters, or to comment on a story's setting or tone or resolution. In any case, understanding exactly what you are expected to do will make your writing task easier.

When you write about literature, you use all the skills you bring to any writing assignment: your goal is to make a point and support it with appropriate references to the work under discussion or to related works or secondary sources. However, because literary criticism is a discipline with its own special requirements, you must follow the conventions your audience expects.

* Use present tense verbs when discussing works of literature: "The character of Mrs. Mallard's husband *is* not developed. . . . "
* Use past tense verbs only when discussing historical events ("Owen's poem conveys the destructiveness of World War I, which at the time the poem *was* written *was* considered to be. . . . "), presenting biographical data ("Her first novel, published in 1811 when Austen *was* 36, . . . "), or identifying events that occurred prior to the time of the story's main action ("Miss Emily is a recluse; since her father *died* she has lived alone except for a servant").
* Support all points with specific, concrete examples from the work you are discussing: briefly summarize key events, quote dialog or description, describe characters or setting, or paraphrase ideas.
* Combine paraphrase, summary, and quotation with your own interpretations, weaving quotations smoothly into your paper.
* Be careful to acknowledge all sources, including the work or works under discussion. Introduce the words or ideas of others with a reference to the source and end with appropriate parenthetical documentation. Enclose the words of others in quotation marks.
* Use correct reference form for fiction, poetry, and drama. When citing a part of a short story or novel, supply the page number (168); for a poem, give the line numbers (2–4); for a play, include act, scene, and line numbers (I. iv. 29–31). When quoting more than four lines, follow the rules for setting off lines of prose or poetry (see 30e).
* Avoid subjective expressions like *I feel, I believe, It seems to me,* and *In my opinion.* These weaken your paper by suggesting that its ideas are "only" your opinion and have no inherent validity.
* Do not rely on excessive plot summary. Your goal is to draw a conclusion about one or more works and to support that conclusion with pertinent details. If a plot detail supports a point you wish to make, a *brief* summary alluding to a particular event or arrangement of events is acceptable. But plot summary is no substitute for analysis.

lit
42c

- Use accurate literary terms (see 42f). For example, be careful to avoid confusing *narrator* or *speaker* with *author*; feelings or opinions expressed by a narrator or character do not necessarily represent those of the author. You should not say, "In the poem's last stanza, Frost expresses his indecision" when you mean that the poem's speaker is indecisive.
- Identify works of literature correctly in your text: *underline* titles of novels and plays; set titles of short stories and poems within quotation marks.

42d Writing About Fiction

This section traces the writing process of a student, Carla Watts, preparing a paper on a 1983 short story by Gary Gildner.

Sleepy Time Gal

In the small town in northern Michigan where my father lived as a young man, he had an Italian friend who worked in a restaurant. I will call his friend Phil. Phil's job in the restaurant was as ordinary as you can imagine—from making coffee in the morning to sweeping up at night. But what was not ordinary about Phil was his piano playing. On Saturday nights my father and Phil and their girlfriends would drive ten or fifteen miles to a roadhouse by a lake where they would drink beer from schoopers and dance and Phil would play an old beat-up piano. He could play any song you named, my father said, but the song everyone waited for was the one he wrote, which he would always play at the end before they left to go back to the town. And everyone knew of course that he had written the song for his girl, who was as pretty as she was rich. Her father was the banker in their town, and he was a tough old German, and he didn't like Phil going around with his daughter.

My father, when he told the story, which was not often, would tell it in an offhand way and emphasize the Depression and not having much, instead of the important parts. I will try to tell it the way he did, if I can.

So they would go to the roadhouse by the lake, and finally Phil would play his song, and everyone would say, Phil, that's a great song, you could make a lot of money from it. But Phil would only shake his head and smile and look at his girl. I have to break in here and say that my father, a gentle but practical man, was not inclined to emphasize the part about Phil looking at his girl. It was my mother who said the girl would rest her head on Phil's shoulder while he played, and that he got the idea for the song from the pretty way she looked when she got sleepy. My mother was not part of the story, but she had heard it when she and my father were younger and therefore had that information. I would like to intrude further and add something about Phil writing the song, maybe show him whistling the tune and going over the words slowly and carefully to get the best ones, while peeling onions or potatoes in the restaurant; but my father is already driving them home from the roadhouse, and saying how patched up his tires were, and how his car's engine was a gingerbread of parts from different makes, and some parts were his own invention as well. And my mother is saying that the old German had made his daughter promise not to get involved with any man until after college, and they couldn't be late. Also my mother likes the sad parts and is eager to get to their last night before the girl goes away to college.

So they all went out to the roadhouse, and it was sad. The women got tears in their eyes when Phil played her song, my mother said. My father said that Phil spent his week's pay on a new shirt and tie, the first tie he ever owned, and people kidded him. Somebody piped up and said, Phil, you ought to take that song down to Bay City—which was like saying New York City to them, only more realistic—and sell it and take the money and go to college too. Which was not meant to be cruel, but that was the result because Phil had never even got to high school. But you can see people were trying to cheer him up, my mother said.

Well, she'd come home for Thanksgiving and Christmas and Easter and they'd all sneak out to the roadhouse and drink beer from schoopers and dance and everything would be like always. And of course there were the summers. And everyone knew Phil and the girl would get married after she made good her promise to her father because you could see it in their eyes when he sat at the old beat-up piano and played her song.

That last part about their eyes was not, of course, in my father's telling, but I couldn't help putting it in there even though I know it is making some of you impatient. Remember that this happened many years ago in the woods by a lake in northern Michigan, before television. I wish I could put more in, especially about the song and how it felt to Phil to sing it and how the girl felt when hearing it and knowing it was hers, but I've already intruded too much in a simple story that isn't even mine.

Well, here's the kicker part. Probably by now many of you have guessed that one vacation near the end she doesn't come home to see Phil, because she meets some guy at college who is good-looking and as rich as she is and, because her father knew about Phil all along and was pressuring her into forgetting about him, she gives in to this new guy and goes to his hometown during the vacation and falls in love with him. That's how the people in town figured it, because after she graduates they turn up, already married, and right away he takes over the old German's bank—and buys a new Pontiac at the place where my father is the mechanic and pays cash for it. The paying cash always made my father pause and shake his head and mention again that times were tough, but here comes this guy in a spiffy white shirt (with French cuffs, my mother said) and pays the full price in cash.

    And this made my father shake his head too: Phil took the song down to Bay City and sold it for twenty-five dollars, the only money he ever got for it. It was the same song we'd just heard on the radio and which reminded my father of the story I just told you. What happened to Phil? Well, he stayed in Bay City and got a job managing a movie theater. My father saw him there after the Depression when he was on his way to Detroit to work for Ford. He stopped and Phil gave him a box of popcorn. The song he wrote for the girl has sold many millions of records, and if I told you the name of it you could probably sing it, or at least whistle the tune. I wonder what the girl thinks when she hears it. Oh yes, my father met Phil's wife too. She worked in the movie theater with him, selling tickets and cleaning the carpet after the show with one of those sweepers you push. She was also big and loud and nothing like the other one, my mother said.

    Carla's assignment was to select a short story from a list supplied by her instructor and write an essay exploring a central idea of the story. Carla began by reading the story through quickly. Then she reread it more carefully, highlighting and annotating as she read. A portion of the highlighted and annotated story appears below.

When do events take place?

    In the small town in northern Michigan where my father lived as a young man, he had an Italian friend who worked in a restaurant. I will call his friend Phil. Phil's job in the restaurant was as ~~ordinary~~ as you can imagine—from making coffee in the morning to sweeping up at night. But what was ~~not ordinary~~ about Phil was his piano playing. On ~~Saturday nights~~ my father and Phil and their ~~girl-friends~~ would drive ten or fifteen miles to a ~~roadhouse~~ by a lake where they would ~~drink beer~~ from ~~schoopers~~ and ~~dance~~ and Phil would play an old beat-up ~~piano~~. He could play any song you named, my father said, but the song everyone waited for was the one he wrote, which he would always play at the end before they left to go back to the town. And everyone knew of course that he had written the song for his girl, who was as pretty as she was rich. Her father was the banker in their town, and he was a tough old German, and he didn't like Phil going around with his daughter.

    My father, when he told the story, which was not often, would tell it in an offhand way and emphasize the ~~Depression~~ and not having much, instead of the important parts. I will try to tell it the way he did, if I can.

Sat. nights = special- dancing, beer, etc.

fal fal sti

    Carla's instructor required the students in the class to keep journals of their progress. In her journal, Carla recorded notes to which she could refer when she wrote her paper. These notes expressed her reactions to the story.

    First, she made a brainstorming list to help her find ideas. Before she could decide on a topic for her paper, she had to decide on one area on which to focus. To do this, she found it helpful to brainstorm separately on plot, character, setting, point of view, and tone and style, to see which suggested the most promising possibilities. Then she brainstormed further to explore the story's theme and the way each of its elements contributed to that central idea. Carla's brainstorming list appears below.

Brainstorming List

Plot
Flashback—narrator remembers story father told.

Story: Phil loved rich banker's daughter, wrote song for her, girl married someone else, Phil sold song for $25.00, married another woman.

Ordinary, predictable story of star-crossed lovers from different backgrounds ("Probably by now many of you have guessed. . . . "), but what actually happened isn't important.

Characters
Phil—Italian, never went to high school, ordinary job in restaurant, extraordinary piano player.

Girl—no name, pretty, rich, educated

Narrator—?

Mother—romantic

Father—mechanic; gentle, practical

Setting
"small town in northern Michigan"

Past—when narrator's father was a young man

In woods—near lake

Roadhouse—dancing, drinking, beat-up piano

Point of View
Narrator tells story to reader, but there's a story inside this story.

Father tells his story, mother qualifies his version (she's "not part of the story" but has heard it), narrator tells how they told it.

Point of view keeps shifting—characters compete to tell the story ("I would like to intrude further . . . ").

Father's version: stresses Depression, hard times

Mother's version: stresses relationship, "sad parts"

Reader encouraged to find own point of view; narrator of story addresses readers.

Three characters invent and reinvent and embellish story each time they tell it.

Tone and Style

Conversational style—narrator talks to reader ("Well, here's
    the kicker part.")
Like fairy tale (girl = "as pretty as she was rich"; father = a
    gentle but practical man)
Casual speech: contractions, "well," "some guy," etc.

Theme

Which is "real" story?
Subject of Phil's story = missed chances, failure.
Subject of narrator's story = the past? Values of different
    characters? Conflict between real events and memory?

When Carla looked over her brainstorming list, she saw at once
that character and point of view suggested the most interesting possibilities for her paper. After she reviewed her brainstorming list and her annotations, she went on to brainstorm further about the story's title because she felt sure that it could be an important source of material. She was so interested in the significance of the title that she asked around until she found someone who told her that it was the name of a real song—and supplied the lyrics.

lit
42d

Brainstorming List—Title

"Sleepy Time Gal" = name of song. Mother says Phil got
    inspiration for song from the way his girl looked when
    she got sleepy.
Does title of story refer to girl or to song?
Date of song? Lyrics?
Song = fantasy about the perfect married life that should
    follow the evenings of dancing: in a "cottage for two"
    wife will be happy cooking and sewing for her husband and will end her evenings early. She'll be happy
    to forget about dancing and be a stay-at-home wife.
Lyrics describe what Phil wants and never gets.

When Carla's brainstorming was complete, she decided to identify patterns by **listing.** She arranged some of the most useful material from her brainstorming lists and her annotations into the following lists of related ideas, reflecting the three versions of Phil's story presented in "Sleepy Time Gal."

Mother's Version

Likes the sad parts and the details of the romance: the
   way the father made the daughter promise not to get
   involved with a man until she finished college, the
   way the women got tears in their eyes when Phil
   played his song.
Remembers girl's husband had French cuffs.
Remembers Phil's wife = "big and loud"
Notes people were trying to cheer Phil up
Remembers girl resting head on Phil's shoulder, and how he
   got idea for song.

Father's Version
Depression/money: mentions Phil's patched tires and engine,
   how he spent a week's pay on new clothes, how girl's
   husband pays cash for a new Pontiac
Times were tough

Narrator's Version
Facts of story—but wants to add more about Phil's process
   of writing song (because he, like Phil, = artist?), more
   about romance ("you could see it in their eyes").
   Wants to embellish story. *"I wish I could put more*
   in. . . ."
Wonders about parts father doesn't tell—e.g. what girl
   thinks when she hears song.
Talks to reader about his creative process: "I couldn't help
   putting it in. . . . "

Carla's notes and lists eventually suggested a possible thesis for
her paper: "'Sleepy Time Gal' is a story that is not about the 'gal' of the
title or about the man the narrator calls Phil but about the different viewpoints of its three narrators." Guided by this tentative thesis, she went on
to draft, write, and revise her paper, following the process detailed in
Chapters 2 and 3. The final draft of Carla's paper begins below. Annotations have been added to identify the conventions that apply to essays
about works of fiction.

```
                    Whose Story?

Midway through Gary Gildner's short story         Title in quotation
                                                  marks
"Sleepy Time Gal" the narrator

acknowledges, "I've already intruded too
```

much in a simple story that isn't even
mine" (215). But whose story is "Sleepy
Time Gal"? It is presented as the tale of
Phil, an ordinary young man of modest
means who falls in love with a rich young
woman, writes a song for her, and loses
both the woman and the song, as well as
the fame and fortune the song could have
brought him, apparently because he is
unwilling to fight for either. But
actually, "Sleepy Time Gal" is not Phil's
story, and it is not the story of the girl
he loves; the story belongs to the three
characters who compete to tell it.

The story they tell is a simple one;
it is also familiar. Phil is a young man
with an ordinary job. He has little
education and no real prospects of doing
anything beyond working in a restaurant
doing menial jobs. He is in love with a
girl whose father is a rich banker, a girl
who goes to college. Phil has no more
chance of marrying the girl than he has of
becoming educated or becoming a
millionaire. He has written a song for
her, but he is doomed to sell the rights
to it for twenty-five dollars. Phil may
be a man with dreams and expectations
beyond the small Michigan town and the
roadhouse, but he does not seem to be
willing to struggle to make his dreams
come true. He never achieves with his
"gal" the happy married life his song
describes; his dreams remain just dreams,
and he settles for life in the dream world
of a movie theatre.

Quotation introduced

Parenthetical documentation

Thesis

Brief plot summary combined with interpretation

**lit
42d**

   The character who seems to be the
author of Phil's story is the narrator's
father: he is the only one who knew Phil
and witnessed the story's events, and he
has told it again and again to his
family. But the story he tells reveals
more than just what happened to Phil; it
says a lot about his own life, too. The
father is a mechanic who eventually leaves
the small Michigan town in which the story
is set for Detroit. As the narrator
observes, he is "a gentle but practical
man" (214). We can assume he has seen some
hard times; he sees Phil's story only in
the context of the times, and "times were
tough" (216). The narrator says, "My
father, when he told the story, . . .
would tell it in an offhand way and
emphasize the Depression and not having
much, instead of the important parts"
(214). In the father's version, seemingly
minor details are important: Phil's
often-mended car engine, "a gingerbread of
parts from different makes" (215), and
incidents like how Phil spent a week's pay
on a new shirt and tie, "the first tie he
ever owned" (215), and how the girl's
husband paid cash for a new Pontiac.
These details are important to the father
because they have to do with money. He
sees Phil's story as more about a
particular time (the Depression era) than
about particular people. Whenever he
hears Phil's song on the radio, he
remembers that time.

   The narrator's mother, however, sees

*Father's
perspective*

*Past tense used to
identify events
that occurred
before story's
main action.*

*Ellipses indicate
words omitted
from quotation.*

lit
42d

Phil's story as a romantic, timeless story
of hopelessly doomed lovers. She did not
witness the story's events, but she has
heard the story often. According to the
narrator, she "likes the sad parts and is
eager to get to their last night before
the girl goes away to college" (215). She
remembers how the women in the roadhouse
got tears in their eyes when Phil played
the song he wrote. The mother's selective
memory helps to characterize her as
somewhat romantic and sentimental,
interested in people and their
relationships (the way the girl's father
made her promise to avoid romantic
entanglements until after college, the way
Phil's friends tried to cheer him up) and
in visual details (the way the girl rested
her head on Phil's shoulder, the French
cuffs on her husband's shirt). In the
interaction between the characters she
sees drama and even tragedy. The
sentimental story of lost love appeals to
her as the story of lost opportunity
appeals to the father.

The narrator knows the story only
through his father's telling and retelling
of it, and he says, "I will try to tell it
the way he did, if I can" (214). But this
is impossible: he enhances the story, and
he makes it his own. He is the one who
communicates the story to the readers, and
he ultimately decides what to include and
what to leave out. His story reflects
both his parents' points of view: the
focus on both characters and events, on

Mother's perspective

Point supported by specific references to story.

Narrator's perspective

lit 42d

romance and history. In telling Phil's
story, he tells the story of a time,
recreating a Depression—era struggle of a
man who could have made it big but wound
up a failure; however, he also recounts a
story about people, a romantic,
sentimentalized story of lost love. And,
he tells a story about his own parents.

  The narrator, like Phil, is creative;
he needs to convey the facts of the story,
but he must struggle to resist the
temptation to add to them: to add more
about how Phil went about writing the
song, "maybe show him whistling the tune
and going over the words slowly and
carefully to get the best ones" (214–15),
more about the romance itself. The
narrator is clearly embellishing the
story—for instance, when he says everyone
knew Phil and the girl would get married
because "you could see it in their eyes"
(215), he admits that this detail is not
in his father's version of the story—but
he is careful to identify his own
contributions, explaining, "I couldn't
help putting it in there (215). The
narrator cannot help wondering about the
parts his father does not tell, and he
struggles to avoid rewriting the story to
include them. Sometimes, he cannot help
himself, and he apologizes for his lapses
with a phrase like "I have to break in
here . . ." (214). But, for the most
part, the narrator knows his place, knows
it is not really his story to tell: "I
wish I could put more in, especially about

Narrator's
perspective
continues.

lit
42d

the song and how it felt to Phil to sing
it and how the girl felt when hearing it
and knowing it was hers, but I've already
intruded too much in a simple story that
isn't even mine" (215).

    Phil's story is, as the narrator
acknowledges, a simple one, almost a
cliché. But Gary Gildner's story, "Sleepy
Time Gal," is much more complex. In it,
three characters create and recreate a
story of love and loss, ambition and
failure, each contributing the details
they feel should be stressed and, in the
process, revealing something about
themselves and about their own hopes and
dreams.

Conclusion:
reinforces thesis.

Works Cited

Gildner, Gary. "Sleepy Time Gal." Sudden Fiction:
    American Short—Short Stories. Ed. Robert
    Shapard and James Thomas. Salt Lake City: G. M.
    Smith, 1986. 214—16.

**lit
42d**

Carla's paper focuses on the story's shifting point of view and the contributions of the three central characters to Phil's story. She supports her
thesis with specific references to "Sleepy Time Gal"—quotations, summary, and paraphrase—and interprets the story's events in light of the
points she is making. Her paper does not include every item in her notes,
nor should it: she selects only those details that support her thesis.

    The following checklist can guide your analysis and inter-
pretation of works of fiction.

Checklist for Analyzing and Interpreting Fiction

Plot
- How do events relate to one another?
- How do single events relate to the work as a whole?
- How are events arranged in time?

- How does the arrangement of events in time compare to the order in which events are presented in the story?
- What conflicts occur in the story?
- How do these conflicts move the plot along?
- How are these conflicts developed and resolved?
- How are events juxtaposed? How does this juxtaposition affect the development of the story?
- Does the story include flashbacks? foreshadowing?

Characters
- What conflicts exist between the protagonist(s) and the antagonists(s)?
- What traits, feelings, and values are exhibited by the characters?
- How do the characters relate to one another?
- What do the characters say? What do they *not* say?
- Are the characters fully developed? stereotypes?
- Are the major characters changed by events? How?
- Do the major characters learn from experience? How?
- Does this knowledge affect the other characters and the plot? How?

Setting
- When and where does the action take place?
- What is the relationship between the setting and the plot?
- How does the setting create the mood of the story?
- How does the setting affect the characters?

Point of View
- Is the story told in the first person ("I") or in the third person ("he," "she," or "they")?
- How much does the narrator know about the events in the story?
- Is the narrator detached or involved?
- Is the narrator a character in the story?
- Does the narrator understand the full signficance of his or her statements?
- Is the narrator trustworthy?

Tone and Style
- How would you characterize the tone of the story (light, serious, bitter, etc.)?
- Does the narrator's tone reveal approval or disapproval?
- Is there any apparent discrepancy between the narrator's stated
- feelings and the feelings and attitude of the author?
- Does the work include any examples of irony?
- What words or phrases are repeated throughout the work?
- Does the work include any language that is unusual or that highlights a particular character or event?
- Does the work include figures of speech? symbols? patterns of imagery?

Theme
  • What is the central or dominant idea of the work?
  • What issues are considered in the work?
  • What conflicts are presented in the work?
  • How does each element of the story contribute to its theme?

42e Writing About Poetry

When you write a paper about poetry, you follow the process you use when you write any paper about literature. However, you concentrate on the elements poets use to create and enrich their work: voice, form, sound, meter, language, and tone. Each of these elements contributes to the poem's central idea, or theme.

Daniel Johanssen, a student in an introductory literature course, followed this process as he planned an essay about Delmore Schwartz's 1959 poem "The True-Blue American."

DELMORE SCHWARTZ (1913–1966)
The True-Blue American

Jeremiah Dickson was a true-blue American,
For he was a little boy who understood America, for he felt
    that he must
Think about *everything;* because that's *all* there is to think
    about,
Knowing immediately the intimacy of truth and comedy,
Knowing intuitively how a sense of humor was a necessity   5
For one and for all who live in America. Thus, natively, and
Naturally when on an April Sunday in an ice cream parlor
    Jeremiah
Was requested to choose between a chocolate sundae and a
    banana split
He answered unhesitatingly, having no need to think of it
Being a true-blue American, determined to continue as he
    began: 10
Rejecting the either-or of Kierkegaard, and many another Euro-
    pean;
Refusing to accept alternatives, refusing to believe the choice of
    between;
Rejecting selection; denying dilemma; electing absolute
    affirmation:
    knowing
        in his breast   15
            The infinite and the gold
            Of the endless frontier, the deathless West.
"Both: I will have them both!" declared this true-blue American
In Cambridge, Massachusetts, on an April Sunday, instructed

By the great department stores, by the Five-and-Ten, 20
Taught by Christmas, by the circus, by the vulgarity and gran-
    deur of Niagara Falls and the Grand Canyon,
Tutored by the grandeur, vulgarity, and infinite appetite grati-
    fied and
        Shining in the darkness, of the light   25
On Saturdays at the double bills of the moon pictures,
The consummation of the advertisements of the imagination of
    the light
Which is as it was—the infinite belief in infinite hope—
    of Columbus,
        Barnum, Edison, and Jeremiah Dickson.

■   Daniel's assignment was an open one; his instructor had asked only
that each student choose a poem and react to it. After he chose his poem,
Daniel read it several times. Then he read it aloud, paying special attention to the sound of the poem. As he read, he highlighted and annotated
the poem, as illustrated below.

DELMORE SCHWARTZ (1913–1966)
The True-Blue American

Jeremiah Dickson was a (true-blue)   = *loyal; faithful*
    American,   (*also = "red white*
For he was a little boy who un-   *+ blue"?*)
    derstood America, for he felt
    that he must

lit
42e

Think about *everything*; because
    that's *all* there is to think
    about,
Knowing immediately the intimacy
    of truth and comedy,

why? Knowing intuitively how a sense   *intuitively*
    of humor was a necessity   5
For one and for all who live in   *natively*
    America. Thus, natively, and   *naturally*
Naturally when on an April Sun-
    day in an ice cream parlor
    Jeremiah
Was requested to choose between
    a chocolate sundae and a
    banana split
He answered unhesitatingly, hav-
    ing no need to think of it
Being a true-blue American, deter-
    mined to continue as he
    began: 10

Rejecting the either-or of Kierke-   ?
   gaard, and many another
   European;
Refusing to accept alternatives, refusing to believe the choice
   of between;
Rejecting selection; denying dilemma; electing absolute
   affirmation: ?
   knowing
     in his breast
       The infinite and the   15
        gold
       Of the endless fron-
        tier, the death-
        less West   *rhyme*

ambition, refusal "Both: I will have them both!"
to settle for half.   declared this true-blue
Or just greed?   American
In Cambridge, Massachusetts, on
   an April Sunday, instructed   *What do all*
     By the great department   *these things*
     stores, by the Five-and-Ten,   *teach?*
Taught by Christmas, by the cir-   20
     cus, by the vulgarity and
     grandeur of Niagara Falls
     and the Grand Canyon,
Tutored by the grandeur, vulgarity,
   and infinite appetite gratified
   and
     Shining in the darkness,
   of the light
On Saturdays at the double bills of,
   the moon pictures, = *movies*
The consummation of the adver-   25
   tisements of the imagination
   of the light
Which is as it was—the infinite
   belief in infinite hope—of
exploration —Columbus,   *light*
circus   — Barnum, Edison, and
   Jeremiah Dickson. *— Why part of this*
               series? Irony?

    On first reading, Daniel saw the poem as a patriotic catalog of all
the things that made America great; in fact, its seemingly patriotic theme
was what made him select this poem to write about. The closer he looked,
however, the more clearly he saw how deceptive his initial impression
was. As he studied the poem, he saw how all its parts contributed to one

impression: a critical look at American greed and materialism. Even though he did not like what he found, he could not just choose to ignore the clues to the poem's theme; the paper he finally wrote would have to interpret the poem in light of these clues.

As Daniel read and reread "The True-Blue American," he expanded his annotations in his journal, brainstorming and listing to find ideas for his paper. He began by brainstorming in a systematic fashion, considering voice, form, sound, meter, language, tone, and theme one by one. His brainstorming on the first four of these categories was not very productive: he concluded only that the poem's speaker was an anonymous voice, not identified as a particular person; that line length varied quite widely and did not seem to follow a particular pattern; and that the poem did not seem to have a regular rhyme scheme or meter. When he brainstormed about language, tone, and theme, however, he was able to discover some interesting ideas. The sections of Daniel's brainstorming list that pertain to language, tone, and theme appear below.

Language
Repetition: true-blue American (3 × + title), Jeremiah Dickson (first and last words of poem), vulgarity, grandeur, infinite, light
Parallelism: "Knowing immediately . . . knowing intuitively";
         "Rejecting. . . . Refusing to accept . . . refusing to believe. . . . Rejecting . . . denying . . . electing . . . knowing";
         "instructed by . . . taught by . . . tutored by. . . ."
Imagery: "moon pictures"—glowing in the dark

Tone
Speaker's attitude seems angry, bitter, disillusioned—why?
What does it mean to be "American"? to understand America? Is being "true-blue" a positive or a negative goal?
Is title ironic?

Theme
Poem's stated subject = true-blue American, but what *is* true-blue American?
Is poem's real subject what it means to be an American?
What is meaning of America? Is America great, full of possibilities? or corrupted by materialism and greed?
What is significance of names of people and places? How do they fit in with poem's theme?

After he had finished his brainstorming, Daniel made a more focused list to organize some of the poem's key ideas and allusions.

Places
America: ice cream parlor, West (frontier), Cambridge Mass,
        department stores, Five-and-Ten, circus, Niagara Falls,
        Grand Canyon, movie theatre

People
Kierkegaard (?), Columbus, Barnum, Edison (+ Jeremiah
        Dickson, typical average American)

Miscellaneous
chocolate sundae, banana split, Christmas, advertisements

Contrasting ideas
Positive
Promise of western frontier (infinite/endless/deathless)
grandeur
gold
imagination
light
hope
Negative
vulgarity
greed
appetite
darkness

Daniel's notes suggested many interesting paper topics. He could contrast the poem's superficial patriotism with its actual pessimism or explore the relationship between language and theme. He could pursue the idea of making choices, or the contrast between positive and negative images. He could do some research in order to consider the poem in the context of the United States in 1959, when it was written, or to consider how Delmore Schwartz's life or other works, or the works of his contemporaries, might be pertinent. He could examine the specific people and places mentioned in the poem and consider their possible significance. Finally, he could compare the poem to another poem with a similar—or contrasting—theme. Any of these possibilities would be perfectly appropriate. However, Daniel knew that it made sense to focus on a thesis his notes could support, and this eliminated some possible topics—for example, those focusing on the poem's sound or form.

As Daniel proceeded to find a thesis and an effective arrangement for his ideas, he followed the general process outlined in Chapters 2 and 3 of this book.

The following checklist can guide your analysis and interpretation of poetry.

Checklist for Analyzing and Interpreting Poetry

Voice

- Who is the speaker?
- What point of view does the speaker assume?
- Is the speaker a particular person? a representative figure? an anonymous narrator?

Form

- Is the poem's form open or closed?
- Does the poem have stanzas?
- Are all the stanzas about the same length?
- Are all the lines about the same length?
- Do variations in form place emphasis on particular words, phrases, or ideas?

Sound

- Does the poem use rhyme? If so, is the rhyme regular and predictable?
- Does rhyme appear only at the ends of lines, or does the poem include internal rhyme?
- Does the poem use alliteration? assonance?
- How does the rhyme scheme (or the lack of a rhyme scheme) influence your interpretation of the poem?

Meter

- Does the poem have a regular meter?
- Are there any departures from the dominant metrical pattern?
- What is the effect of these departures on your interpretation of the poem?

Language

- Is the style of the poem formal or conversational?
- What figures of speech are used? For instance, does the poem use similes, metaphors, or personification?
- What ideas does the poet emphasize through the use of figurative language?
- Is there a group of related images in the poem?
- Are any terms used symbolically?
- Does the poet use repetition or parallelism to enhance ideas?

Tone

- What attitude does the speaker convey about the subject of the poem?
- How does this attitude influence your view of the poem's subject?
- Is the speaker's voice distant or intimate?
- Does the poem make use of irony?

Theme
* What is the poem about?
* What ideas does the poem consider?
* What main idea does the poem convey?
* How does each element of the poem contribute to its theme?

The following checklist can guide you as you revise an essay about a literary work.

Revision Checklist for Writing About Literature

* Reconsider your topic. Is it specific enough? Do you focus on the concerns of your assignment?
* Does your introduction provide readers with the background or context they need to understand the discussion to follow? Would your introduction benefit from a quotation from the work? an overview of your research? a summary of your points?
* Do you clearly state your thesis? Does your thesis reflect your purpose? Does it clearly identify the aspects of the work you will discuss?
* Do you discuss the most pertinent points in your essay? Would other points about the work help you make a better case?
* How effective is the organization of your essay? Would your discussion be more effective if you arranged your points in a different order?
* Do you support your interpretations and judgments about the work? Would more support strengthen your case? Do you include too many points? Do you include a wide enough range of examples from the work and from your research? Do your examples actually support your points?
* Have you supplied the transitional words and phases you need to reinforce the logical connections among your ideas?
* Have you included any plot summaries or definitions of literary terms that your readers need to understand your discussion?
* Does your conclusion reinforce your main points? Would a different strategy improve your ending?
* Have you documented all words and ideas that are not your own? Have you followed MLA documentation style?

☐   **EXERCISE**

Review "The True-Blue American" and Daniel Johanssen's notes on pages 697–98. Brainstorm further if necessary, and arrange your material into lists of related ideas. Next, develop a thesis your notes can support, and write a paper about the poem. Finally, revise your paper according to the revision checklist above.

42f   Using Literary Terms

When you write about literature, you use a vocabulary appropriate to the discipline. The following glossary defines many of the terms you may use.

Glossary of Literary Terms

alliteration   repetition of initial sounds in a series of words, as in "dark, damp dungeon."

allusion   an unacknowledged reference to a historical event, work of literature, Biblical passage, or the like that the author expects readers to recognize.

antagonist   the character who is in conflict with or in opposition to the *protagonist*. Sometimes the antagonist is a force or situation, such as war or poverty.

assonance   repetition of vowel sounds in a series of words, as in "fine slide on the ice."

blank verse   lines of unrhymed iambic pentameter in no particular stanzaic form; approximates the rhythms of ordinary English speech.

character   the fictional representation of a person. Characters may be *round* (well-developed) or *flat* (undeveloped stereotypes), *dynamic* (changing and growing during the course of the story), or *static* (remaining essentially unchanged by the story's events).

climax   the point of greatest tension or importance in a play or story; the "turning point" at which the story's decisive action takes place.

closed form   a poetic structure characterized by a consistent pattern of rhyme, meter, or stanza form.

conflict   the opposition between two or more characters, between a character and a natural force, or between contrasting tendencies or motives or ideas within one character.

consonance   repetition of consonant sounds in a series of words, as in "the gnarled fingers of his nervous hands."

denouement   the point in the plot of a work of fiction or drama at which the action comes to an end and loose ends are tied up.

end-stopped line   a line of poetry that ends with a full stop, usually at the end of a sentence.

enjambment   a line of poetry ending with no punctuation or natural pause so that it runs over into the next line.

exposition   the initial stage of the plot of a work of fiction or

lit
42f

drama, where the author presents basic information readers need to understand the story's characters and events.

figurative language language whose meaning is not literal. The most commonly used figures of speech are *hyperbole, metaphor, personification, simile,* and *understatement.*

free verse poetry that does not follow a fixed meter or rhyme scheme.

hyperbole a figure of speech that depends on intentional overstatement or exaggeration.

imagery use of sensory description (description that relies on sight, sound, smell, taste, or touch) to make what is being described more vivid. A *pattern of imagery* collects a group of related images in order to create a single effect.

irony the use of language to suggest a discrepancy or incongruity between what is said and what is meant (*verbal irony*), between what actually happens and what we expected to happen (*situational irony;* also called *tragic irony*), or between what a character knows and what the reader knows (*dramatic irony*).

lyric poetry poetry that expresses a subjective response to the world. Lyric poems are usually short.

metaphor a comparison that equates two things that are essentially unlike.

lit
42f

meter the regular pattern of stressed and unstressed syllables; each repeated unit of rhythm is called a *foot*. An *anapest* has three syllables, the first two unstressed and the third stressed; a *dactyl* has three syllables, the first stressed and subsequent ones unstressed; an *iamb* has two syllables, of which the second is stressed; a *spondee* has two syllables, both stressed; and a *trochee* has two syllables, the first stressed and the second unstressed. A poem's meter is described by naming the kind of foot (iamb, dactyl, and so on) and the number of feet in each line (one foot per line = monometer, two feet per line = dimeter, three feet = trimeter, four = tetrameter, five = pentameter, and so on). Thus a poetic line containing five feet, each of which contains an unstressed syllable followed by a stressed syllable, would be described as *iambic pentameter*.

monologue an extended speech by one character.

narration the recounting of events in a work of fiction. When an event that has already occurred is recounted in a later sequence of events, it is called a *flashback;* when something that will occur later in a narration is suggested earlier, the suggestion is called a *foreshadowing.*

open form a poetic structure that is not characterized by any consistent pattern of rhyme, meter, or stanza form.

paradox   a seemingly contradictory statement.

persona   the narrator or speaker of a story or poem; the persona's attitudes and opinions are not necessarily those of the author.

personification   the assigning of human qualities to non-human things.

plot   a connected series of events occurring in a work of literature.

point of view   the perspective from which a story is told. A story may have a *first-person narrator*, who may be a major or minor character in the story. A story may have a *third-person narrator* who does not figure in the story's action. This narrator may be an *omniscient narrator*, who knows the thoughts and motives of all the story's characters, or a *limited omniscient narrator*, who sees into the minds of only some of the characters. A narrator who cannot be trusted—because he or she is evil, stupid, or self-serving—is called an *unreliable narrator*. The objective point of view that is limited to information you would get from watching the action unfold on stage is called the *dramatic* point of view.

protagonist   the principal character of a work of drama or fiction.

rhyme   the repetition of the last stressed vowel sound and all subsequent sounds. *End rhyme* occurs at the ends of poetic lines; *internal rhyme* is the rhyming of words within a line of poetry.

rhythm   the pattern of stresses and pauses in a poem; a poem's meter.

setting   the background against which the action of a work of literature takes place: the historical period, locale, season, time of day, interior decoration.

simile   a comparison of two essentially unlike things using the word *like* or *as*.

soliloquy   a convention of drama in which a character speaks directly to the audience, revealing thoughts and feelings that the play's other characters, even if they are present on the stage, are assumed not to hear.

stanza   a group of lines in a poem, separated from others by a blank space on the page, that forms a unit of thought, mood, or meter. Common stanzaic forms include the *couplet* (two lines), *tercet* (three lines), *quatrain* (four lines), *sestet* (six lines), and *octave* (eight lines).

stock character   a stereotypical character who behaves consistently and predictably and who is instantly recognizable and familiar to the audience.

symbol   an image whose meaning transcends its literal or denotative sense in a complex way. Its associations give it significance beyond what it could carry on its own.

theme   the main idea of a work of literature, made concrete by the work itself.

tone   the attitude of the speaker toward a work's subject, characters, or audience, conveyed by the work's word choice and arrangement of words.

understatement   intentional downplaying of a situation's significance, often for ironic effect.

43

Writing Business Letters and Memos

Everyone writes business letters from time to time—to request information, to order a product, to complain about something, or to apply for employment. Many of the principles we have been discussing apply to this kind of writing.

43a Composing Business Letters

(1) Planning your letter

Before you sit down to write a business letter, you should think carefully about your purpose. Decide in advance why you are writing your letter and keep that objective in mind as you write. You should also evaluate your audience. Are you writing to a single person? Will a group of people see your letter and act on it? What information and what approach should you use to influence this audience? When you have answered these questions to your own satisfaction, do some brainstorming or some research to gather the information that you will need to write your letter.

(2) Organizing your material

Once you have the information that you want to convey, you should organize it into broad categories and then put those categories into a logical order. This arrangement becomes the structure for your letter. For example, a student in a work-study program who had to write a letter to a potential customer explaining the advantages of the Apple IIe as a word processor over a conventional typewriter did some research and brainstorming and assembled this list of information.

> The Apple IIe has a text editor.
> The Apple IIe system costs $3700.
> Deadlines disturb routines.
> Employee morale is down.
> Rental typewriters cost $873 per year.
> The Apple IIe does not make errors.
> Floppy disks are $24.95 a box.
> The Apple IIe is four times faster than manual typing.
> Floppy disks make storage easier and cheaper.

Reviewing her list, the student realized that she could group her information under two topics: cost and efficiency. As she did this, she discarded some points and added others.

> *Cost*
> The Apple IIe system costs $3700.
> Floppy disks are $24.95 a box.
> Rental typewriters cost $873 per year.
> Total savings first year: $3373.

> *Efficiency*
> The Apple IIe is four times faster than manual typing.
> The Apple IIe has a text editor.
> The Apple IIe does not make errors.
> The Apple IIe makes deadlines easier to meet.
> Floppy disks make storage easier and cheaper.

**bus
43a**

After putting her subpoints in logical order, she was ready to write her first draft.

(3) Writing and revising your letter

Most businesses receive hundreds of letters each day, so your letter should be brief and to the point. Important information should appear early in the letter, and you should not digress. Be concise and try to sound as natural as possible. Stilted or flowery language gets in the way of clear communication, and so do legalistic terminology *(in re: your letter)* and business jargon *(in regards to, herewith enclosed).*

The first paragraph of your letter should introduce your subject and mention any relevant previous correspondence. The rest of your letter should present your reader with the facts needed to understand what you are saying. If the matter is complicated, you may want to list information in numbered points. Your conclusion should reinforce your message, and the whole letter should communicate your goodwill.

Type your business letter on good-quality 8½″ × 11″ paper. Leave wide margins, at least an inch all around, and balance your letter on the page. Type your letter single-spaced and use an acceptable format. One of the most common, the block format, is illustrated below. (The semiblock format appears on p. 711, and the indented format on p. 714.) The **block format** letter begins every line at the left-hand margin and separates paragraphs with a double space. Double-space between the inside address and the salutation, between the salutation and the text, between paragraphs, and between the text and the complimentary close.

After you proofread your letter, you may have to retype it. The appearance of your letter affects your reader's response to it. A neatly typed letter, free of smudges and errors, makes a favorable impression. A sloppy letter or one with misspellings or corrections made by hand presents you and your case badly. (See 43a.4 for more information on the format of business letters.)

Sample Letter—Block Format

Heading   6732 Wyncote Avenue
Houston, Texas   77004
May 3, 1988

*Inside
address*   Mr. William S. Price, Jr., Director
Division of Archives and History
Department of Cultural Resources
109 East Jones Street
Raleigh, North Carolina   27611

Salutation   Dear Mr. Price:

Thank you for sending me the material I requested about the pirates in colonial North Carolina.

Body   Both the pamphlets and the bibliography were extremely useful for my research. My instructor said that I had presented information in my paper that he had never seen before. Without your help, I am sure my paper would not have been so well received.

I have enclosed a copy of my paper, and I would
appreciate any comments you may have. Again, thank

Compli-
mentary
close

you for your time and trouble.

Sincerely yours,

Written
Signature

Kevin Wolk

Typed
signature

Kevin Wolk

Additional
data

Enclosure

(4) Understanding the conventions of a business letter

The format of a business letter may seem arbitrary and prescrip-
tive, but remember that this format has evolved in response to
the special needs of the business audience. Using an inside address, for example, seems pointless until you consider that business letters often circulate to people other than the recipient,
and to these readers knowing the original recipient is important.
Dates are also necessary. Letters frequently become part of a permanent record, filed for some future use. These letters can have
uses weeks, months, and even years later that no one could have
originally predicted.

By conforming to the following conventions when writing
business letters, you will be less likely to forget an important bit
of information—and of course your readers will know where to
look for it in your letter.

bus
43a

The Heading The **heading** of a business letter consists of the
sender's return address, but not his or her name, and the date
the letter is written. If you use letterhead stationery, supply only
the date, typing it two spaces below the letterhead. Each line of
the heading falls under the one above it, flush to the left.

Spell out words like *Street, Avenue, Road, Place, East,* and
West in full. You may, however, abbreviate the names of the states
using the postal list of abbreviations found in many college dictionaries. Be sure to punctuate the heading correctly. Commas
separate the name of the city from that of the state and the day
from the year. Do not, however, use punctuation before the zip
code or at the ends of lines.

The Inside Address The **inside address** cites the *recipient's* name and address. It begins at the left margin four to six lines below the heading, depending on the need to use space for a balanced page. Include an appropriate title (Mr., Ms., Mrs., Miss, Dr.) with the recipient's name and the recipient's full address. Previous correspondence should be your guide to your recipient's correct name and title.

The Salutation The **salutation** ("Dear _____") appears two spaces below the inside address, flush to the left margin. In business letters the salutation almost always ends with a colon, not a comma. It includes the person's title followed by the last name as it appears on the inside address.

If you do not know how to address a person in a specific profession—a judge, for instance—consult the index of a college dictionary such as *Webster's Ninth New Collegiate Dictionary* for a list of proper forms of address.

Addressee	*Form of Address*	*Salutation*
Federal judge	The Honorable John Smith, United States District Judge	Dear Judge Smith:

If you are on a first-name basis with someone, you should still use his or her full name and title in the inside address. You may, however, use the first name, followed by a comma, in the salutation.

If you are writing to a woman, refer to previous correspondence and use the title that she uses. If you do not know her preference, use *Ms.* If you know someone's initials but do not know whether the person is a man or a woman, you might call the company switchboard and ask. You can also use a neutral form of address—*Dear Editor* or *Dear Supervisor*, for example.

If you are writing to someone you do not know—the Director of Personnel, for example—you can avoid the awkward phrase *To Whom It May Concern* by routing your letter to a specific department or by referring to a particular subject.

bus 43a

```
College Department
Holt, Rinehart and Winston
111 Fifth Avenue
New York, NY  10003

Attention: Director of Personnel

                or

Subject: Sales Position
```

Keep in mind that salutations such as *Gentlemen* and *Dear Sirs* should be used only when you are certain that your audience is male. To use these salutations as general forms of address may offend some readers and should be avoided.

The Body The **body** of your letter contains your message. Begin this section two spaces below the salutation, and single-space the text. In a short letter of two or three sentences, you may double-space throughout. In a block format letter you do not use paragraph indentations; in some other formats you indent paragraphs five spaces from the left-hand margin (see p. 43d).

If your letter takes more than one page, place the addressee's name, the date, and the page number in the upper left-hand corner of the second page.

The Complimentary Close The **complimentary close** appears two spaces below the body of the letter and flush to the left.

The most common complimentary closes are *Sincerely yours*, *Yours truly*, and *Yours very truly*. If you are on friendly terms with the recipient, *Best wishes* or *Cordially* is appropriate. More formal letters to high government officials, members of the clergy, or diplomats might call for *Respectfully yours*. Note that only the first word of the complimentary close is capitalized.

bus
43b

The Signature Leave four spaces below the complimentary close, and type your name and title in full. Sign your name, without a title, above the typewritten line.

Additional Data Indicate additional information below the signature, to the left.

Enclosures *(Material enclosed along with letter)*

cc: Eric Brody *(Copy sent to the person mentioned)*

SJL/lew *(The initials of the writer/the initials of the typist)*

43b Writing Letters Requesting Employment

When you request employment, your primary objective is to interest a prospective employer enough so that he or she will schedule an interview with you. Before you write, collect all the information you need for your letter—previous employment, employers, dates, and relevant courses, for example. Then consider why you want the job and what about you might interest a prospective employer. You will want to make a scratch outline before you begin your rough draft.

Begin your letter by stating which job you are applying for and where you heard about it—in a newspaper, in a journal, from a professor, or from the school job placement service, for instance. Be sure to include the date of the advertisement and the exact title of the position. End your introduction with your thesis: a statement of your ability to do the job.

The body of your letter provides the information that will convince your reader of your qualifications. Mention any relevant courses you have taken and any pertinent job experience. Take care to address any specific concerns mentioned in the advertisement. Above all, emphasize your strengths. If you are applying for a sales job, for example, stress your ability to communicate effectively, not your limited experience. If you have special skills or training, such as word processing, be sure to mention it.

Conclude by referring to your résumé. State that you are available for an interview, listing any dates on which you cannot be available.

As always, your letter should be smooth, natural, and free of errors.

Sample Letter of Employment—Semiblock Format

**bus
43b**

```
                          246 Hillside Drive
                          Urbana, Illinois  61801
                          October 20, 1988
```

```
Mr. Maurice Snyder, Personnel Director
Guilford, Fox, and Morris
Eckerd Building
22 Hamilton Street
Urbana, Illinois  61822
```

Dear Mr. Synder:

```
My adviser, Dr. Raymond Walsh, has told me that you are
interested in hiring a part-time accounting assistant. I
feel that my academic background and my work experience
qualify me for this position.
```

I am presently a junior accounting major at the University
of Illinois. During the past year, I have taken courses in
taxation, trusts, and business law. I have worked with a
microcomputer and have developed my own tax program. Last
spring, I worked in the department tax clinic and gained
much practical accounting experience.

After I graduate, I hope to get a Master's degree in
taxation and then return to the Urbana area. I feel that
my experience in taxation as well as my familiarity with
the local business community would enable me to contribute
to your firm.

I have enclosed a résumé for your examination. I will be
available for an interview any time after midterm
examinations, which end October 25. I look forward to
hearing from you.

                                        Sincerely yours,

                                        Sandra Kraft

                                        Sandra Kraft

                                        Enclosure

**bus
43c**

☐ · **EXERCISE 1**

Look at the employment advertisements in your local paper or in the
files of your college placement service. Choose one job, and write a letter
of application in which you outline your qualifications and achievements and discuss why you want the position.

43c Writing Résumés ─────────────────────

The letter of application presents your qualifications and interest
in a specific job. The résumé that accompanies the letter provides an overview of what you have already done. It focuses on
your education and your work experience. A résumé should create one dominant impression: that you are a motivated person
who has the ability and maturity to do a job well.

Before you compose your résumé, list all of the pertinent
information about your education, your job experience, your
goals, and your personal interests. Then select the information
that is appropriate for the job you want, emphasizing the accomplishments that differentiate you from other candidates. If you

have received academic honors or awards, or if you have financed your own education, include this information as well.

There is no single correct format for a résumé. Whatever its arrangement, however, it should be brief—one page is sufficient for an undergraduate—easy to read, and well organized. An employer should be able to see at a glance what your qualifications are. Many résumés contain the following sections.

The *heading* includes your name, school address, home address, and phone number.

The *education section* includes the schools you have attended, starting with the most recent one and working back in time. After graduation from college, do not list your high schools unless you have a compelling reason to do so.

The *summary of work experience* starts with your most recent job and works back.

The *background section* lists special interests and community service. (Just a few examples will suffice.)

The *references section* lists the full name and address of at least three references. If you already have a full-page résumé, a line saying that your references will be sent upon request is sufficient.

If you can, include an *honors section* in which you list academic achievements and awards. In addition, you may include at the top of the page a statement of your *career objective.*

Remember that federal law prohibits employers from discriminating on the basis of age, sex, or race, and you need not include this information in your résumé.

**bus
43c**

Sample Résumé

Michael D. Fuller

Address	Home	Campus
	1203 Hampton Road	27 College Avenue
	Joppa, MD 21085	College Park, MD 20742
	Telephone:	Telephone:
	(301) 877-1437	(301) 357-0732

Education 1985-1987	University of Maryland, College Park, MD (sophomore). Biology major. Expected date of graduation: June 1989. Presently maintain a 3.3 average of a 4.0 scale.
1981-1985	Forrest Park High School, Baltimore, MD. Basketball team, track team, debating society, class president, mathematics tutor. Graduated in the top fifth of the class.

Experience 1986–1987	University of Maryland Library, College Park, MD. Assistant to the reference librarian. Filed, sorted, typed, shelved, and catalogued. Earnings offset college expenses.
1985–1986	University of Maryland Cafeteria, College Park, MD. Busboy. Cleaned tables, set up cafeteria, and prepared hot trays.
1984 Summer	McDonald's Restaurant, Pikesville, MD. Cook. Prepared hamburgers. Acted as assistant manager for two weeks when manager was on vacation.
Background	Member of University Debating Society. Tutor in University Program for Disadvantaged Students.
References	Ms. Stephanie Young, Librarian Library University of Maryland College Park, MD 20742
	Mr. William Czernick, Manager Cafeteria University of Maryland College Park, MD 20742
	Mr. Arthur Sanducci, Manager McDonald's Restaurant 5712 Avery Road Pikesville, MD 22513

bus 43d

☐   **EXERCISE 2**

Prepare a résumé to include with the letter of employment you wrote for Exercise 1.

43d   Writing Follow-up Letters

It is a good idea to send a brief follow-up letter a week or two after an interview. Thank the people whom you met for their time, and restate your interest in the job. Such letters show both courtesy and professionalism.

Sample Follow-up Letter—Indented Format

17 West Third Street
New York, New York   10003
April 7, 1989

Mr. Thomas Crawford, Manager
FDS Capital Corporation
Two World Trade Center
New York, New York 10015

Dear Mr. Crawford:

    Thank you so much for interviewing me for the
work-study position and for showing me your offices on
March 25th. Your computer department was very interesting,
and the information I obtained will help me focus my
career goals.

    I especially enjoyed seeing how you use computer-
generated graphics in your investment division. I now feel
certain that I want to enter this field after I graduate
in 1990. Any work I could do for you this summer would
help me prepare for this rapidly developing field.

    Again, thank you very much.

Sincerely,

Sara Katz

Sara Katz

☐   **EXERCISE 3**

Assume you were interviewed for the job you applied for in Exercise 1.
A week has passed. Write a follow-up letter thanking the person you
saw.

**bus
43e**

43e   Writing Letters to Graduate or Professional Schools

Graduate and professional schools routinely ask applicants for
autobiographies or statements explaining why they have applied.
These personal statements reveal a great deal about you, including your goals, your maturity, and your ability to communicate.
They are read carefully, and they help to determine whether or
not you will be accepted.

    Do some soul searching before you begin planning a per-
sonal statement. Write down your reasons for wanting to enter
your intended profession and the qualities that suit you for this
profession. Study this material, and organize it into an outline.
Next, write a rough draft quickly, without worrying about how it
looks or sounds. Keep in mind that personal statements are difficult to write, and that you may have to do a number of drafts.

As you revise, concentrate on what distinguishes you from others who are applying to the school. Be specific, offering examples from your experience to illustrate the points you make. Everything in your statement should underscore your thesis: that you are committed to the field and should be admitted to a program.

Sample Personal Statement

During my sophomore and junior years in college, I worked part-time for a law firm in Cincinnati. I began as a file clerk and eventually was promoted to the research department of the firm. This experience was a turning point in my life. It helped me decide to become a lawyer and to take courses that would prepare me for this goal.

The firm in which I worked does general practice and also a good deal of community legal work. After being there for eight months, I was given the responsibility of screening legal-aid clients and assigning them to one of three lawyers. I consulted with attorneys and, at times, discussed specific cases with them. Eventually they allowed me to be present when depositions were taken.

I learned a great deal about the legal profession from my job. One case stands out in my mind. An elderly man had been run down by a bus and was partially disabled. He had no hospitalization and no income other than Social Security. The firm took his case and arranged for the bus company to pay all medical bills and for the man to begin physical therapy. As a result, our client is now able to live at home with the help of a visiting nurse. While doing research for the attorney who handled this case, I saw how much good a lawyer can do and how important it is for those in the legal profession to help those who cannot help themselves.

My experiences with a law firm have given me a realistic picture of what the practice of law is and have enabled me to make a mature, informed decision to become a lawyer. I am certain that as a result, I will be an understanding and compassionate attorney, one who puts her clients' interests before her own.

To prepare for my legal career, I have majored in political science and minored in business. My grade point average has been good: 3.35 on a 4.0 scale. I have taken courses in political theory, government, accounting, and constitutional law. I have also taken a number of courses in sociology, psychology, and business writing. In

**bus
43e**

addition, I am a member of my school's pre—law society, and I won honorable mention in a regional moot—court competition held last spring.

This past year I was the student representative on a search committee for a new dean of the College of Liberal Arts. I worked closely with the former dean and with faculty members from various departments. I have found that this experience has increased my confidence and has made me an effective negotiator. I have learned to state a position clearly and forcefully and not to be intimidated by the arguments of others.

My background has made me realize my responsibility to the legal profession and to society. My involvement with the legal profession has provided me with the motivation to pursue a career in law. My academic record and my experience with legal work make me certain that a career in law is a realistic goal for me.

☐   EXERCISE 4

Assume that you are applying to one of the following graduate programs.

Law school
Medical school
Business school
Journalism school
Social work school
A graduate program in an academic field

Write a personal statement in which you tell the admissions officer what led you to choose your field. Be specific in describing your motivation, your experience, and your aspirations.

43f Writing Letters Requesting Information

Students often have to send letters requesting information from a person or a business. For instance, you might ask an instructor for a recommendation or write to an expert in a field to gather information for a research project.

Before you write such a letter, decide just what information you need. Make a list if necessary, and eliminate questions that you can answer yourself. Think about what you need the information for and how much time you have to get it. Usually you can limit your request to a few questions that can be answered quickly and easily.

bus
43f

Write a courteous and concise letter. Introduce yourself, and say clearly what information you want and why you want it. Be specific; your reader will be doing you a favor by responding, and you should not waste his or her time. If you have several requests, number them—and keep them simple.

Sample Letter Requesting Information

17 Maple Drive
Clinton, Mississippi   39058
December 2, 1988

Dr. Norman Murphy
English Department
Louisiana State University
   at Shreveport
Shreveport, Louisiana   75115

Dear Dr. Murphy:

I am a third-year English major at Clinton College, and I am interested in pursuing a career in scientific and technical writing. Dr. Stewart Lage, my adviser, thought that you could give me advice about schools that have graduate programs in this field.

Although I prefer to stay in the South, I am willing to go to school in any part of the country. I am particularly interested in schools that have internship programs that would allow me to gain practical experience in industry. I have already written to Stanford University and am waiting for its catalog.

I am currently at home and will be back at school on January 6th. I would appreciate any information you could mail to me or to Dr. Lage.

I hope to hear from you soon.

Yours truly,

Daniel Howell, Jr.

Daniel Howell, Jr.

It is always a good idea to thank the person who responds to your letter. An example of such a letter appears on p. 707.

bus
43f

☐   **EXERCISE 5**

For a research paper on television situation comedies, write a letter requesting information from Alan Friedman (38 University Place, New York University, New York, NY 10003), a noted authority on this subject. Ask him four questions you would like him to answer. Remember that Dr. Friedman is very busy, but he will probably answer a sensible, interesting short letter.

☐   **EXERCISE 6**

Three weeks have passed, and Dr. Friedman has not answered. Write a follow-up letter in which you gently remind him of your request and of your deadline.

43g   Writing Letters of Complaint

Often the only way you can solve a problem or rectify a mistake is to complain in writing. Many companies realize that it takes some effort to write a letter of complaint, and when they receive one, they respond. If you feel that you have been treated unfairly or incorrectly, a letter may help to remedy the situation.

Before you write a letter of complaint, you should list the facts that are important to your case. Exact names and dates are extremely important; so are serial numbers and warranty provisions. Reconstruct the facts of your case, keeping events in chronological order. As you look over your list, eliminate details that are not central to your purpose. The fact that a salesperson was rude, for instance, may be less important than his or her misrepresentation of a product.

bus
43g

The purpose of writing your letter is to get satisfaction or redress. To achieve this end, you should make sure that your letter maintains a rational tone. Present yourself as a reasonable person who sees both sides of the issue and who expects to be taken seriously. Anger or sarcasm undercuts your cause, and neither has a place in an effective letter of complaint. The merit of your claim and the clarity of your presentation are what lead a company to act in your favor.

Revise your first draft with your reader in mind. If your reader is unfamiliar with your case, begin your letter with an overview, not an involved discussion of your problem. Make sure that you explain the facts clearly. Put events in logical order, with transitions that make their sequence apparent, and tell your story without editorial comment.

Make certain that your tone is firm but reasonable and your

request for action is appropriate to the problem. Finally, try to end on a positive note—at least by asserting your belief in the goodwill of the company.

Sample Letter of Complaint

2133 Northridge Avenue
Los Angeles, CA   90024
May 8, 1988

Time, Inc.
Subscription Department
Rockefeller Center
New York, NY   10020

Subject: Canceled subscription

On November 5th I sent a letter to you canceling my subscription. Since then, I have continued getting magazines despite my efforts to stop them.

**bus
43g**

On March 2nd I sent a second letter, this time by certified mail; I enclose a copy of my receipt. On April 11th I got a letter (copy enclosed) from the Eastern Collection Agency telling me to pay your bill or risk legal action. I called Eastern (at a cost to me of $3.65) and was told by their manager, Mr. Wolfson, that he could do nothing until I paid the bill or until you told him the bill was canceled.

I am disturbed for two reasons. First, should not one letter be enough to cancel my subscription? Must I write three letters if I want you to take action? Second, surely you do not expect me to pay for magazines that you sent after I canceled my subscription. As far as I am concerned I did not order these magazines, so I should not be responsible for them.

I am certain that Time, Inc., values its good reputation and will want to settle this matter fairly.

Yours truly,

Suzanne Cozmo

Suzanne Cozmo

☐   **EXERCISE 7**

Your college or university owes you a $250 refund from your tuition. Apparently they charged you twice for a student activities fee. After discovering the error you go to the registrar, who tells you that as a matter of policy all refunds are credited to the next semester's tuition. After a day and a half of hearing the same story at one office after another, you decide to write a letter to the president of the school. In this letter tell the president why you think the school should reimburse you. Make a strong case, and present the facts clearly and logically.

43h   Composing Memos

The process of composing memos is much the same as the process of composing business letters. Unlike letters, however, memos communicate information *within* a business organization. They can communicate brief messages of a paragraph or two, or short reports or proposals. Their function is generally to convey information or to persuade. Whatever their function, most memos have the following general structure.

The Opening Component   The **opening component**—*To*, *From*, *Subject*, and *Date*—replaces the heading and inside address of a letter (see sample, p. 722). This section establishes at a glance the audience and the subject of your communication. Because a memo often circulates beyond its original audience, all names and titles should be stated in full. The *subject* line, which exists to give your reader a clear idea what your memo is about, should include more than one word. "Housing" means very little to readers unfamiliar with your subject; "Changes in Student Housing Policy" states the subject more precisely.

**bus
43h**

The Body   The **body** of your memo should begin with a purpose statement containing key words that immediately convey your message. Some people like to present the purpose statement as a separate component with its own heading. In any case, the purpose statement should include a word that clearly defines your intention—for example, *evaluates*, *proposes*, *questions*, *reports*, *describes*, or *presents*.

The first paragraph of the body summarizes your conclusions; the rest of your memo tells readers how you arrived at your conclusions, backing them up with facts and figures. Often each paragraph of a memo has a heading that identifies its subject. These headings guide readers through the body of your memo.

The Conclusion The **conclusion** of your memo should contain a detailed restatement of your conclusions. If its purpose is to persuade your readers of something, you should include a list of recommendations. Because readers remember best what comes last, you should end your memo with a summary of the action that should be taken or the conclusions that should be drawn.

In the following memo from the editor of a college newspaper to the dean of freshmen, the writer states his reason for writing the memo in the first sentence and then goes on to explain how the editorial board reached its decision. The short memo reports information but does not make recommendations.

TO: Donald Abrams, Dean of Freshmen
FROM: Alex McCullough, Editor, the Triangle
SUBJECT: Printing the Freshmen Orientation Schedule
DATE: April 23, 1988

As editor of the Triangle I would like to report the decision the editorial board made concerning your request to print the Freshman Orientation Schedule in our August 5th issue.

During our conversation on April 3rd, you asked if the Triangle would print a four-page pull-out of the Freshmen Orientation Schedule. As you suggested, I brought up this matter with the editorial board and our faculty adviser. The editorial board agreed to print the schedule, but asked that the university pay the cost of printing and that the pull-out not be counted in the eight-page limit the university placed on the Triangle last year.

I hope you find our decisions satisfactory. I will be glad to answer any questions you may have about this matter.

bus
43h

The following memo deals with a more complicated subject. The student who wrote this memo uses headings to identify the major divisions of her discussion and emphasizes her recommendations by presenting them in list form. Her purpose is to persuade her audience; therefore, she discusses her reader's major concerns—cost, ease of construction, and projected benefits—and she ends with a list of recommendations.

```
TO:        Ina Ellen, Senior Counselor
FROM:      Kim Williams, Student Tutor Supervisor
SUBJECT:   Construction of a Tutoring Center
DATE:      November 10, 1988
```

The purpose of this memo is to propose the construction of
a tutoring center in the Office of Student Affairs.

BACKGROUND
Under the present system, student tutors must work with
students in a number of facilities scattered across the
university campus. This situation has a number of
drawbacks, including a lack of contact among tutors and
the inability of tutors to get immediate help with
problems if they need it. As a result, tutors waste a lot
of time running from one facility to another—and often
miss appointments. Most tutors agree that the present
system is unwieldy and ineffective.

NEW FACILITY
I propose that we build a tutoring room adjacent to the
Office of Student Affairs. The two empty classrooms
adjacent to the office, presently used for storage of
office furniture, would be ideal for this use. Incurring a
minimum of expense and using its own maintenance workers,
the university could convert these rooms into ten small
offices. We could furnish these offices with the desks and
file cabinets already stored in these rooms.

**bus
43h**

BENEFITS
The benefits of this facility would be the centralizing of
the tutoring service and the proximity of the facility to
the Office of Student Affairs. The tutoring facility could
also use the secretarial services of the Office of Student
Affairs, ensuring that student tutors get messages from
the students with whom they work.

RECOMMENDATIONS
To implement this project we would need to do the
following:

> 1. Clean up and paint rooms 331 and 333 and connect
>   them to the Office of Student Affairs
> 2. Use folding partitions to divide each room into
>   five single-desk offices
> 3. Use stored office equipment to furnish the center

I am certain that these changes would do much to improve
the tutoring service that the Office of Student Affairs
now offers, and I look forward to discussing this matter
with you in more detail.

☐   **EXERCISE 8**

Your duties at your summer job with a public utility in your area include reading correspondence that goes from your division to the public. While reading a pamphlet that discusses energy conservation, you come across the following words and sentences: "Each consumer must do *his* part," "*repairman*," and "*Mothers* should teach their children about energy conservation." With the approval of your supervisor, you decide to write a memo to John Durand, Public Relations Manager, explaining to him that this language could offend some readers. In your memo explain to Mr. Durand why the language should be changed and what words and phrases he could use in their place. Mr. Durand is your superior, so maintain a reasonable tone.

Appendix **A**

Composing on a Computer

Lately, much has been made of the computer's ability to make writing easier. Despite the obvious exaggeration of some claims, the computer can help you to improve your writing. However, composing on a computer does present some problems. The first is the cost of both hardware and software. Even though prices have been dropping, a computer, printer, and word-processing program can cost thousands of dollars.

Time can also be a problem. A person does not just sit down and begin to use a computer. Like any complicated machine, the computer takes time to learn and more time to master. In addition to learning about the computer itself and developing keyboard skills, you also have to become familiar with the programs you are going to use. Too often people learn just enough to type and print and do not master the subtleties of their software. The result is that they never realize the full potential of the computer.

Once you are accustomed to your equipment and your software, the ease with which you can draft and revise lets you do more work in less time. Keep in mind that even with these advantages, it is *you* who composes your papers. Your likes and dislikes will determine the way you integrate the computer into your own writing process. Some of the following suggestions will be of immediate help to you. Others will help you develop your own ideas for using the computer creatively to plan, shape, and write and revise your essays.

A1 Using the Computer to Plan Your Papers

Because of its ability to record and store information, the computer can help you plan your writing. The computer can also keep a neat record of

725

all your preliminary notes so you are able to sort through this material easily when it comes time to write a draft.

(1)   Freewriting

Freewriting (see 1b.2) on the computer enables you to get down ideas more quickly and with less fatigue than if you used pen and paper. The computer keyboard lets your fingers keep up with your mind. If you pause to correct typing errors, however, you will lose this advantage, so try to ignore the screen. If you are unable to do so, turn down the brightness until the screen is dark, or turn off the monitor if it has a separate switch. When you cannot see the words, they cannot distract you. Free from such distractions, you may capture some important ideas.

If your freewriting yields an interesting idea for a paper, you can move this idea to the end of your text, rephrase it as a sentence, and freewrite on it for another set period of time. If the sentence moves off the screen, move it back to the top. Keeping your main idea constantly on the screen helps you to stay focused as you generate ideas.

(2)   Creating a question file

With a computer you can save any questions you use to find something to say. You might, for example, type these questions to help you focus on your purpose and audience.

> Who am I writing to?
> Do I want to entertain, convey information, convey my attitude, convince readers to do something?
> What is my purpose?
> How much can I write?

Each time you begin a new paper, you can call up these questions, review and answer them, and save both the questions and the answers for future reference. You can easily refer to the questions you have saved as you prepare to write any new assignment.

comp
A2

Any thought-provoking questions that your instructor recommends—the journalistic questions, for example (see 1b.2)—can go into your question file for recall when you start your next assignment. Some instructors even recommend (or distribute) idea-generating programs for their classes. These programs provide prompts that help students find things to say. After using these programs just a few times, many students report that they are able to generate ideas on their own.

A2   Using the Computer to Shape Your Material

Because of its flexibility, the computer can help you organize your ideas. Its ability to move text easily enables you to arrange and rearrange ideas as you shape your essay.

(1) Outlining

Some instructors may ask for an outline (see 2d) of your ideas. If you use the computer to construct an outline, you can easily insert new ideas and rearrange the ideas that you have already typed. Working on the computer is especially efficient for preparing outlines because you can make major changes and still have a clean and legible draft.

If you find that outlining is a valuable part of your writing process, you may want to use a special outline program. Many of the commercially available outline programs can help you arrange your ideas into an outline format. They often work inside your word-processing program, enabling you to organize ideas, write, and revise all at once.

Some word-processing programs enable you to keep several windows on the screen at once. If yours does, you may want to keep your outline on the screen as you write your paper. This technique will allow you to keep track of your paper's organization as you write your rough draft.

(2) Using paper: hard copy

Writing out ideas on paper is still useful, of course. As you begin to shape your essay, you may not want to view your preliminary notes on the video monitor. Instead, you may find it easier to print out the notes you have prepared and refer to this **hard copy** as you start to put your ideas in order.

If new ideas come to you as you work, jot them down on the printout sheets rather than going back to the computer. This technique enables you to see all your notes at once and to add and cross out information without actually deleting material.

A3 Using the Computer to Write Your Rough Draft

When writing a rough draft you should try to get your ideas down as quickly as possible. Using a computer does not automatically eliminate the problems that can occur at this stage of your writing, but it can offer you some unique ways of surmounting them.

(1) Overcoming writer's block

If you find yourself staring far too long at a blank screen, just as you would at a blank sheet of paper, try turning down the screen's brightness and start freewriting (see A1). This strategy gives you a chance to concentrate on ideas rather than on the "look" of your sentences. Many people find this "invisible writing" a useful way to overcome writer's block.

Another technique that may help you to overcome writer's block is to make two or three starts. Begin your paper and name the file "paper

1." Do as much as you think would make a good beginning; then stop and read through what you have written. Now start over again, naming your new work "paper 2." Continue starting over until you have captured the idea you want to convey. If after several revisions you find that your first version was best, go back to "paper 1" and continue writing from there. Or you may find a good sentence in "paper 1," two good sentences in "paper 2," and a good transition in "paper 3." Select the best elements in each and merge them as a new version, "paper 4," and then proceed.

(2) Getting clean copy

One clear advantage of using a computer is that you always have clean copy. The push of a key lets you erase, transpose, replace, and rewrite single words or whole sections of text. The very ease with which you can perform these operations may encourage you to revise a great deal as you write, but keep one caution in mind: If you erase an idea, it is lost forever, and you have no way to review it should you want to. Take out anything you like, but keep a copy of each of your drafts on disk until your paper is finished.

A4 Using the Computer to Revise Your Papers

Revising a paper involves reconsidering many of the decisions that you made when you wrote your first draft. Revision involves adding, substituting, moving, and deleting material. (For detailed information on revision, see 3c–3e.) Although these operations can be tedious when carried out with pen and paper, they are relatively simple when you use a computer.

comp A4

(1) Adding

When you reread your writing after a day or two, you may find that certain paragraphs do not have enough supporting evidence or detail, that your introduction lacks a clear thesis, or that your conclusion proceeds from unproven assumptions. In short, you may need to add material.

Computers make adding easy. If you print out your draft with a wide margin and double-spaced, you can use the margin and blank lines for handwritten notes about the additions you need. You can then type in your additions when you return to the computer.

```
            For most students, university writing will

        now include more than pen, paper, and typewriter.

        As computers become common and inexpensive, more
```

```
students will prepare academic papers on a
microcomputer processor linked to a university's
mainframe computer system or on a personal
computer at home.  In addition to easing the
drudgery of preparing typed papers, computers can
be valuable writing aids.
```

(2)   Substituting

The "find" and "replace" commands help when you substitute one word or phrase for another. But suppose you want to replace one example with another, stronger one. Rather than deleting and then replacing, you should insert the new example, read the whole paragraph, and then move the rejected example, if it is rejected, to the end of your document. You can delete it later if you decide not to use it anywhere. If you do find a place for it, however, you will still have it on disk.

(3)   Deleting

Deleting unwanted material from a paper is easy with a computer. But this benefit can sometimes cause you to erase information that may prove useful later. For this reason, some writers use the end of their papers as temporary storage space as they revise. Only when they finish their papers do they delete this material. Other writers make hard copies of every draft they write. Remember that hasty deletion means loss of material, so keep even the material you have rejected until you are ready to hand in your paper.

(4)   Checking organization

The computer cannot organize your essay for you, but it can help you see whether or not you have stayed on your topic.

comp
A4

After you complete a draft, move the topic sentences of each paragraph. Move these sentences, which form a rough outline of the paper, to a new page. Keep them separated so you know where the paragraph breaks are. You can then check this outline for logic, completeness, and coherence.

If you have digressed from your thesis anywhere in the paper, the outline will show you where. You can then revise either the thesis or those paragraphs that have wandered from the point.

(5)   Checking paragraphs

If you suspect that certain paragraphs of an essay are less fully developed than others or are not coherent, you can use the computer to help you chart paragraph structure as you did in Chapter 4. You need not follow this procedure for every paragraph, but you can certainly use the computer to help you with your weakest sections.

To analyze paragraph structure, move each sentence so that it begins on a new line and so that the paragraph will not automatically reformat when you insert characters. (With most word-processing programs, you will have to include a blank line or some special character next to the sentence.) Then pick out the topic sentence of your paragraph, and put a *1* beside it. Mark more detailed sentences *2* and indent them five spaces to the right. Mark the most detailed sentences *3* and indent another five spaces.

Once you have charted a paragraph in this way, you can restructure it either by adding or deleting material or by rearranging sentences.

(6)   Revising from checklists

You can also use your computer to make a revision checklist that includes questions about audience, purpose, thesis statement and topic sentences, details, transitional elements, and any other points your instructor suggests (see 3d.3 for a sample revision checklist).

You might also add to your list notes about the grammatical or stylistic problems that your instructor identifies on your papers. Copying specific sentences or phrases from earlier papers into this list might help you in revising later papers. The computer's memory thus serves as an active notebook that reminds you of your most common problems.

(7)   Revising for style and mechanics

As you revise for style and mechanics, the global "find" and "replace" commands are especially useful. If you tend to overuse certain words— *very* or *really*, for example—you can search for their every appearance and delete empty usages. Or you can call up every comma in a graded and returned paper and review those you misused.

The computer is especially helpful to you when you study punctuation because unlike the human eye, it skips nothing. Although you may tire of checking punctuation, the computer does not.

comp
A4

(8)   Revising on a printout

Many writers find it hard to make revisions that affect the whole paper while they are sitting at the computer terminal. For one thing, most screens show only twenty-one lines of single-spaced text at a time. Paragraph length, an important indication of paragraph development, is difficult to judge when text moves off the top of the screen. Furthermore, it is hard for most of us to remember what preceded and what follows when we can see only twenty-one lines at a time. We are more accustomed to leafing through the pages to recall what we have written. When we cannot do this, many aspects of the paper, particularly connections, are bound to become fuzzy.

Therefore, you should always do at least one revision—perhaps the next to last—on paper. Many printers are able to print a draft-quality copy at very high speed, and this copy can be used for revising and editing. (Use only a daisy wheel, laser, or high-quality dot matrix printer for any work that you intend to submit.)

(9)   Proofreading

When you have completed your final draft, be sure to proofread carefully. Always proofread *both* on the screen, *and* on paper before you submit a final draft. And be sure to tear off tractor feed edges and separate pages before handing in your work.

A5   Revising and Editing Aids ——————

(1)   Spelling checkers

Computers are particularly good at identifying patterns, and they can quickly locate words that violate expected patterns—that is, words that are misspelled or mistyped. Some word-processing programs include dictionaries that check spelling, but more often you must purchase such programs separately.

Spelling checkers have limited word lists, and they do not identify words that are not in their programs. Most programs let you add to your computer's dictionary, and the user's manual should tell you how. Keep in mind that spelling checkers will not identify a word that is spelled correctly but used incorrectly (*there* used instead of *their*, for example). For this reason, you still need to read for spelling errors even after you have used a spelling checker.

Before you even think about using a spelling checker for your college work, be sure to get approval from your instructor.

(2)   Text-analysis programs

Text-analysis programs, which scan for other errors, are also available. Most of these are proofreading and style checkers that look for simple punctuation placement errors.

**comp
A5**

INCORRECT: "John", he said painfully, "I've been shot".

CORRECT: "John," he said painfully, "I've been shot."

Almost all identify overused or misused words—and some look for wordy, vague, or sexist language. A program might highlight wordy phrases, or it might give you this message.

Check line 10 for *due to the fact that;* consider using *because* to reduce wordiness.

Other text-analysis programs do more elaborate stylistic checking and analysis. If you are interested in trying text-analysis programs, be sure to ask your instructor for permission.

Appendix **B**

Preparing Your Papers

A clean, neatly typed or handwritten paper is a courtesy that you owe your readers. Sloppily typed or smudged papers not only make reading difficult but also detract from your ideas. Some of your instructors will give you specific guidelines for preparing a paper—and of course you should follow them. But others will expect you to be familiar with the conventions for preparing a paper suitable for submission. The following instructions are standard and, in general, are consistent with those found in the MLA style sheet (2nd ed).

B1 Typed Papers

Submit typed papers whenever possible. Because typewritten papers are easier to read and to correct, they are worth the extra effort—even if you are a slow typist. Before you type, make sure that your keys are clean and that you have a fresh black ribbon. Do not use "fancy" type, such as script, that could distract your readers. Be sure to make a carbon or photocopy for your files in case your instructor mislays your paper.

Use white, twenty-pound weight $8\frac{1}{2}'' \times 11''$ bond paper. Avoid both erasable paper and "onionskin." Not only do they smudge, but they are also difficult to read. In addition, it is hard to make corrections in ink on coated paper. If you feel that you must use erasable paper, make a copy of your finished paper on uncoated paper and submit the photocopy. Remember, never use paper that is not white or that is smaller than $8\frac{1}{2}'' \times 11''$.

Double-space your paper throughout. Single spacing does not leave enough room for instructors' comments or corrections.

B2 Handwritten Papers

If you have permission to submit a handwritten paper, use $8\frac{1}{2}'' \times 11''$ wide-lined paper. Do not use narrow-lined paper, unlined paper, or paper larger or smaller than 8½″ × 11″. Your best choice is paper that you can easily and neatly detach from a tablet. Do not use paper that leaves a ragged edge when torn from a spiral-bound notebook. Leave wide margins, write on every other line, and be sure to use only one side of each page. Use black or dark blue ink, never colored ink or pencil.

Make certain that you write clearly and that you form each letter carefully. If your handwriting is sloppy, try printing. Keep in mind that your instructor has many papers to mark and does not appreciate having to struggle with handwriting that is difficult to read.

B3   Format

Leave a one-inch margin at the top and bottom and on both sides of your paper. Indent five spaces for each new paragraph and ten spaces for a long quotation set off from the text.

Many instructors do not require a separate title page. If yours does not, type your name, your instructor's name, the course number, and

First Page of Manuscript Without a Title Page

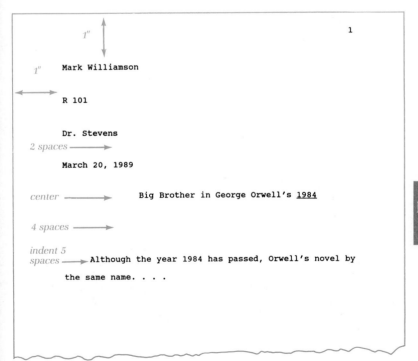

prep
B3

the date (all double spaced) one inch from the top of the first page of the paper, flush with the left-hand margin. Double-space again and center the title. If the title is longer than a single line, double-space and center the second line below the first. Capitalize all important words in the title, but not prepositions, conjunctions, articles, or the *to* in infinitives, unless they begin or end the title. Do not underline the title or enclose it in quotation marks. Underline words in the title if they are underlined in your paper (for example, book titles). Never put a period after a title, even if it is a sentence. Double-space twice between the last line of the title and the first line of text.

Number all pages of your paper consecutively in the upper right-hand corner one-half inch from the top. Do not put *p.* before the page numbers, and do not put periods or any other punctuation after them. To ensure that your instructor will be able to replace separated pages, put your name next to the page number of all pages other than the first (which already includes your name).

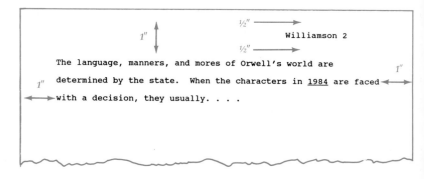

Subsequent Page of a Paper

prep
B3

Some instructors, however, prefer a separate title page and an out-line like the ones appearing with the paper at the end of Chapter 40 (page 630). The title page carries the title; your name, course, and section number; your instructor's name; and the date you submitted your paper. When you use a title page, repeat your title on the first page of your manuscript. Subsequent pages follow the format for a paper without a title page. If your paper includes an outline more than one page long, number each page with a lower-case Roman numeral (i, ii, etc.). A single-page outline need not be numbered. All pages of the text include your last name and the page number.

First Page of a Manuscript with a Separate Title Page

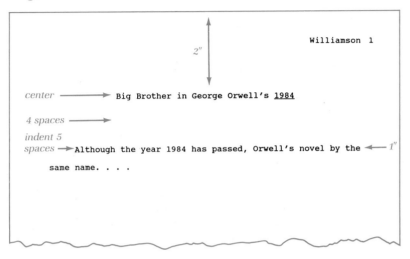

center ──────▶ Big Brother in George Orwell's <u>1984</u>

4 spaces ──────▶

indent 5
spaces ──▶Although the year 1984 has passed, Orwell's novel by the ◀── 1"

    same name. . . .

(2" at top margin; 1" right margin; Williamson 1)

B4   Tables and Illustrations ─────────────

Tables and illustrations aid readers by summarizing material that is being presented. In order to carry out this function, tables and illustrations should be placed as close as possible to the part of the paper in which they are presented. Graphic aids should be integrated into the text, not just dropped into the middle of it. You can achieve this end by introducing tables and illustrations and by explaining their meaning to readers. For example, you might include a sentence such as "Table 3 shows the year-by-year increase in the national debt from 1980 to 1988."

Tables should be headed *Table* and given a number and a descriptive caption. Type the heading and the descriptive caption flush left on separate lines. Give the full citation for the table (if it is not yours) and any notes below the table beginning at the left-hand margin. Double space the table text and the notes.

prep
B4

Table 2

Reading Miscues Based on the Reading Comprehension Test

Reading Miscue Inventory	Percentile
Total miscues	53
Semantically inappropriate miscues	60
Miscues which alter meaning	51
Overall loss of comprehension	40
Retelling score	20

Source: Adapted from Alice S. Horning, "The Trouble with Writing Is the Trouble with Reading," Journal of Basic Writing 6(1987) 46.

Illustrations—graphs, charts, line drawings, and photographs—should be labeled *Figure* (abbreviated *Fig.*) and given a number. Type the label, a descriptive caption, and the full citation below the illustration beginning at the left-hand margin.

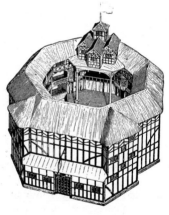

prep B5

Fig. 1. Etching of the Globe Playhouse from Thomas Mark Parrott and Edward Hubler, Six Plays and the Sonnets (New York: Scribner's, 1956) 2.

B5   Editing Your Final Draft

After finishing the final draft of your paper, proofread it carefully and correct any errors. If a page is messy or if you have to make extensive corrections, retype the entire page. Make minor corrections with correction fluid. Never make corrections in the margin or below the line. If

your instructor gives you permission, you may make some corrections
in black ink. Use the following proofreader's marks in moderation to
indicate your changes.

Proofreader's Marks

Mark	Mark in text
∧	add; insert a here (word)
℘	delete; take a a word out
⌣	close up; one w ord
℘	delete; and close up
#⁄∧	add a space
(stet)	disregard change (stet)
¶	¶ Begin new paragraph
/	lower-case Letter
≡	capital letter
∽	transpose lettres
—(ital)	italics (ital)
∽(bf)	boldface (bf)
⌐	You can also indicate that you do not want to begin a paragraph. Draw a line to connect the two sentences.

B6   Submitting Your Paper

When you are ready to submit your paper, fasten the pages together
with a paper clip or a single staple in the upper left-hand corner. Do not
staple the paper together like a book or use a binder that cannot easily
be removed. Remember that your instructor cannot write comments on
your paper if he or she cannot separate the pages.

B7 Typing Punctuation

The following table illustrates the conventions that determine the spacing of typed punctuation. Be sure to follow them consistently throughout the paper.

Type of Punctuation	Typing Conventions	Examples
1. apostrophes	Leave no space before or after the apostrophe unless the apostrophe ends a word.	Turner's landscapes The writer's local color novels
2. commas and semicolons	Leave no spaces before commas or semicolons; leave one space after commas and semicolons.	In fact, the story. . . . her son; in England. . . .
3. colons, question marks, and exclamation points	Leave no spaces before these punctuation marks; leave one space after a colon and two spaces after a question mark or exclamation point.	. . . the following: plot, character, and theme. Was he correct? The debate. . . . Never! Tyranny can never. . . .
4. quotation marks	Leave no spaces between quotation marks and the words or punctuation marks they enclose.	The short story "The Gold Bug" is by Poe. "I come to bury Caesar," said Mark Antony, "not to praise him."
5. periods	Leave no space before a period at the end of a sentence. Leave two spaces after the period.	. . . since 1938. The fight for intellectual freedom. . . .
6. hyphens or dashes	A hyphen is one stroke; a dash is two unspaced hyphens.	quick-witted Ford was born poor-- not rich--on a farm. . . .

Type of Punctuation	Typing Conventions	Examples
7. ellipsis marks	Separate all periods of an ellipsis mark by one space. Do not leave a space before the period at the end of a sentence that is followed by an ellipsis mark.	It was . . . a bitter satire of the motion picture industry. The report examines many classes of people. . . .
8. italics	Underline words to indicate italics. You can use a single line or underline each word separately.	The Sun Also Rises The Sun Also Rises
9. parentheses, brackets	Leave one space before opening a parenthesis and after closing a parenthesis. Do not space between the enclosed words and the parentheses. If the parentheses contain an entire sentence, leave two spaces before and after the parentheses. Brackets follow the same conventions as parentheses.	Charles Lindbergh attended the University of Wisconsin (1920–22) but left to learn how to fly. In 1907, Luther Burbank wrote *Training of the Human Plant.* (The pamphlet dealt with environment and human development.) In 1909. . . .
10. slashes	Leave no space before or after a slash except if the slash separates lines of poetry. In this case leave one space before and after the slash.	The object travels at 800 m/sec in a parallel direction. "Nature's first green is gold / Her hardest hue to hold." (Robert Frost)

prep
B7

Glossary of Usage

This glossary of usage provides you with a list of words and phrases that often give trouble to writers. As you use it, remember that this glossary is intended as a guide and that nothing in it is absolute. Language is constantly changing, so throughout this glossary an effort has been made to reflect current usage in college, business, and technical writing. When a usage is in dispute or in flux, the alternatives are discussed along with the advantages and disadvantages of each. In addition to the advice you receive from this glossary, your own sense of the language, as well as your assessment of your audience and purpose, should help you decide if a particular usage is appropriate. Remember, however, that this glossary is not a dictionary; whenever you need more information about a word, you should consult one of the general-purpose or specialized dictionaries described in Chapter 18.

a, an Use *a* before words that begin with consonants or words that have initial vowels that sound like consonants.

> *a* primitive artifact   *a* one-horse carriage

Use *an* before words that begin with vowels and words that begin with a silent *h*.

> *an* aqueous solution   *an* honest person

accept, except *Accept* is a verb that means "to receive." *Except* is a preposition or conjunction that means "other than." As a verb *except* means "to leave out."

> The auditors will *accept* all your claims *except* the last two.

> Aliens who have lived in the United States for more than five years are *excepted* from the regulation.

advice, advise *Advice* is a noun meaning "opinion or information offered." *Advise* is a verb that means "to offer advice to."

> The king sent a messenger to the oracle to ask for *advice*.

> The broker *advised* her client to stay away from speculative stocks.

affect, effect *Affect* is a verb meaning "to influence." *Effect* can be a verb or a noun. As a verb it means "to bring about," and as a noun it means "result."

A severe cutback in federal funds for student loans could *affect* his plans for graduate school.

The arbitrator tried to *effect* a settlement that would satisfy both the teachers and the school board.

The most notable *effect* of the German bombing of London was to strengthen the resolve of the British.

afraid, frightened   See **frightened, afraid.**

all ready, already   *All ready* means "wholly prepared." *Already* means "by or before this or that time."

During the thirties President Roosevelt made the country feel that it was *all ready* for any challenge that might confront it.

By the time Horatius decided to call for help, it was *already* too late.

all right, alright   Although there is a tendency in the direction of *alright*, current usage calls for *all right.*

allusion, illusion   An *allusion* is a reference or hint. In literature it is a brief reference to a person, place, historical event, or other literary work with which a reader is expected to be familiar. An *illusion* is something that is not what it seems.

In *The Catcher in the Rye* the main character makes an *allusion* to *The Return of the Native*, a book by Thomas Hardy.

The Viking landing proved that the canals of Mars are an *illusion* caused by atmospheric and topographical conditions.

among, between   *Among* refers to groups of more than two things. *Between* refers to just two things. The distinction between these terms seems to be fading, and it is becoming increasingly acceptable when speaking to use *between* for three or more things when *among* would sound awkward. In formal writing situations, however, you should maintain the distinction.

The three parties agreed *among* themselves to settle the question out of court.

By the time of his death in 323 B.C., Alexander's empire encompassed all the territory *between* Macedon and India.

amount, number   *Amount* refers to a quantity that cannot be counted. *Number* refers to things that can be counted. Always use *number* when referring to people.

Because he had missed several payments, the bank called in the full *amount* of the loan.

Seeing their commander fall, a large *number* of troops ran to his aid.

an, a.   See **a, an.**

ante-, anti-   Many students confuse these prefixes. *Ante-* means "before" or "in front of," and *anti-* means "against" or "opposed to."

usage

antebellum   *anti*aircraft

apt to   See **likely to, liable to.**

as . . . as . . .   In such constructions, *as* signals a comparison. To avoid awkwardness, you must use the second *as.*

> AWKWARD: John Steinbeck's *East of Eden* is as long if not longer
>   than *The Grapes of Wrath.*

> CLEAR: John Steinbeck's *East of Eden* is almost *as* long *as The
>   Grapes of Wrath.*

Traditionally *as . . . as* was used for a positive comparison and *so . . . as* for a negative one. Current usage, however, accepts *as . . . as* for both.

> The winters in England are not *as* harsh *as* those in many parts
> of the United States.

as, like   Current usage accepts *as* as a conjunction or a preposition. *Like,* however, should be used as a preposition only. If a full clause is introduced, *as* is preferred.

> In his novel *The Scarlet Letter* Hawthorne uses imagery *as* he
> does in his other works.

> In its use of imagery *The Scarlet Letter* is *like The House of the
> Seven Gables.*

When you use *as* as a preposition, it indicates equivalency or identity.

> After classes he works *as* a manager of a fast-food restaurant.

Like, however, indicates resemblance but never identity.

> Writers *like* Carl Sandburg appear once in a generation.

as, than   When making comparisons, either objective or subjective case pronouns can follow *as* or *than.* To determine case, you must know whether the things being compared are subjects or objects of verbs. A simple way to test this is to add the missing verb.

> Nassim was as tall *as* he (is tall).

> I have walked farther *than he* (has walked).

> I like Jim more *than* (I like) *him.* (*Him* is the object of the missing
> verb *like.*)

assure, ensure, insure   *Assure* means "to tell confidently or to promise." *Ensure* and *insure* can be used interchangeably to mean "to make certain." *Insure,* however, is almost always reserved for "the protection of people or property against loss."

> Caesar wished to *assure* the people that if they surrendered, he
> would not plunder their city.

> To *ensure* (or *insure*) the smooth operation of the mechanism,
> you should oil it every six months.

> It is extremely expensive for physicians to *insure* themselves
> against malpractice suits.

usage

at, to   Many people use the prepositions *at* and *to* after *where* in conversation. This colloquialism is redundant and should not be used in college writing.

> COLLOQUIAL: *Where* are you working *at?*
> *Where* are you going *to?*

> STANDARD: Where are you working?
> Where are you going?

awhile, a while   *Awhile* is an adverb. *A while* consists of an article and a noun that you can use as an object of a preposition.

> Before we continue we will rest *awhile.* (modifies the verb *rest*)

> Before we continue we will rest for *a while.* (object of the preposition *for*)

bad, badly   *Bad* is an adjective and *badly* is an adverb. So used, they should cause you no problems.

> The school board decided that *The Tin Drum* by Günter Grass was a *bad* book and deleted it from the high school reading list.

> For the past five years American automobile makers have been doing *badly.*

After verbs that refer to any of the senses or any other linking verb, use the adjective form.

> He looked *bad;* he felt *bad;* it tasted *bad.*

Bad meaning "very much" is colloquial and should be avoided in academic writing.

> COLLOQUIAL: Jake Barnes felt that he needed a vacation in Spain *bad.*

> STANDARD: Jake Barnes felt that he needed a vacation in Spain *very much.*

being as, being that   Colloquial for *because.* These awkward phrases add unnecessary words and weaken your sentences.

> *Because* (not *being that*) the climate was getting colder, a great number of animals migrated southward.

beside, besides   *Beside* is a preposition meaning "next to" and occasionally "apart from." *Besides* can be either a preposition or an adverb. As a preposition, *besides* means "except" or "other than." As an adverb it means "in addition to."

> *Beside* the tower was a wall that ran the length of the old section of the city.

> The judge pointed out to the lawyer that his argument was *beside* the point.

> *Besides* its industrial uses, laser technology has many other applications.

usage

Edison not only invented the light bulb and the ticker tape, but the phonograph *besides.*

between, among   See **among, between.**

bi-, semi-   *Bi-* is a prefix meaning "two" or "having two" (*bi*valve, *bi*carbonate, *bi*lingual). *Semi-* is a prefix meaning "half of" or "divided by two." The use of these prefixes, however, is not regular. Thus, *biennial* means "happening every two years" and *biannual* means "happening twice in one year." To avoid confusion, consult a dictionary. Or avoid the situation altogether and say "happening every two years," or "happening twice in one year."

bring, take   *Bring* means to transport from a farther place to a nearer place. *Take* means to carry or convey from a nearer place to a farther one.

In the late nineteenth century many Russian Jewish immigrants were able to *bring* to this country only the clothes they wore.

Take this message to the general and wait for a reply.

can, may   *Can* denotes ability and *may* indicates permission.

Can (are they *able* to?) freshmen participate in the work-study program if they have not completed composition?

May (do they have permission?) registered aliens collect unemployment benefits?

censor, censure   To *censor* is to label as undesirable passages of books, plays, films, news, essays, etc. To *censure* is to condemn or criticize harshly.

Recently Studs Terkel's book *Working* was *censored* by a school district in Pennsylvania.

In 1633 Galileo was *censured* by the Inquisition for holding that the sun was the center of the universe.

center around   This common colloquialism is acceptable in speech but not in writing. You may write *revolve around* or *center on* but never *center around* (which is not accurate).

The report *centers on* (not *around*) the effects of cigarette smoking on the circulatory system.

cite, sight, site   *Cite* means "to quote or mention as an example." *Sight* means "spectacle or view," and *site* means "location or place." Because these words sound exactly alike, they can be confusing.

usage

Ordinarily the Supreme Court allows a half-hour to an hour for lawyers to *cite* cases that will support their arguments.

Several days before their first *sight* of land Columbus's crew attempted a mutiny.

The engineers surveyed the *site* before they began the plans for the new office complex.

compare, contrast   *Contrast* means to show differences. *Compare* means to show both similarities *and* differences.

Ernest Jones wrote a book in which he *compared* Hamlet and Oedipus. (He discussed their similarities and differences.)

The company's earnings this year *contrast* sharply with its earnings last year. (The earnings are different.)

compare to, compare with   Formal usage calls for *compare to* when you want to stress similarities, and *compare with* when you want to analyze similarities *and* differences. Many instructors do not insist on this distinction, but you should be aware of it for formal writing situations.

In one of Shakespeare's sonnets, the speaker *compares* his beloved *to* a summer's day.

This study *compares* Nat Turner's revolt *with* other slave revolts that occurred in the eighteenth and nineteenth centuries.

complement, compliment   *Complement* means "to complete or add to." *Compliment* means "to give praise."

A double-blind study would *complement* their preliminary work on this anticancer drug.

Before accepting the 1949 Nobel Prize for literature, William Faulkner *complimented* the people of Sweden for their courtesy and kindness.

conscious, conscience   *Conscious* means "having one's mental faculties awake." *Conscience* is the moral sense of right and wrong.

With a local anesthetic a patient remains *conscious* during this procedure.

During the American Civil War, the Copperheads followed the dictates of *conscience* and refused to fight.

consensus   "Consensus of opinion" is redundant because *consensus* means an "agreement of the majority." Never write "they reached a consensus of opinion." Using "they agreed" or "the majority view was" eliminates any possibility of misunderstanding.

continual, continuous   These words are frequently confused. *Continual* means "recurring at intervals." *Continuous* refers to an action that occurs without interruption.

A pulsar is a star that emits a *continual* stream of electromagnetic radiation. (It emits radiation at regular intervals.)

A small battery allows the watch to run *continuously* for five years. (It runs without stopping.)

could of, would of   In speech, the contractions *could've* and *would've* sound like the nonstandard constructions *could of* and *would of*. Spell out *could have* and *would have* in college writing.

Macbeth *would have* (not *would of*) defied his wife if he *could have* (not *could of*).

council, counsel, consul   Because of their similar pronunciation and spelling, these words are commonly confused. A *council* is a noun

usage

meaning "a body of persons that passes laws or gives advice." *Counsel* is a verb meaning "to give advice." Thus, a counselor is a person who gives advice. *Consul* is a noun meaning "a representative of a country who lives in a foreign city."

couple of   *Couple* means "a pair," but *couple of* may mean loosely "several" or "a few." When you designate quantities, avoid ambiguity. Write "four points," "three reasons," or "two examples" rather than "a couple of" or "several."

criterion, criteria   Although many people use these singular and plural words interchangeably, *criteria*, from the Greek, is the plural of *criterion*, meaning "standard for judgment."

> Of all the *criteria* for hiring graduating seniors, class rank is the most important *criterion*.

curriculum   *Curriculum*, from the Latin, is a noun meaning "a course of study." The correct plural form is *curricula*.

> The premedical *curriculum* at this university is extremely demanding.

> There are three *curricula* you can take in the college of business.

data   *Data* is the plural of the Latin *datum*, meaning "fact." In everyday speech and writing *data* is used for both singular and plural. In college writing preserve the distinction.

> The *data* discussed in this section *are* summarized in the graph in Appendix A.

You can avoid the problem by using *facts* or *results* instead of *data*.

device, devise   *Device* is a noun meaning "a thing adapted for a particular function." *Devise* is a verb meaning "to invent."

> Simple *devices* like the zipper or the safety pin can make their inventors rich.

> A common theme in folklore and fairy tales is young lovers *devising* a plan to outwit an evil parent or guardian.

different from, different than   *Different than* is used extensively in American speech. Stylists, who point out that *different than* indicates a comparison where none is intended, prefer *different from*. In college writing, use *different from*.

usage

> His test scores were not much *different from* (not *than*) mine.

discreet, discrete   *Discreet* means "careful or prudent." *Discrete* means "separate or individually distinct."

> Because Madame Bovary was not *discreet* with her lover, her reputation suffered.

> Current research has demonstrated that atoms can be broken into hundreds of *discrete* particles.

disinterested, uninterested *Disinterested* means "objective or capable of making an impartial judgment." *Uninterested* means "indifferent or unconcerned."

> The narrator of Ernest Hemingway's "A Clean, Well-Lighted Place" is a *disinterested* observer of the action.

> Finding no treasure after leading an expedition from Florida to Oklahoma, Hernando de Soto was *uninterested* in going farther.

economic, economical *Economic* refers to "things maintained for profit or for business." It can also refer to the science of economics. *Economical* means "thrifty and avoiding waste."

> A depression is a period of *economic* crisis characterized by falling prices, tightening of credit, lowering of production, and increased unemployment.

> Silas Marner was *economical* to the point of being a miser.

effect, affect See **affect, effect.**

elicit, illicit *Elicit* means "to draw out" or "evoke." *Illicit* means "unlawful" or "forbidden."

> Some psychiatrists will hypnotize patients to *elicit* responses from them.

> Mata Hari was a German agent who obtained *illicit* information from French officials by seducing them.

emigrate from, immigrate to *To emigrate* is "to leave one's country and settle in another." *To immigrate* is "to come to another country and reside there." The noun forms of these words are *emigrant* and *immigrant*.

> In 1887 my great-grandfather *emigrated from* the Russian city of Minsk and traveled by ship to Boston. During that year many other *emigrants* made the same trip.

> The potato famine of 1846–1847 caused many Irish to *immigrate to* the United States. These *immigrants* became builders, politicians, and storekeepers.

ensure, assure, insure See **assure, ensure, insure.**

enthused *Enthused* is a colloquial form of *enthusiastic* and should never be used.

> President John F. Kennedy was *enthusiastic* (not *enthused*) about the United States space program.

usage

equally as good A redundant blend of the two phrases "equally good" and "as good as." Use one or the other, but not *equally as good.*

etc. *Etc.*, the abbreviation of *et cetera*, means "and the rest." The construction *and etc.*, therefore, is redundant. Although *etc.* is common in popular writing and speech, do not use it in your college writing. Say "and so on" or, better, specify exactly what *etc.* stands for.

UNCLEAR: Before beginning a research paper you should have paper and pencil, *etc.*

REVISED: Before beginning a research paper you should have a pencil, bond paper, and a clean typewriter ribbon.

everyday, every day *Everyday* is an adjective that means "ordinary" or "commonplace." *Every day* means "occurring daily."

In the Gettysburg Address, Lincoln used *everyday* words to create a model of clarity and conciseness.

In *The Canterbury Tales* Chaucer depicts a group of pilgrims who tell stories *every day* as they ride from London to Canterbury.

except, accept See **accept, except.**

farther, further The distinction between these words as adjectives has all but disappeared. In formal writing, however, some stylists still prefer *farther* to designate distance and *further* to designate degree.

The Pioneer 10 Space Probe has traveled *farther* in space than any other man-made object.

Critics of the welfare system charge that government subsidies to the poor encourage *further* dependence.

Two uses of *further* are still very much with us. As a conjunctive adverb *further* means "besides." As a transitive verb, *to further* means "to promote" or "to advance."

Napoleon I was one of the greatest generals in history; *further,* he promoted liberalism through widespread legal reforms.

Tom Jones, the hero of Fielding's novel, is a poor boy who is able to *further* himself with luck and good looks.

fewer, less Use *fewer* with nouns that can be counted: *fewer* books, *fewer* people, *fewer* dollars. Use *less* with quantities that cannot be counted: *less* pain, *less* power, *less* enthusiasm.

Fewer young families than ever can afford the high interest rates on home mortgages.

Sufferers of arthritis often take large quantities of aspirin so they will have *less* pain.

figuratively, literally See **literally, figuratively.**

firstly (secondly, thirdly, . . .) Archaic forms meaning "in the first . . . second . . . third place." Use *first, second, third.*

usage

former, formerly, formally *Former* as an adjective means "preceding" or "previous." As a noun it means "the first of two things mentioned previously." It is often used in conjunction with *latter.*

The *former* residents of this area, the Delaware Indians, were forced to cede their land in 1795.

Two books mark the extremes of Herman Melville's career: *Typee* and *Moby-Dick.* The *former* was a best seller; the *latter* was generally ignored by the public.

Formerly means "just before" or "in a time past."

> *Formerly,* tonality, as it evolved in the seventeenth century, was considered the natural law in music.

Formally means "ceremonially" or "in a manner required by convention."

> Before assuming their duties, ambassadors have their credentials *formally* accepted by the president.

freshman, freshmen   *Freshman* is singular and *freshmen* is plural. Even so, only *freshman* is used as the adjective form: *freshman* composition, *freshman* registration, *freshman* dormitories.

frightened, afraid   Much confusion surrounds the prepositions that follow these words. *Frightened* should be accompanied by *at* or *by; afraid* by *of.*

> Dolley Madison, wife of President James Madison, was *frightened at* the thought of the British burning Washington.

> In Charles Dickens's *A Christmas Carol,* Scrooge is *frightened by* three ghosts.

> Young children are often *afraid of* the dark.

further, farther   See **farther, further.**

good, well   *Good* is an adjective, never an adverb.

> The townspeople thought the proposal for a new municipal water plant was a *good* one.

Well can function as an adverb or an adjective. As an adverb it means "in a good manner." Correct usage requires "He did *well* (not *good*) on the test" and "She swam *well* (not *good*) in the meet."

> *Well* is used as an adjective with verbs that denote a state of being or feeling. Here *well* can mean "in good health": "I feel *well.*" If you mean that your sense of feeling is acute, however, "my feeling is good" leaves no ambiguity.

good and   This colloquial phrase meaning "very" is not appropriate in college writing.

> After escaping from the Iroquois, Natty Bumppo was *very* [not *good and*] tired.

got to   *Got to* is slang and not suitable in college writing. To indicate obligation use *have to, has to,* or *must.*

> INAPPROPRIATE: Anyone who takes a literature course has *got to* get a copy of *A Glossary of Literary Terms* by M. H. Abrams.

> REVISED: Anyone who takes a literature course *has* to get a copy of *A Glossary of Literary Terms* by M. H. Abrams.

hanged, hung   Both *hanged* and *hung* are past participles of *hang.*

Hanged is used to refer to executions. *Hung* is used in all other senses meaning "suspended" or "held up."

> Billy Budd was *hanged* from the mainyard of the ship for killing the master-at-arms.

> The pictures in the National Gallery were *hung* to take advantage of the natural lighting in the various rooms.

he, she   Traditionally *he* has been used in the generic sense to refer to both males and females. To acknowledge the equality of the sexes, however, avoid the generic *he*. Efforts in the direction of a new neutral pronoun have not caught on. And constructions such as *he or she* or *he/she* are cumbersome, especially when used a number of times in a paragraph. To avoid problems, use the second person singular or first and third person plural pronouns when possible.

> TRADITIONAL: Before registering, *each student* should be sure *he* has received *his* student number.

> REVISION: Before registering, *you* should receive *your* student number.

> REVISION: Before registering, *we* should receive *our* student numbers.

> REVISION: Before registering, *students* should receive *their* student numbers.

hopefully   The adverb *hopefully* should modify a verb, an adjective, or another adverb. Increasingly, however, *hopefully* is being used as a sentence modifier meaning "it is hoped." At present, some stylists object to this use, so to be safe and unambiguous, use *hopefully* in its traditional sense.

> AMBIGUOUS: *Hopefully*, scientists will find an alternative energy source by the end of the century. (Who is hopeful? Scientists or the writer?)

> REVISED: Scientists *hope* they will find an alternative energy source by the end of the century.

Here is an acceptable use of *hopefully*.

> During the 1930's many of the nation's jobless looked *hopefully* to the federal government for relief. (*Hopefully* modifies *looked*.)

illicit, elicit   See **elicit, illicit.**

illusion, allusion   See **allusion, illusion.**

immigrate, emigrate   See **emigrate, immigrate.**

imply, infer   *Imply* means "to hint" or "to suggest." *Infer* means "to conclude from." When you *imply*, you *send out* a suggestion; when you *infer*, you *receive* or draw a conclusion. You should maintain this distinction in your writing.

> Mark Antony *implied* that Brutus and the other conspirators had wrongfully killed Julius Caesar.

The crowd *inferred* his meaning and called for the punishment of the conspirators.

in, into   Use *in* when you want to indicate position. Use *into* when you want to indicate "motion to a point within a thing."

As he stood *in* the main burial vault of the tomb of Tutankhamen, Howard Carter saw a wealth of artifacts.

Before he walked *into* the cave, Tom Sawyer grasped Becky Thatcher's hand.

In 1828 Russia and Persia entered *into* the Treaty of Turkmanchai.

infer, imply   See **imply, infer.**

ingenious, ingenuous   *Ingenious* means "clever at inventing or organizing." *Ingenuous* means "open" or "artless."

Ludwig van Beethoven is recognized as one of the most *ingenious* composers who ever lived.

For a politician the mayor was surprisingly *ingenuous.*

insure, ensure, assure   See **assure, ensure, insure.**

irregardless, regardless   See **regardless, irregardless.**

its, it's   *Its* is a possessive pronoun. *It's* is a contraction of *it is.* Remember this distinction, and do not use these words interchangeably.

The most obvious characteristic of a modern corporation is the separation of *its* management from *its* ownership.

It's not often that you can see a collection of rare books such as the one housed in the Library of Congress.

-ize, -wise   The suffix *-ize* is used to change nouns and adjectives into verbs: *civilize, industrialize, Westernize, immunize.* The suffix *-wise* is used to change a noun or adjective into an adverb: *likewise, otherwise.* Unfortunately, business, advertising, and government people, along with professional educators, use these suffixes carelessly, making up words as they please: *finalize, prioritize, taste-wise, weather-wise,* and *policy-wise,* for example. Be sure to look up suspect *-ize* and *-wise* words in the dictionary to make sure that they are standard usages.

judgment, judgement   The American *judgment* is preferred over the British spelling *judgement.*

kind of, sort of   *Kind of* and *sort of* to mean "rather" or "somewhat" are colloquial and should not appear in college writing.

COLLOQUIAL: The countess was surprised to see that Napoleon was *kind of* short.

REVISED: The countess was surprised to see that Napoleon was *rather* short.

Reserve *kind of* and *sort of* for occasions when you categorize.

Willie Stark, a character in Robert Penn Warren's *All the King's*

usage

Men, is the *kind of* man who begins by meaning well and ends by being corrupted by his success.

latter See **former, formerly, formally.**

lay, lie See **lie, lay.**

lead, led The verb *lead* (rhymes with *feed*) means "to guide or direct." As a noun, *lead* (rhymes with *bed*) denotes a metal.

> You can *lead* a horse to water, but you can't make him drink.

> For centuries alchemists searched for the formula that would enable them to change *lead* into gold.

Led (also rhymes with *bed*) is the past tense and the past participle form of the verb *lead.*

> The remarkable Indian woman Sacajawea *led* the Lewis and Clark expedition across the high Rocky Mountains.

leave, let *Leave* means "to go away from" or "to let remain." *Let* means "to allow" or "to permit."

> Many missionaries were forced to *leave* China after the Communist revolution in 1948.

> As the liquid boils away, it will *leave* a dark brown precipitate at the bottom of the flask.

> In London it is illegal to *let* dogs foul the footpath.

led, lead See **lead, led.**

lend, loan See **loan, lend.**

less, fewer See **fewer, less.**

let, leave See **leave, let.**

liable to See **likely to, liable to, apt to.**

lie, lay *Lie* is an intransitive verb (one that does not take an object) that means "to recline." *Lay* is a transitive verb meaning "to put" or "to place."

Base Form	Past	Past Participle	Present Participle
lie	lay	lain	lying

> Each afternoon she would *lie* in the sun and listen to the surf.

> *As I Lay Dying* is a novel by William Faulkner.

> In 1871 Heinrich Schliemann unearthed the city of Troy that had *lain* undisturbed for two thousand years.

> The painting *Odalisque* by Eugène Delacroix shows a nude *lying* on a couch.

Base Form	Past	Past Participle	Present Participle
lay	laid	laid	laying

> The Federalist Papers *lay* the foundation for the American conservative movement.

In October of 1781 the British *laid* down their arms and surrendered to George Washington at Yorktown.

After he had *laid* his money on the counter, he walked out of the restaurant.

We watched the Amish stone masons *laying* a wall without using mortar.

like, as See **as, like.**

likely to, liable to, apt to *Likely to* implies a strong chance something might happen. *Liable to* implies that something undesirable is about to occur. *Apt to* implies having a natural tendency.

Medical researchers feel that in fifty years human beings are *likely to* have a life span of over a hundred years.

If we do not do something to correct the poor drainage in this area, we are *liable to* repeat last year's flooding.

Old books are *apt* to increase in value if you protect them from heat and moisture.

literally, figuratively *Literally* means "following the letter" or "in a strict sense." *Figuratively* is its opposite and means "metaphorically" or "not literally."

Literally, the Declaration of Independence is a list of grievances that the English colonists had against their king.

Figuratively, the Declaration of Independence is a document that elevates the rights of the common man above the divine right of kings.

loan, lend American usage prefers *lend* as a verb and *loan* as a noun. "He offered to *lend* me his car." "I negotiated a *loan* with the bank."

loose, lose *Loose* is an adjective meaning "not rigidly fastened or securely attached." *Lose* is a verb meaning "to misplace."

The barons turned King John *loose* after he agreed to sign the Magna Carta.

The marble facing of the building became *loose* and fell to the sidewalk.

After only two drinks, most people *lose* their ability to judge distance.

mad, angry In American colloquial usage, *mad* has become a synonym for *angry*. In writing, however, you should maintain the distinction between these words. *Angry* means "annoyed" or "irritated" and *mad* means "insane."

COLLOQUIAL: The librarian was *mad* when they returned the books six months late.

REVISED: The librarian was *angry* when they returned the books six months late.

usage

The term *lunacy* derives from the ancient belief that the light of the moon can drive people *mad*.

majority, plurality   These words are often confused. *Majority* denotes more than half. *Plurality* means a larger number but not necessarily a majority. A candidate with a *majority* has over 50 percent of the votes cast. A candidate with a *plurality* has more votes than any of the other candidates, but not over 50 percent of the total. Use *most* rather than *majority* when you do not know the exact numbers.

> INCORRECT: The soprano got the *majority* of the applause.

> CORRECT: The soprano got *most* of the applause.

man   Like the generic pronoun *he*, *man* has been used in English to denote members of both sexes. Certain words, especially those describing occupations, disturb those concerned with the status of women: *policeman*, *chairman*, *postman*, and *fireman*, for example. In recent years, neutral terms that refer to *both* men and women have emerged: *police officer*, *chairperson*, *letter carrier*, and *fire fighter*. Other terms, such as *police person* and *statesperson*, seem awkward and are not widely used. When you write, be sure to consider your audience and use words that will not offend.

may, can   See **can, may**.

media, medium   *Medium*, meaning a "means of conveying or broadcasting something," is singular. *Media* is the plural form.

> Television has replaced print and film as the *medium* of communication that has the most profound effect on our lives.

> A good business presentation uses a number of *media* to make its point.

might have, might of   *Might of* is not the written form for the contraction of *might have*. Do not use it in your writing.

> John F. Kennedy *might have* (not *might of*) been a great president had he not been assassinated.

number, amount   See **amount, number**

on account of   Use *because of.*

> The Ford Motor Company had to recall over a million Pintos *because of* (not *on account of*) their faulty gasoline tanks.

passed, past   *Passed* means "left behind," "threw," or "attained a certain standard."

usage

> Even though we were going sixty miles an hour, another car *passed* us as though we were standing still.

> Last season the Dallas Cowboys' quarterback *passed* for over a thousand yards.

> After trying for nearly four months, my brother finally *passed* his driver's test.

Past has several meanings. As a noun, *past* means "a time gone by."

> Recent discoveries of fossils in Africa tell us a great deal about our *past.*

As an adjective, *past* refers to a previous time.

> In Stephen Crane's novel *Maggie: A Girl of the Streets*, the main character, Maggie, pays dearly for her *past* mistakes.

As a preposition, *past* means "beyond in time or place."

> The space shuttle has been designed to operate *past* the upper level of the earth's atmosphere.

per   Acceptable for technical and business writing, *per* is considered colloquial in academic writing.

> The minimum wage was raised to $3.35 *an* (not *per*) hour.

percent, percentage   *Percent* indicates a part of a hundred when a specific number is referred to: "10 *percent* of his weekly salary"; "5 *percent* of the monthly rent." *Percentage* is used when no specific number is referred to: "a *percentage* of the people"; "a *percentage* of next year's receipts." In technical and business writing it is permissible to use the % sign after percentages you are comparing. Write out *percent* in college writing.

persecute, prosecute   *Persecute* means "to harass or worry, especially for political or religious beliefs." *Prosecute* means "to institute legal proceedings against."

> Quakers were *persecuted* in England until the passage of the Toleration Act of 1689.

> Because of the suspect's age, the district attorney decided not to *prosecute.*

personal, personnel   *Personal* means "one's own" or "private." *Personnel* means "people who are employed in a business firm or in the military."

> Years ago many people kept journals in which they recorded their *personal* experiences.

> The first person I met when I arrived at the plant for my interview was the *personnel* manager.

> The military transported the troops to battle in armored *personnel* carriers.

phenomenon, phenomena   A *phenomenon* is a single observable fact or event. It can also refer to a rare or significant thing. *Phenomena* is the plural form.

usage

> Metamorphosis is a *phenomenon* that occurs in many insects, mollusks, amphibians, and fish.

John Stuart Mill was a *phenomenon*. He could read classical Greek at the age of five.

Comets are celestial *phenomena* that have been regarded with awe and terror and were once taken as omens of unfavorable events.

plurality, majority   See **majority, plurality**.

precede, proceed   *Precede* means "to go or come before." *Proceed* means "to go forward in an orderly way."

Robert Frost's *North of Boston* was *preceded* by another volume of poetry, *A Boy's Will*.

In 1532 Francisco Pizarro landed at Tumbes and *proceeded* south until he encountered the Incas.

principal, principle   As a noun, *principal* means "a sum of money (minus interest) invested or lent" or "a person in the leading position." As an adjective it means "most important."

If you cash the bond before maturity, a penalty can be subtracted from the *principal* as well as the interest.

The *principal* of the high school is a talented administrator who has instituted a number of changes.

Women are the *principal* wage earners in many American households.

A *principle* is a rule of conduct or a basic truth.

The Constitution embodies the fundamental *principles* upon which the American republic is founded.

quote, quotation   *Quote* is a verb meaning "to speak or write a passage from another." *Quotation* is a noun meaning "something that is quoted."

Be sure to use appropriate documentation when you *quote* one of your sources.

In "Politics and the English Language," George Orwell offers several *quotations* (not *quotes*) as examples of bad prose.

raise, rise   *Raise* is a transitive verb and *rise* is an intransitive verb. Thus, *raise* takes an object and *rise* does not.

A famous photograph taken during World War II shows American Marines *raising* the flag on Iwo Jima.

As Babe Ruth ran the bases after hitting a home run, he would *raise* his cap to the crowd.

The planet Venus is called the morning star because when it *rises*, it is brighter than any light in the sky except the sun or moon.

It was only sixty-six years from the time the Wright Brothers' plane first *rose* into the air until the first moon landing.

real, really   *Real* means "genuine" or "authentic." *Really* means "actually." In your college writing, do not use *real* as an adjective meaning "very."

usage

With its ducklike bill, flat tail, and webbed feet, the platypus hardly looks *real*.

When news of the bombing of Pearl Harbor was first broadcast, many people did not believe that it had *really* happened.

COLLOQUIAL: The planaria is a *real* flat worm that we studied in biology class.

REVISED: The planaria is a *very* flat worm that we studied in biology class.

reason is that, reason is because   Most authorities still insist that *reason* be used with *that* and not *because*. *Because* is redundant here and should be avoided.

The *reason* he moved out of the city *is that* (not *because*) property taxes rose sharply.

regardless, irregardless   *Irregardless* is a nonstandard version of *regardless*. The suffix "-less" means "without" or "free from," so the prefix "ir-" is unnecessary.

SLANG: *Irregardless* of what some people might think, drunk drivers kill more than twenty-five thousand people a year.

REVISED: *Regardless* of what some people might think, drunk drivers kill more than twenty-five thousand people a year.

respectively, respectfully, respectably   *Respectively* means "in the order given." *Respectfully* means "giving honor or deference." *Respectably* means "worthy of respect."

In this paper I will discuss "The Sisters" and "The Dead," which are, *respectively*, the first and the last stories in James Joyce's collection *Dubliners*.

When being presented to Queen Elizabeth of England, foreigners are asked to bow *respectfully*.

Even though Abraham Lincoln ran a *respectable* campaign for the United States Senate, he was defeated by Stephen Douglas in 1858.

rise, raise   See **raise, rise.**

semi-, bi-   See **bi-, semi-.**

set, sit   To *set* means "to put" or "to lay." To *sit* means "to assume a sitting position."

Base Form	Past	Past Participle	Present Participle
set	set	set	setting
sit	sat	sat	sitting

After rocking the baby, he *set* it down carefully in its crib.

Research has shown that many children *sit* in front of the television five to six hours a day.

shall, will   *Will* is swiftly replacing *shall* to express all future action.

should of   See **could of, would of.**

sight, cite, site   See **cite, site, sight.**

usage

sit, set See **set, sit.**

site, sight, cite See **cite, sight, site.**

sometime, sometimes, some time *Sometime* means "at some time in the future." *Sometimes* means "now and then." *Some time* means "a period of time."

> In his essay "The Case Against Man," Isaac Asimov says that *sometime,* far in the future, human beings will not be able to produce enough food to sustain themselves.

> All automobiles, no matter how well constructed, *sometimes* need repairs.

> At the battle of Gettysburg, General Meade's failure to counterattack gave Lee *some time* to regroup his troops.

sort of, kind of See **kind of, sort of.**

stationary, stationery *Stationary* means "staying in one place." *Stationery* means "materials for writing" or "letter paper."

> When viewed from the earth, a communications satellite traveling at the same speed as the earth appears to be *stationary* in the sky.

> The secretaries are responsible for keeping departmental offices supplied with *stationery.*

take, bring See **bring, take.**

than, then *Than* is a conjunction used to indicate a comparison, and *then* is an adverb indicating time.

> The new shopping center is bigger *than* the old one.

> He did his research; *then* he wrote a report.

than, as See **as, than.**

that, which, who Use *that* or *which* when referring to a thing. Use *who* when referring to a person.

> In *How the Other Half Lives,* Jacob Riis described the conditions *that* existed in working-class slums in nineteenth-century America.

> *The Wonderful Wizard of Oz, which* was published in 1900, was originally entitled *From Kansas to Fairyland.*

> Anyone *who* (not *that*) visits Maine cannot help being impressed by the beauty of the scenery and the ruggedness of the landscape.

themselves, theirselves, theirself *Theirselves* and *theirself* are nonstandard variants of *themselves.*

> Pioneer families had to build their shelter and clear their land by *themselves* (not *theirself* or *theirselves*).

then, than See **than, then.**

there, their, they're Use *there* to indicate place and in the expressions *there is* and *there are.*

usage

I have always wanted to visit the Marine Biological Laboratory in Woods Hole, Massachusetts, but I have never gotten *there*.

There is nothing that we can do to resurrect a species once it becomes extinct.

Their is a possessive pronoun.

James Watson and Francis Crick did *their* work on the molecular structure of DNA at the Cavendish Laboratory at Cambridge University.

They're is a contraction of *they are.*

White sharks and Mako sharks are dangerous to human beings because *they're* good swimmers and especially sensitive to the scent of blood.

thus, therefore   *Thus* means "in this way," not "therefore" or "so."

In Joseph Conrad's *Heart of Darkness*, Kurtz becomes a man-god to the natives. *Thus,* he is able to collect a fortune in ivory.

INCORRECT: Throughout the past year interest rates have dropped dramatically. Thus, businesses are able to buy the equipment they need to modernize their operations.

REVISED: Throughout the past year interest rates have risen dramatically, so businesses are unable to buy the equipment they need to modernize their operations.

to, at   See **at, to.**

to, too, two   *To* is a preposition that indicates direction.

Last year we flew from New York *to* California.

Too is an adverb that means "also" or "more than is needed."

"Tippecanoe and Tyler *too*" was William Henry Harrison's campaign slogan during the 1840 presidential election.

The plot was *too* complicated.

Two expresses the number 2.

Just north of *Two* Rivers, Wisconsin, is a petrified forest.

try to, try and   *Try and* is the colloquial equivalent of the more formal *try to.*

COLLOQUIAL: Throughout most of his career E. R. Rutherford was determined to *try and* discover the structure of the atom.

REVISED: Throughout most of his career E. R. Rutherford *tried to* discover the structure of the atom.

-type   Newspaper and television reporters, among others, frequently add *-type* to adjectives. Deleting this empty suffix eliminates clutter and clarifies meaning.

usage

COLLOQUIAL: Found in the wreckage of the house was an *incendiary-type* device.

REVISED: Found in the wreckage of the house was an *incendiary* device.

COLLOQUIAL: It was a *cancer-type* tumor.

REVISED: The tumor was *cancerous*.

uninterested, disinterested   See **disinterested, uninterested**.

unique   *Unique* means "the only one," not "remarkable" or "unusual."

COLLOQUIAL: Its undershot lower jaw makes the English bulldog *unique* among dogs.

REVISED: Its undershot lower jaw makes the English bulldog unusual among dogs.

CORRECT USAGE: In their scope and unity, Michelangelo's paintings are *unique*.

Because *unique* means "the only one," it can take no intensifiers. Never use constructions like "the most unique" or "very unique."

used to, use to   *Used to* is the standard form; *use to* is not.

Before factories many women *used to* (not *use to*) be limited to work they could do at home.

wait for, wait on   *To wait for* means "to defer action until something occurs." *To wait on* means "to act as a waiter."

COLLOQUIAL: I am *waiting on* dinner.

REVISED: I am *waiting for* dinner.

CORRECT: The captain *waited on* the head table himself.

(a) wake, (a) waken   Like *lie* and *lay*, these two verbs are easily confused. As a transitive verb, *wake* means "to arouse from sleep," and as an intransitive verb it means "to cease sleeping." *Waken* is usually used as a transitive verb that means "to arouse from sleep."

Base Form	Past	Past Participle	Present Participle
(a) wake	woke	waked	waking
(a) waken	wakened	wakened	wakening

The alarm clock *wakes* Jim up at 6:30 every morning.

Jane Pauley of the *Today Show* says that she *wakes* up at 3:30 every morning.

After entering the castle, the prince *awakened* Sleeping Beauty with a kiss.

weather, whether   *Weather* refers to atmospheric conditions such as rain, snow, wind, or hail. *Whether* can introduce an indirect question or mean "in either case."

Space shots are often postponed because of unfavorable *weather* conditions at the launch site.

usage

Whether or not the country will have a tax increase is up to Congress.

well, good See **good, well.**

were, we're Some people pronounce these words alike, and so they confuse them when they write. *Were* is a verb; *we're* is the contraction of *we are.*

The Trojans *were* asleep when the Greeks climbed out of the wooden horse and took the city.

We Americans are affected by the advertising we see. *We're* motivated by the ads we see to buy billions of dollars worth of products each year.

which, who, that See **that, which, who.**

who's, whose Use *who's* when you mean *who is.*

Who's going to take calculus?

Use *whose* when you want to indicate possession.

The writer *whose* book was in the window was autographing copies in the store.

will, shall See **shall, will.**

-wise, -ize See **-ize, -wise.**

would of, could of See **could of, would of.**

your, you're Because these words are pronounced alike, they are often confused. *Your* indicates possession and *you're* is the contraction of *you are.*

You can improve *your* stamina by jogging two miles a day.

You're certain to be impressed the first time you see the Golden Gate Bridge spanning San Francisco Bay.

usage

Glossary of Grammatical Terms

absolute phrase   See **phrase.**

abstract noun   See **noun.**

acronym   A word formed from the first letters or initial sounds of a group of words: NATO = North Atlantic Treaty Organization.

active voice   See **voice.**

adjectival   A word or word group used as an adjective to modify a noun: *dancing* bear. **25a; 25d**

adjective   A word that describes, limits, qualifies, or in any other way modifies nouns or pronouns. A **descriptive adjective** names a quality of the noun or pronoun it modifies: *junior year.* A **proper adjective** is formed from a proper noun: *Hegelian philosophy.* Other kinds of words may be used to limit or qualify nouns, and they are then considered adjectives: **articles** *(a, an, the)*: *the book; a peanut;* **possessive adjectives** *(my, your, his,* and so on)*: *their apartment, my house;* **demonstrative adjectives** *(this, these, that, those)*: *that table, these chairs;* **interrogative adjectives** *(what, which, whose,* and so on)*: Which car is yours?;* **indefinite adjectives** *(another, each, both, many,* and so on)*: any minute, some day;* **relative adjectives** *(what, whatever, which, whichever, whose, whosever)*: *Bed rest was what the doctor ordered.;* **numerical adjectives** *(one, two, first, second,* and so on)*: Claire saw two robins.* **21d; 25a**

adjective clause   See **clause.**

adverb   A word that describes the action of verbs or modifies adjectives, other adverbs, or complete phrases, clauses, or sentences. Adverbs answer the questions "How?" "Why?" "Where?" "When?" "To what extent?" and "To what degree?". Adverbs are formed from adjectives, many by adding *-ly* to the adjective form *(dark/darkly, solemn/solemnly),* and may also be derived from prepositions *(Joe carried on.).* Other adverbs that indicate time, place, condition, cause, or degree do not derive from other parts of speech: *then, never, very,* and *often,* for example. The words *how, why, where,* and *when* are classified as **interrogative adverbs** when they ask questions *(How did we get into this mess?).* See also **conjunctive adverb. 21e; 25b**

terms

adverb clause   See **clause.**

adverbial   A word or word group that is used as an adverb to modify a verb, an adjective, another adverb, or complete phrases, clauses, or sentences: *The sun rises in the east.; Our vacation begins Saturday.*

adverbial conjunction   See **conjunctive adverb.**

agreement   The correspondence between words in number, person, and gender. Subjects and verbs must agree in number (singular or plural) and person (first, second, or third): *Soccer is a popular European sport.; I play soccer too.* **24a–h** Pronouns and their antecedents must agree in number, person, and gender (masculine, feminine, neuter); *Lucy loaned Charlie her car.* **24i–j**

allusion   A form of **figurative language** in which the writer describes a subject by referring to a famous historical or literary person or event which the reader is expected to recognize. **17e.5.**

analogy   A form of **figurative language** in which the writer explains an unfamiliar idea or object by comparing it to a more familiar one: *Sensory pathways of the central nervous system are bundles of nerves rather like telephone cables that feed information about the outside world into your brain for processing.* **17e.3**

antecedent   The word or group of words to which a pronoun refers: *Brian finally bought the stereo he had always wanted.* (*Brian* is the antecedent of the pronoun *he.*)

appositive   A noun or noun phrase that identifies, in different words, the noun or pronoun it follows: *Columbus, the capital of Ohio, is in the central part of the state.* Appositives may be used without special introductory phrases, as in the preceding example, or they may be introduced by *such as, or, that is, for example,* or *in other words: Japanese cars, such as Hondas, now have a large share of the U.S. automobile market.* In an **inverted appositive**, the appositive precedes the noun or pronoun it modifies: *The singing cowboy, Gene Autry, became the owner of the California Angels.* **7f.4**

article   See **adjective.**

auxiliary verb   See **verb.**

balanced sentence   A sentence neatly divided between two parallel structures. Balanced sentences are typically **compound sentences** made up of two parallel clauses (*The telephone rang, and I answered.*), but the parallel clauses of a **complex sentence** can also be balanced. **9c**

cardinal number   A number that expresses quantity—*seven, thirty, one hundred.* (Contrast **ordinal.**)

case   The form a noun or pronoun takes to indicate how it functions in a sentence. English has three cases: **subjective** (or **nominative**) **case:** A pronoun takes the subjective case when it acts as the subject of a sentence or a clause: *I am an American.* **22a; objective case:** A pronoun takes the objective case when it acts as the object of a verb or of a preposition: *Fran gave me her dog.* **22b; possessive** (or **genitive**) **case:** Both nouns and pronouns take the possessive case when they indicate ownership: *My*

terms

house is brick; Brandon's T-shirt is red. This is the only case in which nouns change form. **22c**

clause   A group of related words that includes a subject and a predicate. An **independent (main) clause** may stand alone as a sentence *(Yellowstone is a national park in the West.)*, but a **dependent (subordinate) clause** must always be accompanied by an independent clause *(Yellowstone is a national park in the West that is known for its geysers.)*. Dependent clauses are classified according to their function in a sentence. An **adjective clause** (sometimes called a **relative clause**) modifies nouns or pronouns: *That philodendron, which grew to be twelve feet tall, finally died.* (the clause modifies *philodendron*). An **adverb clause** modifies single words (verbs, adjectives, or adverbs) or an entire phrase or clause: *The film was exposed when Bill opened the camera* (the clause modifies *exposed*). A **noun clause** acts as a noun (as subject, direct object, indirect object, or complement) in a sentence: *Whoever arrives first wins the prize* (the clause is the subject of the sentence). An **elliptical clause** is grammatically incomplete—that is, part or all of the subject or predicate is missing. If the missing part can be easily inferred from the context of the sentence, such a construction is acceptable: *When (they are) pressed, the committee will act.* **7d.2**

climactic word order   The writing strategy of moving from the least important to the most important point in a sentence and ending with the key idea. **9a.2**

collective noun   See **noun.**

comma splice   A **run-on sentence** that occurs when two independent clauses are incorrectly joined by a comma. **13a–13e**

> COMMA SPLICE: The Mississippi River flows south, the Red River flows north.
>
> REVISED: The Mississippi River flows south. The Red River flows north.
>
> REVISED: The Mississippi River flows south; the Red River flows north.
>
> REVISED: The Mississippi River flows south, and the Red River flows north.

common noun   See **noun.**

comparative degree   See **comparison.**

comparison   The form taken by an adjective or an adverb to indicate degree. The **positive degree** describes a quality without indicating comparison *(Frank is tall.)* The **comparative degree** indicates comparison between two persons or things *(Frank is taller than John.)* The **superlative degree** indicates comparison between one person or thing and two or more others *(Frank is the tallest boy in his scout troop.)*. **25c**

complement   A word or words that describes or renames a subject, an object, or a verb. A **subject complement** is a word or phrase that follows a linking verb and renames the subject. It can be an adjective (called a **predicate adjective**) or a noun (called a **predicate nominative**): *Clark Gable was a movie star.* An **object complement** is a word or phrase that

terms

describes or renames a direct object. Object complements can be either adjectives or nouns: *We built the treehouse out of wood.*

complete predicate   See **predicate.**

complete subject   See **subject.**

complex sentence   See **sentence.**

compound   Two or more words that function as a unit, such as **compound nouns:** *attorney at law; boardwalk;* **compound adjectives:** *hard-hitting editorial;* **compound prepositions:** *by way of, in addition to;* **compound subjects:** *April and May are spring months.;* **compound predicates:** *Many have tried and failed to change his mind.*

compound adjective   See **compound.**

compound noun   See **compound.**

compound predicate   See **compound.**

compound preposition   See **compound.**

compound sentence   See **sentence.**

compound subject   See **compound.**

compound-complex sentence   See **sentence.**

conjunction   A word or words used to connect single words, phrases, clauses, and sentences. **Coordinating conjunctions** *(and, or, but, nor, for, so, yet)* connect words, phrases, or clauses of equal weight: *crime and punishment* (coordinating conjunction *and* connects two words). **Correlative conjunctions** *(both . . . and, either . . . or, neither . . . nor,* and so on), always used in pairs, also link items of equal weight: *Neither Texas nor Florida crosses the Tropic of Cancer.* (correlative conjunction *neither . . . nor* connects two words). **Subordinating conjunctions** *(since, because, although, if, after,* and so on) introduce adverb clauses: *You will have to pay for the tickets now because I will not be here later* (subordinating conjunction *because* introduces the adverb clause). **21g**

conjunctive adverb   An adverb that joins and relates independent clauses in a sentence *(also, anyway, besides, hence, however, nevertheless, still,* and so on): *Howard tried out for the Yankees; however, he didn't make the team.* **21e**

connotation   The emotional associations that surround a word. (Contrast **denotation.**) **17c.1**

contraction   The combination of two words with an apostrophe replacing the missing letters: *we + will = we'll; was + not = wasn't.*

coordinate adjective   One of a series of adjectives that modify the same word or word group: *The glen was quiet, shady, and cool.*

coordinating conjunction   See **conjunction.**

coordination   The pairing of similar elements (words, phrases, or clauses) to give equal weight to each. Coordination is used in simple sentences to link similar elements to form compound subjects, predicates, complements, or modifiers. It can also link two independent

terms

clauses to form a compound sentence: *The sky was cloudy, and it looked like rain.* (Contrast **subordination**.) **8a**

correlative conjunction   See **conjunction**.

cumulative sentence   A sentence that begins with a main clause followed by additional words, phrases, or clauses that expand or develop it: *On the hill stood a schoolhouse, paint peeling, windows boarded, playground overgrown with weeds.*

dangling modifier   A modifier for which no true headword appears in the sentence. To correct dangling modifiers, either change the subject of the sentence's main clause, creating a subject that can logically serve as the headword of the dangling modifier, or add words that transform the dangling modifier into a dependent clause. **14e–14g**

> Dangling: Pumping up the tire, the trip continued.

> Revised: After pumping up the tire, they continued the trip.

dead metaphor   A metaphor so overused that it has become a meaningless cliché. **17f.1**

declarative sentence   See **sentence**.

demonstrative adjective   See **adjective**.

demonstrative pronoun   See **pronoun**.

denotation   The dictionary meaning of a word. (Contrast **connotation**.) **17c.1**

dependent clause   See **clause**.

descriptive adjective   See **adjective**.

direct address   A word or phrase within a sentence that indicates the person, group, or thing spoken to: *Remember, <u>scouts</u>, to do a good deed today. <u>Drivers</u>, start your engines.*

direct object   See **object**.

direct quotation   See **quotation**.

double negative   The illogical use of two negative words within a single sentence: *She <u>didn't</u> have <u>no</u> time.* Such constructions are nonstandard English. Revised: *She had <u>no</u> time* or *She <u>did not</u> have time.*

ellipsis mark   Three spaced periods used to indicate the omission of a word or words from a quotation: *"The time has come . . . and we must part."* **31o–31q**

elliptical clause   See **clause**.

embedding   A strategy for varying sentence structure that involves changing some sentences into modifying phrases and working them into other sentences. **11b.3**

expletive   A construction in which *there* or *it* is used with a form of the verb *be*: *<u>There is</u> no one here by that name.*

faulty parallelism   See **parallelism**.

figurative language   Imaginative comparisons between different ideas or objects using common figures of speech—**simile**, **metaphor**, **analogy**, **personification**, and **allusion**. 17e–17f

figure of speech   See **figurative language**.

finite verb   A verb that can stand as the main verb of a sentence. Unlike **participles**, **gerunds**, and **infinitives** (see **verbal**), finite verbs do not require an auxiliary in order to function as the main verb: *The rooster crowed.*

fragment   See **sentence fragment**.

function word   An article, preposition, conjunction, or auxiliary verb that indicates the function of and the grammatical relationship among the nouns, verbs, and modifiers in a sentence.

fused sentence   A **run-on sentence** that occurs when two independent clauses are joined either without suitable punctuation or without a coordinating conjunction. Fused sentences can be corrected by separating the independent clauses with a period, a semicolon, or a comma and a **coordinating conjunction**; or by using **subordination**. 13f–13i

> FUSED SENTENCE: Protein is needed for good nutrition lipids and carbohydrates are too.
>
> REVISED: Protein is needed for good nutrition. Lipids and carbohydrates are too.
>
> REVISED: Protein is needed for good nutrition; lipids and carbohydrates are too.
>
> REVISED: Protein is needed for good nutrition, but lipids and carbohydrates are too.
>
> REVISED: Although protein is needed for good nutrition, lipids and carbohydrates are too.

gender   The classification of nouns and pronouns as masculine *(father, lad, he)*, feminine *(mother, girl, she)*, or neuter *(radio, kitten, them)*.

genitive case   See **case**.

gerund   A special form of verb ending in *-ing* that is always used as a noun. *Fishing is relaxing* (gerund *fishing* serves as subject; gerund *relaxing* serves as subject complement). Note: When the *-ing* form of a verb is used as a modifier, it is considered a **present participle**. (See also **verbal**.)

gerund phrase   See **phrase**.

headword   The word or phrase in a sentence that is described, defined, or limited by a modifier.

helping verb   See **auxiliary verb**.

idiom   An expression that is characteristic of a particular language and whose meaning cannot be predicted from the meaning of its individual words: *lend a hand.*

terms

imperative mood   See **mood**.

indefinite adjective   See **adjective**.

indefinite pronoun   See **pronoun**.

independent clause   See **clause**.

indicative mood   See **mood**.

indirect object   See **object**.

indirect question   A question that tells what has been asked but, because it does not use the speaker's exact words, does not take a question mark: *He asked whether he could use the family car.*

indirect quotation   See **quotation**.

infinitive   The base form of the verb preceded by *to*, an infinitive can serve as an adjective *(He is the man to watch.)*, an adverb *(Chris hoped to break the record.)*, or a noun *(To err is human.)*. See also **verbal**.

infinitive phrase   See **phrase**.

intensifier   A word that adds emphasis but not additional meaning to words it modifies: *much, really, too, very,* and *so* are typical intensifiers.

intensive pronoun   See **pronoun**.

interjection   A grammatically independent word, which expresses emotion, that is used as an exclamation. Interjections can be set off by a comma, or, for greater emphasis, they can be punctuated as independent units, set off by an exclamation point: *Ouch! That hurt.* **21h**

interrogative adjective   See **adjective**.

interrogative adverb   See **adverb**.

interrogative pronoun   See **pronoun**.

intransitive verb   See **verb**.

inverted appositive   See **appositive**.

irregular verb   A verb that does not form both its past tense and past participle by the addition of *-d* or *-ed* to the base form of the verb. **23a–23b**

isolate   Any word, including **interjections,** that can be used in isolation: *Yes. No. Hello. Good-bye. Please. Thank you.*

linking verb   A verb that connects a subject to its complement: *The crowd became quiet.* Words that can be used as linking verbs include *seem, appear, believe, become, grow, turn, remain, prove, look, sound, smell, taste, feel,* and forms of the verb *be.*

main clause   See **clause**.

main verb   See **verb**.

mass noun   See **noun**.

metaphor   A form of **figurative language** in which the writer makes an implied comparison between two unlike items, equating them in an unexpected way: *He rode the subway, coursing through the arteries of the city.* **17e.2**

misplaced modifier   A modifier that has no clear relationship with its headword, usually because it is placed too far from it. **14a–14d**

terms

MISPLACED: By changing his diapers, Dan learned much about the new baby.

REVISED: Dan learned much about the new baby by changing his diapers.

mixed construction   A sentence made up of two or more parts that do not fit together grammatically, causing readers to have trouble determining meaning. **16f–16i**

MIXED: The Great Chicago Fire caused terrible destruction was what prompted changes in the fire code. (independent clause used as a subject)

REVISED: The terrible destruction of the Great Chicago Fire prompted changes in the fire code.

REVISED: Because of the terrible destruction of the Great Chicago Fire, the fire code was changed.

mixed metaphor   The combination of two or more incompatible images in a single figure of speech: *During the race John kept a stiff upper lip as he ran like the wind.* **17f.2**

modal auxiliary   See verb.

modifier   A word that adds information to a sentence and shows connections between ideas.

mood   The verb form that indicates the writer's basic attitude. There are three moods in English. The **indicative mood** is used for statements and questions: *Nebraska became a state in 1867.* **23g** The **imperative mood** specifies commands or requests and is often used without a subject: *(You) Pay the rent.* **23h** The **subjunctive mood** expresses wishes or hypothetical conditions: *I wish the sun were shining.* **23i**

nominal   A word, phrase, or clause that functions as a noun.

nominative case   See case.

nonfinite verb   See verbal.

nonrestrictive modifier   A modifying phrase or clause that does not limit or particularize the words it modifies, but rather supplies additional information about them. Nonrestrictive modifiers are set off by commas: *Oregano, also known as marjoram and suganda,* is a member of the mint family. **27d.1** (Contrast **restrictive modifier.**)

noun   A word that names people, places, things, ideas, actions, or qualities. A **common noun** names any of a class of people, places, or things: *lawyer, town, bicycle.* A **proper noun,** always capitalized, refers to a particular person, place, or thing: *F. Lee Bailey, Chicago, Schwinn.* A **mass noun** names a quantity that is not countable: *sand, time, work.* An **abstract noun** refers to an intangible idea or quality: *bravery, equality, hunger.* A **collective noun** designates a group of people, places, or things thought of as a unit: *Congress, police, family.* **21a**

terms

noun clause   See clause.

noun phrase   See phrase.

number   The form taken by a noun, pronoun, demonstrative adjective, or verb to indicate one (**singular**): *car, he, this book, boasts;* or many (**plural**): *cars, they, those books, boast.* **16d**

numerical adjective   See **adjective.**

object   A noun, pronoun, or other noun substitute that is influenced by a **transitive verb, verbal,** or **preposition.** A **direct object** indicates where the verb's action is directed and who or what is affected by it: *John caught a butterfly.* An **indirect object** tells to or for whom the verb's action was done: *John gave Nancy his butterfly.* An **object of a preposition** is a word or word group introduced by a preposition: *John gave Nancy his butterfly for an hour.*

object complement   See **complement.**

object of a preposition   See **object.**

objective case   See **case.**

ordinal number   A number that indicates position in a series: *seventh, thirtieth, one-hundredth.*

parallelism   The use of similar grammatical elements in sentences or parts of sentences: *We serve beer, wine, and soft drinks.* Words, phrases, clauses, or complete sentences may be parallel, and parallel items may be paired or presented in a series. When elements that have the same function in a sentence are not presented in the same terms, the sentence is flawed by **faulty parallelism. 9c; 15a–15b**

participial phrase   See **phrase.**

participle   A verb form that functions in a sentence as an adjective. Virtually every verb has a **present participle**, which ends in *-ing (breaking, leaking, taking)*, and a **past participle**, which usually ends in *-d* or *-ed (agreed, walked, taken)*. Note: When the *-ing* form of a verb is used as a noun, it is considered a **gerund.** (See also **verbal.**) **Present participle:** *The heaving seas swamped the dinghy.* (present participle *heaving* modifies noun *seas*); **past participle:** *The aged deserve respect.* (past participle *aged* is the subject of the sentence)

parts of speech   The eight basic building blocks for all English sentences: *nouns, pronouns, verbs, adjectives, adverbs, prepositions, conjunctions,* and *interjections.*

passive voice   See **voice.**

past participle   See **participle.**

periodic sentence   A sentence that moves from a number of specific examples to a conclusion, gradually building intensity until a climax is reached in the main clause: *Wan and pale and looking ready to crumble, the marathoner headed into the last mile of the race.*

person   The form a pronoun or verb takes to indicate the speaker (**first person**): *I am/we are;* those spoken to (**second person**): *you are;* and those spoken about (**third person**): *he, she, it is; they are.* **16d**

personal pronoun   See **pronoun.**

terms

personification   A form of **figurative language** in which the writer describes an idea or inanimate object in terms that imply human attributes, feelings, or powers: *The big feather bed beckoned to my tired body.* **17e.4**

phrase   A grammatically ordered group of related words that lacks a subject or a predicate or both and functions as a single part of speech. A **verb phrase** consists of an auxiliary (helping) verb and a main verb: *The wind was blowing hard.* A **noun phrase** includes a noun or pronoun plus all related modifiers: *She broke the track record.* A **prepositional phrase** consists of a preposition, its object, and any modifiers of that object: *The errant ball sailed over the fence.* A **verbal phrase** consists of a verbal and its related objects, modifiers, or complements. A verbal phrase may be a **participial phrase** (*Undaunted by the sheer cliff, the climber scaled the rock.*), a **gerund phrase** (*Swinging from trees is a monkey's favorite way to travel.*), or an **infinitive phrase** (*Wednesday is Bill's night to cook spaghetti.*) An **absolute phrase** usually consists of a noun or pronoun and a participle, accompanied by modifiers: *His heart racing, he dialed her number.* **7d.1**

positive degree   See **comparison.**

possessive adjective   See **adjective.**

possessive case   See **case.**

predicate   A verb or verb phrase that tells or asks something about the subject of a sentence is called a **simple predicate:** *Well-tended lawns grow green and thick.* (*grow* is the simple predicate.) A **complete predicate** includes all the words associated with the predicate: *Well-tended lawns grow green and thick.* (*grow green and thick* is the complete predicate.) **7a**

predicate adjective   See **complement.**

prefix   A letter or group of letters put before a root or word that adds to, changes, or modifies it. **19e.2**

preposition   A part of speech that introduces a word or word group consisting of one or more nouns or pronouns or of a phrase or clause functioning in the sentence as a noun: *Jeremy crawled under the bed.* **21f**

prepositional phrase   See **phrase.**

present participle   See **participle.**

principal parts   The forms of a verb from which all other forms can be derived. The principal parts are the **base form** (*give*), the **present participle** (*giving*), the **past tense** (*gave*), and the **past participle** (*given*).

pronoun   A word that may be used in place of a noun in a sentence. The noun for which a pronoun stands is called its **antecedent.** There are eight different types of pronouns. Some have the same form but are distinguished by their function in the sentence. A **personal pronoun** stands for a person or thing: *I, me, we, us, my,* and so on. (*They broke his window.*) A **reflexive pronoun** ends in *-self* or *-selves* and refers to the

terms

subject of the sentence or clause: *myself, yourself, himself,* and so on. *(They painted the house themselves.)* An **intensive pronoun** ends in *-self* or *-selves* and emphasizes a noun or pronoun. *(Custer himself died in the battle.)* A **relative pronoun** introduces an adjective or noun clause in a sentence: *which, who, whom,* and so on. *(Sitting Bull was the Sioux chief who defeated Custer.)* An **interrogative pronoun** introduces a question: *who, which, what, whom,* and so on. *(Who won the lottery?)* A **demonstrative pronoun** points to a particular thing or group of things: *this, that, these, those. (Who was that masked man?)* A **reciprocal pronoun** denotes a mutual relationship: *each other, one another. (We still have each other.)* An **indefinite pronoun** refers to persons or things in general, not to specific individuals. Most indefinite pronouns are singular: *anyone, everyone, one, each,* but some are always plural: *both, many, several. (Many are called, but few are chosen.)* **21b**

proper adjective   See **adjective.**

proper noun   See **noun.**

quotation   The use of the written or spoken words of others. A **direct quotation** occurs when a passage is borrowed word for word from another source. Quotation marks ("") establish the boundaries of a direct quotation: *"These tortillas taste like cardboard," complained Beth.* **30a** An **indirect quotation** reports someone else's written or spoken words without quoting that person directly. Quotation marks are not used: *Beth complained that the tortillas tasted like cardboard.*

reciprocal pronoun   See **pronoun**

reflexive pronoun   See **pronoun.**

regular verb   A verb that forms both its past tense and past participle by the addition of *-d* or *-ed* to the base form of the verb. **23a–23l**

relative adverb   See **adverb.**

relative clause   See **clause.**

relative pronoun   See **pronoun.**

restrictive modifier   A modifying phrase or clause that limits the meaning of the word or word group it modifies. Restrictive modifiers are not set off by commas: *The Ferrari that ran over the fireplug was red.* **27d.1** (Contrast **nonrestrictive modifier.**)

root   A word from which other words are formed. An understanding of a root word increases understanding of other unfamiliar words that incorporate the root. **19e.2**

run-on sentence   An incorrect construction that results when the proper connective or punctuation does not appear between independent clauses. A run-on occurs either as a **comma splice** or as a **fused sentence.**

terms

sentence   An independent grammatical unit that contains a subject and a predicate and expresses a complete thought: *Carolyn sold her car.* **7a** Sentences can be classified in any one of four ways: A **simple sentence** consists of one subject and one predicate: The season ended. **7e;** a

compound sentence is formed when two or more simple sentences are connected with coordinating conjunctions, conjunctive adverbs, semi-colons, or colons: *The rain stopped, and the sun began to shine.* **8a**; a **complex sentence** consists of one simple sentence, which functions as an independent clause in the complex sentence, and at least one dependent clause, which is introduced by a subordinating conjunction or a relative pronoun: *When he had sold three boxes* (dependent clause), *he was halfway to his goal.* (independent clause) **8b**; and a **compound-complex sentence** consists of two or more independent clauses and at least one dependent clause: *After he prepared a shopping list* (dependent clause), *he went to the store* (independent clause), *but it was closed.* (independent clause) **8c**

sentence fragment   An incomplete sentence, phrase, or clause that is punctuated as if it were a complete sentence. **12a–12h**

shift   A change of *tense, voice, mood, person, number,* or *type of discourse* within or between sentences. Some shifts are necessary, but problems occur with unnecessary or illogical shifts. **16a–16e**

simile   A form of figurative language in which the writer makes a comparison, introduced by *like* or *as,* between two unlike items on the basis of a shared quality: *Like sands through the hourglass, so are the days of our lives.; The wind was as biting <u>as his neighbor's doberman.</u>* **17e.1**

simple predicate   See **predicate.**

simple sentence   See **sentence.**

simple subject   See **subject.**

split infinitive   An infinitive whose parts are separated by a modifier. **14d**

> SPLIT: She expected *to* ultimately *swim* the channel.

> REVISED: She expected ultimately *to swim* the channel.

squinting modifier   A modifier that seems to modify either a word before it or one after it and that conveys a different meaning in each case. **14a**

> SQUINTING: The task completed simply delighted him.

> REVISED: He was delighted to have the task completed simply.

> REVISED: He was simply delighted to have the task completed.

subject   A noun or noun substitute that tells who or what a sentence is about is called a **simple subject:** *Healthy thoroughbred <u>horses</u> run like the wind.* (*horses* is the simple subject.) The **complete subject** of a sentence includes all the words associated with the subject: *<u>Healthy thoroughbred horses</u> run like the wind.* (*healthy thoroughbred horses* is the complete subject.) **7a**

subject complement   See **complement.**

subjective case   See **case.**

subjunctive mood   See **mood.**

terms

subordinate clause   See **clause.**

subordinating conjunction   See **conjunction.**

subordination   Making one or more clauses of a sentence grammatically dependent upon another element in a sentence: *Preston was only eighteen when he joined the firm.* (Contrast **coordination.**) **8b**

suffix   A syllable added at the end of a word or root that changes its part of speech. **19e.2**

superlative degree   See **comparison.**

suspended hyphen   A hyphen followed by a space or by the appropriate punctuation and a space: *The wagon was pulled by a two-, four-, or six-horse team.*

tag question   A question, consisting of an auxiliary verb plus a pronoun, that is added to a statement and set off by a comma: *You know it's going to rain, don't you?*

tense   The form of a verb that indicates when an action has occurred or when a condition existed. **23c–23f**

transitive verb   See **verb.**

verb   A word or phrase that expresses action *(He painted the fence.)* or a state of being *(Henry believes in equality.).* A **main verb** carries most of the meaning in the sentence or clause in which it appears: *Winston Churchill smoked long, thick cigars.* A main verb is a **linking verb** when it is followed by a **subject complement:** *Dogs are good pets.* An **auxiliary verb** (sometimes called a **helping verb**) combines with the main verb to form a **verb phrase:** *Graduation day has arrived.* The auxiliaries *be* and *have* are used to indicate the tense and voice of the main verb. The auxiliary *do* is used for asking questions and forming negative statements. Other auxiliary verbs, known as **modal auxiliaries** *(must, will, can, could, may, might, ought (to), should,* and *would),* indicate necessity, possibility, willingness, obligation, and ability. *It might rain next Tuesday.* A **transitive verb** requires an **object** to complete its meaning in the sentence: *Pete drank all the wine.* (*wine* is the direct object) An **intransitive verb** has no direct object: *The candle glowed.* **21c; 23a–l**

verb phrase   See **phrase.**

verbal   (nonfinite verb) Verb forms—**participles, infinitives,** and **gerunds**—that are used as nouns, adjectives, or adverbs. Verbals do not behave like verbs. Only when used with an auxiliary can such verb forms serve as the main verb of a sentence. *The wall painted* is not a sentence; *The wall was painted* is. **21c**

verbal phrase   See **phrase.**

voice   The form that determines whether the subject of a verb is acting or is acted upon. When the subject of a verb performs the action, the verb is in the **active voice:** *Palmer sank a thirty-foot putt.* When the subject of a verb receives the action—that is, is acted upon—the verb is in the **passive voice:** *A thirty-foot putt was sunk by Palmer.* **9e; 16b; 23j–23l**

terms

Acknowledgments

Index

Numbers in **boldface** refer to sections of the handbook; other numbers refer to pages.

index

index

Guide to the Plan of the Book

The table of contents that follows highlights key elements of the contents on pages xv to xxiv and gives a more detailed overview of the entire book. Use this guide when you are looking for a specific subject or a discussion that you know is part of a specific chapter. Your instructor may also use this guide to direct you to a particular topic within a chapter.